The Territory of Montana
Secretary's Office,
Helena, M.T. Jan 30th 1886

The District Court
SECOND JUDICIAL DISTRICT — STATE OF MONTANA
. WILKINS, CHIEF DEPUTY
E LEONARD
BOOTH
A HARDCASTLE, DEPUTIES
RMOYLE,
Butte, Montana.

D. W. FISK, TREASURER.   A. J. FISK, SECRETARY.

Helena Herald.
ESTABLISHED 1866.
na, Montana, July 1897

oice,
Agency,
1882

GENERAL OFFICE
— OF —
William A. Clark.
Butte, Montana.

I. N. HAZLETT
LTON & HAZLETT
DEALERS IN
L MERCHANDISE

Agency, M.T. July 20, 1882.

C. A. Broadwater & Co.
POST-TRADERS
Fort Assinniboine, M.T.

Parrot Silver & Copp
Mines and Reduction Works at
Butte City, Mont.

Hon. S. T. Hauser
Helena

Montana Live Stock Excha
Custer County.
Miles City, M.T. Sept

OFFICE OF THE
WHITLATCH UNION MINES,
52 Bridge Street.

OFFICE OF THE
HECLA CONSOLIDATED MINING CO.
INCORPORATED 1877.
SMELTER   MINES
MINING, SMELTING & REDUCTION OF
GOLD, SILVER & COPPER ORES.
RAILROAD & TELEGRAPH STATION
MELROSE, SILVER BOW CO., MONT.

Glendale, Beaverhead Co. Mont. Aug. 9 1883

Mr. Hauser, Bank

D1737301

ROCKY MOUNTAIN HUSBANDMAN
SUTHERLIN BROS., PUBLISHERS.
White Sulphur Springs, M.T. Aug 25 1883

Mr. S. T. Hauser

Historical Society of the State of Montana.
Incorporated by the Legislative Assembly, February 2d, 1865.
FICERS AND EXECUTIVE COMMITTEE.
ent, GRANVILLE STUART, Helena.
esident, CORNELIUS HEDGES, Helena.
onding Secretary, WILLIAM E. CULLEN, Helena.
ng Secretary, HENRY N. BLAKE, Helena.
a F SANDERS, Helena.
an, WILLIAM F. WHEELER, Helena.
S. RICKARDS, Governor, State Ex. Com., Helena.
WITT, Secretary of State, State Ex. Com., Helena.
J. HASKELL, Att'y Gen., State Ex. Com., Helena.

HELENA, MONTANA, Feby 24 1895

ton James Fergus
Post Quartermaster,
Fort Shaw, Montana Territory.
February 24th 1882.

J. SULLIVAN, Grand Receiver, Helena, Montana.
12-5-80
D. THORBURN, Grand Recorder, Ogden, Utah.
JURISDICTION OF NEVADA
Ancient Order of United Workmen
J. W. KINSLEY, G. M. W., Ogden, Utah.

E. L. BONNER, PRESIDENT
R. A. EDDY, VICE PRESIDENT.
MONTANA IMPROVEMEN
[LIMITED]
General Manager's O
Missoula, Mont

S. T. Hauser Esq

OFFICE OF
The Maginnis Mining Company,

HELENA AND JEFFERSON
MILLS BUILDING

NOT IN PRECIOUS METALS ALONE

A MANUSCRIPT HISTORY OF MONTANA

Library of Congress Cataloging in Publication Data

Not in precious metals alone.

Bibliography : p.
Includes index.
I. Montana — History — Sources.   I.   Montana Historical Society
F731.N88   978.6   76-18976
ISBN 0-917298-01-2 (Hardbound)   0-917298-02-0 (Paperback)

Copyright © 1976 The Montana Historical Society, Helena, Montana 59601
Bound by Hiller Book Company, Salt Lake City, Utah
Printed by Color World of Montana, Inc., Bozeman, Montana
First Edition

Not in Precious Metals Alone

A manuscript History of Montana

Notwithstanding the richness of the Rocky Mountains in gold it is not in the precious metals alone that it presents attractions to the seeker after fortune.

JAMES FERGUS, BANNOCK CITY, M.T.
TO JAMES L. FISK, JANUARY 1, 1863

COMPILED AND EDITED
BY THE STAFF OF
THE MONTANA HISTORICAL SOCIETY
HELENA, MONTANA

DEDICATED TO
THE PEOPLE OF MONTANA

PREFACE

The Montana Historical Society has statutory responsibilities to preserve the history of Montana through collection and publication. Gathering and arranging began soon after the Society's inception in 1865; publication commenced a decade later. In 1876, Volume I of *Contributions to the Historical Society of Montana* appeared to meet the Society's public responsibility. Nine other volumes followed in the series, the last appearing in 1940. Subsequently, in 1951, the Society inaugurated the prestigious quarterly journal, *Montana, the magazine of Western History,* interspersing its publication with occasional monographs and papers in decades which followed. *Not in Precious Metals Alone* perpetuates the opportunities and responsibilities of publication begun a century ago in that first volume of *Contributions.* Inclusion of limited selections from the series in these pages serves to reinforce that continuity.

Fortuitously, the Centennial of Society publication coincided with the nation's Bicentennial in 1976. *Not in Precious Metals Alone* represents, in part, Montana's observance of this 200-year milestone and received the encouragement and financial support of the State Bicentennial Administration. Additionally, private monetary assistance for this book came from the Ila B. Dousman Trust, Leif Erickson, trustee. Both sources deserve public gratitude for their crucial aid in preserving Montana's history and making it available for all to enjoy.

Not in Precious Metals Alone is, however, more than an anniversary celebration. It is a vehicle to share diverse historical materials the Society has acquired in the past one hundred and eleven years and the equally diverse heritage of a territory and state with roots extending beyond Montana's formal creation. Readers of text books, articles, and essays often miss the charm, the elucidation, the immediacy, found in original diaries, letters, and other manuscripts which form the basis of history. Few people have the occasion to visit and use archival repositories, and, in consequence, do not realize the vast amounts of original materials preserved therein. This book, if only in a finite manner, allows anyone interested in the state's history or the American West, to enjoy the experiences, observations, successes and disappointments of the men and women who shaped Montana. Society administration and staff feel this is vitally important because our role, programs, and holdings, as well as those of similar institutions, can be fully understood only when such collections are shared with the people on whose behalf they have been preserved.

Add education to collection and publication as a significant Historical Society objective and a motivation for this work. Students in Montana's schools face a dearth of materials when studying the history of their state. The paucity is most acute in available primary readings. In concert with present texts and resources, we envision utilization of *Not in Precious Metals Alone* as a valuable tool in providing information necessary for young historians to better understand their heritage as Montanans and Americans.

Any volume designed to span centuries in time and diversity of audience is open to the vicissitudes inherent in such breadth. The compilers acknowledge that general readers, serious scholars, and students will differ in their appraisals. To some the approach will be too broad, cursory to the point of oversimplification; to others, it will appear parochial to the limit of obfuscation. We have tried to follow the tenuous trail between the two. Each reader must judge whether the volume succeeds in this attempt. Above all, we make no pretense that this is an exhaustive treatment of Montana history.

No matter how often repeated, no institution is better than its staff. In this sense, the Historical Society has been continually fortunate. *Not in Precious Metals Alone* could not have appeared without the intense interest and effort of earlier librarians and curators who preserved much of the material now published. The talent and expertise of the present staff, among them Brian Cockhill, Jeffrey Cunniff, Kenneth Korte, Carolyn Mattern,

Harriett Meloy, Delores Morrow, Rex Myers, and Vivian Paladin, combined to achieve this publication. Credit and culpability for it rest with them, but their efforts alone would not have sufficed to complete the project, and the other divisions of the Society were likewise involved.

With few exceptions, materials on the following pages are in the collections of the Montana Historical Society, a fact determined by the Society's responsibility to publicize its holdings and thus share these irreplaceable items with the public which made the institution and its programs possible. The result is a volume which reflects the strengths and weaknesses of those holdings, and a staff keenly aware of documentary short-comings and anxious to fill the "holes." Where the institution's holdings did not document a major theme, event, or area sufficiently, it became necessary to tap other materials or attempt a more balanced treatment through chapter and manuscript introductions. Conversely, an abundance in Society holdings created selection problems in other areas, necessitating a choice of the "best" relevant document and leaving a quantity of interesting material unused because of space limitations. The documents which follow include many previously unpublished items, rarely seen or used.

The variety of incidents, events and personalities and the ramifications of each in Montana's history presented additional problems, not the least among them, one of space. The result is a compromise among multiple themes, colorful incidents, and limited pages. In consequence, much remains unsaid. Consistent throughout the preparation of this work was an effort to achieve ideological, economic, chronological, and geographic balance. Striving for such balance left much untreated — worthy subjects for future research and publication.

Original writings, the heart of this book, present the danger of intruding on personal feelings, especially with documents from the recent past. Such perspectives are a challenge to historian and editor alike. If there is insult or glorification, attack or praise for any individual or interest, they are unintentional sins of commission and omission which eluded the editing and revision processes. This is not to say that all which follows is positive or complimentary — Montana's history has not always been so, and any portrayal of that heritage can only mirror those events.

Perspectives of the past change with the historians who write and the sources that survive. The answer or rebuttal to the shortcomings of this volume and, certainly, the source for any future work of this kind, lie in the collection or resurrection of all materials illustrative of the past. The Montana Historical Society, along with other archival repositories in the State, encourage all readers to assist in the collection of Montana source materials. Should you possess or should you know of diaries, letters, reminiscences, financial records, and the like, which would enhance the Society's collections, or those of other Montana repositories, we encourage you to take action that will insure their deposit and preservation. Now, for example, is the time to collect Twentieth Century documentation, which might otherwise be destroyed.

Our more recent past needs to be documented as thoroughly as the Gold Rush Era, if future publications in history are to be accurate and complete. Only an interested public can assure that the history of Montana is interpreted with a basis in fact. Complaints of biased history are valid only if sufficient documentation exists for future writers and researchers. All elements of society benefit when the story is properly told.

BRIAN COCKHILL
REX C. MYERS
FOR THE STAFF OF THE MONTANA HISTORICAL SOCIETY

HELENA, MARCH, 1976

INTRODUCTION

If you wish to be confused, go to a thick Webster's and look up the words "manuscript" and "document." On second thought, don't. The definitions are, in fact, limiting, narrowing, and constricting. A far better way to get at the whole matter is to read this book. Or perhaps it would be a wiser adjuration to say that one should "savor" this book — which is to say, "relish" — or to "partake of the quality."

Historians, of course, are utterly dependent upon manuscripts and documents. They study them, ponder them, adhere to them, are skeptical of them, criticize them, endorse them, analyze them — and from all this they write a narrative of things that have happened.

The trouble is that in this complicated process all too often the life is bled from the living manuscript. Not always, of course; the better the historian the less he leaches out the color. The more adept he is at *not* reading today into yesterday the more of yesterday he conserves.

But what we historians do too often (and sometimes because in the interests of space we must), is reduce to a footnote the glowing description and the real living matter in the diary or the letter; reduce it to an *ibid.*, an *op. cit.*, or a *passim*. These may, indeed, be the necessary devices of scholarship; nonetheless, they all too often bleed out the color or reality.

What the historian has to offer is perspective, and cause and effect, which contemporaries usually could not see. They, after all, were present at the moment or at that event. And, as with us today, they could rarely divine that the event was part of a large picture, not a small one. One can see only to one's horizon. It is true that today our horizons are vastly greater than once they were. We see the world through the media as once we could not see it. Yet the irreducible unit of history remains the accounts of men and women who were there — who saw what they saw, felt what they felt, and endured what they had to. The eye, mind, and memory are all imperfect instruments. The result is that manuscripts, letters, diaries, reminiscences, and all manner of accounts do not necessarily reflect what actually happened. But it is vital to remember that in the affairs of mankind we are as often, if not more often, guided by what we *think* is happening than by what, in fact, *is* happening.

Moreover, as you savor this book, you will observe that in many instances, the accounts are descriptive, not judgmental. And what these people described, often in very rich detail, is lost and gone forever — except in accounts such as these.

Compendiums of manuscripts are hardly rare in historical literature. It is, after all, a relatively simple task to concoct an outline, dig out some manuscript pertinent to the outline and have the whole thing printed up into a book. But *good* manuscript histories are rare. They are rare because the task of putting one together with balance, judgment and solid knowledge of the whole period is not a simple task at all. It needs the same sense of structure, organization, judgment and taste employed by the skilled historian, novelist or journalist. These are skills hard to come by. They are abundantly demonstrated in this book.

It is, however, in the matter of choice that the key to excellence lies. To begin with, the documents in this volume have been carefully chosen from thousands. To be more exact, the final potential manuscript list contained more than two thousand items from which those published were meticulously chosen.

It is always tempting in compiling a book such as this to use the atypical rather than the typical, or, to put it another way, to concentrate on the bizarre and romantic aspects of a region's history. In Montana, especially, this poses a serious problem because, in fact, the history of this state *was* so often bizarre and romantic. The editors were fully aware of this — but they were equally aware of the fact that these aspects of our history do not really explain what we were — and hence became. The admixture herein, then, is not random, certainly not careless, but a carefully calculated one.

This book is unusual in another sense. It covers the period from the earliest writings to the present day. It would have been a far easier task to stop short of events which are current or near current; easier and safer. It is one thing to pick manuscripts which best depict the era of the 1860's; it is quite another to choose from the material which depicts the 1970's. Yet it is a far better book because its editors chose the harder way.

Montana is a young state as states go. It is often the case with the younger western states that they have, understandably, thin and irregular manuscript collections. We may never really know whether it was simple fortuity or some combination of peculiar factors which led Montana into a strikingly early and very intense manuscript collection program. Not, indeed, that the enterprise was ever heavily supported by territorial (or for that matter, state) subsidy. The fact remains that the Montana Historical Society was founded in 1865 and that it has been diligently collecting the raw stuff of history for more than one hundred years.

Emerson might well have used the Society as an example of his contention that what is accomplished is usually not accomplished by the many but by the "passionate few." Those familiar with the Society's splendid collections, quarters, and facilities today may be unaware of just how new the quarters and facilities are. Let me digress for a moment.

In the late 1940's I was doing research at the Society, then quartered on the east end of the ground floor of the Capitol building. I was astounded by the size and diversity of the collection. I was also astounded at the staff. I worked there for several weeks before I began to understand how such a small staff could engage in collection activities, to say nothing of processing the material collected, and serving numerous researchers. The first thing I observed was that they worked with intense devotion. My second discovery was that there seemed to be a constant coming and going of people bringing in all manner of materials. My third realization was that these people came not merely from Helena but from all over the state.

Later, early in the 1950's when I became Director of the Society and we were ensconced in fine new quarters, I realized that for over a period of many years the Society had established an amazing statewide network of collectors, informants, collaborators, and dedicated volunteers — the "passionate few." And this, indeed, was a very old formula. A formula applied, expanded, until the Society's present collections form an invaluable store of historical material.

The Society was to blossom in its new quarters; it was to launch what was to become the finest magazine of its kind in America, and it was to create a new museum. But all of this was rooted in the collection which has been building steadily for a century. This book is likewise rooted there — and so its roots go very deep.

A word about utility. The purpose, of course, of collecting manuscript material is not merely to collect it; it is to use it. It is not a hobby. The Society's publications began early and were continuous. All of these publications have had one aim: the dissemination of knowledge about the history of Montana. Moreover, the collection has spawned many books and articles representing the work of researchers and writers from all over the United States.

In this Bicentennial year, nothing could be more appropriate than the publication of this book. That assertion need not be accepted at face value and needs some explication. Obviously, many appropriate things arise from various national and state anniversaries. Often, however, such celebrations produce far more ephemera than substance. There is nothing wrong with ephemeral entertainment, but there are few things better in the name of celebration than those things which combine entertainment, education, and lasting utility. This book has those three attributes. It has one more.

Thousands of students in the state's schools take courses in Montana history annually. In spite of rather valiant efforts over the years to provide teachers with adequate tools to teach the course, we have been only partially successful. Few things appeal to students quite like the "you are there" approach. And this is a book, essentially, which "puts them there." Because of its diversity the teacher can be highly selective — as to time, place, and events. It can help greatly.

Many books require specific approaches on the part of the reader. You cannot dip lightly into many volumes, nor skim others, nor begin in the middle and make sense of most. Yet to this book you may take any approach you wish. You can even read it backwards. You can dip or plunge or read it in a day or over months. But however you approach it, this is a book to savor — and to keep.

K. ROSS TOOLE
HAMMOND PROFESSOR OF HISTORY
UNIVERSITY OF MONTANA

MISSOULA, MARCH, 1976

TABLE OF CONTENTS

Book I
First Arrivals:
A Land to Subdue
1804 - 1866

PRELUDE TO SETTLEMENT

ROMANCE AND EXCITEMENT have characterized much of Montana's history, but the initial contact of the white man with the new land and its original inhabitants during the fur trade period, which lasted a scant half century, has provoked the richest material for folklore. In spite of the pronounced interest it has inspired, the fur trade had limited impact upon Montana's future development, and its tracks and written record are dim indeed. Framed in a wilderness setting, this was a highly competitive and extractive business with overtones of intense international rivalry. Canadians representing the British Hudson's Bay Company and the Scottish North-West Company first entered Montana during the late Eighteenth Century and came to dominate the trade in the western Montana mountains. After the Lewis and Clark Expedition confirmed the claim of the United States to the region, American firms entered the competition. International aspects of the rivalry declined after the War of 1812, and although the trade became primarily a field for private endeavor, competition remained its outstanding characteristic.

To obtain the valuable furs, the British companies sent out large expeditions of engages after rejecting the use of Indian trappers. During the 1820's the American Rocky Mountain Fur Company introduced the rendezvous technique to an already colorful industry. This system, which had little need for established posts, relied upon free trappers who congregated annually to barter.

During the 1830's the decline of the beaver trade — a change in men's hat fashions played a surprising role — and the rise in demand for buffalo robes, led to some important changes in the industry. The robe trade, while never as important as the beaver trade, placed a new significance upon the plains of eastern Montana, where the buffalo was plentiful and upon the Indians, who much preferred hunting buffalo to trapping beaver. At the same time, the introduction of steamboats on the Upper Missouri reduced both the expense and effort of transporting robes to eastern markets. By capitalizing on these changes, the American Fur Company was able to dominate the Montana trade until the 1860's.

Coincident with their quest for furs and robes, the traders and trappers explored most of Montana and mapped out many important wilderness trails through the interior. Contact with the traders also prompted some western tribes to seek information about the white man's religion, an invitation to which the Society of Jesus, the ubiquitous Jesuits, responded enthusiastically with several mission establishments which became Montana's first pockets of white settlement and civilization.

Other than these somewhat tenuous roles, however, the itinerant men of the fur trade contributed little of a positive or permanent nature to the development of Montana. Through them, their superiors introduced the extractive use of her resources and an outward flow of the fruits of exploitation, a pattern which was to continue for many years and in many fields. An equal tragedy was inherent in the traders' relations with the Indians. Exposed to liquor and disease, the tribes were started on the road to dependence and degradation. Nevertheless, the fur trade quickened the nation's imagination about the West and set the stage for subsequent waves of development.

St. Ignatius Mission, 1865

3

PRELUDE TO SETTLEMENT
Exploration, Fur Trade, Missionaries, 1804-1861

On May 14, 1804, Meriwether Lewis and William Clark and their small "corps of discovery" set forth up the Missouri River on one of the great enterprises of American history — exploration of the vast Louisiana Territory. Although an expedition to explore the West and establish a trade route to the Pacific had long been a dream of Thomas Jefferson, purchase of the territory from France in 1803 made the expedition to establish the limits of the new American empire a necessity. President Jefferson was fully aware that he was sending the men to face grave dangers in the wilderness. Thus before the expedition departed, he penned a letter of international credit to be used in the event the party had to return by a different route, possibly by sea and possibly at the whim of a foreign government.

WASHINGTON, U.S. of AMERICA
JULY 6, 1803

DEAR SIR:

In the journey which you are about to undertake for the discovery of the course and source of the Missouri, and of the most convenient water communication from thence to the Pacific ocean, your party being small, it is to be expected that you will encounter considerable dangers from the Indian inhabitants. Should you escape those dangers and reach the Pacific ocean, you may find it imprudent to hazard a return the same way, and be forced to seek a passage round by sea, in such vessels as you may find on the Western coast but you will be without money, without clothes, and other necessaries; as a sufficient supply cannot be carried with you from hence, your resource in that case can only be in the credit of the U.S. for which purpose I hereby authorize you to draw on the Secretaries of State, of the Treasury, of War and Navy of the U.S. according as you may find

your draughts will be most negociable, for the purpose of obtaining money or necessaries for yourself and your men and I solemnly pledge the faith of the United States that these draughts shall be paid punctually at the date they are made payable.

I also ask of the Consuls, agents, merchants and citizens of any nation with which we have intercourse or amity to furnish you with those supplies which your necessities may call for assuring them of honorable and prompt retribution, and our own Consuls in foreign parts where you happen to be, are hereby instructed and required to be aiding and assisting to you in whatsoever may be necessary for procuring your return back to the United States. And to give more entire satisfaction and confidence to those who may be disposed to aid you I Thomas Jefferson, President of the United States of America, have written this letter of general credit for you with my own hand and signed it with my name.

TH JEFFERSON

TO CAPT MERIWETHER LEWIS

Lewis and Clark returned from the Pacific in 1806 to report, among many things, the existence of a fortune in furs in the Upper Missouri drainage. One of the first groups organized to reap this wealth was the Missouri Fur Company, a partnership comprised of some of St. Louis' most enterprising entrepreneurs. Under the leadership of Pierre Menard and Andrew Hunt, the company's first expedition established a post near the Three Forks of the Missouri during the spring of 1810. An attack on the camp on April 12 indicated that local Indians would be hostile to the company's intrusion on their lands. A few days later Menard described the action in a letter to his brother-in-law and business partner, Pierre Chouteau. At the same time, writing in French, he explained the impact it could have on future prospects of the venture.

THREE FORKS OF THE MISSOURI
21 APRIL, 1810

MR. PIERRE CHOUTEAU ESQ.

DEAR SIR AND BROTHER-IN-LAW:—

I had hoped to be able to write you more favorably than I am now able to do. The outlook before us was much more flattering ten days ago than it is today. A party of our hunters was defeated by the Blackfeet on the 12th inst. There were two men killed, all their beaver stolen, many of their traps lost, and the ammunition of several of them, and also seven of our horses. We set out in pursuit of the Indians but unfortunately could not overtake them. We have recovered forty-four traps and three horses, which we brought back here, and we hope to find a few more traps.

This unfortunate affair has quite discouraged our hunters, who are unwilling to hunt anymore here. There will start out tomorrow, however, a party of thirty who are all *gens a gage* [armed men], fourteen *loues* [hired men] and sixteen French. They go to the place where the others were defeated. I shall give them only three traps each, not deeming it prudent to risk more, especially since they are not to separate and half are to remain in camp.

The party which was defeated consisted of eleven persons and eight or nine of them were absent tending their traps when the savages pounced upon the camp. The two persons killed are James Chique [Cheeks], and one Haire [Ayres], an *engage* [employee] of Messrs Crow [Crooks] and McLannell [McLellan] whom Messrs Silvester [Chouteau] and Auguste [Chouteau] had equipped to hunt on shares. Besides these two there are missing young Hulle who was of the same camp, and Flyharte [Freehearty] and his men who were camped about two miles farther up. We have found four traps belonging to these men and the place where they were pursued by the savages, but we have not yet found the place where they were killed.

In the camp where the first two men were killed we found a Blackfoot who had also been killed, and upon following their trail we saw that another had been dangerously wounded. Both of them, if the wounded man dies, came to their death at the hands of Chique for he alone defended himself.

This unhappy miscarriage causes us a considerable loss, but I do not propose on that account to lose heart. The resources of this country in beaver fur are immense. It is true that we shall accomplish nothing this spring, but I trust that we shall next autumn. I hope between now and then to see the Snake and Flathead Indians. My plan is to induce them to stay here, if possible, and make war upon the Blackfeet so that we may take some prisoners and send back one with propositions of peace—which I think can easily be secured by leaving traders among them below the Falls of the Missouri. Unless we can have peace with these [malefactors] or unless they can be destroyed, it is idle to think of maintaining an establishment at this point.

Assure Madame Chouteau of my most sincere esteem as well as your dear children and believe me always your devoted

PIERRE MENARD

We are daily expecting to see the Blackfeet here and are desirous of meeting them.

5

Significant by-products of the fur trade in Montana included the detailed mapping of terrain and the establishment of trails through the wilderness. The diary of Alexander Ross, a clerk for the Hudson's Bay Company, illustrated the manner in which geographical knowledge increased as a result of the search for furs. In 1824 Ross led a caravan through the mountains of western Montana to establish a new post in the Snake River country. His journal depicted some of his dedicated labors as he explored this forbidding but beautiful area, a part of which — Ross' Hole — is named in his honor.

MARCH 11, 1824: . . . . Late in the evening, when our hunters who had been in advance of the camp, arrived, they had a sad story to tell. "We have been," they said, "at the end of the river; our traveling in that direction is at an end; the mountains surround us in all directions and are impassable; the snows everywhere beyond the banks of the river are eight to ten feet deep, and without a single opening or pass to get through, so we may as well turn back without going any further, for we shall have to go by Hell's Gate at last." Discouraging as these accounts were, we made preparations to advance, for I was determined not to turn back while I could advance. . . . [We] proceeded in various directions, often making several traverses through the ice and snow. . . . [Finally] we made a pause and all gazed at the bold and stupendous front before us, which in every direction seemed to bid defiance to our approach. This gloomy and discouraging spot we reached on the 12th of March, 1824, and named the place "The Valley of Troubles,—Ross' Hole."

MARCH 14:—During this day I got six of my most trusty men ready with snowshoes and provisions for four days, and sent them across the mountains to ascertain the depth of the snow, the nature of the pass, and the distance to the other side. . . .

MARCH 15: . . . . With all the difficulties of the undertaking pressing on my mind, I assembled the head men of the different parties, and several others, and we held a council on the steps to be taken in order to cross the mountain. But our council was very discordant. . . . Nettled at their obstinancy, I instantly checked their remarks, by observing that I did not call them together to decide the possibility or the impossibility of making a road, having settled the point already in my own mind, but simply to have their opinions of what they might consider the easiest and best way of doing it, for do it, we must; the sooner we became unanimous, the better. . . .

MARCH 20: Notwithstanding the conflicting opinions regarding the road, and the unlooked for fall of snow, I ultimately succeeded in getting fifty-five men to start with eighty horses, to begin the road. . . . [A]fter a good deal of maneuvering, one man on snowshoes, took the foremost horse by the bridle, while another applied the whip and urged the animal on. When it had made several plunges forward, it became fatigued and would neither lead nor drive; so there we left it in the snow, with nothing to be seen but its head and ears above the surface. The second was then whipped up along side of the first and urged forward and made several plunges further on; and then it lay in the snow some six or seven yards ahead of the other. The third did the same, and so on, until the last, when nothing was to be seen of our eighty horses but a string of heads and ears above the snow. We then dragged out the first, the second, and so on, until we got them all back again. The difficulty in getting them extricated was greater than that in urging them forward; but we were partly recompensed by the novelty of the scene, and the mirth and glee which the operation diffused among the people. All this was very well for a while, but the men and horses soon got tired of it. The single operation for which we only went over all the horses once, occupied nine hours; but we got 580 yards of the road half made, and returned to camp after dusk.

Our first attempt, although an arduous one, produced no very flattering results — scarcely a quarter of a mile of road; but I represented to the people that it was far beyond my expectation; though in my mind the task appeared beyond our means of accomplishing, and so one of the most discouraging undertakings I had ever attempted. And if so hopeless under the shelter of the woods, what would it be in the open plain where the road would be liable, from every blast, wind, drift or snow, to be filled up in as many hours as we would spend in opening it? . . .

MARCH 21: . . . . With various degrees of success, we continued doing more or less each day until the twenty-seventh (27th) when we reached the extremity of the woods. . . . I proposed as an improvement, that there should be a week's respite from labor, in order to lay in a stock of provisions and give time for the snows to decrease in the mountains and on the other side. . . . And as the horse plan did not succeed well, I proposed that we should adopt a more efficient and expeditious plan of proceeding, which was this: We should get mallets and wooden shovels made, two men with mallets would break the crust of the snow, the shovel men would follow and shovel it away, while the greater part would be behind packing the snow down with their feet. Twenty men would be thus employed and the others would guard camp and provide food; and those who worked in the snow one day would remain in camp the next. . . .

Even John Grey seemed to adopt my views, an Iroquois halfbreed, from Montreal, and educated, had no small influence over his countrymen; but he was unfortunately a refractory and base character. . . . I know that Grey was disseminating an ill feeling in the camp, and I was of course preparing, in the isolated position in which I stood, to counteract it. Nothing, however, declared itself openly until the second day in the evening. I had hoped his mechanizations would have failed in their effect; but a little before sunset he came to my tent, saying he wished to see me. I told him to come in, and after sitting down for a few minutes, he said, "He was deputed by the Iroquois, and other men, to let me know that they regretted their promise made at the council, and could not fulfill it, — they were all resolved on abandoning the undertaking, and turning back." He urged that by remaining to make the road, they would lose the spring hunt; and besides they were tired of remaining in the large party, and wished to hunt apart; moreover, they did not come to this country to make roads—they came to hunt beaver. "As for myself," said John, "others may do what they please, but I shall turn back, and I suppose I can do as I please."

. . . I got all out of patience, and interrupted him, by observing, "Whatever you have got to say, John, on your own behalf, I am ready to hear, but not one word on behalf of any one else.

"This," I continued, "savours very much of a combination to defraud the Company and disappoint me. We have all taken the wrong view of things. Every rose," I continued, "has its thorn, John, so has hunting of beaver. You say that by remaining to make the road, you will lose the spring hunt; you will do no such thing; but by turning back, you will not only lose the spring, but the fall hunt. The spring here

is later by a month than in any other part of the country. Your plan is a bad one, even were it your choice, which is not the case. Follow my advice, John. I alone am answerable for your hunts. . . ."

As usual I got up early in the morning, and soon afterwards, sure enough, as he said, John collected, saddled and loaded his horses ready for a start, and every eye in the camp was directed to witness his departure. Affairs had now come to a crisis; the success or failure of the expedition depended on the issue. I was determined now to act, resolutely went up to him, and with a cocked pistol in my hand, ordering him either to pay his debt, or unsaddle his horses and turn them off with the others, or he was a dead man. John seeing no person interfere, unsaddled his horses, and I returned to my tent. Not a word was spoken and here the affair ended. . . .

APRIL 3: At six o'clock in the morning, after an interval of seven days, I set out with forty men and seventy horses, with shovels and mallets for each—John Grey among the number—to resume our labors on the road. After reaching the place, however, the weather turned out so bad with sleet and snow that we were forced to return home without doing much, and what was still worse, many parts of the road already made, were filled up again. This was a very discouraging circumstance, and seemed to cause a good deal of murmuring. . . .

APRIL 8: I set out at sunrise this morning with every man and boy I could muster, leaving five men to guard the camp, and not a murmur was heard. Our success now depending on dispatch, several of the women were in attendance to carry us back at night. During the last day, six men who had volunteered their services, had only made about fifty yards. This day, to our annoyance, there fell a good deal of drizzling rain, which wetted us to the skin; in the evening our clothes froze on our backs and became stiff; but the people, notwithstanding, camped at the edge of the woods, instead of going home, so as to begin early in the morning,—I and another man only returning to the camp. . . .

APRIL 12: At five o'clock in the afternoon of this day, I, with four others, after a day of severe toil, reached the other side on horse back; but being too late, and our horses too tired to return, we encamped there. . . . On the 14th we raised camp, bidding farewell to the "Valley of Sorrows," where we had been kept in anxious suspense for thirty-three days.

Although romantic aspects of the fur trade have captured the popular imagination, the industry was first and foremost a business, and financial success demanded administrative ability and prodigious efforts. Pierre Chouteau, Jr., the principal figure of the St. Louis firm of Pratte, Chouteau, and Co., dominated the Montana trade for many years. Keenly concerned about the smallest detail, Chouteau was kept informed about the employees and affairs of every post under his authority. The following report from J. Archibald Hamilton, bourgeois at Fort Union, is typical of the mass of correspondence which passed between Montana outposts and Chouteau's headquarters in St. Louis.

FORT UNION
JULY 18, 1835

MESSRS. PRATTE CHOUTEAU & CO.

GENT.

I enclose Bill of Lading [for] . . . packs of Buffaloe Robes pr. boats Julia, Jane, Margaret & Isabella under charge of J. E. Brazeau bound for St. Louis to touch at Fort Pierre &c. You will also find an abstract of Furs &c remaining on hand, to be sent forward in September. Inventories, men's accts. and so forth are addressed to Fort Pierre to be looked over. B. Bourdalone No. 21 on the List, who works his passage down, came on here half dead, from a Division of Captain Bonneville's party under Montero, who has been for the last year with 50 men trapping & trading in the Crow country. he tells a woefull tale of the leading features whereof Mr. Tulloch has previously heard from other quarters. The river has been higher during the whole month and to this day than at any period during my long residence here, full to the banks on every part, this I attribute to the incessant and constant rains, no rise generally called the Mountain rise has been decernible. I beg to refer you to Mr. Lamont for Fort Cass & Fort McKenzie news, and am

Gentlemen

Yours Very obediently

(SIGNED) J. ARCHIBALD HAMILTON

──────────────── LIST OF MEN ────────────────

R. Bouche	Good	J. Rouelle	not very good
L. Guinard	Good	J. Praal	good to look after cows
A. Guinard	Not worth his meat	J. B. Leclerc	old
F. Desmay	Not worth his meat	H. Robert	Good
H. Labusiere	willing but slow & sleepy	L. V. Mayotte	Good
E. Labusiere	willing but slow & sleepy	M. Prepey	Good
J. Bolingstone	willing and active, but ignorant	A. Lacroix	Good
M. Helvich	willing and active, but ignorant	A. Solomon	Good
T. Harris	good, but slow	R. Harpan	Good
A. Smith	good, but not very industrious	L. Bacarasse	strong, lazy, often sick

> *While the beaver declined in importance during the 1830's, commerce in buffalo robes rapidly replaced it, and the economic rivalry which characterized the fur trade from its earliest days revived as fierce and unrestrained as ever. Because the robe trade relied upon Indian hunters, the traders introduced all sorts of trickery to win favor and support among the tribes. Liquor, which had particularly demoralizing effects upon Indians, quickly became the most potent trade item. In 1834, the federal government sought to prevent the importation of liquor into the western territories, but the traders devised many ingenious ways of circumventing regulations. Alexander Culbertson, Chouteau's agent at Fort Union, received the following letter which indicated how easily — and usually intentionally — liquor found its way into Indian hands.*

FORT UNION
MAY 5th, 1835

MR. A. CULBERTSON

DEAR SIR

On the 24th ult. our friend Mr. Kipp arrived here in safety with the Fort McKenzie boats and their respective cargoes, had he made the voyage in the accustomed number of days, I think the new equipment would at this time been half way to the Marias river. I have made every exertion to dispatch the Keel Boat with the least possible delay, she has a good crew, is well found, and under the command of J. B. Lafontaine in whose prudence and judgment I have the utmost confidence, nothing doubting that should no unforeseen circumstances interfere, he will make a successful trip. . . .

I have engaged Mr. Harvey for another year having a high opinion of his integrity and bravery (the latter a very desireable quality in this wild country). he professes his willingness to render himself useful in any and every way that you may direct. I hope you will find him a good aid. Mr. J. B. Moncrevie has been five years in the employ of the company and for the last 18 months has had charge of the Stores here, he has moreover considerable medical & surgical skill, he is conversant with the routine of business here & I trust you will find his assistance valuable; he has perhaps too much confidence in his own powers, there is scarcely anything he will not undertake, and it would be [a] mirical if he universally succeeded, he has many good qualities has rendered himself very useful here & his faults are very venial. . . .

The two seasons in which Mr. Kipp has conducted the Blackfoot trade the results have been favourable far exceeding other years, you have had opportunity to profit by his long experience in the Indian trade & I feel assured have not failed to improve it; a very valuable outfit is selected for you amounting at St. Louis prices to $11200 & upwards without any charge for commission or transportation. . . .

The company is desirous to push the robe trade in order to attach the various nations in your District to the Missouri. they are aware a considerable portion of cloth & Blankets must be supplied although the only profitable part of the trade is made in beads, ammunition & Tobacco, for Liquor cannot be obtained on any terms without open war with the President & his army and risking forcible expulsion from the country.

I send you two Barrels of Alcohol and six of wine. make the most of it and do not sell a single drop of it to the men, we have long ceased to do it here; explain to the Indians that our supply of liquor would have been larger had not the Steam Boat been kept here all winter for lack of water, and consequently unable to return here in time sufficient for this outfit which is necessarily sent away at this early date to avoid a rencontre with the Crows. Should the Crow Indians come near you again this summer do not spare them tooth or nail. . . .

In the article of white beads we are sadly deficient and as you may find a supply thereof absolutely [necessary], I would suggest your sending down here in the fall all your spare horses under charge of some trustworthy person (no one better than Mr. Harvey if you can spare him when your first trade is over) and whatever is now wanting shall be furnished so far as your requests can be complied with. I would not advise your keeping more horses than are requisite for the use of the Fort. Horses are but of little value here, 12 or 15 Robes is the most we can get for them but I know in your Piegan trade you will be compelled to take a few horses & I believe you would have more difficulty in keeping them than we have here. . . .

Sell traps cheap to Indians say two Robes each rather than loan them. Beaver packs should not go under the press. Articles in great demand by Indians should not be sold to the men. . . .

As the Beaver trade for the last three years has been regularly declining notwithstanding every facility & encouragement we have given the Piegans, it appears to me that our sheet anchor will be the Robe trade and by encouraging the Blood, Blackfeet & others to make Robes, articles which they now obtain as luxuries will become necessaries and they will be compelled to remain on the Missouri in order to procure them. Rats are a poor trade, those you have sent down this year will scarcely sell at 10¢ each.

As the present fort will scarcely last over the present year select a place suitable for renewing it: Mr. Kipp strongly recommends the mouth of the Marias River, examine the spot and report thereon, there are some hundred logs of fine timber I understand lying there, and an abundant supply can be obtained a few miles up the river and floated down if a boom were thrown across the width of the Marias, if possible employ your spare hands when Indians have left you, preparatory to this object. I presume it has been subject of conversation between you and Mr. Kipp and that you are in possession of his view & the advantages attending the site he recommends. . . .

I will take care some newspapers will be forwarded you in the Fall. Mr. Hamilton and Mr. Kipp have this instant joined me in drinking your health with best wishes that every success may attend you, I know that you deserve it and I hope you may attain it and believe me to be

DEAR SIR

Very truly yours
&c &c
(Signed)

Severely handicapped by inadequate appropriations and insufficient authority, the Indian Service was unable to check the excesses of the fur traders in their commerce with the tribes. Moreover, the patronage system frequently subjected personnel to the whims of partisan advantage. As a result, even the most sincere and dedicated public servant was likely to become discouraged. A typical example is the case of John F. A. Sanford, who served from 1826 to 1834 at the Mandan Subagency, then the most remote outpost of federal authority. Although initially conscientious about his responsibilities, years of inadequate funds and support caused Sanford's enthusiasm to wane as this frustrated report to Superintendent William Clark indicated.

SAINT LOUIS
JULY 26, 1833

GEN. WM CLARK
SUPERINTENDENT IND. AFF.
SIR:

I have just returned from visiting the remote tribes on the upper Missouri to communicate to you in a brief manner the situation of affairs in that remote region.

The Arikara's have abandoned the Missouri river since last fall and where they are gone to or where they are at present I am unable to say. I could not learn from either their friends or enemies. But it is presumed that they are some place in the Black Hills or on the Great Platte. During the last winter a war party belonging to that nation came on the Yellowstone below the Big Horn where they fell in with those men belonging to the Fur Co. who they treacherously killed.

Two of these men had been dispatched from Fort Cass (a new Fort mouth of Big Horn) in the morning with the expert to go on to Fort Union (mouth of Yellowstone). The third was a free man, a veteran trapper, who was accompanying the other as far as a camp of white hunters some short distance below the Fort. They scalped them and left part of the scalps of each tied to poles on the grounds of the murder. Large party of Crows went in pursuit of them the same evening or the next day but could not overtake them. The names of the men killed are Rose, Menard & Glap. The same party killed another young man this spring by the name of Mitchell. There are probably some others, but these were all that I knew when I left that country.

Another party of Arikara's came into a camp of hunters this spring, eat with them, etc. At a concerted signal they all rose gave the yell & succeeded in running off all the horses belonging to the hunters, who however succeeded in making three of their young men prisoners. One of these three they sent after the party to tell them if the horses were not returned immediately they would put to death their prisoners. The party laughed at them, supposing that they would not dare to put their threat in execution. The horses were not given up & they killed those they had in possession—Good!! Is it not time that the government should put in execution some of their numerous repeated threats against the band of robbers & Murder[er]s?

I had a talk with the Crows made them a small present as usual. Gave a large sized medal to the principal Chief (Rottin Belly). They are as friendly as ever, but complain much of the whites being permitted to trap Beaver in their country. They say their country is over run with trappers who distroy everthing before them. They say if it is not stopped it will be productive of mischief between us. I told them to wait for awhile & I would see what the Govt. would do, for myself, I had not the means, else the trappers would long since have been out of their country. When the Indians became acquainted with the value of the fur & know the use of the trap to have traders in their country it is both just & polite that the trappers should be kept out of it. . . .

The Blackfeet have killed only 18 or 20 the last winter but who they are I can't say. They kill them generally to the S.W. of their country, but they are all Americans. This is not greater than usual. This does not surprise me at all, as long as whites are trapping in that country it will be the case. The Blackfeet chiefs have told me that I must never expect anything else so long as the whites were trapping in their country. They

said if "You will send traders into our country we will protect them," that they will, "But for your trappers — NEVER."

Since 18 months a trading post has been established (the first that ever was) in their country where they come to trade amicably. It is the first attempt ever made by American citizens to trade with them, and thus far has succeeded very well. They are very numerous & inhabit a rich region for furred animals. It is now the best East of the Rocky Mountains. It has been reported to me that the traders of the Hudson Bay Co. come within our lines. Its for the purpose of trading with those Indians who formerly traded with them. I should like to know what course I must pursue in this matter, whether take them, their property, or what? It is correctly the duty of the Government to protect its citizens from the competitions of Foreigners in their country particularly when the one pays an enormous duty & the other none at all.

As it regards the relation of the Indian tribes or Nations towards each other, I will only say that they are (as usual) at war with each other, & will always continue so. They are hereditary foes and the facility with which they procure food gives them ample leisure to indulge in their hate & propensity for war. It is as well so, as otherwise as their country. I once was a pipe bearer amongst them and patched up a peace frequently (as others do sometimes & are doing) but the clouds of smoke has hardly time to disappear before a war party was out expecting to find their enemies off guard. Finding that it availed nothing, but that I was in a fair way to get *hammered,* for my parental advice, I thru up my vocation. . . .

The Indian trade has not been as good this year as the last.

This comprises everthing necessary for the Government to know. And indeed so I hardly believe that any part of it is absolutely necessary, for I cannot & do not believe that she will ever support her citizens in that country. There has been to many reports of murder here for this to have any effect. I might have enlarged this to a considerable size, but of what avail.

With Great Respect
I am yr. obt. serv.

JOHN F. A. SANFORD
Asst. Ind. Aff. on the head
Water Upper Missouri

Early Indian agents frequently did little more than make speeches and present gifts to the tribes under their authority, both the speeches and the presents being aimed at securing the Indians' trade and allegiance, convincing them of the superiority of white civilization and preventing hostilities, so the fur trade might be carried on peaceably. By the 1850's, future trends in Indian-white relations were already visible, and the integrity of Indian lands emerged as a much more important focus for concern. For example, when Upper Missouri Agent A. J. Vaughan distributed the following annuities to the Crows in 1854, his purpose was to cement agreement to the recent Treaty of Fort Laramie so that white emigrants might safely cross Indian lands.

We the undersigned Chiefs and Head men of the Crow Indians, parties to the Treaty of Fort Laramie executed on the 17th September 1851 do hereby acknowledge to have received from Alfred J. Vaughan Indian Agent for the upper Missouri Agency the following articles of Merchandise, Provisions, & Ammunition Amounting to Three Thousand Three Hundred & Twenty 62/100 Dollars in full of our proporting (proportion) of the Annuity . . . stipulated to be paid under the 7th Article of said Treaty. . . . having signed our receipts this 18 day of September 1854.

15	pairs 3 pt Scarlet Mack Blkts
40	pairs 3 pt White
91¾	yds Surliest Scarlet Cloth
100	yds Surliest Blue Cloth
2077½	yds Unbleached Shirtings
3473¼	yds Calico
63	Flannell Shirts
1½	Doz. Cotton Shawls
2½	Doz blk Silk cravats
22½	lbs. Vermillion
2942	yds Geo Stripes checks & plaid
1156¼	yards Ticking
211½	lbs Wht Beads
104½	lbs Blue Beads
17½	lbs Ruby Beads
70	lbs Black Beads
45	North West Guns
3	Doz Scissors
12	Hoes

21	Doz Knives
1½	M Gun Flints
2	Doz Fry pans
1	M Needles
½	Gross Gun Worms
77½	lbs Brass kettles
24	Files
1	String Bells
4	Doz Looking Glasses
2	Nests Jap'd Kettles
1	Gro Buttons
1	Box Tobacco
25	Bags Flour
2	Bags Rice
10	Bags Coffee
35	lbs Hoop Iron
25	Bags Sugar
10	Bags Corn
5	Kegs Powder

BAT SAI ET SA KATCH   his X mark

BU - ROOK US   his X mark

CHEE SEE POOSH   his X mark

IST-A-NAK-A SHOOSH   his X mark

WITNESS:

R. MELDRUM, INTR.

JAS. H. CHAMBERS

F. V. HAYDEN

ALFRED J. VAUGHAN

IND. AGT.

Despite the record of the unscrupulous trader, the fur trade provided a setting within which contacts between whites and Indians could take place in a natural and amicable manner. Free trappers frequently lived with the tribes, adopting their clothing and many of their customs, and sometimes taking an Indian wife. Others, such as Alexander Culbertson, who rose to become chief agent for all of Chouteau's posts on the Upper Missouri and Yellowstone Rivers, found acceptance and even friendship because of their fair treatment of the Indians. The government frequently took advantage of the Indians' esteem for these men. In 1853 Washington Territorial Governor Isaac I. Stevens appointed Culbertson as a special agent to urge upon Washington officials the importance of entering into a treaty with the Blackfeet. Culbertson's report to Stevens on the condition of the Indians on the Upper Missouri follows.

The Blackfoot nation occupy the country from the Rivers Assiniboine and Sascatchawine on the northern boundary, to the base of the Rocky Mountains on the West and South — thence East down the banks of the Missouri on both sides as far as Muscle Shell river, and sometimes as far as Milk River. They are divided into three distinct tribes each about eaqual in numbers say 400 total amounting to 1200 lodges which computing eight souls to the lodge would make 9600 persons. Of these 2700 may be said to be Warriors, being fit to bear arms, from the age of fifteen upwards. The above tribes are known by the name of Piegans, Blackfeet, and Blood Indians.

The Grosventres of the Prairie also reside amongst these people, and although speaking a different language have been living with them on friendly terms for many years beyond the recollection of anyone living. They number about 400 lodges, and the population per lodge is much the same as the others. These Indians intermarry with the other tribes, but seldom if ever encamp with them. Each follows the Buffaloe, & hunts separate from the others, tho when they meet the greatest harmony exists and tokens of friendship are exchanged. By long residence and frequency of communication, many of the Grosventres have learned to Speak the Blackfoot language and thereby make themselves understood, also their family relationship tends greatly to preserve the good terms on which they have heretofore lived.

The bands known by the name of Piegan inhabit the country bordering on the Missouri and its tributaries on both sides of the river. The Blackfeet and Blood Indians visit the Forts of the Hud Bay Co in the summer, but move to the Missouri in the fall and winter at or near Fort Benton. The residence of the Grosventre of the Prairie both in the fall and winter is principally on Milk River and the Bears Paw Mountain. The last named tribe being

at peace with the Assiniboines enables them to come nearer the borders of those Indians than the others.

The entire country of the Blackfeet is perhaps the best buffaloe country in the N.W. Territory — indeed there is seldom a season of scarcity — and possessing numbers of horses they are usually well supplied with meat. In the winter season they apply their time to procuring & dressing the hides of Buffaloe, by which they are to supply themselves with Guns Am[munition] . . . from the white traders. The number of Horses belonging to these Indians is great — some owning 70 to 100 head each — others less — upon the whole I should imagine 15 head to each lodge to be a fair average.

Their country throughout is particularly adapted to the raising of Stock—as the grass appears to be more nutritious than in the other parts of the district. The seasons are generally milder than further down the Missouri—and I have no hesitation in saying that horned cattle, Horses, & Sheep would thrive if well taken care of.

Since the year 1838 no Small Pox nor any other infectious or contagious disease has appeared among them. At the time mentioned however, a great many Blackfeet were destroyed by the Small Pox, and even yet have not recovered from its effects. The absence of disease of this description is mainly to be attributed to their isolated residence & infrequent communication with White Emigrants.

Of all the western Indians these appear to be the most warlike—indeed with the Young men war seems to be their principal occupation & amusement. At all seasons and times — parties are out in Various directions—mostly upon the Assiniboins, Crow, & Cree Indians; from whom they steal numbers of horses, and

Kill men whenever an opportunity occurs. Should any whites turn up on their warpath—if not numerous enough to defend—they would undoubtedly share the same fate.

The implements used in War are Guns, Bow & Arrows, war Clubs, Battle Axes & Lances—the use of all of which having been so often explained by different writers, it is unnecessary for me to mention. They shoot well, ride well; are wary, energetic & Savage — consequently are likely to succeed whenever anything like a favorable opportunity presents itself, and being more numerous than surrounding tribes have decidedly the advantage.

The same instruments used in war serve to hunt, tho most of the Buffaloe (their principal Game) are Killed on horseback with Bow and Arrow—Smaller animals on foot with Guns. Polygamy is general amongst them, having from [2] to ten wives, seldom less than two;—women forming a portion of their wealth, and being of great service in dressing skins, culinary departments &c.

Regarding any means that might be brought into opperation for the bettering of their condition and that of the Various tribes with which they are at war, I cannot with confidence advance any decided opinion. Nevertheless something might and should be done. Most of the tribes included in the treaty at Laramie in 1851 were previously nearly as bad as they in all respects, and the consequence of the treaty has been to subdue them, making them friendly to each other and respect the whites. It is therefore but fair to infer that some such course pursued with the Blackfeet would be attended by a like result. I think also if a portion of each tribe was taken to the States, shown the principal cities—holding council with their Great Father the President, and convincing themselves of the power of the Government to reward & Punish—this with an annual donation of ten or twelve thousand dollars in goods, judiciously distributed . . . councils held with them would no doubt in a short time bring them to as orderly a state as possible, compatible with the present life of this wild people. As to Agricultural opperations they are not to be thought of as long [as] Game is abundant. Indians will not work unless their necessities compel them — it is beneath their dignity — and it is evident the day is yet far off when the Blackfeet will turn the Swords into the Ploughshare and make the wilderness bud & blossom like the Rose.

Under the system of commerce devised by the American Fur Company, traders resided at established posts and waited for the Indians to bring in their furs and robes. Life on these posts was singularly dull and uninteresting with few diversions to enliven the routine of baling and pressing furs, preparing the winter express to St. Louis, receiving Indians, keeping records, and cutting wood. Such is the life described in the journal of Andrew Dawson, an employee of Pierre Chouteau at Fort Benton during the 1850's.

SEPTEMBER 28 [1854]—About noon much to the delight of all in the Fort, Mr. Culbertson, Lady, and three men arrived from Fort Union. Received him with a proper salute. Hunter and man got back with the meat of two deer. Game very scarce — 1290 Dobbies [adobe bricks] today — 4 loads wood. . . .

OCTOBER 2 — Busy today putting up another equipment to send to Flat Heads and traded the man's gold that arrived yesterday $160 in all. We hear the FlatHeads have still a good lot of Beaver and some gold, and in the morning shall send there the equipment put up today. . . .

FRIDAY 13 — Again clear and considerably warmer. Had Dobbie makers make up their mud into bricks and bring in all their tools as we have to stop making any more from the lateness of the season and are anxious to get what we have made put on our building. . . .

SATURDAY [NOVEMBER] 4 — Fine pleasant weather, at length finished the dobbie work of our two story Kitchen and now all our fears about this building are ended as the Carpenter work can go along smoothly at any time. Traded a little meat and a few Robes from the Indians that arrived yesterday also a few more came today from whom got some more horses and a little more meat. . . .

NOVEMBER 19 — Waggon and Cart arrived loaded with Meat from the Gros Ventres, Michels two Waggons arrived loaded with 209 Robes etc. etc.

Munroe with his two Waggons arrived loaded with Meat and Robes so that notwithstanding the day this has been one of the busiest we have ever passed in the Country. Put up two equipments to start in the morning, one with Michel to his Camp and another to the Gros Ventres. . . .

FRIDAY [DECEMBER] 29 — Wind throughout the past night so very strong as to alarm a good many of us. Even our solid Dobbie walls shook under it, and the whole of the pickets on the SW side were blown down. Put these up again but the wind still continues so strong as to prevent our other out door work. . . .

TUESDAY [JANUARY] 2 [1855] — More snow fell through-out the night and Ther. at 10° below zero and on this we have not a stick of firewood in the Fort—Late to recover our Oxen and it was dark before we got any wood home. Our Blackfeet also keep hanging on and begging much to our annoyance. . . .

TUESDAY [JANUARY] 9 — A few lousey Pagans from Little Robes band arrived with a horse and a Robe or two to trade and shortly afterwards Cadot arrived with the good news of having found the Oxen and that they and the Wagn. would be here towards evg. but in this latter party our hopes were only raised to be blasted—The Oxen and men arrived but the Wagn. remains upset at the Teton. and thus again is this valuable lot abandoned to Wolves and Inds. . . .

THURSDAY [FEBRUARY] 1 — Tiresome times all sick Hauled two loads fire wood. . . .

MONDAY [FEBRUARY] 5 — Dull times and very mild. Our black spotted Cow gave us a calf last night. In the evg. a party arrived from war with a number of horses. . . .

FRIDAY [February] 23 — Unable to find our Oxen till too late to start Wagn. for Revais [Rivet] — About noon three men arrived from Ft. Union with three horses—Mr. Culbertson and party arrived there safe 25th Ultimo. Bufl. plenty and good prospects for trade in the lower country, but no news lower than Ft. Union.

MONDAY [MARCH] 5 — Put up a few goods for Pagan Camp and sent them per M. Champaign in an Ox Cart. Some few N. Blood Indians arrived with a good many Robes say 25 or 30 packs, every one of whom went to opposition Fort, much to our chagrin. . . .

SATURDAY [APRIL] 7 — North Pagans, some Blackfeet & Blood Indians arrived and are camped on Teton so

that the Fort is full of loafers. A small party headed by the White Cow against the Bank arrived from whom traded 105 Robes on order and 73 Robes they brought—A wagn. also arrived from Michel with 300 Robes. . . .

MONDAY [APRIL] 8 — Another busy day trading with these Indians 441 Robes.

TUESDAY [APRIL] 10 — At it again but the trade is now about over — 170 Robes today Revais [Rivet] also arrived with 246 Robes he traded with North Pagans at Clarks Houses. . . .

FRIDAY [SEPTEMBER] 21 — Mr Culbertson started to the Piegan Camp with two waggons to trade for meat to feed the hands on the Cordelle when the boats shall have arrived. Mr Jackson who was Sent by the Commission as a messenger to the Blood Indians in the North returned to day about 3 o'clock. Mr Bird returned with him — He was unable to find the Principal Camp of the Bloods but about 8 miles from the Fort overtook a small party of them. Three Piegans came to the Fort to day. In the evening the party of Bloods seen by Mr Jackson (consisting of three men & three women) arrived at the Fort. When on the hill back of the Fort they called a halt — commenced firing their guns & raised their colors and spread them to the breese. Mr. Monroe went forth to meet them and to extend to them the hospitality of the Fort. They report their encampment still a long ways off but making their way in this direction. The fore-noon was clear and pleasant but towards night it clouded up and looks much like rain. This morning per request of Col Cummings I took a letter to Mr B De Rochi Bourgeois of Fort Cambell authorising him (if he desired it) to send out to the Indians to trade for *"Meat"*. An important event which I forgot to mention transpired to day. It was that a yellow bitch belonging to the Fort had a fine litter of puppies. Who know but that some of them which now lie with their eyes unopened *may* in their day prove them-selves worthy of the travoise. About sun set it commenced to rain but soon ceased. . . .

SUNDAY [SEPTEMBER] 23 — This day has been remarkably bright clear & pleasant. . . . It was as quiet as usual in the fort during the whole day and though it was the Sabath not an inmate of the fort attended Church. Late in the evening some four or five Blood Indians arrived from the North. They paid their respects to their "Big Chief" Col Cumming soon after dark and indulged themselves freely in the use of *weed.* . . .

TUESDAY [SEPTEMBER] 25 — The wind blew hard all last night but lulled this morning just as *old Sol* peeped over the hills. The day was very fine the sun shining forth with unusual brightness making quite a contrast between today and yesterday as regards the weather. Early this morning Mr Monroe sent an Indian to drive up the horses to send for a load of wood. It was sometime before they could be gotten up but they finally came, when Henry & Demos took the wagon and George the horse cart and brought in wood from the Teton. The two horses sent out a couple of days ago to the Marias for fresh meat was brought back today well packed with fat cow meat which was very acceptable as we have been living on dried meat for several days passed. The Indians who went out after meat also returned today well supplied. They killed I learn one hundred and seventy six cows. If this aint slaughtering buffalo by the wholesale you can "take my hat", but my advise is "To go it while you are young" for when you "get old" you will have no buffalo to kill as Gov. Stevens railroad hands will consume them all. It being his project to feed his hands upon them so soon as the road goes into opperation which in the opinion of "your humble Servant" *will never be.* . . .

FRIDAY [FEBRUARY] 15 [1856] — A large party of Blackfeet arrived under their chiefs the Old Sunn, Big Sun, Bull Sitting Down and The tail that goes up the Hill, being their first formal visit since the Canon was fired on them. They were well received firstly by the fort, and secondly by the Agent who made them a very handsome present. Traded from them 300 Robes and from the Gros Ventres 200 — a pretty busy day. . . .

WEDNESDAY [MARCH] 19 — All quiet about the Fort for the first time for many a day. Arranged Stores for the reception of Comp Wagons and preparatory to making Packs. Sawing plank for a new Boat. Cadot arrived from Wagons and started back again, they being much closer than we had anticipated. . . .

MONDAY [APRIL] 14 — Very high wind. Commenced on the only Boat we intend to build this year 85 ft by 12½. Hauled up to Fort our last years Boat but the wind blew too strong for us to bring up the large Keel. Had her cleaned, however. . . .

THURSDAY [MAY] 1 — Set 8 Men to Caulking New Boat and got through with half of it. Put up our Tongues in Bags, 1581 in all for this year, but we have sold some 300 to different parties. Hauled one load of wood. Sent after and got 6 loads fresh meat. . . .

SUNDAY [MAY] 11 — Fine day and got through with loading all our Boats satisfactorily. Men sleep on Board and tomorrow intend making an early start with our 1540 Packs and three Boats.

MOUNDAY [MAY] 12 — Fine day. Our Three boats started for the Yellowstone with heavy loads and full crews. had the fort cleaned out, received a band of Blood Indians and traded a fiew robes and one mare from a Pagan. . . .

Invitations from the Indians themselves prompted Jesuit missionary Pierre-Jean deSmet to establish St. Mary's Mission in the Bitterroot Valley in 1841. In a book published two years later, deSmet described the enthusiastic reception the Jesuits received from the Flatheads and their neighboring tribes. After the great missionary's departure in 1843, however, relations between the remaining Jesuits and the Indians deteriorated and by 1850 conditions forced the fathers to close the mission. Despite this discouragement, the Jesuits ultimately returned to St. Mary's and succeeded in establishing missions to many other Montana tribes.

The 1st of November — All Saints' Day — after having celebrated the Holy Sacrifice under a large poplar tree, we proceeded on our journey through a defile of about six miles. At the ford of the Great Clark's Fork, we met two encampments of the Kalispel tribe, who having heard of our approach, had come thither to see us. Men, women and children, ran to meet us, and pressed our hands with every demonstration of sincere joy. The chief of the first camp was called Chalax. I baptized twenty-four children in his little village, and one young woman a Koetenaise, who was dying. The chief of the second camp was named Hoytelps; his band occupied thirty huts.

I spent the night amongst them; and, although they had never seen me before, they know all the prayers that I had taught the Flat Heads on my first journey. The fact is, on hearing of my arrival in the mountains, they deputed an intelligent young man to meet me, and who was also gifted with a good memory. Having learned the prayers and canticles, and such points as were most essential for salvation, he repeated to the village all that he had heard and seen. He had acquitted himself of his commission so well, and with so much zeal, that he gave instructions to his people during the course of the winter. The same desire for information concerning religion, had communicated itself to the other small camps, and with the same cheering success. It was, as you can easily imagine, a great consolation for me to hear prayers addressed to the great God, and his praises sung in a desert of about three hundred miles extent, where a Catholic priest had never been before. They were over-joyed when they heard that I hoped before long to be able to leave a Missionary amongst them. . . .

It is amidst the poor tribes of these isolated mountains that the fire of divine grace burns with ardor. Superstitious practices have disappeared. . . . Speak to these Savages of heavenly things; at once their hearts are inflamed with divine love; and immediately they go seriously about the great affair of their salvation. . . .

They came from all parts, and from great distances, to meet me on my way, and presented all their young children and dying relatives for baptism. Many followed me for whole days, with the sole desire of receiving instructions. Really our hearts bled at the sight of so many souls who are lost for the want of religion's divine and saving assistance. Here again may we cry out with the Scripture: "The harvest indeed is great, but the laborers are few." What Father is there in the Society whose zeal will not be enkindled on hearing these details? And where is the Christian who would refuse his mite to such a work as that of the "Propagation of the Faith?" that precious pearl of the Church, which procures salvation to so many souls, who otherwise would perish unaided and forever. During my journey, which lasted forty-two days, I baptized 190 persons, of whom 26 adults, sick, or in extreme old age; I preached to more than two thousand Indians. . . .

Crossing a beautiful plain near the Clarke or Flat Head river, called the Horse prairie, I heard that there were 30 lodges of the Sklazy or Koetenay tribe, at about two day's journey from us. I determined whilst awaiting the descent of the skiff, which could only start six days later, to pay them a visit, for they had never seen a priest in their lands before. Two half breeds served as my guides and escorts on this occasion. We gallopped and trotted all the day, travelling a distance of 60 miles. . . .

They assembled immediately on my approach; when I was about twenty yards from them, the warriors presented their arms, which they had hidden until then under their buffalo robes. They fired a general salute which frightened my mule and made her rear and prance to the great amusement of the savages. They then defiled before me, giving their hands in token of friend-ship and congratulation. I observed that each one lifted his hand to his forehead after having presented it to me. I soon convoked the council in order to inform them of the object of my visit. They unanimously declared them-selves in favour of my religion, and adopted the beautiful custom of their neighbours, the Flat Heads, to meet night and morning for prayers in common. I assembled them that very evening for this object and gave them a long instruction on the principal dogmas of our faith. The next day, I baptized all their children and nine of their adults. . . .

I left the Koetenay village about 12 O'clock, accompanied by twelve of these warriors and some half-blood Crees, whom I had baptized in 1840. They wished to escort me to the entrance of the large Flat Head lake, with the desire of giving me a farewell feast; a real banquet of all the good things their country produced. The warriors had gone on ahead and dispersed in every direction, some to hunt and others to fish. The latter only succeeded in catching a single trout. The warriors returned in the evening with a bear, goose and six swan's eggs. *Sed quid hoc inter tantos.*

The fish and goose were roasted before a good fire, and the whole mess was soon presented to me. Most of my companions preferring to fast, I expressed my regret at it, consoling them however by telling them that God would certainly reward their kindness to me. A moment after we heard the last hunter returning, whom we thought had gone back to camp. Hope shone on every countenance. The warrior soon appeared laden with a large elk; and hunger that night was banished from the camp. Each one began to occupy himself; some cut up the animal, others heaped fuel on the fire, and prepared sticks and spits to roast the meat. The feast which had commenced under such poor auspices continued a great part of the night. The whole animal, excepting a small piece that was reserved for my breakfast, had disappeared before they retired to sleep. This is a sample of savage life. The Indian when he has nothing to eat does not complain, but in the midst of abundance he knows no moderation. The stomach of a savage has always been to me a riddle.

The plain that commands a view of the lake is one of the most fertile in the mountainous regions. The Flat

Head river runs through it and extends more than 200 miles to the North East. It is wide and deep, abounding with fish and lined with wood, principally with the cotton, aspen, pine and birch. There are beautiful sites for villages, but the vicinity of the Black Feet must delay for a long while the good work, as they are only at two day's march from the great district occupied by these brigands, from whence they often issue to pay their neighbours predatory visits. A second obstacle would be the great distance from any post of the Hudson Bay Company; consequently the difficulty of procuring what is strictly necessary. . . .

On the 16th of April, after bidding adieu to my travelling companions, I started early in the morning, accompanied by two Canadians and two savages. That evening we encamped close to a delightful spring, which was warm and sulphurous; having travelled a distance of about fifty miles. When the savages reach this spring they generally bathe in it. They told me that after the fatigues of a long journey they find that bathing in this water greatly refreshes them. I found here ten lodges of the Kalispel tribe; the chief, who was by birth of Pierced Nose tribe, invited me to spend the night in his wigwam, where he treated me most hospitably. . . .

Both missionaries and Indian agents (but not the fur traders) shared a common desire to end traditional warfare between the tribes, settle them on reservations, and introduce an agrarian way of life. Efforts in this direction were particularly successful with the Pend Oreilles, who were members of the Flathead confederation. Under provisions of the Stevens Treaty of 1855, the Pend Oreille settled on the Jocko Reservation near St. Ignatius Mission, and, guided by the Jesuits, adopted some aspects of an agricultural life. Nevertheless, both tradition and necessity dictated continued reliance upon the wintertime buffalo hunt. In 1860, a band of Assiniboine and Cree warriors savagely attacked the Pend Oreilles under Alexander as they moved eastward toward the buffalo hunting grounds. John Owen reported his efforts to relieve tribal distress in a letter to E. R. Geary, Superintendent of Indian Affairs for the northwestern territories.

OFFICE FLATHEAD AGENCY
FORT OWEN
BITTER ROOT VALLEY W. T.
DEC. 21, 1860

SIR

I ret d last Evening after an absence of two weeks to the Jocko Reservation.

While there I heard of Alexanders approach with his defeated & shattered camp. I went to see him. My feelings were shocked at the scene his camp presented. Women with their children hung upon their backs had traversed the whole 400 Miles on foot from the point on Milk River where they had been defeated. They were literally Exhausted & Worn out. The loss of horses they sustained by the attack of the Assinnaboines & Crees was so great that most of their Camp Equipage had to be abandoned on the battlefield. They were destitute of provisions & clothing. I immediately ordered the Ind. Dept. pack train from the Jocko to this place for stores. I issued them four head of oxen.

Alexander had lost a Son in the fight, a young Man of Much promise some 20 yrs. of age. He found his sons

body in a horribly Mutilated State, scalped, striped, & heart Cut out. Some of the Wounded have since died. Dr Mullan was prompt & Efficient in sending assistance to the Wounded that succeeded in reaching here. They Numbered some Eighteen. Operations of a difficult Nature had to be performed, Extracting Arrow points, Bullets &c &c. The Pond's Orilles had twenty killed twenty-five wounded (five of the latter since died) and lost 290 head of horses.

Mr Ogden a ½ breed who was one of the party gave me a thrilling & interesting account of the attack & the battle. He says the Assinnaboines numbered some two hundred or thereabouts. They were a war party all on foot & unincumbered with families, Lodges, horses, &c &c. Nothing in the world saved the complete and Entire Extermination of Alexanders camp but the amt. of plunder the attacking party had come in possession of — the 290 head of horses which they were Eager to secure beyond a doubt.

The Pond's Oreilles Made Every Effort that a brave & gallant band could do to recover some of the animals they had lost. But they were overcome by numbers & had to quietly submit to their fate & beat a retreat toward their far distant home. It was hard. They had just reached the Buffaloe. They were in fine spirits. On the Evening of the night of the attack the tired Camp on bended knees offered their thanks to almighty God for the prospect then before them. Alexander in a short harangue told his camp that here we will Make our winter Meat & return. Secure four fleet horse for tomorrows chase &c &c.

Little did the unsuspecting camp know what awaited them. Before the dawn the camp was surrounded & between the report of the rifle the wailings of the women, the neighing of the horses at the picket & the sheet of fire that Encircled the Camp from the rifles of the attacking party You can form but a slight conception of what followed.

Mr Ogden says it was about one hour before day when the attack was made. Alexanders camp was still asleep. The attacking party approached the Lodges, Cut an opening with the Knife through which they thrust their rifles & discharged their deadly contents. The heart bleeds at the thrilling story. Alexander thirsts for revenge. He talked to me with Moistened Eyes. He says he must visit the sleeping place of his son & people. I tell him I appreciate his feelings. I sympathize deeply with him. I had a long talk with him. I have no doubt myself but that there will be a large war party in the field this Spring. I have had to purchase ammunition for the camp, none having been sent up with the Annuity goods from the East.

JNO OWEN
[Agent to the Flatheads]

Drawn by a sportman's love of adventure, the wealthy and eccentric Englishman, Sir St. George Gore, conceived an elaborate hunting expedition to eastern Montana and Wyoming. In 1854 he outfitted the largest and most lavishly equipped private expedition ever seen in the West. After wintering at Fort Laramie, Gore spent the summer of 1855 along the tributaries of the Yellowstone River. Ultimately his senseless slaughter of large numbers of game aroused the anger of the Indians whose complaints are summarized here by Agent A. J. Vaughan.

FORT UNION
JULY, 1856

SIR:

I had the honor of apprising you by the return of the St. Marys of all matters pertaining to my official duties. Since she left, the entire nation of Assinaboines have assembled at this place showing by every act and action the most unbounded gratitude to their Great Father for the presents which they annualy receive. They are a kind noble and generous people showing every wish and inclination to abide their treaty stipulations and heed their Great Fathers advice. I do assure you Sir, it affords me much pleasure to have the means at my command to bestow upon a people struggling from their barbourous and bemuddled conditions to the habits and maners and customs of the Anglo American. They remained amongst us five days, all was peace and harmony. . . .

The English gentleman [Sir George Gore] whom you granted a pasport to pass in and through the Ind[ian] country will return to your city in a month or so, having been in the Ind. country from the time you granted him a pasport up to the present time. The pasport you granted

him the 24th May 1854, from my construction of the intercourse laws, he has most palpably violated it. He built from his own confession and that of many of his Employees, which was forty-three in number, a fort in the Crow country (same 100 feet square and inhabited the same nine months) carrying on trade and intercourse with the Crow tribe of Inds, trading them all kinds of Ind goods, Powder & Ball.

He states, also his men [state] that he killed 105 Bears and some 2000 Buffalo, Elk, & Deer. 1600, he states, was more than they had any use for, having killed it purely for sport. The Inds have been loud in their complaints at men passing through their country killing and driving off their game. What can I do against so large a number of men coming into a country like this so very remote from civilization; and doing & acting as they please, nothing, I assure you beyond apprising you of the facts on paper. Should I return from the Crow country safe I will avail myself of the earliest opportunity of apprising you of all the particulars of my trip.

Very respectfully your Obt. St.

A. J. VAUGHAN, IND. AGT.

Not only the love of adventure and the desire for wealth drew men to the West; the unknown land also excited interest among the nation's scientists. Subsidized by a small grant from the Smithsonian Institution, in 1850, Princeton graduate Thaddeus Culbertson, a half brother of Alexander Culbertson, made a journey up the Missouri River to collect specimens of animal and plant life and to observe Indian culture. Although he died during the course of his journey, Culbertson's incomplete journal was of sufficient scientific interest to warrant publication by the Smithsonian in its 1850 report.

FRIDAY — JUNE 14 [1850] — We are still in the Big Bend which we entered last night and will not be out of it until we reach the Knife River. . . . This morning we had for snack one of the dainties of this country — the milk gut of buffalo roasted on coals; it tastes somewhat like our white pudding having in it a substance that when cooked has the appearance of their stuffing. Mr. Picotte in speaking of the dislike persons in the states have to such things says that in the north the dung of the reindeer is eaten and very much relished and that he himself has eaten it. It is good because the peculiar weed eaten very much by them is taken out of them before being completely digested. . . .

MONDAY — JUNE 17TH — Yesterday afternoon at 4 Oclock the boat landed at Fort Union having made the trip of 2500 miles in 36 days, 4 hours, the quickest one ever made. We were received very kindly by the gentlemen of the post, Wm E. T. Denig and Ferdinand Culbertson. They showed me quite a good collection of stuffed skins made by them for Prof Baird at the request of my brother. This must have cost them a great deal of labor and considerable expense and they deserve many thanks from the students of natural history for whose benefit this was made.

Fort Union is very much like Fort Pierre in its structure and about the same size, the principal difference being that here they have stone bastions and a cannon mounted above the gate. A room also is built against the wall by the gate, in which they used to trade through a small hole about one foot square in the wall. Now however they trade at the retail store inside of the fort.

The Assiniboines and the Crees are the people principally trading here. The Crees are from the British possessions, and are then called Ke-nis-te-nos; they visit the Missouri but once a year. About six lodges of the Assiniboines are encamped at the opposition fort a few miles below and they were all here when we arrived. . . .

The Assiniboines here are the worst dressed and meanest looking indians I have seen, but this is partly owing to their being in mourning for the young man whom the Crows Killed the other day. The peace was broken in this way; a war party of the A- - attacked some Crows mistaking them for Blackfeet and killed a couple; they tried to settle the difficulty but the Crows killed a young A- - who had strayed from the camp while the negociations were going on and now war is declared fully.

TUESDAY — JUNE 18 — 2 o'CLOCK — I have just returned from a short excursion to Elk Horn prairie about 80 miles from the fort, the object of attraction was the pile of Elk Horns on this prairie. . . .

The report was that all the horns were attached to the head and that the pile was of a wonderful size. The distant view of it, for it was sure like a white monument several miles off, tended to confirm these reports and I thought that here at least there had been no exaggeration. However on close examination I thought it to be no more than 15 feet high and 20 or 25 in circumference, but even this was a wonderful pile to be made exclusively of Elk horns. There was not a single head there but the horns were piled close together to that height, and as there were no heads they probably were all horns that had been shed. What a great number of Elk must have been there to have furnished such a number of horns. As to its origin no certain information can be gained. Old traders say it has been there to their knowledge for 20 years and how much longer they can't tell as old indians say they are ignorant of the time or the occasion of its being made. There were orginally two piles but for several years past these two have been put into one.

The prairie is from 2 to 6 or 10 miles wide on the south side, many miles long & on the south side. It is further remarkable for being the place where the steamer Assiniboine belonging to the company wintered several years ago. She had got this far up and could not get down again because of low water. In the spring she passed down and was burnt, intentionally it is said, below the Mandans. Therefore we are now higher up the Missouri than any other boat has ever been. . . .

WEDNESDAY — JUNE 19 — Ten o'Clock. — Had a long talk this morning with Mr. Clark on the subject of Indian customs. I was surprised to hear what he told me of the language of signs used by nearly all the tribes except the Sious and Assiniboines. It must be as perfect and expressive as the language of mutes with us; by these signs one Indian can tell another the principal events of his whole life and will be perfectly understood. And this does not come from the barrenness of their own language for it is sufficiently expressive, but Mr. Clark thinks it to have originated principally from the fact of the Indians not knowing when they meet a man, whether he be a friend or an enemy; they do not know whether to let him approach or not and by these signs he can learn all about him, though he be too far off to converse with the tongue. It is therefore the language of caution and defence. These signs are beautiful and poetic; the rude figures which we see sometimes on buffalo robes are not mere awkward attempts at ornament, but they are hieroglyphics, as easily read by an intelligent Indian as words by us, and perhaps containing a whole history of some great event.

The Blackfeet do not place their dead on scaffolds but either in a hole well covered to keep off the wolves, or they leave them in the lodge with everything just as it is when they die. In that case the wolves of course eat their bodies very soon; and I am told that in this way the body of nearly every Blackfoot is disposed of. When one of them is in mourning he puts white earth on his head and goes out before his lodge wailing most piteously; as soon as the neighbors see that they all rush to his lodge and take it and everything it contains, leaving him nothing but his horse. The death of a relation is, therefore, a very serious affair, since a man loses all his property as well as his friend. How different with us—where a man frequently gains property with the death of a relative.

A Blackfoot has complete control over his wife; if he finds her unfaithful, he generally cuts her nose off, but he can shoot her down if he chooses to do so, and it is said it is very common to see good-looking young women going about *noseless.* . . .

THURSDAY, JUNE 20 — A large band of buffalo cows with their calves were crossing just above the mouth of the Porcupine, but Mr. Picotte would not allow the men to shoot; we passed very close to them all and it was amusing and touching too, the very great fear they exhibited as they in vain struggled to get up the steep bank. I noticed here for the first time, what I had been told before, that the buffalo grunt almost exactly like a large hog. The men tried to catch some calves with a lasso but did not succeed. The buffalo have been seen in great bands for several days past; last evening probably five hundred were in sight at one time on the river banks. I have seen paths beaten by them which look like traveled roads in a thickly settled country, and paths of this kind are seen at almost every landing. . . .

I really feel very thankful that my life and health have been spared me during this journey. I have reached a point to which few except traders have attained, and I hope that I have gained some valuable information as well as restored my health. But it is a long distance, nearly four thousand miles to my home, and no one can tell what may befall me, but my duty is clear and I hesitate not to go even at the risk of the cholera. Should it please Divine Providence to restore me to my home and my studies, it is my sincere prayer that it may be to employ my powers and my knowledge as a minister of the Gospel.

Huzza for home! Here we are driving at half past three o'clock down stream as fast as steam will let us. Our shouts of farewell have hardly ceased to ring in these old hills that so seldom resound with the voice of the whites, and now for the first time have heard the puff of a steamboat. We stopped at twelve o'clock several miles above Milk River on the southern bank, landed all the freights for Fort Benton and have turned our face homeward. It was a picturesque scene as we rounded to, all the hands on the hurricane deck—the crew singing one of their peculiar songs—the cannon firing and ourselves giving three good hearty cheers while the shore with its green carpet was covered with merchandise—the different families bivuacking under the scattered and venerable trees, and the men who were bound for the Blackfeet, returning our cheers and salute with hearty good will.

A harbinger of the changes that were to come to Montana was evident in increased migration into the Bitterroot Valley during the 1850's. One of the earliest white settlers was John Owen, who purchased St. Mary's Mission from the Jesuits and went into competition with the Hudson's Bay Company. In 1852 Owen hired John F. Dodson, a California-bound emigrant, to work for him at Fort Owen. Dodson's diary recorded aspects of daily life at that remote outpost of white civilization. Its final entry indicates that the tedium of making bricks and mowing hay was fraught with real and present danger.

4TH [SEPTEMBER 1852]. — We rode to fort Owen by 4 oclock   Distance 25   I saw something that was queer   there was snow all around us and roses in full bloom in the valley where we rode

5TH — [SUNDAY] — I have not done much this morning but eat my breakfast. Fort Owen is situated on a graduel slope to the west and very prettyly situated too I think. there are some mountains all around and St Marys river running to the north. this is a pretty stream and there is plenty of fish in it. When we came here yesterday they [gave] us a room and I expected to find it some thing like living in but we went in and found it dirty as the ground and nothing to clean it with. I asked for a broom and they showed me a bunch of willows.

6TH — we have been working in A brick yard or what they call one here where they make adobes or Spanish bricks. I have fixed a dam and a vat. . . .

7TH — I have been making bricks today and very nice work it is as we have to take the mud in our hands and put it in the moulds. weather warm. a small shower about two oclock. . . .

11TH — I have laid a bed all the morning and been very sick by spells. Mr. Owen had five horses stolen last night by the black feet indians. I suppose as they commit great depradations on the whites at this fort.

13TH — I have been mowing today. weather cloudy. a small shower this evening.

14TH — I have been fixing ox yokes and hay rigging. help[ed] to haul one load of hay. weather fair.

15TH — [*entry made by John Owen*] — The poor fellow [Dodson] was killed and scalped by the Blackfeet in sight of the Fort.

Because of his residence among the Flatheads, John Owen received an appointment as Indian Agent in 1857. Ill-equipped by the government to meet his responsibilities, Owen waged a discouraging five-year struggle in the tribe's behalf, frequently meeting the Indians' needs from his own pocketbook. Increasing pressure from whites moving onto the Flathead's Bitterroot lands added to Owen's difficulties. Even further complicating the situation was the fact that although some of the Flatheads had agreed in 1855 to move to a reservation on the Jocko River, others of the tribe refused to leave their homelands. In a letter to Governor Stevens' secretary, Owen expressed the Indians' dissatisfactions and his own disenchantment.

FORT OWEN W.T.
APRIL 25, 1857

MY DEAR DOTY —

Many thanks to you for your very interesting and lengthy letter. . . . The news very satisfactory, Buchanan is elected and governor Stevens sustained by the administration and Ind. Dept. at home. May the snows of Many winters rest lightly on his brow. When I wrote you from the Agency I expected ere this to have been on my way down the Mo. bound for the land of Oysters in the Shell. I did not discern it prudent to leave. . . .

Our Camp has been in a state of excitement all winter. Some of the hostile and dissaffected Indians from below have passed the winter in the jurisdiction of this agency, but what could be done with them. The Flathead Indians say that we are dogs. They say that two years ago they made a treaty with their great friend Gov. Stevens, and have never heard anything of it since. The Same year Some moons later a treaty was made with the Blackfeet which was responded to immediately by their great Father in the shape of Blankets, Guns, Groceries etc.! Why Should the Blackfeet stand so much better with the Great Father than we who have never shed the blood of a white man?

I was called up from the agency some three weeks since by Victor for the purpose of holding a council with the Flatheads. I was far from well but still I came, and in my office at the fort, Victor told me that he was sorry for one thing that they had promised the governor, which was to vacate the Bitter Root valley if it was thought best for them and have the reservation elsewhere. They now say they will never leave this valley. They say we have buried our fathers and children here which endears to us this soil. They went so far as to warn some white men here from fencing and farming, telling them you are only tiring yourselves for nothing, you will sow the crops but we will reap them.

On Easter I killed two Beeves and gave them a feast here and made a short speech to them—it was shortly after Finley returned and they were anxious to hear the news. I did it without authority but the good effects of the feast and the talk is plainly to be seen. told them you are not forgotten by your great Father for by his order I give you this feast. They harped upon the treaty not being satisfied. I told them to be patient and that all would turn out well yet. But they say our big friend Inta-Ki-as-Kin (Gov Stevens) said we would hear our Great Father speak long before this about our lands. . . .

It would have taken but a very little to have Kindled the war Flame in this camp last winter. The Ponderrilles [Pend Oreilles] are not to be trusted too far as a body. There has been some unprincipled white men prowling through this section of country and by their talk and conduct are well calculated to poison the Indian mind. one Johnny Crapeau of Dalles notoreity and a most consummate scoundrel was one. I ordered him out of the country. Still I believe he is prowling about the mission at this time. . . .

There will be the tallest kind of a mess here when the reservation is settled particularly if it is removed from the vicinity of the Mission. There is an under current at work and the peaceable foundations of this little community will be under mind and the fabric will fall with one stupendous crash. New timbers should now replace old and roting ones before it is too late to save the Bargain. An Agents duty is unpleasant as things are, law is impotent, you are not sustained in things you may deem for the good of the Indians for want of troops to enforce the laws. In fact we talked seriously of organizing a vigilance club here this winter for the protection of the few law abiding people here. . . .

I would like to see the Governor and yourself together and talk these things over. I am far from being an alarmist neither do I wish to be frightened by a shadow, But I do assure you my own position may not be tenable long and that among the friendly Flatheads. They are Indians and have their sympathies with other tribes that have never done them any harm. My own people have been cautioned this spring about riding too far from the fort without cause. I hope that in seven years sojourn among these people I have been able to attach to my interest some few stern friends who would give me timely notice of approaching danger. I wish there was more of them. I shall leave for the agency this week although report reached me yesterday of a feast having been given in that vicinity by a Nez Perces & Cayuse Frank and a general invitation sent to the Spokanes & Ponderrills, the object of which was to consult about the policy of their coming and killing me at the agency simply because I was acting agent and was writing to the Governor about them. As for the truth of the report I know not, but I think the party at the agency far from being safe at this time. God send that the Doctor or someone else soon arrive to relieve me.

I can't for my life see why the doctor selected such an out of the way place neither farming land nor grasing land and the Snow Falls deeper and stays longer than in any other section of the mountains. A much better location could be found on the Jocco [Jocko River] further up where he would have a plain some twelve miles in length by an average breadth of from five to seven with favorable wintering ground. But rest assured that these Indians will never yeald cheerfully to being moved. They say this is all our country and that the Ponderrills are merely here on sufferance. Their country is below the Lake and why should we be moved because they are living near the Mission. It is due us as the Flathead Tribe to have more to say about the reservation than they have. If things remain quiet this summer you may see me below. . . .

JNO OWEN

Except for the fur traders who came upriver on the Missouri and a few settlers who reached the Bitterroot via Utah, the main western movement bypassed Montana. This relative isolation decreased, however, with the onset of military exploration and road building during the 1850's. In 1853, Governor Stevens surveyed a route across Montana for a possible northern trans-continental railroad. In 1858 Congress authorized funds to the Army for a more practical project — construction of a wagon road from the head of navigation on the Missouri to the head of navigation on the Columbia. Under the supervision of Lt. John A. Mullan, construction began almost immediately. Although Stevens had decided the general route in 1854, a party of topographers preceded Mullan's construction force to determine the precise location of the road. One of these engineers was P. M. Engle, whose official report of exploration from the Bitter-root Valley to Fort Benton follows. Work on the Mullan Road ended in 1863, just in time to become a significant avenue for thousands of gold miners seeking access to Montana and Idaho.

BITTER ROOT VALLEY
FORT OWEN, W.T.
JANUARY 8, 1860

DEAR SIR:

In conformity to your instructions of November 5, 1859, to make a reconnaissance eastward from the St. Regis Borgia river to Fort Benton, in order to ascertain, in detail, the character of the line for the proper location of the military wagon road, and in order to arrange the working parties for spring operations, and at the same time collect data regarding the climatology of the main range of the Rocky Mountains in midwinter. I left your camp November 7, 1859, then established at Eleven-Mile prairie, on the St. Regis Borgia river, with Major John Owen, Indian agent for the Flathead nation, and reached Fort Owen, after seven days' march, on the 13th, estimating the distance at one hundred and thirty-two and five-tenths miles. . . . The 22d of November, . . . I left Fort Owen accompanied by C. C. Irwine, Esq., two laboring men, with six riding and four pack animals. . . .

November 23 — . . . . At 11 a.m. I made the upper Hell's Gate crossing, at which place the river is divided by an island. The stream was heavily floating with ice, and the crossing rendered difficult by a strong ice cover extending from both shores some twenty feet into the river. The day was cold, and a strong wind blew from and through the canon. . . .

November 24 — . . . . Beaver-Tail Point . . . forms a single spur of half a mile in width, terminating at the river in a perpendicular bluff. The present wagon road makes here two crossings of the river to avoid this place, . . . then one mile and a half over prairie bottom to the river crossing. . . . This crossing might be avoided by keeping the road on the right bank, but it would require some earthwork, and the bridging of a little creek which runs in a steep ravine. This creek has been named "Gold Creek," as Colonel Lander is said to have found gold specimens in it. . . .

November 26 — Started at half past eight a.m.; two mules have strayed off; cold morning; snowed heavily; travelled one mile through a bottom; . . . The wagon road . . . at Deer Lodge valley leaves the river, and cross-ing the valley takes to a gently sloping side hill, and after a mile and a quarter strikes the Little Blackfoot river about a mile and a half above its junction with Deer Lodge creek. From the top of said hill the junction of these waters can be seen, and also the lower portion of the big valley. None or very little work will be required to bring heavy wagons up to the top of the hill without doubling teams; but it may be that some winding about in the descent would be necessary, as some deep hollows cut up the easterly slope. . . . We encamped one-half mile from the foot of the hill in the bottom of the Little Black-foot valley, having made eight and a half miles. Mr. John Grant has settled near the junction of the two branches of the Hell's Gate river and built two log houses. It snowed since 4 a.m., and for some time pretty heavily. At 11 a.m. it cleared off. The snow is not so deep here as below, measuring three inches on a level.

November 27 — ... After ascending a gently sloping hill, I followed its rolling surface for two and a quarter miles, and then began the very steep descent. Here a careful examination of the ground would have to be made to find the best location for the wagon road. This descent of about 350 feet offers one of the greatest difficulties on the whole route. Of the two ravines to the right and left of the trail, one or the other may be adapted to the purpose; if not, considerable work, similar to the descent to the St. Joseph's river, will be found necessary. After reaching the foot of the hill, the road passes up the river bottom for three-quarters of a mile and crosses at the end of that distance the Little Blackfoot river at a point where it forms a timbered island one-quarter of a mile in width. Both crossings are good and with gravelly bottoms; depth of water, about one foot and three-quarters; and width, from fifteen to twenty feet. The opposite hill, which the road has to cross, is called the Mountain, and is said to be more formidable than the divide of the Rocky Mountains. From the foot to the top of the hill the distance is one-eighth of a mile, and I am confident that by two turns, which will involve some side hill cutting, a good and easy grade can be attained. The present road does not ascend the hill at the place where the trail is located, but keeps for one mile further up the valley, which forms here a kind of canon, and then ascends a hill by taking advantage of a coulee which runs up to the top of the mountain. With a little work it is said that a good road can be made there; but it will make four river crossings necessary. . . .

November 28 — Started at 9:20 a.m.; cold but clear morning. . . . The trail, which runs along the right bank, crosses a half a mile from the last rocky hill spur, a creek, which runs in a valley leading north to a spot where the Little Blackfoot valley is strongly bending to the east. Should the road be kept on the right bank of the river, the work is loose rock around the point where I propose to make the crossing, and would extend from fifty to sixty feet. From there, for two and three-quarter miles, no earthwork would be necessary. A corduroy of thirty-five feet, over a wet place formed by a spring coming from a hill spur, would be needed. Two hundred and sixty yards from there another wet place, originating in the same manner, can be avoided by keeping close to the creek where the ground appears to be dry. I think it necessary that this portion of the road should be carefully examined, because the valley is said to be miry in the extreme during spring and summer, and probably here it will be inevitable to have to cut the road high up on the side hills. . . .

Ascending a hill a quarter mile long, from the top of which we enjoyed a fine view of the Upper Missouri valley, the gate of the mountains, and a small portion of the Rocky Mountains. Heart mountain can be distinctly seen, and also the direction of the wagon road for 10 or 11 miles, to a point where it crosses Soft Bed creek. . . . Made today 19¾ miles. Our animals are getting weak; the want of sufficient nourishment commences to tell on them. . . .

December 2 — The wind blew a perfect gale during the night. The morning is very cold and our animals appear much reduced. The snow in the valley is four inches deep and covered with a hard crust, which makes pawing the grass for the animals difficult. . . .

December 3 — It has been a windy night. Our tent was blown down, and we were fearful that some of the shallow-rooted trees would be blown upon us. This morning it is quite mild. Started at 7:45 a.m. to make Sun river in good time. . . .

December 4 — The weather had not moderated in the least, and I judged that the thermometer must have been at about forty degrees below zero. It still snowed, but not so heavily as yesterday. We were undecided whether to push on to Sun river or go back to the Dearborn. To retrace our steps seemed the most sensible in our present condition, as we would have the wind in our backs, and in a short ride could reach shelter and food in a large Pend d'Oreille camp which we left at the Dearborn river; but then the snow might fall to such a depth that we would be cut off from Fort Benton. At 10 a.m. we decided to try to reach Sun River Farm, and at 11 a.m. started for that point. It was terrible weather, and we could distinguish nothing at a distance of 100 yards. After a ride of three and a half hours we reached Sun River Farm, which was twenty-three and seven-tenths miles distant from our last night's camp. We were all more or less frostbitten, and had suffered extremely. Colonel Vaughan, Indian agent for the Blackfoot nation, received us very kindly, and with his well-known hospitality, offered us accomodations at the agency for any length of time that we might wish. . . .

December 8 — Started at 9 a.m. . . . The day was clear and warm. After a ride of 28 miles, during which we crossed the Grand and Eight-Mile coulee, and descending near Discovery Butte into the Missouri River valley, we arrived at Fort Benton, and were most kindly received. There was scarcely any snow here, but the river was frozen solid, which was a fortunate circumstance, as we could drive across our animals, that would have starved on this side. . . .

photo by W. H. Culver

26

THE RUSH FOR GOLD

EGEND CLOUDS the first discovery of gold in Montana, but facts confirm that within a few short years of the first authenticated strike, the glittering metal transformed Montana from a backwater region, peopled by Indians, traders, and a few farmers to a booming frontier anxious for statehood. Because gold had already drawn hordes of prospectors to California, Colorado, Nevada and Idaho, it was inevitable that tales of strikes on creeks in western Montana should side-track some Idaho-bound adventurers. The disappointing sparseness of gold reported further west caused prospectors to spill out into the neighboring valleys and in no time a rush was on. The first sizeable strike in Montana came in July, 1862, along Grasshopper Creek. As the camp rapidly attracted population it became known as Bannack and during its brief hey-day the town served as Montana's first territorial capital. Bannack's inhabitants were a restless lot, and they quickly deserted the town when they learned of richer diggings in Alder Gulch. Soon known as Virginia City, the new strike rapidly spawned a host of satellite camps and by the end of 1863 it boasted a population of several thousand.

From Virginia City the placer miners spread out to comb the highly mineralized valleys of southwestern Montana, using their portable, unsophisticated equipment. In the Prickly Pear Valley (Helena), Confederate Gulch (Diamond City), the Yellowstone Valley (Emigrant Gulch), and along Silver Bow Creek (Butte), a few lucky prospectors found the bonanzas of which they dreamed. The great majority of gold seekers, however, found only discouragement and wasted efforts.

Life in these hastily constructed gold camps was rough, crude, and violent. The passion for wealth so consumed the miners that all else became secondary. On the other hand, life was exciting, frenzied, and surprisingly cosmopolitan. The gold attracted a heterogeneous population and, at least in its early stages, it was a great democratizer. When it became evident that not everyone was going to get rich, prejudice and crime set in. The unsuccessful either left the territory or turned to other areas of economic endeavor.

Montana's placer mining frontier died almost as quickly as it began, leaving behind a legacy of ghost towns and disappointment. Even during its zenith the Montana rush never equalled the size or wealth of the earlier strikes in California, Colorado or Nevada. The degree to which these few frenetic years served as a positive stimulus to Montana's development is still disputed; yet it is clear that the 1860's initiated patterns in business, agriculture, transportation, and politics that flourished long after the prospectors had gone.

PLACER MINING NEAR LEWISTOWN, 1888

THE RUSH FOR GOLD
First Major Migrations and Settlement, 1862-1867

News of the gold strikes in Montana spread fast, and visions of more, perhaps richer diggings drew hordes of prospectors to comb western Montana's mountain gulches. Regardless of whether they were unsuccessful miners fresh from Colorado and California, discouraged mid-western farmers, down-on-their-luck New England shopkeepers or disgruntled fugitives from both the Union and Confederate armies, they all came with the dream of bettering their condition. Official sources, such as Commissioner of Emigration Francis M. Thompson, issued optimistic but moderate encouragement concerning Montana's prospects; nevertheless, the heady visions of streets paved with gold, of instant wealth, persisted for "bummers" and loafers as well as for those willing to work.

Turning to a large map of the Western and Pacific States and Territories, and putting your finger upon the city of St. Louis, if you will follow up the Missouri River, you will find, at the mouth of the Yellow Stone, the Eastern boundary line of Montana Territory.

Following on up the Missouri, just above the mouth of the Maria's, is Fort Benton, an American Fur Company trading post, but now grown into quite a town, containing many stores and store-houses, for this is the head of navigation on the Missouri River. Upon the arrival of the steamboat will be found hundreds of great wagons called "Prairie Schooners," and immense droves of cattle, awaiting the merchandise and machinery annually brought by steamer up this great natural high-way, to within sight of the snow-clad peaks of the Rocky Mountains. On my way down from Fort Benton, which place I left June 1st, I met twenty-two steamers bound for Montana, loaded down with passengers, merchandise and machinery. Here the emigrant may, if he chooses, find employment as a teamster, or take passage upon the coach for the mines. For the most of the way the road to the mines from Fort Benton is good, and after crossing the Dearborn River, ninety miles from Fort Benton, upon the headwaters of nearly every stream running from the mountains, mining operations are going on.

Extending along the base of the mountains upon the eastern slope, for two hundred miles, are miners' camps. Sometimes the solitary prospecter, in his camp under the shade of the willow brush — sometimes a "city" of two or three log cabins, and, again, towns and cities, in fact, of from 3,000 to 10,000 population, while in every little valley are the cattle "ranches" and the grain and vegetable raising farms. 160 acres of the unoccupied land is free to any claimant who occupies and improves it, and it is secured to him, by legislative enactment, against all but the United States Government. Upon the western slope of the mountains, in the Deer Lodge and Black Foot valleys, are rich and extensive mining camps, and as a farming region it is hardly excelled in any country. No country can compare with Montana as a grazing country. Cattle, horses, and even sheep, winter easily without food of any kind except what they find on the hill-sides and prairies, and with such shelter as they find in the brush along the streams. I have ridden a horse four hundred miles in eleven days, in the month of February, with no other feed but what he picked up on the way. . . .

Thousands of streams run down from the mountains, making their way through fine valleys, affording unparalleled advantages for mill and mining purposes, and for irrigation. Nearly all crops which can be raised successfully in New England can, with proper attention, be raised here. . . .

So far in our history the discovery of new Placer diggings has kept pace with the increase of population, so that the laborer has always been able to obtain ample remuneration for his toil; and as not one-tenth part of that portion of Montana which is supposed to contain rich mines has been prospected, it is fair to suppose that this state of things will continue for years to come. . . .

But it is not to the Placer diggings that the friends of Montana look while contemplating her future wealth and prosperity. All along the foot of the hills extend Lodes of Gold and Silver-bearing quartz, which are inexhaustible in wealth, and will yield forth their treasures, for ages to

come, giving employment to immense capital, and thousands of willing hands. . . .

The United States Government have made an appropriation for building a road direct across the plains to Montana, from near Sioux City, Iowa, and the survey is now being made. For men who expect to work for success, and for capitalists, there is no better place than Montana; but for "bummers" and loafers, it is the worst place in the world. I would refer the latter class to the report of the Vigilance Committee, for encouragement and information.

RESPECTFULLY,

F. M. THOMPSON
COMMISSIONER OF EMIGRATION
FOR MONTANA

JULY 26, 1865

Many of Montana's gold seekers quite literally followed in the wake of the fur traders. Just as the Missouri River had served the trappers and traders as their principal highway, the river carried hundreds of prospectors to Fort Benton, the head of navigation, and thence overland to the goldfields. Every fall, throughout the 1860's, the steamboats carried tons of ore (and many disappointed gold seekers) back downstream to St. Louis. Although infinitely more comfortable than wagon or ox-cart, steamboat travel was not without its disadvantages. A typical journey might include groundings, fires, wrecks, and Indian attacks. One less harrowing journey is described in the journal of Daniel H. Weston, who ultimately became territorial treasurer. Weston had been unsuccessful in his earlier attempts to find the glittering metal in Colorado and Idaho, and prudently included in his cargo on this journey a load of goods with which to open a bootery in Virginia City.

TUESDAY — [JUNE] 12TH — [1866] — . . . . Sunday morning early we passed the mouth of the Yellowstone and shortly after Fort Union. Yesterday we spent nearly all day cutting ash wood and have the boat loaded down with this fine fuel. . . .

FRIDAY — [JUNE] 15TH — What a beautiful morning! Doubly beautiful after our long, cold, stormy weather. Great floods of yellow light pour over the river and tree-green shore. The sky is of that light soft blue so bewitching. I have been sitting in my little room facing the wide open door to take in the glorious light, and richness of this rare morning, and reading one of Dickens' stories. Although I greatly admire his books I cannot sit long unmindful of this charming day, and so I come here to my nook on the guard to revel and rejoice in the sunshine and kindly sky. . . .

Nearly Sunset — This afternoon we had an exciting time with buffalo of which we have seen large herds today. Right under a steep bank which they could not climb and just at the water's edge we came upon seven, and as the boat approached they took to the river. I fired twice and have the credit given me of bringing down one with the shot that killed him. Others were wounded but only one was killed and he was after some difficulty hauled on board by means of the derrick. He was a large noble looking fellow and his flesh now it is dressed looks finely. It will be quite a luxury to us, which is the first buffalo we have killed. Just as we had got the animal on board the steamer "W. B. Dance" met us and rounded to. We just had time to scribble notes to send by her and I sent one to Father and Mother. The "Sunset" boat has overtaken us and now lies in sight. We have had more trouble today getting upon and over bars than for a long time and now the yawl is out sounding for the channel. . . .

SUNDAY [JUNE] 17TH — Another lovely day—soft, still and full of sunlight. We are in the worst part of the river we have seen yet. There seeming to be no channel at all and we have been since day before yesterday vainly trying to pass. We are now laid up at the bank and will doubtless have to lighten our load in order to get over this shallow place if we get over at all. I do hope we shall not be stopped here for it would be very difficult and expensive to try to get goods through from here overland. Yesterday we were nearly all day upon a bar but toward supper time got off with much sparring. Broke a spar and derrick. . . .

WED'Y [JUNE] 20TH — We got over the bar all right by lightening the cargo, and got reloaded and a fair start Monday forenoon. . . .

THURSDAY [JUNE] 21ST — We passed the mouth of Milk River yesterday and stopped not far above at a large grove of dead cottonwoods to collect wood. We staid till morning and laded the boat heavily with wood.... This forenoon we passed Fort Copelin and the "Dry Fork of the Missouri." We feared much trouble by low water at places today passed but got over. . . . I think we are over the worst of the river and now looks as though we should reach Fort Benton of which I have of late had fears. . . . Passed this forenoon a [place] where three men were killed by Indians last year who went on shore from the "U.S. Grant." . . .

FRIDAY [JUNE] 22ND — We made a good run yesterday, though stopping several times for cutting wood. We ran till midnight and made at least eighty miles. Saw the first pine trees since leaving the States. . . . The ridges are very high and may really be called ranges of mountains with serrated tops and corrugated sides.

SUNDAY [JUNE] 24th — Yesterday we passed the mouth of Muscleshell, the terminus of the projected road from Va. City and Helena. A few men were there, at a cabin and stockade. A town called Kercheval is laid out there but it will be quite a while ere it obtains metropolitan importance. . . .

THURSDAY [JUNE] 28TH — We are at the moment passing some of the most unique and imposing scenery I ever saw. Great jagged towers, pinnacles and ramparts rise out of the long ranges white and grand. White sandstone is the rock. Palisades circle around detached bluffs like pillars against their sides with rounded capitals. One immense rock like rusty iron rises from

the white battlements of a great fortress. One rock called "Steamboat Rock" bears some resemblance to a steamer. . . . Yesterday we made slow progress being in rapids nearly all day. We were many hours at "Drowned Man's Rapids" and soon after we got out of them by "cordelling" with a hawser we struck Pablo's Rapids. At both I went with the other passengers ashore and tugged at the hawser to get it above the rapids and make fast while the capstan slowly drew us through. We just passed Pablo's Rapids last night and lay there till morning. . . .

Yesterday morning we wooded at the mouth of the Judith in a most charming spot amid so much desolation. It was a green grove of cottonwoods whose floor was green with grass and fragrant with acres of wild roses. I wandered long in the grateful shade and balmy, bracing air, gathering at times wild strawberries. I found the remains of many Indian camps and it seem[s] a favorite haunt of the red man. They show their good taste to frequent such a lovely spot. An antelope was wandering like me listless and absorbed not far off. We often see deer and mountain goats flying up the steep cliffs while many a vain bullet is sent after them.

Afternoon. We have a fine deep river and are making a steady run. The river of late has been becoming clearer until now it is quite clear enough to drink without settling though it has a yellowish tinge. . . . We have passed today "Hole in the Wall" and "Citadel Rock," the latter a pinnacle rather than a citadel rising sheer from the water to about the height of two hundred feet. . . . We are seventy miles or so from our steamboat journey's end and tomorrow or next day ought to reach Fort Benton. We are now sixty five days from St. Louis.

FRIDAY [JUNE] 29TH — Afternoon. At last we are in sight of Fort Benton. It is in plain view three or four miles ahead with three steamers lying there.

It is sixty-seven days since I bade goodbye to friends at Boston and this boat left St. Louis the same day. Thus our long journey up this great river for over three thousand miles from its mouth draws to a close. Through dangers by navigation and hostile savages we have safely passed through delays and doubts and fears. We have nearly reached the end of a river journey such as the world elsewhere does not afford. Thankful to a kind and forbearing Providence for all care and protection to unworthy mortals we welcome the end, and look back to the memories of our journey.

Originally the only overland route to Montana was via the Oregon Trail to Fort Hall and then north on the Idaho-Utah trail. For the anxious gold seeker, a shorter road was clearly necessary. In 1863, John M. Bozeman marked a trail from Fort Laramie across the base of the Big Horns and the Yellowstone Valley to Virginia City. Although the route shortened the journey by a tempting 400 miles, it also cut across Sioux hunting grounds. In 1865, in an effort to halt the increasing tide of migration, Chief Red Cloud launched a series of attacks upon travelers on the Bozeman Trail. The next year the government negotiated a treaty and built three forts to protect travelers, but the Sioux continued to attack at will. Methodist minister W. K. Thomas, traveling with his young son and two other men, witnessed enough fresh graves to give them pause; yet when a broken wheel halted the wagon train, Thomas disregarded the military's advice and moved on alone. Several days following the last entry in the minister's diary, another traveler came across his wagon and its four scalped occupants.

JULY 31 — [1866] — So [is] the inexpressible gift of God. We are now among the hills. . . . I . . . find myself by the side of a little silver skirted lake at the foot of the mountains bordered round about with long entangled grass resting its drooping head upon it placid busom. For a moment I stand gazing at the lofty peaks, now at the rigid rocks, while my mind runs even then at the wild seines of nature that spread out before my eyes. I am meditating upon the adventure that I am about to take — counting the cost — Summing up the danger. cold chills run through my blood. . . .

AUG. 2 — Thursday at 2 o'clock the Train of a hundred and twelve wagons moved from Fort Phillip Kearney the intention is to drive out five miles to Creek and camp — but accidently one of the wagon wheels in the train gave way which caused such delay that we did not reach the place desired. . . .

AUG. 3 — Friday morning at five O clock we drive about a mile around way to where there is plenty of water and breakfast with orders to wait until government train of fourty wagons comes up & two companies of Infantry about a half a mile drive from camp. this morning on the hill side to the left of the road is a grave containing the bodies of five men who were killed a few days ago by the Indians. as I passed by the grave I saw that the Wolves had made an opening to the inmates and had torn the flesh from the bodies and left their ribs exposed. Such is the haste and depravity of Man out here that he will hardly take time to pay his last respects to the dead — but leaves him for the wild beasts of the field to cry and howel over and often to feast upon. . . .

AUG. 7 — Tuesday mourning at about 5 O clock we leave Camp North Tongue River. the road is very good to day. we passed over a few small hills and several nice little streames and through a beautiful country to day well supplied with grass. just before we cross trout Creek to the left of the road is a lone grave. the inmate was deposited in July last. we could not make out his name. part of head board being gone. he left Chamberburg Pensylvania May 8th 1866 and was killed here by the Indians. The poor fellows remains had not been left in peace to moulder away into dust—but as his life had been taken by merciless Savages—so had his body been disturbed by the wild wolves. . . . they had dug down until they had left the inmate half uncovered and nawed the flesh from his face. we could see that he had been scalped. A sad sight to look at — but worse to reflect upon . . . .

AUG 17 — Friday morning the train started at about 6 Oclock over rather a sidling and hilly road, one of the freight wagons broke down about an hour after leaving camp. My wagon and two other Citizen's wagons passed, went together two or three miles, they stoped behind thinking it safer to wait for the train. I determined trusting in the Lord to go ahead. We moved on beaver Creek about ten miles from where we left the train. drove about eight miles in afternoon. we saw plenty of antalope and Buffalo.

AUG 22 — Wednesday morning at 6 O clock we left Thomas's Spring drove the branch a mile cross it. took over the hills & within four miles we crossed a river a mile further we crossed another river. drove three or four over the hills & nooned at a little Creek, afternoon drove five miles, crossed a river. while crossing it we lost our coffee pot — drove three miles from there and camped for the night on a nice little branch. Broke our Champaigne bottle.

The rush to Montana's goldfields kindled hopes on the part of Minnesota businessmen that they, too, might profit. The focus of their ambitions was an overland wagon route across the northern plains from Minnesota to Montana. As the result of heavy lobbying, the Minnesotans secured government appropriations to pay for a military escort on the proposed road. In 1862, James L. Fisk, the most energetic and widely-known propagandist of the scheme, led the first of four expeditions west to establish the route. One of the members of this first expedition was James Fergus, who was to become one of Montana's most prominent pioneers. Fergus spent the winter of 1862-63 in Bannack, by no means prospering. Nevertheless, he penned an optimistic description of the conditions for Fisk to use in promotion of the 1863 expedition.

BANNOCK CITY
BEAVERHEAD COUNTY
DAKOTA TERRITORY
JANUARY 1, 1863

. . . . There is no doubt of the existence of gold in greater or less quantities in all the mountain ranges comprising and connected with the great Rocky Mountain chains from Caribou to Mexico. Besides the Colorado mines (Pike's Peak) it is found on the head-waters of the North Platte, of the Yellow Stone, and Missouri proper, East of the Mountains and on nearly all the head waters of the Columbia and Colorado on the West. Paying diggings are now worked at Prickly Pear, Big Hole, Rattlesnake, and this place, on the East side of the Main range, and at Deer Lodge, Fort Lempe and other places on the west side.

Large parties have been prospecting all the fall, and some are still out on the headwaters of the Yellowstone and Snake Rivers, where gold is supposed to exist in large quantities, and where rich diggings are looked for by next Spring.

The diggings here are the best that have been found since the Salmon River discovery. Of course a great deal of time has been spent prospecting and opening claims which have paid nothing.

But as high as a pound weight of gold has been taken out in one day by three men in the short cold days of November and some claims have paid as high as one dollar to the pan. Of course these are exceptions to the general rule. Notwithstanding the lateness of the season some of the miners are still at work taking gold from the bars and dry gulches where it was easiest to get at, and the diggings are improving daily. . . .

The bed of the creek and low flats, however, are supposed to be much richer and parties are preparing to work them next summer. Some quartz lodes have been discovered, which will be worked as soon as quartz mills can be got here.

Wages for common labor is four dollars per day, without board; flour $20 to $25 pr hundred (supplied from Salt Lake); beef, the best I ever saw, 20 to 25 cts per; lumber, 20 cts pr foot; goods, owing to the want of supply, have been very high. We have now some half a dozen stores, however, and prices are more moderate viz: — nails — $1 pr lb; glass — 8 x 10 $1 each; sugar — $1 per lb.; Coffee — $1; tea $4; boots, $15 to 20 pair; etc, etc. . . .

Notwithstanding the prospective richness of the Rocky Mountains in gold it is not in the precious metals alone that it presents attractions to the seeker after fortune. The mountain ranges in this lattitude are low; the valleys broad, level and well watered affording millions of acres of excellent pasturage.

Bitter Root, Deer Lodge, Prickley Pear, the Sun River Valleys, and the Three Forks of the Missouri, Beaverhead, and Horse Prairie are favorite grazing localities with the Indian tribes where they winter thousands of horses without hay or shelter.

The American Fur Company have a large grazing range on Sun River where they send their spare horses and cattle, both summer and winter to fatten. . . . Several half breeds and Canadians are also engaged in raising cattle and horses in Deer Lodge Valley. Most of the beef used here is from their herds; and notwithstanding the good quality of Minnesota beef, that sold here is certainly far superior. . . . I think the valleys of the Rocky Mountain region and of the streams running from it must eventually become the great grazing country of the United States. There is so little rain that the grasses do not loose their fattening qualities when they become dry.

Little or no hay is needed in winter; the snows are very light and seldom lie long—the first this season commenced yesterday — and the water is excellent. Notwithstanding the excellent grazing qualities of this region, I do not, however, think they are inviting fields at present for the general emigrant. There are a great many hardships to encounter in all new countries, and they become greater the further they are away from the borders of civilization. Few localities are low enough to grow the cereals to perfection and the mountains are still in possession of numerous bands of roving Indians, who are here today and there tomorrow and who look upon any settler in their territory as an intruder, his goods lawful plunder and his scalp a lawful prize. Even the seeker after gold is not always rewarded but often, after enduring hardships that he would be unwilling to endure in an old settled country, goes home poor in purse and broken in health or toils on in search of the phantom fortune, which it may never be his lot to find.

RESPECTFULLY YOURS

JAMES FERGUS

Illusions died rapidly upon first glimpse of the shanties and tents that comprised Montana's mining camps. Engrossed by the importance of working their claims, the miners simply had no time to worry about life's amenities. In 1863, F. E. W. Patten came to Montana and after visiting Bannack, settled in the newer, richer diggings in Alder Gulch (Virginia City). He noted that the natural beauty of the area contrasted markedly with both towns and their unattractive log shacks, refuse-littered streets and crude sanitation. Yet both communities were lively and bustling, buoyed by the expectation of sudden wealth. After only one day of labor on another man's claim, Patten decided his fortune would have to be made in the freighting business.

THURSDAY, JULY 30, '63: . . . . This is decidedly the most beautiful part of the Rocky Mountains I have ever seen. The valleys are broad and fertile by being irrigated from the streams running through them. The climate is fine, and one would not realize from the air that he was so elevated, as is generally very discernible to persons when thus elevated. Travelled thirty miles and encamped about ten miles on the Missouri side of the range. After some counciling we all concluded to go by Bannock City to Virginia City. Pleasant evening; good water; grass and brush for wood. . .

FRIDAY, AUGUST 14, '63: Have ten miles to go to get to Bannock City, where we are all anxious to get, as we have quite a disposition to see this gold region on the headwaters of the Missouri River. About eleven o'clock, after travelling over some good road, until the last two miles, which is very hilly, we came in view of the Golden City, which is not by any means prepossessing, and is nothing more than a mining or gulch town, covering some four or five acres of ground. There are log houses, mostly covered with dirt. There is rather a flat where the town is built, one main street running through. There are several hewn log business houses and miners huts. The mining commences at the lower end of the town, where the bluffs close in, and the gulch is some five to seven miles in length, where mining is done. There are several good log business houses under way, but nothing seems to have been done for some time upon them, as business has so fallen off here since the discovery of Stinking Water diggings, which has caused a great stampede from here to there.

The mines and town here are on Grasshopper creek, a small stream that heads in the main snowy range about thirty miles west, and runs into Beaverhead creek about fifteen miles below Bannock City. There have been a number of fine quartz leads discovered here, though little worked. There is in operation one small four stamp water mill, which, though a very inefficient one, does a fine business. The quartz leads are said to be very rich, and when good mills can be gotten in operation no doubt this will become a point noted for quartz mining. There are, as I have before said, a number of business houses here—auction and commission houses, livery and feed stables, boot and shoe shops, two or three express offices, one exchange office, buying gold dust, and black smith shops; and a variety of houses and shops doing a varied business.

This seems to be a healthy location, surrounded mostly by mountains and hills, and has a population of some one thousand persons, with a number of families, which looks odd here upon the headwaters of the Missouri River. We remained overnight, and sent our mules out three miles to graze. Considerable prospecting is going on here at this time. There is some excitement occasioned by some discovery nearby, and large numbers are going out every night to ascertain the locality of the same. Many valuable discoveries, it is thought, will yet be made in this part of the country. Thirty miles west a discovery was made sometime since, though water is so scarce that mining is obstructed, and the richness of the same cannot well be tested this fall. This is known as Horse Prairie diggings.

AUGUST 15, 1863: In accordance with former intentions we started east to Stinking Water diggings, seventy miles, being now the most extensively populated place, the richest and most extensive gulch, and now attracting the greatest attention. . . .

MONDAY, AUGUST 17, '63: . . . . The country along the road is very destitute of vegetation, and as I now write we are on a hill in view of Stinking Water creek, a beautiful stream in appearance, running through a beautiful valley, nicely lined with trees and shrubbery. It runs in a northwest direction and soon empties into Beaverhead Creek and this into Jefferson's Fork. . . . I have with my wagon just descended a very steep hill, or precipice, I might say, into the valley of the stream in question. The train is now so engaged, and will have a difficult time getting down. One hour later, all down safely. They let the wagons down by ropes. We have encamped on the eastern bank of the stream. . . .

WEDNESDAY, AUGUST 19, '63: . . . . After going up the gulch, above where mining is being prosecuted, came to the first village or town called Nevada City, a considerable village, generally built of pine logs with roofs of dirt. It has more than otherwise the appearance of a gulch mining town, and is constantly and continually building up. Tarried here but a few minutes; discharged a little freight; visited the express offices in search of letters; received none. Then moved on up to next village or town, Virginia City, a larger place, but not so well located, the first, Nevada City, being located upon level ground, and the latter on a ridge gradually inclining to the creek or mining gulch. This place is built at an angle of ninety degrees from the creek, and has one principal street that runs square off from the creek, upon which there is and will be the principal and heaviest business done. This is a rich and very remarkable gold locality, surpassing perhaps any ever discovered in America,

length and extent considered. Virginia City is about five miles above the beginning of the mining district. . . . This gulch or mining district is said to be fourteen miles in length, and is richest upon nearing the source, and the gold coarser in quality and size of particles. . . .

This village, Virginia City, is fast building up. There are mostly log houses, covered with earth. It has a growing population, living in all manner of ways and localities, some families and messes of men living in houses, some in wagons, some in tents, some in bush arbors and some under clusters of trees. All are more engaged in searching for and obtaining gold than preparing for comfort, or for the approaching winter, which in this latitude and elevation must be hard and heavy. Yet all this manner of living is pleasant thus far, as the weather is fine, and there is no rain falling.

Many men are to be seen selling merchandise in tents, under bush arbors and in wagons, and, upon the whole, all here presents quite a novel appearance. Here in this northern latitude, at the head of the great muddy Missouri River, which a few years ago was looked upon as being very remote and difficult of approach, is now peopled with civilized people, towns spring up, business is done, large herds being kept, families interspersed over the country, and everything being engaged in, and moving on, American-like. . . .

MONDAY, AUGUST 31, '63: This morning I witness a sad sight. A man said to have been of sober, moral, steady habits, named Woods, (I know not where from), committed suicide by shooting himself dead with his revolver about daylight while sleeping between two other men in a bush arbor, the ball entering the forehead. He had, the day previous, received a letter from a young lady in the States, whom it is said he was addressing, and disappointed love is supposed to have been the cause. He had been an aspiring man, but had been unfortunate, and this morning had to go to work by the day to live.

TUESDAY, SEPTEMBER 1ST, '63: Today mined for Mr. Mathews as an experiment, it being the first in my life. Day fine and pleasant. The labor being the first made me very sore. . . .

THURSDAY, SEPTEMBER 3RD, '63: Today not engaged, having become so sore and crippled from the past two days of mining had to be discontinued. Day passed quietly. I concluded to go to Salt Lake City after freight. Sent to ranch for my mules, and began to make the necessary preparations. . . .

Quite by accident, Emily and Frederick Meredith spent the winter of 1862-63 in Bannack. In a letter to her father the following spring, Emily described the tenuous but fast-paced existence she witnessed. Mrs. Meredith, who was well-educated and one of the few women in the camp, did not care much for Bannack's lack of religion, its predominantly southern character, or its immorality and violence; nevertheless she bravely faced up to the discomforts. The price of mining claims was already highly inflated (as was everything else) when the couple arrived and Meredith, a printer by trade, did not attempt any prospecting. Instead he herded cattle and the following year he took his wife to a farm in the Gallatin Valley.

BANNACK CITY, IDAHO
APRIL 30TH 1863

DEAR FATHER,

I have felt so uncertain about the reception of the various letters I have written home since my arrival here, that I have thought when I had a good opportunity I would write you a kind of abbreviated history of my wanderings since I left Bridger, at which point I know you heard from us. Such an opportunity seems to be presented for Dr. Hoyt proposes leaving here for Minnesota; he may never reach there, but as he will probably travel in a large company I consider him a safer carrier than the express. . . .

I think it was on the sixth of September we arrived here & for more than a month after that no one felt certain enough that they could remain here to build. Many anticipated a severe winter because we are so near the top of the range; others thought the Indians would not allow us to stay, or that if white people enough came in to obviate that difficulty there would be actual starvation, some thought the mines themselves would be exhausted in two or three months, or at best it would be impossible to work them longer than that, until quite late in the spring.

Fortunately none of these forebodings were prophetic. We have had a very mild winter; the Indians have done nothing more than steal stock & kill stragglers; there has been plenty of provisions at prices which although exorbitant every one has been able to pay; the mines have been worked all winter — & not until within the last three months has their real richness been suspected.

I know of one claim bought last fall for a set of house logs cut in the woods fifteen miles from here & sold this spring for $3000. cash. Claims which could have been had for the taking when we came in & which could have been purchased last winter for $100, or $200, now rate

from $1500. to $2000. I know one bar claim which sold for $7000., but the risk of buying at such prices is so great that would much sooner be the seller than the buyer. Nevertheless it is not strange that claims should rate so high when they occasionally prove so inordinately rich. In one claim $2500. was washed out in about three hours. I saw the gold washed out of one wheelbarrow full of dirt taken from another claim weighed & it weighed exactly two ounces (36$). These sound like regular Salmon river stories, but they are true, but in neither case would this be the average yield.

It is difficult to know just how to write home about this country. A list of the prices of things here would make most persons in the states suppose there must necessarily be suffering; if we say that people pay $25. per 100 lb. for flour as easily as $1.50 at home the general opinion would be that money must be quite plenty & people getting rich fast. Neither opinion would be quite correct. Every one seems to be getting along, very few are discouraged, but comparatively few have, to use a westernism "made their pile." . . . anyone who is shrewd & *has money* can make money here now. How it will be with those who come in I know not; unless there are other mines struck they will have but a poor chance, but in all probability there will be other mines struck.

There are but few things a man can do here now. Freighting, teaming & ranching are profitable but risky on account of the Indians; gardening will pay extremely well if anything can be raised, but no one knows yet whether there is any night in the year free from frost. (There were heavy frosts in August when the mines were first found). The name by which this stream is known, Grasshopper Creek, seems to indicate the presence of another foe. Mining does very well for those who have claims but if I had one or two thousand dollars spare cash I should not like to put it in the ground for fear it might prove as you say "a permanent investment." I never would advise anyone to come to a new mining country because there is a great deal to risk & a great deal to endure, nevertheless many persons undoubtedly will come here this summer & make more than they could in years at home. And they ought to, a person ought to make money pretty fast here to pay them for living in such a place.

I should like to see a pagoda or a mosque or anything to indicate that there is a religious principle in man. If "labor is worship" this is a most worshipfull community, but of any other kind of worship there is no public manifestation whatever. I verily believe two thirds of the people here are infidel and "Secesh."

I don't know how many deaths have occurred this winter but that there have not been twice as many, is entirely owing to the fact that drunken men do not shoot well. There are times when it is really unsafe to go through the Main Street on the other side of the Creek, the bullets whiz around so, & no one thinks of punishing a man for shooting another. What do you think of a place where men will openly walk the streets with shot guns waiting for a chance to shoot some one against whom they have a grudge & no one attempt to prevent it?

EMILY R. MEREDITH

One of the chief attractions of placer mining was that it required little in the way of knowledge, equipment or capital investment. It was, however, back-breaking labor that usually offered discouragingly limited rewards. Andrew Jackson Fisk arrived in Helena on October 5, 1866, and began working a claim with three other men. In only one day they built the sluice boxes necessary to wash their diggings. When that claim failed to pan out, the four optimistically moved their equipment to two more claims. Despite characteristic confidence that the pay streak must be there, none of their claims paid more than a pittance. In November, Fisk determined to form a partnership with his brother, Robert, to purchase the HELENA HERALD.

OCTOBER 9 — [1866] — "Our claim" dont pay "by a long shot." This morning "Ed" [Owen] washed out $2.25 from our yesterdays work. We concluded that we would try it another day—but todays work was worse than yesterdays—only took out $2.00. The dust is very fine — almost as fine as flour — but its the best looking dust I have seen in the place. There is a claim open above here about 300 yards and we think we will give that a trial for a couple days. . . .

OCTOBER 10 — We moved our Sluice Boxes to the upper claim this morning — got all ready to "run through" by noon. Ed Owen then went up to "Dry Gulch" to see if he could not get us a good claim. Van [Hayden Fisk, brother] & him are going up tomorrow to see about it. . . .

OCTOBER 11 — We took out tonight after a hard day and a half's work—$10—and although it pays better than the lower claim it don't one-quarter pay wages. Van and Ed were up to "Dry Gulch" today and bought a claim for $120.00—pay part in labor at $5.00 per diem and the balance in dust when we take it out—over and above our expenses. Ed thinks the claim will pay about $6 per day to the man. If it will pay that I will be satisfied for a while — till something turns up better. Our old Docter who came over with us is sick down to Widow Dergan's.

OCTOBER 12 — Van and George [Burson] moved up to "Dry Gulch" today. We think we will try this claim a couple days longer as we think we have got a "pay streak". We went to work "Stripping" this morning and stripped about 12 by 16 feet and this afternoon we run through some. I worked a couple blisters on my hands. Van and George are going to work tomorrow for the man we bought our claim off. A cold drizzling rain set in about dark and it is still raining quite hard. Our tent dont leak much but it is getting mighty disagreeable this camping out.

OCTOBER 13 — Rained all last night and all day today—except this afternoon it has got cold and it has been snowing for several hours. It has been impossible to work on the claim. The boys all went uptown & left me to keep house and I went to bed to keep warm. . . .

OCTOBER 14 — Widow Dergans Ranche. Got up this morning—found the [ground] covered with snow and concluded I would come down here and spend the Sabbath in Bro. Jim's [James Fisk] warm tent. . . . Snowed some all day. This evening we spent over to Mrs. Dergans. She is a great talker. Goodie gave me a splended dinner—oyster soup, butter, cheese and *such* a piece of *mince pie. Lord* but twas good.

OCTOBER 15 — At camp on claim. Came up today about noon and found nobody here so I went up Town and loafed arround all the afternoon. Times are getting quite dull in the City — to what they were a week ago. So many have left for the States and still they are going. It is still storming—snow is a couple inches deep on the flat—and most as many feet on the mountains. Its mighty cold tonight—coldest night of the season.

Poten and English are going back to the States. They are one of the "Danville Boys" and the motto on their waggon was "Montana or Bust" & now they ought to hang out — "Busted by G - d."

> *If patience and persistence counted for anything in placer mining, James H. Morley should have been a rich man. Taking little time to seek out saloons, hurdy-gurdy houses or other diversions, Morley doggedly worked his claims — first at Gold Creek, then Bannack, Virginia City, and finally Helena — but on none of them did he find his bonanza. Equally methodical with regard to his diary, Morley described his situation with equanimity and good humor. On one occasion he even included a full description of his Alder Gulch "mansion," copying it from a letter he had sent to his wife, Virginia.*

SUNDAY, MAY 22, [1864] — In A.M. wrote to V. In P.M. went to town. Clear and cool. Settled lumber bill. (Extract from letter mentioned above:) "In reply to your question how we live, I will give you an idea of the modus operandi. Our work is two miles up the gulch from town. On our ground is a nice little clear stream of pure water, coming down a precipitous ravine, into the main gulch. Within twenty feet of this limpid water is our mansion, embracing a suite of one room, twelve by fourteen feet. In one corner two bunks as in a steamboat, the lower one occupied by your huge, loquacious brother-in-law, the other by his brother. In one corner is a nice cheerful fire-place. On one side a window, composed of three panes of "10 by 14" glass, side by side; on another side a valve swings on wooden hinges and is fastened by a wooden latch, with a hospitable latch string which is usually out "for all that are honest and true", the whole arrangement being commonly called a door. Tin plates, cups, camp kettles, shovels, picks, clothing &c. &c. are to be seen in the various parts of the apart-ment, the latter of a quality a Broadway pedestrian would be unlikely to don. Also newspapers, magazines and novels strew the shelves, from which you will infer we have still preserved a taste for letters. Now as to cooking, "grub" is the mountaineer's appellation for food, we do that by turns weekly. Bacon, beef, bread and coffee are the staples. We get potatoes and dried peaches, however occasionally. Our cabin outwardly presents the appearance of a Missouri stable, being built of rough logs, but the roof is different, being composed of small poles laid close together, covered with pine boughs, then over the whole about nine inches of dirt, the lower strata being worked into a mortar before putting on. This makes a roof warm and tight for winter. . . .

SUNDAY, SEPTEMBER 25. In morning made survey for Anderson of his drain drift. In P.M. to town. A "bull fight" in corral back of Virginia Hotel, with a large crowd in attendance. No fight in the bulls, being some old stags, who have hauled goods over the plains. but the getters up got their $2.00 a head from a large crowd of fools. This continues to be a great country.

SATURDAY, NOVEMBER 12. Just one year ago today we started drain ditch. . . . I took a long walk toward the mouth of the gulch. It surprises me to see how rapidly this country improves. First, two miles below here is Virginia City. a thriving village with many business houses; then one mile farther down is Central City, not quite so large; then in another mile you enter Nevada, as large as Virginia; then about a mile and half further brings you to Junction City. The road connecting all these "cities" is bordered with dwellings, on both sides all along. I shouldn't have the patience to count the business places, but can say that the market is so well stocked that all necessaries and many luxuries can be obtained in the stores. Recalling that only eighteen months ago this was a "howling wilderness," or rather a howling desert, which the deer, elk, mountain sheep and wolf occupied unmolested, and where the busy beaver built and sported along the thicket bound streams, truly truth is more wonderful than fiction, and excels in marvellousness even the Arabian Nights' entertain-ments. but truth and the marvellous go hand in hand when Young America finds a good gold gulch.

The shrewd money-makers of Montana's gold rush era did not waste time washing gravel in stream beds. Instead, realizing the miners' almost total dependence upon outside sources of supply, these men turned to merchandising. Because of the long overland haul and limited supply, they could, and did, charge all the traffic would bear. During the early spring of 1865, for example, heavy snows completely isolated Virginia City and drove the price of flour to over $100.00 per hundred. Residents of Alder Gulch retaliated by systematically seizing the merchants' hoarded flour. Observing the rise in prices during the winter, newcomer M. J. Morsman advised relatives in Iowa on how to profit in the mercantile trade if they should decide to immigrate to Montana.

VIRGINIA CITY, M.T.
JANY 20TH, 1865

DEAR FATHER:

Your's of the 18th of Dec. came to hand last night, and thought I would answer it immediately so that the answer might return in the next mail, which leaves tomorrow, but I am very much afraid that this will not get through before spring, as the indians are again committing depredations along the Platte river. . . .

In regard to Harley's case I would say that "on the whole" although I have *not* been successfull here so far, I think that if he can get in with a *good* company, with a team of his own, loaded with staple goods, and has no trouble or unusually bad luck that he might make at least one thousand dollars (in cy) [greenback currency] off from the trip, and return next fall to the States, which I think would be the best plan for him, as there is no work or employment for but a very few men here in the winter. I could get fifty men in a days time if I wished who would gladly work until spring for their board.

If there is a large emigration to this place the coming season, there will be a big "stampede" back to the States again next fall just as there was last season, and with a four mule team he could probably make two hundred and fifty to three hundred dollars (cy) by taking passengers back in case he did not sell his "outfit" here. . . .

Although I would *like* very much to see a *big* immigration here, I would not advise any body to come here expecting to make a *big thing*. Although many will undoubtedly make "lots of money" by far the greater number will probably "fail to realize their expectations." There has been quite a number of new discoveries made this winter which are reported *very rich* and I guess *are* but they cannot be proved until spring, if they turn out good, it will make employment for a great many more than are here at good prices, if they do not, there are about as many people here as can make a living except

such as come prepared to make this their home and go to farming or stock raising which is the best business here now for a "poor man with a family," by all means.

In case Harley should come I will give what little information I can in regard to "outfitting" and the route to take.

In the first place the middle of Apr. is soon enough to leave the Mo. River, as there is *no feed* on the Platte before the 1st of May, any season, and sometimes not as early as that.

If the indians have not destroyed the Ranches and prevented the making hay, the South Side of the Platte River is the best road as far as Julesburg which is the *best* crossing. He can find out at the river what the chances are for getting hay and grain along the road, if he comes, and comes that way. . . . From Julesburg to Ft. Larimie (170 miles) there is no trouble for water . . . but *wood* is decidedly scarce all the way from Ft. Kearney, in fact there is a *general* scarcity of wood all the way except Sage Brush. At Larimie any necessary shoeing can be got done by paying well for it. From Larimie the best way is to go to the Upper Bridge on the *North* Platte (about 150 miles) there is two bridges across the North Platte, six miles apart, by all means cross at the upper bridge even if there *is three or four* dollars difference in the Toll as that six miles is "awful" from Platte Bridge to Red Buttes (10 miles) here the Bridger Cutt off leaves the main road. *(Turning to the right* but I would not recommend loaded teams to take that route though many came that way this last year.) Said to be a good road for feed and water except the first 75 miles. . . . There are two roads — one keeps on the South side of the Sweet Water and the other on the North side most of the time but crosses the Sweet Water three times at what are called the "Three Crossings." This latter is the *best* road, if the river is not too high to ford. We came on the South side on account of the high water, *around* the "three Crossings" there is twelve miles of the worst sand road out of doors.

At South Pass Station, "Lander's Cutt off" leaves the main road, the main road keeping on the South Side and the Cutt off on the North side of the Sweet Water. This Cutt off is the nearest road and said to be a good mountain road and plenty of feed and water but the early trains had a great deal of trouble getting through the snow, while the later ones had no trouble except with the Indians, but supposing he comes the *main* or Telegraph road from South Pass Station to Green river (distance forgotten) ferry at Green river, ferry loaded teams *should* take the Ft. Bridger road. . . . Soda Springs is the next point at this place the road divides to two ferries on Snake river, the road to the upper ferry is sixty miles nearest and was a *very* good road and good feed and water when we came over it. On this road you make a junction with Lander's Cuttoff at the crossing of the "Black foot." *Excellent fishing here.* After crossing Snake river at the upper crossing it is nine miles to where the road leaves the river, six miles from here is a lake of stagnant water which is the last water for twentyfive or thirty miles, and the road is terrible as far as *dry* creek (which *is* dry) after crossing this *desert* there is no trouble the balance of the way here.

The Telegraph follows the road *pretty much* all the seventy miles, and by making inquiries at these places and at the ferries the "Pilgrim" can keep pretty well posted.

Four mules are much more profitable and safer than two for if a man should lose *one* he has still got a *team.*

Should Harley *come,* with a team, he should by all means bring one or two passengers to assist in keeping guard, driving, etc. in case he did not feel well, last spring men paid from 75 to 150$ for the privilege of "driving out" (they being boarded of course).

An ax, ½ inch chisel, and a brace and awger bits and *one* shovel are all the tools *necessary.* An extra pair of *lead bars,* not ironed, are very good for a four horse *rig.*

It is quite important that mules should be at least 5 *years old,* as younger do not stand the trip well.

For a wagon the best is a wide track "Schutler" *new,* with a *good* cover, and provided with a California Brake & Rough lock for four mules, and a very light narrow track for two. Schutler wagons will always bring ten or twenty dollars more than any other kind in this market, and are about the *best* wagons which come across the plains.

Thirty hundred, aside from *grain* is a big load for Four *good* mules, *every* effort should be made to keep the stock up in the early part of the trip, and grain or flour feed when possible. The *necessary* expense of my team (2 mules) for grain and Toll was about $80.00 besides one sack of Flour. A few *shoes,* horse shoe nails (ready pointed) and a few cut nails. . . .

If I could sell out my ground I should be tempted to come back to the States and try freighting again this coming season. At any rate I shall sell out at *some* price this summer if I do not get them, the claims, to paying something *pretty* big for I am nearly "played out" on mining. . . .

        E. M. MORSMAN

Merchandising in the gold camps was not without its difficulties; if the profits were enormous, the attendant risks were equally great. Thomas Conrad, a Missouri merchant who immigrated to Montana in 1864 to recoup Civil War losses, established a business in Virginia City. After the mines in Alder Gulch declined, Conrad moved his operation to Helena, where he eventually prospered. A religious man, Conrad found the necessity of doing business on Sunday and the forced separation from his family to be among the chief disadvantages of the trade.

        VIRGINIA CITY
        OCT. 2 1864

MY DEAR MARY

I will write, but in doing so I shall perform only a mechanical opperation. Having received nothing from you Since July, I have no Spirit — no Enthusiasm to inspire me and to write under these circumstances is a laborious task. My desire to hear from you grows greater every day — Some times I imagine you Sick or in want, or the children Sick or dead and after indulging them awhile I brush them away and pursue my daily occupation.

We are now prepared to meet trade and the winter blasts, but competition runs so high that we do not get as big profits as we anticipated. Yet I am not discouraged—I expect to make Some money in case we do not burn out during the winter. We are still in debt about 3000$ which I expect to be able to pay by the 1st of November — after that what money we receive we may call our own.

I commenced boarding this morning with Capt Rogers—it is more convenient to our shop but not any improvement on my old boarding house. I have a good Straw bed and a good house to live in. . . .

Being free from the houndings of the military we have no undue excitement and are annoyed only by the orgies of the frequenters of the Whiskey Saloons. The Vigilance Committee take charge of all bad cases. . . .

I wish I knew how you are prepared for the coming winter — I hope to hear as soon as a mail gets through. I would like to go to church once more — I don't like the Sabbath breaking habit of this country — yet I have hopes of it being speedily stopped. We keep no sign out Sunday but still we have to sell some — I wish to quit it altogether. . . .

OCT 11TH 1864

MY DEAR MARY

I did not write on Sunday last as usual, but I wrote a few days before and Sent it by Mr Sanders. I was too much occupied on Sunday with church affairs to find time to write. The Rev. father Reverdy from Denver paid us a visit and is taking Steps to build a church at once. He is a Frenchman and cannot speak much English. . . .

After this is done I Suppose the father will leave, taking Steps to have us regularly provided for. We need a good English Speaker. We have in this city & vicinity two or three thousand Catholics and many others would attend if we had a good preacher. On Sunday evening we held a meeting appointed a committee to raise funds and another to Select ground and Superintend the building of a Small Church. I am on the last named committee and Spent the forenoon yesterday in its Service, but have arrived at no conclusion yet—the most desirable ground is all occupied—Still there is plenty left—the main thing is the money and I think we can raise that without any trouble. I dont think the people are quite as craving here as they are in the States. If we get a church and Priest here, will you be willing to come out? I think if the war continues you will have to do it. . . .

JAN. 15TH, 1865

MY DEAR MARY

I am in receipt of your favours of Dec. 11-15th & 18th and I am more amused than offended to find your finances in such a bad condition. . . .

I think your experience will have taught you that it is an easier matter to spend money and harder to make it, than you had any idea of before. Your experience will be no loss, I am rather pleased with it and hope that if I fail to make a fortune you will not seek a divorce on account of my poverty. . . .

"When will I come home to stay?" God only knows. You cannot desire me to come more than I desire to go, but so much depends on circumstances, that I fear to promise you anything. But I will promis you this. I will come just the very first moment that I can do so, without to much detriment to my interests here. . . .

"Don't ask you to come to Virginia." You already know that I have left it an open question for you to decide yourself. If you do not wish to come and think you can live in peace where you are, by all means just remain where you are. But surely you would not have to sacrifice my prospects here after making this trip, without giving them a fair trial. I cannot believe you desire that. I shall therefor pursue my investment here as best I can in the hope that I may realize enough to give us a support in darker days for I see no hope of peace or prosperity in Missouri.

But if you should conclude to come out here, I must assure you that I have no fears about the Indians, or their "shields" for I have told you that I never will drag you over the plains, but if you come, you *must* come by Boat up to Fort Benton where I will meet you. And if you kept yourself & Children in the cabin there would be but little danger from the bullets of the Indians. I feel very sure that a large number of persons here have made arrangements for their wives & children to come up the Missouri river in case Capt. Kercheval succeeds in getting a boat. Your greatest trouble would be in preparing to come and parting with friends.

I again repeat, judge for yourself and I shall never complain of your decision, only you must allow me the same privilege. And in case you have any apprehensions about your health you must let me know, and in that case I will Sacrafice anything to get home to see you. . . .

AFFECTIONATELY YOURS

THOS CONRAD

Franklin Kirkaldie arrived in Virginia City in the fall of 1864, anxious to make a fortune so that he might return home quickly. He soon realized prospecting was not for him, but after noting the high prices which farm products commanded, he put his earlier farming experience to use rather than return home in defeat. Kirkaldie settled on a 160-acre farm in the Gallatin Valley, where problems arising from the unfamiliar climatic conditions beset his best efforts. The following years, he tried again on a farm near the new diggings at Confederate Gulch. This time his problems included glutted markets and low prices. Undaunted, Kirkaldie turned to grain farming at Deep Creek. In subsequent years he never achieved the success he hoped for, but despite his struggles, Kirkaldie developed a strong faith in Montana's future and in 1869 brought his family to the territory to settle permanently.

GALLATIN VALLEY
6TH DEC., 1864

DEAR FAMILY:

As it is a stormy day today and we cannot do much out of doors I will write you another letter. I often look at all your pictures — Mama's and yours, and the babies, and wish I could see you all — or even hear from you oftener than I do. And when I cannot do either — all I can do is to write you another letter. . . .

Our cabin is quite warm and comfortable although it would not look much like a house in Joliet. It has no window; but we have a piece of white cotton cloth spread across the upper part of the door which admits considerable light; but we cannot see through it. However, we do not spend much of our time during the day in the cabin and at night we have candles as well as the fireplace which gives a good deal of light. We had no boards or plant [planks] for a floor so I cut down a tree and cut off logs the right length and then split them in the middle and hewed the pieces as flat as I could on one side and we have them laid down the flat side up — and they make a very respectable floor. They are called puncheons.

All our dishes are tin and iron. We eat off from tin plates and drink our coffee from tin cups. Our food is mostly bread and meat and coffee. We have had no potatoes or turnips or beets or cabage or butter for five or six months. We are having plenty of venison now though which is very good meat — but we would like first rate to have some potatoes to eat with our meat and some butter to put on our bread. We have beans once in a while and dried apples or peaches stewed for sauce and sometimes we have some doughnuts or dried apple pies. But we have good appetites and get along very well. I hope to raise some potatoes and other vegetables next summer and then I can have some to eat. . . .

GALLATIN VALLEY
24TH JAN. 1865

MY DEAR WIFE:

. . . . I have endeavored in my letters to you—to give you as correct an idea of this country as I could—partly because I thought it might interest you partly because I had not much else to write about. As to the gold I shall most assuredly use my best endeavours to secure all I can of it honorably—in asmuch as that was my sole object in coming here—But I have not yet secured it and I am fully convinced—as indeed I always have been—that in my case at least, it will require time. I have not the faith to believe that I shall "strike a big thing" and get a fortune in a hurry—It is true a good many have done that—but it is only a very small proportion of those who have run the venture and I do not consider that I have the right to venture all I have and also the comfort and maintenance of my wife and children on an absolute uncertainty—especially if there is anything else which promises a fair and tolerably sure return. Mining even in good mining countries is *uncertain* business. Probably not more than one in fifty of the mining population ever get rich at it, while farming in a good mining country has almost universally proved profitable. . . .

NEAR CONFEDERATE GULCH
30TH AUGUST 1866

. . . .I am offering to sell my ranch & crop here very cheap & it is *possible* I may find a buyer & sell out the whole thing. If I do it will not amount to much — but I had rather do it than to be obliged to stay here all winter to sell what few potatoes I shall have. But it is quite uncertain whether I shall be able to sell or not—Farmers have had such times last year & this year with grasshoppers . . . I fear there will be more sellers than buyers in the market. . . .

I was over at Helena since writing you last—That town is now unquestionably the metropolis of the territory. There are a good many fine large stone & brick business buildings—some of them finished & occupied filled with heavy stocks of good—& others in process of erection—some of them costing many thousands of dollars. I remained there over Sunday — And the scene presented in the streets on that day would astonish beyond measure — anyone who had always been accustomed to observe the Sabbath & seeing the community about him observe it as a sacred day — Here in those mining towns — it is a great day for business — such as buying & selling & pleasure — Every public place — shops — saloons — billiard room & bowling alleys — gambling houses etc. are in full blast & the streets are thronged. The sunday I was there there were 3 auctioneers selling horses — two selling clothing — and there may have been others — but these were all on the main street & within a few rods of each other — then there were several gambling houses with tables arranged for all the different games — some of them with piles of gold & silver coin upon them & surrounded with men playing. These rooms are some of them georgeously fitted up — with a bar & with musicians who are discoursing splendid music, at the back end of the room — In the afternoon there was a horse race somewhere outside of the town & numerous hacks & coaches drove through the street crying for passengers to the race ground. The town — especially the main street was crowded with men nearly the whole day — And strange and awful as all this would appear to one unaccustomed to such sights — it seems to be regarded here as a matter of course. And in all this crowd — and during the whole day — I saw no fighting or quarreling & but one or two drunken men — Nearly all were perfectly civil & seemed disposed to mind their own business. . . .

Near the mouth of Deep Creek, M.T.
16th Dec. 1866

Since writing to you last, I have removed to this place which I expect to make my home— or rather my stopping place until next fall—and as "Indian Creek" is much more convenient to this place than Diamond City—you will please direct letters for me to that place via express from Helena as before. . . . I had the misfortune to lose my memorandum book which contained all the family likenesses—I miss them very much—and if you can afford the expense—I would be very glad if you will have the picture taken which I mentioned to you last summer and send it as soon as is practicable—I feel lost without even the shadow of my family to look at occasionally. . . .

There have been several new discoveries of gold this fall & winter and it is generally thought that business will be very brisk in the mining camps as soon as spring opens—and miners wages as high or higher than ever before. I hope the country may be prosperous & that in my *third* attempt at farming I may be more successful than in the two preceeding ones. . . . Love to the children & yourself.

F. L. KIRKALDIE

In view of the high demand for food products in Montana's isolated gold camps, it was inevitable that the mining industry spurred the development of territorial agriculture. To supply these lucrative local markets a number of disappointed miners turned to the many fertile and easily irrigable valleys of southwestern Montana. By the end of the gold rush era they had been joined by immigrants who came to the territory with the principal intention of farming or ranching. George Thomas was one of the earliest immigrants to make the transition. In a letter to his grandmother, Thomas' eight-year-old son, Homer, described the family's overland trip and the first days on their Gallatin Valley ranch.

Dec. 17, 1864

Dear Granma:

I thought your would like to hear from us all so I have thought I would write you few lines, to let you know that I have not forgotten you all yet. . . . I have got away out here in the Indian & gold country, where there is plenty of gold, but it is hard to get hold of it.

Well I guess I will tell a little about our trip, as it was a very long one. When we left St. Louis, we went to St. Joseph, there loaded our wagons & hitched on the teams & started for Omaha City. . . . When we left Omaha City we struck the old Platte River. We travelled on this river for a long time & came to Fort Kearney, & then away farther up the river is Ft. Laramie. These places have Government soldiers stationed there for to fight the blamed Indians. There is where we had trouble with the Missouri River Sioux Indians. I tell you granma, if you had been there to see us fight the Indians, you would have thought it better for them to stay away or they would get killed. . . .

We had an awful time on the Plains. I don't like that kind of travelling. I would rather take the cars or a steamboat let the old slow oxen go. On the Platte, the musquitoes half eat us up & it was as hot as fire & mighty dusty. I am mighty glad you didn't come with us, you could not stood it, for it was mighty hard for me to stand. If I had known what this kind of a country, & so long a road was, I bet you I never would have come out here to see Virginia City.

It's a very poor city—it is more than half as big as Belleville & crowded with old ox wagons. You don't see any nice horse teams & buggies like you see at home—& most of the men are dressed in old dirty & ragged clothes; they do not look nice, like at home. I wish I was back to get some of your good things to eat & so I could have some apples & cider. There is not any out here in this mountain country. Still I have had some nice antelope, deer and elk meat. I think elk is the best of all, and there is some big bears out here too, but we have not killed any, but some of the hunters kill them.

We did not stay very long at Virginia City. Father took a notion to go down to the Gallatin Valley and take up a ranch. That is what we used to call a farm at home. So we come down and father bought a nice place, and we built a good log cabbin & father put a floor in it, too. I tell you we got a good cabbin. There are not any of them got floors but ours and Mr. Thorp's, and he just put his in today. He lives right close to us, about a quarter of a mile below and has got a little boy about my size, and we have fun now with our sleds, pulling them through the snow. We have two little calves—they are pretty little fellows. One is mine and one is Georgie's. We will have plenty of milk just as soon as it gets a little warmer. It's so cold now father lets them have most of it, so they will get fat & grow big.

Well Grandmother it is pretty near Christmas time and I do not expect to get many things this year, for it is not like home, because old Santa Claus do not come out here to give children things, because he thinks all the children too smart to come to this old place. Well, I can do without any nice toys this year, but I want you to save me some nice things so I can have them when I come back home. I tell you Georgie has grown mighty fast & is

getting pretty big now. He can almost say everything. He says "I want to go Ganma's & get some cake." He don't know anything about apples or I bet he would want some of them, too. . . .

Well, I can't write much this time but I want to write a long letter for I cannot get to write very often & it is hard to send letters to the office, as we live sixty miles from Virginia City & a mighty bad mountain road I tell you. It is called the Bridger Cutoff. Well, to tell the fact, if I was back there, I think I would stay there awhile, but now I am out here I think I will make some money to bring home with me. I have one dollar in silver—two quarters & a half. Father has got lots of gold dust, that is the kind of money we have out here, none of your greenbacks but plenty of gold & the nicest kind, too. I haven't got any gold yet, but when I sell my calf I will get it all in gold. . . .

We built our house out of cottonwood logs. Well, Granma, they build houses funny out here, they put poles or kind of rails on the top, then mix mud & put over them, then they put about three or four inches of dry dirt upon that & it makes a mighty warm roof. . . . I tell you a person learns a good many things by coming out in this country. I expect this will be a great country some day, but I don't care for that, just as soon as I can get enough gold, I bet you I am coming back, for I think I have learned enough of this country to last me, for a while anyhow, for we travelled most all over the mountains & went to most every place except Salt Lake City & I do not care much about that old place, for nobody lives there but the old Mormons anyhow.

Tell Uncle Jim this is the very country for him, if he was out here, he might make something out of himself. Tell him to write to us, we have had no letter since we left home. Father says he don't know what is the matter that none of you don't write to us once in awhile. Tell Aunt Jen, & Aunt Liz, & all of them to write to us, for we do not get any news out here. Tell us all about the war & every thing else, we don't know a thing about what is going on in the states since we have been living in this Golden Territory. I tell you, Granma, butter is a mighty big price out here. It is worth one dollar & a half a pound. Everything is high. Father sells sugar & coffee for 80¢ a lb., in gold at that. Father thinks this is a bully country.

Well I must stop for this time, I will write every chance I get & I want you all to do the same.

GOODBYE GRANMA,

HOMER THOMAS

While Montana's isolation spawned violence, immorality and harsh living conditions, it also lent an importance to glee clubs, debating societies, and theatrical performances that cultural activities have seldom since enjoyed in Montana. Typical of the schizoid character of life were the recollections of Henry J. Bose, a placer miner who arrived in Helena when it was still a "hell-roaring camp," full of temptations and dreams. Bose clearly indicated that he enjoyed having a good time, but he was greatly relieved when the influential Masons found him worthy of membership.

.... I must mention right here when we got to Last Chance, it was certainly a Hell-roaring Camp, wild I had never seen the likes before as we went up the Gulch. The claims were all working hard.... We walked along, on corner of wood Street, Jo and Frank's Corner and across was Dan Florey's [Floweree] large place. We went in. Two Faro Tables running one Spanish Monti and 2 more large tables all running. 2 round tables of Poker, and the bar with 2-3 Barkeepers all busy. It was a great sight, but no rowdiness I noticed at the Faro Tables. Lots of well-dressed men. Men that looked like business men, lawyers or other professional men, all playing, sitting along side common miners in blue flannel shirts, no coats.... it was good to look at, occassionally you would see a fellow get up, and go off rather looking a little blue, but not a word.

In the Spring..., to my great surprise our claim paid fairly well. I had some money "Dust." Mr. Kleinsmith in the Bank made me to open an account and I became a man miner, a self Riser, as all were called that came from the Pacific. There were three distinct classes of People here. First the Self-risers, the ones from Colorado, and the poor trash Tenderfeet that came from the East. Pike's Peakers, the ones who came from Colorado. The Self-risers . . . were principal old miners....

As I did not drink, although I was no angel, I fooled my money away, but not too much. But could a poor miner help it? Here was a town all full of temptation, gambling, dance halls, etc., and us poor miners had to help them keep up and many a one especially if they drank went to excess....

The winter . . . was a cold one. I came to town, and rented a good cabin with George Booker. We were good chums, and spent a pleasant winter. In the Spring I got a claim in Blue Cloud Gulch.... My claim in Blue Cloud paid good wages, but nothing big, and it was worked out during the season. I went to a couple of stampedes, but found nothing. Of Course, we miners never worried about how to get our next claim. We thought there was no end to it. We always lived in a dream of finding it rich

and make our pile. It is the life of a Placer Miner. Well I was doing well, had good health, always working. I was respected and I appreciated all.

I always thought a lot of Free Masons. Had a talk with Mr. Hedges about it once and shortly afterwards, Mr. T. H. Kleinsmith and Mr. G. Woods, a Storekeeper, offered to make out my Petition, and I was very glad of it, and although I was very much afraid for I heard that there was more rejection than admittance, although there was nothing against my character, or my past, but as I found out afterwards so many of the rough element, gamblers and tin horns, when they needed a raise, would try and get in. I was certainly glad and well pleased when I heard after about a month, that I had been accepted and to hold myself in readiness for my initiation.... I took my degrees in the Masonic Lodge and was well pleased and very proud of it....

One of our neighbors, a good young fellow, got sick and none of our medicines helped him. We had the Horse Doctor down from Bear Town. He relieved him some, but he lingered on. We all done our best for Mike Flynn was a good fellow, and well appreciated as a neighbor. Word came that Mickey Finn [Flynn] died. A meeting was held and it appeared that his partners had promised him before he died, that they would bury him by a Priest and in consecrated ground. Now the nearest Priest and Church was in Deer Lodge. Mickey had been a strict churchman. Of course, we all had to go to the funeral... We started out one morning from Mickey's Cabin. We had the corpse rolled up in a blanket and thrown over an Arapahoe pack saddle....

Near the mouth of the Bear Creek, we found a man who had his rip-saw set up in the woods. Some of us stayed there to saw enough lumber to make a coffin for poor Micky, while some of us went into Bitter Root to Baron O'Keefe to borrow an old democrat wagon and harness....

Well, we put the corpse in the coffin, and placed it in the wagon in the back. Next morning when we got ready to pull out for Deer Lodge we had another circus getting the horses started, but after breakfast the procession started, those on horseback going ahead. It was quite a procession. We traveled until we got to Gold Creek. At Pioneer bar there was some ground sluice and we found there was a saloon. As it was late in the afternoon some of the boys went in and had a drink, and pretty soon they went in and had another drink. Then we concluded that as poor Micky had never had a wake we should bring him in and hold a real Irish Wake. We got some candles and brought the coffin in and sat it on two beer kegs. We took off the lid and lighted the candles and there was poor Micky a layin' in there. We had some real good singing and drinking all night. . . .

In the afternoon the storekeeper said to me and Jim to ride on ahead and see the Priest and tell him we were coming and to dig the grave for Micky. So the two of us spurred up our horses and got to Deer Lodge and saw the Father, and told him to show us the place to dig the grave. He was very kind to us and gave us some supper. . . .

As we were waiting for the procession we finally saw it coming down the valley. All of us stood in respectful position ready for the burial of poor Micky. And finally as the wagon pulled up, Lord and behold the corpse was gone. I tell you we sure felt badly. The two drivers said that coming down the hill the wagon had run up on the horses' hind quarters and of course they reared around acting as though they wanted to shake hands with the driver. We all felt pretty bad and were ashamed of ourselves. The Father said for us to go to Deer Lodge for the night and in the morning some of us could look up the corpse and bury it. . . .

The next morning Jim and I and two more started out from Deer Lodge in the wagon. At the top of the hill we found the place where the horses had acted up and after a long search we finally found the coffin down in the creek bed where it rolled. And there was poor Micky standing on his head. We had an awful time getting the water out of the coffin, but we brought the body up to Deer Lodge and buried it with proper ceremonies. . . .

The ratio of women to men in the early gold camps of Montana has been generally underestimated, but the problem for Mary Edgerton, wife of Montana's first territorial governor, was not the scarcity of women, but the scarcity of women of the proper sort. When she arrived in Bannack, Mrs. Edgerton noted the presence of prostitutes and dance hall girls, although she was too polite to mention the fact in letters to her family in Ohio. Her many messages home made it clear that she found little female companionship outside her family and that her life was one of loneliness and homesickness. Mrs. Edgerton was undeniably pleased to leave her log cabin "executive mansion" to return to Ohio in 1865, but she faced her life in Bannack with the resourcefulness and courage typical of most pioneer women.

BANNOCK, JAN. 1ST, 1864

[NO SALUTATION]

I wish you all a "happy, happy, new year." Wouldn't I like to see you all to night? I have been very busy today getting things ready for Mr. Edgerton. have been baking gingersnaps, and ironing fine clothes. I am ashamed to have you see his white shirts (I say white shirts because he wears his woolen ones all the time here). the bosoms look so badly. if I had not so much to do I would wash them over. they are just as I brought them from Omaha. . . .

Sunday Jan 7th. we rec'd a package of letters from home yesterday over which there was a great rejoicing. Letters from home do us a great deal of good. In one of

your letters you wonder how I get along without butter? If you were here you would be astonished to see how we get along about cooking without a great many things. I have bought seven lbs of butter at $1.25 pr lb & expect it to last all winter. But precious little do I use about cooking, & have bought one doz of eggs at $1.50 per doz—have been without milk most of the time since we have been here; when I do get any I have to pay twenty five cents a quart. I get along very well without it. I want to tell you how I prepared the juices of lemons so it has kept until now & I presume would any length of time. I bought a doz of good lemons at Omaha and pressed all the juice into a pitcher, then made it thick with sugar and put it into bottles and corked it tight. put a large spoonful in a tumbler of water & it makes good lemonade. I used one bottle when Mattie was sick &

have one left. The lady that told me how to prepare them said grate the rind of the lemon into them but I did not do so for I had no grater. I think it is full as good without. It would taste too strong of the lemon. If you can get the lemons before Mr E comes back I wish you would prepare some that way and seal it up and send to me. You can fix them so for yourself & keep any length of time. be sure to have good lemons or it will not make good lemonade. try it. Hattie has just been in & says that I am mistaken about grating the rind into the juice but that the lady said grate the rinds by themselves & put sugar with them & bottle to flavor custards or anything we wished.

I want you to send some school books for the children; Greenleaf's higher arithmetic such as was used in the academy. Town's highest reader for Wright & a geography suitable for him. . . .

BANNOCK, MARCH 6TH '65

DEAR SISTER:

. . . . Mattie is holding baby while I write, & I will have to hurry while she (baby) is quiet. She has worried more during the last ten days than [at any time] since she was born. She took cold, sitting on the floor & was *very sick* four days & is not well now but so much better that we think her about well. her teeth trouble her now. We did not wash today but attended the funeral of a lady, the wife of one of our nearest neighbors. She was taken with convulsions about ten hours after giving birth to a child & had them as often as once every half hour for twenty four hours when she died. The child is doing well. . . .

GOOD NIGHT,
MARY

The most popular interpretation of the prevalence of violence on Montana's gold frontier suggested that crime and lawlessness flourished to such a degree under the secret leadership of Bannack Sheriff Henry Plummer that responsible citizens had to take the law into their own hands. The diary of miner James Morley contradicted some of these assumptions. Morley felt the rudimentary governmental authority exercised by the informal miners' courts and meetings was sufficient to suit his needs and he expressed only passing interest in the vigilante activities. Although he supported the Vigilance Committee, Morley's response to the first appearance of territorial government in Virginia City suggested that he preferred the unorthodox law enforcement methods of the Vigilantes chiefly because they represented savings to the taxpayers.

THURSDAY, OCTOBER 16 [1862] — Finished work putting on cabin roof. Weather fine. Moved into cabin in evening. . . .

SUNDAY, OCTOBER 19 — Being now in cabin . . . we therefore spent A.M. in the luxury of a good bath. At noon attended miners' meeting. Weather fine, clear and warm days, with frosty nights. . . .

FRIDAY, NOVEMBER 21 — . . . A very cold night, but warm and pleasant after ten A.M. Pitcher, Jule and self out all day hunting stray oxen. Quite a stampede for new mines said to have been discovered some fifteen miles to the north. . . .

SATURDAY, NOVEMBER 22 — Pitcher, self, Underwood and Bozeman went to new mines, some fifteen miles north and found everything exaggerated. Camped on Fifteen Mile Creek. A fine pleasant day.

SUNDAY, DECEMBER 21 — A miners meeting called to pass the odious code of civil laws gotten up for benefit of a few pettifoggers, but they were rejected by a two-thirds majority to adjourn until spring. Spent day at home.

MONDAY, DECEMBER 22 — At home in A.M. In P.M. Pitcher and self worked stripping claim. In evening had meeting of some twenty in our cabin to organize a town association to operate at Three Forks of Missouri River. Was elected chairman of meeting.

TUESDAY, DECEMBER 23 — Spent most of day in getting up articles of association for organizing the town Co. having been appointed last night on a committee for that purpose. In evening a meeting was held in our cabin which adopted the articles of association. Pitcher worked on claim. Weather continues fine. Elected one of the trustees of the town association and president of the board.

WEDNESDAY, DECEMBER 24 — A.M. spent up town. In P.M. Mandeville and self continued stripping claims. In evening some of the share-holders of the town association met at our cabin to make arrangements about going down to view townsite at Three Forks. . . .

THURSDAY, DECEMBER 25 — Spent this Christmas Day at home. Weather fine. . . .

WEDNESDAY, JANUARY 21 [1863] — The shooting last night made this a day of excitement. Three Indians reported dead and one white, and others not expected to live. A committee appointed to pursue the desperadoes in morning, who started in pursuit accompanied by four of the Indians. Visited the Indian lodges in morning, but the only tenant was a dead Indian, an old man, the whole camp having left during the night. Six of the squaws returned while I was there, one of whose child was killed, and set up a piteous wailing. Four of the men came in soon after. At night the committee returned with the prisoners, among whom was Plummer, the man who shot the man on Wednesday the 14th, he having left this morning, fearing the excited state of feeling among the miners. A guard was posted around them through the night, anticipating a rescue of the prisoners.

THURSDAY, JANUARY 22 — Plummer tried today before a jury and "honorably acquitted," the man shot having been proved a desperado and outlaw, said to have belonged to Watkin's band in California and who had pursued Plummer for purpose of taking his life, said Plummer having served as an officer in California, to the detriment of said Watkin's schemes. The other two prisoners, Charley Reeves and Moore, also Bill Mitchell, still in custody. Was notified to appear at court in morning as one of forty-eight jurors, from whom twelve are to be chosen to try case of Mitchell.

FRIDAY, JANUARY 23 — Was chosen one of twelve jurymen, from the forty-eight of yesterday, in morning, and sat on case of Mitchell all day. Verdict returned this evening and sentenced to banishment for two years beyond one hundred miles of mines. Evidence showed him a man of "reckless conduct."

SATURDAY, JANUARY 24 — Spent day at home. Cases of Reeves and Moore tried before a jury. H.M.M. on jury.

SUNDAY, JANUARY 25 — Verdict rendered in case of Reeves and Moore, which was that they were guilty of "manslaughter in the first degree." Sentence was banishment six hundred miles with punishment of death if found inside these limits.... The culprits had three hours in which to leave, and they made good use of their time leaving before it expired....

TUESDAY, JANUARY 27 — Spent the day in getting up report of our expedition to Three Forks to the shareholders. Messrs. Burr and Bostwick made their report to trustees. Citizens talking a good deal of getting up a military organization to be prepared for Indian depredations....

THURSDAY, JANUARY 14 — [1864] — At windlass all day. Jule in drift. A stream of men going by to town all A.M., which returned late in P.M., among which were our neighbors Cole and Co., from whom I learned five men were hung in Virginia City today for being implicated in highway robberies and murders. One was Lyon, the man who barely escaped hanging in the same place 30th of June last. Also hear of Plummer and others having been hung at Bannack, some at Rattle snake, Deer Lodge, and two down Stinking Water for same crime. Also that Copley had been shot dead at Bannack while attempting to arrest one of the robbers. Such wholesale hanging ought to rid the country of these desperadoes who have rendered travelling so dangerous. Weather warm and pleasant....

SATURDAY, FEBRUARY 27 — .... Report says the first U.S. Mail will be in in a few days. The desperadoes being pretty well annihilated now, letters will go more safely. The number of the desperado gang now hung in this region, by the vigilance committee, is not less than thirty. So the roads are now pretty well cleared of them, as they have been of Indians, that is hostile Indians, some time ago....

WEDNESDAY, MAY 4 — In A.M. resumed [my] work of yesterday. Quit at noon and dismissed our drifter, whose experiences is not equal to his work. He has worked one and one half days and made no advance, taking out nothing but top stuff which comes in faster than it can be taken out....

SUNDAY, MAY 8 — ... Since the summary proceedings of the Vigilance Committee order and quiet prevail throughout the country and one feels as safe, if not safer, than in the States. The miners are a well disposed class and are all intent on getting fortunes. Goods and provisions are beginning to arrive in wholesale quantities, so that the market is becoming well stocked and prices are greatly reduced....

SUNDAY, JUNE 19. In A.M. wrote to V. In P.M. went to town. No letters. Great crowd in town; horse racing and auctions. all bustle and excitement. Emigration continues to flow in and as there have been no new mines found, labor is abundant and many are disappointed. "Pilgrims" find gold can not be found in every stream by merely the trouble of picking it up, an idea many have until they come and learn for themselves: Every thing is safe and quiet so far as Indians and desperadoes are concerned.

SATURDAY, JULY 16. . . . The weather is delightful, cool nights and bright, sunny days, with pleasant breezes. We have a new territory now and a Governer has been appointed. Today a collector made his appearance in the gulch to "stick" us for a four dollar poll tax, as he said, to raise $5000.00 to build a jail. That seems to be of primary importance in organizing government in these latter days. I more than half wish, when I see such officers and the scores of "pettifoggers" going about "seeking whom they may devour" in the country, that Uncle Samuel would let us severely alone, for it is a fact that miners can make their own laws so as to get along smoothly with each other, better than government laws enforced by such men.

Summary justice at the hands of Montana Vigilantes began its most dramatic and bloody chapter with the December, 1863, murder trial of George Ives in Virginia City. The chief prosecutor before the informal miners' court was the ambitious young lawyer, Wilbur Fisk Sanders. As a result of Sanders' forceful presentation and his determination that the punishment be carried out immediately, Virginia City residents executed Ives on December 21. A few days later, Sanders wrote to his sister about the episode, which had as its most dramatic result the formation of a Vigilance Committee to rid the territory of all criminals.

VIRGINIA CITY
DEC 26TH, 1863

MY DEAR SISTER

I wish you from the bottom of my heart a merry Christmas and many a happy New Year and not to you only but all who

"____ grow in *beauty* and side by side.
"And filled one house with glee
"Whose homes are severed far and wide
"By Mount and stream and sea."

I have a chance to send this hearty wish by Mr. Charles M. Davis who . . . is going to Friendship, Allegheny Co. and who if you see can tell you more than I know or can hope to tell concerning myself. I am here practising Law the only Lawyer of the Union persuasion in this Territory east of the Rocky Mountains and of course I think the best. I have just closed one trial of a highway man and murderer and we closed the trial not before a Court but before the people (miners) with passing my motion that "we now proceed to execute the defendant by hanging him by the neck until he be dead," which by nice moonlight we proceeded to do.

Then we tried and convicted a man for harboring highway men & murderers knowing them to be such, found him guilty and upon my motion it was "resolved that the defendant have ten days to close his business and that if at the end of that time he was found in the Country it was the privilege and duty of each and every citizen to shoot him at sight." The first trial took three days the second, one.

The people were tickled at the way I tried the case and I had reason to feel satisfied though I was not paid for the next day. The friends of the other murderers are highway men who were being pursued, came to me in the expectation that they would be caught and said if I would agree to defend them if caught they had raised $500 to pay me. I was so mixed up with the prosecution that I could not defend, and then they said if I would go over to Bannack where Hattie & the boys are and not prosecute or defend but keep still they would then pay me the same money in gold which proposition after consideration I felt compelled to decline.

The people have raised between $200 & $300 and talk of buying for me a watch and chain as a present for what I have done. So I hope I have "struck a lode" as they say here among the mines. I am well, up to Christmas there had been no snow to speak of and no day that boys were not playing ball in the streets and unless I am compelled from now out to modify my opinion, this desert mountains Country has the finest climate in the world.

I have not been to Bannack in a month but go tomorrow. It is 70 miles west of here on the north side of Jefferson Fork. I hope Philo & Jennins of whom I have not heard since I came, will . . . come here next summer. I think we are all well. For myself I was never better. Hattie was not very well two or three weeks ago but had recovered at the last accounts. My Love to all. How is mother and father and Beverly & family & Sophia. How much I rejoice in the hope not so doubtful now, of realization that before Long I may return to see you all well. Adieu.

W. F. SANDERS

Address me at East Bannack City via Salt Lake.

Most of Montana's mining communities flourished briefly, only to die when the placer diggings played out. In the few that survived, notably Helena, Butte, and Virginia City, violence gradually gave way to law and order, and a sense of community and permanence emerged. Many who had arrived in Montana expecting to make their fortune and quickly depart, found that the new land grew on them. One of those who decided to cast his lot with Montana was Cornelius Hedges, a Yale and Harvard Law School graduate who arrived in Helena in July, 1864. After a year working for day wages and giving only intermittent attention to his law practice, Hedges determined to remain in Montana one more year. Then, regardless of his prosperity, he planned to return home. During that year Hedges realized that new opportunities lay in the territory's developing economy, and although he did return home in 1866, his intention was to escort his family back to Montana to make a permanent home.

HELENA CITY
SEPT. 13, 1865

DEAR PARENTS—

I presume you have not forgotten your boy in the Rocky Mountains & would like to hear from him & know of his welfare. I am comfortably situated in this city where I have been since last winter. I am still practicing law though business has been rather dull of late—I have held my own & been steadily advancing since I have been here. I have a third interest in three lots on Main St. on two of which we have houses. One we rent for $30 a month & we rent part of our office where we are to the county for $75.00 a month. We rent the other lot without improvements for $30.00 a month—I have two cabins of my own besides that rent for $10. a month, one—the other is not finished.

I have 300 feet of gulch claims to which we have been running a Drain that has cost me already $400. in gold & it is not finished yet. I dont know as the claims will be worth anything but hope & think so—I have about 10,000 feet of Lode claims that may prove rich but nothing is known yet—In fact nothing is sure here but what one has in his hands. Perhaps I couldnt sell all I have here for $1,000. but I know I wouldn't take $5,000. for it.

I am going to stay here one year more & see what I can do in that time. If I cant make anything in that time I shall come home anyway—I have seen about as much of the mountains as I desire without I get some good pay for it. It is a hard life at best, full of self denial & hardship. Living is very high without any luxuries—We hardly ever see any fruit—vegetables are scarce—potatoes are pretty cheap now, only 10 cts a pound, milk is 25 cts a quart & butter $1.75 a pound—Flour is $24.00 a hundred—So we live—Yet

there is some constant excitement. Everyone expects to make a fortune any minute. . . .

It is a pretty hard country to get a start in, but after being once started it is pretty easy to make headway, if one is careful—I am satisfied with what I have done since I came up here—I lost all I made last season entire—But I learned by it & will try to keep clear in the future—

Life is full of danger here—We have lots of men who are ready to murder for a few dollars. Only yesterday a man was shot not half a mile from a town in open day & robbed of all his money—He started on foot a few minutes ahead of the stage & was to get aboard when it overtook him—They found him lying in the road — Twenty men were out hunting the murderer yesterday but have not found him yet if found he wont see sunrise again—Civil law is but little guarded—Men protect themselves & hanging or shooting is the general remedy. . . .

I wish I could have some apples & cider once in a while—I dreamed the other night of eating apples. It is the nearest I have come to having any for a long time—This is the season of the year that I always loved at home, I would like to help father through his fall work, gathering corn & potatoes & apples—How strange it all seems—I never see a fruit tree of any kind—There is nothing but pine here—I am one of the county commissioners here now—I was candidate for District Attorney on the Union ticket—I expect I am defeated as the secesh are much the strongest in this section—I would like to hear from you very much & all the neighbors & relatives. . . .

WITH MUCH LOVE YOURS TRULY

CORNELIUS HEDGES

Book II
A Society Evolves: Securing the Land..
1866 - 1910

photo by L. A. Huffman, Huffman Pictures, Miles City, Montana

INDIAN — WHITE RELATIONS

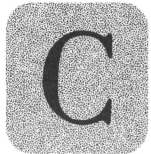

ULTURES IN CONFLICT best describes the causes and realities of the Indian-white encounters which took place in Montana during the last half of the Nineteenth Century. The westward expansion of the country, a product of western civilization's values, brought Indian and white cultures into confrontation. One way of life had to give way, physically, philosophically, and spiritually, in the ongoing process which had touched most of the world since the first voyages of European exploration. Inevitably, the course of expansion reached Montana, and with her unusual opportunities for the ambitious and the energetic, a flood of whites entered the land of the Salish, the Assiniboine, the Crow, the Blackfeet, the Sioux, and the Gros Ventres.

To early trappers and traders, the presence of a large Indian population was an economic blessing, a source of furs and wealth. As mining, agriculture, lumbering, small industry, transportation and supportive commerce developed, however, the tribes became impediments. At best, Indians were white society's responsibility, to be christianized, educated, and shown the joys of the life of the small farmer. At worst, they were marauding savages: raiders, horse thieves, and capricious murderers, occupying land rich in gold, grass, and timber.

Inconsistency forever plagued federal Indian policy, reflecting changing demands forced by the ever-increasing white population entering the Indian lands. The Indian and his culture were always the poorer for these shifts in policy. At different times, bureaucrats, politicians, religious bodies, grafters, and soldiers administered policy. Peace was always the object, but in different guises. Initially, the government viewed tribes as sovereign nations, but this approach was eventually replaced. It gave the Indian too much land, too many prerogatives, and the treaties arrived at were largely unenforceable, or too quickly superseded.

The administration of Ulysses S. Grant determined to treat the Indians as individuals, and to seriously begin the process of acculturation. Grant's visionary "Peace Policy," however, was doomed from the start. White fears, coupled with increasing demands for more land, and encroachment on reservations, forced a conflict which could be handled only by military means. The Indian Wars of 1876-1877 resulted from the pressures, dishonesty and mistakes of the preceding ten years. In Montana, they marked the end of the Indian as a major, disruptive force. The defeats and deprivations of this period forced the tribes to the reservations, there to be managed by agents of the government. The virtual extinction of the buffalo, for which the Indian must share responsibility, in the early years of the 1880's, removed all chance for the old life.

By the late 1880's executive orders, commission agreements, and deceit forced the constriction of the reservations to approximately their present boundaries. The government, usually helpless in the face of local pressures, ignored virtually all treaties made with Montana Indians. These actions left the tribes with little of their former homelands and no other resource. The good intentions of the government or of individuals never had sufficient time or support to be beneficial. The United States, by the early Twentieth Century, provided for thousands of destitute wards, lacking skills, education, or even the necessity of the common language. They were hapless wards in a limbo between a culture lost and one not yet attained.

SUNDAY MORNING AT THE MISSION, ST. LABRE'S MISSION, ASHLAND, 1901

INDIAN — WHITE RELATIONS
Encounter, Conflict, and Subjugation

Much Indian history prior to the arrival of the white man remains obscure to historians because of the absence of a written language. Nevertheless, Indians possessed a well-developed historical sense which they passed from generation to generation through the oral tradition and a conventionalized form of pictorial representation. In contrast with the calendar-like winter counts which depicted tribal experience most accurately, history combined with legend in auto-biographical drawings of a heraldic nature. By depicting his own heroic deeds on clothing and possessions, the warrior sought to gain stature in the eyes of his peers. Here the pencil sketches drawn during the 1880's by the Gros Ventre Elk Head vividly depict two aspects of traditional life of vital importance to the warrior — the hunt and warfare.

Indian culture, though rich and varied, embodied different experiences and values than that of white civilization. After initial encounters, a process of modifying or destroying the native way ensued, often unconsciously. Convinced of their superiority, whites assumed that the Indian culture should give way. Pierre Pichette, through the Indian oral tradition, recounted his grandmother's search for a vision. This experience, so central to Indian life, established the future place of Mary Sdipp-shin-mah (Fallen From the Sky) with the Salish.

The story of my grandmother *Mary Sdipp-shin-mah* (Fallen from the Sky) is as follows — I am telling and writing this just exactly as it was told to me by my grandmother — here is what she said:

During those days of long ago when the country was still free from the clutches of the law of the Whites during those days the attitude of the Indians of their children is to see that they are well brought up, properly taken care of as to the customs of the tribe which is to be honest, friendly, and courteous to all and also their anxiety is to see that their children become real good faith-doctors or medicine men which is a gift obtained from Nature through the beasts of the wilderness and through trance or visions, and now beginning she says.

When I was a little girl of about six or seven years old one day my mother told me that we are going to take a ride up on the mountains to look for some huckleberries of which I was very much delighted and before long we was on our way climbing up the mountains riding double and we went up and up until it was getting pretty late in the evening and believe me all during this time I was sure enjoying the ride and the scenery and just then while we was moving along I could see a nice patch of huckleberry bushes heavily loaded with nice big huckleberries, and me telling mother look there is some nice big huckleberries and plenty of it and she said my child have patience a little further up is the place where we will get our berries.

So we went on and on until when the sun was just about going down she stopped our horse and said here is the place where we are going to pick our huckleberries and she put me off the horse and she got off also and she went around plucking huckleberry bushes loaded with berries and put them on the ground and she said come my child sit here and help yourself on the berries while I am going down here a little ways to see if there is a lot of berries around there too and stay right here I will not be long, be a good little girl and don't be afraid nothing will harm you and she spread out my little robe and I sat on it and began helping myself on the berries.

And she mounted on the horse and away she went saying as she was going my child remember stay right here and don't go anywhere I will be back pretty quick. And she disappeared in the brushes and there I was alone and not frightened as I was sure having a feast eating huckleberries and while doing so I was busily looking around enjoying the scenery, trees, etc., and talking to myself about all the scenery around me and at last I learned that night was just about falling on me and my mother still away yet. Surely then I was frightened and called and called for mother but no sign of her and again calling and calling through sobs as I was already crying bitterly not knowing what to do. So I cried and cried, called and called for my mother during the night. But there was no use as she had left me and went back home leaving me alone on the high mountains. Well I cried and cried until I could not cry any more then I got up and took my little robe and walked away not knowing where I was going and it was in the night yet and so very dark. I went on and on until I got tired and sleepy, then I laid myself down for a sleep and weeping now and then but at last I was sound asleep and when I awoke the sun was way up already nice and warm and me thinking that I was sleeping with mother at home and finding myself high up in the wilderness alone and not knowing of my whereabouts and where to go.

I was sure a lost child and again began crying and as I stopped crying I stood and walked away, and on my way I sure got pretty busy eating huckleberries as I was sure getting hungry. I kept on and on until I got to a place where I sat down for a rest facing a deep gulch fully covered with trees and while I was sitting there resting I thought of home and my old folks and began weeping bitterly and as I was weeping I barely heard a sound which aroused my attention promptly thinking it was a sound of a human being's voice and after listening closely for a while and hearing nothing more, I thought to myself it must be a cry of a bird or something anyhow. But just then I heard a sound again and as I was listening I heard it again and again and this time distinctly the voice of human beings laughing and talking loudly way down to the bottom of the gulch. And I could not see them as it was covered all over with trees and bushes of various kinds and as I was watching I could tell that it was coming towards me as the sounds were getting louder and louder.

Just where I was sitting was the summit of a ridge and below on the hillside is an open bald space and the sounds was coming right straight for it so I was watching closely which sure surprised me with joy to see a woman and two youngsters coming. I was sure happy finding myself thinking with someone I must know from my tribe and while they were themselves running and chasing each other laughing and shouting and when they came pretty close I saw the woman was a very handsome woman, well clothed all in buckskin and clean and this was the mother of the two children. One of them was a little boy and the other was a little girl, pretty little fellows and also well dressed also all in buckskin. And as they came up to me the mother said to me pitifully, poor little girl this is not a place for you especially to be alone out here in this wild rough country and I am sure you are thirsty by this time. Come with us and we will bring you down to the stream for you to drink. And as she turned around she said children you must not bother your little sister, she is thirsty and tired. And while we were going down the little boy and girl were sure happily chasing

each other laughing and playing and they sure wanted me to play with them, and the mother always stop them telling them that your little sister is tired so leave her alone. And when we got to the stream we all had a good drink.

I was the last one that finished my drink and as I stood, turned and looked, instead of seeing my little sister and my little brother and mother, there was sitting mother bear and her two little cubs. I was sure frightened but Mother Bear said to me in a low loving voice, don't be frightened my little child, I am your Mother Bear and here is your little brother and sister. We will not harm you.

Well, my child said Mother Bear to me, listen closely and carefully as I am going to grant you medicine power by which you will be a great help to your people in the future which will be after you pass middle age, but remember you must not try to do more than I am allowing you or granting you because if you do, it will be nothing more than false and you will be responsible to sufferings and even to death, and one of my gifts from Mother Bear is that I am to be helpful to the women especially to those that are having hard times and suffering of giving the birth of a child. And after all this I was brought back safely to my people by Mother Grizzly Bear and little grizzly brother and little grizzly sister.

Horse stealing, to the Indian more sport than thievery, caused continuing problems. Whites, raised in an acquisitive, goods-oriented culture, could not comprehend the Indian attitude toward such expeditions and protested strongly to local authorities. Victor, a friend to the whites, attempted to maintain good relations between his people and the encroaching newcomers. To forestall conflict, he returned the white man's property. In his letter to Governor Edgerton, however, his desire for peace mingled with his resentment at the loss of his homelands. An imprecise treaty, signed in 1855, appeared to him to secure the Bitterroot for his tribe, but whites chose to interpret it differently. The Salish resisted continuous pressure to move to an agency on the Jocko. Begun with the first white settlement, this demand finally forced the Indians' exodus, in 1891, from the Bitterroot Valley.

Four horses have been stolen by some of our young men, but I cannot find them in the camp. Therefore I, Victor the chief, send you four horses of our own, . . . and I . . . send to you the Chief of the whites, a horse of mine, which I present you with for yourself.

I send back also five oxen found, not stolen by our men, from below the Marias. You will see to whom do they belong. . . .

Now I address myself to you the Great Chief of the Whites of this country. Some of the big men among the

white settlers in this our land, spoke to drive us away from our country. This thing vexed a great deal me, and all the other Chiefs, and all my children. I, Victor, therefore do send you the horse above mentioned to pray you to take pity on us, and to put an end to such talkings, and to stop the whites from building themselves houses in our land guaranteed to us by Treaty. We are almost given to dispondency seeing every day new houses started up, and farms taken by whites in our land. We got this spring some ploughs from [the] Government, and we are all busy, and in great earnest to make ourselves fields; but after a little while there will be no more room for us in our own country, if you do not stop the whites. . . .

I, Victor, spoke already to my children not to go to war. But you must tell your white children to give nothing to eat to these warriors or horse stealers both Snakes, or Flatheads, but to let them starve. Though our boys go not much to war, . . . other indians of other tribes go, and say to the whites that they are Flatheads, because we are good friends with the whites.

The last favor that I and all my fellow Chiefs beg from you, is, that you would give order to the whites settled in our valley to sell no wisky to our boys, who go to buy it against our will. I, Victor, an old man already, . . . could not sleep all the winter, because the whites and indians, both drunk, were always fighting in the camp. My heart was broken seeing the whites compelling by force our boys and girls, young men and women, to drink; you know for what purpose. . . .

From the Flathead camp in Bitterroot Valley, Apr. the 25th, 1865.

VICTOR
THE CHIEF OF THE FLATHEADS
[AND SIGNATURES OF 5 OTHER CHIEFS]

Generally good Indian-white relations prevailed, until 1866, when increasing population pressures in Montana caused local tribes to react to their loss of homeland, hunting grounds, and freedom of movement. The acts, or depredations, which triggered the first Indian scares were scattered and, with hindsight, predictable. To the settler, what had been an annoying situation suddenly became a threat to his livelihood and territorial progress. The answer was force, whether federal troops or locally raised militia. Frank Elliott, an Irish immigrant who joined the gold rush, displayed the attitude which rapidly developed in Montana's new communities — a determination to fight. Negotiation and agreement did not suffice and solution to the problem lay in final elimination of the Indian. It was a simplistic answer to a complex issue, but typical of the singleminded attitude of the frontier.

MADISON VALLEY
MAY, 1867

DEAR FATHER:

. . . I have but little news as I have been writing for several days & my news bag is about empty. We have had a very hard snow & plenty of winter . . . it has been as cold as 57 below zero. In the Salmon river mines of which at present there is little known . . . the snow is so deep they cannot prospect.

I thought some of going over their myself but the darn Indians have to be tended to. They killed one of the most prominent citizens of Galatin Valley a few days ago & wounded another while on their way to fort Smith on the Big Horn river. Mr. Bozeman killed, [Apr. 18, 1867] Tom Cover wounded. . . .

Some of the most prominent citizens in Virginia City are getting up Independent Companys to chastise them in the way of killing every thing in the shape of Indians they meet—besides $200 a scalp bounty. I am going with them. They take every thing in the shape of plunder [they] can find, ponies, Robes, etc. etc. . . .

I care but little but some one has to go & I feel [it] is my duty to go.

If some thing of this kind is not done they will make many a poor white man bite the dust [since] they spare neither women or children. . . .

General Meagher, our [Acting] Governor, is going [so are] Judge Therroman [Thoroughman], Judge Davis & several more.

I have said but little in regard to the Indian question. but their is but one way to treat them & that is extermination. . . . They are a great draw back, in prospecting our rich territory. Many are the hardships & exposures which the pioneer has to undergo on their acct. . . .

Making treatys with Indians will not do. Uncle Sam ought to have found that out by this time. Something has to be done and immediately. . . . I tell you we are getting hostile. The Indians have to be chastised & we are going to give them the best in the shop. We have stood it long enough. . . .

FRANK

White civilization contributed to the Indian's demoralization and attacks upon his culture. Firearms, disease, cheap trade goods, and whiskey — especially whiskey — changed his way of life. To the keepers of peace, the whiskey trade was as troublesome as it was to the tribes. Lieutenant Gustavus C. Doane, recognized explorer and experienced western cavalryman, undertook a reconnaissance of the Judith Basin region to determine its suitability as a possible new reservation for the Crows. His subsequent report to the Secretary of the Interior commented on the effects of the liquor trade and possibilities for controlling it.

Since the suppression of the Monopolies in the Fur Trade enjoyed by the former large companies of the north west, this branch of our commerce had not only shrunk very materially in importance, but its revenues have been greatly subdivided. Not only are traders licensed for each tribe of Indians, or for each agency, but there are special licenses given and each of these licenses of every kind can be, as it were, subdivided, so as to cover a number of trading posts. At least so it is managed whether so intended or not.

The Indians, finding great competition between the traders, conceive therefrom an exaggerated idea of their own importance, as manufacturers and producers. They come to think that the whites are dependent of them, for articles of necessity; and actually believe that the buffalo robe is "King" to a great extent, and will grant them immunity for any depredations, if they will only afterward consent to trade. The government policy as to traders, in a miniature sense, is made by them to appear, like the old status political, at times previous to 1861 the subservient many to the arrogant few.

Thus it may be seen, the Indian trade conveys to the Indian a wrong impression at the outset, and one which has a tendency to place him in hostility, rather than dependence. . . .

The above consideration however grievous, sinks into utter insignificance, in comparison with the *whiskey trade.* This great evil is directly encouraged and allowed by licensing traders. . . . *As long as traders are allowed to penetrate the Indian Country at random,* far from the immediate supervision of the agents, *so long the whiskey trade will be kept up.* It is in full blast now all along the Missouri River, openly and publicly from Fort Benton to the mouth of the Musselshell. . . . So long as the trader is allowed under any circumstances to trade away from the agency, so long these people will laugh at the futile efforts of the Government to break up the whiskey trade.

But even the restriction of trading to the agencies would not produce the effect desired and attainable. The agency trader is not there as a missionary, he is there to make money, and the money made is not from dealing in articles of use, but from proceeds of sales of trash.

The Indians are eminently notional. They have most absurd tastes, and are made to pay a most extortionate price for the gratification of these tastes. Observe what "Blackfoot," the most intelligent of the Crows, and probably the most eloquent Indian alive, says the Crows want: *"Mexican Blankets, Elk Teeth, Beads, Eagle Feathers, and Panther and Otter Skins.* We like fine horses and needle guns. These things are to us what money is to you . . ." His vitiated taste is encouraged to that extent that he strips himself of his warm winter coverings, to stand around under a load of brass beads, shells and other gew gaws. . . .

If the government would establish something corresponding to the "Sales to Officers" in the Commissary Department of the Army, and invoice to each agent such articles as the Indians desire, selling them under fixed rules for robes at prices which would re-imburse the expense of purchase, carriage, clerk hire and wastage, and *abolish all Indian trade in every form,* the department would be master of the situation at once. The Indian is a shrewd trader, in his way, and the low prices of the government goods would soon "freeze out" all illicit trade, when combined with enforced rules against those who, under cover of licenses for goods now deal in whiskey and ammunition in defiance of the law. Simple location in the Indian country could then be made "prima facie" evidence of guilt, when suspicion attached, but under the licensed traders system, this cannot be. $500,000 would more than move the annual robe crop and the government need not lose a cent by the transaction; while the Indians would be immensely benefitted, and the labor of the department much simplified and certainly its responsibilities and cares greatly lessened in magnitude.

G. C. DOANE
1st Lt. 2nd. Cavalry

COPIED BY CORPORAL SHEA
Co. "G" 2nd. CAVALRY.

Coupled with unremitting pressures of white immigration, the failure of the Bureau of Indian Affairs to deal efficiently with conditions, left many tribes without livelihood or future. Indians, like the Bannocks, could not compete with larger tribes for the remaining game and received little consideration from the federal government. This neglect eventually led the Bannocks to a minor rebellion, in 1878, which Montana troops quickly put down. Territorial Governor Benjamin F. Potts saw the injustice of the situation and asked Secretary of the Interior Columbus Delano to intercede on behalf of this minor tribe.

NOVEMBER 9 [1872]

Personal
HON. C. DELANO
WASHINGTON, D.C.

SIR:

In behalf of suffering Indians, I make this appeal to you. Ten Doy, head chief of the Bannacks, Sheep Eaters, Shoshones and other Indians, called on me yesterday and asked me to make an appeal to the authorities in behalf of his suffering tribes.

Ten Doy and his band have no reservation, and therefore no home that they can call their own. They are told that the "Lemhi" Agency in the Montana Superintendency, is their home where supplies are to be issued them; but Ten Doy Says when he goes there, nothing is issued them by the Agent, Save a few blankets and Some Calico. . . . He and his band have to go into the Mountains without food or blankets and hunt or Starve.

He Says his band numbers about 500 Indians; that only ten sacks of flour have been issued by the Agent at Lemhi this fall, to his Indians. . . . Because of this failure to supply them with flour and blankets, his band has been compelled to break into small parties and go into the low, warm valleys for protection from the Severity of the Winter and hunt small game to keep from Starving. He says his people cannot go to the Yellowstone this year to hunt buffalo because their arms are so inefficient and defective, as to render them unable to cope with the Sioux or to be successful in killing buffalo.

Ten Doy is very solicitious for the welfare of his people this winter as many are without blankets or robes; he fears they will perish if the winter is Severe. Their condition now appeals strongly to the humane policy of the Government for aid. I Know of no Indians save the Flathead, that are so friendly to the whites as Ten Doy's people, and while the Flatheads and other tribes not so friendly obtain large annuities and have their broad acres

for a home and a hunting ground, Ten Doy's people have no reservation or hunting grounds; and from Ten Doy's statement they receive little or nothing as annuities. No Indians deserve more sympathy or support ·from the Government than Ten Doy's people and none would learn the arts of peace sooner, if they were provided with a reservation and a good Agent who would take an interest in their welfare instead of the one they now have, who Ten Doy does not hesitate to denounce as dishonest and unworthy and who takes no interest in the Civilization of the Indians under his charge. Ten Doy pleads for a home, says his people are tired of roaming about and want to be treated like the Crows and Flatheads. Ten Doy is a good man and deserves better treatment than he has so far received or is likely to receive in this Superintendency. I commend him and his people to you and recommend that the condition of his people be invested by some party outside of the Indian Department of Montana, if you deem an investigation necessary. The other Indian tribes of Montana have engrossed the attention of the Government and their wants have been liberally supplied but Ten Doy and his people, much more meritorious than many others have been neglected and what has been intended for them by the wise and humane policy of the Government, has from Ten Doy's Statement been diverted. I feel that I can not appeal too strongly to you in behalf of these unfortunate people. I have ventured to Say this much in regard to these Indians, at the risk of being charged with interfering with the affairs of another and separate Department of the Government. When the condition of Ten Doy's people became personally known to me and no redress could be obtained here, I thought it my duty to Say this much to you in their behalf.

I am with high regard,

YOUR FRIEND AND OBEDIENT SERVANT,

B. F. POTTS

An early major conflict between native Montana tribes and the Army was the Piegan War. Frustrated young men of the Piegan tribe raided throughout north central Montana. Constriction of their hunting lands, clashes with settlers, and the maddening effects of whiskey forced them to the warpath. Only a minority of the tribe involved themselves in the warfare, but the Army and the Indian Bureau believed all Piegan bands must be taught a severe lesson. The result was the Baker Massacre of Heavy Runner's band on the Marias River, January 23, 1870. The blow fell on the followers of a friendly chief, but it made an impression. The Piegan never rose again. An official report of the Military Department of Dakota, in reaction to criticism in the East, differed substantially in tone and emphasis from the recollections of Bear Head, a young boy who survived the assault.

FROM THE REPORT

As is known to the authorities, certain bands of the Blackfeet Nation, generally living in the extreme Northern unsettled portion of Montana or just north of the National Boundary in the British Possessions, had for two or three years prior to this event, been a constant terror to the settlers, especially of the Gallatine Valley. On frequent occasions during this period their war parties had dashed into the settlements and after killing the inhabitants of . . . exposed ranches . . . and burning the houses, had easily made their escape through the passes in the "Little Belt Range" driving before them all the stock they could collect. In general all efforts to overtake them and recover the stolen stock were fruitless.

Their severe chastisement had long been a positive public necessity. . . . On the morning of the 23rd of January, [an expedition under Maj. E. M. Baker] surprised and attacked a Camp of the Piegans band of Blackfeet located on the Marias river to the northwards of Fort Benton. One hundred and seventy three Indians were killed, over one hundred women and children and three hundred horses captured. . . .

It is to be regretted that in the attack on the Camp some women and children were accidentally killed but the number was very greatly overstated in the newspaper account published throughout the country, emanating from unreliable sources of information in Montana. As is well known to all acquainted with Indian fighting, a certain proportion of accidental killing will always occur in affairs of this kind, especially when the attack is made in the dim light of the early morning and when it is a necessary element of success, to fire into the lodges at the outset to drive the Indians out to an open contest. It is believed that not a single woman or child was killed by our own people outside of the lodges, although, as is also well known a good many of the women on such occasions fight with and as well as the men. From the most reliable information I have been able to obtain I am satisfied less than forty of the number killed were women and children. . . .

As much obloquy was heaped upon Major Baker, his officers and men owing to the exaggerations and mis-statements published in relation to the number of women and children killed, I think it only justice to him and his command that the truth should be fully made known to the public. Recollecting the season of the year in which the expedition was made, the terrible cold through which it marched day after day, and the spirit with which the troops engaged an enemy whom they deemed as strong as themselves, I think the command is entitled to the special commendation of the Military authorities and the hearty thanks of the Nation. . . .

BEAR HEAD'S STATEMENT

. . . Our Camp was on the Marias river Heavy Runner was the chief of this camp. Most all of the able bodied men were out on the hunt leaving only the women and old people in the camp. Myself and about ten other boys of various ages were sent out to round up the camp horses in the morning. After we had got the horses all rounded up we cut the bunch in two the better to handle them on account of their being so many — so we made two herds of them.

When we were moving the two herds of horses in towards the camp and had got them within sight of the camp and were on top of a ridge we saw approaching on another ridge quite a little distance away many riders and wagons. . . . When we saw them to be soldiers all of the boys became frightened and all of them except myself made off in the opposite direction.

I alone stayed with the horses, when the soldiers came up with me one of them pointed his gun at me and made as if to shoot but evidently seeing that I was a boy did not do so. I called out to him "How" to which he responded "How" and kept on going but the next soldier who came up caught my horse by the rein and led it along with him with me still on the horses back. . . .

By this time we could see the main body of the soldiers approaching the camp and getting off their horses . . . which some of them held while the rest scattered out into line. . . . We could plainly hear the sound of their guns and see the smoke as they began firing into the camp.

When the party who had me with them came up to the ones who were firing into the camp, I tried to get off my horse and go into the camp but they held me back and made signs to me to stay where I was or they would kill me. One man said to me in Piegan "Is this Mountain Chiefs Camp." I told him "No his camp is further down this is Heavy Runners camp." He replied, "That is Strange, we have two Indians with us who told us that this is Mountain Chiefs Camp." I said to him "Let us go over to them." We went over to where they were — two Blood Indians with their wives and they were being guarded by a soldier. . . .

The man who spoke in Piegan again asked me if it was not true that this was mountain Chiefs Camp and I again told him No this is Heavy Runners Camp. By this I knew that these two Blood Indians had misdirected the

soldiers to Heavy Runners camp instead of to that of Mountain Chief. . . . I hear one of them say to the other, "I told you that if we took them to Mountain Chiefs camp they would turn us loose but you said if we took them to the first camp we would be allowed to go the sooner." One of the women spoke up and said, "We were to take them to Mountain Chiefs camp and they told us that when they got through with Mountain Chiefs camp they would give us what horses and other stuff there was left as our pay.

After the soldiers had made their camp and the one who was guarding me gave me a cup to go [to] the river for water and as I went . . . to where there was a hole cut in the ice, I saw the body of "Black Eagle" lying on the ice and just above him lay the body of Chief Heavy Runner. The soldier gave me some food and made signs to me . . . to run away which I did as fast as I could. I went to our lodge which was also Heavy Runners lodge and which had not been burned and where the soldiers had taken all of the wounded indians. All of the lodges except this and one other had been burned and all of the robes and subsistence of the camp and everything else which belonged to the camp had been burned. The soldiers camped there for a couple of days and when they moved away, they took with them all of the Horses. . . .

BEAR HEAD   his
X
mark

Increasing white settlement in the Bitterroot and the Valley's obvious attraction as a desirable agricultural area caused steady demands for removal of the Salish to the Jocko Reservation. Governor Benjamin Potts recognized the legitimacy of the tribe's insistence on remaining in their homeland, but argued that the Indians should be removed to make way for progress and white utilization of the Bitterroot. Potts was not inhumane in his attitude; he honestly reflected the beliefs of the era. Indians should be well taken care of, but they should not be allowed to hinder white expansion. Such arguments resulted in the loss of the greatest part of the Indians' land by 1890.

VIRGINIA CITY
SEPTEMBER 8, 1871

To THE HONORABLE
COMMISSIONER OF INDIAN AFFAIRS
WASHINGTON, D.C.

SIR,

Permit me to call your attention to the importance [of] taking immediate steps to secure the removal of the remnant of the Flathead Tribe of Indians from the Bitter Root Valley to the Jocko Reservation. . . . I have recently

made . . . a thorough investigation into the right and propriety of the said remnant of Indians remaining longer in the said Bitter Root Valley and I hereby recommend that the President direct the removal of said Indians to the Jocko Reservation and I beg leave to submit the following facts in support of said recommendation.

First: The Flathead tribe proper is almost extinct. The number of the tribe and those connected with them heretofore reported to the Department is largely in excess of the actual number. I was present in the camp of the whole tribe near the Village of Stephensville about ten days ago and I am satisfied that one hundred and fifty . . . would embrace the entire tribe. . . .

Second: The Bitter Root Valley has now a population of about One Thousand . . . white Settlers located upon Substantial farms and well improved. . . . The Valley is rapidly settling up and in a short time will be filled to its utmost capacity. . . .

Third: But few Indians remain in the Valley during the entire year. The bulk of the tribe are absent on their Spring and fall hunts consuming about the whole year. . . .

Fourth: The [Jocko] reservation . . . contains about six thousand . . . square miles of land absolutely equal if not superior to the best in Montana; is walled in by mountains on all sides; is entirely isolated from all lines of travel; is covered with Game; and is in all respects the proper place for these Indians . . . to protect them from the vices incident to a . . . connection with the Whites.

Fifth: The Agent of the confederated Tribes as well as the Catholic Flatheads . . . have expressed to me their strong desire that the Flathead Indians be removed to this Reservation. . . .

Sixth: The cultivation of the Bitter Root Valley by the Whites is absolutely necessary for the support of the people [who] . . . raise most of the Grain and Vegetables which feed and support nearly one half of our people.

Seventh: The . . . Stevens Treaty of 1855 forbade the settlement of this Valley by Whites, until the President should decide whether any part of it should be set aside as a separate Indian Reservation. The President never having made any decision . . ., the presence of the Whites there is in some sense a Trespass. . . . On the other hand the said Indians have never objected to white settlement in said Valley, but have always invited Settlers among them, as a protection against their hereditary Enemies the Snakes and Blackfeet, who were constantly making incursions into [the] Valley. . . .

Eighth: . . . The Flatheads admitted that they understood from the Stevens Treaty that in case the President should decide that the Bitter Root Valley was not as well adapted to their wants as the Jocko Reservation, they were to remove to [the] Reservation. . . .

For these reasons I cannot too strongly urge you to recommend as follows: First: to obtain action by the President as provided by . . . Stevens Treaty of 1855. . . .

Second: To authorize the Superintendent of Indian Affairs for Montana to make an arrangement with the remnant of [this] Tribe [for] . . . their immediate removal to the Jocko Reservation; . . . such arrangement being substantially upon the basis of establishing them upon said Reservation in as good condition as they now are. Believing that this is the most humane course which the government can pursue toward these Indians, I have the honor to be

VERY RESPECTFULLY

B. F. POTTS

Property taxation provided an illustration of cultural incompatibility between the two races. Missoula County officials deemed Flathead property in the Bitterroot subject to assessment and taxation. Prevalent white opinion saw these Indians as freeholders, not living under the care of the federal government on a reservation. The MISSOULIAN stated, "If an Indian is favorably impressed with civilization and desires to dwell . . . in its light, he should cheerfully take upon himself the burdens which his choice imposes. . . ." Bitterroot Flatheads differed with this argument, seeing their occupation of the land as natural and not something for which they must pay the white tax collector. One chief expressed their displeasure with this further incursion on tribal freedom.

Yes, my people, the white man wants us to pay him. He comes in his intent, and says we must pay him — pay him for our own — for the things we have from our God and our forefathers; for things he never owned and never gave us. What law or right is that? What shame or what charity? The Indian says that a woman is more shameless than a man: but the white man has less shame than our women. . . . No, no; his course is destruction; he spoils what the spirit who gave us this country made beautiful and clean. But that is not enough; he wants us to pay him besides enslaving our country. Yes, and our people besides that degradation of a tribe who never were his enemies. . . . My people, we are poor; we are fatherless. The White man fathers this doom — yes, this curse on us and on the few that may see a few days more.... He says his story is that man was rejected and cast off. Why did we not reject him forever? He says one of his virgins had a son nailed to death on two cross sticks to save him. Were all of them dead then when the young man died, we would all be safe now and our country our own.

But he lives to persist.... Pay him money? Did he inquire how? No, no, his meaness ropes his charity, his avarice wives his envy, his race breeds to extort.... Why thus; because he himself says he is in a big debt, and wants us to help pay it. His avarice put him in debt — he wants us to pay him for it and be his fools.

Did he ask how many a helpless widow, how many a fatherless child, how many a blind and naked thing share what little we have. . . . No, no, his crimes to us are left untold. But the desolater bawls and cries the dangers of the country from us, the few left of us. Other tribes kill and ravish his women and stake his children, and eat his steers and he gives them blankets and sugar for it. We the poor Flatheads who never trouble him he wants now to distress and make poorer.

I have no more to say, my people; but this much I have said and close to hear your minds about this payment. We never begot laws or rights to ask it. His laws never gave us a blade nor a tree nor a duck, nor a grouse, nor a trout. No; like the wolverine that steals your cache how often does he come? You know he comes as long as he lives, and takes more and more, and dirties what he leaves.

The defeat of Custer's 7th Cavalry represented the height of tribal resistance. While the war of 1876-1877 ultimately proved disastrous to the Indian way of life, their victory at the Little Big Horn mitigated fifteen years of frustration. In a rapidly altering world, the Sioux's martial success seemed to reaffirm the "old ways." Thomas J. Mitchell, Sioux agent at Fort Peck, reported a version of the events of June 25, 1876 as presented to him by Little Buck Elk, an Uncpapa dog soldier.

MILK RIVER U.S. INDIAN AGENCY
FORT PECK, M.T.
SEPTEMBER 25, 1876

HON. J. Q. SMITH
COMM. OF INDIAN AFFAIRS,

SIR,

Little Buck Elk, an Uncpapa, and chief of the soldiers band arrived here on the evening of [Sept.] 23, . . . six nights out from Sitting Bull's camp, bearing a message from him to myself.... Sitting Bull sent him to ascertain whether I would allow the hostiles to come in and trade for ammunition.

I dispatched a messenger to his camp informing him that they could get no ammunition here, or on this reservation, but if they desired to come in, surrender their arms and all Government property in their possession, I would treat them kindly, and provide for them until I could receive instructions from you. I will receive a reply from Sitting Bull within ten days or two weeks.

Little Buck Elk stated that he was in the fight in which Gen. Custer and all of his men were slaughtered; and that eleven different tribes were engaged in the fight.

He stated that the Indians were as thick as bees, at the fight; that there were so many of them, they could

not all take part in it; that some men call the soldiers cowards, but they were not; they were all brave men and fought well.... Some of them, when they found themselves surrounded and overpowered, broke through the lines and tried to make their escape, but were pursued and killed miles from the battle ground. One soldier who had a faster horse than the rest, made his escape into the bad lands, and after he had ridden seven or eight miles from where the fight took place, accidentally ran into a war party of Indians and was killed by them. This soldier rode a big horse with flaxin mane and had a Government saddle with grey saddle blanket; but it was not known whether he was an officer or not.

[Little Buck Elk] stated that they captured six battle flags and that no soldiers were taken alive, but after the fight, the women went among the dead bodies and robbed and mutilated them.

That after Custer and his men were "wiped out" they attacked Reno, and surrounded his command on a hill. . . . The soldiers dug holes and got into them and fought the Indians, but if Gen. Terry's forces had not came up when they did, Reno with his entire force would have been "wiped out" also.

He states further that there were plenty of watches and money taken from the bodies of the dead soldiers, and that the young men are now wearing them in their shirts and belts.

He promised me that if the watch belonging to Lieut. Crittenden could be found he would deliver it to me.

He says they have tried to keep the number lost by them from being known, but that it is no use of lying about it, for the truth will come out some time. . . . They had over one hundred Indians killed in the fight; but it was not known at the time of the fight that Gen. Custer was in command and was killed.

I told him I had understood that Lieut. Crittenden was the only child of his parents; and that his death had almost broken their hearts. His answer was . . . you say that the parents of Lieut. Crittenden loved him, that he

was their only child, and that they are sorely grieved at his death, you can judge of the grief and anguish of the parents of the nine young men found by the whites after the battle, lying dead in the lodge. They were all brave and good — yes fine young men, and the grief of their parents is great. . . .

If the relatives of the soldiers who were robbed of their watches and other valuables after they were killed, would send a description of the same to me, I think I might recover at least a portion of the captured articles. . . .

Will keep you advised as to movements of hostiles in this direction.

VERY RESPECTFULLY,
YOUR OBEDIENT SERVANT,
THOS. J. MITCHELL

Federal Indian policy shifted with varying conditions and demands. It suffered from lack of continuity, inefficiency and, ultimately, corruption. When U.S. Grant became President, he determined to alter Indian policy, deal with reality, and eliminate corruption. His initial plan left the administration of affairs to the Army, but Congress would not accept this. Grant then decided the nation's religious denominations should direct Indian relations and administration, in combination with the Bureau of Indian Affairs. Grant's "Peace Policy," as it was called, enjoyed little more success than had earlier approaches. The religious bodies, Catholic and Methodist in Montana, could not control the flow of immigration onto the Indian's land or the graft and corruption which remained prevalent. E. G. Brooke, Whitehall rancher and stage station operator, voiced his skepticism with the administration and effectiveness of the religious denominations. He insisted to Territorial Delegate Martin Maginnis that only the Army understood and therefore could administer the tribes. Brooke's was not a humanitarian view but it was realistic.

WHITEHALL
DEC. 6TH 1877

HON. MARTIN MAGINNIS
WASHINGTON CITY

DEAR SIR:

It is with pleasure I write to congratulate you on your grate speech made on the Indian and army question. On seeing it as published in the Helena papers I at once ordered 2 doz coppys for distribution among my neighbors who do not receive the Helena papers. All . . . here regardless of Party endorse it and say well don *good and faithful servant, you are in the right place and we will with your consent, return you as our delegate to Congress.*

You have made a ten strike, and our people say with one voice Amen. I am in hopes that the present Congress

will make a Radical Change in our (the Government) Indian Pollacy of placing them under the exclusive controll of the army, let those who have them to fight feed them. So far as the Religious training of the Indians is concerned, the Roman Catholic church is the only one that has made any progress in Christianising the Savage. All Protisent denominations have made a failure and today the indians under their controll complain most bitterly of [being] swindled by agents. This to you may sound strange comeing . . . from a member of a Protisent Church. Never the less it is my honest conviction after 12 years watching the working of the different agencys. . . .

Please remember me kindly to Mrs Maginnis.

VERY TRULY YOUR FRIEND

E. G. BROOKE

Corruption and graft in the Indian Service resulted in constant privation on the reservations. Tribesmen, hungry, without clothing, and lacking adequate shelter, had to leave the reservation on hunting and raiding forays. White victims of such marauding bands cared little about the causes, only demanding action from the military. The military recognized the problem and attempted to halt abuses in the supply system. Major James S. Brisbin of the 2nd Cavalry worked throughout his career in the West to alleviate this and other problems, soliciting reports and evidence on the subject. In one reply, Captain George S. Browning, a member of the 7th Infantry and supply inspector at the Crow Reservation, detailed his knowledge of conditions among the Crows.

FORT ELLIS, M.T.
DECEMBER 18, 1878

MAJOR JN S. BRISBIN
COMMANDING, FORT ELLIS M.T.

SIR:

. . . I have the honor to state that during my thirteen years service in the Indian country, I have seen considerable of the workings of the Interior Department in connection with the Indians and in that time I have been stationed on two Indian Reservations. My opinion has always been, that there was more or less fraud and mismanagement at the agencies. Since 1870 my only experience has been with the Crow agency which . . . I have visited several times . . . as Inspector of supplies. A large amount of annuity goods are annually sent to this Agency, which are totally unfit for issue to Indians. . . .

In the issuing issued by me in March 1878, there were thousands of dollars worth of such articles as over-coats with velvet collars, Cashmere pants and vests, all of a material too light and fine to be of use to the Indians, and not one tenth part of which were ever used by them, they being almost immediately traded off to Squaw men and other whites at the agency and elsewhere. In the issue of annuities in March of past year, there was an evident attempt to keep back for some purpose a large amount of annuity goods. . . . After the agency had reported to the Inspector, that the annuities were all taken out of the warehouse for distribution, the inspector entered said store-house, and found several thousand dollars worth of blankets, dress goods, cloth, boots and shoes still in the boxes in which they were shipped.

The Inspector had all these goods taken out and distributed. On speaking to the agent in regard to it, he said he thought the annuities with the exception of a small amount for the "Home" were all taken out for distribution. In the issue of rations to the Indians at the agency during the past year, large issues have been made on paper, when the affidavits of interpreters and others, show that not nearly the number of Indians reported . . . were at the agency. . . . In the reported issues of October 1878, . . . the Agents issue book shows an issue to 300 families, and the affidavit of two interpreters at the post show but about 100 families at the agency. Affidavits of two white men living at or near the agency show that supplies of different kinds, were several times during the past year taken from the agency warehouse at night by themselves and others, under the direction of the Agents employed in charge of the store-house. My inventory of Government property at this agency in November showed that nearly one half of the herd of Beef Cattle, were not branded with the agency brand "ID" and the hay purchased was much of it of an inferior quality. The Agent [has also been] under indictment by the Grand jury of Madison County, Montana, for fraud in the receipt of hay for the agency.

One employee Jn Severn made affidavit in November that he had not been paid his salary in about nine months, although a stub in the agents check book showed the agent had drawn money for that purpose from the 1st National Bank of Bozeman in May, 6 months before. Large sums of money [have] been drawn from the Bank for expenditure for [employee salaries] and . . . not been so applied by the agent. This agent received as presents from the Indians several hundred robes, during the past year.

GEO. S. BROWNING

Reservation and agency sites were selected to keep tribes on less desirable land, away from the path of white settlement. By 1880, expansion in mining, farming and ranching made much of this previously undesirable land appealing. As a result, the federal government determined on yet another Indian policy — one that gave each reservation Indian a share of tribal land and forced the new freeholder to the responsibilities of property ownership. The land remaining after allotment was opened for settlement and exploitation. The policy was formalized, in 1887, as the Dawes Act. While little individual allotment took place in Montana, the reservations were severely diminished in size. Tribes north of the Missouri lost 17,500,000 acres by 1888. Paid in installments over ten years, a total of $4,300,000 was granted to the tribes for the ceded lands. Charles A. Broadwater, contractor and partner in post traderships at Forts Assiniboine and Maginnis, sought special consideration in the redrawing of reservation lines. Using his considerable power in the Democratic party, he asked Delegate Martin Maginnis to arrange preferential treatment to improve business at mercantile establishments he controlled. His words typified the expansionist views which led to the acquisition of ever more tribal land.

FORT ASSINNIBOINE, M. T.
DEC. 6 1881

DEAR MAJOR:

By this mail I send you a map of the Reservation showing that portion in which I am more particularly interested. In the event of any change in the Reservation being made I would like the Western line made to conform to the line which I have drawn in Blk Ink. . . . However I have given the whole matter much thought and have talked with a good many about it. The fact is the Valleys of the Bear Paw and the Little Rocky Mountains and all of the country lying between the Mo. River and Milk River is the very Garden Spot of M.T. not excepting Judith or the Yellowstone. On one point it excels them both in being well watered. I have made two trips across the county since I saw you and the more I see it the more favorably I am impressed. Added to this I do not think there is a question about there being good mines in the Bear [Paws]. I have seen some fine specimens of ore from there.

If in the new program of Indian Reservations the Bear Paw should be given the Indians it is only a question of time when there would have to be another Treaty with the Tribe, as the Miners will have it and they cannot be kept off of it. My idea is to throw open to settlement all the country between the Mo. and Milk Rivers as far west as the Coal Banks or Marias (Mouth). . . .

I do hope you will make an effort to accomplish this matter this winter. It would materialy help me in my business by a large increase in my citizen trade & would be a large Feather in your cap with the people of Northern M. T. This and an additional appropriation of $12 M or $15 M to complete the Post and build an additional sett of Barracks making it a 12 Co Post is all I intend to bother you with this winter. Both I must have or damned if I dont go back on you next election. . . .

YOURS TRULY

C. A. BROADWATER

Following final settlement of Montana's tribes on compressed reservations, agents induced their charges to adopt many facets of white civilization: police, courts, codes of law, and other forms of government. While providing self-government and some self-respect, this policy did not confront the reality of a civilization forced to change too rapidly. Tribal codes accepted in this period illustrated the compulsory introduction of a value system strange to their traditions.

At a council of the Blackfeet, Blood and Piegan tribes of Indians, held at the Blackfeet Agency, Montana Territory on the 20th, 21st, 22nd and 23rd days of April, A.D. 1875, an election of chiefs was had and the following Code of Laws adopted.

The council opened with prayer and songs to the

Divine Father, the Indians all kneeling.

The meeting was called to order by Agent John S. Wood, who commenced by saying: . . . "For many years you have been without unity, without a head chief and without laws, roaming over the prairies in small, unfriendly, if not hostile bands, killing each other under the influence of whisky. . . . I want you to elect a head chief who does not drink whisky and who will care for and control his people." . . .

After deliberation and voting the council declared Little Plume elected Head Chief by a unanimous vote, and Generous Woman and White Calf, subordinate head chiefs by a like vote.

Whereupon they adopted the following Code of Laws for the government and welfare of their people, pledging themselves in the presence of the Great Spirit to obey and enforce them.

Art. 1st — The Head Chief and two subordinate head chiefs, together with the Agent, shall constitute a tribunal for the trial of any Indian . . . charged with a breach of these laws. . . .

Art. 2nd — If any Indian shall kill another, he shall be arrested and tried, and if found guilty of murder, shall be hanged by the neck until dead; but in case of an Indian killing a Whiteman or woman, he shall be arrested and given in custody to the civil authorities.

Art. 3rd [and 4th] — If any Indian shall threaten to kill another [or steal from another], he shall be arrested and tried, and if found guilty, shall be punished by a fine of horses, robes or peltries, or imprisoned. . . .

Art. 5th [and 6th] — If any Indian shall strike, beat or bruise another, [or his wife, or any other woman], in anger, he shall be . . . punished by a fine of horses, robes, or peltries or imprisoned. . . .

Art. 7th — If any Indian shall take to himself more than one wife, . . . he shall upon conviction . . . be punished by fine or imprisonment. . . .

Art. 8th — If any Indian shall have carnal knowledge of any woman by force, he shall . . . be punished by fine or imprisonment. . . .

Art. 9th — If any Indian shall sell his daughter, wife, mother, sister, or other woman, to any Indian or Whiteman he shall . . . be punished by . . . fine or imprisonment, . . . and the woman thus sold shall be freed, and no claim be made upon her by reason of such sale or bargain. . . .

Art. 10th — Every Indian accused of any crime or breach of the foregoing laws shall be arrested by the chiefs or Agent. . . .

Art. 11th — If any horses belonging to Whitemen be found by any Indian . . . such . . . horses shall be given to the Agent, and should any Indian conceal or sell such . . . horses, he shall . . . be fined and punished. . . .

Art. 12th — If any Indian . . . receiving rations from the Government shall buy, sell, or keep . . . any spirituous or intoxicating liquor, or . . . use the same, [he] shall . . . be punished by . . . fine and imprisonment.

Art. 13th — The tribunal shall have power . . . to inflict punishment and fines . . . but such punishment shall not be barbarous or cruel, or endanger life.

Signed: LITTLE PLUME . . . Head Chief

[And 19 Subordinate Chiefs/Headmen]

As the turn of the century neared, the Indians of Montana lived with the remnants of their culture, at the mercy of white civilization. In an era of self-assured progress, no thought was given to the uniqueness or viability of the Indian way of life. The dominant culture made several assumptions: the Indian would adapt to white social patterns; through education, agriculture, and the acceptance of new values, he would be assimilated. Major James S. Brisbin, a champion of the Indian cause, demonstrated his humane and concerned approach to the problem. Nevertheless, his suggestions enunciated the values of the Nineteenth Century: fairness, education, and their own farms would make good citizens of tribesmen only recently torn from a different life. Right or wrong, this solution had small hope for success; such a major transition required centuries, not decades.

Fort Custer, Montana
December 18, 1889

. . . It has been my misfortune as an Officer of the Army to be stationed among or within close proximity of various Indian Tribes for more than twenty years, and it cannot therefore be said that I know nothing about Indians. The Truth is I know a great deal about Indians, and especially the tribes of the Northwest. . . . It is only the western man who has to deal almost daily with the Indian, that can understand his wants and necessities and realize fully what is best to be done for him. . . .

First . . . let all the reservations be surveyed at once and the Indians settled on the best lands . . . and this done, let the rest be speedily thrown open to settlement by white men. . . . The Agents should not only encourage them the first year, but *insist* upon their taking farms the second year and *locate lands for all who had not availed themselves of their privilege.*

Of course the Indians should be assisted with oxen, agricultural implements and seed to sow, but I would have it understood that at the end of four years, assistance from the Government in this respect would be withdrawn, and the Indians must become self supporting. . . .

During the last Century, we have done nothing for the Indian worth mentioning unless it has been to rob him of his land and cheat him out of his just dues and rights. Our Indian policy, as a great writer recently said, has been "a century of dishonor." . . . The only safe road out of our Indian difficulties, I believe, is to educate the Indian. Little can be done with the old Indian, but the young ones are easily educated and if we get to work in earnest in two or at most three generations *savages* will have disappeared from the American Continent. . . .

The present salaries of Indian Agents are merely a method for converting an honest man into a thief. The honest Indian Agent can make nothing, cannot even live on the frontier, while the dishonest Agent can in a year or two return home with $10,000, $20,000 or even $50,000.

We should give our Agents salaries commensurate with the danger, duties and responsibilities of their positions. Make their tenure of office during life or good behavior and we would soon have an efficient Indian service. . . .

It is with a faint hope, I may awaken for the Indian some interest in the hearts of good citizens, that I write these words. . . . The shame of having first robbed a people of their lands and homes and then left them to perish in poverty, ignorance and without even a knowledge of God, is ours. . . .

Our churches should move in the matter and each denomination should build up a school for the purpose of educating and christianizing Indian children. These schools should be at or near cities and large towns, where the Indian children would be constantly surrounded by the influences of civilization. . . . To make the education of the young Indians effective they should be separated from their parents and savage surroundings and placed in the midst of civilization where they would be compelled to attend school regularly. When they had learned to read, write, and had acquired a knowledge of the Bible, they should be allowed to go at any trade they might fancy. Indian girls, after a year or two in a good industrial school, would make very good house servants, and the boys readily take to farming, carpentering, blacksmithing and many other trades. . . .

Transition did not come rapidly. The increasingly civilized expanses of Montana still appealed to the Indian. Reservation Indians, caught between tradition and reality, rose occasionally in futile revolt, causing consternation in surrounding towns. Unprovided for tribes, such as the Crees, roamed in search of sustenance. Residents, like Thomas Miles, complained to the Governor about such "interlopers." The Indian, in a rapidly maturing society, became an irritant, not a major threat, dealt with by civil rather than military authority.

SILVER BOW, MONTANA
NOVEMBER 22, 1891

HON. J. K. TOOLE
HELENA

DEAR SIR:

I desire to inform you that there is some Fifteen Lodges of Indians gone into winter quarters near my place. . . . They say they are Crees, none of them "savvy" English altho there are a goodly number of them. They have from one hundred to one hundred and twenty horses and these they have put right onto my winter range and have scared or driven mine off. . . .

Now I am a resident and taxpayer of this place, my home and family are here. My stock which consists of some two hundred head of horses and fifty or sixty head of cattle live and range on those hills that those Indians have appropriated and I as well as all my nabours protest.

Further we have signs of Indian wars every spring, Massiah crazes etc etc. and we here would prefer to be excused and think that if those Indians belong to the U.S. they should winter on their Reservation. . . . If they are British or Canadian Indians they should be compelled to go there. I inquired in Butte yesterday for some authority or person to report to and was refered to you, so hoping your Excelency will give this matter due attention, I will be greatly obliged. . . .

YOURS VERY TRULY,
THOS. O. MILES

As the Nineteenth Century closed, the Indian, once a threat to settlement, became a minor consideration in the development of the American West. Isolated on reservations, the Indian made minimal advances in agriculture and education. But as a curiosity he had value. Wildwest shows, exhibits, and nickles constituted the tribes' contribution to American culture. Arrangements for an exhibit of Montana buffalo and Indians at the Columbian Exposition in Chicago in 1893 reflected this degradation. Indian Commissioner Morgan's concern with authentic costumes and lodges provided a footnote to the end of a culture.

DEPARTMENT OF THE INTERIOR
OFFICE OF INDIAN AFFAIRS
WASHINGTON, APRIL 23, 1892

PETER RONAN
U. S. INDIAN AGENT,
FLATHEAD AGENCY, JOCKO,
MISSOULA CO., MONTANA.

SIR:

Referring to previous correspondence on the subject of having at the Chicago Exposition a herd of buffalo raised upon the Flathead reservation. . . . We have [considered] your proposition that Indians of mixed blood, named Charles Allard and Michael Pablo shall take to Chicago their herd of buffalo to be exhibited during the Columbian Exposition. These men you represent to be capable of managing the entire business without outside assistance.

. . . If it is practicable, it is better that the entire exhibit should be planned and carried out by persons of Indian blood, who will thus furnish an exhibit not only of Indians and of buffalo, but also illustrate and show the capacity of Indians for business. In this connection, however, you would do well to impress upon the minds of these men, that while the exhibit of buffalo may seem a very simple thing to do, there is connected with it, a good deal that might prove an embarrassment to them.

It will be necessary for them to secure from the Committee of Ways and Means at Chicago, a concession for the use of a certain tract of land for which a certain tax must be paid. Moreover provisions must also be made for having the ground fenced, and for food for the buffalo. There must be a gate keeper and a treasurer, the expense of transporting to and from Chicago of the animals and the Indians who care for them [must be paid for] etc., etc.

In short, before they enter upon a scheme of this kind, they ought to think it out in all its details and be perfectly sure of what they are going to do, and what it will cost, and whether they have sufficient capital to undertake such an enterprise without risk of bankruptcy.

[I] consider it desirable . . . that those who care for the buffalo should be dressed in native costumes, and bring with them and erect in Chicago their native habitations; so that those who attend the exhibition of the animals may see as clearly as possible a transcript of life in the Indian country as it used to exist in the days of buffalo hunting.

So far as this office is concerned I am willing to give my indorsement of this scheme to the authorities at Chicago with a view of assisting Messrs. Allard and Pablo in securing the concession already suggested, and am perfectly willing to give [a] permit for such persons to be absent from the reservation for this purpose, as you may recommend. Further than this, however, I cannot go, and cannot assume any responsibility whatever for the financial arrangements or out-come; in so far as it is a business transaction, the responsibility must rest upon the shoulders of those who undertake it.

During the time the Indians may be [in] Chicago under permission from this office, they must conform to any rules and regulations that may be prescribed for the government of Indians at the Columbian Exposition. . . .

VERY RESPECTFULLY,

T. J. MORGAN
COMMISSIONER

THE MILITARY EXPERIENCE

SCENES OF CHARGING CAVALRY have dominated the popular image of the American Army's frontier service. Infrequently, such momentous clashes did take place, but a soldier spent an overwhelming preponderance of his time in far less "glorious" pursuits. Scouting, maneuvers, tracking livestock thieves (Indian and white), road maintenance and security, providing communications, garrison duties, and countless hours of unwelcome idleness constituted the decidedly unglamorous service of cavalry and infantry stationed at Montana posts. One of the military's enduring accomplishments in Montana was its contribution to exploration and establishment of transportation routes — providing survey escorts or actually manning the exploration.

As the large influx of miners, farmers, businessmen, and their families rapidly populated the infant communities of Montana, the demand for the military's presence rose. Security from the Indian menace, often more imagined than real, and guaranteeing safety of transportation and communication were the major responsibilities of men in the garrisons. Major clashes with tribes of the region — Red Cloud's War, 1866-1868; the Piegan War, 1870; the Sioux-Cheyenne War, 1876-1877, and the Nez Perce War, 1877 — demanded heavy commitments of U.S. troops from Fort Ellis, Fort Shaw, Fort Benton, Fort Smith, and Fort Logan.

The cessation of these conflicts marked the virtual end to any serious Indian threat to Montana communities. It did not, however, signal a similar scaling down of the Army's presence in Montana. Several major forts, including Missoula, Assiniboine, Maginnis, Custer and Keogh, were completed well after the conclusion of the campaigns of Gibbon, Custer, Miles, Baker and others. Built to replace outmoded posts such as Ellis, Logan and Shaw, these forts actually increased troop levels in Montana.

This continuing — and largely unnecessary — military commitment in the Territory and State of Montana was a major factor in the development of many communities and areas. The arrival of black troops, the Spanish-American War excitement, and the use of soldiers to quell labor conflicts were some of the more significant aspects of the region's military history in the last decades of the Nineteenth Century.

To the men in the ranks, most service in the years after 1877 presented little more than drudgery and an unchanging view of a forbidding landscape. Boredom, homesickness, excitement and apprehension were all elements in the writings of officers and men serving at the scattered posts in a rapidly maturing region.

SCOUTING NEAR FORT MAGINNIS, 1888

THE MILITARY EXPERIENCE
Contrasts in Adventure and Boredom

Mushrooming populations at gold camps like Bannack, Alder Gulch and Last Chance Gulch began to exert pressure on the Indians of Montana. Native tribes responded with raids, depredations and attacks on small parties and individual travelers. These led to the territory's first major Indian scare with resultant demand for federal protection, and the raising of local militia. Not incidentally, such military efforts proved profitable to local merchants and entrepreneurs. They were among the most vocal in demanding military security. Hezekiah Hosmer, an Ohio Republican, appointed Territorial Chief Justice by President Lincoln, commented on the first flurry of excitement to his friend and fellow investor, Samuel T. Hauser.

VIRGINIA CITY
JUNE 24, 1865

FRIEND HAUSER,

. . . Langford is well & will write you . . . today, by the next mail. Your brother is here, and had a good time dodging Indians between here and Denver. The very d-l will be to pay with the indians in this Territory unless Government lends us a helping hand. They killed twelve men at the mouth of the Marias three weeks ago, and our Governor, and Sanders made a great fizzle over it in getting up troops to send on for the protection of the route from Benton to Helena. We had more Generals and Colonels, etc., etc., than there were in the Army of the Potomac, trying, with beat of drum, a great display of flags, and a most melancholy waste of cheap whiskey, to raise 500 men. The result was, after a fortnight recruiting, boys and all, the company numbered about 30, and broke up in disgust after having pressed into the service, from the Ranches on the Stinking Water, about 90 of the hardest looking specimens of horse and mule flesh you ever laid eyes on. It was a tremendous exhibition of windy patriotism, out of which no Buncombe could be made for any body. . . .

Cortright who was our agent in building ferry boats at Big Horn & other rivers on the route, was attacked by the Indians two weeks ago and he and his party barely escaped with their lives. One was killed. Courtright came in here reduced to [a] mere skeleton and his clothes full of bullet holes. He was without food nearly ten days. His best friends did not know him. It is supposed now that the Indian Confederacy against the white embraces all the indians in the Territory except the Flat Heads. They threaten to attack Virginia City before fall. Government should send us two Regiments.

New gulches continue to be discovered every week of more or less richness. There is no limit to the mineral wealth of the Territory, but the climate is abomniable. We had a snow storm of three days duration last week. . . . I can think of nothing more that is new except that we are making grand preparations for an old fashioned 4th of July celebration. Let me hear from you soon.

TRULY YOURS,

HEZ. L. HOSMER

Increased immigration to Montana, coupled with continued threats of Indian hostilities, forced the federal government to establish permanent military posts in Montana Territory. One of the first, Camp Cooke, at the mouth of the Judith River, proved to be a temporary and ineffectual garrison intended to guard the head of Missouri River navigation and the overland freight routes from the river to the mining camps. Lieutenant Martin Hogan, Irish immigrant and Civil War veteran, served with the force that established Camp Cooke. His letters to Andrew O'Connell, a pioneer merchant and contractor, discussed the routine of frontier military life and mentioned the reconnaissance of the Sun River Valley. This survey eventually led to the establishment of Fort Shaw, headquarters post for the Military District of Montana.

CAMP COOKE, M.T.
AUG. 25, 1866

ANDREW O'CONNELL, ESQ.

SIR:

I wrote to you some time ago and sent the letter by Gov. Meagher who was my guest at this post a short time ago. Not ever having seen you and yet knowing you so well, hearing my sister, Ann, and Mary that is Mrs. M. W. O'Connell, your brother's wife, and Mrs. Michael Hall speak so often of you, also your own brothers and sisters, Mrs. Healy, Mrs. Ryan, Dan, John & M.W.

Mr. O'Kief who will hand you this note, came to the Camp yesterday and on inquiry I learned that you were at Blackfoot. I would like very much to see you to give you all the Terre Haute news of the last 8 or 9 years. I am commanding the Cavalry of this command and will be in Fort Benton and Sun River some time between the 1st and 15th of September. Could you not make it convenient to meet me. I know how much you old miners think of riding a few hundred miles so there are no excuses for you but to come.

I suppose you have heard of me as a child from my brother, John, who, as I understand, stood in years past in the relation of one of your greatest chums, but poor Brother, he found an early grave, his remains like many more of your former acquaintances lies in the Catholic Cemetery of Terre Haute blotted out of this Sphere but not forgotten.

You will perhaps wonder at finding me the youngest of the Hogan family in the regular army and only a few years from Ireland. I entered the Volunteer Army as a private soldier early in 1861 and raised to the rank of Major. After the war was over Andy Johnson thought I was a bully boy and sent me a commission in the regular army as 2nd Lieut. This new Army bill passed by Congress will make me a Captain so I am all OK. I suppose you will be up in this country perhaps for several years. I expect to see you often. We always have in Camp plenty of whiskey, Cigars and fat pork so if you visit me I will neither let you perish from thirst or starvation. I am under the impression that I, with my Cavalry Command, will winter at Sun River, and the Battalion (First Battalion, 13th U.S. Infantry) will undoubtedly move there and build permanent quarters next Spring. Mr. O'Keif was my guest last night and I got on a bust and my pen is somewhat tremulous this morning but, so as you can decipher it, I dont care, for as long as there is need for Military Officers so there will be a demand for whiskey. Judging from this Command of the regular army, especially the officers, has more mortal combats with the Legions of Bourbon than any other Monarch, but enough of this. Let me hear from you.

I have the honor to be, very respectfully,

YOUR OBT SVT

MARTIN E. HOGAN
LIEUTENANT, 13TH U.S. INFANTRY

CAMP OF 1ST BATTALION
13TH U.S. INFANTRY
MOUTH OF THE JUDITH, M.T.
SEPT. 17, 1866

DEAR FRIEND:

A few days ago I had an opportunity to acknowledge receipt of your very friendly and welcome letter of August 28 but only had time to say a few words. It was not for lack of time on my part for, in general, officers of the Army have more leisure hours than any other class of men having little else to do than attach their signature to the official papers after they are prepared by their clerks.

... 'Tis true that the salary of a line officer is not very heavy, a Lieutenant being $140.00 and a Captain $163.00 per month but unless we go to extravagance it is plenty to supply our wants, and if we were very extravagant in this desert, it could not be gratified.

Money in a soldier's pocket in Montana is as useless as so much paper clipped from a corner of Greeley's N.Y. Tribune. We have our commissary and sutler who supplies — with a bountiful hand — our table, but we are entirely excommunicated from our evening social parties, our chit chats with pretty girls and last but not least, our morning bitters and evening hot punchs; but in summing up all, we enjoy life as well as mortals should.

A few days ago I returned from a trip to Sun River. I was ordered by Major Clinton, commanding at this post, to proceed with mounted men to accompany Captain Webb to Sun River for the purpose of reporting on the policy of establishing a military post in that vicinity. We were absent 8 days and had a very pleasant time. Several gentlemen, citizens of Fort Benton, accompanied us.... We visited the old Mission (St. Peters), the government farm, and a great portion of the Sun River Valley. Spent two days hunting and fishing and drinking claret, and

returned to Camp with a report that Sun River is only second to the Garden of Eden.

Captain Webb and myself after returning were immediately detached from the Battalion with orders to make preparations to return to Sun River with our Companys to remain during the winter and, in a few days, we will have the pleasure of bidding a last, but by no means a tearful, farewell to the bleak hills of the Judith. We should have gone there at first to be of any benefit to the people of this Territory as we are no more use here than in St. Louis. It was no will of ours in stopping here; we only obeyed orders from a higher source. I am sorry to say that I won't be able to visit you at your home.... [but] I trust you will do me the honor of spending a few days with me at the Mission at your earliest convenience. Bring any of your friends with you. Myself and the Captain (who is a courteous gentleman) will take the best of care of you — and now I consider your visit a settled matter. ...

OBT. SERVANT

MARTIN E. HOGAN
LIEUT. 13TH U.S. INFANTRY

The opening of the Bridger and Bozeman Trails, in 1864, compounded Indian resistance to the increasing numbers of miners. These cutoffs led through some of the choicest unceded hunting grounds claimed by the Sioux and Northern Cheyenne. In 1866, to protect the routes and immigrants using them, the Army established three forts along the Bozeman Trail: Forts Reno and Phil Kearny in Wyoming, and Fort C.F. Smith in Montana. The posts further infuriated the tribes and the Red Cloud War, 1866-1868, ensued. Tribes attacked immigrants, supply trains, and military detachments indiscriminately. The clashes included the well known Fetterman ambush, the Wagon Box and Hayfield fights. Intense tribal opposition forced the military to abandon the trail and its forts to the Sioux and Cheyenne. Lieutenant Edmond R. P. Shurly, a Chicago native, later wrote of an experience he had commanding the escort for a train of freight wagons ascending the Bozeman Trail between Forts Kearny and C. F. Smith.

GENERAL,

... In the latter part of October 1868 [November 4, 1867] I was detailed to escort [a] waggon train to Fort Phil Kearney W.T. A detail of forty men from the four companies at Fort C. F. Smith was ordered to report to me for duty. The Indians in the Powder River Country ... had been on the warpath for some time, many of the waggon trains unless very strongly guarded had to fight

their way up and down [the Bozeman Trail].... My order was to change trains if I met one between Smith and Phil Kearney. ...

We arrived at a point about six miles from Fort Phil Kearney [and] saw in the distance ... near the Fetterman Masacre ground a train corralled [and] also quite a body of Indians on the Bluffs in the vicinity of the train. We pushed on as rapidly as possible to aid the train in distress. about the time we arrived . . . the Indians left. The train belonged to Wells Fargo & Co. [and] was drawn by oxen [and] composed of 26 waggons heavily loaded. In obedience to orders I took possession of this train. . . .

About twenty two miles west of Fort Phil Kearney near Goose Creek, the trail crossed a deep ravine . . . about 500 yards beyond the ravine there was a bottom. . . . I ordered [that] as fast as a wagon was passed, [through the ravine] it be taken to this bottom and as it arrived, immediately coralled. . . .

I [had a] little Howitzer [which] I kept at the rear of the train, . . . in charge of Corporal Donely. . . . I told him to send a shell at the First Indians he saw. I had passed all the waggons over except three. They had coralled as ordered when bang went the Gun and in less time than I can write it the rear guard, seven men and myself, were cut off from the rest. . . .

Corporal Donely was badly wounded — I saw the situation at a glance. I told the driver of the gun to make for the corall, save the gun at all hazzerds. Those mules flew — The Indians were [on] one side of the wagons, we on the other. . . . Two of my men were killed. I had an arrow through my left foot from an Indian on the other side of the wagon. Bullets and arrows flew lively. Fortunately I had with me a small revolver and an old fashioned colt (horse pistol). . . . The Indian that shot me dashed round the end of the wagon. I shot him in the stomach at the same time [two] other Indians fell by the wagon from Springfield Musket bullets. The Indians were coming down the Bluff rapidly. I said make for the coral. I got Corporal Donely by the arm and how I reached that coral I do not know. The corporal lived only a few minutes after reaching it. We saw the Bluffs were black with Indians.

I was suffering fearfully with my foot, the arrow had passed through so that the point protruded through the sole of my boot, no time for a surgical operation. I caused the sacks of corn to be unloded, piled under the waggons [and] closed the mouth of the circle, so [we had] just room to operate the gun. . . . The Indians kept up their fire but did not come close, we could see about a hundred of them inspecting the wagons [and] . . . they were a prize. I did not know until then that those wagons contained stock for the Post Trader at Fort C. F. Smith, two of them loaded with Red Blankets, more precious than diamonds to Indians.

I was very weak but had pulled out or rather pushed through the arrow and bandaged my foot with my neck tie.

I said bring some amunitin for the Gun. Let the men fill there cartridge boxes; but you may judge of my dismay when I learned that the mules and [ammunition] wagon was gone — in fact run right into a lot of Indians coming from the direction of Goose Creek. Our command consisted now of thirty-one soldiers with about 40 rounds to each man left, 26 drivers, 1 wagon master, Wm Harwood. . . . The drivers had a few revolvers amongst them, it seems they did not expect to come so far, [and] six rounds for the 4 Pound Howitzer.

We had scarsely our arrangements made when we saw the Indians desending from the Bluffs in large numbers. The party numbered about 700 under Red Cloud.

I told the men that the first one that fired without my order I would shoot. Told them the enemy would know that we only had a few rounds of amunitin. On they come as gallent as I have seen in the Army of the Potomac. I did not wish to use the gun if possible except in a great extremety, but saw this charge was to formidable, as a reserve was forming to back up the first, so I concluded to use a shell. Mr. Harwood served the gun and most effective. The shell burst right over the Indians. They went back as fast as they could run.

They continued to annoy us. . . . They made frequent charges on foot, [but] we could generaly drive them back by pointing the Gun at their advance. When to persistent and strong we used a round shot. . . . Slowly the day wore away, not a cartridge wasted.

The welcome darkness came. . . . We had two horses left, the one I rode and the Wagonmasters. We called for volenteers to try and reach Fort Phil Kearney. We thought by following up the ravine leading up to the mountains, the men could get through the Indians. . . . The men got through.

At day light the fight commenced in earnest again, many of our cattle [and] a number of the oxen were wounded or killed; many of the men had slight wounds, five or six serious — three dead. . . .

We repelled a tremendous attack of the Indians, only two cartridges for the gun left. There seemed to be a great comotion amongst them. They disaperred from the Bluff. Huruh! I shall always remember that cheer when Major Dave Gordon, with his Co came trotting up to our camp ahead of the column. [It was] a terrible looking battle field, our shells had kept the Indians from the wagons part of the time, but many a young Buck sported one of Al Leighters Red Blankets that winter. . . .

EDMUND R. P. SHURLY

Indian scares continued throughout the 1860's and the pressure on the military forces in Montana remained constant. Depredations by Piegan bands in retaliation for the murder of two young tribal members at Fort Benton, in 1869, increased the clamor for protection. Recently arrived as commander of the District of Montana, Colonel Philippe Regis Denis de Keredern de Trobriand reported on an inspection trip to Fort Ellis, commenting on the most recent Indian scare, civilian reaction, and the territory's military situation. De Trobriand was a French aristocrat, a veteran officer of the American Civil War, with three years of service on the western plains. His background made him uniquely qualified to observe the situation in Montana, having written at length on American society, culture, and military affairs since his arrival in the United States in 1841.

HEAD QRS. DISTRICT OF MONTANA
FORT SHAW, SEPTEMBER 9, 1869

BVT. BRIG. GENL. O. D. GREENE, USA
ASST. ADJ. GENL. DEPT. OF DAKOTA,
ST. PAUL, MINNESOTA

SIR,

I have the honor to report that I returned yesterday, after an absence of fourteen days, to visit and inspect Fort Ellis. . . .

During my journey to and from Fort Ellis, I saw many different people, had long talks with most of them, and neglected no opportunity of gathering full and reliable information about the *real* facts which gave rise to the excitement in regard to Indian hostilities, — what part was to be attributed to exaggerated reports, and what part to interested speculations. What conclusions I came to, is the principal object of this report. . . .

It is a remarkable fact that whenever there is no apparent danger, and no cause of apprehension, people will think that there is *always too much* of military; while, if a handfull of red-skins appear on the bluffs shaking their buffalo robes, it turns out suddenly that there is *never enough* of it, according to the same people.

In this case I strongly suspect that there was some interested scheme on the part of some parties, to magnify the danger, exaggerate the reports, and through the general excitement to bring the Governor, then just arrived, to issue a proclamation to raise a regiment of mounted volunteers. This, if successful, would have procured some fat jobs to somebody or other, at the expense of the government. But when I broke the subject to Govr. Ashley, I found at once that he had seen through the game, and that no proclamation would be issued, at least not without real necessity. . . .

This report being now complete about my visit to Fort Ellis, I have only to respectfully submit the following conclusions:

1st, The military force in this District is now scarcely sufficient for garrison duty, and entirely inadequate to the exigencies of the service, in case Indian hostilities should assume a serious character.

2nd, As far as the Infantry is concerned, filling up my regiment would be quite enough, especially if the building of a new post at the mouth of Muscleshell River, would bring back to the District the three Companies now detached at Fort Buford.

3rd, Could Fort Buford be garrisoned like Fort Ellis by four Companies of Cavalry, I have but little doubt that those eight companies could well keep in order the hostile Sioux and other Indians on the Yellowstone river, and afford sufficient protection to that region, the most exposed one; while mounted detachments of Infantry could drive away the roaming bands of marauders from the lines of communication on the Muscleshell and Missouri up to the British Possessions.

4th, The land travel for recruits sent to this District is extremely slow, difficult and expensive. All recruits for the garrisons of Montana should be sent in the early spring by steamboats to Benton, which can *always* be done during the months of April and May, and at least part of June.

RESPECTFULLY SUBMITTED,

P. de TROBRIAND

By the fall of 1869, near hysteria reigned in Montana. The looting of a train of freight wagons, the murder of Malcolm Clarke, and other acts of violence in the area between Fort Benton and Helena led citizens to demand action the Army could not possibly implement. Colonel de Trobriand, replying to the clamor of several prominent Helena residents, took a relatively realistic view of the situation. He denied that events, since known as the Piegan War, even constituted a war. His protests were largely unavailing and civilian pressure forced severe government action. De Trobiand's letter foreshadowed those events.

HEADQUARTERS DISTRICT OF MONTANA
FORT SHAW, OCTOBER 6, 1869

MSSRS. A.S. SIMMONS, HENRY THOMPSON,
N.T.A. SMITH, WARREN C. GILLETTE,
H.D. WASHBURN, S. HAUSER, and
M. MACGINNISS

GENTLEMEN,

. . . Without going so far as to apprehend that the depredations and isolated murders lately committed by the Indians may "culminate in a general massacre of our outlying settlements" or as your honorable committee seems to fear, I agree completely with you that some way must be taken as soon and as efficiently as possible to suppress the crimes against persons and properties in this territory. . . .

. . . Let us see the facts as they are and without exaggeration: the first fact which, I think, must be admitted by all is that there is actually *no Indian war* in the territory. Depredations are committed, even murders perpetrated; but by whom? By a handful of roaming thieves and murderous red vagabonds belonging principally to the Piegan tribe, and doing mischief not in any concentrated force, but in small parties of few men. . . .

As for the Indian tribes, as such, the *Pend'oreilles* are friendly and peaceful; the *Blackfeet*, the *Bloods* remain quiet so far on their reservation; so with the *Mountain Crows*; so with the *Bannocks*; and even so with one half at least of the *Piegans* who disclaim any complicity with the small band of their tribe. . . .

If therefore nothing happens to alter the condition of things, the capture or death of these few men is the principal object to be aimed at, and would in my opinion suffice to restore security through the territory. This is what I propose to do as soon as possible, through a cavalry expedition; and to that effect, instructions will be sent without delay to the post commander at Fort Ellis. . . .

My view in . . . respect and in regard to the necessity of a larger military force in this territory have been fully submitted to the proper authority. I have no doubt that the government will reinforce this command as soon as practicable. . . .

In the meantime, gentlemen, there is a French proverb which says that "the prettiest girl can give but what she has." So with any military commander. He cannot furnish more troops than he has under his command. Rest assured that what little I have for the present will be put without delay to the best use, and that no effort will be spared on my part toward restoring security to the white residents and visiting the guilty Indians with the punishment they so richly deserve. . . .

I remain, gentlemen, very respectfully

YR. MOST OBED. SERVT.

P. de TROBRIAND

Negotiations with hostile Piegans failed. By December, 1869, the Army had determined to strike one massive blow against the recalcitrant bands and thus bring a halt to depredations causing so much alarm in the territory. De Trobriand, a moderating influence while the action was planned, insisted the blow fall on hostile Piegans, preferably on the camp of Mountain Chief, one of the major leaders. In a letter to General Alfred Sully, Montana Superintendent of Indian Affairs, he pointed out the friendliness of Heavy Runner's band, whose camp was ultimately the target of the force under Major E. M. Baker. On January 23, 1870, Baker's cavalry troops from Fort Ellis killed one hundred and seventy-three of Heavy Runner's band, including fifty-three women and children. To complete the chastisement, troops destroyed all lodges and baggage, forcing over a hundred women and children onto the plains in subzero cold without protection. As a demonstration of force, the action was successful. The Piegans and the other tribes of the Blackfeet Confederacy never again tempted the wrath of the Army. Baker's action against Heavy Runner's camp, hailed in Montana, met with severe criticism and congressional inquiry in the East. De Trobriand, in his second letter, attempted to present a united front in defense of the military's action. The letter also represented a denial of his previous feelings of fairness and decency for the sake of expediency.

FORT SHAW, MONTANA TERRITORY
DECEMBER 12, 1869

GENERAL,

I am in receipt of your private note of the 9th inst. and according to your wishes, I will give you my views in regard to its contents.

I see that you [denounce] by the general name of *Blackfeet* all the Indians who belong to the agency on the Teton river. Allow me, in order to make the matter more clear and precise, to consider separately the *Blackfeet* proper . . . [from] *Piegans* and the *Bloods.* . . . Two bands — the first led by *Heavy Runner* and the second by *Escapeman* are friendly. Neither had anything to do with the murders or depredations of last summer. . . .

The guilty parties, nearly all of them, are with *Mountain Chief.* . . . This last band numbering no more than about twenty or 25 lodges is on Milk river near the [Canadian-American] line, and is the one we should strike whenever we have an opportunity; the balance of the *Piegans* and *Bloods* being for the present out of our reach on Belly river.

Such being the case, I cannot honestly say that I regret that no action has been taken on your proposition to pitch into those two friendly little bands, to make them pay for others, — principally when they had come to the agency on your invitation. . . .

Now, don't you think, general, that it is preferable to limit the chastisement as much as possible to the guilty parties, their associates, and those . . . Piegans and . . . to leave alone those like Heavy Runner against whom there is no charge that I know of. For my part, I think this is the most honest policy, and the best calculated to secure peace among the white residents of the territory.

I REMAIN &C

PHILIPPE de TROBRIAND

[FORT SHAW, M.T., FEB. 2, 1870]
O. D. GREENE, A.A.G.

SIR,

I have the honor to report that after consultation with Bt. Col. Baker, I concluded to order back to Fort Ellis the four companies of cavalry which have successfully operated against the Piegans under his command . . . [for a] rest well deserved by their gallant conduct and courageous endurance.

The Blackfeet proper are away in the British possession. The Bloods, terrified by the punishment of the Piegans, deem it very fortunate not to have brought upon themselves such a severe retribution, and will carefully avoid giving offense to the white residents of the territory. As for the Piegans, they are completely cowed. They had never dreamed of the possibility of such an execution, and the blow is more telling for being so entirely unexpected. Their principal chief *Big legs* has already sent two or three messengers to know what we want him to do. . . .

Mountain-Chief took refuge with his followers in the camp of *Big legs* in order to escape more easily. But *Big legs* in fear of the consequences wanted to shake them off, and said that if they did not go, he would fight them himself. . . . *Eagle's rib* who escaped with three or four others from *Bear chief's* camp is badly wounded by a bullet through the hips, and not likely to recover. *Red Horn* was killed in his camp.

Heavy Runner was also killed, by his own fault. Attracted to the hostile camp by the presence there of some whiskey smugglers . . . he left the trading post where he was perfectly safe, and went to his fate. It is to be regretted that a friendly chief who had met Genl. Sully in council three weeks before, should have perished by our bullets; but at the same time his death is not without some salutary teachings by showing to the friendly Indians what heavy risks they run in keeping intercourse with the hostile ones.

This is well understood by his friends and relatives, as well as by the Bloods in the case of a few of their young men who were killed like *Heavy Runner* under the same circumstances. The chiefs had sent for them to leave the hostile camp, but they would not listen to it, and therefore were served right.

I don't apprehend any new outbreak of hostilities, and I consider the safety of the settlements far better secured now than at any time before. . . .

I AM, GENERAL, &C

P. de TROBRIAND

One campaign has dominated the Indian Wars era — the expedition which culminated in the Custer defeat on the Little Big Horn, June 25, 1876. Three columns, under Terry, Gibbon and Crook, were to converge on the encampment of hostile Sioux and Cheyenne and force them to lay down their arms and return to their agencies. The Montana column, commanded by Colonel John Gibbon, included freight wagons of E. G. Maclay and Company — the well known Diamond R — which had contracted to haul military freight for the expedition. Matthew Carroll, a Diamond R partner and later a cattleman, directed the train as Master of Transportation for Gibbon. Carroll's reaction to the rumors and reality of the Custer defeat are preserved in the diary he kept while on the campaign.

MAY 15, 1876 — E.G. Maclay & Co's train consisting of fourteen teams and twenty-eight wagons . . . with freight . . . left Fort Ellis to-day. Number of men employed, eighteen. Escort under Lieutenant Kendricks of the 7th Infantry. . . .

JUNE 25, SUNDAY — Left camp at 5 A.M. . . . Arrived at Big Horn River after making twenty miles. Watered and made three miles down the river and then nooned. Roads bad and our battery of three Gatling guns had much trouble. Infantry came to camp at 5 P.M. We left as they arrived, and made camp at midnight. . . . Will certainly see Indians to-morrow. They are without doubt watching us. We are one or two miles from the mouth of the Little Big Horn. . . .

[JUNE] 26 — Broke camp at 9 A.M., and, after going two miles, discovered some of our Crow scouts who were with Custer. They reported a big fight on the Little Big Horn and Custer badly whipped. Our Crow scouts left us. General Gibbon joined the command, leaving boat where we nooned yesterday. Conjectures are rife as to the truth of Custer's defeat. He was to meet Terry at the mouth of the Little Big Horn to-day, but no news from him. Nooned on Little Big Horn, a nice stream; has ash growing on it. . . . Bostwick and Taylor were each sent with a note to Custer, going by different routes, and if successful are to get $200.00 each. Both returned reporting plenty of Indians. . . .

[JUNE] 27 — . . . Broke camp early and, after traveling four miles, struck the battle-ground where the big camp had been, but the Indians had all left the night before, leaving lodge poles and any amount of camp utensils. We saw at once that General Custer had been badly whipped. Found Reno some two or three miles higher up, fortified on a hill east of the river. He was glad to see us. Reno attacked the upper camp with three companies of Benteen's and four companies protecting pack-train. Custer, with five companies, attacked the lower camp, but he never crossed the river or got to the camp, as he and all his men were found killed. It must have been a horrible massacre. Reno lost heavily in killed and wounded. The Seventh is entirely used up. Had it not been for our command coming up, Reno would have been cleaned out. Crossed the wounded over to our camp, which is on Reno's battle ground. To-morrow will be devoted to burying the dead, and destroying property. It is my opinion a goodly number of Indians were killed. We found twenty-five bodies and presume we will find plenty more to-morrow. Soldiers were horribly mutilated. The entire affair is fearful to contemplate.

[JUNE] 28 — Went and saw the dead buried. It was fearful. Nearly three hundred and fifty killed and wounded, fifty of whom come under the head of wounded. Spent entire day making litters to carry the wounded. Left camp at sun-down. It took us until 12 o'clock to make five miles, when we camped. We are now going down the Little Big Horn to take the wounded to the boat. . . . What we will do after leaving the sick on the boat, I can't say. What next? Of course, I have my own opinion.

The conflict of 1876-1877 ended in defeat and forced return to the reservations for hostile Sioux and Northern Cheyenne bands. In defeat they had impressed their foes, greatly testing the Army's military abilities. General George Crook, who commanded the southern arm of the three-pronged campaign of 1876, narrowly escaped defeat at the hands of Crazy Horse on the Rosebud several days before the annihilation of Custer's troops. Crook's report on the campaign demonstrated his respect for the Indian's warrior qualities. Most western field commanders rapidly came to agree with his assessment.

HEADQUARTERS DEPT. of the PLATTE
ASST. ADJUTANT GENERAL'S OFFICE
OMAHA, NEBRASKA
SEPTEMBER 25, 1876

GENERAL
MILITARY DIVISION OF THE MISSOURI

SIR,

. . . Of the difficulties with which we have had to contend, it may be well to remark that, when the Sioux Indian was armed with the bow and arrow he was more formidable, fighting as he does most of the time on horseback, than when he got the old fashioned muzzle loading rifle. But when he came into possession of the breech loader and metallic cartridge, which allows him to load and fire from his horse with perfect ease, he became at once ten thousand times more formidable.

With the improved arms I have seen our friendly Indians, riding at full speed, shoot and kill a wolf, also on the run, while it is a rare thing that our troops can hit an Indian on horseback though the soldier may be on his feet at the time. The Sioux is a cavalry soldier from the time he has intelligence enough to ride a horse or fire a gun. If he wishes to dismount, his hardy pony, educated by long usage, will graze around near where he has been left, ready when his master wants to mount either to move forward or escape. . . .

VERY RESPECTFULLY,
YOUR OBEDIENT SERVANT

GEORGE CROOK

Custer's defeat had as its most important result the determination to inflict a series of defeats on the hostiles so severe that the Indians would have no choice but to return permanently to the reservations. The instrument of this policy was Colonel Nelson A. Miles and his 5th U.S. Infantry Regiment. Miles' punitive campaigns of the fall and winter of 1876-1877 broke the power of all the hostile bands but one. Sitting Bull and his followers, after several minor battles and skirmishes, fled to Canada, where they remained until 1881, posing a constant if distant threat. Edwin M. Brown, a trumpeter with Company B, 5th Infantry, in writing his friend, John Penwell, discussed those critical campaigns. The selection below recounted events of October 20 - 22, 1876 through the eyes of a private as much interested in his own safety as he was in the success of the campaign.

We had come to a valley and halted to rest when the Indians . . . appeared on the bluff to our left with a white flag. They sent a Chief in, with a request to Gen. Miles to come out halfway and hold a council. The Gen. granted them this request, who, with a small escort went out to meet the famous Sitting Bull. They held a long pow-wow, but no satisfaction could they gain from the General, who wanted them to surrender on the spot, or fight. . . . They withdrew a few rods and held a pow-wow among themselves; finally a Chief rode up to Gen. Miles asking him to withdraw his troops and give them till the morning to decide the matter. . . .

The request was granted by Gen. Miles, who marched us back eight miles and went in camp. I suppose the General began to think they were shamming and were only asking this request in order to give their camp time to move. Early next morning we pulled out and started in pursuit of them; before we got to them we could see them watching us from the bluffs; Gen. Miles had surmised correct, they were indeed moving their village. . . . They looked like a vast herd of buffalo. The warriors had all stopped back to give us a reception. . . .

An Indian was seen setting the prairie on fire about one hundred yards from the command; the General ordered a scout to go out and put a stop to his work; the scout rode out and shouted at him, but fired at the same time. The Indian rolled over on the burning grass, we did not stop to ascertain if he were dead, but marched straight ahead towards the Indians which occupied the bluffs ahead of us. The bluffs were literally swarmed with the "red varmints." By this time the prairie was a solid wall of fire around us; after the scout had shot this Indian which set the prairie on fire the "opera" commenced. Bullets whistled lively over our heads and around us for a short time; many a strong heart grew weak as our thoughts flew back to the Custer massacre. We began to think our case as hopeless, for indeed the odds were against us; no doubt had we been cavalry they would have killed every one of us, but as we were enabled to fight them on their own principles it was much to our advantage. As we were down in the ravine the "big gun" which was planted on the summit of a high bluff broke loose which scattered them in all directions. . . .

We fought them all that day through fire and smoke which nearly suffocated us; that night we camped on five hills, companies occupying the hills with the wagon train in the valley in the center. As we did not camp with Sitting Bull that night, we *did* camp where he camped the night before. . . .

All night the red-skins could be seen dancing through the flames and yelling like fiends. It reminded one of a representation I once saw of hell, in the panorama of Milton's Paradise Lost. Many was the poor wretch that never shut an eye that awful night. Fires shone all around us, it made me think of "torch light processions."

A fellow was almost afraid to go to sleep for fear he might never waken. I was one of them; all my sins rose up before me like huge mountains; I began to think of the good advice which I had scorned. I began to think of home and friends and almost wished I was back in the Buckeye State once more, far from the scenes of carnage and warfare, where one could lie down peaceably to rest without the fear of his scalp being torn from his cranium by these red and bloodthirsty fiends. I assure you I was not the only one, for I heard more than one remark that they wished we were back in camp at Tongue River. If there ever in this world [was] a case of home-sickness I was the worst case at that time that ever was known.

The morning dawned at last, the Indians were still ahead of us, ready to renew the contest, but not willing to come to close quarters . . . [but] . . . they kept continual watch of our progess. They were surprised at the tenacity with which the "walk-a-heaps" as they call us, followed their trail. . . .

As I am not of a romantic turn of mind I will not try to describe the grand scenery of Montana more than just given; but shall leave it to those of a more romantic nature. But be it romantic to tramp over a wild, barbarious country, with the expectation of losing ones "top-knot" in the bargain I will take none for mine, but shall close this little sketch of the Sioux Campaign and bid you adieu, hoping I have given satisfaction. I am,

MOST RESPECTFULLY, ETC,
EDWIN M. BROWN

Western Indian wars bore no resemblance to formal, gentlemanly conflicts so prized in Eighteenth and Nineteenth Century Europe. Brutality was a factor on both sides. Animosities arising from these encounters color the thoughts of many westerners to this day. The sentiments of William Sellew, a scout for Terry and Miles, were typical of the attitudes of many who populated Montana Territory at the time. The "only good Indian is a dead Indian" philosophy failed to recognize the causes for the raids, for depredations, and conflict. It contrasted markedly with the more gentle attitudes prevalent in eastern states — "bleeding hearts" to many westerners.

DECEMBER THE 9TH - 1876
BIG HORN RIVER
MONTANA TERRITORY

DEAR MOTHER

We are camped on the big horn river. Thare is 3 companies of soldiers, one company of cavelry folowing a Indian Trail. I returned to camp this morning at day break [with] another Scout by the name of Smith. He saved my life while we wer caring dispatches from Gen. Miles to Col Otis. Thare was 3 of us, one man by the name of Gedy. He was kiled. One ball went through his neck and 2 through the body. My cloths wer shot through several times, one ball through under my arm, and one through my shurt, four balls through my legens and pants. My gun stock was cut in too & slightly wounding my hand. I had 2 ribs broken by my horse falling on me when he was shot.... The Indians ... first Jumped us at 11 in the fore knoon and had us coreled till dark. We kiled 8 & skalped 2. We had a crick for brest works after the first 15 minutes. I do not know how many red skins thare was but we wer surrounded. . . .

I first went Scouting in August for Gen Miles & in July for Gen Tery. I had left Powder river with dispatches for Custer & had traviled one night and had met skouts that had escaped from Maj Renoes fight. They said Custer and his men must be al kiled & it was no use to go. But I took the dispatch to Reno. I did not beleve them for they wer Indians employed as Scouts ... but when I got thare I found it was only to true which pen can not discribe horid upon horid. The Crick was full of horses and men cut to peces by the Squaws others burned. It makes one that saw it shuder to think of it. It is a pleasure to chop an Indian to peces after seing that. *I saw a man kill & scalp a squaw and then crush the papooses head with his foot* which looked horid at the time but the squaws are worse than the bucks. . . .

I will folow scouting as long as thare is a red skin on the preary or as long as uncle sam will furnish omnutition. I furst was getting $50.00 but for my bravery and Dependance in what I report when returning from a scout he said he would rase my wages to $90.00. I never report any thing but the trouth to the oficer.

I am in Leutenant Cusics tent.... He is ingaged to a girl by the name of Jonson. She is 17 years old. He shoed me her picture [and] she is very pretty — to much so to waste her lif for an oficer in the U S army, a drunkerd. It is not often that I cn get a pen & paper to rite. . . . It will be a month be fore you get this pleas rite soon, I have not had a letter since last March. . . . I must close with love to all from your afectionate son

W R SELLEW

please excuse mistakes for I have not time to look this over.

Final subjugation of the Sioux and Northern Cheyenne had barely concluded when fleeing Nez Perce precipitated another Indian scare in Montana. Having battled troops from Idaho and Washington to a virtual standstill, the Nez Perce crossed into Montana and descended the Lolo Trail to the Bitterroot Valley. Here, their first encounter was a debacle for the white forces, regulars and volunteers. The Nez Perce easily bypassed the hastily erected fortification designed to halt their progress down the Lolo Trail. Afterward, the tribe spent several peaceful days in the valley trading with the white population. The deceptive ease with which Fort "Fizzle" was outflanked contrasts with the bitter fighting and desperate flight the Nez Perce experienced for the remainder of their passage through Montana. John Martens, a farmer near Victor, was a participant in the first "clash." His diary chronicled the events of that inauspicious week.

MONDAY, JULY 23, 1877 — Wheather clear and hot until the midle of the afternoon. After Breakfast went out to arigate ... I seen Clark and Litter hurrieng toward Tudors. They got there a little before I did. When I got there they told me the news that Johsphefs band of Indian 200 strong were on the LoLo trail at the hot springs; and that they, Clark & Liter, were going to take all the women and Children to Fort Owen ... All hands [went] to Frank's — and there to fortefy ourself and await further results wich we did working all night. At Daylight we were in a position to widstand a considerable atack. . . .

TUESDAY, JULY 24 — . . . A party of four [went] to see if the Road was Clear from here to Town. They came back, ... [and] reported Everything clear and started with the wimen and Chdren to Fort Owen. Lt. Chatfield came in to nieght — no news from the seat of war.

THURSDAY, JULY 26 — Wheather warm and clear. Put up Fence in foorenoon. A little before noon Doc Woodmance came and told me that Carlo [Charlo] the Flathead Chef, had sent word to the People that the Nes Perces wold be in the Vally the next Day at 10 oclok and ... the Cheif advised all of us to go to Fort Owen for protection and we all started. A little above the upper Bitter-Root Bridge we met Mr Wm N. Smith widt orders from the Govenor for all the Men to come to Lo Lo Fork the next Day or else send the Guns. Got to the Fort and staid over nieght. . . .

SATTURDAY, JULY 28 [LoLo] — Clear and bright. Exspected an atack from the Indians but they like senscible falows found a way aroun us and let us alone. About two oclock orders came to move camp which we did going down the creek at a lively rate when we came to the mouth of the canon. The Missoula Vollenteers struck for home and the Regulars soon following which left the People of the Vally no choise but to make pease widt the Indians which they did. I got to Fort Owens late at night. Quite an exitement prevailed.

SUNDAY, JULY 29 — Clear and warm. Spent the Day watching the Indians. They moved up a little way above Carlos and camped. Bass and Jerry Fahey went over to trade widt them, I hope they will do well. . . .

MONDAY, JULY 30 — Warm and clear. People somewhat pusled as to what the Indians will do, wheather they will keep Pease or make war. A number of Indians in Town trading, paying for what they got.

TUESDAY, JULY 31 — Another warm Day. Left the Fort and went to Town to see how things looks. Plenty of Indians in Town and all armed thinking there mieght be a chance for a row. . . . All went on peaseable however. Indians moved further up the Vally to Day.

The Nez Perce almost reached their goal — sanctuary in Canada — after they had fought and fled across much of western and central Montana. Every move the Army made against them they countered, often inflicting severe defeat upon pursuing troopers. Finally they were trapped, just short of their goal, by forces under Colonel Nelson A. Miles, a latecomer to the pursuit. Joseph and his people struggled over seventeen hundred miles to their last battleground at the foot of the Bear Paw Mountains. Rather than freedom, they gained only imprisonment and exile to a reservation that was not their home. Lieutenant Thomas M. Woodruff, a member of the 5th Infantry, described the last battle which took place September 30 to October 4, 1877.

ON BOARD STEAMER GEN'L. MEADE
NEAR FORT PECK, MONTANA
OCTOBER 15, 1877

MY DEAR MOTHER,

. . . About 8:30 [September 30] we came to the high ridge above the village . . . surrounded on three sides by steep bluffs, some 50 feet high. Our line was deployed on the ridge. . . .

We charged; the 7th Cavalry getting way ahead on the right, & the 2nd loosing ground by having to cross the creek. The 7th got into action first, and had to withdraw and dismount, partly on account of the fierce resistance, & partly the steep bluffs. At about 100 yards from the bluffs our battalion dismounted and leading their ponies the men went right up to the edge of the bluffs and settled down to work. We held this position all the time, . . . about 300 yards from the centre of the village. . . .

Being adjutant, I had to go from one point to another, and I remained mounted for some time, and then finding that many men were being killed and wounded just in front of me, and almost at my side, I dismounted. For about 3 hours we had pretty hot work right there.

In the meantime the 2nd Cavalry had passed way off to the left, and had cut off a greater part of the Indian herd of ponies; and two companies of the 7th Cavalry had dismounted, whilst Maj. Hale with the third company was being severely handled about a mile off on our right. Here it was at this time that Maj. Hale and Lt. Biddle were killed together with several of their men.

Finally the Indians took refuge in the holes and ravines in the bluffs and kept up a constant fire on us. But we had them and their families hemmed in, in the village, and the only thing to do was to make a clean sweep by charging along the whole line, and drive them from the ravines and from their village out into the open plains.

. . . Orders were sent [but the couriers were wounded] . . . and the orders never reached those commands. When the order to charge was given, only a part of two companies of the 5th Infty. went forward; this little handful was composed of 15 men of Co. "I," . . . and 10 men of Co. "F," and two or three odd men. I went forward with the line. We yelled and cheered, went over the steep bluffs across a deep ravine, and right into the village. After getting in we could not stay, and had to fall back to the ravine, with a loss of eight wounded (2 afterwards dying). We remained in the ravine until sunset, . . . occasionally firing when an Indian showed himself.

. . . I made my way back across the dangerous space that we had charged over to where Genl. Miles and Capt. Snyder were, and reported to them. . . .

Late in the afternoon . . . I was sent down into the village to withdraw Capt. Carter, & the men there; which was done by crawling on our hands and knees along a little ravine for about 20 yards.

. . . Lt. R[omeyn] unnecessarily exposed himself, and a great many shots were fired at him; his horse received two severe wounds; his field glass case was shot away, and another shot cut his sword belt at the left side, striking the handle of his knife, which with his belt & pistol fell to the ground, & almost at the same moment he was shot through the right lung, lower part.

The 7th and 2nd Cav. were withdrawn from their positions after sunset, . . . keeping strong pickets out to watch the Indians and prevent them from escaping from the village. . . . On the 1st & 2nd, we had partial parleys with Joseph, whom we held in camp on the night of the

1st; unfortunately Lt. Jerome went down to the village, & the Indians kept him until the evening of the 2nd, when we had to release Joseph to get Jerome. We were all very much incensed at him. We had occasional firing both nights. . . .

On the evening of the 5th Genl. Howard arrived, & by his interpreter we made terms with the Indians who surrendered on the 6th about 11 o'clock.

Most of the days of the siege we had very severe weather, snow & rain, & we all suffered a great deal. . . . Our losses were 2 officers & 21 men killed; 4 officers & 42 men wounded. The Indians lost 23 killed & 51 wounded in the village; 5 Indians were killed outside & 11 more were killed over on Milk River by the Gros Ventres & Assiniboines, to whom these 11 had gone for assistance. We captured about 800 ponies, and have Joseph & all his people about 380 souls. It is the greatest victory over the Indians in our history. — Love & kisses to all. . . .

Ever your affectionate son,

MAYHEW

The Sioux-Cheyenne and Nez Perce Wars brought many additional troops into the territory, the construction of several new posts, and the possibility of several more. To Montana business-men this promised financial opportunity as well as security. Samuel T. Hauser, pragmatic Helena banker and mining investor, demonstrated such interest in a letter to Montana's Territorial Delegate, Martin Maginnis. Hauser's desire for a post and troops was clearly economic; he did not mention the question of security.

HELENA, MONTANA
DECEMBER 11, 1877

HON. MARTIN MAGINNIS
WASHINGTON, D.C.

DEAR MC

I have been here now about a week. . . . The town is feeling the good effects of the *Troops here.* There isn't an empty house, and the town is decidedly lively. And quite a [number] of our most prominent Citizens here asked me whether you couldn't bring influence to bear upon Sherman to *secure a small post here,* and get this made *district headquarters. Couldn't Montana — or better* all that

portion west of Yellowstone (Ft Shaw, Ellis & Missoula & Helena post) be made an independent *district,* With Helena *District* headquarters.

If you can accomplish that, our town would be wild with delight, and instead of 150 majority, we will give you 600 next term. It would *real*[ly] *double* the value of our property here. And as we are *Central* I hope you can do it. . . .

Let me hear from you as to a permanent post & District Headquarters.

YRS

HAUSER

Life at frontier posts could not compare with the comfort to be found in established eastern communities. It did include some diversion and, particularly for the officers, many of the comforts left behind. This unpublished article, written for HARPER'S MAGAZINE by an unknown correspondent, in the late 1870's, described some high points of daily existence at Fort Ellis. The officers' life in the 2nd Cavalry Regiment — known as the "Lost Battalion" because of its long uninterrupted service in Montana — reflected more variety than one might expect. What the correspondent omitted were the rigors and hardships that also constituted a part of western military assignments.

. . . Perhaps no Journey on the continent is more tiresome than that from Utah to Montana. . . . The "land of the Mountains," however, well repays one for the fatigue and we doubt if anywhere in the world is to be found a more interesting country than Montana with its wonderful geysers, beautiful valleys and rich gold mines.

It was quite dark when we arrived at the old straggling Cavalry station of Fort Ellis. . . . The old rambling post of Fort Ellis with its low squatty log houses had not impressed us favorably but when we entered the quarters of some of the officers we were astonished to find how roomy and comfortable they were. The ceilings and walls were white-coated and hard finished so they glistened in the light and the floors were carpeted and well furnished. Notable was the house of the Commandante whose tough log exterior gave no evidence of its internal comfort and even elegance. It was quite dark when we called and the lights had been lit. The same orderly who had invited us stood bolt upright before the front door and in white gloves and glittering uniform with profuse politeness ushered us into a wide carpeted hall and thence into large double parlors luxuriously furnished and flooded with light from immense chandaliers. Bronze figures, pictures, rare books and vases were scattered about in profusion and everything arranged in that negligent yet elegant way known only to a lady of taste and a good housekeeper.

We found the Commandante surrounded by . . . four children engaged at play. His wife a beautiful woman of apparently not more than twenty-five summers was laughing heartily at the pranks of a rosy two year old boy who rolled on the floor, while the father held on his knee a little girl of four years whose abundant blond curls fell to her waist. Both father and mother wellcomed us to their home and we spent two or three pleasant hours in this happy family. . . .

The next day after dinner the Commandante told us there would be a theatrical performance in the evening at the theater and sent his orderly to get us tickets. The theatre is owned by the soldiers and was built and furnished entirely by their own labor and money. It has a good stage and would seat comfortably about two hundred persons. The stock company was made up entirely of soldiers and their acting was fully as good as that seen in the cities at variety theaters. Several of the performers were very good indeed and, we were informed, had played engagements in former years at the best theaters in the east. We asked how such men came to be soldiers and were told trouble and more often drink drove them into the army. The Fort Ellis troup is one of the best variety companies we have ever seen and would draw crowded houses any where. They give a performance once every two weeks during the winter season charging a merely nominal admission fee sufficient to pay expenses. Once each month by permission of the Commandante they go to Bozeman or some other town in Montana and give an entertainment charging a dollar and even two dollars fee for tickets and never fail to sell every seat in the house.

Next evening there was a soldier's ball given in the mens quarters and we were of course invited to attend. The ball, or *baile*, as the soldiers call it was held in L company 2nd Cavalry barracks and all the men of the company were hosts. The dancing took place in the company mess room which was beautifully decorated with evergreens and draped with flags. About sixty persons could dance at one time and the floor was kept constantly full. Many of the guests had arrived when we reached the building and dancing was already going on. We were politely received by a venerable sargeant in full uniform who conducted us to the entrance of the ballroom where five young men in gorgeous cavalry coats white gloves and eppaulets took charge of us and conducted us [to] a little platform with chairs where we had a good view of the dancers.

About nine o'clock there was a great stir at the door and it was announced the Commandante with the Officers and ladies of the garrison had arrived. The Captain of the company giving the entertainment assisted by his lieutenant received the Commandante and his party in the outer room and the old Sargeant, the five young soldiers and Sargeant Major marshalled the procession to the platform. A young soldier with a small white rod distributed programmes of the dances and then presenting himself before the Commandante asked if he would dance. The Commandante did not dance but said perhaps some of the ladies and gentlemen would. The young soldier then asked each lady and gentleman and received from them a reply in the affirmative. A part of the room at the end next [to] the musicians was cleared and the officers and their wives formed a separate set.

These dances as well as the presence of the officers and their wives at soldiers balls are merely matters of ceremony and intended to show their good will and respect. The officers and their wives seldom dance more than one set and generally retire at the end of half or three quarters of an hour. Such a thing as a soldier Sargeant or even Sargt Major dancing with the wife, sister or daughter of an officer would not be thought of. Neither do officers dance with laundresses, their daughters or soldiers wives. A young Lieutenant who danced one set with the pretty daughter of a laundress was ordered to come to the office of the Commandante where he received a sound scolding and was informed if he ever again participated in a soldiers ball he would be placed in arrest and brought before a court martial. . . .

Next day was muster and at 10 o'clock a.m. all the soldiers appeared in full dress on their company parades in front of the quarters. They were first inspected by their company officers and then followed a minute inspection by the Commanding officer who examined their arms, clothing, quarters, mess and beds. Several soldiers who had dirty ears and neck were sent to their quarters and the surgeon directed to examine their person. Others who had too long hair or unkempt beards were ordered to have them cut. Those who passed had their names called from the muster roll and were marked for pay. The others were ordered to report to the Adjutant in the evening after they had put themselves in proper order when if they passed inspection their names would be called for pay. [This] occurrs six times a year on the last day of the months of February, April, June, August, October, and December. . . .

In contrast to the relative gaiety pictured in the HARPER'S article, the life of a private soldier after the conclusion of the major Indian wars offered little diversion and long periods of inactivity. Private Andrew McKeon fled famine-struck Ireland for opportunity in the new world. He joined the U.S. Army to obtain security he had not found as a civilian. McKeon, like many immigrant soldiers, was sent west, serving at Fort Custer and Fort Assiniboine. He adjusted poorly to the often harsh Montana climate and spent much of a generally dull enlistment fighting germs rather than Indian marauders. From his sickbed he wrote to his brother, Patt, in Ireland. Unhappy with military life, Andrew later joined the Canadian Mounted Police and eventually returned to Ireland.

CUSTER STATION, M.T.
SEPTEMBER 20, 1886

MY DEAR PATT

I am learning to die in this place. I am almost confined to my bed for the last two months. . . . I was so ill on arriving here that I could not proceed to . . . Fort [Custer] thirty-five miles from here south. I was taken to a room in the station house where everything is nice, clean and tidy, with a soldier to attend me, and Doctor from Junction comes to see me every morning and when I was bad he used come twice a day. I am far from being well yet, but the doctor gave me permission to get up today for an hour to write this letter. I am a complete wreck. They weighed me this morning and I weigh only one hundred and twenty-four pounds. The Doctor gives a half pint of brandy and as much milk or lemonade a day as I want. He sometimes brings me a bundle of newspapers and Reading books. But he wont allow any of the Railroad people to come into my room on any conditions.

I am better today than I have been for some time but I wont quit this place until I am perfectly well again. By the way for Blankets and quilts on my bed I have Buffalo skins of enormous size. The fellow that was left here to attend me is seldom here, he is rambling about all day long, or out shooting but doing very little duty. Only that he happens to be an Irishman, I'd have him relieved. Nearly all the company is Germans, and I applied for him as attendant to get him an easy job. He calls himself Denis O Flaherty, Irish American. I attempted to write this on two previous occasions and miserably failed, before I could finish four lines I'd get so weak I'd have to throw it in the fire stove and get to bed again. . . .

It is not homesickness that is on me, but it must be I can see they are not able to fight the world, because it is nothing less than fighting a hard battle to live in this world. I was [so] tired of it that when I was very ill in Helena I wished from my heart that I might die. But I still linger on and the Winter is coming and I have great fears of it. It is not that I am afeared to die, but I'd like to live longer for others sake. . . .

It has been very warm here during the summer, and I hear it does [get] very cold indeed in the winter. The thermometer stood this summer at 110 in the shade and I am told that in the winter it goes down to 50 below zero. This place and all around where I am now is an Indian Reservation, no White man is allowed to settle on it. You will after getting this write to me without delay and send me a good long letter. . . .

PS dont tell anybody at home or elsewhere that I'm sick. Hoping you are well.

I AM YOURS AFFECTIONATELY

ANDY

Applied ingenuity has always been America's pride, even at frontier military posts. Colonel C. S. Otis, commander of the 20th Infantry and the Military District of Montana, headquartered at Fort Assiniboine, spent an inordinate amount of time describing his post's "facilities" to the commanding officer at Fort Custer. Most of the men of Otis' command may have been served by this exercise in military verbiage and efficiency, but pity the poor Post Scavenger!

FT. ASSINABOINE, M.T.
AUGUST 3, 1888

COMMANDING OFFICER
FORT CUSTER, M.T.

SIR:

To the enquiries contained in your communication of the 23rd inst. I have the honor to reply that the barracks closets are double, are constructed of brick and are thirty feet long and eight and one half feet wide. The seat is continuous along the back wall and the boxes beneath it are made of one inch plank, are three [feet] long, twenty inches wide and nine inches high, outside measurement. The boxes are shoved in place from [the] outside . . . on a light frame work, which extends about two feet beyond the wall on [the] outside, and on which the boxes rest when pulled out, for the purpose of being emptied. The post scavenger, who is furnished with a cart having a tight tank, nightly pulls these boxes out, shovels the contents into the tank, throws a little dry earth into the boxes, and shoves them back into place.

The urinals are separate, consisting of a trough about six feet long, which empties into pails made of kerosene oil cans placed beneath the trough. When one pail is full it is replaced by another. A Company makes use of five or six of these cans daily, and the contents are emptied into the tank of the night cart, by the post scavenger, and the cans placed back in the building for the next days use. Every post has a great abundance of these cans, so that they can always be obtained.

The room orderly or company police is obliged to visit the closets frequently, throw a little dry earth into the closets and replace the cans which are full. The dry earth is furnished by the post scavenger. . . . It is simply sandy loam from the surface of the prarie, which, when dry, is an excellent disenfectant. Formerly the urinal trough discharged into a wooden box, outside of and in rear of the building beneath the surface of the ground, but this was found unsatisfactory in cold weather, as the pipe discharging into it would freeze and it was also difficult to take out the contents of the box. As now arranged the pails are readily emptied and if broken in the attempt it makes little difference as more can be obtained without expense.

The seat boxes are emptied by means of an axe and shovel, in cold weather, into an open cart. The scavenger dumps his loads on the surface of the open prairie — a good distance from the post, scattering the filth so that the atmosphere soon carries off all stench. . . . It is necessary to watch the closets closely in Summer time, to avoid stench, but with the use of plenty of dry earth, and care to keep plenty of pails at the urinals, there is no trouble. . . .

The system has its advantages and disadvantages. The expressed view of those officers who have been stationed at Fort Maginnis that the closets are very uncomfortable during the extreme weather of Winter,

because of the constant rushing of cold air into the boxes, beneath the seats, are correct, and I doubt not that many men delay in attending to calls of nature for that reason. We can however always maintain a good state of police with proper care. . . . The system gives considerable work, but the old back house stench with the necessity of periodical removal of buildings over new excavations, and the accumulation of filth which must result from many years occupation of a post, are avoided. I am Colonel Very Respectfully

Your Obedient Servant

C. S. OTIS
COLONEL 20TH INFANTRY
COMMANDING

The Spanish-American War was the last of the "popular" wars. The rush of volunteers after the sinking of the MAINE and the final declaration of war, overwhelmed the staff at the Governor's office. Montana's National Guard was immediately offered for service. The federal government accepted, designating it the First Montana Infantry Regiment. For Montana's troops, the service was ultimately disappointing. They did not serve in Cuba but were, instead, transported to the Philippine Islands to put down a native insurrection which followed the Spanish defeat. To most Montanans, fighting against these tribesmen was not why they volunteered, and they constantly longed to return home. Casualties were inevitable. Second Lieutenant Eugene S. French, of Helena, Company "L", First Montana Infantry, was killed in action on February 23, 1899. Lieutenant Fred Yaeger, a former sergeant in Company "L" was promoted to fill French's position. Yaeger wrote his friend's widow to extend his sympathies, his letter revealing the frustrations of Montanans who had gone so patriotically to war and were so disappointed in the foes they ultimately faced.

MALOLOS, PHILIPPINE ISLANDS
APRIL 18, 1899

MY DEAR MRS. FRENCH:

. . . I surely appreciate the pain, anxiety and distressing feeling you must have experienced at the news of this sudden loss but was powerless to send a cable. Wrote you a long letter giving a description of the affair which has reached you long ere this. Capt. [Louis P.] Sanders, who was in Manila at the time, saw that the body was properly embalmed and placed in a vault awaiting shipment to the United States. I trust that it arrived in good condition but the long voyage and length of time it remained in this tropical climate may have had a bad effect on it.

Am satisfied that Eugene had no thought that he would receive a fatal wound as we had often spoken of the enemy's poor marksmanship and least of all expected it while we were protected by a dyke. On several occasions our advance had been over open ground and always in plain sight of the enemy yet up to this time we had but one man hit. . . .

Under ordinary conditions & circumstances the promotion to 2nd Lieutenant on the field would have been hailed with delight, yet no such feeling came over me because I knew that it was gained on account of the loss of my dearest friend. I would clearly & gladly give up commission, hopes, or anything within my power could it but restore his life & bring him back to his family. The loss to me is that of a brother. . . .

You have well said that this entire archipelago with its horde of savage, dirty, diseased people is not worth his life. My greatest pleasure in life will be to board a transport for home, never again to set foot on these accursed islands. The glory & honor gained in killing these reptiles falls as flat on us as rice cooked without salt. The only satisfaction is that we are fighting for the stars & stripes and partly avenging the deaths of those

gone down before us. . . . Yesterday I was offered the appointment to go into the regular army but I declined. One dose is enough for me. Give me back friends and civilization and anyone can have my share of this archipelago. . . .

SINCERELY YOUR FRIEND

FRED S. YAEGER

By the turn of the century, military establishments in Montana had long outlived their usefulness. Serving strictly in a garrison capacity in a peacetime army compounded the drudgery and boredom of duty at isolated western posts. A little noticed and seldom published aspect of such service was the presence of black troops at several Montana forts between the mid-1880's and 1911. Monotony led to racial frictions that might not have existed under more demanding circumstances. One incident was typical. The night of August 20-21, 1902, at the Montana Concert Hall in Havre, one black private, John W. Traylor, Company "F", 24th Infantry, and one white private, Edward Poag, Troop "G", 13th Cavalry, were shot during a racial confrontation. Traylor died of his wounds, Poag recovered. Private Everett Wall, also of Troop "G", and Poag were charged with deliberate manslaughter of the black private. Another black, Corporal Joseph Brooks, of Company "E", 24th Infantry, was charged with assault with intent to kill. The incident stemmed from the imposition of a color line across the length of the dance hall, intended to segregate the soldiers. Traylor violated the "color line" and fought with Poag before the shooting. Racial tension had, according to witnesses, been of long standing and threats issued several times from both sides before the shots. The confrontation was ugly, but a natural outgrowth of attitudes and forced idleness of the garrison troopers during the period.

BAGLEY STATEMENT

My name is J. L. Bagley of H. Troop 13th Cavalry. I was there in the Concert Hall when the shooting occurred. On the morning of the 21st of August, 1902, Charlie Hilton and I went up to the bar. As we turned around I saw Ed Poag taking hold of a colored fellow, trying to get him to set down. He kept persuading him, and finaly got him to set down. He no more than sat down when the colored man got up and shot the pistol off in the ceiling. . . . I didnt see the colored man fire but one shot; that went into the ceiling. If he had fired any more I think I would have seen him. Private Walls of G. Troop was the only man I saw shoot any after that. I dont know exactly how many he shot, but he shot more than one. The pistol was pointed in the direction of the colored man, I never saw Poag shoot at all. . . . The colored mans back was to Poag when Walls was doing the shooting. I have no idea where the shot came from that hit Poag in the back. If Poag had shot at the colored man, he would have shot him in the back, unless he had changed his position, which he did not do.

COOPER STATEMENT

My name is Joel Cooper member of G. Troop 13th Cavalry. I was in the [Havre] Concert Hall when the first shot was fired. I saw a colored man on the white side of the color line, and Poag, a member of our troop walked to get him to go around on the other side. The colored man was sitting down. He got up and fired into the ceiling. I was sitting at the lunch counter at the time. . . . As soon as the first shot was fired I wheeled around in my chair and went out the side door in the end of the room close to the lunch counter. As I went out I saw the colored man going towards Poag with a revolver in his hand, pointed at Poags back, and just as I went out the door I heard the report of a pistol. The colored fellow was about ten feet from Poag over near the slot machines. I did not know the colored man; the best I could tell he was a colored Corporal.

I never saw him after that. . . . That is all I know about the matter. I went right away from there and never went back. I saw that colored Corporal before. I think I could identify him if brought before me.

photo by F. Jay Haynes, Haynes Foundation, Bozeman, Montana

FOOD FROM THE LAND

EMANDS FOR FOOD in growing mining camps of the early 1860's provided an impetus for agricultural and accompanying livestock developments. The mountain valleys of the Gallatin, Prickly Pear, Bitterroot, Madison, and Deer Lodge took on new importance. Agriculture expanded as a supportive link to feed both the mining communities and the military garrisons protecting them. High prices encouraged production and farmers purchased new implements, usually at exorbitant interest rates. Still, profits rose at a rate which encouraged further farm settlement. The livestock industry had small beginnings in southern Montana valleys, but expanded in the 1850's to supply beef for the westward immigration. When mining boomed, the industry prospered on unlimited free range, covered by lush grasses, and aided by burgeoning markets. So rapid was this expansion that by 1865 an act to regulate "marks and brands" passed the Territorial Assembly.

Predictably, profits and growth attracted outside investment. Cattle drives from overcrowded Texas ranges began in 1866, when Nelson Story pushed the first trail herd to Montana. By the late 1870's, large herds appeared in the fertile valleys of the Sun, Smith, Musselshell, and Yellowstone Rivers, and the Judith Basin region of central Montana. New markets and the completion of the Northern Pacific Railroad spurred expansion after 1883 onto less crowded eastern Montana ranges. This eastward movement accompanied a simultaneous importation of large sheep flocks, eventually resulting in overstocked grazing lands.

The "hard winter of 1886-1887" remedied the problem of overcrowding, as well as other range questions. Some stockmen recorded losses in excess of fifty percent. Substantial profits registered by large livestock corporations vanished. The decline of open range grazing gradually followed. New ideas — winter feeding, reduced herd size, fenced ranges — became the norm. More farms, protected by a network of barbed wire, dotted the landscape. The cowboy, a symbol of the open range, had to change, much to his own disgust. Repairing fences, gathering hay for winter feed, digging ditches and post holes, although not in the image of Hollywood romanticism, became routine activities.

No less important was the homesteader's appearance. Lured to the West after the enactment of promising land laws, the newcomers soon competed with ranchers for Montana's fertile river valleys. Initially small irrigation systems watered the fields, but by the 1880's, promotion of dry-land farming methods made these pioneer settlers more flexible. They moved to the arid plains of eastern Montana and again found themselves in direct competition with livestock growers.

Diversification of livestock and agriculture was the key to eventual stability. Ranchers and farmers became managers of the land, not exploiters. Emerging organizations, such as the Grange and livestock associations, formed a well-defined political base to challenge western Montana's mining interests. More significantly, making a living from the land evolved into a respectable business, rather than a speculative scheme or a romantic interlude for outside investors.

Potts and Harrison Horse Ranch, Townsend, c. 1885

FOOD FROM THE LAND
Livestock and Agriculture in the 19th Century

From small beginnings, Montana's agriculture rapidly expanded to meet the needs of hungry miners. Thomas W. Harris, one of Montana's first commercial farmers, supplied these new markets in the mining camps. A Kentucky native, Harris settled at Fort Owen in the Bitterroot Valley in May, 1852, and for the next decade worked for John Owen, engaging in small scale subsistence farming on the side. From his property at Three Mile Creek, near Stevensville, he sold gold seekers harvests of grain and potatoes.

MAY 13 — [1860] — Still Cold. west winds, and nothing growing. this evening I was up to look at Lompreys wheat which looks much worse than mine. he says the Indian wheat looks still worse than his. . . .

JULY 4 — . . . To day Irvine, Tipton and Mr. Chase & family took dinner with me. we had a half dozen chickens Fried — the first this season — and a nice Rubarb Pie, becides a vareity of other good things with a glass of good old Whiskey which has been Saved by Mr. Chase for the occasion since last winter. . . .

OCTOBER 2 — . . . men Thrashing wheat. myself & Gregway hauling Hay. Mr. Higgins wagon arrived from Benton with Howitzer. fired five rounds — the first Canon Shot in the Bitter Root Vally.

JANUARY 1ST — [1862] — To day has been clear and pleasant. to day I went deer hunting but saw nothing. This evening Maj Owen and myself played crib and Backgamon for amusement. I beat him at Backgamon he beat me at crib

JANUARY 2 — Today cold and blustry. strong north wind this evening. the express got in with some old letters and old news papers. no news of importance, only that the war is still going on and no hopes of pease very soon. . . .

MARCH 4 — Clear & pleasant, a regular spring day over head. this evening Mr McClairin arrived from the mission at which place he says a great many head of cattle and horses have died by starvation — . . .

APRIL 28 — Clear & warm. to Day sowed three Bushels wheat. Thornton Plowing it in. To day Maj Owen, Maj Grayum & Mr Adams left for deer lodge. Maj Grayums Horse threw him below Rogues fork. the Horse ran back to the fort. Mr. Adams after him. . . .

JUNE 14 — Cloudy and rainey all day. this evening I eat first mess of Strawberries and cream — today the last of the Indians left for Camash and Bulls. . . .

AUGUST 15 — Clear & warm. men hauling Hay. This evening killed a beef. Major Grayum got in from Deer Lodge. he says he has found new gold diggins over the Mountains on the waters of Missouri and most every one is leaving Deer Lodge.

AUGUST 16 — Clear and warm. men hauling hay. to day some miners passed for Deer Lodge from Elk City. . . .

DECEMBER 31 — Since the 28th the weather has been quite unsettled altho not very cold — The Old year is now at a close and I thank god for the health that we have all been blessed with. also for our pease and prosperity and prey that the same blessing may be extended to us during the new year. . . .

JANUARY 1 — [1863] — This Morning cloudy but clear this evening & pleasant. this evening the settlers from Willow creek are all hear on a wedding party — Mr Cone & Miss Johnson from Willow creek are to be married and worse than all no minister nor Justice to perform the surimony, so I will have to do it myself being the only one present legally autherised.

FEBRUARY 3 — Clear & pleasant. still putting up Ice — it is very fine about 30 inches thick. last night the Indians that started with the express got back. Snow so light they cant walk on snow shoes. this evening Chatfield got back from Hellgate. he was unfortionate in his trip to Hellgate as he got badly whiped and nose bit. fortunily not bit off. a man by the name of Campbell whiped him. . . .

MAY 22 — Cloudy & cold. this morning a heavy frost. Potatoes and corn bit to the ground. to day eleven Elk City miners got in on their way to Banack City. also Mr Clark in from Banack reports between two & three thousand emigrants already in from Pikes Peak, the States, and Salt Lake, and that the road behind is lined with emigrants and wagons. . . .

DECEMBER 25 — Cloudy & cold. This evening in order to keep up the name of Fort Owen I have invited all that is about the Fort to take dinner with me, and I must say that Lesette has given us a very good dinner. I have a little whiskey but all hands are sober, I suppose from the fact that it is to mean to drink. . . .

DECEMBER 31 — Cloudy. cold & snowing most all day. This being the last day of the year I thank almity God for the health happiness & prosperity granted myself & family for the past year and prey God that we may be in like manner blessed in the year coming & until death when we hope to meat at thy right hand in heaven.

APRIL 16 [1864] — . . . today I moved out to my ranch on 3 Mile Creek & buid farwell to Fort Owen as a home at which place I have been so long that it was like drawing my eye teeth to leave. but I am now at home which I have never been before since I have been in the Vally. I now prey to almighty God for a continuation of good health, peace, happiness and prosperity & the same for my family and Maj. John Owen. My Rhumatism is still very painful but I trust in God that I will now soon be well.

JULY 2d — [1865] — Back home from Fort Benton. I had a very pleasant trip. . . . I am thankful that my crop is good also Brother Bens, but am sorry that the crops in the country are very poor. most all distroyed by Grasshoppers and bugs. I am also thankful to find my Family all well, and my stock all in a thriving condition.

MAY 23d — [1867] — Last night & this fore noon a good rain. Today I set out about fourteen hundred cabbage plants & 40 or 50 Tomatoes. Ambros tells me to day that the Grasshoppers are more plentiful down in the vally than he has ever seen them & that they have already commenced on the wheat. God knows I hope they will not visit me, as yet there are none.

JUNE 11 — Warm & Cloudy most of day. this evening a light shower. to day I have been laying adobeys for the first [time] in my life, but no man knows what he can do until he tryes. to day Farnham sick. Grant Mason commenced work by the day at 2$ per day.

JUNE 14 — Clear & Pleasant. to day laying adobeys. To day Mr Adams got back from resivation & mission in company with Louis Brown. They both say my crop is the best in the country. . . .

JUNE 18TH — . . . To day all hands busy killing crickets. they came down this morning from toward 8 mile creek as thick as they can. will lay on the ground [and] unless I can turn them they will soon take all my crop. to night I have 2 rollers running to try & kill them while they are laying in piles. I intend to give them the best fight I can and trust to God for his blessing to turn them from me. I have the best prospect for a crop I have ever had since I have been in the country — if Crickets & Grasshoppers will let it alone. . . .

JULY 1ST — Clear & very warm & sultry. I have caught cold and am quite unwell. Still I have not time to lay up. to day have been working in garden. Musquitoes getting very bad. last knight and to knight a very long & bright comit seen in the north west. . . .

JULY 4 — This morning Farnham fiared two rounds with the Howitzer, but the American Flag has not been seen as a Bloody Englishman is in charge. I suppose if he had of had a flag with god save the Queen on it or much less her Back side it would have gone up with the Sun. As it is myself, Chatfield & Brook have drank Sunday Julips. . . .

JULY 9TH — . . . to day all hands killing crickets. it seems as if they are determined to have my crop. I dont think I would exagerate to say that we have killed to day five large wagon boxes full. we have been fighting them now almost every day for a month — and still there seems to be no end to them. . . .

JULY 14 — Clear & very warm. to day myself & wife hunting cattle. This evening Dr Atkinson arrived from Fort Benton & reports the steamer blown up some six days sail below Benton. every thing on board lost but no lives. he also hears that Maj Owen has been removed & the new agent [of the Flathead Agency] is on his way up by Benton. . . .

JULY 16 — Clear & warm. to day working in garden and irrigating. some corn beginning to shoot. Oats about all headed and are rank and fine. Dr. Atkinson & Chatfield [went] fishing but musquitoes drove them home. River nearly fordable. . . .

JULY 28TH — . . . Still all hands fighting Crickets. it seems that they are coming thicker than ever. tomorrow I shall commence digging a ditch on the South Side of my farm, which I hope will turn them. . . .

JULY 29TH — . . . Stewart and Lewis digging ditch. All the rest of us fighting Crickets. God knows I am getting very tired of it but still they come as thick as ever. . . .

SEPTEMBER 27 — Since the 23d Maj Grayum, Lomprey and myself have been up the Vally prospecting for gold but found none. The week past has been clear & pleasant. my Potatoes are all dug and put away. in all 155 Bushels. . . .

NOVEMBER 1ST — Cloudy & snowing on mountains. to day Dr Atkinson got back from Deer Lodge. thinks he has found gold diggins that will pay ten or fifteen dollars per day. this evening I put out more Stricnine

NOVEMBER 2 — Clear & pleasant to day. Maj Grayum got back from Deer Lodge. reports favourable of the gold diggins. this evening Batchalder got in with the express. reports Major Owen on his way home.

DECEMBER 31 — Cloudy & cold this fore noon. last night about 4 inches snow. to day Mr Blake went to Hellgate after express from Walla Walla. today I have been making a chair — Our Christmas is about gone and every thing has passed off very smoothly and quietly. This has been a year to me of health to myself and family. also pease & happiness and prosperity. hoping the next may be equally so. I now bid farewell to old year with thanks to our heavenly farther for past favours.

As Montana matured after the gold discoveries, agricultural opportunities grew accordingly. Like many immigrants, Joseph Bumby first served in the Civil War, then was enticed to locate in Montana under the Homestead Act of 1862. The prospects of settling on 160-acre tracts (free, except for a $25 filing fee), and attractive livestock profits drew the ambitious westward. In letters to his parents and family in Huddersfield, England, Bumby described Montana's advantages, its agricultural outlook, and the profitability of cattle raising. His optimism was strong enough to persuade his father, William, to immigrate.

SILVER STAR, MONTANA TER.
MAY 21, 1871

DEAR FAMILY,

. . . I suppose I must say a little about my own farming. I guess if any of you could see me this morning, Sunday, as I am set on the ground in my rags, writing this note, it would cool the emigrating fever. It is nothing to me, but I can fancy what it would be to a person just from the comfort of an old settled country, but that is not describing my farm. I have put in 3 acres of oats, 3 1/2 acres of wheat, 2 acres of Barley, 2 acres of Potatoes and perhaps 1/4 acre of Ruta Bagas. The small grain is all up but does not look as well as I should like it, perhaps I watch it with too anxious care. . . .

I think I have as good a stock farm as there is anywhere. It is a beautiful place here in pleasant weather, thousands of acres of thick, green, luxuriant bunch grass . . . all around you with the thickly wooded snow capped mountains in the distance. . . . Sometimes I almost get discouraged, here all alone camping out amongst the wild beasts, without any fence around my grain, at present. I am now building one. I have more to do than one person can attend to. After harvest I shall know what to do. . . . If I don't grow anything I shall leave it and don't know what I shall do next, but I am in strong hopes of making a good farm here. . . .

AUGUST 4TH, 1871

. . . Montana is a beautiful country & very healthy but no society. . . . It is just the place for you all & am satisfied . . . about 500 pounds, put . . . into stock [would purchase] . . . a few hundred head of cattle. They increase very fast here. . . . Spanish cattle can be bought [in Kansas City] for about $12.50 a head. Now is the time to put money into stock for when this place is settled then will be the time for selling it. . . . I am sure there is no better place for stock raising in America. . . .

AUGUST 20, 1871

The stock business is a mania in Montana. Everybody that has a dollar or two are into it and accumulating in number rapidly, while the prices are as high or higher than ever. What are called American Cows sell from 50 to 75 dollars. Texas cows can be bought for 30 to 40. I do not think this state of things will always last — If I am not mistaken before very many years some man will be caught with a lot of dead or worthless cattle on his hands. It has been so in Cal. & Tex. & I think will be so here; but it is well enough for a man if he has the money to take advantage of this apparently unlimited pasture while it lasts. . . .

JEFFERSON VALLEY, MARCH 2, 1872

. . . You will notice by the heading of this letter that we have changed our location since you last heard from us. . . . I guess I had better . . . try and explain our circumstances to you more clearly, as I am led to think you do not . . . understand our situation.

When I commenced to put in a crop last spring, I had in money and property . . . from five to six hundred dollars, besides a good horse and saddle worth $175.00. . . . The money was all used during the summer in buying team, tools, seed and provision, and a very poor outfit I had as far as regards tools. Well, I did not grow enough for our next years living and should have had to have worked for wages again in order to get . . . a little money for incidental expenses as well as some provisions. . . . Well I looked around and found another location

with the intention of putting in a crop this spring. . . .

We have had a rough time of it ourselves this winter, the storm caught us before we had finished building our cabin. We lived in a "root house" in a cellar dug in the ground to keep roots. The roof is made of pine poles with about 2 feet of dirt on the top. A quarter of the roof was torn off. . . .

A great many farmers are looking for grass hoppers this year. To a beginner to be eat[en] out with them . . . would be ruinous, while to those that have got started it falls not so heavy. He would have his own cows, his hens, his pigs, and his garden he would be able to save. I have seen a large garden in a bad year kept in flourishing condition by having a lot of hens with broods of young chickens. Take an open box and tie the old hen so she can't get out and the young chickens eat the grasshoppers. You may think what with frost, grasshoppers, and need of irrigation this is not a desirable place to farm, but there are drawbacks in every country. . . . I am satisfied Wisconsin never offered the inducements to settlers that this country does. . . .

With kind love to all, I am yours, etc.

JOE BUMBY

Irrigation has historically been one key to successful agriculture. In Montana, irrigation began simply as a series of short, small ditches along river bottoms. These systems were a common denominator in reducing many farmers to simple ditch diggers. John P. Martens, a Victor area farmer, typical of early irrigators, recorded some of the back-breaking vicissitudes.

SUNDAY, JUNE 25 — [1877] — Whaether cloudy. Arigated Pease and wheat all Day. Seen Frank Tudor, he was in the same busisenes. . . .

TUESDAY, JUNE 26 — Whaether cloudy, raining some in the forenoon. Did not do much of anyting. Wm. N. Smith and Blake was here. I took them around and showed them the difrendt kind of crops. . . . After Dinner went with Blake to look at his crop — it looks well. . . . I went home and made a Triangel and coments to survey a Dich on my upper line, south of the Ravine. It coments to rain hard and I quit. . . .

SATTERRDAY, JULY 21 — Clear and verry warm. Termometer standing 106 deg. in the shade. Went to the Feild before Breakfast and regulated the Water on the Beans and Wheat, then came in and got Breakfast and done the chores. . . .

MONDAY, JULY 23 — Whaether clear and hot until the midle of the afternoon. After Breakfast went out to arigate. Regulated the water on my own Feild then went down to Tudors. He was getting ready to start [on a trip.] . . . I went home, done some moore arigating. After Dinner went and turned in moore water in my own and Clarks Dich. Came down home, met Blake, he telling me that Nelsons feild was full of Hogs. We went back up again but did not find any Hogs. Came on down together back of the feild. At the uper end of my feild we parted. . . . I seen Clark and Litter hurrieng toward Tudors. . . . I got there . . . and while they were talking a storm came on. It was moore than a storm it was a Tornado acompanied by Hail. It lasted between 10 or 15 minutes but the destruction of Property was tirreble. . . .

Agricultural discontent in the late 1860's led to the formation of the national "Patrons of Husbandry," or more commonly, the Grange. The first Montana chapter, organized in December, 1873, was led by Robert N. Sutherlin. As editor of the ROCKY MOUNTAIN HUSBANDMAN, Sutherlin called for the cooperation of Montana farmers. Inadequate transportation facilities and constricting local markets underscored the need for unity. However, numerous problems served to forestall the movement's growth. The Grange's failure, in 1876, to work out a cooperative marketing plan for supplying military posts intensified dissatisfaction. Crop failures, the result of unusually heavy grasshopper infestation, added to the disillusionment and despair. Undaunted, Grange Secretary P. B. Mills renewed the call for unity.

BOULDER VALLEY, MT.
DECEMBER 15, 1876

DEAR EDITOR:

What are you grangers doing now? The order in this Territory is not dead is it? What is the Grange doing now to benefit the farmer? Has the Grange any business schemes or plans of co-operation? What objects has the Grange in view for the future? . . .

Every Patron in the Territory may ask himself the above questions and answer them if he can. Although we may safely attribute the absence of any well directed . . . organization . . . to the ravages of the grasshoppers, yet it does not follow that the hope, energy and vitality of the farmers [is] sapped to the core. . . .

It is true that the order is in too reduced circumstances to engage in gigantic undertakings with any hopes of success, but it should not deter us from our purpose or diminish our confidence, or embargo a free discussion of business schemes and plans. . . .

The farmer has been for all time the ass that has bore the burdens of low prices and oppression; of suplicatingly inquiring how much will you give for my produce, and how much will you take for your wares? But the time has arrived when the farmers as a class, through education, sound judgment and fraternal unity, can protect their own interests. . . .

The work before us is of no little moment. The issue now, is between capital and labor, between monopoly and competition, and every guarantee to capital at the expense of the agriculturist and producer. Capital combines and forms great manufacturing combinations. . . . and we the lords of the land, and to the manor born, have to foot the bills. . . .

While I do not wish to disparage or underate the moral, social and educational features of our order; yet I do claim it is high time that Patrons should be educating themselves to . . . become independent.

P. B. MILLS

Since settlement of western lands in the last century was a prime concern of the federal government, Congress passed a succession of land laws: the Preemption Act of 1841, the Homestead Act of 1862, and the Timber Culture Act of 1873. In one form or another, these statutes allowed settlers to file on 160-acre plots. Based on the eastern concept that such a tract could support a family, the laws were unrealistic in the arid western states. Finally, in 1877, the Desert Land Act permitted a person to buy an entire section of land — 640 acres — at $1.25 an acre. An owner must only promise to irrigate within three years. In practice, the measure led to widespread abuses; more than a few stockmen had their ranch hands file on land, and then had it assigned to themselves. There were other methods as well. A stageline owner named S. S. Huntley detailed his own scheme in the following letter. Huntley's plan succeeded. The next year he formed a partnership with P. B. Clark to raise horses.

SALT LAKE CITY
NOVEMBER 22, 1877

FRIEND CLARK,

. . . Since leaving Montana learn that one can take up desert land. Now I want you to post yourself immediately on this matter and take up all the land you can for us.

You can not get to much — would like at least four or six sections. One in your own name — One in Tom Shirleys — and the others in any reliable persons names who will turn the land over to us soon as they get the proper papers. Would take up in my own name but can not being absent.

For our purpose Crow Creek Valley is the best in Montana. We must controll every acre in it possible. Prevent others from getting land there, and if possible freeze out *stock men* now living in the vally. A few years from now land desirable will not be so easy to get as now. Do this quietly, and loose no time about it. I think we are on the right track now and must stick to it.

HASTILY YOURS

S. S. HUNTLEY

No time to loose — am afraid the law will be repealed this congress . . .

As ranges to the south and west filled and were depleted, massive trail herds began entering Montana's grasslands. The life of a cowboy on these cattle drives was anything but uneventful. From 1866 to the late 1880's, hundreds of cowpunchers signed on for the long drives from Texas to Montana, and some of them stayed. H. J. Rutter, later a Hinsdale rancher, joined one of these last drives as a "cocky youth." Indians, rustlers, lightning storms, and mad dashes to turn the herds were only a few of the trail crew's problems. Yet some of the longest hours were spent on more tedious duties. Long stretches in the saddle, sleepless nights, and a monotonous diet were the norm.

We started north in 1884 just after the spring breeding season with a herd of about three thousand head a part of one of the last big cattle drives from Texas. Our herd was about a fourth of the whole herd which came up in four sections . . . making about 12,000 head. . . .

All cattle starting north on the trail were given a trail brand and there would be a man left at the central points along the way for a number of days after the herd had passed through; this man would look over the other herds that came in and he could claim all the cattle bearing the brand of his outfit no matter who brought them in. . . .

We had a crew of ten or twelve cow-boys to handle 3,000 cattle. When it was near time to bed down for the night the point men would lead the herd off the trail, the swing men would allow the cattle leeway and the herd would start grazing. The trail boss usually had the camp spot picked out hours before it was time to turn off the trail. . . . Having a watering place spotted we could judge the rate of speed the herd would have to make. Within about two miles of the camp spot the crew threw them off the trail and the cattle started grazing and by the time the spot was reached the cattle were full and the leader was ready to lie down. Then the swing men closed in and sometimes the entire herd would follow the leader and lie down. That was a sight to see a herd of 3,000 stretched out over several acres but this was unusual as it was generally a slow job to crowd the herd into the bedground so gradually that they were all given time to lie down.

Besides the crew of cow-boys and the trail boss there was the cook and the horse wrangler. The horse wrangler, usually a young boy, looked after the remuda which might consist of from five to ten horses to the man. Besides this he was expected to rustle wood for the cook. . . . The remaining member of the crew was the cook and he was a character.

His official position while we were on the trail was at the helm of the . . . mess wagon. . . . It often had to be loaded for as many as three hundred miles and that meant a limited supply of everything and careful vigilance on the part of the cook. For the most part the supplies consisted of coffee, bacon, beans and flour. The coffee that was carried was unparched coffee bought in 100-pound containers. Part of the kitchen equipment was a dutch-oven and the cook used this to roast the coffee as it was needed. The oven was really built for service and even the familiar beans and bacon weren't so bad when they were baked in it.

The fire was burned down to bright coals then the coals were raked out and the oven was buried in the embers, full of beans and bacon while the live coals were heaped over it. When the contents were done the red-hot lid had to be lifted off with long tongs.

The cook never had to sound the dinner gong more than once. When we heard the first bang of his big cooking ladle on the dish pan we were ready to line up and by the time the echo was dying away we were ready for beans and bacon.

The daily schedule was much the same. . . . During the day I kept far enough ahead of the herd to know where the next watering hole would be. We tried to regulate the speed of the herd so as to bring them on water at noon; then we grazed them until two o'clock. At two we threw them back on the trail and would make about seven miles to some dry ridge where we would set up a dry camp. The number of miles the herd could make in one day depended on the grass and water supply. It was usually between 15 and 20 miles a day.

Lack of food or water, strange noises or prowling animals kept up the constant hazard of a stampede at night so the night watch was a very important part of a trailman's duty. The first guard went on at 10 o'clock, the second at mid-night, the third at two, and the fourth . . . from four until morning. If a member of the crew was responsible, . . . if he had imagination, if he was highly sensitive or had a depth of emotion the night guard brought it out and gave him some of the greatest experiences of his life. . . .

What did it take to run a large, successful ranch during the height of the open range cattle boom? Granville Stuart provided an inventory for the DHS Ranch and thereby an insight into the era. With investors A. J. Davis and S. T. Hauser, Stuart formed the DHS Ranch in the Judith Basin. He had been an early placer miner and mercantilist until 1879, when he entered into cattle raising. After that he served as general manager for the DHS while it expanded to become one of Montana's largest cattle companies.

FORT MAGINNIS, MONTANA
SEPTEMBER 10, 1884

S. T. HAUSER, ESQ.
HELENA, MONTANA

Have been too ill to fix up lists for incorporation, but get out of bed to Send you following memorandum.

15,318 Cattle (fall roundup in progress, may go [up] 1400)
    79 Horses (worth about $6000)
  400 Acres Scrip land. All Hay, with fences & improvements Cost about $9000.
      4 Wagons & Harness
      2 Mowing Machines
      1 Horse Rake
      5 Saddles
      3 Stoves
    13 Corrals on Range
  250 Tons Hay
      6 Winchester Rifles

I am not able to come to Helena now, but am improving, & may be soon. Write me fully what is required more, if anything. . . .

Reeces party were *surprised* in the night by a strong force & the 5 horse thieves taken away from them near mouth of Musselshell. Dont know what became of them — too bad, wasn't it. . . .

YOURS &C

GRANVILLE STUART

Hunger and the necessity for survival forced Indian bands off their reservations in 1881. The scarcity of wild game and the inconsistency of government food issues were the catalysts. Provided with passes from reservation agents, the tribes journeyed to central Montana hoping to intersect the last remnants of the once-massive northern buffalo herd grazing in the Musselshell region. In this letter to Sam Hauser, Granville Stuart was apprehensive about the situation, realizing that individual stockmen were helpless in controlling the roving Indian bands. He felt punitive and organized action was needed, and in the following year, local cattlemen began forming "protective associations" to share the work of policing central Montana ranges. The Indians returned to the reservations, their last bid for freedom to hunt gone, along with the herds of buffalo.

FORT MAGINNIS, MONT.
JUNE 28, 1881

S. T. HAUSER, ESQ.
HELENA, MONT.

DEAR SAM,

Tom Power was awarded the beef contract at this post at $5.94 per hundred delivered on the block, or in other words cut up into steaks &c in a regular butcher shop. I know he cannot make a cent at that figure & doubt if he can keep even. . . . I write this to post you so that if Weston or anybody else wants us to fill this contract we will do it for seven (7) cents pr lb. provided they will allow us a month to put up shop, slaughter house etc., & to go out & hunt up a competent butcher, get tools & fixtures, and we wont do it for any less because we can do nearly that well selling them out on foot. . . .

I have always ordered our men to not let any war party of Indians come up to them on the range, as once in camp in force they are liable to rob or kill them. . . . On the 24th as Ben Farrar & John Cabler (a mighty good man) were going down Box Elder Creek on the E. side of the range to see what the cattle were doing they saw 12 Indians on foot coming to their noon camp. Cabler ordered them to keep away but they would keep coming on, so he opened fire on them, knocking three down the first round, but I am sorry to say that they were not killed, but all got into the coulee's & got away. The boys poured the lead into them so lively that they stood not on the order of their going but went at once, only firing a few shots from their little rim fire Henry Carbines in return. The boys held the field & then went on around the range & did not get back to the ranch for two days & a half afterwards. . . .

I see by the papers that the whole Flathead tribe recently passed thru Helena on their way to the Mussleshell, & not a single d-d paper has a word to say about what an outrage it is to let these lazy devils come from their reservation out into this country under pretense of hunting, when there is not half game enough for them to subsist upon & when in reality they come to gratify their propensity for rambling, & to get whiskey, and eat our cattle, & often steal horses too. . . . Now we protest against the continuance of this sort of thing, and demand that all the Indians be made [to] stay on their reservations, and unless something is done about it *soon*, we will be compelled in order to save our property, to cease protesting, and begin protecting ourselves. . . .

We want no Indian war, for we know that the fault lies not wholly, nor yet half with the Indians, but we do want common justice & that protection for our lives & property to which we are entitled and we propose to have them, though it should cost us, (sad thought) the displeasure of all those rich, but silly, old women *of both sexes*, in the States whose ancestors have exterminated the superior races of Indians who once owned the Eastern States, their descendents who now own the plunder, think that by way of compensation the western Indians should be allowed to exterminate the toilworn pioneer who is engaged in unlocking the vast treasures of the mighty West. But alack & alas for poor Lo, the contract is too hefty for him, even with the aid & comfort derived from the idiotic stupidity of the general government in its administration of Indian affairs, and as Bohm remarked of the Helena Smelter "The dividend is the udder vay."

It waxeth late, & the voice of the mosquito is heard too numerously, therefore, with respects to Mrs. Hauser, goodnight.

GRANVILLE STUART

The location of the DHS Ranch near Fort Maginnis provided distinct advantages — military protection from Indians (however limited), and favorable beef contracts to supply the garrison. This proximity also had its disadvantages.

FORT MAGINNIS, MONT.
DEC. 6TH, 1881

DEAR SAM,

. . . I have had my hands full or I would have forwarded report ere this. . . . On the 3rd a company of soldiers left here for Keogh and as two of our men was coming up from below . . . they meets two soldiers who had the hind quarters of a freshly killed beef behind their saddles. They saw our men & dodged out of the road, and as the boys were each driving a hay team they of course could do nothing then, but they came & told me, & next morning we went & took their tracks & followed them to where they had shot a fat 2 1/2 year old steer & cut off the hams leaving the rest lying with entrails all in & spoiled & we poisoned it for the wolves.

One of our men who lived near Fort Logan while the soldiers occupied it says it is the regular thing with them & they all do it, & do it plenty too. The most of them are coming back again & we think we can identify them & will go for them, but its only petty larceny anyhow — a month in jail and $100 fine. . . . This is pretty rough hav[ing] to watch them too, & from this [time] on they will be worse than the Indians. They most probably killed one for each mess (4 or 5) before they got off the range, as each looks out for itself. They draw rations of beef, but it is only about half enough. . . . It would not surprise me if there was some soldiers found dead on the range before long as there are war parties of Indians prowling around.

RESPECTFULLY YOURS

GRANVILLE STUART

As a young woman, Grace Bendon came with her family from Missouri to Glendive. Three years later, in 1883, she met her first husband, Edward Marron, at the city's "pioneer ball." The following December, the young lovers were married by an army chaplain from Fort Keogh. Everything at the ceremony was imported, she reflected, from the "minister to the turkey dinner." Years later she reminisced before the Glendive PTA about her first year of marriage. Her words revealed that the cattle range was not solely a man's realm, although young white brides were scarce indeed.

Now for the bridal trip and honeymoon. The 1st. week was spent at a hotel, waiting for the weather-man to get over his New Years celebration. Then we started for our future home, sixty miles away, over the bleak snow-covered planes, coolies, bad lands, & a mountainous divide. . . . It was a "long, long trail" and I thought we would never reach our journey's end. . . .

Finally we arrived at the ranch and found six cowboys and a Mexican cook anxiously waiting for us. Soon a piping hot dinner was on the table which consisted of baked beans, raw tomatoes served in the can, bacon and sour-dough biscuites. For desert we had, what the Cowboys called *spotted dog* and was boiled rice with raisens in it. In those early days we ate nothing that was not dried, fried, canned or condensed. If that sort of food contained the proper amount of *Vitamins,* the old timers certainly got their share of the "basic" food we hear so much about these days.

We had several thousand cows on the range, still we freighted all kinds of canned vegetables, meat, and condensed milk sixty miles. . . .

With the coming of the white squaw, things changed a wee bit. We soon had a garden and raised all kinds of fresh vegetables. We built a log chicken coop, and had all the spring friers we could eat. We broke several wild cows, which we milked by 1st tying their hind feet to one post and their front feet to another. We put up ice (in a dugout) useing hay for sawdust. Thus we had ice-cream, and all the delicacies that go with rich, fresh milk, cream, butter and eggs. And what do you think we did with the thousands of tin cans we had piled high in a cooley nearby. First we had our log-cabin home fenced — Then we had gravel walks running in all directions and angles. Then tin cans were reserected, paper labels taken off and then sorted and carefully placed on each side of our gravel walks forming a protective curb. When finished they shone & glittered in the sunshine like a silver band, and when it rained — the pitter-patter of the rain drops on the tin sounded like a symphony orchestria outside our log cabin home. . . .

I shall never forget the reception I received when I arrived at the ranch. The cowboys would ride miles to see the bride, and when they arrived at the ranch, half starved and partly frozen, they were to shy and bashful to even speak to her. White women were a real curiosity in those day's. One winter I was the only white woman on a stream 90 miles long and I did not see a white woman for six months. Still, I can look back today to those ten years on a frontier cattle ranch with a great deal of joy. . . .

Sheep raising in the latter half of the 1870's grew into an extremely lucrative business. From 1875 to 1880 the number of sheep in Montana increased six-fold, to over 385,000. Favorable grasses and high profits encouraged men with little or no experience in woolgrowing to decide on the gamble. One of these converts was John H. Stoutenburg, who had spent three months driving sheep from Nevada in the summer of 1877. In 1878 he settled in the Judith Basin country. In this reminiscence he gave his impressions of the advantages of the sheep business and some of its hardships.

. . . Our idea was to take sheep on the shares. . . . With $1,500.00 cash in hand we went to Tim Collins, a Benton Banker, and after a heart to heart talk induced him to lend us $1,500.00 at 12 per cent per annum, he taking a chattle mortgage on the thousand grade yews bought with the $3,000.00. This arranged, Barney and I started for Helena and after looking over herds held in that vicinity for sale, finally secured a thousand good yews at $3.00 per head. Then we headed for Sage Creek.

The winter of '79 and '80 was remembered by sheep and cattle men as the hardest winter since white man's time — the coldest and with the most snow. The Judith Basin was only half stocked to capacity. There was an abundance of grass but it was covered with from eighteen inches to two feet of snow. . . . One could hear the snow fairly squeel as cattle drifted by the cabin at night in search of feed. Our mercury thermometer was faithful, ever on the job, but laid off work at 40 below. . . . [We had] four men to care for a paltry bunch of 1,000 sheep, with a good warm shed, and plenty of hay. . . . We had the time of our life, [each] cooked [for a] week about, and played cards between times. . . .

It was my week to cook. We had a young elk that was pretty good eating. We had a big iron pot which we used for making stews and we all enjoyed the stews made from the elk meat flavored with bacon. I took great pains in preparing this one and cooked it until it was just right. We all ate and pronounced it perfect. At each meal they said it was better than before. On the second or third day when Albert was loading his plate from the pot, he reached with his fork nearer the bottom for a piece of elk. He drew out on his fork not a piece of meat but half of a fifty pound flour sack. Holding it up before us all he asked, "What the Hell is that?" After coming out of the trance I said, "I'll be darned if it isn't that old dish rag that I have been looking for the last three days."

A good third of the stock on the Judith Range died that winter. It was almost a clean sweep for sheep men unprepared with hay and shelter. . . . The Sage Creek sheep went through the hard winter of '79 and '80 with the loss of only one sheep, an old toothless ewe. Hamilton fed her gruel, made her hay tea, and sat up with her a few nights but her time had come. Anyway 999 sheep saved out of 1,000 was the banner record of Montana for that year. Of course we ranged the herd all winter when it didn't blizzard. . . .

It was on the 23rd of February, the thermometer registered 33 below that morning. I was with the herd a mile or so from the sheep shed. . . . At about 3:30 p.m. the wind suddenly changed . . . [and became] so warm that it made one gasp for breath. A fog rose where the warm air met the cold and changed the ice particles into mist. . . . Then all of a sudden the wind let up for a few minutes. When it returned it was with a velocity of fifty miles per hour and a temperature of 55 above. That night before going to bed our thermometer showed 58 above. . . . Anyone who has never witnessed a chinook can form no idea as to what it will do to snow. A hundred degree July sun without wind can't hold a candle to it. Snow melted before a chinook like greese on a hot stove.

Another novice sheep raiser was James H. Blake, who formed a partnership with his brother, Helena dentist John M. Blake. Like Stoutenburg, the Blakes located their ranch in the Judith Basin, at the foot of the Big Snowy Mountains. Here Blake wrote sarcastically to a friend, C. E. Stone, about his brief herding experience after weathering a severe winter.

Sunless Ranche
March 24, 1881

Friend Stone,

. . . The Winter has near disappeared and I am very glad of it. I can safely say that this is the most disagreeable winter that I ever put [in] & I hope to go to *H-ll* if I ever put another in like it. I have been out with the sheep every day but one, that day I went to the Post Office. I say that it is good calculation to higher men and do all the hard work your self because they only cost $20 per month. . . .

I think that sheep herding is the nicest business that I ever struck. It [is] so delightful to go out in the morning after gitting breakfast, stay till dark, then come in [and] git [supper] for some lazy S - n of B - - ch because he [was] higherd for $20 per month — it is so *damnd* nice to have higherd [someone] and have to do all the work yourself. . . .

The Grass is starting a little and the sheep run like grayHounds. It is fun you bet to herd them. When Dock comes over he will be in a *H - ll* of a stew to [see] that thare has not been a shed made to shear in and building built to keep the hides in, but if I am as tirard then as I am now, a very little growling will cause me to take a walk. . . .

Five years ago Jim Horbuckle bot 2500 sheep, 2000 of these Yews. Thare [have] not been any sold out of the band and there is only 600 left — how is that looking on paper, . . . less than 25 percent. . . . Beverage's band . . . are all dead. Hatch has lost over half of his. Moule has lost 2/3 of his 2500. Severance has not lost but a very [few]. He had sheds & hay and pays a man $50 per month for herding. . . .

Old Dick Barnes came over here in Jan. & the *Damd* old *pawper* has been here ever since. He went out . . . to kill some Elk and a [herd] of 103 run over him and it is a Damd pitty that it did not kill him. It put his shoulder out of Joint.

J. H. BLAKE

The Montana Stockgrowers Association held its third annual meeting in Miles City, Montana's self-proclaimed "cow capital." The Territory's most prominent livestock owners had joined together, in 1885, to work out common range problems. One factor they could not control was the weather. Russell B. Harrison, son of U. S. President Benjamin Harrison and the Association's recording secretary, reported on the industry's problems after the disastrous winter of 1886-1887. Heavy losses in sheep and cattle forced revolutionary changes in the livestock industry and marked an end to the cheap grazing on the open range.

APRIL 19, 1887

With this meeting, our Association enters upon the third year of its existence. . . . Since we last met . . . the range business has had three severe trials:

1st: The unprecedented drought that prevailed last Spring and Summer, causing a great shortness of food, and making the cattle poor in flesh. . . .

2nd: The low price of beef that ruled in Chicago during the fall, shrinking our receipts materially.

3rd: The very severe winter which has just passed, which brought general loss, more or less severe, depending upon circumstances, to every member. . . .

These reverses were sufficient to try the patience and fortitude of every one throughout the range country, and as you are aware, has demoralized the business and turned the tide of investment from us to other directions. That the trials through which we have

passed were remarkable, not only for their severity, but particularly because they followed each other so closely, is universally admitted: A drought without parallel, a market without a bottom, and a Winter, the severest ever known in Montana, formed a combination, testing the usefulness of our Association and proving its solidity.

Thinking that these trials were not sufficient for our industry, Congress, in its wisdom, has added a fourth, the Inter-State Commerce law, which has seriously interfered with the attendance at this meeting, owing to the difficulty of securing reduced transportation, and which threatens to interfere seriously with the necessary rights and privileges of cattle men of the far West, in transporting their quota of the food supply of the Nation to Eastern markets.

Yet, notwithstanding these difficultues, we have reason to congratulate ourselves upon the very large attendance and the Interest taken in the proceedings.

After 1887, Montana's livestock industry gradually changed character. Cattle raising returned to more local ownership and reduced herds. Cowboys who once served large companies either departed Montana, changed their life style or ventured out on their own. No longer "riding the line" for $40 a month, those who remained became range managers on their own spreads. Albert Ronne, one such cowhand, started anew at Woody Island Creek on recently opened Indian land. Some vestiges of the open range still remained north of the Milk River and he availed himself of this opportunity. His operation also incorporated techniques more accepted by the industry — cutting hay and irrigating land.

NOVEMBER, 1892

MR. JAMES FERGUS

OLD FRIEND,

It has been my intention to write you for a long time [and] give you a short sketch of my eventfull & dissipated career, since leaving your Ranch. On arriving at Chinook, the Round Up was about to start out. So thinking it would be a good chance to see the country, as well as to gain a few needful specimens of "the allmighty," my services were engaged to "Sleepy Tom," Foreman for the Broadwater Cattle Co., and done the Wild West Cowboy act from May 20th. . . .

The evening of the 3rd July, when being seized with an uncontrollably patriotic desire to celebrate, I sent in my resignation, which was promptly accepted, and ten oclock that evening found me in Chinook. After the celebrations were over with, (and my head once more assumed its normal size) I started out north with a pack horse & saw some fine country, also found a suitable location which I afterwards returned to and am now living on.

We (Ronne Sr. & ditto Jr.) have each taken up 320 acres on what is called "Woody Island Creek." It is a running stream of pure spring water, which heads at the international boundary line and runs southeast into Milk River through the finest range in Montana. But Nature has been rather too parsimonious in the matter of timber, it being 25 miles from where we live. . . .

We certainly have a good location, being right in the heart of a Virgin Range with plenty of fine water & land which can all be irrigated. Since coming here on August 12, we put up about 40 tons of hay also a house & stable etc. Have done lots of hard work & expect to do a great deal more, having demonstrated to my entire satisfaction the *Darwinian* theory of the struggle for existence.

I shall sorely miss your library this winter, as I have allready suffered from mental starvation having nothing to read. However, I have made the acquaintance of the Lady teacher in Chinook who is the most intellectual woman I have met in Montana, and she has promised to loan me some of her books. But if you will kindly send me a bundle of "Investigators, Ironclads," etc. they will be gladly accepted. . . .

We are having a cold spell [of] weather here just now, with the usual fall winds, & several small snowfalls. There is a large amount of cattle here, one outfit from New Mexico turned loose 15,000 head of steers, but as there is a large scope of country extending north & east with plenty of grass there is lots of room for more. But I must close for fear a too lengthy letter will give you "that tired feeling." . . .

ALBERT RONNE
CHINOOK, MONT.

As agriculture and stock growing diversified, old methods of operation were discarded. Land resources became even more important and control of public lands spurred wide debate. Some advocates felt public domain leasing would help alleviate overcrowding and other range problems. Small ranchmen and new settlers feared large stock owners would use leasing to squeeze them out. Paris Gibson, best remembered as a founder of Great Falls, long supported open settlement for homesteaders. While campaigning for the U.S. Senate, he freely expressed his views to Governor R. B. Smith. After his election, Gibson worked energetically, albeit unsuccessfully, to secure the repeal of what he viewed as "obnoxious" land leasing laws. Later legislation did address these diverse demands concerning the West's public domain.

GREAT FALLS, MONTANA
APRIL 2, 1900

HON. R. B. SMITH,
GOVERNOR OF MONTANA

DEAR SIR:

I wish it were possible to ascertain the views of all the voters of Montana on the question of leasing the federal lands or of ceding them to the States, for it is not alone the stockmen and farmers who should have something to say on these matters, but laboring men of all classes and professional men have an interest in the disposition of the public domain.

I am in favor of maintaining our federal land laws just as they are, and keeping the public lands untrammelled by leasing measures, so that they may be taken hereafter by actual settlers, as such lands have always been taken. At the rate immigrants are now pouring into the North West, it will be scarcely a year before all the government lands east of the 100 degree of longitude, fit for settlement, will be taken. After that, immigrants in large numbers will settle in Montana. . . .

To give Montana the control of the public domain within its borders would at once create a political issue hitherto unknown here, and it could not fail to have the most corrupting tendencies. I am ready to believe that the stockmen of Montana, wealthy, active and vigilant, would get control of all the best of Montana's farm-lands as fast as they were offered, having shaped legislation to suit themselves. . . .

If all leasing measures are deferred for ten years, I am confident the public domain lying in Montana, now so little appreciated for agriculture, will furnish homes for forty thousand farmers. . . . Let Congress adopt a leasing measure and no possible safeguards can be thrown around it that will prevent our best farm lands passing at once into the control of capitalists and large stock companies. . . .

It is the man with the plow that we should now seek for to settle upon one hundred and sixty acre tracts, and not the man who will control a large body of land that he never will improve. . . . Knowing what I do of the agricultural advantages of this part of the West, I cannot but deplore the efforts that are now being made to hold Montana as simply a pastoral and mining state.

PARIS GIBSON

SPANNING THE DISTANCES

ONTANA HAS BEEN both blessed and cursed by the vast abundance of its space. In its excesses lay the beauty and isolation of Territory and State. The problems of distance were nowhere more apparent than in transportation; the lack of it or the need for it. Coexistent with the difficulties of distance was the interwoven relationship between transportation and the development of the region's society or economy. Formation of even the smallest or most basic socio-economic unit — mine, mining camp and the like — produced a demand for improved transportation. Similarly, isolation retarded or forestalled growth and made immigration or importation of heavy machinery arduous. Economic maturation and diversity were practical only if transport and communication were possible. Transportation, then, provided a skeletal framework for any territory, and Montana was no exception.

Moreover, there existed a step-by-step progression unique to Montana. First came river-borne traffic. From the exploration of Lewis and Clark, through the fur trade era and into the first decades of mining, principal access and egress followed the course of the Missouri and its tributaries. River traffic was seasonal at best, and confined to limited passageways. The need for distribution beyond the river banks spurred construction of overland routes — private and public. John Mullan built one of the first; but there were others — the Bozeman Trail, the Corinne-Virginia City road, toll roads, and more.

Even well-defined roads lay exposed to seasonal hazards. Snow, mud, or choking dust often made overland freight and passenger travel rigorous. Railroads ranked foremost among suggested remedies. Congress chartered the transcontinental Northern Pacific a few days after it organized Montana Territory; but almost two decades lapsed before rail transport became an accomplished fact. From the arterial routes — Union Pacific, Northern Pacific, and later, Great Northern — subsidiary branch lines probed the most remote canyons to seek out freight and passenger revenue. In urban areas, street railways served a similar branch line capacity, providing dependable, flexible, in-city travel while funneling passengers to the local depot.

For the Nineteenth Century, the steam locomotive was the ultimate in transportation sophistication. Yet it was but an integral part of a communication system, or network, and an ongoing process of sophistication. Bicycles, electrification (urban and long haul), and internal combustion engines appeared, each in turn, as part of an experimental and developmental process as society sought increased efficiency and mobility. Transportation was the indispensible tool for Montanans working to overcome the handicaps of space and isolation and finally secure the land.

STEAMER ROSEBUD ON THE UPPER MISSOURI, 1886

SPANNING THE DISTANCES
Transportation in the 19th Century

Winter compounded Montana's isolation. Ice and low water levels dried up river traffic while mountain ranges caught the winter storms, clogging valleys and passes with drifted snow. Infant industries and communities lay dormant, awaiting the reopening of commerce each spring. Periodic thaws might provide a respite from winter seclusion, but prolonged bad weather meant both isolation and potential commodity shortages. Joseph C. Walker's account of winter freighting illustrated the problems. Deepening snow had closed his Virginia City sawmill operation and in the process of leaving Montana for the season, he encountered another Alder Gulch businessman engulfed in the futility of winter travel.

PLEASANT STATION
DEC. 6, 1864

We were looking to the south in hopes of seeing some of the stage people coming. We saw some footmen come in sight a little more than a half mile away, and until there were thirty of them. They were walking or rather wading in the snow in double file form, each one having a shovel upon his shoulder, and in their rear was five yoke of oxen slowly drawing one wagon. The oxen were following these trails these footmen were making for them. They came on, and camped on the creek a little below the station. Shortly after a man came wading through the snow up to the station. He proved to be William L. Bullard. . . .

He informed us that he had thirty ox teams loaded principally with flour for Alder Gulch, but that he was snowed in at the foot of the mountains twenty or more miles away, and that he was now attempting to take his drivers through to Alder Gulch; that he had selected five yoke of his strongest oxen and hitched them to one wagon, and put into that wagon provision and bedding that would weigh about fifteen hundred pounds, and by arming these thirty men with shovels . . . to walk in front of the oxen and break trails for them, he had thought he could surely get over the range, but he said he had had a hard time in even getting that far. He came to the station to see if any one there could tell him of the conditions of the snow ahead. . . . He was wonderfully pleased at meeting our party of five, who were as direct from Virginia City as it had been possible for us to be. . . . We told him the snow was one foot deep when we took the stage at Virginia City and detailed to him our trip. He decided that it would be far better for him to abandon the attempt to go farther.

Then he wanted to know about the flour market. When we told him that flour was above thirty Dollars per one hundred pound sacks, and that every half inch of snow added one dollar to the sack; that merchants were getting up early and before putting on their pants they would look out, and if there had been as much as a half inch of snow fallen during the night, they would call out, one dollar more on flour; and it became proverbial all over the camp. . . .

When we had given the state of the flour market to Mr. Bullard, he having perhaps nearly a thousand sacks of flour within one hundred miles of Virginia City, and knowing that he could not get one pound of it to Virginia City before spring, and expecting to lose the greater part of his oxen where they were, made his eyes almost go shut. . . . Mr. Bullard then decided to let his oxen rest one day before starting back to his train. . . . He then asked the station keeper if he could get meals for himself at the station for that one day. The station keeper told him no. He saw that Mr. Bullard received his answer with much surprise. The station agent then said that he had signed a written contract with Ben Holliday to forfeit his position and a portion of his salary if he sold anything from the station or fed man or beast not stage passengers or employees of [his] line.

Mr. Bullard went to his camp and soon came hiking back to the station with a Christmas turkey under his arm and presented the same to the station keeper's wife. He then got his meals at the station for the day he lay over. This turkey Mr. Bullard had gotten in Utah and by arrangement was taking it to a man at Virginia City and was to get fifteen dollars for doing so. Our party left earlier the morning Mr. Bullard was to leave. I heard afterwards that Mr. Bullard lost all of his oxen but one.

Pleas for improved overland travel secured a two-fold response from the federal government. Congress authorized funds for the survey and construction of two roads to Virginia City — one from Niobrara on the Missouri River in Nebraska, the second from Snake River headwaters at Lewiston, Idaho. The magnitude of both projects, coupled with the paucity of public funds, proved overwhelming. Mismanagement did not help. Wellington Bird served as director of the Lewiston-Virginia City project during its most active phase. An Iowa native and totally unfamiliar with western conditions, Bird had secured the road's superintendency through a political appointment. He arrived in Lewiston during the spring of 1866 and found the scenery enthralling, but the task awesome. During the late spring and throughout the summer, he explored the trails between proposed termini. In the fall he returned to Lewiston and eventually home — Mount Pleasant, Iowa — amid accusations of incompetence and malfeasance. His summer's work, which absorbed half of the total $50,000 Congressional pittance, left nothing more than a pack trail and frustration. The Niobrara project ended similarly while Virginia City and Montana remained isolated.

JUNE 18, 1866

LT. COL. J. H. SIMPSON
CORP OF ENGINEERS
WASHINGTON CITY, D.C.

DEAR SIR:

I am making slow progress. . . . The trail I am following is an old one, the same indeed as that by which Lewis and Clarke first passed from the Missouri to the Columbia River in 1803 and is known Every where in this country as the LooLoo [LoLo] fork trail. The trail in many places is impracticable as a route for a wagon road, but . . . no insurmountable barriers are yet encountered. I think a road can be made on this route by diverging Every now and then from the trail when better ground can be found. . . .

After crossing the Clear Water the Country is covered by a very dense forest of Evergreen Trees and underbrush which in many places is almost impracticable. This, with the incessant rains we have had here [this] |spring, makes a survey of the line of the old trail for any new route very slow and tedious work.

I last week took with me a couple of men and visited in person the top of the mountain range some 25 miles in advance of our present position. It is undoubtedly a very elevated range to make a road over, not less certainly than Six thousand feet, and I found for five or six miles before reaching the summit [an] abundance of snow.... This I am informed by Col. Craig will probably continue on our course for a distance of thirty miles. If it would freeze and remain frozen for a few days I could travel over the snow, but when it is thawing it would be rather hazardous to attempt to take animals over it. . . .

I might work on the road between this and Lewiston but for the fact that finding the people of Lewiston nearly Equally divided as to the merit of two routes viz. The LooLoo fork and the Elk City route. I conclude to make a preliminary survey of both routes before commencing any decided road work. . . . After I conclude as to which route to take, I will first cut out a narrow road on the proper line for a permanent wagon road which will at least serve as a pack trail, and as such will be a great benefit to the business of both sides of the Bitter Root Mountains. . . . and afterward I will expend the money left . . . [and] work on the road as far as it will go.

My present opinion is that a road on this route is practicable. . . . If you could stand where I did last Friday and see before you for forty miles the stupendous mountains, all broken up in masses and peaks and see the country I have already passed over, you would be likely to think that fifty thousand dollars was but a pittance and yet I really think that a road made on the line I am now travelling would be worth to the country all it cost. . . .

As it will be some weeks before grass will be sufficiently green to sustain any stock on the route before us, I am making arrangements to carry food with us for about 3 days and shall start as soon as I think the snow can be safely crossed.

We are obliged to cut the trail out before us almost constantly before our pack mules can get through on account of brush & fallen timber.

I am very respectfully

YOUR OBEDIENT SERVANT

W. BIRD

Congressional funds and Corps of Engineer efforts focused on river improvements as well as road construction. When it became obvious the Northern Pacific was not immediately forthcoming, Montanans exerted what little Congressional leverage they had to secure navigational improvements on the Missouri and its tributaries. Physical work centered principally on clearing rapids, or, "blast out a few boulders," in Achilles Lamme's words. Also of necessity was a secure passageway. Stories and realities of Indian attacks hampered river trade, if only to a minor extent. As a dynamic Bozeman merchant, Lamme saw in Yellowstone navigation a means of improving his source of supply and developing the Gallatin Valley. He shared his desire for additional military posts on the Yellowstone with other area residents, all the while skeptical of military capabilities in light of mounting Indian hostilities. Later in 1876, Congress authorized construction of two new military posts in central and eastern Montana. Federal funds also financed Missouri and Yellowstone surveys and, albeit modest, river improvements.

WASHINGTON, MO.
FEBRUARY 9, 1876

FRIEND MAGINNIS

DEAR SIR:

I have thought some time of writing you; believing it to be a duty to represent our wishes to our Representatives. . . . And the matter in which very many of your friends and constituents are particularly interested in is the opening the route up the Yellowstone river to Eastern Montana instead of going around to the West Side and then coming back to get to the Eastern part of the Territory as had been the case since the settlement of the country. We wish to have the shortest and most direct route, and the one Nature has made and left only to be utilized; but till now, it has been almost impracticable and only for the reason of the failure of an ordinary effort on the part of the people who are to be benefitted by it to put it in practical operation.

Now a few of us have taken note of the matter and are now building a steam boat especially adapted to the navigation of the Yellow Stone River. . . . and we ask your co-operation and efforts to have us some protection in the enterprise. We would like to have one or two small military posts established — say one about the mouth of Powder River and another somewhere in the vicinity of the mouth of the Big Horn or what may prove to be the head of navigation on the Yellow Stone River. More particularly for the protection of goods and

transportation at that point. That would give us a line of posts all along between the hostile Indians and whites, and open up to settlement the most inviting country of the Rocky Mountains. . . . The early settlement of the Black Hills will necessarily force the hostile Sioux to that border which will make it the more necessary for some protection.

And furthermore for a very small outlay to blast out a few boulders in two or three places in the Yellow Stone River, we can have a better river to navigate than the Missouri. . . . I see by the papers you have introduced a bill for the improvement of the upper Missouri and Yellow Stone, hope you will be successful in your efforts to accomplish that important object. A very small outlay judiciously expended in the Yellow Stone would certainly make that a good navigable river for a long ways up.

I would be pleased to cooperate with any party for the purpose of improving the navigation of that river. There will be plenty of transportation on that river next spring to effect any effort that would be advisable to be made for the improvement of that River. We want and must have, some facilities for shipping out some of the rich quartz of the Upper Yellow Stone and that is the proper channel for it to go.

Hoping to hear a favorable report from you soon I am as ever

YOUR FRIEND
A. LAMME

My address at present and will be 'till the 15th of April is Washington, Franklin Co., Missouri.

From the river boat landings, roads wound through the expanses of Montana. Out of Fort Benton, Judith and Musselshell landings, Carroll, or a dozen other impromptu and permanent ports, freight and passengers radiated out to many destinations. Freight wagons and stages became indispensable. On June 2, 1885, one of David Browne's mule teams, with a freight wagon and its cargo, sank as a result of an accident at the Fort Custer ferry on the Big Horn River. In his unsuccessful efforts to secure reimbursement, Browne disclosed several interesting elements of overland transit. Like road projects and river improvements, government ferries constituted a means of federal assistance on the transportation frontier. Also notable was the equipment and cost for a single freight wagon — right down to the oats for the mules and the tobacco for the driver.

FORT BENTON, MONT. T.
FEBRUARY 23, 1886

H. S. CUMMINGS, ESQR
WASHINGTON, D. C.

DEAR SIR,

. . . I herewith enclose you a claim against the Govt which ought to be easily collected.

While my mule train was enroute from Fort Benton Montana to Fort McKinney Wyoming and was being ferried over the Big Horn river at Fort Custer Montana on the Government Ferry, the tripod of the Ferry broke and the boat sunk with four head of mules and a wagon loaded with freight consigned to John H. Conrad & Co., Buffalo Wyoming.

The accident was no fault of mine or anyone in my employ, but was the fault of the owners of the boat who charged toll for crossing teams, and should have had the boat in better repair. The officers at Fort Custer who had charge of the boat at the time said that I ought to be paid and would do all in their power to see that it was made good to me. The amount of the loss was:

Mules wagon &c merchandise paid,	1208.00
J. H. Conrad & Co.	492.69
	$1700.69

Since the above bill was rendered the wagon was taken out of the river and turned over to me in a much damaged condition and perfectly worthless to me. I trust you will push this matter as soon as possible and should you desire any further information will furnish it promptly on receipt of your communication. Please let me know what you think about the claim as to its being collectible.

YOURS VERY TRULY,

DAVID G. BROWNE

FORT CUSTER, MONT.

GOVERNMENT FERRY
FORT CUSTER, MONT.

June 2 To property lost by Govt. Ferry at Ft. Custer, M.T.

1 — 2½ inch Fish Iron Axle Wagon	265.00
4 head mules	700.00
1 set Wheel Harness	60.00
1 set Lead Harness	50.00
1 pr Double Trees	5.00
1 pr. Stretchers	4.00
1 Tongue Rod	2.50
1 Coughling rod	4.00
3 Rough Locks	18.00
3 Lock Chains	15.00
1500# Oats	37.50
1 Lot Blankets and Bedding	35.00
1 Jack screw	4.50
2 Monkey Wrenches	2.50
6# Tobacco	5.00
	1208.00

I solemny swear that the above valuation is just and true to my best knowledge and belief.

DAVID G. BROWNE

Romanticism has pervaded the popular history of river boating much as it has other facets of the westward experience. T. C. Power and his Bismarck superintendent, I. P. Baker, knew the intimacies of river boat commerce on the upper Missouri. Both knew the problems that low water, burst boilers and accidents could bring to Fort Benton trading companies. They experienced the frustrations of unpredictable pilots and deck crews (Roosters) as well as the profitability of government supply contracts and states-bound cargoes. It was all business for Power and Baker — the romantics were elsewhere.

BISMARCK, D.T.
JULY 12, 1884

T. C. POWER, ESQ.
HELENA, M.T.

DEAR SIR:

Helena has been here since 8th inst. repairing Boilers. Had to put new Sheet in after end of Starboard Boilers. It had been patched ever since first year after she was built and had become so leaky we were forced to put in new sheet.

Sent you list of Cargo of the *Helena & Benton*. Considerable government freight on the *Benton*.

Had a tough time with Crew — Officers of the *Benton* — The Captain . . . would not go unless I put different Engineers on the Boat which I tried to do but none were here to be had. [He] refused to go pilot either so I put John J. Barr in command. McArthur too refused to go on the *Benton* so I put him on the *Helena*, & Keenan

went out in the *Benton* for the trip. Capt Johnson was unwell & could not go. The Roosters all struck the last thing so it looked blue until Barr & I talked them back to work and the old *Benton* left in good time with nice trip last night. The Entire crew from Captain down struck one by one and I am glad they all have gone. Roosters wages on both of these Boats, $35.00 per month.

Will try and hold off departure of next Boat until 15th to 20th Aug. The *Helena & Benton* cleaned up everything here — private & government included.

Think the *Batchelor* should meet the *Benton* and take the *Benton's* [cargo] and help the *Helena* at the same time. The *Batchelor* is light draught and can carry the load without trouble I think. The *Benton* can bring out the wool & take load of Oats to Yates.

YOURS,

I. P. BAKER

Alma Coffin captured in writing the rigors of early passenger travel in Montana. In the summer of 1878, she and two of her sisters journeyed from the family home in Mankato, Minnesota, to visit their father, who had taken employment as a mine superintendent at Glendale. By river steamer they traveled to Fort Benton where they transferred to horse-drawn stage. The trip was an adventure for the young ladies, but mud spattered, windblown, thirty-two hour rides converted even the casual visitor to the advantages of improved transportation and railroads.

AUGUST 7, 1878

We lost no time. Our baggage was conveyed to the hotel. We were allowed only twenty-five pounds each on the stage, so we worked half the night unpacking, repacking and trying to decide what articles to take and what to leave in the trunks. . . . The trunks are to be forwarded by ox-freight and we may not see them again until mid-winter.

The stage proved to be a "jerky" and well worthy of the name. There were two seats inside facing each other, with room for three on each seat. The coach springs were not very good or, perhaps, too good, for one's head sometimes bumped against the top.

In the Sun River Valley the roads were bad in many places. The passengers climbed down and out, the men helping to pry out the wheels. Once when we offered to walk, the driver called cheerily, "Sit still ladies! Sit still! And we'll all be buried together!" When we began to climb the hills clad with evergreen amid the rocks, the view was beautiful and we all wished it were possible to ride outside. . . .

Of the country between Benton and Helena we saw but little for we traveled all night. No wonder our vehicle bounced and jolted all the way, for it drew up at the Grand Hotel four hours ahead of schedule time. If mud splashed us the first part of the journey, dust covered us the last part. Sunburned, windblown and weary, after thirty-two hours without rest we were glad to escape to a quiet room. . . .

I know now why people love the West. The beauty and grandeur of the mountains, rocks and trees, canons and dashing streams! The vast landscapes revealed in the clear atmosphere are beyond all description. The people are friendly and hospitable. New comers are warmly greeted for do they not brings news from "The States?"

Stagecoaches augmented rail as well as river travel. Routes varied depending on the upper limits of river navigation or the progression of a railhead. T. C. Power, although long identified with Missouri river trade, responded to railroad potential for freight and passenger revenues. As Northern Pacific construction moved into Montana and up the Yellowstone Valley, T. C. Power stages met the end of track and trans-shipped personnel and property. The railroad company founded a new community — Billings — early in 1882, and set out to develop it as a distribution point. Walter Burke served as Power's agent in establishing a stage route between Billings and Helena/Fort Benton via the Musselshell. He laid out the road, made provisions for stock and clientele, and reported back. Despite his lack of expertise with the written word, his work was efficient, his assessment of Coulson's future vis-a-vis that of Billings, notably preceptive. Until rails reached the Musselshell Valley years later, the stage continued to be the vehicle of transport and commerce for central Montana.

MR. T. C. POWER

MARTINSDALE, MT.
JULY 4, 1882

DEAR SIR:

I Reseved your Letters of 25 [and] 27, This morning as I came in on The stage From Coulson. For our First Trip we got in in good time and Left in Due time for Coulson which is only one Hour after ariving from Martinsdale. . . .

I wil Now Tell you What I Have don when I Arived at Martinsdale. I Found out that Horses wer very scarce and in Fact there wasent Non For Sale. I Had with me Three Head that I Pict up on the Road From Benton. I made arrangments with Mr. Clendenin Before I Left in Regard two the Ceaping of the Station and two be agent For the Line.

Mr. Power what Do you in Tend to do in Billings in Regard two a Barn and a place For the Horses. Lots ar seling at one Fifty at the cheapest. You cant Leace one Short of [$] 8 or 9 per month in any Place in Town or Rent one For Now Reasonable Figure. You can get A Lot For one Fifty That wil Be close a Nuff to Town For a Barn an that is the cheapest that is For Sale. Logs are worth $1.50 per Log. Lumber is worth From [$] 60 to 70 [per] Thousand But Lumber wil Be cheaper after the Track Reaches Billings. . . .

I went up two Billings. There I met with a Nold Friend of mine that . . . is ceaping Hotell & Resturant. He agrees two Furnish Meals at 25 cents per meal and a place For The Driver two Sleep. The Horses while in Billings ar cep in the Horse Hurd day [and] Night For $2.50 per Head and the use of the Barn while Harness-

ing. There is so much Stealing Going on in Billings & Coulson that you Have to Ceap Every thing Lock up or it wil Be Stoleint.

Billings is Just one Mile From Coulson. Billings is Building up very Fast and it is Opinion that Coulson wil Die out in the Course of one year or two and that it wil Be Nothing But Billings and For that Reason [along] with High Prices that I Didn't stop at Coulson. The Post office & Express office is at Coulson yet. The Post master E. D. Alderson is the agent in Coulson. He agrees two do as Follows: Meals at Twenty Five cents per meal, Barn Free of charge with a Pasture connected. Hay at $10 per Ton the year around.

After I had arrang with Clendinin I started Four Coulson [and] as I went I Arranged with the Ranches a Long the Road two take care of the Stock. The First Station From Martinsdale is Ballard & Stone. He agreed to tak care of the stock four $20 per month; meales at 33 1/3 cents per meal. The Next Station is Jenifer. He wouldent take care of the Horses For Less than $30 per month; meales 33 1/3. The Next station is al olden Place, that is the Home Station For the Drivers. Meales 33 1/3 cents. Drivers take care of there [own] stock. The Next comes Bull Mountain. He agrees two take care of the Horses at $20 per month & meals 33 1/3 cents. From there two Coulson is Thirty Five Miles.

Now Pashingers Rates as they wer — $16. Express Rates, six cents per lb Two Coulson. If you want any Change Let me Now.

YOURS RESPECTFULLY
WALTER BURKE

In many ways, the career of Charles Higgenbotham spanned the era of stage transportation. He claimed, with pride, to have driven the first scheduled coach into Butte shortly after the Highland Gulch excitement began in the 1860's. Several decades later, he handled the reins on the last stage, after rails replaced the four- and six-horse teams. Thereafter he toured with Buffalo Bill Cody's Wild West troupe, driving wagons and stagecoaches at world-wide shows. His memoirs attested to both the multiplicity of routes necessary to serve Montana in the mid-1880's, and the varied nature of the driving profession. He endured inspections, accidents, holdups, and inclement weather — all part of overland transportation in early Montana.

While I was driving [The Silver Star Route] there happened to be a stock-tender whom Gov. [Pollinger] had it in for. Gov. came along one day.... At Fish Creek he [Pollinger] got down and walked into the barn while the horses were being changed. He put his hand on one of the animals, and, apparently petting him, rubbed down along his hip and leg. The stableman [stock-tender] said, "Who put his dirty hand on my clean horses?" and Gov. replied, "I did." ... After a half mile he remarked, "Well, I caught that fellow dead to rights, didn't I? He been 'galvanizing' those horses long enough, instead of properly currying and brushing them."

To "galvanize" a horse is to wipe it down with a wisp of damp hay. It shines the outside of the animal, but doesn't cleanse him. Next day he sent a stocktender to relieve the fellow.

Gov. played the same kind of a trick on me eventually. I used to stop at Fish Creek and get into a poker game. He caught me at it, after two years and two months work on his line . . . .

⸻

I drove a night route from Sun River to [Eagle] Rock for seven years and eight months. I never missed a run, and had but one accident. . . . On the banks of the Birdtail creek, with a wet road, a badly-loaded stage and a bad side-hill, I threw the wagon clear over a 30-foot cut-bank. It killed three of the right-hand horses, but we got off without a wound, tho there was 26 fellows on the load. . . .

Two weeks after this accident, I was pulling a steep hill. . . . It was muddy and I had a lady and a 13-year-old girl on the seat with me. Ten or twelve men were walking ahead while I stopped to tinker with the brake-block. . . . When I came to the top of the hill, I halted to replace the blocks to ease the wagon down the hill. . . . I was wearing my black gum coat and had just replaced the blocks, when three fellows, masked in the traditional manner, stepped around from the off side of the team and one of

them threw a double-barreled shot gun down on me. There were still several passengers aboard, tho about a dozen, as I have stated, were walking ahead.

The road agents relieved my party of $700 or $800. One [passenger] who walked ahead happened to have about $14,000 on him, which, of course, the robbers missed. The woman on the seat screamed, and I said to the leader of the hold-ups, "Let me get hold of these lines, or we'll all be afoot." He said "All right," and I leaped and grabbed the lines. As I did so, my rubber coat came open and showed a heavy gold watch chain that I was wearing around my neck, attached to a $600 watch. These pieces of jewelry really belonged to a lady friend of mine in Helena. They promptly attached the articles and then silently and swiftly disappeared. . . .

⸻

While driving on the Benton road, a fellow by the name of Wallace Taylor was on his way to his folks at Helena to spend the holidays with them. I picked him up at Sun River Crossing, and he bought a bottle of 11-year-old whiskey for him and me.

We got to Fort Shaw, five miles further, when a fellow came around the corner, clad in a Scotch plaid suit, and with his ears and hands done up in cotton-batting. You'd have thought he was just out of a hospital somewhere. . . .

The Weather Bureau man had failed to mail his day's report to Washington, and he happened along, just at that moment. It was 57 degrees below. When he passed my lead horses he said, "Driver, get down into your furs; the Thermo's 57 below, and still a-fallin'."

Just then the cotton-battin' man stepped up and asked if this was the Helena coach. "Yes, get on your overcoat, it's cold," I said. The gentleman in the ice-cream suit with cotton-battin' trimmins replied curtly, "I've paid my fare; I can stand it if you can!" "Well," said I, from the depths of my buffalo coat, "[you haven't] clothes enough to flag a hand-car!" The fellow insisted that he was drest warmly enough, so I took him under protest, and on his own responsibility. He piled in on the sleigh, and sat on a bare board, tho there was lots of hay in the bottom of the sled.

We drove 12 miles to supper at Eagle Rock. Wallace's whiskey had frozen up, and we couldn't manage it. But there was a saloon at Eagle Rock, and there we warmed up, outside and in. When supper was announced, we had shed our buffalo coats and pants, but our prize passenger of the cotton-battin' wrappings sat by the stove and wouldn't come in to eat. . . .

It was the 23rd of December, just before Christmas, and a number of sheepmen had come in, somewhat early, to celebrate. Already they were as well lit up as the station was. . . .

"Come in and drink!" yelled Long Shorty, a six-footer who seemed to be the leader of festivities . . . but Cottin-battin . . . replied, "I don't drink, thank you."

Shorty reached forth a long arm and grabbed him by the collar; a friend seized him by an arm, and they lifted and dragged him into the saloon. . . . "I never took a drink in my life," remarked [cotton-batting], virtuously. "By gad! you'll take one now!" cried Shorty, and the fun was on.

They mixed him a hot one, and they used a funnel to pour it down him; then we staged a walk-around the stove, till another called, "Halt, bellies to the mahogany!" Cotton-battin' drank that time, with no special invite. . . .

At rock Creek at breakfast I turned him over to the tender mercies of Mose Gebo, a Frenchman. Mose hauled him as far as Silver City, 12 miles out of Helena, but would not take him any further. He was by this time pretty near frozen, and had to lay over to thaw out. . . .

Multiple routes meant rivalry. As stage and wagon lines joined Montana's transportation network, competition developed among companies. Rails of the Northern Pacific were in Montana by 1886, while the vestiges of the Missouri River trade still supplied the northern portion of the territory. Between the two, a lattice work of roads and trails served the more remote regions. Sources of passenger traffic peppered the expanse of land, at best. With their constant turnover of personnel, Montana's military installations constituted a good source of fares for stage lines. The Benton and Billings Stage Company courted this military business — at Fort Assiniboine, for example — and Private H. K. Weeden, Company "C", 20th Infantry, served as T. C. Power's "inside" contact in competition for the soldier's traveling dollar.

Fort Assinniboine, M.T.
May 7, 1886

T. C. Power and Bro.
Benton, M.T.

Sirs:

I have deferred untill now answering your letter. It is with regret that I inform you that blackmailing reports have spread through the garrison regarding the Benton and Billings Stage Line. The substance of which is as follows: That the road is unsafe to travel upon on account of the frequent robberies committed by Road Agents; That the accommodation is poor and dangerous, particularly at the all night rendevous, where the ranch is infested with cow boys who try all means available to reach the pocket books of passengers; and other such foolish rumers which grow the futher they travel. I have a very good and I believe accurate idea of who started this report. But as I could not prove the same perhaps it would be better to mention no names. Suffice it is to say he is an old residenter. . . .

Do not think by the tone of my letter that I am in any way discouraged, for on the contrary, it pushes one to still greater efforts in your behalf. If any one in this post can be of any use to your line in promoting its advancement and patronage, I am conceited enough to think I can. But I would like a letter from you refuting the charges referred to in the commencement of this, also a corrected list of rates to all principal points east and south. . . .

It would be a good idea for you to question Corporal Bayard on his return and if you find him satisfied with his trip from Benton to Billings (which I have no doubt he was) why [not] give him a good strong hint to let men whose time is short, know that there is but one way to reach the railroad, and that by the B. and B.S.C. Line.

Trusting to hear from you by mondays mail and apologizing for my long silence, I am

Very respectfully yours &c
WEEDEN

Railroads would answer all Montana's problems of transportation and isolation — or so many residents thought. Initial optimism focused on the transcontinental Northern Pacific, but political and financial problems appeared or reappeared, delaying construction. It also became obvious that the initial right-of-way would provide a limited corridor of commerce: up the Yellowstone, to Bozeman, through Helena and the Continental Divide at Mullan Pass, then down the Clark's Fork River, past Missoula, and out of Montana to the west. Delays and distance from the proposed line provoked disillusionment in many quarters. New proposals arose — a narrow gauge connection (the Utah Northern) with the Union Pacific at Ogden; a feeder line from Fort Benton south to Helena and Butte. Proponents of each venture extolled the virtues of their route from public rostrums and in newspaper columns. They also advocated economic subsidies in the form of territorial bonds for construction. In 1873 and again in 1876, legislators obliged with proferred aid, subject to public referendum. Competing interests waged vigorous campaigns for or against each proposal. Their efforts proved mutually detrimental. Taken with a national recession, the result was no territorial aid and no railroads during the 1870's. At the time, Judge O. B. O'Bannon and Sam Hauser were strong advocates of the Utah Northern. Their correspondence reflected the emotion of the contest.

DEER LODGE
MARCH 13, 1876

DEAR SAM:

Your telegram was rec'd this evening, and I am truly sorry to learn the non-acceptance by the U.N.R.R. . . . I hoped the U.N. would accept, if for no other reason than to help us beat the infernal N.P. It has more supporters here than I had any idea of — especially in the Northern camps of the County, and now that the U.N. is out of the way I am fearful it will receive strong support at Butte and other Southern camps. . . .

We would have carried this town and the Southern part of the County handsomely for the U.N. Mills has leanings for the N.P. but I feel sure he will not do much of anything in his paper in its favor. Dixon, Robinson, Dick Kennon, Zener, Bob Kelly and several others are strongly against any subsidy. Clagett, Knowles and every County officer (except Dick Kennon) and *all* the Irvine family are strongly for the Narrow Gauge, but will all oppose the infernal N.P. If possible, Granville and I will make a raid into the Northern camps and do what we can against the infernal fraud. . . .

Granville and I have both been to Butte on other business, but whilst there, each of us did all in our power in favor of the U.N. . . . We got that camp into good shape, but I am now fearful that the overwhelming desire for a Railroad of some kind will induce very many to vote for the infernal fraud, simply because it is the only proposition before the people. . . . It looks to me as if it will take the best efforts of all of our way of thinking to prevent the N.P. subsidy from carrying. If there is not some united resolute effort, I fear we are gone.

IN HASTE YOUR FRIEND,

O. B. O'BANNON

Utah Northern rails first entered Montana from the south on March 9, 1880. Northern Pacific track crews crossed the eastern border of the Territory, along the Yellowstone, in December. Although N.P. construction proceeded simultaneously from west and east, not until September of 1883 did rails join near Gold Creek. Acute interest in construction progress existed in "the states" as well as in Montana. To cover the story, an eastern journal sent a correspondent to visit railhead communities. Under the sobriquet "Prospector," the journalist detailed life along the line. In the process, he discovered an intimate relationship between railroads and beer — two bulwarks of civilization.

MAY 22, 1882

Speaking about prices . . . I will give a few of the quotations from the new city of Billings for other than eatables. As Billings is a community, that will derive its future growth to the agricultural developments of this part of the country it may be of some value to compare them. In Billings [it] costs —

Washing the piece	20 cents
One cigar (miserable weed)	25 cents
One bottle of Lager beer	50 cents

In regard to the latter beverage, I wish to give a striking observation, which is quite interesting and comes from the Beer supply agent of the Northern Pacific Co. To build a mile of railroad it needs 2640 ties and as the laborers, during each mile, drink 110 cases of beer at 24 bottles each, one bottle comes to each tie. One railroad tie costs fifty cents and so does a bottle of beer.

One might therefore say that there exists a mystic connection between Railway and beer, strange as it may look at the first glance, yet not without a natural definition. As known, Railroads are the bearers of civilization. The German, however, who finds one of his principal tasks in making propaganda for his beloved barley juice, named the beer the bearer of civilization. The laborers of the Northern Pacific Rail Road, no learned professors but, practical men, prove that both theories are right by the fact, that they instinctively imbibe exactly one bottle of beer to every tie. . . .

Rails, rivers and roads provided, at best, a primitive transportation network or system in Montana. Until additional rail service — main or branch lines — reached more Montana communities, a journey to all but a few cities involved steam and horse drawn travel. Combinations of rail and river were not uncommon, however, particularly in the early 1880's. Roy M. Cobban typified immigration to Montana. As a young man, he left his family in Wisconsin to pursue his fortune in the West. He went by rail to Bismarck, a rowdy end-of-track camp on the Northern Pacific. There he boarded a river steamer to Fort Benton. He concluded his trip by wagon to the Judith Basin, where he remained briefly. Ultimately, he established himself in Butte, where he built and operated a planing mill. The journal of his trip depicted the varied means of transportation in Montana.

DEAR MOTHER:

Thinking perhaps a connected account of my trip, from the time of starting to the present, with a discription of what I have seen and learned might be of interest to you. I shall commence such an account tonight, hoping it will when finished, give you pleasure. . . .

April 19, 1880 . . . At half past nine the call "All aboard" brought us to our feet and with hasty good byes we were soon rushing along leaving those who were dear farther and farther away, each moment adding so much more to the distance between us.

I have seated myself in one of the first class cars but this will not do. Thaddie comes with a request from Mr. Pound that I come in to the pallace car where most of the others are.

This is the first time I was ever in a palace car, how nice everything is, but I soon get tired of this and I go out on the platform where I can see everything along our way. . . .

Soon the country changes and it is a beautiful rolling prairie which we see, with nice farms and tasty houses to meet the eye every little way. perhaps just over some little swell in the prairie we can see the church spires pointing Heavenword where some little village has half hid itself. Hudson at last is reached and here we cross lake St. Croix. . . . Now we are in Minnesota, soon the smoke and steam from numerous factories are seen and long before we reach the St. Paul depot we have passed many large factories of different kinds.

Minneapolis is reached and passed and darkness gathers around . . . I spread out my blankets on the seat and try to take a little sleep but I am soon awakened by the shrill cry of the train boy "'n apples 'n figs." It is getting cold and I straighten up and look out of the window although I can see but a rod or two. I can see there is a little snow on the ground. . . . Again I compose myself to try to get a little sleep. This time I am awakened by a man just across the aisle who has asked Mr. Shaw if he wont take a lunch. As soon as I look up the man holds out a loaf of rye bread in one hand and a knife and big chunk of pork in the other and kindly invites me to lunch . . . but I am not so inclined. . . .

April 20, 1880 — At last I get a little sleep but am awake at day light, but what a sight meets my eyes. I need not discribe the scene inside the car for you have often seen a car full of sleepy tired travelers so I leave you to imagine that — but outside as far as the eye could reach a smooth level prairie covered with about a foot of snow. Every little while we would pass a little village.

About seven oclock we reached Fargo a very pretty place with some fine buildings. Everything had the air of neatness and cleanliness and this is realy the last nice place I see until Helena is reached. Here [Fargo] we took breakfast. Moving on the snow gets deeper and on one side track was a train of flat cars that most of which were entirely covered with snow only the break sticking up to show where the cars were. But about eight oclock there is a change and at nine we can see but little snow. . . .

From [Jamestown] we strike the plains or bad lands and here we first see the bones of the buffalo that have been killed along the road. Numerous lakes are seen and all of them filled with geese and ducks which rise in a black cloud as we come rushing along. And now we begin to see the alkali the cactus and the sage brush of which we so often read about. . . . Shots are fired at ducks and geese from the car windows every few minutes.

Buffalo bones are growing thicker and antelope and coyotes are often seen. . . . The R. R. stations now are nothing but box cars which are on the ground and answer for depot and dwelling houses. . . .

Bismark at last and at seven oclock P.M. Tuesday eve. we were all seated at supper in the Sheridan house. After supper I started out to see what I could see, and I was indeed disappointed. I had expected to see a thriving city of 5000 or 6000 inhabitants with fine buildings and etc., but instead I found a place of possibly 1,300 inhabitants, hardly any fine buildings most all were one story of wood. The place was lit up, and as I passed down the principal street I noticed that about half of them were saloons, gambling halls, and dens of all kinds. . . .

Of all the places . . . that I have ever seen Bismark beats them all. I was glad to get back to the hotel and shut out part of the noise and sounds of wickedness which could be heard nearly anywhere on the street.

Wednesday [April 21] came bright and fair, but our boat had not yet arrived. . . . We watched the "Rose Bud" a large boat! as she was just starting for Benton, little dreaming then that it would be two weeks before we started up the river. . . .

Monday the 26th . . . [was] warmer. We have been looking all day for the Helena our boat — or rather the boat — we had engaged passage on. About dark a boat came in sight around the bend in the river. we of course thought it was the Helena but it proved to be the Far West. The river is very low. . . .

May 1st. The steamer Key West put in an appearance . . . but there is no tidings of the Helena.

Mr. Pound engages passage on the Key West for the whole party, and now it is all hurry and confusion trying to get things packed and put on the boat for we are going today. About six o'clock we start up the river but only get about 3 miles. . . .

May 6 — The evenings, most of them, are very pleasant and are spent by our party on the upper deck where Ida Pound entertains us with playing the violin. It is so pleasant to sit there listning to the music and watching the ever changing banks of the river. When the music ceases it is as quiet as death almost only the dip of the water wheel or the plunge of a beaver breakes the stillness. Then when it gets dark we all retire to the cabin where often there is dancing until ten o'clock. . . .

Sunday, May 9 — Wolf Point is reached . . . and here we tie up for the night. The indian agency here lies back from the river about half a mile. . . . Before dark we had a great deal of amusement with the little indian boys, who had their bows and arrows. We would put five and ten cent pieces in split sticks and let them shoot at the money the one who was fortunate enough to knock it out had it for his trouble. Then I took a stroll around the indians, to see what I could. Several of the indians had fine swords which probably were got at the time of the Custer Massacre for a good many of these indians were there. . . .

May 11 — Getting along nicely today. . . . The scenery is grand. In some places the banks are one or two hundred feet heigh perpendicular walls of stone. In some places where the stone is soft and has washed a way a good deal one can imagine here an old cathedral, here the ruins of a fine bridge and one thing which looks so funny is large stones resting on pillars. . . . This is caused by the caps being of harder stones than the pillars. . . . Sometimes you can see great rocks that look like steamboats ballanced on little pillars.

May 14 — Cow island is reached today. It is an old deserted military post but only a few little shanties and dug outs are left. we stayed here about two hours. . . . The government has done a little work here in improving the river.

About a mile above Cow island is a rapids I think it is *dofan* rapids but am not quite sure. When we got to the rapids the Capt'n asked the men if they would not as soon walk for about a half mile until he got over the rapids saying it would only take a few minutes. of course we were glad to get off and take a ramble. The worst of the rapids was only for two or three rods. A line was put out and the boat was drawn allmost over when the rope pulled loose and away the boat shot down the river and came near being smashed on the rocks. Again the boat was straightened up and the line stretched again. The boat was nearly over when the line broke and away went the boat. It was now a good while after dinner and it had turned cold and was raining but we could not get on board until about two o'clock. You may be sure we had a good appetite for dinner. While we were at dinner the line was again stretched and this time we were taken over, and were soon going along as though nothing had happened.

Sunday, May 16th — A bright beautiful day, and we expect to get to Benton by noon. of course we are all busy getting ready to leave the boat the first part of the morning then we all gather on the upper deck to get the first sight of Benton.... At last we are there and our boat comes to the landing.... Benton lies on the east bank of the river. It has a few nice buildings. The residence of Mr. Conrad is the finest building in the place. I. G. Baker & Co. have a fine large brick store. Kleinschmidt Bros. have a large stone store but it is too low to look well. Murphy Neill & Co. also have a large store. The old fort is in the lower part of the town and is built of *dobies* (or unbaked brick) with plenty of mud. We could see many places where the bullets which had been fired at it has struck. What tales that old fort might tell if it could speak. . . .

Railroads were neither an economic panacea nor an unmixed social blessing. With the completion of the Northern Pacific came accusations of land grant abuse and monopoly. As a result, Montanans welcomed James J. Hill's St. Paul, Minneapolis and Manitoba Railroad for the competition it offered. Hill extended the broad gauge line along the Missouri River from Minnesota to the Great Falls, where he established a townsite. From there the narrow gauge Montana Central built south to Helena — and, ultimately, Butte. In the early 1890's, Hill constructed westward and formed the transcontinental Great Northern Railroad. The Hill companies opened new parts of Montana to reliable, year-round transportation, and Great Falls became one of the state's major communities. W. R. Sellew was not alone, however, in his disgust over railroad practices — to him reprehensible harbingers of civilization.

GREAT FALLS
JUNE 21ST 1888

DEAR MOTHER:

Times are very quiet here at present & have bin all spring. it has bin rainy for 2 months staidy almost & cold. . . . I am teaming but still living on the ranch. will move to town as soon as the weather gets clear tomorow or the next day as my work is mostly thare.

I would send you more of the Falls papers But there is not a word of truth in them in regard to the Falls and country around here. I used to think it would make a good town and county but the climate and soile will not permit. the R R and the town site company are all the same and they own the paper and are trying to boom the town. . . .

There is 160 achers in my place here. The rail road runs for 3 quarters of a mile rite through the center of it and also my crop wich you may say spoiled al of it. they traviled at the rate of 8 mile a day when coming through here. I was out to snd cooley [Sand Coulee] cuting grain for the other people at the time. no one at home. they opened my fence and thare stock at night spoiled what they did not. when I come home the R R was only 50 feet from my house. it shakes the house when they go by. grain does not so well here when the R R gets to any country. . . . I am hunting for a country wher there is none. . . .

The papers say this is the turminous of 4 R R but it is the turminous of none. the M T Central and the Manitoba are al the same road. the Misourie and Great Falls is only a side track runing to the Smelter. the sand cooley branch is a road runing to their cole mines 5 miles by the wagon road and about 12 by the RR so you see how they miss lead suckers. . . .

Billings had the distinction of being the first Montana city with street railway transportation — a horse car line begun in 1883. This particular line was of short duration, but the need for urban transportation was not. Seven Montana communities had street railways, spanning the period from 1883 to 1951. They employed diverse means of motive power — horse-drawn and steam-driven, cable, electric power. E. D. Edgerton was president of the Helena, Hot Springs and Smelter Railroad — a steam (or motor) street railway line. As the company's name suggested, proposed termini included public facilities (Broadwater Hot Springs in this case, but cemeteries and fair grounds were also popular), and places of heavy employment (here, the East Helena smelter). The line laced these facilities together with subdivisions, business districts, and always, the railroad station. Indeed, getting people from the depot to business or residential sections was an essential motivation for construction of every line. A railroad's interest in urban travel was often more than casual, as this letter implied. The Helena, Hot Springs and Smelter's successors finally electrified, as did all Montana street railways. In their prime, trolley cars formed an indispensable part of Montana's transportation facilities.

OCTOBER 4, 1889

MR. N. P. TERALL
ASSISTANT TO THE PRESIDENT
N.P.R.R. [St. Paul]

I have heard nothing from you since leaving St. Paul. . . . I have not received the motor yet, and it seems very strange; it left Philadelphia on the 17th of last month, and I have telegraphed all over the country. I have reduced the operating expenses from over a thousand to $881, and shall make a further reduction next month. The total [monthly] receipts [are increasing.] . . . This in connection with the reduction of the operating expenses makes a very nice showing, I think, but we do need more rolling stock. I shall have to buy at least two more cars, am also thinking very seriously about equipping it with electricity. There are a good many reasons why . . . it would be better. There is no doubt in my mind, that a road down to our ground, equipped with electricity, would enhance the value of our property more than a steam line. . . .

I do not wish to experiment any, as we are not strong enough to afford it. And by the way, I will say that while our receipts are going up, we have too many improvements to make; . . . it keeps us hard up for money, and we must sell some bonds. . . .

I must have money enough from the sale of the bonds to build a line and equip it to the Fair Grounds, as well as to equip our line from the depot to the hotel. I am very anxious to get this matter through. . . . I must either go ahead and get some more cars, and sell the bonds, and put in a motor line to our ground, either this fall or early in the spring, or else make our plans to put in electricity, with the same results. . . .

The service is not very good at present, owing to a lack of motive power. Northrop and I did think of making a change in the superintendents, but the more I looked into the matter, the more I am convinced, that our . . . manager is as good as any one we can get. . . .

VERY TRULY,
E. D. EDGERTON

High wheelers and two wheelers appeared across the country in growing numbers as the Nineteenth Century closed. Bicycles offered a means of economical, personal transportation to an era that preceded the automobile. They were more than a craze. National and state chapters of the American Wheelmen and similar organizations became vocal advocates for sympathetic laws and better roads. Even the U.S. Army considered using two wheelers as a replacement for the horse. To Montana and the nation, the bicycle's potential deserved serious appraisal as a means of better transportation. For Eugene May, like many others, it was a fad — and fun.

. . . Billings, on the Northern Pacific Railroad, is fifty-three miles west of Custer Station and fifty-five miles northwest of Fort Custer. Thitherward was I bound. No wheelman had ever been over this road, and reports concerning its nature was very conflicting. Some thought it fair for a bicycle, others held it to be quite impracticable. At a bright, early hour I set out. . . .

I had barely covered twelve miles when I was overtaken by a shower. It was scarcely a heavy sprinkle, yet it rendered me quite helpless in less time than is taken to record it. The soil there is called gumbo. Its adhesiveness, when moist, is not excelled by that of any soil the earth affords. . . . I tried the bicycle on the grass, in the road, on the embankment and on the ties of the new railroad then building. It was a complete failure and I consumed an hour in pushing the wheel a single mile. . . .

[Then] the rain came down more freely. . . . My wheel would not turn twice around without clogging. To ride was impossible, to push was impossible, to walk and carry the wheel was impossible! Discomfited and discouraged I discerned a wagoner approaching. With four horses to his empty wagon he was making slow progress and kindly consented to carry me and my bicycle to the railroad boarding train, two miles distant. . . .

Here [I] lay idle for twenty-four hours. . . . The clouds . . . cleared away . . . and I [resumed] my journey. The road is dry, but rough, the wind is against me, my wheel runs heavy and progress is slow for a number of miles. . . . After a few hours of varying fortunes I came to the banks of the . . . Prior's Fork River, a branch of the Yellowstone. Here I had my first fording experience with a bicycle. The river is about 100 feet wide, not very deep at this point, but recent rains had swollen it; the waters were icy cold, and the bottom was rough with pebbles and stones. With wheel and pack and shoes on my shoulders, a weight of sixty-five pounds, I took a foot-bath that I would gladly have avoided. Three times in three miles I was compelled to ford this river. . . .

It was getting late in the day, and yet no Billings appeared to my anxious view. Long ago, according to my best calculations, I should have arrived there. Evidently I had lost my way. . . . "It never rains but it pours." I had barely crossed the third ford of the river when my rear tire gave out. It was now late twilight and too dark to see to repair it. There would be an hour or so of moonlight, but I was now getting anxious to find a refuge for the night. Fortunately I had supplied myself with ample

lunch, and now dined off it for the second time. . . . After lunch I traveled for about a mile in a broken-down way, when I discovered a camp-fire half a mile from the road. Rejoiced at the sight, I pushed rapidly towards it. . . . I proceeded to investigate. . . . I met one of the supreme surprises of my life. There seated in a circle . . . were ten Indians — three squaws and seven braves. . . .

I could get no information from them as to the way to Billings, or anywhere else, and prepared to depart. The savages were in their war-paint and were returning from some of their wild dances on the reservation. . . . I mounted my wheel and made the best mile on record on an airless rear tire! . . . [A]fter two hours Billings appeared. . . . I had wandered some twenty miles out of my way, and rejoiced to get back to civilization again. . . .

New railroads aroused excitement. When the Chicago, Milwaukee and St. Paul projected a transcontinental extension early in the 1900's, enthusiasm bubbled throughout Montana. The same competition, evident in the 1870's, resurfaced. Each community or valley wanted to be included on the route. Helena was no exception — case in point, INDEPENDENT editor John S. M. Neill's suggestion. Alas for Neill's efforts, the railroad bypassed Helena, taking a more direct route to Butte's copper industry. More important, the Milwaukee opened large portions of central and eastern Montana (principally the Musselshell Valley) to homesteading and settlement. For Montana, then, the significance of the Milwaukee lay in its reaffirmation of the relationship between distance, transportation and regional development.

DEC. 29, 1905

MY DEAR GOVERNOR [HAUSER]:

I hand you herewith copy of The Independent containing an editorial and article by Mr. Raftery suggesting the proper course for the main line of the Chicago, Milwaukee & St. Paul railroad through Montana; also a map in which I have traced said proposed line in RED.

You will notice that we propose to have them construct their line from Miles City . . . to Martinsdale . . . to White Sulphur Springs, thence down the Smith river valley to White's gulch, [then west to] the Missouri to Trout Creek, then across the river coming to Helena on the old "Harlow" railroad bed; from Helena to Rimini, from Rimini to Basin, and thence to Butte and westward.

They would cross the Missouri river at Trout creek between the Canyon Ferry dam and the new dam. A wonderful location for their shops because they would have 25,000 horse-power available for their business. . . .

In addition to creating a business between Basin and Rimini, the enormous tonnage of low-grade ore at the latter point could be hauled to the river for Concentration.

A point on the river between the two dams would be a most desirable location for the smelter of Mr. Clark, Mr. Heinze and, possibly, the Amalgamated Copper company when they find it necessary to build a new smelter as soon as the present capacity of the Washoe smelter at Anaconda is exhausted.

Upon receipt of this letter, I wish you would consult Senator Clark and both, jointly, see Mr. H. H. Rogers and enlist his influence in bringing the necessary pressure to bear on the chief engineer of the Chicago, Milwaukee & St. Paul railroad and have the definite location of the main line made via White's gulch . . . to Butte.

If this line, as indicated, should be taken it would be very easy to . . . build due south along [the Shields River] valley to Livingston where they could secure their share of the traffic to the national park. And, if they desired to go to Great Falls, it would be very easy to build from a point on the east side of the range at White's gulch. . . .

I trust you will get to work at this immediately. Any delay may mean that Helena will be cut out from the main line. Kind regards. I wish you a happy New Year.

SINCERELY YOURS,

JNO. S. M. NEILL

MERCHANTS AND MINERS

MOST TRADERS WERE Montana's earliest businessmen. They met the region's first needs, fur trapping and Indian trade. Trailing behind came waves of small operators, the placer miners and merchants. By the mid-1860's these groups were over-shadowed by entrepreneurs who developed the larger financial pursuits — the banks, lumber companies, quartz and copper mines, and general mercantile firms. As soon as placer deposits played out — and this came soon — more technologically sophisticated procedures followed. These required substantial investments, signaling a dramatic growth throughout the business sector, particularly banking. Mercantile companies moved into the mining districts, and beyond. Many, originally established in Fort Benton as local business and import houses, extended their reach to support mining. These commercial concerns also came to serve the military, Indians, farmers, livestock companies, lumbermen and railroad lines. With enlarged markets came competition, sometimes fierce and brutal.

Financial expansion, coupled with the railroads' arrival, also brought trade diversity to a maturing territory. Smaller, more specialized businessmen ventured west to meet the commercial demands. In came the tailors, grocers, jewelers, druggists, harness makers, undertakers, and those in the professions — the lawyers, doctors, and dentists.

While commercial ventures flourished, the predominant industry, mining, sank its roots deep in Montana's mountains. The boom in gold and silver confirmed the permanence of many camps — Marysville, Boulder, White Sulphur Springs, Helena, Butte. Mine owners took on an aura of respectability, predicated on their wealth.

Among them all, Butte was unique. Silver and gold gave way to copper, and before long in Montana mining, copper reigned supreme. Two dominating forces arose in the industry: William A. Clark and Marcus Daly. From 1888 to 1900, all Montana was a sparring ground for their personal and economic feud.

As copper barons consolidated their mine holdings, they inadvertently gave rise to a new force — labor unions. Beginning as small, occasionally effective alliances, unions, like the Western Federation of Miners, established a powerful base from which the laboring class could demonstrate its strength. Miners demanded better working conditions, a reasonable wage, and safety in the mines.

Montana stepped — or rather stumbled — into the next century, monopolized by a single industry as it was when the fur traders dominated. Copper mining, directly or indirectly, affected the majority of citizens. For many years, its influence was all-pervading: as the copper industry went, so went Montana.

MINERS PREPARING TO DESCEND, BUTTE, C. 1900

121

MERCHANTS AND MINERS
Business and Industry in the 19th Century

Not all Montana's pioneers came to make their fortune in mining. In 1863, Anton M. Holter and Alexander Evenson established a primitive water-powered sawmill near Virginia City. Demands for lumber by Alder Gulch miners soon pressed the capacity of their business to its limits. A little "Yankee ingenuity," luck, and hard work were ingredients of success, as Holter, later to become a leading Helena businessman, detailed in this reminiscence.

Mr. Evenson and I finally selected a location for our sawmill, and after considerable hardship we reached the top of the divide between Bevin's and Ramshorn Gulches on December 7, [1863] where we went into temporary camp, with no shelter beyond that afforded by a large spruce tree. . . . We made a hand sled with cross beams extending outside the runners far enough, so when necessary with a hand spike on each side we were able to nip it along. With this hand sled we removed our outfit to the creek and we did all the logging this way during the entire Winter. We first built a cabin and a blacksmith shop, but this soon became more of a machine shop, for when we came to erect the sawmill we met with what seemed insurmountable difficulties.

As I knew nothing about sawmills, I had left the purchase of the outfit to Mr. Evenson, who claimed to be a millwright by profession, but it developed that he had either been very careless in inspecting this machinery or he had not understood it, for so much of it was missing that it seemed impossible to get a working mill out of the material on hand. As there was no foundry or machine shop in this part of the country we were at a loss to know what to do, but were determined to erect a sawmill of some kind. So [we got] out of our rubber coats and whipsawed lumber. We made a blacksmith bellows, then we burned a pit of charcoal, while a broad axe driven into a stump served as an anvil.

Mr. Evenson knew a little about blacksmithing, so I began to feel somewhat at ease, but soon discovered what seemed to be the worst obstacle yet. This was that we had no gearing for the log carriage, not even the track irons or pinion — and to devise some mechanism that would give the carriage the forward and reverse movement, became the paramount problem. After a great deal of thought and experimenting we finally succeeded in

inventing a device which years later was patented and widely used under the name of "rope feed." . . .

These were strenuous days and we worked early and late in the face of the most discouraging circumstances. We manufactured enough material for the sixteen-foot overshot waterwheel, the flume, etc. As we were short of belting, we made it out of untanned ox hides, and it worked well enough in the start. We finally got the mill started and sawed about 5,000 feet of lumber before we ever had a beast of burden in the camp.

Before we could get any of this lumber out we had to employ some help, and the first thing necessary to do was to grade a wagon road on the side of the mountain to get to the top of the divide. It required a great deal of labor to get a road in shape to put teams on. . . .

Now as the mill had been tried and proven satisfactory, a crew [was] employed and the mill started. I felt at ease, as I imagined all obstacles had now been overcome so I left the mill and went to Nevada City, a flourishing camp three miles below Virginia City, and opened a lumber yard.

When I got the yard opened at Nevada City, the lumber commenced arriving from the mill and was disposed of as fast as landed. When we began selling lumber we made only two grades, namely, sluice or flume lumber, which we sold at $140 per M. and building lumber . . . for which we got $125 per M. in gold dust.

The demand for lumber was greater than the supply, and quite often some of the larger mining companies would send a spy out on the road, in order that they might be informed when a load of lumber was approaching. Then they would have a crew of men arrive at the yard simultaneously with the load of lumber, and when the team stopped, without consulting me at all, they would unload the lumber and carry off every board to their mines. Soon a man would come to me with the pay for the lumber, and they always settled according to the bill of lading of the load at the established price so that no loss was incurred by this summary method of marketing our product. . . .

News was a precious frontier commodity. Montana, in a surprisingly short time, had the means for its dissemination, with newspapers speaking for every segment — Democrats, Republicans, independents, and agrarians. Quite naturally, these publications wielded a great deal of influence, both in the business community and in the political arena. They were the instruments of news, but also the tools for special interests. In this account, the editor and publisher of the WEEKLY MISSOULIAN, *Chauncey Barbour, gave his impressions on the alternative of starting a daily Democratic newspaper in Butte to compete with the weekly Republican* MINER. *His plan hinged on the financial backing of one interest — Jay Gould's northward advancing Utah Northern Railroad.*

MARCH 4, 1878

(CONFIDENTIAL)

S. T. HAUSER, ESQ.:-

DEAR SIR:

Intimations have been conveyed to me from Butte that some of the able-bodied citizens of that place desire that I should start a daily paper there, and I desire, if anything should come of it, there should exist between us some such a silent partnership as was suggested last spring. It has occurred to me that you could manipulate the thing and have a say in such [a] projected paper without the investment of a cent.

I am persuaded from our former conference, that you can induce Jay Gould to place $5,000 in a vigorous railroad paper at Butte. . . . From $3,000 to $5,000 can be relied on to be subscribed by Butte. . . . The people of Butte must be brought to feel that a creditable newspaper in their place is a judicious investment, and will return to them in the same manner that money ungrudgingly subscribed to an institution of learning returns to all who are within its influence.

The publication of a newspaper is not altogether a legitimate business enterprise: people tacitly admit this by continually going down into their pockets to start such enterprises and to keep them on their feet after they have become involved. . . . People everywhere . . . need to have a more vivid conception of the fact that a journalist is working as well for the place and people as for himself. Besides, a local journal, to be efficient, must not be a half-starved thing, destitute of respect and wanting in influence. An editor cannot make a good newspaper without tools any more than a carpenter can build a house with a jack knife. . . . I firmly believe that the people of Butte can be made to see that it is to their interest to have a newspaper of which they need not be ashamed. . . . A thrifty, vigorous daily newspaper will do them good. . . .

I have made a close estimate that a fully equipped daily office cannot be laid down in Butte short of $8,000. As an enterprise of this kind cannot be expected to pay from the start, at least $1,000 should be held as a reserve. Of this amount Jay Gould can comfortably afford to let go $5,000 from the million and a half that the paper will be expected to help him to, and could assist in the transportation of the material. The Butte people will, I believe, add enough to this to put the office on an independent financial footing. . . .

I understand that it is the general preference in Butte that the new paper shall be Democratic. The best papers in the country are independent, and it is my judgment that independent journalism is best adapted to a forcible presentation of the railroad question. . . . So long as I remain in Missoula county it is my solemn duty to oppose all aid to railroads. The people are so far away from any beneficial influence that a railroad would bring that their position makes them anti-subsidy. . . . A journalist is bound to reflect the sentiments of his immediate patrons. If he goes among another people he must reconstruct, so to speak. There is truth on both sides of every public question; and I know of no law of ethics that makes it a crime for an editor to present arguments for a measure which a community esteems for its best welfare. . . .

I have marked this "confidential" [because] . . . a knowledge of these negotiations would injure me at home, and I impart to you the matter in this letter *on the square,* for you to accept and use as such.

FRATERNALLY YOURS,

CHAUNCEY BARBOUR

The slaughter of the American bison is one of the saddest chapters in Western history. It was a return to the traditional form of exploitation as practiced during the fur trade era. Making money, as much of it and as quickly as possible, was the only key. In Montana this systematic annihilation started in 1876, when hunters had decimated the southern herd of its four million animals. Professionals moved north to continue their business at an average of two to four dollars per hide. Once begun, the destruction by Indians and whites alike swiftly reduced the northern herd from a million and a half animals to mere thousands in less than a decade. It was estimated that the Northern Pacific Railroad, in 1882, shipped from the Miles City-Glendive region 200,000 hides. Two years later, not more than a hundred were freighted. A major reason for this complete obliteration was the "still hunt." W. T. Hornaday, one of the earliest authorities on the buffalo slaughter, described it as "... mere butchery of the ... most cruel kind, [and] of all the methods that were unsportsmanlike, ignoble, and utterly reprehensive [the still hunt] was ... the worst." It was also highly efficient. The buffalo's rapid destruction was testimony to that. Here, H. J. Rutter, an early cattleman, gave his impressions.

The last of the big herds of buffalo had been killed off in this territory in 1881 and 1882. . . . It was a very profitable commercial affair and the methods used were most efficient. [Buffalo hunters] would establish their camp . . . in a thickly populated buffalo country. The partners were the killers and they would hire a crew of about twelve men as professional Skinners. Having established themselves in a buffalo area the two leaders scouted until they located a herd on a big flat. If the wind was from the east the killers would work around to the west side of the herd. Equipped with rest sticks, heavy guns and ammunition the men would dismount a mile from the buffalo and approach with extreme caution to a point where they might be visible to the animals; from here (perhaps from 500 yards) they would crawl on their stomachs to within 150 or 200 yards of the edge of the herd. Here they would set up their rest sticks. These consisted of two sticks crossed about two thirds of the way up and bound together at this point with a buffalo thong. When set up in the ground the sticks formed a rest for the heavy guns and insured steady aim. The gun rest was very essential for the steadiest shot when you consider that they often waited a half an hour for the shot they wanted.

If you know the habits of the buffalo you understand why the men had to be sure of their shots. If the first failed to kill a buffalo but wounded him he would start a deafening bellow and start running. That was the cue for the rest of the herd and they would be off at a gallop and the hunting for that day would be over. For these experts there wasn't much danger of the first crack

out of the barrel not being a dead shot. If the first shot broke the buffalo's neck or back or pierced his heart he would fall without a struggle and the other animals at the scent of blood would mill around the dead one in confusion.

The rest of the marksman task was simple. If the herd was a large one the killers might shoot down 200 animals. . . . If the herd consisted of from twenty five to a hundred and fifty the hunters would probably drop them all on the one spot.

When the slaughter was finished the killers moved on to locate another herd; the paid skinners went to work on the dead herd and there was no time lost. The only meat used from all this accumulation of flesh was the tongues and humps. The hunting party used the humps and the tongues were shipped to eastern markets.

The skinners carried a sack of pegs and after skinning a buffalo they turned the hide flesh side up in the sun, pegged it down and allowed it to dry. In a month's hunt these men would amass one thousand buffalo hides. The hides were piled on a hay rack and taken to the head camp which would probably be on the Missouri River and from here were shipped down the Missouri and Mississippi to St. Louis or New Orleans and sold at a good profit. The buffalo bones left to bleach on the plains were often gathered some time later by the breeds of the locality.

[A few years later] while we were exploring for a camp site [where] . . . Hell Creek . . . enters the Missouri, . . . there on the banks of the Missouri was a solid wall of had a gasoline engine they powered it with, and they had an expert to run this gasoline engine. Ordinary guy didn't know anything about them, and if anything would happen, why they had to get this expert in there, and God, we'd look at him like he was some kind of magician! There was a lot of trail bands went out through here at that time. J. B. Long ran a lot of sheep up here, . . . and they'd bring these wintering bands about shearing time, which was usually the last of June and in July, and then they'd trail them on down to Dakota and ship them out of there. . . . They'd have about three bands of sheep and one camp tender, and he'd have about three trail bands of them, pretty big bands most of them, about 2,000 to 4,500. . . .

There was mostly professional sheep shearers. . . . Some of them was what they called "high rollers" and they'd knock out a couple of hundred a day there. Some of them would count out 200 strings in the morning and when they got their 200 knocked off, they'd quit, and sometimes they'd quit four o'clock in the afternoon, some of them. . . .

I washed the combs and cutters — that is, part of the clippers. . . . [I'd] brush them in cans of water and I had to wash them up before they could grind them. They got gummed up from the grease from the wool.

Well, I graduated from that pretty early. One summer was all I put in. My heart wasn't in the business. I wanted to get to punching cows as soon as I could. . . . I went to work for the Circle Diamond as horse wrangler in 1909. . . .

Frank Brock was cooking, and I was horse wrangler, and old Frank was a fine feller. . . . I used to have to flunkey for him and help him wash the dishes and chop wood and pack water to him besides watch those horse herds. . . . I remember Frank was quite a philosopher. One day he was making what they called a son-of-a-gun-in-a-sack. . . . It was really a suet pudding, and Frank was always kidding me and talking to me, and he said, "Now kid, I'll tell you something, kid. The meat might be burned or the biscuits might not be just right, but you give them something to taper off on and keep the sweet taste in their mouth, and then you get away with it all right. If you have dealings with a man, even if you have to take a little the worst of it, why, leave him with a sweet taste in the mouth." . . .

As early as the 1880's, before the use of internal combustion engines, some Montana ranchers raised horses exclusively. These animals gained acclaim for their stamina and quality, and the outbreak of World War I placed a premium on their supply as artillery and cavalry mounts. European army representatives attended the Miles City horse market — one of the world's largest — to fill their needs. Helena banker Samuel McKennan visited the community and enlightened T. C. Power on the brisk international sales.

HELENA, MONTANA
APRIL 23, 1915

One of the interesting sights which came to my attention at the Miles City stockyards was the inspection of horses by representatives of the French Government. . . . The morning I was present they were selecting light weight horses for the cavalry and were paying an average price of $135 per head for horses approved. As the horses were led into the yards, the officers looked them over critically and after say five minutes examination either accepted or rejected the animal. If accepted, they passed immediately into the branding chute, where they were branded with the proper brands of the French Army. They are able to pass on from 40 to 60 horses per day, I am told. . . .

Last week was an interesting one at the yard. Three countries were purchasing — Great Britain, France and Italy. Great Britain and France were purchasing artillery horses at an average price of about $175 per head and Italy was purchasing lighter horses at about $140. The stock was first offered to the English inspectors and all those not accepted by the English were then offered to the French and those not accepted by the French were later offered to the Italians. The result was that . . . over 900 horses were accepted during the week. At an average price of $140 per animal, the week's purchases amounted to $126,000. . . .

Approximately 225,000 horses have already left the United States for the foreign countries now at war. The average life of a horse, they tell me, is but seven days from the time it enters the army service at the front.

S. McKENNAN

After the buffalo vanished from the plains, predatory animals increasingly plagued stockmen. A long program of eradication began, aimed primarily at wolves and coyotes, with the state even paying bounties to hunters. This was only mildly successful and stockmen devised other methods for removal, including the dispersal of selected animals infected with mange or other diseases. Thomas C. Power wrote his representatives at the Judith Mercantile and Cattle Company detailing how to distribute several infected animals. This method, too, proved to be unsuccessful.

HELENA, MONTANA
OCTOBER 18, 1913

GENTLEMEN:

Will ship you Wednesday afternoon by Express, One (1) Big Strong Grey Wolf, in a single cage, and three cages of Coyotes, containing 9 Coyotes. . . .

Be extra careful in handling the Wolf as he is a bad one, and is liable to put up a fight and a good one too. . . . Place the cage on the ground at the point you desire to unload him, open the cage door and drive away for 15 or 20 minutes and give him time to get out and away.

Believe you had better start distributing the Coyotes from the 79 ranch, as the hub of a wheel, and a common center, distributing them South, east and west there from, a few miles apart in locations where there are no settlers.

Would advise the immediate distribution of these infected Coyotes as they have been penned up some time. Spare no expense, sending only good reliable men, interested in the stock business, that will see to it that the work is thoroughly done.

Remember the Bounty hunters will be after these Coyotes in order to kill them wherever possible to prevent the spread of the infection.

Make no noise about this distribution . . . and ask every one connected with the distribution to keep the thing quiet.

Coyotes to be fed but once a day on raw meat and watered while in captivity. . . .

VERY RESPECTFULLY,

T. C. POWER

Small family cattle operations declined during the 1920's, but after the catastrophic failures of the homestead period, the remaining cattlemen expanded operations. Many had no pity for those who went bankrupt, maintaining that the homesteaders had failed because of their own stupidity and cupidity. Quick to criticize, but quicker to capitalize, stockmen eagerly bought up tax-forfeited homestead land. Robert T. Pound, Lavina cattle rancher, wrote Evan Hall, newly appointed Milwaukee Railway agricultural agent, about livestock's economic role in Montana.

LAVINA, MONTANA
NOVEMBER 17, 1926

DEAR MR. HALL:

Individuals connected with this firm have been running livestock in Montana since 1886. Our experience is that natural grass has no superior as an income crop. . . . The short grass sections . . . of the state are best grazed by sheep, while the longer grass goes best with cattle. . . .

Perhaps the most remarkable thing we can say

about livestock in this section, or in Montana for that matter, is that cattle and sheep are today paying the losses of men who have been engaged in banking, storekeeping, oil drilling, mining, and a dozen other enterprises that suffered in the post war deflation. The livestock business is the major enterprise of this section of the country, and doubtless will remain so. . . .

YOURS SINCERELY,

ROBERT T. POUND

William H. Donald's struggle epitomized the plight of Montana cattle ranchers during the Depression. On his Melville ranch he bred Hereford stock and augmented his income with a dude ranching operation. Besides contending with the "usual" bad weather, Donald faced the problem of most Montanans — a lack of money. Continued confrontations with banks and federal loan officials compounded Donald's concerns. His diary disclosed a trying ten years and reflected more contact with bureaucrats than cows.

FRIDAY, MAY 6, 1927: Snow, Slush, Mud & Hell. Coldest & wettest spring that ever I saw. Rode thru G. cows. Thank God no cow presented this fiendish weather with a calf, though Fannie lay down in front of me & had a fine foal. . . .

SATURDAY, MAY 7, 1927: Weather man still turning loose a lot of snow. You'd think the son of a bitch would run out of stock some time. Stumbled thru G. cows in storm. Tagged three wet & chilly calves. . . .

SUNDAY, MAY 8, 1927: WOW! BASTARDLY BLIZZARD. Never Saw a Storm Like This In May Before. Blinding, Whirling, Howling Snowstorm On. One poor chilled calf dropped but seemed to be doing well. Storming so hard did not dare leave shelter of brush for fear of being lost. Sat around house & cursed weather. . . .

MONDAY, MAY 9, 1927: Weather Broke!!! Thank God!!!

SATURDAY, MAY 28, 1927: Rain! God Damn It, Rain!!! Started out with Herb to move yearlings on Upper Ranch. . . . New man up there, some cowboy. Doesn't care which side of a horse he gets on or off nor does he know a cow from a steer. Cold, wet, slippery work. Couldn't get out the cattle we wanted but after a lot of trouble put 176 head in Sec. 33. . . . Lunch U.R. & home wet, cold & tired. Warm house with furnace going . . . sure made a person appreciate a cozy home.

MONDAY, NOVEMBER 18, 1929: Up to Upper Ranch in Truck, worked calves around and started them out for Big Timber, 111 head. Cold raw day. John met us at 10 mile with truck and cooked lunch. John went with calves and I took truck and went on in to B.T. leaving boys [to] bed at Hathaways. . . .

TUESDAY, NOVEMBER 19, 1929: Got car started early and down after calves. Picked them up a few miles out from Big Timber. Took horse in tow and went on to bridge where I took horse and helped cross river and R.R. tracks. Led horse with car up to Stock Yards, set gates and got cattle in. Weighed up one load. Sure would of lost my shirt had I sold . . . by the pound. . . .

MONDAY, DECEMBER 9, 1929: Haircut. In and saw Eddie Phillips for a while. Talked with accountants keeping Ranch Books, and then in to see my "Big Hearted (?!*) Bankers." Same old story. I am carrying too big a load and got to cut down loans. . . . Came right down to it, though, the bull market is a bit slow. I really am just about holding my own despite a pretty poor year in the cattle business and I take quite a bit of comfort in that. . . .

SUNDAY, APRIL 20, 1930: Easter. Pretty nice day outside. . . . It was about as blue a day as I put in all winter. Not having Billy I guess is what made it seem so extra cheerless. . . . Money is awfully tight and business is rotten. Have over $4,000 worth of stuff to sell and can't move a thing nor have I paid a bill in the last three months. Last week was a particularly discouraging one. Billy getting the measles was discouraging enough. Losing 7 head of cows and four of them registered did not help much. . . . On top of that had a very discouraging talk with the Scandanavian-American Bank. . . .

SUNDAY, NOVEMBER 11, 1934: Chicago. We come racing in to Chicago & land at the Stock Yards at 9:20 A.M. Best & fastest run I ever had in to Chicago. Up to Walters & Dunbar Office, Get mail, Change clothes. Out in yards . . . get Sam Scott to inspect my cattle. Cut out Bangs reactors. Lunch. Up to Hotel, bath & cleaned up & feel fine. Wander around & invest in a few drinks. It beats the band the way all these cocktail bars are crowded — and high priced drinks too. . . .

MONDAY, NOVEMBER 12, 1934: Chicago. Out to yards fairly early. It is a rotten market. Few top cows at 4¢, top calves 5¢. Don't weigh. Most of cows around [$]2.75. . . .

TUESDAY, JULY 13, 1937: Cow Camp. Got the crowd out by 4 A.M. sharp. Bkfst 4:30 & riding by 5:15. Had cattle all corralled & cows cut from calves by 9 A.M. 5 extra cars down there & about 18 extra people. . . . Grand chicken dinner about 5:30. Big and noisy ball game. Most of the crowd went home in cars but about 12 of us still in camp.

WEDNESDAY, JULY 14, 1937: Breakfast at 6 A.M. By 7:30 we broke camp & riding home. It began to rain & everybody got well soaked. Home 10:30. Stormy looking day. Looked around ranch. Tried to nap. . . .

TUESDAY, AUGUST 24, 1937: Dam, badly worried: Regional Agr[icultural] Cr[edit] Corp. notified me a new man in Helena Office & come in & see him. Same time Federal Land Bank notified me they are so exasperated at Regional turning down my interest & taxes they are starting foreclosure. Whew! . . . Start [to] Helena in car about 10, in by 2. . . . See Gribble (new man in Regional). Nice enough guy, but put in there to be tough & he is. Politely assures me he is quite certain Regional will not renew in fall & will have to sell out. Will let me know later. Leave Helena. . . .

WEDNESDAY, SEPTEMBER 15, 1937: Helena. Lit out after breakfast for Helena. Raced the North Coast Ltd. from Big Timber to Livingston. Helena 10:30. Talked with Paul Raftery. Doc Butler is sure fighting with me against the Regional. Has U.S. Sen. Jim Murray all lined up too. . . . In to see Gribble, of the Regional at 3. Between he & Kitting from Washington was with them till 6:30. Very unsatisfactory. My chief desire was to get the Land Banks foreclosure on the lands stopped. They would not allow me the money out of sales to stop that & only conclusion I could draw was they were doing it for the deliberate purpose of forcing me to sell my cattle to protect my land thus being able to say "We never foreclosed on

Bill Donalds cattle." Sure mad when I left there. . . .

WEDNESDAY, OCTOBER 27, 1937: . . . Having this summons & complaint slapped on me regarding the foreclosure on my land — in which there is a big equity — certainly looks like the RACC would have me sacrifice that so they could say it was the Federal Land Bank closed me out & not the RACC. Yet it was the RACC put the Land Bank in position where they had to do something. Fight drought & grasshoppers for 3 years. Buy feed & pasture to hold the herd together. Then this God Damned RACC is going to have me foreclosed because I borrowed too much money to buy feed & pasture.

MEMORANDA — 1937: Was a tough one & a year of great disappointments to me. First place, was just beginning to get around pretty well on my broken leg. Had flu & a bad relapse again. Nearly cut a finger off & rendered it useless in a buzz saw. Another bad infestation of grasshoppers cut down my summer pasture badly. We had a fair number of Dudes, but strung out very erratically & when I came to figure out how I had done, found I was in the hole. Didn't charge enough. In late August the RACC nearly put me out of business entirely & tried to force me to sell out. Had a mean automobile wreck where a fellow ran in to me. Bill came down with appendicities & had to be operated on. Cattle market was good up to Oct. 1st, but I overstaid my market & did not get in on the good market. Calves still unsold [because] the RACC, the Fed. Land Bank started an action to foreclose my lands. Only consolation I had was Billy was able to be with me till Xmas. One Hell Of A Year Says I.

As the Milwaukee Railroad's agricultural agent, Evan W. Hall was headquartered at Miles City. Besides promotion work, his main assignment was the development of sound agricultural techniques on land served by the railway. Poor range conditions, overgrazing, abandoned homesteads, drought and hard winters had denuded 108,000 acres between Mizpah and Pumpkin Creeks. Hall suggested to stockmen that this public domain be blocked off and leased. They agreed, and formed a cooperative grazing district, with authority of federal legislation. This was a significant step toward intelligent management of the public domain, and proved so successful during dry years that Congress used it as an example when it passed the Taylor Grazing Act in 1934.

MR. ALVA A. SIMPSON
U.S. FOREST SERVICE
DILLON, MONTANA

DEAR ALVA:
    R. W. Reynolds tells me that you are contemplating writing a brief history of the Mizpah-Pumpkin Creek

Grazing Area, on which the legislation incorporated in the Taylor Bill was based.

    It is very interesting to note the progress which has been made in the past eight years to bring about this legislation which has been needed so long. Our original aim has been accomplished . . . to establish a demonstration which would show the western states and prove to Congress that the Public Domain which was strictly grazing land, could be handled in a practical way by using the grazing district method. . . . It has certainly served its purpose in bringing about the passage of the Taylor Bill.

The day on which the Mizpah-Pumpkin Creek Grazing Area was originated was Wednesday, June 16th, 1926. I had suggested to Paul Lewis, County Agent for Custer County, that we call together four or five substantial farmers and stockmen, to get their suggestions as to the real needs in Custer County and southeastern Montana in order that I might work intelligently on the problems facing us. . . . The things that came up most often [were] the need for more grass, . . . better control of grazing, . . . [and] stabilizing . . . business by control of grazing land at a reasonable cost. . . .

The thought came to my mind "why not get this district under control and have the Public Domain blocked, with the private ownership and lease on a ten-year basis to the stockmen along the two creeks?" . . .

I presented the idea to the stockmen . . . to . . . Congressman Scott Leavitt, and . . . in December, 1928, to . . . E. C. Finney, Asst. Secretary, Department of Interior. . . . The support given [by] Congressman Leavitt [and] E. C. Finney was what finally secured the passage of the legislation making the Mizpah-Pumpkin Creek Grazing Area possible. . . . [They] performed a real service to the livestock industry by putting over the Mizpah-Pumpkin Creek Grazing legislation. . . .

SINCERELY,

EVAN W. HALL

By mid-century, trail drives and cowboy traditions were dim memories, but survivors of the open range era attended reunions to relive vicariously the old times. On July 1, 1951, the Montana Cowboys Association held a roundup and "branding bee" on a horse ranch near Glasgow. At the gathering were cattlemen and cowpunchers from outfits out of Montana's past, such as the Circle Diamond, XIT, 76, N-N, Turkey Track, Mill Iron, and others. Ailing Con Price could not attend, but acknowledged his regrets.

NAPA, CALIFORNIA
JUNE 2, 1951

FRANK MESSENGER
SECRETARY-DIRECTOR
MONTANA COWBOYS ASSOC.
GREAT FALLS, MONTANA

DEAR FRANK:

Well, you tell me they are going to have a big blow out in Glasgow July 1st. And how I would like to be with you all, and go among you fellows and squeeze your old Paws, and even look at your old hoofs to see if you were getting tenderfooted.

Sure will be lonesome to-day thinking of you old Scalawags. I knew most of you from the Rockies to the Dakota line, from Canada to Wyoming. But Hell, my saddle is wore out, and that part of my body that I used to sit on it, is about wore out too, so I can't make the trip. If I were there, the only sadness I would feel, would be in working the old herd. I would miss so many of the old

bunch that has crossed the big Devide, but damn it, I can't feel they are gone forever. They just went to work for another outfit on another range. . . . May have to go to work over there myself before too long. I am sure the big Range Boss up there has cut that old Montana Herd in a bunch by them selves. I feel there is no State in the U.S. that has your brand of people. And if it wasn't for your tough winters, I sure would go back there and finish my last roundup.

But old Dad time has put his Hobbles on me, I couldn't even trot fast enough to keep warm and I don't seem to shed off anymore, you old boys know that is a bad sign. . . . Guess I better unsaddle and quit.

Hoping the Sun shines on all of your trails to the jumping off place. Wishing you health and happiness all the way. So Long — Good Bye — and Good Luck.

SINCERELY,

CON PRICE

> *Adaptation and diversification have always characterized Montana agriculture. Livestock owners expanded and changed to keep pace, and theirs became a significant industry, rather than a romantic interlude as it was during parts of the Nineteenth Century. Ralph Miracle, as Secretary of the Montana Stockgrowers Association, discussed the evolution and local dependence on the livestock business.*

I think everybody realizes how much the cattle industry meant in the early days of Montana, that it was the cattle industry primarily and the livestock industry as a whole that built Montana. . . . But that was a long time ago — been a lot of changes since then — the industry's changed — everything's changed . . . but in the process . . . the cattle and livestock industry is even more important today. . . . And it involves more people.

In the real early days of the open range we had a few large cattle owners that utilized the range. . . . Today, almost everybody that has a ranch or farm property owns some livestock and has some cattle and has a cattle brand and utilizes the facilities that have developed over the years for marketing their cattle and utilizing the information that's available to them from their educational institutions, and from the organizations that serve the industry. . . .

When you start talking about the importance of the cattle industry you're not only talking about the value of the ranches and the value of the cattle and the value of the equipment that they have, but you're also speaking of all the people and all the businesses that are related to that industry. . . . If you take in the related industries, the amount of equipment and the amount of fertilizer and the amount of feed and all the different supplies that go into the cattle industry, it becomes a tremendous industry affecting so many people. . . .

We hear many people talking today about urban and rural conflict, that they're entirely different kind of people and put their hats on a different way and they don't get along with each other and they're opposed. But when you get to Montana, and you start talking about urban Montana, we're really talking about people who are just about as close to the ranch as they can be without living on it. They're in the automobile business, they're in the hardware business. If it's feed, or if it's any other type of business, or even if it's hotels and motels and all the other things that are combined, they're real close to the industry which is agriculture and which livestock is the big part of it in the state of Montana. . . .

> *Exportation of goods has historically been essential to bolster markets for Montana's agricultural products. Better foreign markets meant more production, particularly for high protein wheat. Bob Brastrup of the Montana Department of Agriculture addressed the export issue before the Senate Finance and Claims Committee in 1974. His support of a portion of H.B. 746 called for funding of an eighteen-month foreign export study, and reflected the state's search for new market opportunities. Despite Brastrup's testimony, the bill failed to pass.*

I appear today to support [a portion of] House Bill 746. . . . I'm really not here as a matter of self-interest, because of all Montana's products, agricultural and otherwise, wheat already produces practically all of the dough in Montana's present export trade. . . . Of $208,900,000 worth of agricultural commodities exported from Montana in fiscal year 1972-73, . . . 72 percent was represented by wheat alone. . . . In effect, then, what I'm saying is that as far as the export market is concerned, Montana has been living by bread alone. For nearly 10 years, wheat has represented two-thirds of the total exports from Montana. . . .

As promised in the Governor's State of the State address, the Foreign Trade Potential Committee will develop the information necessary for all Montana products — not just wheat — to take better advantage of expanding opportunities in international markets. It is certainly true, as the Governor said, that increased foreign export offers a definite possibility of improving the state economy. [We need to] . . . inventory products suitable for export, locate markets, improve transportation arrangements and apply innovative new approaches in foreign commerce. . . .

I say to you as strongly as I can that I am a "true believer" — we are and have been selling at least 60 per cent of our wheat to foreign nations. I'm afraid the only alternative in many past years would have been to plow it up. Certainly Montana should explore the possibility of selling its various other products in the same manner and quantity. The market awaits our action. . . .

Many have viewed rural life as more healthful and wholesome than an urban existence, and have deplored the decline of a pastoral way of life. Yet in Montana, as elsewhere, the move away from the farm has been a constant reality. In 1945, a Lewistown group under the auspices of the Montana Study, met to evaluate the situation in that community and heard Ann Mather, a farm wife, voice her feelings.

Quite often city folk consider farm folk peculiar, but the farmers are just like anybody else.... [I do feel] that moral, religious and educational standards are easier to maintain on the farm than in town, because neighbor children live farther away, frequent meetings do not occur and discipline is easier.... Most farm children are kept busy by chores and cannot get into trouble....

[I] worked during the depression in the Roundup area with farm families who were in need of loans. In these families, many lacking the necessities of life, [I] found that the wives were very devoted to their husbands. With so few material comforts ... they might be expected to find fault, but . . . they did not. . . .

The farm woman ... is tremendously important. A farm wife who desires a social life in the city cannot be a successful partner. Many farm wives are forced to move to the city for the education of their children, thus causing a disruption in the normal activities of the farm family. Nine of the twelve months are thus spent away from the real home. . . .

Rural children should consciously be taught the value of their birthright. Urbanization brings a decay in the moral fibre of people. . . .

Formal religion has ... largely disappeared from the rural community because of the disappearance of the "little red school house." Rural community clubs and other activities have [also] grown less active because of [its] disappearance. . . . Now many organizations take the time of farm people [and] draw them away from the farm to the city. Young people are drawn away in the same manner, leaving the old folks on the farm.

Small farming and livestock interests were not always compatible. Often at issue was the conflict of life-style and economics. In 1973, the Montana Legislature saw the groups in opposition over this question — farmers speaking through the Farmers Union versus the livestock associations. House Bill 132, referred to as the Family Farm Act, attempted to place control on corporate farming, calling for limits on corporation shares, a return to family control, and an end to factory-type operations. Theoretically, it would have preserved Montana's rural environment and helped slow the out-migration of the state's young people. Clyde Jarvis spoke unsuccessfully for the bill's approval at a committee hearing.

The Montana Farmers Union supports House Bill 132, the Montana Family Farm Act of 1973, both from an economic and a philosophic basis. This legislation not only will prevent economic injustices, but also it will preserve the social benefits of rural life. . . .

The family farm or ranch ... provides the best rural environment for the growth of individual personality and character, for stability of family life, and for the strength of the rural community and all of its institutions — churches, schools, businesses and local governments. . . .

This legislation would stop tax-loss farming by so-called conglomerates and prevent them from putting excess profits into large agricultural operations as a tax shelter. . . . It is aimed at stopping corporations from buying farms or ranches for an investment. . . .

These major corporations . . . put extremely little back into Montana from a financial viewpoint, yet are capable of using unlimited funds from out-of-state to compete against young Montanans seeking agricultural livelihoods. Thus, our own young people are squeezed out despite the fact they have the expertise. [Montana] has the resources, and the financing could be found, to permit them to stay and flourish in the Treasure State.

From yet another economic viewpoint, it is significant in considering this legislation to note many studies indicate smaller units in agriculture are the most efficient and economical. Almost all such research shows well-managed one- and two-man farms and ranches are the most efficient when measured by the cost per unit of output. . . .

With these observations on the Montana Family Farm Act of 1973, I have no hesitancy in recommending that your committee support its passage. . . .

CLYDE JARVIS, PRESIDENT
MONTANA FARMERS UNION

photo by N. B. Cresswell, Kansas City *Journal Post*

COLLISION OF INTERESTS

HE PATTERN OF personal constituencies and the dominance of corporate interests continued to color the fabric of Montana politics during much of the Twentieth Century. Comprised of diverse elements and subject to a host of disruptive influences — including considerable voter independence — both major parties were but loosely structured. The result was that if politics in the state were frequently unpredictable and fraught with a kind of schizophrenia, they were always complex. For many years, the Anaconda Company, often in concert with other corporate interests, wielded overwhelming influence on politics in the state. Although eminently successful in its objectives, this corporate influence was unlike that of the traditional political bossism, for it cut across party lines with such subtlety that the influence was sometimes barely perceptible. It was a domination that continued, albeit in more benign guise, well into the century.

Beginning in the 1940's, however, changing internal conditions brought corporate politics into competition with other highly influential pressure groups, including farm, labor, education and other sectors. With reapportionment still in the future, rural areas continued to wield a large influence, much of it generating a conservatism and a demand for economy and reorganization in state government.

In contrast with the generally conservative tinge of politics at home, Montana voters elected a host of liberals to national office. Because of the political affiliations of such men as Senators Thomas J. Walsh, Burton K. Wheeler, James E. Murray, Mike Mansfield and Lee Metcalf, Montana reaped proportionately more from federal spending programs than it paid out in federal taxes. At the same time, the state's congressional delegations have a number of times risen to great influence and renown in national affairs, out of proportion to the small electorate they represented.

Recent improvements in communication, together with the "liberation" of the state press, permitted national influences to become an increasingly prominent foundation for state decision making. The resultant focus upon issues rather than personalities and a number of important structural changes, including a new constitution, pointed to the development of a sophisticated political alignment more in tune with national patterns.

B. K. WHEELER CAMPAIGNING FOR THE VICE-PRESIDENCY, 1924

COLLISION OF INTERESTS
Politics in the 20th Century

Montana's political history has traditionally been a complex of varying ideological beliefs, interests, and factional loyalties — all intertwined to weave a tangled network. Although he spoke with reference to presidential politics of 1948, the attitudes of Missoula lawyer Emmet Glore were equally applicable to Montana politics during most of the century.

MISSOULA, MONTANA
OCTOBER 10, 1947

MR. PRESCOTT COOKINGHAM
PORTLAND, OREGON

DEAR MR. COOKINGHAM:

Our mutual friend has asked that I write you briefly concerning the . . . situation in Montana as it may affect Senator [Robert] Taft's possible candidacy for the republican presidential nomination. The Montana political situation stinks; and not briefly. Unless Montana's few delegates and votes are imperative to Senator Taft, in my opinion he will be better advised to seek his support elsewhere. . . .

Montana politics can be understood only by Montana politicians. This is a rugged state. So are its politics. So far as I know, only one [columnist] had even a passing conception of what was going on in the Wheeler-Erickson senatorial shuffle that ended, to the amazement of all hands, with the election of Zales Ecton. . . . The republican people's governor [Ford], a potent Baptist every Sunday, is a company-bound disciple of the ex-democrat senator [Wheeler] . . . who was originally elected as the people's advocate and promptly went over to the company. This ex-senator was defeated last fall in Montana, by one Leif Erickson because his opinions on Germany offended some of the wealthy Jews in New York City. All the Butte chaws and cousin-jacks voted for Erickson. Does this make sense? Absolutely in Montana. [Wellington Rankin, a republican] now expects to defeat the incumbent democrat [Murray] with the assistance of [Ford] and this same ex-democrat senator's machine, which, incidentally, elected this republican people's governor. . . . It's all fascinating and on one's better days, hilarious. . . .

If he must have Montana, my advice to Senator Taft is to buy it: from B. K. Wheeler, Sam Ford, Wellington D. Rankin and J. Burke Clements, and from the Monopoly. In Montana politics, that approach is most direct, least expensive and best understood.

YOURS FOR HONEST ELECTIONS,

EMMET GLORE

During the early decades of the Twentieth Century, Montana politics took on a new variety that caused consternation in many quarters. Primarily centered in the mining regions and paralleling the concern of agrarian radicals in eastern Montana, the Montana Socialist Party became a sizeable minority which served as a framework for social criticism. Although many of its ideas are today routinely accepted, the party was undeniably radical in its time, and at the peak of its influence it found an able spokesman in Lewis J. Duncan. When he wrote the following letter to Utah Socialist William Brown in 1911, Duncan had just won a resounding victory in the race for mayor of Butte. A decade later, the Socialist Party in Montana was all but extinct.

APRIL 12, 1911

WM. THURSTON BROWN
SALT LAKE CITY, UTAH

DEAR COMRADE:

My election will make a vacancy in the office of state secretary. . . . I want you to have the position, and I know the comrades at Butte and Great Falls will nominate and try to elect you, if you will consider the proposition.

To mention the least important matter first, the salary is : . . . $100.00 per month. The really important matter is the cause in Montana. This I am certain will appeal to you. For the first time, the socialists have [an] opportunity to demonstrate their methods and efficiency before the people of Montana. This demonstration will be in the strongest organized labor town in the state, where, if we make good, we shall be able to get the practical support of the industrial organizations in our political efforts. It was the labor vote that carried us into power this time and it can do it every time if we can retain the confidence of the workers. This situation is going to result in a clear class alignment in future political fights—organized labor with the socialists on one side and the Amalgamated with the old political machines on the other side. . . .

This condition will center the attention of the whole state on the socialist administration in Butte. . . . We have a fine body of workers that are enthusiastic . . . but we are short handed for speakers and writers. We mean to keep up the education at even greater pace than during the last four months. We want to make the paper a weekly. We want to carry on weekly propaganda meetings in the local and outside the local. I am about the only one competent to take the platform with the kind of propaganda message that is required, and the duties of the mayoralty, will be even more onerous and time consuming than those of state secretary. Another man of culture is needed and you are the man we want. . . .

Should we prove convincing in city affairs, we shall be able to get the county at the next election and send representatives to legislature. We might even be able to get state officers next year. We have got to have men for these positions. We must import and make them. We want you first of all as one of those to assist in developing the right kind of material in the ranks of the comrades and of organized labor. . . .

Yours Comradely,

DUNCAN

After a long struggle, Montana women won the vote in 1914, part of the victory attributable to the Progressive crusade to make political institutions more representative. A majority of the responsibility, however, lay with Jeannette Rankin who formed a sophisticated organization and marshaled a host of dedicated campaigners to visit every part of the state. During the campaign, Rankin reported on the progress to Anna Howard Shaw, president of the National American Women's Suffrage Association. Although the suffragists — and their opponents — declared that women would reform and/or vastly change politics, women as members of the electorate altered the character of Montana politics very little.

[DEAR DR. SHAW,]

I had been asked to come by the suffrage workers [but after] I consented they found that the people did not want me on the program because they did not want a political speech. However, the governor was billed to speak so I said I would go anyway and if there was a chance alright and if not alright. When I arrived it was still said that I would not be allowed to speak, but there were several men very determined so when the speaking was over they called "Miss Rankin." The men helped me on the platform but the chairman shook his head so I got down. Then they started to call again and as the chairman had left and the crowd started to leave, I got up and a man introduced me and the crowd came back. I talked a few minutes telling my best stories and the people thought it was a great joke that I finally got on, and they were all very good-natured. . . .

We had an interesting time in a little . . . village where we held an open air meeting. There were very few people in town [as] they were preparing for a big celebration the next day. The men sat around the saloons and insisted they would not come to hear the speaking, but a few women and children mixed in with our crowd made a beginning and after that the men gradually came until we had a good audience. . . . We did not try to take up a collection but told them we had some Votes for Women buttons to sell. A woman in the audience who was the assistant postmaster came out in front and said, "Here, come buy these buttons," and the men came up and we sold all the buttons we had. We felt that we had gained quite a victory.

The country districts are coming forward most wonderfully. We had a very interesting time at our State Central Committee at Lewistown. . . . Women from all parts of the state made their first suffrage and open-air speeches at the same time and the audiences enjoyed them very much. There was one anti in Lewistown. . . .

One woman . . . said that the antis reminded her of the old jingle about the purple cow: — "I never saw a purple cow. I hope I never see one, but I can tell you anyhow, I would rather see than be one."

[JEANNETTE RANKIN]

The Progressives' desire to reform government gained momentum from the enthusiastic boosterism of the period to produce the phenomenon known as county-splitting. As Montana population sky-rocketed during the homestead era, the creation of additional counties seemed an admirable idea, one calculated to bring people closer to their government while providing impetus for economic development. Thus, from 1910 to 1925, Montana counties frenetically divided and redivided until twenty-eight new government entities emerged. With the onset of drought and depression the population trend dramatically reversed, leaving a legacy of overly expensive local government.

Nov. 2, 1922

Flathead county has been much excited, perturbed, agitated and aggravated recently over the matter of county division, as well as a wild scheme to remove the county seat from Kalispell to Whitefish — or elsewhere. . . .

The movement started in Polson to create a new county out of portions of Flathead and Missoula counties . . . which the people of this vicinity generally recognized as a fair division, and little if any opposition was made.

But the county divisionists had a specialist on the job, who gets so much per division, and the next move was a petition to bring the north boundary of the proposed county of Lake nearly to Somers, and to . . . [propose] the creation of still another new county out of northern Flathead and eastern Lincoln counties, removing the county seat from Kalispell entirely.

The Columbian designates this threat . . . as a "form of reprisal," . . . to force the people of Northern Flathead to accede to the proposed new line of division near Somers.

County division fights are always nasty, and this one is no exception. Already it is beginning to bear fruit in the way of abuse and criticism, just at a time when the different communities should be working together for the common good.

As we see it, the people of the southern part of the county want, and are entitled, to a county seat. There has always been complaint of the hardship of traveling the fifty-odd miles to Kalispell during the winter months. . . . But conditions would not be improved if a division were made whereby the people from . . . the north end of Flathead lake were compelled to travel to a county seat at Polson. . . .

The only logical division would be about midway of Flathead lake, . . . and it impresses us that the sane method of procedure would be for the factions to get together and agree upon a division which would be reasonable and best for the interest of all concerned.

The division is bound to come some day, and we may as well have it over and done with it. . . .

L. D. SPAFFORD, EDITOR
KALISPELL INTERLAKE

In the heat of hysteria during World War I, there was an ever-present threat to personal liberties throughout the country. It was especially apparent in Montana, where the Council of Defense sat in Helena to enforce sedition laws and stave off what it considered anti-American action. As the following letter indicated, Attorney General Sam C. Ford became increasingly alarmed, and although his complaint dealt solely with juridical matters, Ford perceived that the Council, together with many of its zealous supporters, possessed a dangerous potential for crushing all political dissent.

MAY 27, 1918

MONTANA COUNCIL OF DEFENSE,
HELENA, MONTANA

GENTLEMEN:

As Attorney General of the State of Montana, I feel it my duty to call to the attention of your honorable

body, recent violations of the state constitution and laws in a number of counties of the state . . . which in my opinion, are matters of tremendous importance to every citizen of the state.

The right of free speech [has] been denied individuals . . . by violence and in direct violation of law. . . .

Furthermore, it is common knowledge that in many cases members of county councils of defense participated in these unlawful proceedings. . . . The persons so misused have been met by self-constituted committees and informed that they would not be permitted to make addresses. . . . If they attempted to make addresses they might subject themselves to violence. . . .

The freedom of the press, and the unrestricted right of public assemblage and free speech are absolutely necessary for the maintenance of a republican form of government. . . . It is true that we are at war and that the life of the nation is at stake; and that these conditions may so effect the minds of over-zealous patriots and persons of hysterical tendencies as to lessen their power to clearly analyze civil rights; and to perceive the importance of the strict respect that should be given the same; nevertheless, it is also true that the primary purpose of this war is to uphold the fundamental principles of freedom and to prevent autocratic grovernment, the rule of might, from being established on this continent.

A cloud has arisen upon Montana's horizon that threatens dire consequences to the people of the state. Class is being arrayed against class, and . . . if the lawlessness cited is not put down, and the right to free speech is not rescued from the disrepute thrown upon it, in my opinion, conditions may follow that will do the people and the fair name of the state incalculable injury. . . .

I am constrained to suggest to your honorable body that you take steps to reinforce and assist the ordinary authorities in repressing those engaged in these infractions of the law and in the punishment of the offenders. . . .

SAM C. FORD
ATTORNEY GENERAL

During the early years of the century, corporate influence was still dominant in Montana politics. To achieve legislative goals, their methods included bribery, election fraud, almost total control of the state's press and both major parties. The result was even further complication of an already involved political alignment. In 1919 a group of Butte Republicans, parroting the Company "line," ironically raised the issue of election fraud in order to challenge an anti-Company slate which had captured the Democratic nomination.

At a meeting called for the purpose of . . . informing the public as to the conditions of political affairs and frauds perpetrated for the sake of securing so-called Democrats immunity in office, [the Republicans of Silver Bow County stated the following facts:]

Butte . . . filled up in past days with adventurous souls to whom the lure of the silvery dollar appealed in raucous tones. . . . Time has passed and Butte has changed, and — for the better — as to morals, but not as to elections. . . .

Matters have so come to pass with us that secret jugglery of the ballots, forgeries, the casting of ballots by dead men and women, purposeful miscounts, . . . have developed. A political democratic machine, nearly as efficient as that of Tammany has been built up, and its leaders are influenced by money or ambitious designs for power. . . .

The Republicans, numerically inferior in Silver Bow County, aided, however, at times by popular sentiment when things became too "raw" have been the backbone . . . of the forces fighting for principles. . . . Our men and our women candidates for office have at all times been people of most excellent citizenship and seldom, if ever, has one been chosen against whom reproach could be cast. . . .

The last Election presented strange anomalies here. One man . . . was declared elected. . . . Then the voters seem suddenly to have switched and . . . votes went in overwhelming numbers to his antithesis. . . . Only peculiar methods could produce such peculiar results. . . . We believe desperate methods were resorted to to accomplish some of the results. . . .

We believe the great majority of public sentiment here demands that the Republicans, . . . particularly every Republican in the Senate and House of Representatives of this state, "go through" to the finish on this question of fraud. . . . This is not a partisan issue but a matter of good citizenship. . . . We now ask the Legislative Assembly to . . . stand against hydra-headed fraud in Elections, and help us stamp into the ground the viperous heads raised treasonably against good government. . . .

LEE HAWLEY
D. J. CHARLES

Progressive ideas tended to disrupt both major political parties. Such fragmentation is well exemplified by the career of Joseph M. Dixon, one of Montana's most outstanding but over-looked politicians. As a United States Senator, Dixon split with orthodox Republicans in 1912 to support Theodore Roosevelt's Progressives. Although he later rejoined the party, conservatives were loath to forgive Dixon, even after he won the governor's race in 1920 in a heated campaign against B. K. Wheeler. In a letter to Congressman Carl Riddick, Attorney General Ford, himself a disappointed aspirant to the governorship that year, urged that the party put factionalism behind and move forward as a united party.

HON. CARL RIDDICK
MEMBER OF CONGRESS
WASHINGTON, D.C.

HELENA, MONTANA
DECEMBER 23, 1920

MY DEAR CARL,

. . . Under ordinary conditions I think perhaps your plan would work out fairly satisfactory but we should not forget that extraordinary conditions prevail in Montana. The republican party is as much divided to-day as any. We still have the old would-be leaders, the most reactionary set of men to be found in the state, whose interest in politics is largely personal and selfish and who have seldom, if ever, assisted a party in the state. And there is a young progressive element who believes in honesty and fair dealing in politics. . . . [who] resent the unscrupulous and contemptuous method of the old wing and believe that party interest should come before personal interest. In 1912, some, but by no means all, of the more liberal in the party joined the progressive party and during the campaign just closed an effort was made to get these republicans back into the party. . . . Now that they are back are we going to keep them or drive them out by surrendering all to the reactionary crowd? . . .

Some of the prominent republicans throughout the state are ready, willing and anxious to trade off the entire ticket from president down in order to save Senator Dixon. . . . Personally I cannot subscribe to such a policy. I would never permit these men who have no interest in you or Senator Harding to make a single appointment but on the other hand those who honestly and conscientiously did their part should receive due consideration. . . .

If we use just a little common sense we can reach no other conclusion but that the future success of the party in Montana depends upon a progressive, forward-looking set of men and the sooner we get the elements which you propose to give recognition to . . . the sooner the party will be on a firm foundation with bright prospects for the future. . . .

SAM C. FORD
ATTORNEY GENERAL

In contrast with the generally conservative aspect of politics within Montana, the state's voters sent a long line of liberal representatives and senators to Congress. One of the most distinguished was Thomas J. Walsh, who served in the Senate from 1912 to 1933. A superb politician, Walsh proved adept at bending to the company at home — as evidenced in this letter to Bozeman newspaperman Walter Aitkin — while furthering liberal legislation in Washington. Perhaps best known for his exposure of the Teapot Dome scandal in 1923, Walsh was appointed Attorney General by Franklin Roosevelt, but was denied this honor by a fatal heart attack.

MR. WALTER AITKIN
BOZEMAN, MONTANA

WASHINGTON, D.C.
APRIL 8, 1932

DEAR WALTER:

. . . I am in a rather embarrassing position concerning . . . Penwell. . . . Miles Romney has been my consistent friend and supporter, in person and through his paper, ever since I have been a seeker after public office. He was belligerently so at Livingston in the convention of 1910, a crucial test. In the campaign a year ago last fall I twice appealed to Erickson to take the stump for me. In both instances he responded with alacrity. Under these circumstances, intimate as my relations with Penwell have been, I do not feel warranted in throwing the weight of any influence I may have in favor of him as against either of the other two.

Then another situation is embarrassing to me. No one conversant with the matter can hesitate in the belief that the Anaconda Company and its allies have been exercising a dominating influence over our public life. I had to encounter that opposition to come to the Senate in the first place. I dare say it and the Montana Power Company have been escaping their just share of the heavy burden of taxation . . . but I am not keen just now to assail the Anaconda Company when every day the probability grows more and more imminent that it will be forced to shut down. . . . I think every one must realize that since copper fell below seven or eight cents at least all of its operations have been carried on at a loss. If it were making money I should have every disposition to get into a fight to compel it to bear its fair share of the cost of government, by whomsoever the effort to attain that end might be led. As it is, as indicated, I am not keen about a fight on them just now.

SINCERELY YOURS,

T. J. WALSH
U.S. SENATE

In theory, appointive powers permitted an elected official to reward his friends and strengthen his party; in practice, patronage tended to please only the few, while disappointing the many. In this case, the rivalry between eastern and western portions of the state disrupted Governor Cooney's attempt to carefully balance all significant interests.

GLENDIVE, MONTANA
APRIL 21, 1933

HONORABLE F. H. COONEY
HELENA, MONTANA

DEAR MR. COONEY:

In reply to your letter of April 19th concerning the appointment of a gentleman from Missoula to the State Highway Commission. I must say that the people of Eastern Montana feel deeply hurt at your action.

If you will take a map of Montana and draw a line East of Butte and Great Falls, Montana, you will find that over half of the State of Montana was overlooked. . . . I assume that you selected an able man, yet it has been my experience that people in Western Montana have never realized what Eastern Montana is. . . . I am writing you in this manner for I feel undoubtedly three years from now you'll be a candidate to succeed yourself, and political experience and policy should suggest to you that Eastern Montana must at all times be considered. . . .

YOURS VERY TRULY,

DESMOND J. O'NEIL

Senator Burton K. Wheeler, one of the most powerful politicians in Montana's history, possessed an unblemished reputation as a liberal during the early years of his career. After jousting with the Anaconda Company and the Council of Defense, Wheeler won election to the Senate in 1922. Within two years his fame was such that he received the vice-presidential nomination on Robert LaFollette's Progressive ticket. Senator Wheeler at first staunchly supported the New Deal, but he later broke with Roosevelt, first over the court-packing issue and later over foreign affairs. Wheeler's isolationism was unquestionably based on principal, but it, along with this break with the President, convinced many Montanans that he had become a reactionary with pro-German sympathies. In 1946 Wheeler lost his bid for re-election in the Democratic primary, an event foreshadowed before the fact in Walter Aitken's letter.

BOZEMAN, MONTANA

MR. BURTON K. WHEELER
UNITED STATES SENATOR
WASHINGTON, D.C.

MY DEAR SENATOR:

I have received from you a copy of "The United States and the Peace." . . . Perhaps you are right in assuming, as you do in your covering letter, that the inclusion of your speech in a compilation of other speeches and documents of real importance is something of a compliment to you, but it seems more likely that the real purpose is to enable readers to make comparisons and contrasts with speeches by other senators on the same general subject. . . . If that is done it is not going to enhance your reputation either as a speaker or a patriot. . . .

Your speech was not intended to be helpful in devising some workable means whereby the world may hereafter be reasonably free from the scourge of war, but to put obstacles in the way of accomplishing that most desirable purpose. . . . Considering the satisfaction with which that speech and some others by you have been received, quoted and used by the enemies with whom our country has been and is now at war . . . the conclusion is logical [that your statements are] close to, if not actually and legally, treasonable.

Of my own knowledge there are many among your Montana constituents, formerly your political friends and supporters, who now regard you as a traitor. . . . Many . . . myself among them, distrust you for the friends you have made, in Montana, throughout the Nation and abroad. . . .

[We recall] one of your early [statements], "When they support me, my friends, you may be sure that I have betrayed you." . . . They are supporting you and praising you, Senator, those predatory special interests in this state which you at one time so roundly and vehemently

denounced as public enemies and worse and who in turn characterized you as . . . a "Russian-loving communist," "political upstart," "dangerous demagogue, agitator" and other familiar epithets. . . .

If and when you again become a candidate in Montana for re-election . . . it will be a test of whether the people of Montana, including the farmers and the railroad employes, regard material profit or genuine patriotic loyalty as the higher and more enlightened self-interest. . . . There are many Montana voters who have voted for you three times, including myself, and some of them four times, but who nevertheless have good memories and, remembering, are "fed up" with you. They no longer trust you or believe in your sincerity or loyalty to anything but your own not over-scrupulous self-aggrandizment and self-seeking, and you are going to have a hard time fooling them again. . . .

WALTER AITKEN

Although the New Deal produced a political realignment in the nation as a whole, in Montana the impact of Roosevelt's New Deal politics was only temporary. During the first years of the 1930's, Montana Democrats experienced solid victories and an ideological shift to the left. This trend culminated in the 1936 election to Congress of Jerry J. O'Connell, who represented the extreme left-wing of the party. In subsequent years, however, the liberal coalition collapsed as a result of state and national pressures and the party reverted to a more typical pattern of personal constituencies. Ironically, the same 1940 election which marked O'Connell's second unsuccessful try for re-election, also witnessed the appearance of Mike Mansfield, who was to establish the greatest political constituency in Montana's history.

HAMILTON, MONTANA
APRIL 9, 1940

H. S. BRUCE, EDITOR,
THE PEOPLE'S VOICE,
HELENA, MONTANA.

DEAR CAP:

. . . I do not know whether you have been following Caverly's paper. . . . If you have you will notice that Tom time and time again, has taken little pot shots at me in a rather clever way. This is obviously because he is for Mansfield for Congress. Naturally I resent it, particularly because on the basis of my record I feel I do not deserve it even for somebody like Mansfield, who is absolutely untried and has no record. . . .

If you fellows get together and decide who the liber-

al candidate for Governor is, what assurance have I that you have not already done so as far as the congressional race or any other race is concerned. From present indications, it looks pretty much to me that you have already decided on Mansfield, untried, no political experience, and God only knows what he would do if he were elected. I know he says he is a liberal, but why doesn't he run for the state legislature, show us what he's got, and then if he withstands the heat, let's give him his chance. In the face of all this, I have only one conclusion to make, and that is that your crowd has decided to write me out of the picture; if that is so then I have only one alternative, to take the situation to the rank and file of the progressive organizations, and I think you know I can do a fair job. . . .

SINCERELY YOURS,
JERRY

Three constitutional conventions dotted the history of Montana Territory. Spurred by Democratic desires to correct problems inherent in a system of territorial tutelage under a Republican Congress, an abortive convention met in Helena in 1866. Its efforts came to naught. By 1884, bipartisan support for statehood produced a second convention. In November, voters endorsed the finished product by a 4-1 margin, yet statehood was not to be. Political concensus in Montana mattered little to a politically divided Congress and Montana's second effort failed. Territorial Secretary (Acting Governor) William B. Webb described the more local, partisan considerations of statehood in a letter to Governor S. T. Hauser while the latter was absent from Montana in 1886. As it turned out, the Territory (and the Democrats) had three more years to wait.

HELENA, M.T.
JANUARY 30, 1886

MY DEAR GOVERNOR:

. . . I mail you today . . . copies of the Butte Inter Mountain on the inside page you will find marked an editorial on "Montanas Admission." The Republicans here are inclined to be angery at the Inter Mountain for giving their "snap" away. . . .

Met Broadwater on the street the other day, he professes to be violently opposed to Montanas admission at present time. Says he is doubtful if we could carry Montana just now for state officers. He also said that the increased expense of State government would largely increase taxes. Think the majority of the Dem. Central Com. and prominent Democrats out here are afraid to advocate admission as a state until we have had another general election in the Territory and find out what our party strength is, and if we should loose the first election for state officers as they did in Colorado, it would be very hard to regain it for many years. . . .

Everything is looking bright for a lively season during 1886, and through the Territory and especially in Helena the general impression seems to be one [of] extreme confidence in all branches of business. . . . Affairs in the Executive Department are moving smoothly. I have granted but two pardons during your absence. . . . The work on Penitentiary is about completed and the contractors have received their money. . . .

With very best regards for yourself. I am

SINCERELY

WM. B. WEBB

A lame duck Congress, in February, 1889, finally agreed to the "omnibus" admission of Montana and her neighboring territories. In consequence, on July 4, 1889, the Territory's third Constitutional Convention met in Helena. The body was generally harmonious, and in six weeks it had a final document ready. Again, territorial residents approved, and with the signature of President Benjamin Harrison, on November 8, 1889, Montana joined the Union. Henry Blackwell, a suffrage advocate from Boston, was on the scene to offer one of many petitions the 1889 delegates considered. He was unsuccessful. The right of suffrage fell to adult males only (county and local school elections excepted). Montana's women did not receive the right to vote until 1914.

COL. W. F. SANDERS

JULY 17, 1889

DEAR SIR:

I am here as Sec. of the American Woman Suffrage Association to ask the Const. Convn. to insert a clause: "The Legislature is empowered hereafter at its discretion to extend Suffrage to all citizens 21 years of age, of sound mind, not convicted of crime, without regard to sex."

Will you please see *Gen. Warren* who is a strong Republican friend and Judge Bickford and Mr. McAdow who are strong Democratic friends, & do what you can to help us. They have the names of 19 friends. The point is to get 19 more. I bring letters from the leading public men, copies of which I enclose.

YOURS TRULY

HENRY B. BLACKWELL

P.S. I go to Washington Territory today. Please see our friends here at once. This is *important* for if the Constitution shuts the women out without appeal to the Legislature the cause is *put back* for many years until a majority of the voters are converted to equal rights.

Statehood was by no means a cure-all for political skullduggery. In truth, the 1889 election witnessed political chicanery, charges, counter-charges — and, ultimately, an irreconcilable, partisan division of Montana's first state legislature. The controversy focused on Precinct 34 in Silver Bow County. Matt McGinnis' testimony speaks for itself on the validity of the issues. Unfortunately, investigation did not resolve the controversy. Legislation was confined to political bickering, and the state's initial legislative session was anything but positive or productive.

JANUARY 18, 1890

[I], Matt McGinnis, . . . was at work on the grade of the Northern Pacific and Montana R. R. from the 15th day of August, A.D. 1889 to the 20th day of December of the same year. [I] was present at the Precinct No. 34, the whole of election day the first day of October, A.D. 1889, [and] . . . was well acquainted with . . . J. Morrison, who was one of the Judges of the election at said precinct. . . .

During the whole . . . day and as long as the polls were open, . . . I was engaged, at the request of . . . Morrison in getting the men to go to the polls and vote the Democratic Ticket. . . . After the closing of the polls, . . . Morrison came to me and asked me to come with him into the polling place, and help him count the votes. I went with him into the store where they were going to count the ballots. There were two other men in there at the time I went in with Morrison. . . . Morrison suggested the putting of . . . paper on the windows saying that it would prevent anyone from seeing what was going on. After the paper was put on the windows and the door locked, Morrison dumped the ballots out of the ballot box, onto the table, and after carefully examining them one at a time, he set aside a large number, about fifty or sixty as near as I could judge, from the bulk of them. He took the pile up and wadded them in his hands, and at the same time said to me, "Now you keep your mouth shut about this. There is money in this for you as well as for me." Morrison then took some ballots from some that had not been used, and began stamping them with the official stamp. . . .

I then left . . . and went to bed and do not know what more was done in the matter. I voted that day at the precinct but was not registered. Morrison told me to vote in the name of a registered voter, by the name of A. Gilles, that he had gone away, and it would be all right. [He] said if I would do it that I would be well paid for doing it. So I did go into the voting place and voted the Democratic ticket. . . . I gave my name at the time I voted as A. Gilles, and my ballot was accepted without question and I saw it put in the ballot box. . . .

MAT. McGINNIS

Capital maneuverings during Montana's territorial period were almost pristine compared to the affray which arose in 1894. The prize was the permanent seat of state government and the principal contestants were Helena and Anaconda. Deep in the matrix of the contest was economic as well as political rivalry. William Andrews Clark was a financial power in Montana — a mining millionaire — and so was Marcus Daly, head of the Anaconda Copper Company. Their economic rivalry and affluence spilled beyond the confines of their corporate interests, and permeated all Montana politics. Naturally, Daly's sympathies and finances favored Anaconda as capital. Likewise, Clark rose to the challenge. No businessman or politician was exempt from the ramifications of the feud; no expense or county spared in the struggle. Missoula entrepreneur and lumber magnate A. B. Hammond discussed the campaign's status in western Montana, illustrating how local issues, like county seat fights, became means to statewide political ends.

MISSOULA, MONTANA
NOVEMBER 1, 1894

HON. S. T. HAUSER
HELENA, MONTANA

MY DEAR SIR: —

. . . I find the situation in Ravalli County very discouraging. Daly has had that thing almost entirely to himself. I think fully one-half of the voters in that county, and there are some 2000, are employed directly or indirectly by him. The republican organization also is under his control; his lawyer, Robert O'Hara, being Chairman of the County committee. Some of the oldest, and heretofore most influential citizens are canvassing the county in the interest of "Anaconda for the Capital." Some of these parties receive $5.00 per day for their services, which includes a horse and buggy. I do not consider that any work has been done in Ravalli County in the interest of Helena, so far as I could see. The registration has not even been watched at Hamilton or Darby; at least, this is the information I got on the subject.

There are three political parties in the field — Populists, Republicans and Democrats. There is also a County Seat contest going on, and, in my opinion, the only show that Helena has, is to get up a row. I believe the Populists could be induced to support Helena, as I was informed that there was much discontent in that party, because of their suspicion that Anaconda would fight their ticket. The people at Corvallis, and in that section want the County Seat. Anaconda has promised to be neutral in the contest between Corvallis and Stevensville and the Corvallis people can readily be induced to go against Anaconda in retaliation. If I was to advise your committee on this subject, I would suggest that these different elements be worked against each other in the interest of Helena, and to do this, it will require $1500.00. If you will send one or two Helena men over here to look after it, we will be glad to give them the information they need, and, if necessary, send a man with them who understands the situation fully.

In regard to Missoula County, it has been well managed up to the present time, and is in good shape, but they should have at least $3500.00 from Helena with which to finish the campaign. Now, when I say, $1500.00 and $3500.00 I mean just what I say. The Anaconda Company has probably spent $60,000.00 already in this County. Your committee sends Mr. McLeod $300.00 for the whole of Ravalli County, while they give a common healer on the streets $500.00 to do business with.

Now, in regard to your telephone message, I have this to say: Besides suffering heavy losses in our business on account of the stand we have taken in favor of Helena, we have been assisting your committee here with money. We are doing this on general principles, and will continue to do so, providing that your committee makes the proper exertions here. . . .

We will continue to do as we have been doing, providing that you send this money for Missoula and Ravalli counties; it should be here by Sunday. Of course, the greater portion of it will not be needed until the day of election. The money for Missoula County should be sent to McConnell as usual; the money for Ravalli County should probably be sent down here with a Helena man who should confer with McConnell and ourselves as to the best course to pursue.

VERY SINCERELY YOURS,

A. B. HAMMOND

Denied the vote, but far from devoid of influence, Montana's women readily took sides in the capital fight of 1894. To the political novice, the dichotomy of issues was simple: The Helena Hog vs. The Copper Collar. Women of Helena labored long in their community's behalf, financed through the largesse of Helena's supporters. After the election, Mrs. Davidson praised the efforts of her colleagues, reveled in their success, and took comfort in the just nature of Helena's cause. Unquestioned went the vast expenditures on both sides, unchallenged the fact that political spending and degradation had reached new heights.

LADIES:

. . . For the benefit of some who may have been absent, I will state that Mesdames Kirkendall, Spaulding, Curtis, N. W. McConnell, Priest and A. Kleinschmidt visited Missoula and Deer Lodge. At Missoula a Club was formed, which entered enthusiastically into the work. At Deer Lodge, no club was formed, but the women were much interested and pledged themselves to exert their personal influence. Mrs. Carter and Mrs. Lang made a tour of the Bitter Root Valley in company with Mr. Carter, and lost no opportunity of saying a word for Helena in the midst of the enemy's strongholds. . . .

Mesdames H. W. Wheeler and Nettie C. Phillips visited Basin where a Club was organized. On their return they held an informal meeting with the women of Boulder. Mesdames Kirkendall and Curtis visited Marysville to counsel with the Club already formed there. [The Howey party] visited Miles City, Billings, Livingston, Bozeman and Butte . . . via Logan. . . . [They then] proceeded to Great Falls. From there Mrs. Howey returned to her school at Lewistown, and the others returned to their homes in Helena, on Saturday Nov. 3rd. Our own Club was in existence less than five weeks, but in that time, inspired by our organization, Clubs were formed at Miles City, Livingston, Bozeman, Basin,

Missoula, White Sulphur Springs, Marysville and Sand Coulee.

You have already been informed through the papers, of the enthusiastic meetings held by our women at Basin, Miles City, Missoula, Livingston, Bozeman and Great Falls. In the other towns, they had to adapt themselves to circumstances, being largely guided by the state of public feeling, and always consulting with the Helena Capital Committees of each town. . . .

We are indebted to the Helena Capital Committee for transportation for our women on the Northern Pacific Railroad. The Northern Pacific Express Company . . . carried our packages free. The Great Northern granted us half fare. We sent from our rooms, 25,000 copies of our own circular letter, 10,000 copies of the Capital edition of the Butte Miner, 1300 copies of the Daily Herald, given us by that firm, 3500 copies of an address written by Rev. J. H. Crooker, and given to us by private parties, a speech delivered by Hon. J. K. Toole, an article by Hon. J. M. Quinn, Helena's Pay Roll, Last Appeal to voters, pamphlets &c furnished us by the Helena Capital Committee. In all, nearly 60,000 pieces of printed matter, not including our subscriptions to newspapers, which amounted to $544.16 and were mailed direct from the printing offices.

I must not forget to mention our 45,397 badges. In addition, in two days of the week preceding the election, 20,000 badges were made in our rooms for the Helena Capital Committee. . . . For our celebration, the whole decoration of the Auditorium was assigned to this Club. . . . How well [the] work was done needs no further expression as it has been universally praised. Some of our women trimmed a carriage with flowers for the use of our honored guests, which formed an attractive and unique feature of the procession. . . .

Truly the wives, mothers, and daughters have *all* aided by their presence at our rooms, by the work of their hands, and by their words of encouragement. . . . We entered upon this work, believing our cause to be just. We invoked the blessing of God, and we have daily asked His care and guidance. No matter what scoffers have said or may say we still trust our God. . . .

MRS. J. J. DAVIDSON
CHAIRMAN EXECUTIVE COMMITTEE

William Andrews Clark made a fortune extracting copper from the Butte hillsides. In 1888 he aspired to one thing more — high political office. He secured the Democratic nomination for Territorial Delegate, which, given past Democratic successes, seemed tantamount to election. Yet Clark lost. He saw in the Republican majority the sinister influence of his economic rival, Marcus Daly. The incident presaged a political donnybrook between the two which historians called "The War of the Copper Kings." It ran its rampant course through all Montana to the end of the Nineteenth Century and into the early years of the next, setting a tone of political conflict and corruption. In the Spring of 1893, Clark renewed his political aspirations. State legislatures appointed U.S. Senators and Clark sought the Montana designation. Elizabeth Chester Fisk, wife of the HELENA HERALD editor, watched the theatrics.

MARCH 5, 1893

MY DEAR MOTHER:

. . . Last week has been an exciting one, in political circles. We spent a part of two evenings at the Legislature and were also present when the final ballot was taken for U.S. Senator. It was the most exciting scene I ever witnessed. As the roll was called . . . the Senators responded to their names. When Hatch, a man whom every one supposed was a staunch Republican, an upright incorruptible man, gave his vote to W. A. Clarke the hall resounded with cheers, groans and hisses.

As the roll call proceeded and Dixon Democrats changed their votes to Clarke and five other Republicans went back on party pledges, principles & good name and also voted for him; people fairly held their breath till the official count was announced.

And still Clarke failed to receive the requisite number of votes and no maneuvering on the part of his friends could secure a second ballot. The immense Auditorium was packed from floor to ceiling. The excitement was intense. Senator Matts, a Dixon man, slowly rose and took off his overcoat, and turning faced the assembled multitude. Then he told his party what he thought of them, of their conduct for nearly sixty days, on any one of which they might have elected a Senator. You can read his speech in the Herald, but can have no idea of his manner, his face white with suppressed anger.

Then the Populists asserted themselves and they too were angry, and when the vote was taken to dissolve the joint session and the gavel fell, the wildest excitement prevailed. The renegade Republicans were publicly arraigned as traitors and charges of bribery and corruption were freely hurled.

No Senator having been elected, it became necessary for the Governor to appoint and many were the seekers for the position. Col. Sanders was anxious to be his own successor and felt, as did many of his friends, that his appointment by [Governor] Rickards would be a complete vindication of the conduct of both in regard to Precinct 34 about which we heard so much two years

ago. Tom Carter assured the Governor if he was appointed his, (the Gov.'s) political future was assured.

But Lee Mantle of Butte was the fortunate man and on Saturday noon his name was given to the people. He is a man of some ability, a self-made man, but a most immoral one. The best women of Butte do not recognize him, so open and notorious are his violations of decency. What combination, sale or bargain led to his appointment has not yet transpired. . . .

With much love,
YOUR DAUGHTER

Politically, W. A. Clark failed in his first two efforts to win a seat in Congress, but another Senatorial appointment loomed in 1899. This time Clark determined to secure the prestige of a U.S. Senatorship at any cost. John S. M. Neill was the outspoken editor of the Democratic HELENA INDEPENDENT. *Samuel Hauser's prominence in banking, mining, and Democratic politics was long-standing. For party and Clark, all things were possible — at a price, of course. Clark was willing to pay the costs, a fact well documented by Editor Neill.*

Hon. S. T. Hauser
City

HELENA, MONTANA
NOVEMBER 16, 1898

MY DEAR GOVERNOR:

I called at your office just after you had left for dinner, and realize that it will be impossible to see you before you take the train for Butte. I regret this exceedingly, because I desired to talk further with you in regard to Mr. Clark's plan of campaign.

You will recall the fact, that when we went over to see Mr. Clark last summer, he agreed to carry out the following plan on the advice of yourself, Mr. Davidson and other friends.

1ST He would contribute the necessary amount of money to carry the primaries.

2ND If we should then come to him and say that we had been successful in controlling the delegates to a sufficient number of county conventions, that he would then contribute the necessary funds for these various nominees for the legislature to make their canvass with.

3RD If after election, we should say that we had elected a sufficient number of members who stood a reasonable chance of being opposed to Mr. Daly, that he would contribute further funds for the purpose of "holding them in line."

The primary and election are both over. As you know, Mr. Clark contributed every dollar that was

necessary for us to have. So far as general results are concerned, we have won a sweeping victory. We now come down to the third proposition, and it is for Mr. Clark himself to say whether or not he will go to the United States Senate this winter. If his campaign is properly managed, and backed up financially, he can go, and you know it.

I would suggest that we put forward Mr. E. C. Day of Lewis and Clarke County as the anti-Daly candidate for speaker. It would be necessary that some one *at once* should cover the State for the interest ostensibly of Mr. Day for speaker, but wherever he succeeds in securing a sure vote for *Day* for speaker the same man should be able to also influence this same member to cast his vote for Mr. Clark for the U.S. Senate, and if necessary, should then and there give this member the first installment of "expense money."

It would be well to impress upon the mind of Mr. Clark that he entrust his campaign to as few as possible, that he have one principal confidential man, and only one. We can not manage this campaign without a head. In order to be in shape to win, we must win the speakership fight, and in order to commence our campaign, we must bend every effort to win our speaker. Having succeeded in this, the fight is half won.

VERY TRULY YOURS,

JNO. S. M. NEILL

Money bought William A. Clark not only selection to the U.S. Senate, but also trouble. His financial high handedness with Montana's legislators ultimately provoked a U.S. Senate inquiry into his fitness for office. Before an investigating committee, Clark and Marcus Daly traded charges and countercharges. Sliced clean of personal animosities, the episode illustrated deep corruption in Montana politics. The Senate finally judged Clark unfit to join the august body. In an impassioned speech, Clark resigned his seat and defended his honor. He did more. Through some not-so-subtle manipulation, he arranged to have himself reappointed to fill the vacancy his resignation created. Wilbur Fisk Sanders outlined this phase of chicanery in the letter below. Even the most staid solons were aghast at the treachery. Summarily they denied the Montana millionaire his seat once more and the state's congressional delegation was without one Senator until the next election. More effectively this time, Clark relaid his groundwork. Montana's legislature appointed him a second time in 1901. Clark finally won public office, but Montana's political morality lost once again.

My Dear Sir: May 19, 1900

I take advantage of a brief lull in the comedy or travesty of our senatorial escapade to write you the situation. . . .

The Governor and Lieutenant-Governor of this state were elected by the Populists and Democrats, they both having been placed on the ticket as Populists. The Governor, heretofore and now identified with the Democratic party, and I presume the Lieutenant Governor pretending to be a Republican. The Lieutenant Governor has been understood to be a friend of the Clarks, and he was manager of the Ruby mine, which belonged to the Clark Bros. . . . You probably are aware that he has been a month or two in Washington City, having spent that time in the early part of this year in the interests of Mr. Clark. Thomas Hinds also spent some time there, he also being an active supporter of Senator Clark, and his reward for that service (as is usually done in Butte) being the taking of leases of mining ground from the bribers, which pay large profits to those thus bribed. . . .

From the beginning of the controversy (certainly since the adoption by your committee of the report) some of us have believed that Mr. Clark would escape the castigation by resigning; but all his friends in Montana, and the newspapers owned and controlled by him, have stoutly affirmed that he would never resign, and have repeatedly published alleged interviews by special dispatch and associated press reports, that he would not resign. Under date of May 12th a dispatch was sent to the Montana press, and published in Montana papers, stating that he emphatically denied that he would resign. This dispatch was given great significance by the Helena Independent, published at the Capital, and controlled and doubtless owned by Senator Clark, who has upon it a

mortgage of more than it is worth. . . . This is dated the day on which he says he sent in his resignation, but it is published in Montana the following morning.

The letter of resignation, signed by Mr. Clark was not sent by the ordinary avenues of correspondence, but was brought from Butte by Chas. W. Clark and E. L. Whetmore, Mr. Clark's son and hired man, whom you will doubtless remember. An examination of the letter of resignation shows that the date, May 11th was printed thereon with other type and ink from that of the body of the letter, and a close inspection of the head line shows clearly, I am advised, that the word "April" and the figures indicating a date, had been erased, and May 11th printed thereover. . . .

Sitting in the Silver Bow Club on the Evening of the 18th inst., Charles W. Clark, in company with Mr. Whetmore, joined our coterie, whereupon Gen. Chas. S. Warren . . . addressing Mr. Clark, said: "Charlie, you tell Jack Hoey not to show that telegram which he had from Tom Hinds." Whereupon Mr. C. W. Clark asked him "why not?", to which he replied that it showed collusion, whereupon Mr. Clark said "All right". Subsequently I met General Warren, and he told me that Mr. Jack Hoey had shown him the closing paragraph of a telegram from Tom Hinds from Grass Valley, California, in which he had telegraphed to Mr. Hoey, who was his partner and confidential friend, that he had landed his fish, or words to that effect, understood and intended to be a boast that he had lured the Governor out of the State at the pivotal and agreed time. . . .

The Lieutenant Governor was a delegate to the Populist Convention at Sioux Falls, and went to the Omaha dinner, and Sioux Falls. He remained at Sioux Falls long enough to hear the convention called to order, and then started for home, arriving here May 11th, on the same day on which Clark's letter of resignation is dated. . . . I do not personally know, but am told that he came home responsive to a telegram sent him. The letter of resignation was delivered personally to the Lieutenant Governor by Chas. W. Clark, probably Tuesday noon, and Tuesday night at 8 o'clock, the Lieut-Governor mailed his certificate of appointment of Mr. Clark, and wrote him a letter urging him to reconsider his determination to eschew public life, and enter upon the discharge of public duties, as I am advised.

Every circumstance of this transaction brands it as a conspiracy, for however far apart were the actors, their actions dovetail into each other with such minuteness as to show concerted action, and it does not seem possible that all these coincidences could have occurred accidentally. . . .

W. F. SANDERS

Newspapers provided significant avenues to public sentiment. William Andrews Clark realized this and used the columns of his BUTTE MINER without hesitation to vilify Marcus Daly and the Anaconda Copper Company following his first political defeat in 1888. The lesson was not lost on Daly. In 1889 he established the ANACONDA STANDARD to vent his views. As in all things, Daly bought the best, including Dr. John H. Durston, editor. Soon the STANDARD was among the best in western journalism as well as the public organ of the Anaconda Company. Whatever the issue — Montana's capital or Clark's candidacy — Daly used the STANDARD to express his ideas. When F. Augustus Heinze interloped amid the confrontation of copper magnates, it was only expected that Daly's opinions and frustrations would flow through the pen of John Durston. Heinze's style included corrupt judges (William Clancy and E. W. Harney, to be specific) and courts cluttered with nuisance litigation designed to constrict Anaconda profits. He had his own paper, too — THE REVEILLE. The anti-Heinze campaign which Daly inaugurated continued unabated after his death in November, 1900. Standard Oil's Amalgamated Copper Company succeeded Daly in control of Anaconda and the contest with Heinze. In 1906, ten million dollars purchased Heinze's interests and removed his nuisance from Butte mining and Montana politics. It was just another installment in the saga of boodle and ballot — Montana politics.

MR. J. H. DURSTON,
WASHINGTON, D. C.

NEW YORK
JANUARY 19, 1900.

DEAR SIR: —

Send word to Walsworth to have a talk with Scallon and then go to work getting in readiness to write up the history of Heinze in Butte, showing that he is a black-mailer, a thief and a most dangerous and harmfull man to the business and property interests of Butte. Have him go through the whole story, from Heinze's first suit with Jim Murray, tell how he took leases on mines adjoining good properties with the deliberate intent of using their workings only as a means of stealing ore from adjoining mines. Then tell of the Boston & Montana receivership case, his numerous injunctions, preventing the working of valuable properties, then and I think this should be made the basis of the main attack, tell of the closing of the Anaconda Mine under Clancy's order in the "Copper Trust" lode case, and show the possibilities that might follow his operations, based in every case entirely on blackmail, attempted intimidation and robbery, and not in a single instance on legitimate business reasons. Take up Judge Clancy then, and the manner in which he has violated all dignity and honesty of his official position at the bidding and command of Heinze, and particularly in the "Copper Trust" decision. Make the denunciation of his methods as definite and scathing as is possible. . . .

You should certainly remain in Washington as long as you feel you can accomplish anything. The long fight has reached the decisive battle and this is the crisis. The case is strong, and impressive on testimony already given. Now, my idea is that we should make every effort to force it through as rapidly as we can while it is in its full strength and before it gets stale and any possible political changes occur that they might trade on. . . .

YOURS TRULY,

MARCUS DALY

P.S.   I fully agree with your idea of writing up the 1893 campaign. Can't you get some of those fierce attacks the Inter Mountain made on Clark at that time, accusing him of bribing members of the Legislature away from Mantle. It seems to me they would be good stuff. . . . They certainly would go a long way to show the Clark methods, and discredit his talk of persecution. . . .

photo by A. J. Lawson

PORTRAIT IN DIVERSITY

ARAH RAYMOND introduced formal education to Montana in Virginia City's Union Church and Thomas Francis Meagher drowned at Fort Benton. Marshal Thomas Irvine watched the ice skaters and whores in Miles City, and Hum Fay defended his rights in Butte. All these people were Montanans. Each immigrant, each resident, reflected both unique personal contributions and the new amalgam that was Montana life and culture. Changes were many and dynamic in Montana between 1864 and the Twentieth Century. From the milieu of Indians, immigrants and infant industry consolidated by Congress into a territory, to the proud and prosperous state of 1900, one trait predominated — diversity. Indeed, the only characteristic that always stood out in Montana's society was its conglomerate nature.

Mineral rushes lured fortune seekers as different in background and scattered in origin as the gulches they inhabited. A few came to settle, more came to extract what riches they could and return to "the states." Some tried to import eastern values and culture; others sought escape from them. If consistency existed it was only in the opportunity frontier Montana presented to all comers. Failure and disillusionment turned or returned many. Death, too, punctuated each era. Those who stayed — or survived — built Montana, gave it color, character, and culture. Indian, Oriental, "secesh," saint, pioneer, coward — each touched Montana, leaving a social montage defying generalization.

Extant records of life in Nineteenth Century Montana vary greatly. Too many visitors and residents left no trace. Others left only a rotting cabin frame, an unmarked grave, or an empty glass on a long-forgotten bar. A minority kept diaries, made speeches, preserved letters, took photographs, and composed memoirs. By default, the task of chronicling Montana's heritage for its literate progeny fell on the few authors of the pioneer era.

Assembled, the parts and pieces filled Montana's frame, but the picture presented little continuity. Montanans made their fortunes, mitigated their failures, met their futures, in a land as diverse as the experiences they brought to it, as different as the records and heritage they left for it.

FOURTH OF JULY PARADE, HELENA, C. 1900

PORTRAIT IN DIVERSITY
Life and Culture in the 19th Century

Schools, public and private, gave a community stability and permanence in the frontier perspective. The school district, companion to the mining district, formed a basic unit in territorial government — significant beyond the walls of the classroom. Sarah Raymond arrived in Virginia City on September 5, 1865, after a venturesome trek from Missouri. Her courage and sense of adventure sustained her the following spring when she opened the first public school in the territory. Her first class consisted of fifty to sixty unruly students of all ages. In the classroom she encountered discipline problems and a paucity of textbooks; but during her brief tenure she earned the community's esteem. She left the "tedious tiresome life of a school teacher" in 1867 to become the bride of James Herndon, an early and successful Virginia City merchant.

THURSDAY, JANUARY 25, 1866 — . . . I have applied for the female department in the district school in this city. Mr. Willard is one of the trustees & I think he will do all he can for me yet I shall be kept in suspense until I know whether or not I succeed. . . .

FEBRUARY 5, 1866 — . . . Mr. Willard called this eve & told the welcome news that I would be employed to teach the school. Oh! I feel so grateful for his efforts in my behalf, shall endeavor to prove my gratitude & hope he may never regret aiding me in getting a start. . . .

FEBRUARY 7, 1866 — . . . They have offered me the School but I do not like the terms & hardly think I will accept. . . .

FEBRUARY 23, 1866 — . . . Mr. W [Willard] says the school commissioner will be here tomorrow to examine me, preparatory to my opening the district school, says they will want the school to commence the first Monday in March. How I long for the examination to be over with & yet how I dread his coming! What would I do if I should fail to get a certificate, I should die with mortification.

FEBRUARY 24, 1866 — Mr. Thrasher — the commissioner — has been here. I have passed through the trying ordeal & come out Successful. Mr. T. seemed well pleased with my qualifications, complimented me by saying that I passed a good examination, that I did exceedingly well. Oh! I am so glad it is over with, don't think I shall ever dread it again as I have. . . .

FEBRUARY 26, 1866 — . . . Bought some gingham to make me a sunbonnet to wear to school. They are to pay me $125 per month for teaching. Will open the school next Monday. . . .

MARCH 5, 1866 — An eventful day. The Legislature met today. . . . I opened the district school, had over fifty pupils, & the worst set of children I ever saw or heard tell of. Am almost afraid that I never can bring them under subjection. We were expecting Mr. Thompson to take the male department but as he didn't come, I had to send for Mrs. Farley to come & assist me this afternoon. . . .

MARCH 6, 1866 — Another days work is done & I feel as tired as if I had been mining, yet I feel contented for I know that something has been accomplished to-day. The children did some better than yesterday, feel somewhat encouraged. . . .

MARCH 9, 1866 — One weeks work is done. My school has improved very much, had a real good, attentive & obedient school today. Had a spelling match this afternoon, came home very tired, feel as though I can scarcely move. . . .

MARCH 10, 1866 — . . . I was introduced to Miss Bell today — the lady who is to help me. Like her appearance very much but feel sorry for Mrs. F [Farley] for she really wanted the situation. Miss Bell is to go in on an equal footing with me & help bear the responsibility. . . .

MAY 28, 29, 30, 1866 — Oh, this tedious tiresome life of a school teacher, I know I was born for something better. Sometimes I have tried to persuade myself I like it — but it is no use. I am tired to death of it. What merit is there in being a good school teacher? None whatever & if there was I would not obtain any as I am situated at present, for although I am certain that the success of our school is wholly owing to my own persevering energy, Miss Bell seems to claim & receive all the merit. Well I don't care, she is welcome to all the praise for I think there is but little honor attached to a pedegogues career. I feel tired & lonely this evening. . . . Oh this is such a lovely moonlight night. I am writing by the light of the moonbeams, which are shining full upon me as I sit by the window and are helping to dispell the cloud that was overshadowing my heart.

Andrew J. Fisk and his three brothers led a wagon train from Minnesota to Last Chance Gulch during the spring and summer of 1866. As a young bachelor, A. J. Fisk availed himself of the community's many social activities — including the young ladies. Working on the staff of the HELENA HERALD, *he became involved in the rudiments of newspaper printing, community development, and Territorial politics. He saw in Montana not only the opportunity for advancement, but also the prospects for permanence and a new home.*

OCTOBER 5 — [1866] — Was up to Helena City today. It is not so large a place as I thought it was — but it is the busiest place I ever saw. They have also got a good many fine buildings and one splendid Stone building is in the course of construction. The streets are very narrow. There are a good many Chinese there and all of them (I guess) wash clothes for a living. . . . Invested in several glasses of "Light Beer" 25 cts. In fact they don't look at a fellow for less than 25 cts. Peaches are 50 cts. a piece. The fruit came from Salt Lake. I saw good horses and saddles sold at auction for $40.00. Most all of our boys got pretty good places to work. Ed Owen has jumped a claim and I think of going in with him mining. Potatoes are 3 cents a piece. Green apples are $1.00 per pound. Billiards 75 cts. per game. Almost as warm as summer today.

OCTOBER 7 — . . . This afternoon we went uptown to see the sights. Sunday is the great day here. The town was thronged. Auction store every ten feet — and every auctioneer trying to call the loudest. Any amount of miners drink but must say they were very peacable. Played several games of Billiards — just to see how it would go. . . . In the evening I went around to the several "hurdy gurdys" or "dance houses" where for the sum of $1.00 in funds you could have the pleasure of dancing with a girl and the whiskey thrown in. I did not invest. . . .

NOVEMBER 16 — "The Helena Herald" — first issue — R. Emmett Fisk Editor — came out today — printed on brown paper — and it looked very well *considering*. They expect their paper from Salt Lake next week. . . .

NOVEMBER 17 — . . . Bro. Bob had a regular row down town this evening — concerning a "local" in the paper. He cleaned out a couple of "roughs" handsomely. Bob's face is scratched up some. . . .

FEBRUARY 2 — [1867] — . . . Attended a concert this evening in the Court Room. . . . The room was full — a number of Ladies were present — and the singing was quite a success. Weather changing — getting colder. . . .

FEBRUARY 3 — Spent a pleasant afternoon up home. This evening I attended Gen. T. F. Meagher's Lecture at the Theatre building. Text — "Personal recollections of the Irish Brigade." It dident amount to a great deal. He related some laughable jokes, but that was about all. He had a full house. . . .

FEBRUARY 4 — The Chinese "New Years" is today — and this holliday continues for a week. They are having a big time, celebrating on the 4th of July principle — on a small scale. . . .

APRIL 19 — Still the old cry — no Eastern mail. A slight sprinkle of rain this forenoon. This evening we manufactured about 12 lbs of Printers Ink. We were entirely out. Our case we ordered from Salt Lake not yet having arrived. The job was a nasty one, but it was a success. It is composed of Lamp black, linseed oil, rosin, japan & soap.

APRIL 20 — We tried our Ink today and it did not work according with our anticipation. It clogged up the type after a few impressions. We found a recipe in Ure's dictionary for making printers Ink & we have partly made up a large batch of it. It is a very nasty, dirty job. . . .

APRIL 22 — We finished our Ink today by grinding it or putting it through a paint mill. It is a perfect success — better, if anything, than our Salt Lake Ink, which arrived last night along with a very, small Eastern mail. No letters. . . . I drank nearly two glasses of vinegar this afternoon — for cider. I got hold of the wrong bottle & thought it queer cider. . . .

JULY 3 — The Benton Coach in this morning brought the news of the drowning of Gen. Thomas Francis Meagher on the night of the 1st inst. He had been on board one of the Steamers to visit some of his friends, got on a spree, went to bed, was heard to get up and go out on the guards. A splash was heard and the once brilliant and brave man was seen no more. Another victim of whiskey. . . .

JULY 4 — Well, we have celebrated the 4th of July in a sort of a fashion — and, altogether, had a very pleasant day. O'Brien & I went out to the Hot Springs, took a bath, had a good dinner, came back to the race course, saw a race for $200 in greenbacks between Travis horse and young Eaves' mare. They came out so closely that the judges could not agree or at least had not when we left about 5 P.M. . . .

January 1 — [1869] — A Happy New Year. Helena, Montana. The weather delightfully cool — say down about to zero. . . . A large but select party at John Ming's tonight. Went down the Valley and brought up Miss Sallie Hill. Excellent sleighing, and a pleasant drive with an agreeable partner. . . .

JANUARY 2 — The party last night was An occasion that will be treasured up for many a coming New Year. Danced till quite 3 o'clock. Dancing waltz on a Brussel's carpet was a pleasant novelty. This afternoon I took Miss Sallie home. . . .

THURSDAY, JUNE 10 — THE POST IS DEAD! *After 14 months of bitter fighting, we have cleaned them out! Glory enough for one day!* They came out in an editorial this morning and threw up the sponge.

JANUARY 4 — [1871] — . . . Worked on the books all day. After the "Weekly" was *up* this evening, I dropped in at the "Theatre Comique" to witness the wonderful contortion feats of Mme. Forrestell. She is the best performer I ever saw, and her feats astounded everybo[d]y present and the house was *jammed*. . . .

FEBRUARY 22 — The masquerade ball last night was the grandest affair of the kind I ever attended. My disguise as an Indian was complete, and I received many compliments for the manner in which I carried out the character. My partner, Hattie, was not very well disguised, but was tastefully and elegantly dressed in blue silk. I think I never enjoyed myself so much before in one night's dancing. The ball broke up at 5 o'clock a.m. Bro. Van was there. . . .

MARCH 25 — . . . The petition, which I put in four weeks ago, to join the Masons, was voted upon in the regular meeting to-night, and I was duly elected. Will probably take the first degree some evening next week. . . .

MARCH 26 — This forenoon I had four more cavities filled. Was three long hours in the Dentist's chair. This afternoon, I attended the wedding of Ike Greenhood and Miss Sallie Abrahams, at the residence of Felix Poznanisky. The ceremony was first performed in Hebrew, according to the Jewish faith, and then by a Justice of the Peace. Both bride and groom shed copious tears. The supper was very fine, and champaign abundant. This evening attended a sort of a Sunday School Exhibition or concert at the M.E. Church. . . .

JULY 4 — This is America's great NATIONAL HOLIDAY! Of course, we issued no paper. This afternoon I went out to the Fair Grounds to see the races. They were rather exciting. Broadwater's horse won the trotting race, and "Reuben" the running race. About 600 people were on the grounds. This evening I took Hattie and Clara Wilcox to the Strawberry Festival, at the Masonic Hall, for the benefit of the Helena Library Association. It was a grand success, and we had a big time — you bet!! Five years ago to-day I was killing buffaloes on James River, in Dakota. . . .

SEPTEMBER 11 — This afternoon I called on Mr. Rumley, and told him that Miss Hattie had promised to be my wife — subject to the consent of her parents — and that I had come to ask his consent to our engagement. We had a long talk together. He assured me that he had no objection whatever to me, but that he thought Hattie too young — almost a child, in fact. But he would have a talk with Mrs. Rumley . . . and would give me an answer soon. . . .

SEPTEMBER 13 — This afternoon I called at Hattie's and had a two hours talk with Mrs. Rumley. I cannot give here even an outline of all that was said. But the main thing was this: If Hattie and I were positive that we each dearly loved the other, she would place no obstacle in the way of our marriage — though it would be a great trial to part with Hattie so young. I told her that I desired to marry in four or six months. Altogether it was a pleasant and satisfactory interview. . . .

OCTOBER 14 — To-night, on the road to Church, I placed an engagement ring upon Hattie's finger. We expect to get married about the first of next March.

Preachers went west too. They assembled congregations when and where they could, rode circuit over vast territories, marrying or burying, as necessary. Initially, most early ministers joined the rushes for reasons of personal callings — gold or God. As communities took on permanence, several denominations appointed ministers. At 29, Daniel S. Tuttle became Episcopal Bishop of Montana, Idaho, and Utah. He left a wife and baby in New York, traveled west, and held his first western religious service for a few hundred miners in Virginia City in 1867. Living in a small, one-room cabin situated on a hill above the school, Tuttle composed his sermons, passed lonely hours comforted only by his cat, Dick, and wrote his wife about his successes and failures.

SUNDAY, JAN. 5, 1868

MY OWN DEAR WIFE,

Oh be joyful of the "beautiful day" and mild weather. Last night and today have been stingingly cold. I havn't yet heard report from a thermometer, but Mr. Davis thinks it is 30 below zero. Crazy I (as usual) slept with open window last night, & under my buffalo skin, & this morning when I woke, half of my cabin floor was covered with snow that had blown in, and the water in my tin pail was solid.

Mr. Davis . . . said I wouldnt have to preach today, for no one would come, & to carry out his prediction of course, he didn't come. But at the usual time I went down & . . . began service & preached the sermon on "Here a little & there a little" that I wrote last week. . . . The congregation numbered less than twenty. A collection was made for parish expenses amounting, I think I heard Mr. Everts say, to more than eighteen dollars. We are to be turned out of our "Reception Hall." Where we are to worship next Sunday I know not. I gave notice this morning that "Announcement of the place of worship for next Sunday will be made in Saturday's paper." . . .

3½ P.M. Sunday School is over. It grows no warmer. My window is so frosted that I can't see out. . . . Only three teachers & eleven children were in S.S. Judge Lovell, I am sorry to say, is still continuing his "New Year's" & keeps drinking. My heart is very sad for this. His wife seems almost disheartened. . . . Mr. Gostling has taken the Library books to arrange & inscribe & is going to be Librarian & open for the scholars next Sunday. . . .

Alas! Alas! it does seem as if there [is] nothing human for me to lean upon or stay up myself or . . . work with here. Maybe God means it exactly thus that we may be compelled to remember that all power & goodness comes of Him, & all glory sh'd be returned to Him. . . .

Friday I wrote on my sermon. . . . & dined (!) & spent the eve. at Dr. Gibson's. We dined off a huge & delicious (Mormon) turkey that had been sent up from Salt Lake by Anthony Godbe. The guests were about a dozen. . . . In the eve. I had my delightful two-dollar bath as usual. . . .

I AM YOUR LOVING AFFECTIONATE

HUSBAND

Elizabeth Chester married Robert Emmett Fisk in March, 1867, and migrated to Helena, where Robert managed Montana's leading Republican newspaper, the HELENA HERALD. Upon arriving, Elizabeth shared the excitement of the bustling frontier city and the hard work of her husband's publishing business. Burgeoning frontier towns, like Helena, quickly took on the vestments of eastern urban society. This hurry and culture appealed to the young bride and she soon found herself avidly exchanging social calls with other young matrons. The arrival of "Baby Grace" in 1869 restricted Elizabeth's time and her enthusiasm for cultural amenities. Her impatience of January 6, 1871 proved shortlived, however, for during her forty years in Helena, Mrs. Fisk participated readily in affairs of her church and community.

JANUARY 6TH, 1871

MY DEAR MOTHER:

I did not attempt to receive calls on New Year's. Our house is so small and inconvenient and I did not feel

as if we could well afford the expense to say nothing of the trouble. Two or three of my friends came in, notwithstanding closed doors and darkened rooms. They were not easily frightened, they said.

Receiving calls is a good deal of a farce, under any circumstances. The very people you are most anxious to see are sure not to come and a troop of those for whom you care nothing come in and eat your cake and drink your coffee and never come near you again for a whole year. Such is life — I am a little bit tired of it. I feel as if I would like to come home and rest. People here are growing so dreadfully stylish, nothing but a velvet cloak and silk dress is suitable for a calling costume and I will not have such things till we can afford them.

Yesterday I scrubbed my kitchen floor on my hands and knees. I usually get a Chinaman or darkey to do it for me but this time I thought I would save the fifty or seventy five cents. I felt poor. I had just finished when there came a knock at the front door of which baby apprised me in her noisy way.

I threw off my big apron, pulled down my sleeves and opening the door presented myself to the gaze of Mrs. and Miss Chumasero in their velvet cloaks and hats, handsome furs, spotless kids and elegant dresses. Didn't

I feel the contrast and for a minute consign them in my thoughts to some other place.

However I ushered them in, told them this was one of my busy days in the kitchen, of which every housekeeper found some, and then I talked as well as I knew how to atone for the soiled dress and flushed face. Baby had been helping me and did not look very nice and it is my aim to have her always clean. She had cut her fingers on a broken toy and daubed her face, dress, and white apron with blood.

These are the times when I long for a [maid]. When I go east I shall bring a girl back with me. I think I could keep her for six months perhaps, before some nice young man discovered her charm and enticed her away. Then I might make arrangements with parties in the east to send me another as soon as the first one married and so establish a sort of colonization society.

How easy to do all these things on paper. . . .

Love for father and self from

L. C. FISK

Fires erupted with disastrous frequency in the wood and timber mining camps of the western frontier. Helena, with its mountain gulch setting, was no exception. On January 9, 1874, the most devastating of a series of fires leveled most of the business district along Last Chance Gulch. Wilbur Fisk Sanders was absent the day it happened, attending the 8th Regular Session of the Territorial Legislature in Virginia City. He left behind not only his personal books and papers, but the entire Montana Historical Society collection for which he was trustee. The fire destroyed everything. Hattie Sanders saved what she could and then sat down to tell her husband the extent of his losses.

HOME
JANUARY 9, 1874, 10 A.M.

MY DEAR:

What I have been through this morning I cannot tell. As soon as I got up I sent Jimmie to see where the fire was, he came back and said on upper Main Street. I then put on my things, did not wait to comb my hair and went to your office. The International [Hotel] and Travis' stable were all on fire. I ran up the stairs quicker than ever before and took off my shawl, spread it on the floor and put all the papers that were in the pigeon holes in the large room and most of the papers out of the drawers and got a man to bring them to the house.

Then I told Jimmie to bring some books in his arms and I took two. We had no time to do anything more for the men told us that we must not stay longer. The fire went so quickly that people had no time to save their own and there was no one to help us. Mr. Cullen came in and told me not to take one thing out of the office for it would

not go he thought. I told him I would take the papers and the books I must leave.

When we came down the awnings were falling in all directions and it was with difficulty that we could get through. I had no time to ask what were your more valuable books and caught two and Jimmie two. You will think we might have brought more but I could hardly walk with what I had. The wind — I think I never saw it blow harder.

All there is left of your fine library is "Brightly's Digest, 1787-1857," "United States Digest," "Vol. 11 Equity Digest," and "Bishop on Criminal Law," Vol. 1 and 2.

We made coffee and I took a large pitcher of coffee and bread and butter . . . down to Hall & Hagadorn's for the poor firemen, they were nearly dead, for none of them had had breakfast. Mrs. Fisk and Mrs. Bromley took down coffee too. Ben Dittes brought us home. We made more coffee and baked biscuit and all the ladies made coffee, they came for it in wagons and took it down for the men. When we were coming home we saw that Gen. Blaine's house was on fire from sparks, there was no water and the men were obliged to leave it. Poor Mrs. Blaine. I had not thought till then that we should burn, but then I felt sure, for the wind was fearful and the flying sparks and cinders were thick as hail and the smoke was dreadful. Every minute or two new fires were discovered all about. I came home and the boys and I took everyone of your American Cyclopedias across the gulch [Dry] and over the hill out of danger. I packed nearly everything, tied up the bedding.

Now the fire is over I am only too thankful to have a house to unpack in. Mr. Johnson came up to breakfast. I asked him to telegraph to you for me that your papers were saved. He said that all the clothes he had were on his back. He did not save anything, he thought they would not burn till it was too late to save them. He put his [surveying] instruments in Fox & Lyster's (Bank) and they were all burned. I am so sorry that your library is gone, but just think of others that are so much worse off. Was your library insured at all? . . .

We are all well and have a home, and it might be a great deal worse than it is, so don't be discouraged. Mrs. Sands sent her piano, all her wardrobe, all of her jewelry and everything to a fireproof [building] and everything was burned. Johnny Ward only has his clothes; put his watch in a trunk and it was burned. . . .

FROM YOUR LOVING WIFE,

HATTIE

Cornelius Hedges came to Montana with degrees from Yale and Harvard, and a tenacious belief in the advantages of New England education and culture. During his tenure as Superintendent of Schools for Montana from 1872 to 1878, and again between 1882 and 1885, Hedges worked hard to transplant his standards on the rough territory. His influence on the development of formal education in Montana was profound. He firmly believed his duties required him to travel the territory for at least three months a year, visiting schools, consulting county superintendents, and addressing public assemblies on subjects pertaining to schools. He received $1,200 a year in salary, and $300 for travel expenses. The financial support was minimal, the reception warm, the results prodigious.

NOVEMBER 9 — [1872] — Started at 6 for Deer Lodge, Wheeler was company. . . .

NOVEMBER 10 — SUNDAY — Got up at 3 and took the stage to Missoula. Jack Robinson was company. Weather was stormy & cold & I didn't see [as] much of the country as I expected. Snowed furiously some of the time & way. Reached Missoula about 8 in evening. . . .

NOVEMBER 11 — Spent day making calls & acquaintances, much of time with McCormick. Stormed all day & growing colder. Went with [County] Supt. Dickinson to visit the schools in town; found two, one private & one public — Miss Weedon, teacher.

Tuesday, 12 — . . . Lectured at Court House in evening on School matters — Had a fair audience & severe headache. Went afterwards to Worden's store with McCormick, Knowles & Jack Demars & had champagne & talked Rail Road. . . .

THURSDAY, 14 — Weather extremely cold. . . . Spent most of day at McCormicks writing article on schools for publication. . . .

FRIDAY, 15 — . . . Up & off at 3. . . . Suffered from cold feet in first part of the journey — crowded & cold all the way. Dr. Mitchell got aboard at mouth of Bear. Reached Deer Lodge at 11½ after a hard trip.

SATURDAY, 16 — Went around with Prof. Smith to see school room & new school house. . . . Took dinner at his house & spent afternoon with three school marms: Smith, Reznor, & Lawrence. . . .

TUESDAY, 19 — Up and started at 6, not so severely cold. . . . At Blackfoot several more came aboard & we were badly crowded afterwards. Got home soon after 4 oclock. . . . My trip cost me $87 including $6 for pioneer & $15 paid for my bill at Hotel. . . .

MONDAY, DECEMBER 9 — Started on my school visiting tour, rode outside with driver & heard his stories of mining life & Indian experiences. Got off at Hills. . . . Visited school, Miss Sechorra and Mrs. Addis. Rode up on Robt. Tucker's horse to Jefferson. Visited school there, took supper with Mrs. Putnam. Lectured in evening, had a good houseful.

TUESDAY, 10 — Staid over night at Merrimans, left at 10½, Deegan & another aboard. Dined at Cooks, reached Whitehall & staid over night. Rev. Sanford bedfellow, snored.

WEDNESDAY, 11 — Started at 5, rode to Fish Ck., got there early — visited school taught by Miss Jourdan. Lectured in store in the evening. . . .

SATURDAY, 14 — Spent night on floor in parlor with D. H. Weston. . . . We got up at 2½, to breakfast & start. I was alone to Argenta, very cold & sleepy. Got to Arg. at day light. C. G. Hall teaches school. Stoped two hours, called at Smiths. Started for Ban [nack] 9½. . . Ride very cold, most froze when I got in, didnt get dinner till 3. . . . Called in evening on Mr. and Mrs. Taylor, teacher, elegant educated lady. Ball in Masonic Hall in honor of Fred Peck & Con Bray going to states. Got to bed at 12.

SUNDAY, 15 — Poor Bed but slept well. Took breakfast about 10. Walked out to Plummers gallows & Grave. Heard Hugh Duncan preach. . . . Spent evening at Masonic Hall till late. Had bed to myself. . . .

MONDAY, 16 — Visited school till 11 o'clock. Rode over to Argenta with Duncan, stopped at French's. Spent

evening with Hall & hearing Duncan preach. Had a terrible cold bed. Lay & shivered all night. . . .

WEDNESDAY, 18 — Rode over to Sheridan. . . . Visited school. Rode to Virginia in afternoon & put up at Crescent Hotel. Got no letters from home. . . .

THURSDAY, 19 — Got pants mended $1. Called at office of Montanian, paid $6.00 subscription. Called on Gov. & Rogers. Visited Marshall school in afternoon. . . .

FRIDAY, 20 — Visited school again fore & afternoon. Lectured in even. at Council Chamber. Audience not large, Good Templars overhead made much confusion. . . .

WEDNESDAY, 25 — Met James King on way to States. Maj. Brooks [at Whitehall] treated us all to egg nog. Changed vehicles to lumber wagon. Hard riding but good driver. Fair dinner at Beavertown. Four passengers got on at Jefferson & it became awfully crowded — passengers fell off. Reached Helena about 7½ took supper at Bazaar. Found Wilson & spent rest of night reading letters. So went Christmas for 1872.

Alma Coffin and two of her sisters left St. Paul, Minnesota, on July 6, 1878, to join their father in a remote Montana mountain town. Arriving in Glendale a month later, the three young ladies proved a welcome addition to the predominantly male camp. As for the girls, they were agog with the excitement of living in a beehive of mining activity. Not only was the bustle of the community attractive, but social prospects were inviting. Glendale's opera house hosted Maguire's troupes from Butte once a week while local churches and private homes provided settings for endless socials. That fall Alma Coffin moved to the Beaverhead Valley to teach school. She spent the rest of her life in Montana, always with pleasant memories of her first adventures in Glendale.

SEPTEMBER 1, 1879

Glendale, the mining camp in which our father lived, and the destination of our long journey of a month, is located in the northeastern part of Beaverhead County, . . . on Trapper creek, a small branch which flows into the Big Hole river. . . .

At Glendale [are] located many of the buildings of the Hecla Mining Company including the smelter, a large roaster, office, assay office, warehouse, blacksmith shop, sack-house, iron house, powder houses, coal sheds, stables, and dwellings for the officials. The Hecla Hospital, a clean up-to-date institution [is] also located here, in this seemingly out-of-the-way place.

Glendale has one main street winding up a gulch and a number of little frame houses and log cabins scattered along the stony hillside. The only vegetation is the

prickly pear cactus and a scant growth of low bushes, excepting the willows on the creek which tumbles down the bottom of the narrow gulch.

The smelter gives employment to the community. It reduces the copper and silver ore brought down by freight wagons from the Trapper Mountain mines nine miles above.

Noah Armstrong, the Superintendent, was formerly a resident of Mankato, Minnesota. Having known him there, father decided upon Glendale as his destination when he came to Montana in 1877. Father is building a little two-room house on the hillside. We shall have to go to Virginia City, fifty miles away, for a cook stove and furniture. Meanwhile we are boarding in the home of Phineas Mathews and his widowed mother whom we knew in South Bend, Minnesota.

There are more than a hundred working men about town. Those who have families in the "States" expect either to send for them or to return home. The young men are usually hustling, ambitious fellows, eager to make a stake. "I'm not in the mountains for my health," is a common expression frequently heard. Some are well educated and from good families "back East."

Good, substantial working clothes and unconventional manners are the rule. There are, of course, bartenders and men known to be gamblers, but these are not well received by the better class of citizens, notwithstanding a smooth address and good appearance.

Besides ourselves there are few young ladies here. Miss Armstrong, from Minnesota, is visiting her father. Two girls of fifteen are reported to be engaged to middle-aged men, and one but little older — a newcomer — is receiving much attention and is quite giddy in consequence. Dancing and card playing are the chief amusements.

A little Sunday School is maintained and church services are held once or twice a month by Rev. W. W. Van Orsdel or Rev. Duncan, both of the Methodist Episcopal Church. Bishop Tuttle of the Episcopal Church visits and conducts a service in each community once a year.

Father taught the Glendale school last winter and he often laughs about the only stipulation made by the trustees: "The teacher must not get drunk in school hours." In this instance the teacher had always been a total abstainer.

Gossip is rife, as in most small places, and everyone's affairs are either known or guessed at. Character is quickly read and people rated at their worth.

Prices are high and change smaller than "two bits" is not usually considered. . . .

At best, the life of a United States marshal was difficult — jurisdiction immense, salary meager and not always forthcoming, assistance rare or nonexistent. Thomas Irvine ranched, mined, managed an irrigation project, and scouted for General Miles before his election as Custer County sheriff and subsequent appointment as marshal. He enjoyed not only the duties of his new offices, but the boisterous, gregarious society of early Miles City.

APRIL 12, 1879 — [Miles City] — The weather is beautiful. Times are very dull. Quite a number of strangers in town but no money. Masquarade ball at Reiceses dance house and a coon dance at Annie Turners. I have 7 prisoners in Jail. . . . King and I quit drinking today. Miles Town has about three hundred & fifty inhabitants. Five stores, 20 saloons, about twenty five whores. Lots of gamblers and as many theives as any town of its size in the world. . . .

MAY 7 — Davie Borum, X. Beidler, Frank Murray and I took a coffin and hitched up Xs mules and went below Buffalo Rappids and buried Bob Hammond who was drowned a month ago. He was nearly decayed and smelt fearful. We found $600 in a hankerchief around his leg and six in coin in his pocket. I drank plenty of liquor while handling the corps and got quite full tonight. . . .

JUNE 23 — [Helena] — I was busy until late tonight. Settled with Joe Woolman the territorial auditor for prisoners taken to the penetentiary. He cut down my mileage and wouldnt alow anything for a guard. . . . Received in Territorial warrent $660.80 and sold at par to Cannon. Unable to sell County scrip and deposited it at First National Bank. Knocked around with Granville Stuart for a while and then with Hugh McQuaid. I received my appointment as deputy Marshall but couldnt give bonds and had to send it to Deer Lodge to be filled. Went to Mr. Mahans to see Sallie. Gave her $40.00 and went to the Hotel and to bed.

JUNE 30 — [Fort Assinaboine] — We left Benton in coach in company with Mr. Fish and his wife & child of Ft. Belknap and got to Fort Assinaboine about dark. We stopped in the edge of the encampment and I as spokesman was taken to the officer of the day and from there under guard to the General [Ruger]. He is a fat red looking old rooster and terrible stiff. . . . We put up at the Sutlers Store with Mr. Broadwater. After supper X and I went up to see the general. . . . The whole outfit are shavetails. . . .

JANUARY 22, 1880 [Miles City] — Tried to get my prisoner a hearing but failed. I am deputy U.S. marshal and to save Custer County the expense of the trial I wanted to make a U.S. case. The horses belonged to the Crows and were stolen on their reservation and as that is under the exclusive jurisdiction of the United States Courts the case should be tried in that Court. It is thought that we killed the other horse thief and tis hard to make them think differently. We do not care what they think for I am sorry we didnt kill both of them. I would rather kill a thief than a yellow dog. An old fraud of lawyer by the name of Swift is trying to make it appear that we captured our man in Dakota and is trying to make us trouble on the charge of Kidnapping. If he goes too far we will hang him. . . .

JANUARY 26, 1884 — [Miles City] — Sick all day. . . . I drove up to the brewery in the forenoon with Silverberg after Mrs. . . . The skating rink is all the rage. All classes are equal there. Negros, Whores, Gamblers and our pretended Christians all mix and the women all crazy over skating. If we dont hear of big scandals there then I will miss my guess. I think it will turn out to be a large size whore house. Lots of family jars and divorce suits. . . .

FEBRUARY 7, — Had two hundred cards printed to send to Sheriffs all over the western States and territories advertising a detectives agency that Jim Conly & I have established here. I fixed up a job on Silverberg for cooking my eggs that I left in his house while I went to the Post Office about three weeks ago. . . . He uses Halls hair dye to keep his hair black. I emptied that out and filled his bottle with something that will stick his hair as tight as glue. Wife at rink in foornoon. . . .

MARCH 1 — Louie King went to the brewery and he & Bullard and I shot pistols for the beer. I shot against both of them, used either my right or left hand, and they used both of theirs and I won every time. Then, Ullman, Lansing & Silverberg came up and all played whiskey poker for beer and I am too drunk for my own good and the others are as bad off. I got home late in evening and found wife gone to the rink without me. I went there and when the fun was over we came home.

Western immigrants did not leave their prejudices behind. In Helena, the issue of integrating public schools prompted E. W. Knight, a member of the school board, to request an opinion from the U.S. Attorney General. Perhaps Knight's inquiry stemmed from a sense of fairness or from the political realities of his forthcoming campaign for mayor. Whatever the cause or the reply, Knight won election and Helena residents voted that spring to integrate their school facilities.

HELENA, MONTANA
FEBRUARY 7, 1882

HON. ATTORNEY GENERAL OF THE U.S.
WASHINGTON, D.C.

DEAR SIR,

I should be obliged if not trespassing upon your time and patience too much for your views upon the Legality of our School Law. As one of the School Trustees of this District the Question is presented as to our Territorial Law coming in conflict with 14th Amendment to Constitution of US.

Our section 1120 Reads: "The Education of Children of African descent shall be provided for in Separate Schools. Upon the written application of the parents or guardians of at least Ten such children to any board of trustees, a separate school shall be established for the Education of such children, and the education of a less number may be provided for by the Trustees in separate schools in any other manner and the same laws, rules and regulations which apply to schools for White Children shall apply to Schools for colored children."

When we had some Ten or twelve African Descent children we provided [a] separate school, but when only two such children were attending we provide[d] for a special hour in the morning and like hour in the P.M. But the question I wish to submit is if the Provision of our Terr. Law is carried out and if substantial and equal school privileges are extended under the above law, is it a question that comes in violation of 14th Amendment. . . .

I have the honor to be Yours Respectfully

E. W. KNIGHT
TRUSTEE

Glendive took form as the Northern Pacific track pushed westward late in 1880. Nine hundred people crowded into the railroad camp during its first two years. Excitement prevailed not only among those early residents but in the eastern press, where readers clamored for news about the progress of the transcontinental railroad. "Prospector" was the pseudonym of an eastern journalist sent west to satisfy urban curiosities. His reports not only described the rowdy camps but included sage advice for any traveler — always stay in "the other" hotel.

. . . It was Wednesday evening May 10th when I landed in Glendive and had a formal reception by General Merrill and the prominent citizens of that future capital. The General did not wear his U.S. uniform except the skie blue gold [striped] Trousers, according to his rank; the prominent citizens being mostly proprietors of Saloons, gambling dens or dance houses all showed the signs of their Western frontier civilization, meaning their aversion to the use of soap. Heavy rain poured down and the Hotels on that ground neglected to send out their omnibuses. The General made the remark to me not to go to that Hotel but to the other. Unfortunately I made a mistake and went to "that Hotel." (Dear reader if ever you come to Glendive do not follow my example, but all at once go to the "Other Hotel.")

Late in the evening General Merrill sent for me and invited me to call and see him at the store of his friend Douglas. This store is the best in the place. The general ordered "Mumm's Extra Dry" and we drank on the prosperity of his creation. He handed me a copy of the Glendive Times of May 4th. This paper is printed by the Pioneer Press of St. Paul and is one of these patent inside sheets of which said St. Paul Paper prints about two hundred & thirty [listing] all the printing staff and leaving only space for local gossip & advertisements. Said copy contains the following item. A correspondent

of the "Minneapolis Evening Journal" with the name of Hohl, who lately visited Glendive says that there is no decent building in this place. He lies, there are dozens of them and daily are added to them. He further says that there were hundreds of poor fellows here, who do not own a cent, had to beg for their food and to sleep in empty cars. He again lies. Everybody will find profitable employment in Glendive and laborers of any description are daily wanted. He further . . . proclaimed the Glendive Times to be a "humbug." He again lies. If he had done so, we would have fired him out d.q. (double quick). He complains to have paid in one of our Hotels $14.00 per week. Now, what of it? In New York at Delmonico's you have to pay more than this and nobody will cry over it. He says we had no police. He lies, we have the best police in the world. Should he ever show his face again hereabouts he will learn it.

This article was handed to me with the request to truthfully inform the public about Montana and in a special way about Glendive.

Now as far as Montana is concerned, I have to confirm with much pleasure, that all the good things that have been told lately about this Territory are true. The climate is wonderful, the lower lands fertile, the upper lands fine meadows. The inhabitants are a solid population, frontier mannered, but true and hospitable.

Rapid growth brought increased danger from communicable diseases, particularly smallpox. Butte, with its transient mining population, was no exception. A reported outbreak occurred in 1883, prompting the City Council to take immediate action.

CITY HALL, BUTTE CITY, M.T.
WEDNESDAY, JULY 11TH, 1883.

. . . The subject of Small Pox existing in the City was . . . discussed by the Council at length, and on motion of Mr. Clark it was ordered that the New Brunswick Hotel, the place where most of the disease originated, be closed up for the present time, and that the occupants of said building be required to remove from there forthwith. It was moved, seconded, and ordered by the Council that

Mrs. Baxter, the occupant of said Hotel, be removed to some other building and she be required to remain in said building for a period of thirty days. It was suggested by Mr. McMurphy that there was a shaggy dog at the New Brunswick Hotel that had been frequenting the room where small Pox patients were, and that the animal was liable to carry the disease to persons in the outside. Mr. Clark then moved that the City Marshall be directed to exterminate and kill the said dog; the motion being seconded, it was so ordered by the Council. . . .

A self-assured young man named Roy M. Cobban left Chippewa Falls, Wisconsin in 1880, headed for Montana. One of the persons who bade him farewell was Alice Hardy. After brief stays in the Judith Basin and Wickes, Cobban settled in Butte, where he established a planing mill and prospected the surrounding hills. Loneliness dogged his optimism, however, stimulating a long correspondence with the "girl he left behind." Cobban remedied the solitude and separation in 1887 when he married Alice and brought her to Montana.

ROYSTON, MONTANA
SEPTEMBER 20, 1886

DEAR FRIEND ALICE:

Sunday evening again finds me seated at my desk in the boarding house surrounded by the men. One of them playing "Home Sweet Home" on the violin. There are about twenty men at work for me at present. A good hearted lot but most of them rough. There is as yet but one lady in the place but we hope very soon to have several families, a store, post office etc. . . .

I should like very much to listen to you sing and play and then when we were alone I should like to visit with you for I have many things to say that I fear will never be said if I have to depend on writing. . . . I have thought what a pleasure it would be to be at home for a few months, that we might get better acquainted. Of the pleasant little trips we might plan of a hundred ways to pleasantly pass the time. But with the wish comes the word IMPOSSIBLE if I would make a success in the enterprise I have undertaken. I could plan to be away for the 15th of Dec. until after New Year but no longer. . . . Only a flying visit and back to my western life.

Alice, I should be the happiest of men if I could hope that you would care enough for me, if you could learn to love me and return with me as my wife to my western home. . . . I have no wealth to offer, but a warm heart and a willing hand I have. . . .

Can I hope, Alice, that my wish will be granted? We are both young and strong and can stand it — rough it in the west for a year or two. I should hope that it would not be necessary to do as I am now doing for any great length of time for I should like to go to New England to live near my friends. If here, there would be very few advantages but an occasional ride to Butte to church, only a few women in the place to see and visit with. . . .

I fully realize what I am asking of you. Not only a woman's love but the leaving of home, friends and advantages to go out in the world with, nearly a stranger. Alice, I cannot give their equal, but I will love and cherish and make home as near a little paradise as can be here (poverty permitting). Alice, I shall hope for a speedy reply. . . .

Please don't keep me waiting long.

This I believe would be called a love letter but there is no taffy in it. I should in immagination if I dared, take you by the hand and — well, give you a good kiss.

YOURS TRULY,
ROY M. COBBAN

Colter's Hell had topographical and thermal wonders to impress visitors long before it became Yellowstone National Park in 1872. Lone travelers and official expeditions preceded tourist hordes. Each report, each letter, provoked curiosity and promoted more visitors. Hattie Shober, niece of a prominent Helena attorney, visited Yellowstone fifteen years after it became a park. Even that early, the availability of good meals and comfortable lodging indicated the rapidity with which tourism flourished.

HELENA, M.T.
SEPTEMBER 4, 1887

MRS. MARY SHOBER
DEXTER, IOWA

DEAR AUNT:

I received your welcome letter a few days ago and will now attempt to reply, giving you an account of our trip through the Park, which I enjoyed very much, equally as well if not better than our European trip. I believe there are more natural curiosities in the Park than is to be found in any other territory of the same area in the whole world.

I purloined a few specimens from the Park which I shall divide with you when I return to Iowa. They of course are not so nice as some that are not to be had, but they will give a faint idea of the formation, etc. One can get only those that are loose and easily stolen as guards are on the watch. I felt satisified if caught with my ulster pockets full that I would be ably defended, but I didn't expect to be caught.

We made the round trip from Helena in seven days taking what they call book tickets which gives you five days in the Park furnishing you with conveyance and driver, board and lodging for $40.

The best way to go is to make up a party, hire someone to take his team and take a camping outfit including all the necessaries for camp life, hire a colored boy to do the cooking or do it yourselves if preferable, then get two or even three seated carriages to convey yourself and party. In that way you can stay as long as you like in each place. However the way we went is very satisfactory and very comfortable, hotels are built at proper distances apart to make it convenient to stop for meals and lodging. . . .

About three fourths of the Park is covered with dense forests of pine, fir, spruce and cedar, the pine is very dense and it takes a great amount of time and expense to make roads through it, in many places the forests have been burned, detracting considerable from their beauty, tourists sometimes carelessly leave camp-fires burning and fires originate in that manner but now they are watched pretty closely by the guards, and such accidents are more rare than a few years ago. In some places evidences of cyclones or tornadoes are visible in the fallen timbers in places not a single tree is left standing. I thought if the Iowans had free access to that dry fallen pine, and it was in closer proximity it would soon be removed, a great portion of the road is through large bodies of pine and what a delightful shady road it is. The meadows and hillsides are covered with quite a variety of pretty wild flowers, larkspurs, golden rod,

daisies, dwarf sunflowers and forgetmenots being the principal ones. The Park is rightly called the "Wonderland of America". Its boiling springs, spouting geysers, paint pots, picturesque mts, beautiful valleys, lakes, rivers, canons, gorges, and mountain brooks are all worthy of note.

But if I describe my trip and the main places visited I must not delay longer. We left Helena Aug. 18th about 8 A.M. arrived in Livingstone shortly after dinner where we changed cars taking the National Park Branch Line. . . . [After] passing through [an] interesting region we arrived at Cinnabar the terminus of the R. R. and took a stage for Mammoth Hot Springs six miles distant, and the first stopping place in the Park, this ride is for the most part through a rough mountainous district, and is mostly up grade. We staid at the M.H.S. hotel and spent the next forenoon viewing the Springs and other objects of interest in that locality, walked about 7 miles and strange to say was not tired, had to stop occassionally and puff a while when climbing but after getting a good breath was as good as ever.

These Mammoth Springs . . . are quite deep and the water boils as hard as I ever saw water in a kettle or boiler boil. The water is blue but so clear you can see the coating of the basin in the bottom and on the sides. . . . The brilliancy and the variety of the colors deposited around the pools and the beauty of the formation is indescribable — cream, pink, white, red and brown are seen near the edge of the pools in the coating, the edges of some of them have a delicate frost like formation — too delicate to get specimens of — in fact one cannot carry these beauties away except in the picture gallery of memory's hall. . . .

HATTIE

By 1890, 12,000 foreign born emigrants had settled in Montana's sixteen counties. Mining settlements absorbed the majority of Europeans and Asians — the Cornish, Irish, and Chinese, specifically. Railroading and farming attracted Scandinavians — Danes, Swedes, and Norwegians — who settled along rail lines and adapted to life as best they could, given language difficulties and America's bewildering customs. Bertha Josephson Anderson, her husband, Peter, and their children, were among the first Danish families to settle in the vast farming region close to the North Dakota border. Mrs. Anderson's account of the Atlantic voyage and subsequent adjustment to homestead life echoed sentiments of thousands of pilgrims who settled Montana.

The trip across the Atlantic was very hard, as we had to take steerage, because that was the cheapest, and the ship was very crowded. We had only one bunk for the five of us. My baby, little Dagmar, who was then ten

months old, was cross the whole trip. She was used to nurse my breasts, but being seasick I had no milk. The other two, Mary and Niels, were as good as gold, but it was hard for we could not undress on the whole trip. We did not have a cabin for ourselves, but were in a large room, big enough for one hundred to one hundred sixty or maybe more, which was all filled with two tier bunks — one above the other.

Most of the passengers in that room were Polish or southern Germans, with a very few Scandinavians, but little we cared who they were, just so we were left alone. That was nearly impossible for if the party in the bunk above us felt nauseated, as most of them did, he just vomited right past the bed underneath and down on the floor. There it stayed until twice a day some sailor came and tried to sweep it up with a coarse broom made of birch branches. Many of these people would sit and pick vermin out of their clothes and throw them on the floor. . . .

But all things come to an end and so did that voyage. When we were a few days from New York, we learned that the Danish liner which we had hoped to go with but had missed, was lost at sea. Then I knew why the money was lost and we were delayed. Though we were sick and weary, thanksgiving to God filled our hearts that we were safe. . . .

When we reached Glendive, Montana, our destination, it was not far from midnight. It was only a little border town between North Dakota and Montana. . . . We were in a strange place with three little children, it was midnight, and we could not talk with anyone or make ourselves understood. They finally guessed we were Scandinavians for they sent out to find a Swede they knew lived in Glendive. . . . The Swede finally came and all was well, for he took us to a rooming house.

The next day a Mr. Otis came to take us along with him to Sidney, and he brought with him a letter from my brother Carl. . . . This was the last hop of our journey. It was a lumber wagon loaded with all kinds of boxes, with a spring seat without any backrest. . . . When the time seemed long I sang Danish hymns, and Mr. Otis soon was whistling them, for he, too, knew them in the English language. However, we looked with great longing toward the evening of the second day for the place we were going to call home.

On the twentieth of April, 1889, we had our first meal in our own log shack. . . . It was not easy to get along, since the two rooms were entirely bare except for a little home-made table, but we found a discarded stove and enough old boards lying around to nail together some kind of a bed for ourselves.

The chest we had brought our baggage in from Denmark had split and could not be repaired again. I took the top with its curved lid and used it for a cradle for the baby, for that was what I seemed to miss most. The bottom I used for the clothes we did not wear every day. During the day I folded over [it] the quilts the children slept in on the floor, and that made a place to sit down on. We nailed a bench together for the children, and for the rest . . . we used the ends of trees which were sawed off straight. We had our tin dishes from the ship, and a neighbor loaned us a kettle and a frying pan.

We were not bad off, or at least we got along. We soon became used to the bare log walls and cracks in the floor wide enough to stick a knife or fork through. . . . We got our water from the Yellowstone River which was only a few rods from the shack, but we still had to carry it a long way because we had to go around by a coulee to get down to it. We used only one of the two rooms because we had nothing whatever to put in the other. . . . What bothered us most was how we should get started to earn something. About a week went by before any decision was made, and we had to eat, even if it was sparingly. The settlers from thirty to forty miles around came to see the strange people who had come so far to settle in such a shanty. Luckily we could not understand them. There was one thing we soon got clear: that they nearly all had something they wanted to sell.

As I could milk and there were several companies of soldiers about twenty-five miles north of us at Fort Buford, an Indian reservation, we soon figured out that we should buy cows and make butter and sell at the Fort. Therefore, we first bought ten milk cows, paying down a little and signing notes for the rest. . . . There was no way of starting to farm that spring.

During that summer and also during the winter when we could get time, we studied our Danish-English book and an old Montgomery Ward catalogue which was in the shack when we came there, so by this time we were getting along real well in the English language. . . .

[By early spring] there was literally nothing in the house to eat. Our cupboard was bare. The children had the leavings from the morning meal, and went to bed and to sleep, but sleep wouldn't come to me. I thought it was strange that God didn't in some way interest himself in us. I knew we had tried our best.

When morning came Peter and I got up as usual, but there was no breakfast to get, so I was glad the children slept late. They had just dressed and were asking for something to eat, when a man living near us came riding into the yard, and stopped for a little visit with Peter. When he saw the children crying and us with sober faces he somehow surmised what was the matter. He left at once and inside an hour he was back again, and he brought with him all kinds of necessary things so we could get along until spring. He even brought a couple

dollars in cash, so if need be we could get more. It was the only time we have been without food in this country.

SEPTEMBER 25, 1896

MY DEAR MOTHER,

After laying in a stock of paper like this I found that the writing showed through, so you must not take it as evidence of waning devotion if I write on only one side for a while. . . .

You ask what effect it has upon me to know the depravity of Helena society. . . . I am . . . completely an outsider. I am looked upon as the well-bred pastor of an ill-bred church and regarded with some curiosity. The more I call among my people the more I feel the justice of the social ban that has fallen upon my church. There is only one family of real culture and of real "social" worth in the whole church. People of fine education come to hear me, but they are not my people. And as for the rotten "four hundred," they don't concern me, for they are out of my reach. Either they don't go to church at all, or they go to the episcopal "church" (a church of St. Judas) or to the Unitarian "church," whose platform is occupied by a sort of journalist, who reads editorials on current topics — studiously avoiding religious topics — and who draws the biggest crowd in town. The most worldly people hear him gladly. He is certainly a very able man, but for that reason he does the more harm.

My preaching calls out a great deal of approbation.

People say they like my sermons because they are so "spiritual," and yet Mrs. Lyman tells me they are too much so. She says Helena people are not up to them. When I preached that sermon on a "Portable Christianity," people said "that's just what we want." — that's a "regular Montana sermon" — "If you preach like that these people will come to hear you." I shall work that vein for the present and see what result I get. This is a hard, tough, worldly town, and any device that will reach the people ought to be tried.

Yes, my room is pretty, my bed is perfect, and my board thoroughly good. I never was more comfortable and never had better health. . . .

Looking back over this letter it seems to me I've been a bit too blue. When I say the Lymans are the only people of culture I mean that they are the only people of extreme refinement. They are intellectually and personally the finest of the fine. . . .

Now it is getting dark and I must go to dinner. Love to Grandma — tell her I wish I was back . . . though I am happy enough "down in Montayna." . . . Tomorrow I'm going digging for garnets. . . .

EVER DEVOTEDLY,

ROLLIN

DECEMBER 7, 1896

MY DEAR MOTHER,

. . . This, you observe, is Monday — "Blue Monday" — and I am "enjoying" my usual attack of Mondayishness. You ask how I stand preaching. You ought to ask how I stand Montana. . . .

First, as to nerves. I never felt so well in my life. Yet I have no endurance. . . . I have to limit myself to only 3 hours' writing if I am to get through a day and not

feel collapsed. . . . The one thing that reduces me to wreckage is the detestible Chinook. When the weather is 20 below zero I feel strong and brave and happy, but when that warm wind comes over the mountains I am worse than a limp rag — the only way to work then is to load up on strong tea, which like other stimulants, has more effect up here than elsewhere.

Evening, when I don't have actual work on hand, I play. I belong to two nice sets now — people much like Buffalonians and I have a range of pleasant

64 *Portrait in Diversity*

acquaintances outside these sets. Down at the boarding-house we have sings after dinner every other evening in the week. . . .

Life in Helena is very narrowing. There is nothing to do — nothing to hear or see, nowhere to go. Everybody goes to the theatre here pretty nearly — even ministers — but there isn't a play or an opera once in six weeks. They get up a one-horse local talent concert about once in two months. There are hardly any places to visit — nothing of interest after the novelty of Western life has worn off. The nearest town is 70 miles away and it doesn't amount to anything. Butte is 100 miles off and the toughest town in North America. Consequently our pleasures are all social pleasures and yet the society here is all split up into cliques and people get awfully tired of each other.

Helena is a city of homesicks. The one need of Montana is money enough to get back East. Nobody likes the West. Everybody says he was a fool to come. Of course, this feeling would be different if money was free and plentiful as it used to be.

Doubtless you will want to know how all this strikes my fancy. I confess I never in all my days was so hungry to see or hear something beautiful. It would be worth $1000 to go to a fine picture show or a symphony concert. It would be worth everything to be with intellectual people and in an atmosphere of social refinement. And yet, much as I feel the privation of life in Montana, I find my work so engrossing that there is a real companionship in that. . . .

The work itself remains as encouraging as it has been. The people seem pleasant and the audiences are what we call "good." You understand, of course, that that means I am working my head off for a smaller church than you find in an ordinary New England village. . . . One thing about the personal side of my work. The altitude while not consciously affecting my nerves, does affect my general temperament — so much so that I can't trust myself to speak without manuscript. Hence my bondage to the pen. . . .

EVER DEVOTEDLY,

ROLLIN

Western states often parceled educational and custodial institutions among communities according to geographic distribution and political power. When Montana legislators came to the task in the 1890's, Miles City received the State Reform School. Governor Robert Smith appointed a sheep rancher from the area — B. C. White — as the institution's first superintendent. Perhaps the frustrations of shepherding recalcitrant youth were too much for White. He served as superintendent only two years, then returned to ranching.

MILES CITY, MONTANA
AUGUST 22, 1898

HIS EXCELLENCY ROBT. B. SMITH
GOVERNOR OF MONTANA

MY DEAR GOVERNOR:

. . . I have had a regular *epidemic of runaways* for the past five days. In the first place three boys ran away and I caught them 45 miles below here, and rode 90 miles with a team and neither slept or rested for 50 hours. I brought them back and through the laziness, and disobedience of the night watchman one of them got away again. That man's job is short lived. After I got back from my tiresome trip in the hot sun, and the mercury was over 100 in the shade, two girls made a break, bare headed, to run away, but they only got out to the corn field, and we caught them. The idea of herding these big renegade boys from other states here on the prairie, with only a simple board fence to prevent their

getting away is absurd. I am tied up here so that I can scarcely get to town, and keep a saddle horse ready all of the time, and have to watch the horse to see that he is not taken in a wild break to get away.

There are a few things that the legislature wants to change, or ought to change in the law governing this institution, and there is one thing that the courts of the state will have to be more cautious about if we are going to get the desired results, and carry out the aims of the institution. . . . That is the sending of the big renegade boys from other states here. They are vicious to the last degree, and they know far too much, and corrupt the small boys so far as they can get an opportunity. . . .

The weather is roasting hot down here, but we are all well, except one little fellow sick with the rheumatism. He is around on crutches, however.

SINCERELY YOURS,

B. C. WHITE

Hum Fay owned the Palace Restaurant in Butte. Frank Baldwin waited tables in a white establishment and belonged to the Silver Bow Trades and Labor Assembly. Their clash on the streets and in the courts of Butte represented more than personal antagonisms. Chinese communities grew in Butte, Helena, and throughout the western United States as an urban residual of the mining frontier. They worked discarded mines with profitable patience, served in countless domestic capacities, and formed communities reflecting their cultural background. Oriental uniqueness sparked against a dominant Occidental culture and erupted in heated confrontations throughout the region. In Butte, antagonism took form in a union boycott of Chinese businesses. Hum Fay's recourse through the courts ended the boycott in Butte, but not the prejudice there or elsewhere in the nation. Montanans regarded the "Yellow Peril" with emotional alarm, as did many of their western neighbors. The cry rose in the next century, culminating in a Chinese exclusion act. Montana's heritage reflected the cultural amalgam of gold rush settlement, but she joined the nation in its abhorrence of a "different" way of life.

STATEMENT OF HUM FAY:

... The first part [of] 1897 ... I saw [in] the newspaper [notice of] this general boycott against the Chinese by order of the Silver Bow Trades and Labor Assembly, P.H. Burns, President, George B. Walters, secretary.... I have the paper here. [The witness produced a copy of the *INTERMOUNTAIN* which was introduced into evidence].

"A general boycott has been declared upon all Chinese and Japanese restaurants, taylor shops and wash houses, by the Silver Bow Trades and Labor assembly. All friends and sympathizers of organized labor will assist us in this fight against the lowering Asiatic standards of living and of morals. America vs. Asia, progress vs. retrogression, are the considerations now involved. American manhood and American womanhood must be protected from competition with these inferior races and further invasion of industry and further reduction of the wages of native labor by the employment of these people must be strenuously resisted.

"By order of the Silver Bow Trades and Labor Assembly."

At that time I do a big business. After the last part of 1896 and the first part of 1897, the business fall off, pretty near fallen all off.... Sometimes I sell four or five dollars a day, that is all. ... [The reason for this falling off was] because in the first part of 1897 these delegates stand in front [to] prevent customers from coming in....

STATEMENT OF DON LEN:

Most generally every day ... I come up town by the noon hour to go to the post office, and I always dropped in there. Hum Fay was the first man I got acquainted with when I come to Butte. He kept a restaurant ... on West Broadway.... Used to be he done a good business before the boycott, but afterwards, as soon as those walking delegates kept there in front of his house, ... I believe that his business dropped nine out of ten. That is, hardly was anybody there at ... noon time; used to be a full house at the noon hour before the boycott....

STATEMENT OF QUON LOY:

I went up to the City; I called on Chief Tebo and upon Waters; and I told him; I say "our people pay licenses and pay taxes and poor taxes just the same as other people, and the walking delegate prevent them from trading, and I think the City ought to do something." He told me he was going to see about it, look into it and I wait a few days and nothing happen. ... The walking delegates [were] still going on the streets and the banner going on the streets just the same. ... Then I went and called on the Mayor, Mayor Thompson, and asked him if he couldn't stop that. I said "A wagon [goes] on the streets just insulting our people, and the City ought to stop that." ... While we were talking about it that wagon drove past the City Hall. ... He says "You go and see an attorney, you go and see Thompson Campbell," and he says "You go and see Mr. Wines, see old Wines." That is what he said. I say "The City do nothing to protect our people." So I went away, and then I went again and I called on Detective Dave Meiklejohn; nothing done whatever. The Police officers stand outside the street, the walking delegates stand in front of the Chinese restaurant, and the police only walk close to it. ...

I went and called on the City attorney, but it didn't do no good, and I never go there again. Before ... that a few years ago, Mr. Lee Mantle was the Mayor of the City at that time that boycott was going on too, and I went and saw him. Nothing done and I had a conversation with Governor Toole, too, the Governor of the State. ... He said he couldn't do nothing.

MONTANA THROUGH

The Photographer and His Camera, 1883
— F. Jay Haynes

Among the seekers after fortune who came to Montana in the 1860's was a vanguard of photographers. They came, laden with cumbersome equipment, to bring the "miracle" of photography to the frontier. Part artist and part technician, these early professionals were inevitably also part historian, recording and preserving the passing scene with a truthfulness and fidelity to fact that the written word could not attain.

They documented the physical appearance of the American West as they accompanied government surveys and marched with the Indian-fighting army. Such was the nation's interest in the new land and its inhabitants that the work of a number of these government photographers achieved national renown and spurred the settlement of the region.

Largely itinerant, many of Montana's earliest photographers departed with the decline in mining, but a number stayed to portray the emergence of the territory into a settled community. As Montana diversified, photography became increasingly focused in urban areas and dominated by its more commercial aspects. Whether taking portraits or preparing advertisements, however, the photographer continued to preserve the reality of the material and cultural world around him.

By the turn of the century, professional photographers became an important adjunct to the state's newspapers. Largely as a result of the photographic efforts of the Farm Security Administration during the Depression, photojournalism gradually assumed a unique historical character. The intent of the photographer was no longer to document fact alone, but to comment and interpret.

During the Twentieth Century, technical advances and lower costs brought photography within reach of the general population. Much of the visual documentation of rural life such as the homestead era exists as a result of amateurs and their unpretentious box camera. Although frequently flawed by imperfections, these photographs are full of feeling and the importance of everyday life. In more recent years, photography has grown to become a hobby of such vast proportions that many amateurs rival their professional colleagues in both ability and artistry.

THE CAMERA'S EYE

Main Street, Helena, 1875 — EDGAR H. TRAIN

Cheyenne Village, c. 1879
— STANLEY J. MORROW

Crow Couple at Fort Custer, 1888
— O. S. GOFF

Fort Keogh Trumpeter Sounding Off, c. 1890 — CHRISTIAN BARTHELMESS

First Threshing
On Fallon Flat, 1908
— EVELYN J. CAMERON

Shearing Sheep at Big Sandy, 1895 — DAN DUTRO

Bringing a Calf to the Branding Fire, c. 1900 — LAYTON A. HUFFMAN

Butte, The Richest Hill on Earth, c. 1900 — N. A. FORSYTH

Carnival Day in Lewistown, c. 1900 — GLENN MORTON

Interior, Lou Lucke Company, Havre, 1916 — PHILIP A. BRAINERD

U. S. Forest Service

Tourists in Missoula National Forest, c. 1930 — K. D. Swan

Unidentified Amateur and His Camera, c. 1925
— Edward Reinig

State Championship Basketball Team, Sweet Grass County High School, 1913 — Ben L. Witham

Farm Girl Pumping Water at Fairfield Bench, 1939
— Arthur Rothstein

Eroding Beauty, 1974 — Don Bianchi

Marysville Boarding House, 1975 — WILLIAM POTTS

Book III
New Perspectives:
The Land Mastered
1910 - 1976

DREAMS AND DROUGHT

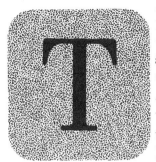

HOUSANDS CAME. Most of them were Easterners, Midwesterners and Europeans, enticed by the blandishments of railroad promoters and news of greatly liberalized homestead laws. Between 1909 and 1916, alluring visions of prosperity brought the hopeful newcomers to the Northern Plains. Advertisements depicted Montana as the "land of milk and honey" — a land where a poor man could make his fortune on his own land, his plow literally turning over the coin of prosperity. James J. Hill, who built the Great Northern Railroad without government land grant or subsidy, hoped to "colonize" the land his rails had penetrated, his hopes given substance by the passage of the new Homestead Acts of 1909 and 1912 which expanded federal policies aimed at settling the public domain. Hill was one of the first to devise a promotion campaign extolling Montana's agricultural potential and salubrious climate.

The Northern Pacific and Milwaukee Railways, not to be outdone, created their own brochures and poster inducements to publicize lands they served. Local and state groups followed their lead. The campaigns proved so successful that in the dozen years after 1910, homesteaders had claimed forty-two percent of Montana's land, and the state's population increased by one-third.

The new arrivals came by many methods, including boxcars, in which they carried tools, machinery, household goods and livestock. A trip from Minnesota to Eastern Montana by this method cost $50.00. At most stations, land locators met the homesteaders, rushed them by wagon or Model T to view a parcel of land, and returned them to town to file on the claim — for a fee, of course. Sometimes it was good land; often it was on a flat, wind-blown plain, far from tree or water. Frequently dubbed honyockers, nesters, scissorbills and sod busters, the settlers took the land eagerly, ignoring warnings about the perils of dryland farming, if they heard them at all.

Building a home was the first order of business. A few copied the Nebraska tradition and constructed sod houses. The majority built $100 tar paper-covered shacks, usually 12 x 16 feet in size, the cracks stuffed with rags and newspapers to keep out the ever-present wind. If a homesteader could afford it, he had a well drilled; if not, he dug it with pick and shovel.

Few of these people had any experience in dryland farming, or any kind of farming for that matter. Until 1917 they struggled, but averaged good yields, particularly in wheat, of up to twenty-five bushels an acre. That year a dry summer struck northern Montana. The next year, and the next, the drought worsened. As it moved south, hot winds parched the land, but still no rain fell.

Everyone suffered — ranchers, merchants and bankers. During World War I farmers bought new machinery to expand their crops and patriotic local bankers loaned them money. After the war, a series of circumstances combined to bring disaster: inflation, poor markets, European recovery, and the devastating drought. Unable to collect their loans, many banks extended even more hoping to recoup. Finally, everything collapsed. Thousands went bankrupt and left. Banks and businesses closed, depopulating homestead towns and newly-created counties. The failures of the period left Montana with incalculable debts and uncertainty as the next decade loomed.

EDGAR SYVERUD HOMESTEAD, DAWSON COUNTY, 1914

DREAMS AND DROUGHT
The Homestead Era, 1908-1921

Enactment of the "three year" Homestead Law greatly expanded settlement of federal lands. The law reduced from five years to three the time necessary to "prove up" a claim and permitted five months' absence from the land each year. For Montana it meant 12,500 homestead entries in the first year alone. Railroads, land speculators, state agencies, and local commercial clubs all capitalized on its provisions. Promotional campaigns, together with the availability of land, an extended wet cycle, and the promise of additional federal land legislation gave the public campaign impetus. Following are excerpts from a typical brochure lauding Montana's advantages and designed to lure even more land seekers.

MONTANA

The state of Montana contains 146,572 square miles and is as large as the combined area of New York, Pennsylvania, Indiana, Maryland, and Connecticut. . . . The population of Montana is only 400,000. It will support in comfort forty times that many. . . . All it needs to make it one of the greatest states is more capital and more people of the right kind. . . .

In the next few years Montana will show the most rapid development ever known in any state. Its mines, its forests, its rich agricultural and grazing lands, its water power, will all contribute to make its settlers independent. Wealth awaits those who, properly equipped, will join fortunes with the state of Montana, and now is the time. . . .

The construction of the Chicago, Milwaukee & Puget Sound Railway, through the state of Montana from east to west, has opened to settlement thousands of acres of farm land that can now be homesteaded or purchased at low prices. These lands in a few years will double or treble in value. . . .

THE KIND OF SETTLERS DESIRED.

The ideal settler for Montana and the one we are trying to reach is the man who has made a moderate success in the East, but who is too ambitious to be satisfied with slow progress and too wise to overlook the great opportunities in the West. . . . The young man especially should go to Montana. That state, while rich in natural resources, is just beginning to be developed, making it an ideal place to get a start. Montana is the last of the good states to be developed, and will be settled with a rush. Land values will quickly increase and make large profits for those who go early.

CLIMATE.

The climate in Montana is excellent. . . . The clear, dry air is extremely invigorating and, one of the most healthful and pleasant in the world. . . . No one need fear the winters of Montana. They are tempered by the warm Chinook winds and by the mountains. . . . The summer days are long and, although at midday the sun is quite hot, sunstrokes are unknown. The nights are always cool and pleasant.

Montana has never known a tornado or cyclone. . . . Montana has no diseases peculiar to the country and its dry atmosphere will cure affections of the nose, throat and lungs. The state has a number of hot springs that are noted. . . . The summers of Montana are noted for the long days, giving many hours of sunlight for the growing crops. Plowing begins in March and ends usually in November.

One important fact will be noted: In Montana more than TWO-THIRDS OF THE MOISTURE FALLS DURING THE GROWING SEASON.

SOIL.

The soil of Montana varies with the different districts, but generally it is an alluvial deposit, a gray loam of extreme fertility, from two to forty feet in depth. . . . No question has ever been raised regarding the fertility of Montana soils. . . .

Another important property of Montana soil is that it is of a proper consistency for a country of light rainfall. It works and pulverizes readily, making the task easy of keeping a dust mulch on top for conservation of moisture. The soil is heavy enough that this dust blanket does not blow away. Besides these advantages, it is a soil that readily absorbs and holds moisture.

Montana furnishes the best of all markets — the home market. So large a percentage of the population is engaged in mining, lumbering, stockraising, etc., that her farmers can not supply the food for the state. . . .

HOMESTEAD LANDS.

There are millions of acres of Government land in Montana open to entry under the Homestead Act. A large proportion of these lands is tributary to the Chicago, Milwaukee & Puget Sound Railway, and is suitable for farming. The lands near the railway are being rapidly homesteaded and haste is necessary in order to get a farm near a town. . . .

For details regarding these lands see our pamphlet "Government Homesteads and How to Secure Them." It will be mailed free on application.

Otto Jorgensen, member of a Danish immigrant family recalled, in detail, two facets of homestead settlement in eastern Montana — construction of a sod house, and education in a one-room school. In 1908, twelve-year-old Jorgensen and his family located at Dagmar. With vivid recollection he detailed the architectural complexities in building their first house. For a school boy who spoke no English, learning the three R's in the "Little Red Schoolhouse" left a lasting impression.

We of course had the all-important problem of getting a house and barn built before the rigors of winter caught us with our "walls down." [We had] no money to buy lumber with, so it was decided to build of sod. . . . Helga and Pa, with the help of Soren and Jens Nickoliasen, were the ones on whom the herculean task fell. Soren was the "sodcarpenter" who in turn had learned to build a sod house that would stand up, from Pete Hendriksen from Nebraska, where sod houses were quite common. . . .

First a strip of good tough prairie sod had to be turned over with a 14-inch breaking plow, about three to four inches deep. If the implement was working as it should, this left a ribbon of sod fourteen inches wide and three inches thick. These were cut up into 28-inch lengths, loaded onto a flat-bed wagon or stone-boat, and hauled to the building site. A tier is then laid the length and breadth of the house, inside measurements, and the succeeding tier laid in a transverse position to the preceeding one, like bricks, until the desired height is reached. There is, of course, a little more to it when it comes to corners, windows and doors, but after the sod is hauled, the whole thing can be done with a square-nosed spade and a strong back. . . .

The house we built was unique in many respects and for all I know, the only one like it ever built. It was 16 by 24 feet; a full-sized cellar, walls 7 feet high, a ceiling, above which rose a peaked roof of unusually high pitch. The sod gables rose clear to the peaks, no small task in itself to accomplish. The sod, for the last part of these, had to be thawed out by the fire and hoisted up with

tackle before they were completed. There were no partitions, the lower floor was a good floor, of three inch quarter-sawed fir, with 1" by 10" joists, 16" apart. The upper floor had 2" by 6" joists about 24" apart, with 6" grooved boards. The roof — get this — the roof had 1" by 4" rafters, 4 feet apart, with 1" by 4" strips nailed crosswise to them about the same distance apart, to which was tacked, running up and down, what was called "resaw" boards 3/8" thick by 10" wide, second or third grade stuff. On this was tacked a layer of tarpaper and another layer of "resaw." That roof, believe it or not, took the worst wind, rain, hail and snowstorms Montana had to offer for four long years. . . .

A sod [school] house had been built the year before we came, a sort of Community meeting-house, Church and school house, about three miles as a crow would fly . . . west and south of our homestead. . . .

Here I met a different breed of barefoot, overall-clad boys, some of them with an accent in their speech. We had no tracable accent, due to the fact that our folks had insisted upon using the Danish language in our home. Dad always said to Ma: "Let's teach the kids the language we are master of; they'll soon enough learn the other, and learn it correctly." . . . In this primitive earth and board structure . . . part of the time was devoted to English and later, entirely so. . . .

[A year before] this schoolhouse was full of children, including the young and buxom Marie Hansen, the teacher. . . . Although it's doubtful [she] ever had any experience with prairie fires, she no doubt had heard them described by early settlers. She was alert at the first sign of smoke, borne by the high northwest wind. There was no firebreak around the building, . . . and as the threatening smoke-clouds increased, she and the older boys did what they could to cover any inflamable parts of the building . . . with dirt. In the meantime . . . she herded all the frightened children inside, closed the door and placed her trust in the sod walls, and her faith in God. . . . With express-train speed, [the fire] swept down upon and over them. It seems to me that this remarkable woman . . . rates with other heroines of the frontier who have earned fame, if not immortality in extraordinary moments of intestinal fortitude, during fires, floods, snowstorms and blizzards. . . .

Schooling, too, was more or less of a hardship — what I got of it, except the few years in Wisconsin, where we only had a mile and a half to walk. Even though this is not my life history, except for the early days in Montana, and what pertains to it, I can't resist a few comments on that institution of learning that we attended in Wisconsin. No doubt everyone has heard of the now, almost legendary, "Little Red Schoolhouse." Well, this was it — just as you see pictures of it — and it was old. There were old grey-haired men and women in that community whose fathers and grandfathers had learned the three "R's" in that same school house. The belfrey, I recall, was pock-marked and battered from the attempts of passing generations at hitting the bell with rocks and stones of various sizes. The schoolhouse itself, measured about 20 or 24 feet, by 30 or 32 feet, and had a row of windows on each side. The only door, protected by a small lean-to shed, or entry, was to the north. This shed served as wardrobe, and clothes locker, consisting of a row of nails driven into the wall, and as storehouse for wood to feed the hog-shaped, hog-bellied stove in the back of the room. The two blackboards — just that — blackboards — some with cracks between them; and the teachers desk, were on each side of the door. Also, the pull-rope for the bell, shelf in one corner for the water

pail and dipper, and a large chart on a tripod, with big paper pages about four feet square, stood beside the teachers desk. This about sums up the equipment and furnishings except for three rows of desks, one on each side, and one in the middle. And last but not least — the teachers' pointer!

The threshold, or doorstep was worn through. The six-inch floor boards at the door and branching out towards the two aisles, were worn down like cow-paths, but the big square-headed iron nails were not; consequently causing many toe-stubbings.

You have all read, one time or another, John Greenleaf Whittiers' poem (or was it James Whitcomb Riley?) "The Little Red School House." — its charcoal frescoes on its walls — the doors' worn sill, betraying — etc. Well, this was it, only it wasn't poetry. I don't recall any charcoal frescoes, but I do remember the paper-wads and spit-balls on the ceiling. Many times, while daydreaming and staring at the ceiling, I used to wonder why it was so rough and lumpy, until I noticed a spot where the plaster had come loose. It showed that layer after layer of what looked like cardboard, but was simply chewed up tablet paper, had been poised on the end of a ruler or stick and snapped with a "splat" against the ceiling. The yearly peltings were simply whitewashed over from one generation to the next. I don't suppose any of you younger people know much about that sort of thing! The present, "well-behaved" youngsters of this day and age would never resort to such rude antics — perish the thought!

There had been a time when there were as many as forty pupils going to that school at one time, but the year we left, there was only one — my sister, Esther. She went one term, alone, and that was after a new and larger school had been built. Why I didn't go that summer is not clear to me; most likely, I had to help with the moving preparation.

Speculation at the beginning of the homestead era drove land prices upward. To secure more land and expand operation it was not uncommon for the newcomers, men and women alike, to seek outside employment. One of them, Addie Stewart, experienced this reality and cooked for a restaurant at Ismay. She and her husband, Cary, enthusiastically planned their future as permanent residents. In a letter to Emma Milnor, a childhood friend, Mrs. Stewart outlined what she considered their promising situation.

ISMAY, MONTANA
OCTOBER 15, 1910

MY DEAR NEGLECTED, EXILED FRIEND,

. . . It would take a volume to tell all the history of the Stewarts since I wrote you last. We came out here

March 22 and landed on our claims March 24. We lived in two tents from then until June 30 when we moved into our 14 x 24 house. We had much beautiful weather and many storms and high winds making tent life here on the plains very disagreeable at times. . . . Cary had to shovel away snow banks from in front of the tent several times before we could pass in and out, and twice we had to seek shelter at a neighbors [who] had their house up. . . .

About 1/2 hour after we got the stove and bedding moved into the house a terrible wind & hail storm broke over us which cut down all our crops to the ground and tore down one of our tents and deluged everything in them. Our corn was knee high, our potatoes budded to bloom, garden all coming fine. There was apparently nothing left, but the corn and potatoes came again and we will have some corn and from 80 to 100 bu. of fine potatoes. We have 60 shocks of fodder and about 10 tons of nice prairie hay. Our barn is about half done. It is made of sod and poles and room for 12 head of stock but we only have 7 head 3 horses and 4 cows.

Cary is painting our new school house while the other men are building the coal house and out houses. The [school] house will be plastered next week and the furniture is ordered. The house is 18 x 24 and the building will be painted white. It is only 1/2 mile from us. There are 18 children of school age within two miles of the house probably 16 to go to school. . . .

3 weeks and 2 days in August I worked as cook in the only restaurant in Ismay. There was only the proprieter and his wife, the dishwasher and I and we cooked for from 20 to 60 a day. The work was too hard, I could not stand it and it was such a worrysome place to work because Mr. Johnson and his wife quarreled so. She did scarcely any work while I was there. . . . Both drank, played cards &c &c and I think she was the most devilish woman I ever saw. I got $27.00 for the time I was there which helped out pretty good in a pinch. . . .

The man who owns the section of land joining us on the west refused $20.00 an acre for it a few weeks ago. The homesteader that comes to our N.W. corner refused $1500.00 for his relinquishment when he only had his barn built. The relinquishment to a half section homestead that is between us and town was sold for $1000.00 this fall. It was raw land. A section a mile north of us sold for $16.50 an acre this fall. Every homesteader around us has a half section and all are here for five years any way. Most of them expect to stay longer. This means better buildings . . . schools, roads &c. . . .

We do not take the *Democrat* now. We had to cut out every expense that was not absolutely necessary. We are facing the hardest winter we ever did. I am sure I dont know how we will come out. I'll tell you better in the spring. . . .

ADDIE STEWART

Homesteaders lived in a variety of dwellings, ranging from tents, log cabins and sod houses to wooden shacks. In many cases wood was not available; when it could be obtained, it was usually too expensive. Consequently, homesteaders had to be content with what they could afford, and what materials were available. For many new arrivals this rigorous life on the dry-land plains lacked appeal. Carroll Graham, Billings state senator, visited his boyhood home near Jordan and recalled one very ingenious residence — a cave house, and its disillusioned resident.

We came to this homestead on the Big Dry in 1916. At the time I was approximately 3 years old. . . . It was . . . about 10 miles from a place called Edwards, which at that time was quite a thriving place having a post office, blacksmith shop, dry goods store and things of this nature. . . .

I very well remember this [dugout cave]. It was in the fall, I think, of 1920 or 21 that I went there with my father and several neighbors to dig coal. . . . It was in November and the weather being rather chilly and I being a young fellow of about 8 years old, . . . got cold. . . . [One neighbor] noticed that I was getting cold and he asked me why I didn't go to his house so I could get warm as he had a fire in there. . . . I said, "I don't see your house, mister." . . . "Right over there," he said, "where that blanket is hanging up on that bank." So I went over there and I stood outside quite awhile, being no door to knock on, and he hollered over and said, "Just go right in through under the blanket." . . . There was a nice fire going in there and this woman greeted me . . . and it was indeed very warm in there. . . .

I remember my father discussing this place. . . . The cave house had no support whatsoever, it was dug in very hard material and there was approximately 3 small rooms that were arched into the clay bank. . . . As I remember, the woman was a younger . . . lady and she was extremely friendly and proceeded to keep me entertained most of the rest of the day so I never went back out. I had a very good chance to visit with her. I learned afterwards from my father that she was a mail order bride. My father said the fellow had advertised for a wife, claiming he was a coal mine owner and operator. She came out to this country which was 50 miles from a railroad and this cave house was what this fellow had to offer. . . .

This woman became very unhappy as time went on and the long winter wore on. When he would leave to go for the mail or buy groceries he would take the only pair of shoes she had so that there wasn't any chance that she would leave until he got back. . . . When spring came and the ground warmed up he went one day for another supply of groceries and took the shoes but when he came back his wife was gone. The weather got warm enough that she could go barefoot, and she struck out across the hills. . . .

> *Heating fuel and water were the two essential commodities on any homestead. Since wood was expensive and scarce, it was used only in a few areas where trees abounded. Many homes burned coal, since the Montana plains provided an ample supply of the surface variety, and it was free for the digging. Water was a different matter. Until a well could be drilled, or dug, water had to be hauled, and depending on the distance of supply, was often the most precious item of all. Paul DeVore recounted his father's coal and water excursions, in 1916, on the family's Wibaux area farm.*

Fuel was free for the taking, but the taking involved no small amount of time and labor. There were outcroppings of lignite coal on most farms, . . . but . . . the better quality coal lay . . . five or six miles to the west. Covered with a few inches to a foot of gumbo, the surface-mined coal could be peeled off like strips of leather, then chopped or broken into chunks small enough to lift over the sideboards of the wagon. The coal usually oozed with water and was heavy, but once exposed to the air it readily disintegrated into small pieces and slack. Piled in the coal shed at home while still wet, the coal held its body for weeks and months and burned quite readily once a good blast had been established in the firebox of the stove. Four or five wagonbox loads in the fall would usually provide fuel for the winter months. . . .

The small, drab house on a knoll overlooking most of the farm's 320 acres of rolling crop and pasture land must have been a shock to my parents, particularly my mother when they arrived that October evening in 1916. . . . But the prospects of amassing a fortune in two or three years outweighed the negative aspects of their new home. The four room house actually was superior to many of the homestead houses in the area, but it was not insulated and its 4-inch board floors were badly worn. A coal range in the kitchen and a hotblast-heater in the living room provided ample warmth for the cold winter months, but the complete absence of shade trees made summer living a bit uncomfortable. . . .

A rectangular granary and a side-hill, straw-roofed barn, with adjoining pole corral, comprised the major building. A side-hill root cellar for refrigeration and storage, a side-hill chicken house and the usual "Chick Sales" outdoor plumbing completed the improvements.

It was two miles to the nearest source of [good] water from their new Montana home. A partially dug-out, board-walled spring on a section of railroad land had, for many years, been the only supply of water for a number of families in the community. Four 50-gallon wooden barrels were needed to haul and store the water. Two or three times weekly Dad drove to the spring with two empty barrels, dipped the water from the spring with a rope and pail and upon arriving home emptied the water, pailful by pailful, into two other barrels kept in the kitchen or adjoining coalshed. A frog, snake or occasional mouse had to be baled out of the spring before filling the barrels, but that was better than drinking the slippery alkali water from a nearby well or from Cottonwood creek which ran through the south end of their place.

Washing clothes with spring water usually necessitated an extra trip to the spring and, actually, the water was not the best for washing. . . . To supplement the spring water, Dad dug a 10-foot cistern at the corner of the house into which he shoveled and packed snow during the winter months. This proved to be a valuable and time-saving asset. . . . [1918] was not a good year for my parents cropwise, but by carrying water from the cistern and irrigating my garden twice a week, I came up with the county championship and a scholarship to the University of Montana . . . which paid most of my fees during my freshman year at the University.

Sue Howells and her husband, Joe, located in Chouteau County, several miles from Graceville, and as she vividly recalled, homestead life could be monotonous and lonely. The new settlers usually lived in one-room tar paper shanties that were cramped, stark, dusty, and cold. Entertainment was sparce, since families usually lived miles from any community. When they went to town — and then only to buy necessities — it was generally little more than a tiny settlement. The resourceful homesteaders thus provided their own diversions, meeting at someone's home. Dances, literary groups, and picnics constituted many of the social gatherings. In this account, Sue Howells fondly reminisced about her first Christmas celebration in Montana.

I have stood in the doorway of our shack, with my heart full of saddness and loneliness and listened to the wind. Even closing the door didn't help a great deal. It is an incessant, screeching, whining and screaming wind and seems to be heard nowhere except in Montana on the homestead. With the wind, I've seen the air dark and thick with tumbleweeds and if you were lucky enough to have a wire fence, you'd have a mile of . . . tumbleweed.

Each year, the Phantom Coulee Picnic was held at our homestead, because we were so centrally located. The neighbors gathered from near and far. They began coming early in the morning and continued coming until it was time for the dance to begin that night. It was a red-letter day and a big time for all of us. . . .

Our first Christmas in Montana and on the plains is one of my cherished memories. Everyone for miles around had congregated. . . . Faces and beards were beaming. Broncos were tied outside or just left by the door. Aunt Lucy Brady had the biggest "sitting room" anywhere in that part of the country, but it surely was none too big that Christmas night. Everyone was buzzing like a bee's nest . . . and all were waiting for the mailman. He arrived about 6:00 P.M., driving two lively cayuses hitched to a bobsled. That sled was "fuller" of mail than any Santa driving his reindeer ever had brought us before or after.

The buzzing ceased. . . . We . . . lined up against the wall and waited for our names to be called. No one was forgotten. Joe played the part of Santa Claus and he did it to perfection, even to the point of putting cotton on his beard so it would look like that jolly old fellow, Santa Claus. . . .

Thus ended our first Christmas Eve on the Plains, where there was not a tree to be had or in sight. Some children who live on the prairies are quite old before they ever see a Christmas tree. . . .

Entrance of the United States into World War I placed great importance on agriculture. Conflict in Europe halted local production and war demands made American farming lucrative. Federal and state governments encouraged expanded yields and bankers did their part by offering farmers additional credit. Montana's patriotic homesteaders, with little or no savings, naturally accepted, going into debt for better farm machinery. Ensuing uears of drought and poor markets eventually forced many farms and banks into insolvency. Half of Montana's banks permanently closed — 214 during the years between 1920 and 1926. But, in March of 1917, optimism still ran high. The First National Bank of Plains assisted farmers, and even managed to remain stable during postwar adversity.

To The Farmers of Sanders County

In the face of the grave crisis now confronting this nation it is the patriotic duty of every citizen to serve his country. . . . The most effective way for the farmer to serve his country at this time is to plant every available acre of land that can be cultivated into some kind of food crop for man or beast. It is our duty to serve the nation by extending such financial aid to the farmer. . . .

We are prepared to assist all solvent farmers in a financial way, not only for the purchase of seed grain and money to get their crop in, but will also agree to finance them thru the growth and harvesting of the crop and until such a time as same can be marketed. . . . Our membership in the Federal Reserve System and our connection with the Federal Reserve Bank of Minneapolis enables us to extend credit freely for the above purpose. The price of grain and hay as well as cattle and hogs is bound to be high for some time to come, and now is the time to prepare to seed every available acre, as well as to increase the number of domestic animals.

Remember, this will not only yield you a big profit, but it is your duty to serve your country in this manner.

Come in and let us talk it over.

THE FIRST NATIONAL BANK OF PLAINS

MARCH 29, 1917

Grasshoppers accompanied grass fires, wind, hail and dust to complete the homesteaders' misery. Farmers tried various methods to control the hordes: burning and irrigating fields, introducing large poultry flocks to eat the insects, and even grasshopper catching machines. All proved unsuccessful. Finally, the State Entomologist devised a poison bran mash solution to spread across the land at a cost of 35¢ to 50¢ an acre. Scheduled "mixing-bees" brought farmers, their wives, and local agricultural agents together to do battle. State Entomologist R. A. Cooley reported on progress to Governor Samuel V. Stewart in 1917. The poison bran method eventually proved too costly to be practical.

HELENA, MONTANA
JUNE 29, 1917

GOVERNOR S. V. STEWART
HELENA, MONTANA

DEAR SIR:

I feel that I should bring to your attention . . . the grasshopper situation in Montana. . . . Grasshoppers are very abundant, and if not killed, will be destructive in parts of Missoula, Flathead, Sanders, Broadwater and Gallatin Counties. In the western part of the State . . . there is a region where grasshoppers hatched this spring in great numbers and more recently we found another patch extending into two counties near Three Forks. In parts of these grasshopper districts the young hoppers are incredibly abundant.

Fortunately, however, there is a good and satisfactory remedy which may be used. Under the State Entomologist fund I have organized the control work in all the known infested localities and the farmers are cooperating beautifully. In fact, in the western part of the State, where the trouble chiefly is, I do not know of a single farmer who is objecting, or who is not cooperating. It is very difficult to say just how much territory is effected. Several hundred square miles anyway are in danger.

In mixing and spreading poison we have actually ordered, or actually used upward of one hundred tons of bran, and much more will yet be purchased. . . . In addition to this, large quantities of lemons, salt, molasses, and arsenic have been used. The smelter at Anaconda has co-operated with us very well and has gone out of its way to aid us in getting the arsenic we need. . . . Without doubt many thousand acres of crops have been saved. I was at a "mixing bee" on the shores of Flathead River in Flathead County, last Monday morning. Ninety farmers . . . mixed something over twelve tons and spread it the same day. The whole program is working very well . . . though we are somewhat uneasy about the possibility of winged hoppers flying in from the surrounding mountainous country and doing damage later on. . . .

The Federal Government has sent in men, Mr. Creek, Mr. Rockwood, and Mr. Taylor, who were sent here from the Forest Grove Laboratory, Forest Grove, Oregon. The work has been divided, and they have been attending to poisoning of Indian lands, power sites, reservoir sites, and other public lands while we have been attending to the poisoning of the lands owned or rented by the farmers.

I shall be pleased to give you all the information I have regarding these troubles, and if necessary, come to your office and talk with you.

VERY RESPECTFULLY,

R. A. COOLEY

Following World War I, drought was a major factor that broke Montana's farmers. It started in the northern counties during 1917 and moved southward. By 1918, Hill County registered precipitation half that recorded the year before. Throughout 1919, over 3,000 county residents were destitute, and countless letters from across Montana reached state agencies pleading for assistance. Governor Samuel V. Stewart finally called a special legislative session in July, 1919, during which lawmakers debated the weather but reached no solutions and adjourned. Ada Abare, a Hill County resident, typified the growing frustrations of homesteaders.

SOUTH TACOMA, WASH.
FEBRUARY 24, 1919

DEAR SIR:

I have been advised to write you in regards to securing a loan from the state so as to put in a crop this spring. I have had a failure the last two years. 1917 I had 40 acres of flax a complete failure and 1918, 40 acres wheat and 20 acres flax not worth harvesting. I was a widow when I took this homestead [in] 1916 and have since remarried. Last April my husband was drafted into the service at Havre, Montana. . . . We are with out funds and want to put in a crop this year. The 40 I had in wheat last year has to be plowed this year at a cost of 4 dollars an acre besides the other work. I can get the 60 acres put to crop on the 50-50 basis if I pay for seed and 160 dollars for plowing of the 40 acres that was broke two years ago. I have still 7 months to live on homestead before I can prove up. I want to know if there is a way to get help from the state. We have nothing to farm with at the present

time — It has taken more than I was able to earn to pay for crops I had put in. My homestead is 30 miles N.W. of Havre Montana. My husband was [just] discharged from Camp Lewis, Wash. That's why we are here. . . .

ADA ABARE

DEAR MADAM:

Replying to yours of February 24th I regret to say that there has been no provision so far for loans by the state to farmers this spring. There is a bill now before the legislature authorizing the Montana Council of Defense to make loans, but it has not passed both houses. If this authority is granted, notice of it will be printed in the newspapers and I would suggest that you write the Council of Defense, Helena, about March 8th and make inquiry as to whether the legislature gave the authority to make loans.

C. T. STEWART
SECRETARY OF STATE

Conflicts between homesteaders and livestock owners were not unknown in Montana, although never as dramatic as sometimes pictured. Some ranchers still considered the public range as their private grazing domain, however, and the arrival of the stubborn homesteaders intensified a long-standing hostility toward farmers. Competition for the land endured throughout the era and subsided only after many of the homesteaders had departed. Here, BILLINGS GAZETTE Editor Leon Shaw informed the State Agricultural Commissioner about one farmer-rancher confrontation.

JUNE 4, 1918

DEAR SIR:

In the Custer district, 40 miles east of Billings, a Wisconsin man has purchased eight or ten sections of land for speculative purposes. . . . There are a number of stockmen in the vicinity and they need the land for grazing purposes. But instead of leasing the land to stockmen, he lets it out section by section to a homesteader with one or two horses at a nominal rental to keep the stockmen off. The stockmen have offered to lease the land at a reasonable figure — $25 a section for dry land, which is regarded as sufficient when it is

considered that the building of reservoirs will be necessary in order to have water.

The homesteaders immediately drive off the stock of the stockmen, and then dog the stock. The Wisconsinian's property is not fenced, and he evidently wants to raise a good stand of grass. On the other hand such action has a decided tendency to curtail livestock operations, and certainly meat is necessary for war purposes. We are at a loss how to proceed. . . .

VERY RESPECTFULLY

LEON SHAW

A young widow, Lulu Benjamin, settled on the Montana plains in the mid-1890's. While raising a son, she ran her small farm in the state's southeastern corner. Unlike some home-steaders of more recent years, she adjusted well to the hardships of the plains. Experiencing homestead problems of two eras, she epitomized those Montanans who weathered adversity and stayed on the land. Mrs. Benjamin wrote frequently to a friend's mother about the beauty and wonders of the Montana landscape.

ALZADA, MONTANA
FEBRUARY 28, 1920

MY DEAR MRS VILAS —

Sometime ago I asked your dear daughter if I might write to you and she told me I could do so. I consider it a great privalege to write to the Mother of the good woman who has tided us over so many rough & trying times. . . . I want to tell you of our wonderful country where we have all work and no play and, until the last two years, no sickness & no death except the very aged or by accident. I will tell you at another time about the people, I mean the natives — the old timers we call them — no such queer specimens anyplace as here so we think. —

The wide scope of these plaines carries a spell-bound sentiment to me through all these years. All sunrise—all sunset—all horizon and beauty every-where because of the greatness and vastness. No trees—no foliage except the cultivated trees & bushes about the ranch homes—from one side of my little house we have a strech of plaines that reaches 40 miles to the next tree. The soil is a sandy lome that is very productive—a very nutritious hay covers the plaines — the growth not very high but forms a perfect wheat top and is very fattening to any sort of animal. The sunshine — O the beautiful sunshine is all glow—so few dark days here & little rain & few storms except mid winter so we have little moisture & all thru the country large reservoirs are built to conserve water. . . .

Here & there are great stretches of land that is barron—this soil is called gumbo. It is absolutely barron except during the month of July. This land is covered with a beautiful little green sprout that developes a gorgeous little lillie about as big around as a silver dollar—called gumbo lillies. . . . The crocus is the earliest flower and the cactus the loveliest of all [and] is the last to bloom in the fall. We grow no crops without irrigation so few crops are grown except [in] the garden spots.

The wild animals are the antilope—porcupine and they are plentiful. [There are] few snakes [on] account of dry land. In my years living here I have never seen one on our place. We live 50 miles to [the] nearest railroad point and 18 miles to inland post office. Houses in this country are low & small, [on] account of much high wind & little money to buy lumber. We go 25 miles across the country into Wyoming & cut spruce trees & haul them 25 miles back for our fuel. Our wood pile is always higher than our house all the time. . . .

SEPTEMBER 17, 1920

. . . Our land lays near the borders of Montana, Wyoming & So Dakota. Our homesteads lay in a flat valley, no trees, no brush except a few here & there on the streams or water holes. 25 miles from our place on the Wyoming side in the hills or Sheep mountains . . . is where we go to get our wood. . . . The hills are thickly covered with wonderful pine trees. This section is all government land and the settlers are allowed to cut the dead or dying timbers & haul pine cones for their supply of fuel.

It is the custom of the settlers to club together two & three families & go in the fall while the good weather is on & camp for 3 or 4 weeks at a time & cut their wood & fence posts for the years supply & then haul it home. . . . Each man has his own supply marked out & no one bothers his outfit no matter how long a time elapses before his hauling is finishing. . . .

The first trip we made to the Pines we joined a party of twelve. I drove my own team [and] rode in my buggy with my son then too small to handle an ax. I had hired a neighbor man to drive my other team & wagon for hauling. He was to do my felling of trees. . . . We located where there was a cute log cabin so I was domiciled there and I agreed to do the cooking for the crowd. . . . They would be far from the camp & all took guns not only for protection but in case of wild game. The men explained to me I must learn to use a gun for my own protection but I thot a signal from the dinner bell would bring me the help I needed if danger came. . . . We were in this camp 3 weeks but I was not left there alone. The other women could handle a gun as well as the men so one of them always stayed with me. In all these years I have not learned to handle a gun. . . .

No federal or state aid was available to assist drought victims. Bankrupt and destitute home-steaders turned to the Salvation Army and the Red Cross for help. Helpless to aid the thousands of homeless, officials of these agencies argued that drought sufferers were a state concern. Shelby attorney W. M. Black witnessed the disaster and wrote Governor Joseph M. Dixon about its proportions. Unable to hang on, many left in despair — one with a poetic sign on his wagon: "Twenty miles from water, forty miles from wood. We're leaving old Montana and we're leaving her for good."

SHELBY, MONTANA
JULY 28, 1921

HON. JOSEPH M. DIXON,
HELENA, MONTANA

MY DEAR SIR:

I have been requested by several responsible persons in this vicinity to place the following situation before you. . . . Owing to continued crop failures due to drouth, cut worms, and grasshoppers in this county and the counties adjacent to this along the main line of the G.N. Ry. a large majority of the people are in very hard circumstances. They have very little to eat and will have very little to wear to keep them from suffering when cold weather approaches. They will also find it almost impossible to obtain fuel in sufficient quantities to keep comfortable. A survey of the situation reveals that several families at present are not getting enough to eat.

I know of three families right now, Governor, where there are a father and mother and from two to four minor children, and either the father or the mother is unable to work owing to illness or infirmity, the children are too young to take care of themselves. In one instance the mother is almost an invalid, she has three children, the father cannot leave her. . . . All they have had to eat for the past two months has been potatoes, last year's crop, bread and eggs. They sold what little butter one cow made in order to buy a little sugar and syrup. The children are almost naked, and are indeed a pitiable sight. Other instances might also be cited, some better than this, others worse. One family of eight, the mother an invalid, only one cot in the single room shack, the oldest child about twelve years of age, no chairs or dishes, only tin plates and spoons. The father is working on the railroad section but cannot meet expenses.

The Red Cross has an agent here, a man, but he does not seem to grasp the situation. . . . A woman could do much better for the reason that she could visit these homes and have personal, heart to heart talks with the mothers in the homes. Many of these people feel proud and in many instances do not feel like soliciting aid, altho they are in dire need. Those of us who are more fortunate believe that a wider and better movement should be set on foot in order to take care of these unfortunate people, and at least these small children. They are really the ones who are suffering. They need more for the upbuilding of their bodies than the food they are now obtaining. They will become our future citizens.

Immediate aid for some is required in the line of food and clothing. A system of relief which can be extended as it is required should be instituted for what will be required in winter weather. We understand that work can be obtained over in Washington on small tracts of land, which may also be rented. But these farmers cannot leave in many instances; some have not the railroad fare. But many could leave and obtain work if they had the transportation. Others might find work in the localities in this State where crops are good if there was a system of finding where this work could be had, and some means of getting the man there. These people are all American born largely, and feel that it is their fault that they are in the condition they now find themselves and do not like to ask for aid. . . .

Now Governor, I have written at length on this as I feel deeply about it. I know these people personally, some are my neighbors. I believe a more extended action should be taken by the Red Cross, or some such organization for this relief. . . .

We feel that the present representative of the Red Cross . . . has not grasped fully the situation which exists. Many of these people donated eagerly what they could from their small living during the war . . . and now, owing to no fault of theirs, they are certainly entitled to relief. . . .

YOURS RESPECTFULLY,

W. M. BLACK

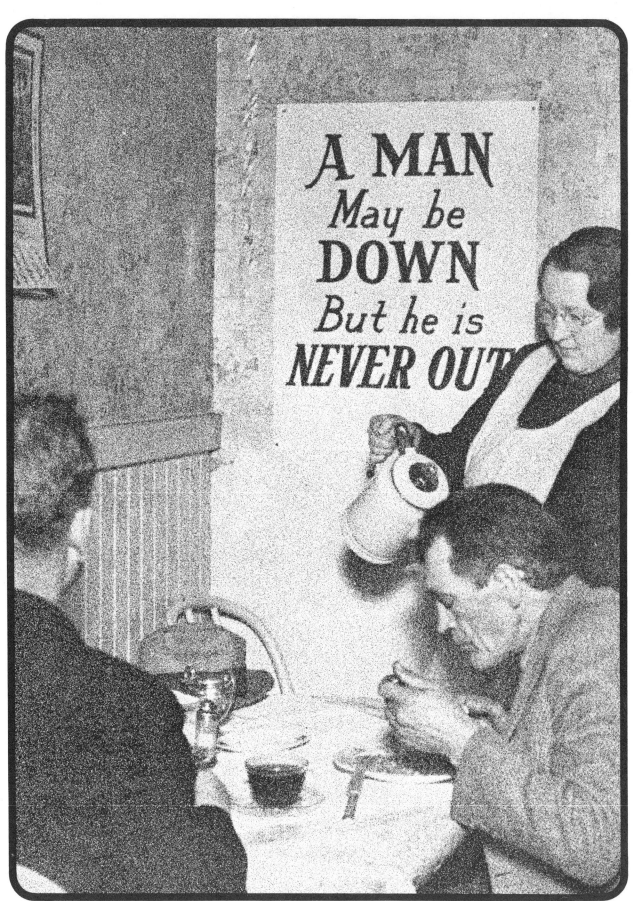

photo by Leslie Jorud

A DECADE OF DESPAIR

THE GREAT DEPRESSION only intensified the distress that Montana's agricultural community in particular had experienced since the "boom and bust" of the homestead period. The mid and late 1920's saw some recovery for Montana agriculture and industry, but financial normalcy had not been fully achieved when the stock market crash of October, 1929, rocked international finance and changed the lives of a generation. Farmers who had survived the trauma of the later homestead years again faced falling markets, restricted credit, overextension and foreclosure. Disastrous natural conditions compounded their troubles. Drought and dust storms, hail and grasshoppers plagued farmers and ranchers in section after section of rural Montana.

As the decade of the 1930's began, farmers were by no means alone in their distress. Montana industry, particularly copper, suffered heavily from falling demand and low prices, resulting in shutdowns, layoffs or shortened work schedules. Rapidly spreading economic contractions were soon translated into severe hardship and losses for every segment of Montana's population.

The depth of the Depression came in 1932. Disenchantment with the apparently ineffective policies of the Hoover Administration brought landslide victory to Franklin D. Roosevelt in November. His assumption of the office brought liberal economic theory to federal policy making. While not a long-term solution to the Depression, the historic federal programs which followed, known broadly as the "New Deal," brought immediate short-term help in the form of relief, agricultural loans, and public works employment. In Montana, government monies built Fort Peck Dam, subsidized many community projects, including storm sewers in Butte, supported publication of a state guidebook, funded county records surveys, relocated bankrupt farmers, and brought hundreds of idle city youths to C.C.C. camps to reclaim lands and repair roads and trails in a pristine atmosphere.

As with most major federal programs, not all the accomplishments of New Deal agencies were positive. Graft, political wrangling, nepotism and favoritism marred the operations of some programs with confusing "alphabet soup" names. Impersonal bureaucracy often frustrated, disillusioned or defeated Montanans seeking relief. President Roosevelt's "pump priming" programs did not solve the ills of the Depression.

In the long term, economic stability returned to the United States — and Montana — through the demands of war. Armament orders from European nations, beginning in 1938 and 1939, and later from the U.S. military, revitalized heavy industry. The positive effects of this upsurge eventually pervaded the national economy. In the same years, the drought ended and Montana agriculture again produced to capacity for more favorable markets and prices.

The Great Depression left Montana and the nation a varied legacy: exaggerated fear of future economic catastrophe, conservative opposition to Roosevelt and his "socialist" doctrines, distrust of big business, and increased reliance on and acceptance of big government in Washington.

A DECADE OF DESPAIR
The Depression Years in Montana, 1929-1939

Following the stock market crash in 1929, the Depression rapidly spread throughout the country, drastically altering the conditions of life for everyone. Major institutions in which society had steadfastly believed during earlier decades failed, taking with them opportunity, options, and the illusions of a generation. For many, government, on all levels, became the only source of hope and salvation to the destitute, whether they lived on a farm or in the city, whether they were young or old. J. E. Finch's plea to Democratic Governor John Erickson typified the growing despair as the Depression deepened.

SUMATRA, MONTANA
JULY 16, 1931

DEAR GOVERNOR ERICKSON:

I am writing you regarding the deplorable conditions existing at the present time. . . . Many people here are now and will be suffering for the necessities of life. Many of us still wish to keep our self respect and wish to get along if possible without appealing to Charity. . . . Is there any place in the State where we people here can go to get State work? Why are not road projects in active operation at the present time when so many of us poor farmers are in such desperate need? Do not the officials of this State realize the desperate financial condition of the people of Eastern Montana? Can you not realize yourself Governor that 90 percent of the cattle, sheep, and horses here will be forced on the market in the next few weeks . . . and that this stock when placed upon the markets will not bring 1/4 of its real value . . . These sacrifices will injure this whole State for the next ten years and at the same time fill up our prisons and lunatic Asylums to a still higher degree. A man who has been driven half crazy by stress of circumstances does not care much about law and order. Or a man and woman who see there accumulation of years foreclosed upon and sold for a song will soon be fit candidates for Warm Springs. . . .

I am an old man, 70 years old. I and my old wife at the present time have one baking of flour left and one pound of coffee. We have no credit and no work. Our 400 acres of crop is utterly destroyed. We had no crop last year and only a very poor yield in 1929. In 1928 hail destroyed our crop with no insurance. In a short time the Bank will take our stock and other creditors our Machinery. We have lived here 20 years and I have paid $3500 in taxes since I have been in Montana and this is the end. What can you or anyone do about it?

VERY SINCERELY YOURS,

J. E. FINCH

Depression devastated all sectors of Montana's economy. Industry in the state, and communities dependent upon it, suffered at least as heavily as their counterparts in the East. Butte's copper mines, the basis of the area's economy, stagnated under falling demand and prices. John E. Corette, Sr., Butte attorney and businessman, characterized the financial climate in the Mining City in a letter to William Taaffe of Newark, New Jersey.

MARCH 20, 1931

DEAR BILL,

Your letter of the 16th arrived yesterday and . . . I was sorry to hear of your financial condition. The business depression there is nothing compared to the business depression here. You probably know that before the crash copper was selling at eighteen cents per pound, and that today it is selling at ten cents, with no market. Our mines are practically closed as our products are copper, silver and zinc, and the price for those products is so low, and in addition there is such a small market, that we are probably going through a harder period of depression than any other section of the country. I am sorry I cannot assist you at this time, but practically every business in which I am interested here is now, and has been, losing money for the past year, and I am myself a heavy borrower, and do not feel that I could borrow more, or take any more burdens myself.

Is it not possible for you to do there as we have done here? Have your company borrow the money from your bank, or borrow money on your life insurance policy. . . . With love to all of you, I am

JOHN E. CORETTE

Depression reality drove many to escapism. The 1930's produced a culture which sought release in new entertainment — it was the golden age of motion pictures, dance marathons, walkathons, flagpole sitters, comic strip heroes and swing music. Events like walkathons offered cash prizes and poverty tempted many to participate on the chance of winning. A Butte resident, irate that such an event could be held, protested to the Governor.

BUTTE, MONTANA
MAY 7, 1931

GOV. ERICKSON
HELENA, MONTANA

DEAR SIR:

I am taking the liberty of writing to you in regard to this Walkton [walkathon] that is being carried on at the Temple Ball room in Butte by some Seattle people. It is a shame and disgrace to tolerate anything like this when there is so many hungry people in Butte. . . . They take in on an average of 1555 dollars every 24 hours. So you can see how much better it would be if that money was left in Butte as there is certainly people that need it worse than giving it to some foolish thing. . . . After this Walkaton is over they are going to have a Rocking chair contest. They have to rock for 50 hours without eating or sleeping or drinking and we as taxpayers in the state of Montana think that it is time that such things are stopped as they all help to take the money out of Montana and it is needed at home badly.

A TAXPAYER

Staggering debt, crop failure, falling prices and the imminence of foreclosure faced many Montana farmers. Some gave up and left, others continued, aided by outside employment. To a few, the frustrations and seeming inequity of the Depression demanded radical solutions. Economic distress fostered a multitude of radical, "leftist" movements in the United States during the 1930's. Some Pondera County farmers chose this course, relying on cooperation and resistance to protect their futures.

The following Resolutions have been adopted by the farmers of Pondera County, Montana, assembled this Twentieth Day of January, 1933, at Conrad. . . .

We are resolved at all hazards to defend the safety of our homes and our access to the necessities of life.

We are resolved that [these things] shall not be taken away from us by the injustice of requiring debts to be paid in an American dollar that has been so mishandled as to make it buy five times as much farm produce as it did five years ago.

We are resolved . . . to prevent collection of debts by legal processes, in terms of a dollar which bears an unjust and fraudulent purchasing power, . . . by . . . the Legislature and Governor of our State, [on] all foreclosures upon farms, farm equipment and homes . . . until such time as the purchasing power of the American dollar in terms of farm produce shall be . . . equal to the purchasing power of said dollar . . . when our farms and homes became involved in debt. . . .

Americans sought explanations for the catastrophe they endured. Some continued to believe that hard work and thrift could answer the financial ills of the country. They viewed the "Roaring Twenties" as a period of profligacy and the most obvious reason for the crash that followed. Charles T. Gadsden, resident manager for the New Mine Sapphire Syndicate, seemed an unlikely proponent of such attitudes, having responsibility for a mining company which had not operated in years because of poor market conditions. Gadsden's views of the Depression and its causes, as expressed in a letter to the company president, represented one view in the nation's search for answers.

YOGO MINES
MAY 31, 1933

MY DEAR MR. WOOD:

I was very glad to hear from you again. . . . Conditions in this country do seem to be improving somewhat except of course in our own particular line and that seems to be quite hopeless. . . . This depression had to come in this country, war or no war. I told you both in 1920 and 1923 that a combination of prohibition and motor cars would ruin any country on earth. When people mortgage their homes and Life Insurance Policies to buy cars to run about and drink Moonshine in, it can only lead to nothing else.

I . . . [know] of only one man who would be in a position to buy the Mine. . . . I explained to him that any reasonable offer would be submitted to the Shareholders and that I would like to see the property all kept in one block so that it would be possible for it to be worked again someday for the good of the surrounding country. . . . I was unable to pay this last installment of the 1932 taxes due today. The Counties have much land

on their hands to sell. . . . I suppose that will probably be the end of this. . . . If the pendulum ever swings back to sparkling gems it will be when wages and salaries are good but not so extravagant, when credit [on] cars is limited, and when sparkling wines are legal. . . .

Think of all the hundreds of thousands of dollars paid out here to men not more than ten of whom ever tried to save one cent. Now we are taxed to keep them. The more . . . they went in debt . . . the less they would ever try to do. No wonder the Robot will replace them. . . . This country is always after the Big Fellow . . . it's the labouring men they should be after. . . .

I can only see disaster in the Government loaning so much money to these so-called farmers. They dont ever intend to pay back and they never will. It is utterly destroying what little independence and moral dependability they possess and that is not much. . . . The Government is in this loan business for ever. . . .

YOURS SINCERELY,

GADSDEN

Fort Peck Dam dominated New Deal public works efforts in Montana. One of the first major national projects of its kind conceived by the Roosevelt Administration, it embodied not only hope for temporary relief but long-term benefits: the great earthfill structure would provide flood control, irrigation, recreation, and, eventually, hydro-electric power. For the Depression, the giant project became a source of jobs, from its beginning in October, 1933, to its virtual completion in 1940. John Pope, a local employee of the Mississippi Valley Water Conservation Commission, commented to Governor Frank Cooney on the project's potential.

JULY 31, 1933

GOV. FRANK COONEY
HELENA, MONTANA

DEAR SIR:

During my trip to the Ft. Peck Reservoir and Dam site I . . . heard a great deal about conditions and sentiment in that part of the State. The sentiment in Glasgow is very favorable to the project on account of the

amount of work which will be done in this vicinity and the employment it will give and this relief is very badly needed. During the last three years Valley Co. has received from $2,500,000 to $3,000,000 in what amounts to charity from the Red Cross and in relief including seed loans, feed loans, &c which will never be repaid. The almost absolute failure of the crops this year due to drought and grasshoppers has made conditions there worse than at any previous time. These people will have to be fed this winter and the continued application of charity has already demoralized the population. . . . Employment for the people will change this almost overnight and kill the communistic sentiment which is largely created by outside influence through paid workers.

The only opposition I found to the Ft. Peck project was from land owners along the Missouri River who are opposed to selling their lands since they have a large amount of range for their livestock principally in McCone Co. . . .

I inspected the Ft. Peck Damsite and the lower 25 miles of the Reservoir site with Murphy, Engineer in charge for the War Dept. The site is favorable for a large storage and the land to be flooded is 85% valueless. . . .

YOURS TRULY,

JOHN D. POPE

Bank failure plagued Montana in the years of agricultural collapse after World War I, and Depression brought closure to another series of banks. While not as severe as the earlier period, over twenty lending institutions closed their doors between 1929 and 1933. These failures brought even more hardship to the largely rural population they served. One of the failed institutions, the Reed Point State Bank, closed because of overextension and under-capitalization. Liquidating Agent T. W. Marshall described the remaining assets of the bank to R. W. Johnson of the State Banking Department.

BILLINGS, MONTANA
DECEMBER 22, 1933

DEAR MR. JOHNSON:

The assets remaining of the Reed Point State bank, in liquidation, consist of a safe, 120 acres of dry land, a small bank balance and some very small notes of doubtful value. I advised one of our directors that I was sending out notices of an annual stockholders' meeting for the second Tuesday in January and he suggested that

I find out if it is necessary. . . . Please advise me.

I thank you for your letter of Dec. 19th and will appreciate it if you will advise me if you have an opening in the near future with the Department, I would be glad if you know of a position with a Montana bank at this time.

YOURS VERY TRULY,

T. W. MARSHALL
LIQUIDATING AGENT

Public works employment often took forms other than major construction. Dorothy Ball found work as an extra employee in the U.S. Land Office at Great Falls. In her case, the enforcement of federal rules made the wages insufficient. This was not uncommon, for relief work often paid little and was inadequate for life's necessities, even at low prices. Mrs. Ball complained to Governor Cooney about the inadequacy of her compensation and the seeming capriciousness of the federal bureaucracy.

GREAT FALLS, MONTANA
FEBRUARY 15, 1935

HONORABLE MR. COONEY:

. . . There are four girls in the office of Tom Corbally and all widows with children, not only doing the work of the day to earn a mans salary, but doing the sewing, washing, ironing and cooking for our families. This has been cut so that we are not making the wages of a Western Union boy. I have been cut to $34.00 per

month giving me 14 working days. My brother on the grazing project cut to $22.00 per month. Would you call $54.00 living wages for educated people...? We were the lowest cut on both projects, the alibi, . . . is we live at home. We . . . can hardly expect our 72 year old Father who has been a tax payer in Montana since 1881, and broke from the strain of it; to keep several families that are grown. . . . To show you the financial condition of my Dad, he is not even in a position to take advantage of the Home Loan.

I feel if the so-called investigators are drawing salaries to make proof of cutting the budgets to the disgraceful sum of $34.00 and $22.00 they have not lawfully gone into our case. . . .

Mr. Corbally has fought for this project for the interest of his office. . . . I feel rather guilty troubling you with this information but there are none on these projects driving or buying new cars, saving money for a college education or enjoying any luxuries of life. We don't want relief jobs if we could get any thing else; but its impossible as you know. . . .

Thanking you for your interest, I am

SINCERELY,
DOROTHY DICKINSON BALL

Work on Fort Peck Dam stimulated the economy of the Glasgow area. At the peak of construction, in 1936-1937, over 7,200 men toiled on the structure. Demands for housing and services led to a series of boom towns in the area not unlike the gold rush camps of the previous century. Orlo Misfeldt, area salesman, itemized these towns for the local newspaper.

GLASGOW, MONTANA
MAY 20, 1935

GLASGOW COURIER
GLASGOW, MONTANA

SIRS:

Enclosed is . . . the final listing of the mushroom towns, which has included the following newly formed temporary residential and business areas:

Park Grove	Idlewild
New Deal	Valley
Wheeler	Martinville
Delano Heights	Sorensons Place
McCone City	Parkdale
Lakeview	Midway

The towns of Cactus Hill, Hiland, Roosevelt, Square Deal, [and] Wilson are not listed for the reason that there are but few people living in them as yet. Some of them are growing and some are losing population, so that this listing is held up until the population becomes less transient.

The list supplied contains the names of some 1600 individuals located in mushroom towns in the damsite area. Nearly every person listed is the owner of his home, however small, and is the father of a family. . . .

YOURS TRULY,

O. H. MISFELDT

While federal programs could provide relief to the destitute and the unemployed, bureaucratic "red tape" also had its place in New Deal agencies. Eva MacLean, writing years after the Depression, did not remember the government's efforts with fondness. Her disenchantment, while not typical, reflected the problems caused by impersonal application of federal directives.

GLENDIVE, MONTANA

Back . . . in 1933, . . . the word "relief" was only mumbled with downcast eyes. . . . While most of us piled up mortgage upon mortgage, kept our worn-out shoe soles firmly on the floor, and saved the sugar for Sunday company, we watched with shocked amazement the ease with which public aid was being condoned by many hitherto proud neighbors. . . . I am inclined to suspect that [my] self-righteousness was tinged with a bit of envy for the ease with which these others were able to make the best of a bad situation. . . .

A year or two after this I had occasion to learn how the shoe felt on the other foot. . . . A job of any sort seemed Heaven-sent in that year of no crops, . . . but [my husband had to] "sign up for relief," [in order to get a W.P.A. job]. . . . We told each other . . . that the money would be more than honestly earned, that it was a matter of community interest.

With our son helping him, my husband put in ninety hours on [the] school house that summer. Since our family was four in number, his wages were doled out to him at the rate of $10 per month in food orders. . . . After receiving one $10. dole as pay for the school house work, we were notified that our son, who was ready for his senior year at high school, was called to the C.C.C. with a note to the effect that relief grants would be discontinued to any family whose son failed to comply.

It had cost us no small sacrifice to put [him] through the first three years, and we had no intentions of being balked in our determination to see him graduate. . . . We simply ignored the imperious summons. Within a few days we were honored by a visit from the relief officer. . . . My expostulations that the food we had received was in payment for services rendered, were met by the argument that relief money was relief money and no family should have it if life could be sustained otherwise by any member thereof. . . . The following month the family's relief check was cut to $7.50. . . .

Subsequent observation and experience with the W.P.A. have convinced me that if the morale of the people has been lowered . . . by their dependence on work relief, it is due . . . to the failure . . . to inculcate a pride and personal interest in the job itself. . . . I have always felt that it should have been easy in the beginning to stimulate pride in this vast program of National improvements. All other branches of federal employ are respected professions, even though they are also supported by taxation.

[Sometime later] my husband [was] hired to work his horses on a C.W.A. road project. . . . Red tape, that omniverous devourer of all public affairs, had delayed the approval of the work until the forty below weather of Montana's early winter had set in earnestly. . . . For the first several weeks there was no time to build camp shelters or sheds for the horses. There was no cook shack nor building of any sort anywhere near the works. . . . My husband left home at five each bitter morning in our decrepit car, in order to give his horses such care as he could and be ready for work by seven. From his departure until his return about 7:30 in the evening, he never saw a fire. Often the lunches the men carried were frozen hard by noon. Only a fortunate few owned vacuum bottles in which to carry their coffee. One man well along in years, must be helped to drink his coffee — his old hands shook so from the cold that he could not guide the cup to his lips. . . . Later, as the work was nearing completion, a small cook car was provided in which a fire could be kept and part of the men could crowd into it for lunch. Some shelter for the horses was also arranged for.

Since then I have seen many W.P.A. workers loitering around fires at all hours of the day. . . . We always exclaim virtuously: "That's the W.P.A. for you!"

Emergency employment extended beyond common conceptions of manual labor. Falling revenues idled thousands of social scientists, artists, historians, and others in fields of higher education and the professions. The government determined to use this pool of expertise in various Works Progress Administration programs. In Montana, several projects received attention: publication of a state guide book; county and state records surveys; plus several other publications, including COPPER CAMP and LAND OF NAKODA. The W.P.A.'s federal headquarters discussed its "white collar" program in a memorandum distributed to its state offices.

The "White collar worker":

Our more modern civilization has stressed the need of education, and we have made it possible for a much larger percentage of the people to train themselves for occupations other than "pick and shovel." We have discovered that there are periods in our present day civilization when an education does not guarantee a job. All that has been accomplished is to lift a certain portion of our citizenry out of the pick and shovel class into the "Pen and ink" group.

When "hard times come a knocking at the door" now we cannot put all of the idle people to work as common laborers. Many of them have been educated and

trained for brain work rather than brawn. They would be more out of place on muscular labor than the laborer would be on a pen and ink job. . . . Today we construct public buildings and highways, dams and landing fields, to keep the men busy. . . . There are many men and women who are better fitted for the class of work required in making economic surveys, gathering data on sociological conditions, etc. . . . to permit a thorough study of the causes leading up to such a condition.

Consequently, the workers who are assigned to "white collar" projects are not only being given an opportunity to earn their living but are helping solve a great problem for future generations. . . .

Agricultural depression and continued severe drought ruined many farmers and ranchers who had survived earlier rainless cycles. The combined problems continued through 1938, particularly in Eastern Montana counties, necessitating massive federal aid. Direct relief, feed and seed loans, or resettlement were stopgaps at best. They could not stop the wind, grasshoppers, and the lack of rain. To many it became apparent that parts of Montana would never be continually productive, for the cyclical moisture pattern made intensive dryland farming impossible. James E. Murray, Montana's junior Senator and a champion of the farmer, received repeated descriptions of Montana conditions. A sampling of his correspondence reflected the despair that ended only with the saving rainfalls of the late 1930's.

OPHEIM, MONTANA
JUNE 28, 1933

. . . It is my conclusion that this territory is "gone to the grasshoppers". The territory north of Opheim . . . has been nearly all destroyed at this time, and another week will take it all. South of here the farmers are putting up a strong fight with poisoned bran. . . . This looks hopeless on account of so much vacant land, where hoppers are breeding . . . faster than they can be destroyed. . . .

WM. J. FLACHSENHAR

GREAT FALLS, MONTANA
MAY 17, 1937

After 26 years of traveling over this State I am accustomed to seeing things look pretty bad but never before in my humble opinion has the prospect looked quite as bad as it is for north and eastern Montana this year. . . . On May 6th, I was in Scobey where the people of that community were celebrating the anniversary of their last rain. . . .

WM. H. BARTLEY

SACO DIVIDE
MAY 27, 1937

We are definitely in the Dust bowl, no rain for eleven months, day after day of dust storms, grasshoppers hatching by the millions, crops all gone and no feed for livestock. Farmers sacrificed everything they had last winter to bring a few head of cattle through for foundation herds and now cattle look worse than they did last winter. Conditions are desperate. . . .

SACO DIVIDE IRRIGATION COMMITTEE

JORDAN, MONTANA
MAY 31, 1937

. . . The past two years I haven't made any crop, last year I had to sell all my cattle, raised nothing to feed them. This is the worst year we ever have had in Garfield County, Montana. . . .

JOHN WOMBLE

HELENA, MONTANA
JULY 13, 1937

North Valley County, all of Daniels and Sheridan, and I was told, most of Roosevelt, McCone, and Richland have had no rain this year. In the parts of these counties I was in the farmers haven't even feed for their family milk cows, let alone for general farm stock. Wheat won't even yield seed. Not a sprig of green not even of weeds, shows in Daniels County. From the highway I didn't see a day's feed for a single cow. Drought, wind, and dust reign. The whole top soil of the county seemed to be on the move. At times we had to drive with car lights on at midday to be safe.

Thirty families have already moved from the county this spring, and many more would leave if they could raise the money. Leading farmers who have farmed there for twenty-five and thirty years told me that conditions are far the worst they have ever seen. . . . Between Plentywood and Dagmar, in that most beautiful stretch of wheat land in Montana, a thinly scattered stand of wheat is already headed when only about five inches high. The fields are so parched that kernels cannot possibly form. The farmers have turned their live-stock into the fields to graze, but even this will furnish feed for about two weeks only. . . .

EUGENE R. ORMSBEE

Rural electrification emerged as one of the New Deal's most impressive accomplishments. The program's promise was enormous: it expended money, mitigating problems of local business and industry, fostered increased employment, and brought to the farm a more comfortable way of life. REA construction of expensive electric systems to scattered towns and farms brought the agricultural community into the Twentieth Century. Begun in 1935, and not finally completed until the late 1960's, rural electrification in Montana was still little more than a dream when Engineer Raymond Floch wrote Governor Elmer Holt.

MISSOULA, MONTANA
JUNE 3, 1936

DEAR GOVERNOR HOLT,

In view of the fact that so much delay has been experienced in connection with the State Rural Electrification Program . . . it has become quite apparent . . . that some steps should be taken to speed up, or at least to follow up and assist in the action taken upon them after they leave our state office.

I believe . . . the time is right for some properly qualified individual to be sent to Washington, D.C., . . . to see that it gets the proper recognition. This fact has been made evident . . . [in] correspondence from Washington. . . . In very few instances are two consecutive letters . . . received by any individual written by the same official. This alone would not be of serious consequence were it not for the fact that already letters and telegrams have been received from the office in Washington which are plainly contradictory.

I firmly believe the R.E.A. is a most worthy Administration, and has been fostered by men with a vision worthy of historic note. It is, I believe, of such value and of such proportions as to merit the very best efforts any intelligent person of intellectual ability can give it. . . . To speak to the point, I want to have the honor of taking the problems of the State Board, and of the needy residents of our rural districts back to Washington with the authority to present them where and when they are most likely to get prompt action. . . .

YOURS VERY TRULY,
RAYMOND C. FLOCH

Political and economic changes brought about by the Depression and the New Deal did not meet complete acceptance. In an immediate sense the era troubled the lives of most citizens, but more importantly, the changes substantially altered American society for decades to come. Many, like pioneer cattleman Wallis Huidekoper, could not accept these alterations, objecting philosophically and politically to the new trends of the 1930's. The frustrations he shared with fellow rancher Dan Casement reflected a desire to return to values and practices he experienced during an earlier time.

MAY 6, 1939

DEAR DAN,

. . . I had to do a lot of plowing this spring as dandelions got my old stand of alfalfa. . . . Am going to let it set until July and then disk and drag and make good for a large seeding of winter wheat. Do not know how the A.A.A. will like this but to Hell with them. I am like you concerning their representatives and have told them to keep off the American Ranch. One A.A.A. agent last year intimated he could get me some money as I had put certain lands back in forage crops instead of grain but what I told him was plenty. . . .

I found among my ranch mail your [article] . . . called "A Farmer on the Farm Problem". I want to congratulate you on this well written and wonderful article and believe it is the very best thing you have ever put in print. . . . There is one thing I find all over the country from California to Montana and I guess in the Middle West and Far East and that is a rapidly growing feeling against the "New Deal" or rather as we say the "Raw Deal." I believe the coming election will end it for it will either be a Republican or an old time Democrat and there is no doubt but what F.D.R. is slipping and even has Congress against him now. We, here in Montana, have taken up with Wheeler and consider he has done some good work in Washington but he, like all others, has an ax to grind. Oh, why can we not have a clean lot of professional business men running our glorious country instead of a lot of bum politicians. Enough of all this for this time. . . .

YOUR AFFECTIONATE FRIEND,
WALLIS HUIDEKOPER

190

A CHANGING SOCIETY

O NLY THIRTY-FIVE YEARS separated the onset of the homestead era from the end of World War II, but despite the short period involved, Montana witnessed many profound and dramatic changes. In 1910, the state still exhibited many vestiges of its frontier beginnings; by 1945, it had fully entered the modern era. During the interim, many sources of the cultural diversity which had characterized the Nineteenth Century died, departed or adapted. At the same time, technological advances brought Montana into closer, more immediate contact with the world beyond its borders. The result was that by 1945 life on even the most remote farm or ranch was not unlike that found in any other part of the nation. Technology had made many changes in Montana prior to 1910, but these changes had been largely confined to business, industry, and transportation. After 1910, technology began to invade the home. Electricity made housework easier, radios brought entertainment and information, and automobiles gave ordinary citizens greater freedom and mobility.

Such advances were not, of course, without their perils. Montana entered the century naively confident that the state's future was bright and that economic, political, or social inequities would inevitably give way before reason and goodness. Tested by twenty years of economic depression and two world wars, Montanans lost much of their earlier confidence in themselves, their institutions, and their future. During the testing process many traditional values and beliefs came under scrutiny. The church and the family, once unquestioned arbiters of manners and morals, declined in influence. At the same time, many of the old distinctions between classes, religions, races, and sexes lost much of their force within society.

One significant value change that deeply distressed many Montanans concerned the belief in the moral superiority of agrarian life. In the face of this traditional view, Montana's rural areas after 1917 witnessed a continuing out-migration as thousands of the state's citizens departed to seek greater opportunities for economic and personal fulfillment in more populated or industrialized areas. Yet this trend had some positive repercussions upon the state's cultural life. In its wake the outward migration left a tested and resourceful population, and the exploitative spirit that characterized early Montana had declined in influence.

During the first half of the Twentieth Century, Montanans paid dearly for their progress. What was more, they realized that even more complex and baffling problems lay ahead. Yet they looked to the post-World War II era determined to have a hand in making their own destiny.

MAIN STREET, KALISPELL, C. 1925

A CHANGING SOCIETY
Life and Culture, 1907-1945

Most white Americans considered the "Indian problem" well on the way to solution once the Indians had been settled on reservations. Until the 1930's official policy dictated that reservation Indians should be assimilated into white civilization and that traditional cultures should be eliminated. To speed acculturation, the government offered the Indians inducements to adopt the agricultural life and placed their children in agency boarding schools. Despite these efforts — or perhaps because of them — most Indians adapted poorly to reservation life. They realized that the old ways were impractical, but the new world remained a baffling mystery. Caught in a world of poverty and disease and robbed of their cultural identity, many Montana Indians of the early Twentieth Century lived lives of quiet tragedy.

CROW AGENCY
OCTOBER 14-18, 1907

My name is Ethel Plentyhawk. I am 16 years old. My home is at Lodge Grass.

When I was about seven years old I learned how to swim. I learned it from the girls.

My mother show me how to sew. And when I came into the school Hazel One Goose show me how to sew on the sewing machine.

Before I came into the school Mr. Greene taught me a few words in English. I know how to write my name before I came into the school too.

When I was about 8 years old I learn how to ride horse back. My mother used to tie me to the saddle, And when I get tired some time I sleep on the horse and after all I learn how to ride. . . .

When I came into the school I didn't know anything and when I get lonesome and cry Rose Old Bear used to say that our folks will be in to see us and then I stop crying. The first time I ever was in the detail they put me [in] the dining room and I used to think that it was very hard to work in there and sometimes I cry over it. After while they put me in the sewing room and after that they put me in the laundry. I always cry over it because I didn't like to work there.

At the turn of the century, Montana's predominate social mores reflected a white, Protestant, middle-class society. "Blue laws," permitted by local option, were only one aspect of the puritanical restraints on society which remained in effect, in varying degrees, until well into the Twentieth Century.

MR. ALBERT J. GALEN
ATTORNEY GENERAL
HELENA MONTANA

COLUMBIA FALLS
MAY 5, 1911

DEAR SIR:

We are in this city running a motion picture show on a good legitimate basis, and as the town is small (612) it is hard to pull a crowd to defray expenses and pay us amply for our work.

We are desirous of opening our house on Sunday nights with a good clean moral show, giving the young

people a place to go and spend the evening, but the city has an ordinance prohibiting it.

Is there a law prohibiting it? I have been informed that Gt. Falls and Missoula carried this case up and got a supreme court decision to the effect that a moral, quiet show could be carried on on Sunday without violating the laws. All of the Saloons are open on Sunday here, also pool rooms. . . .

Please enlighten us in this matter, as 9/10 of the people here are in favor and want us to show Sundays.

HUFF and WOLGAMUTH

Behind the cloak of middle-class respectability, there lurked a good deal that was unpleasant and disquieting. As the state's largest city, Butte possessed many of the social problems common to the nation's urban areas, as well as many unique to the city's economic base. In order to discover the reason for the high incidence of tuberculosis, Silver Bow county health officials examined sanitary conditions in the mines and above ground from 1908 to 1912. Their report

This investigation was undertaken to determine, if possible, the source of the high death rate from tuberculosis in Silver Bow County.... In this work 438 houses with 1,418 rooms and 2,949 occupants were inspected. In the detailed report we mentioned only ... places ... found to be in an insanitary condition.

No. 22 Corra Terrace: 4 people one bed room, 272 cubic feet air space to each person, toilet outside, sewage disposed of in Cess Pool, own cow, never disinfected, very dirty house, cow pen at back door, many flies, no screens, pipes in sink leaking and water dripping from side of house....

No. 137 East Daly: one room one bed room, 980 cubic feet air space, toilet outside, sewage disposed of into street, don't use milk, never disinfected, one tuberculosis April 1912. Very dirty and filthy place, bad odor, woman very unclean and stated had running sores on her hips, her face and hands were covered with pimples, no garbage can and slops ... thrown into street.

No. 21 Plum St.: conditions in vacant half block adjacent to this place is very insanitary, people in streets above, keep hogs and cows, slops and refuse are thrown into alley, rain washes it down into flat where it lodges in an old cellar on flat, close to 21 Plum St., no drainage from this hole and water stands in it until dried up by the sun, cats are drowned here and dead animals are thrown into this hole, people are compelled to keep windows and doors closed on account of the odor from this place....

Mullin St.: Pile of decayed meat in alley near butcher shop. Refuse thrown on street in front of Mullin House. This part of the street is flat and very little drainage. Refuse from Wells and Center Streets washes down and become stagnant here. Some of the people have cows and the manure is very much in evidence....

Ohio St., Hopkins St., New St., Mahoney St.: This Section is what is known as the "Cabbage Patch" and is too filthy to describe. Found but one garbage can covered, many of the garbage cans on the sidewalks and in streets. Houses small, poorly ventilated, alleys filthy. Dead dog found in alley and judging from odor believe had been dead three or four days. Understand many miners live [here] on account of the cheap rent....

Throughout the century a growing number of students attended various units of the Montana University system. The curriculum was gradually broadened and academic standards upgraded, but student life remained generally placid. Like Kyle Jones, a student at Montana State College in Bozeman, most students apparently believed that all was right with the world and their primary concerns were athletics, debates, dances, and — inadequate allowances.

BOZEMAN, MONTANA
FEBRUARY 25, 1913

MY DEAR MOTHER:

We start rehearsals of the "Prof's Malady" again next Wednesday. We are going to put it on in Belgrade on the 14th or 15th. They have a new opera house there. Belgrade is about 10 miles from here and has a population of about 800.

I am taking violin lessons this semester. I take two lessons a week at one dollar a lesson. The college pays for one of the lessons, however, so I get out of it for a dollar a week. They just hired a new violin professor at the beginning of this semester. I like him very much; he is an artist and as jolly as he can be. I got a violin and case and bow which he selected for me; it cost $28.00. If I find that I can do any good at it, I shall get a better one later.

One of the old members of our dramatic club has just written a comedy drama which will be put on here in Bozeman tonight and tomorrow night. The entire Opera House has already been sold for both nights.... He is an excellent pianist and has in the play fifteen or sixteen songs for which he wrote both the words and music. I have bought tickets to the play and will take a young lady friend along; the first one I have taken to anything this year except to the K.N. dance. You see, I am beginning to "branch out" a little in my post graduate year.

I asked a girl whom no one here ever asks to go to

anything. She is a senior and one of the best girl students here. Also she is vice president of our dramatic club.

If I don't get the $30 pretty soon that I asked you for, I'll soon have no boarding place.

LOVINGLY,

KYLE

An important facet of the Progressive political movement was a renewed effort at social reform. In 1916 Sam C. Ford's promise to enforce all laws won him election as Attorney General, and he immediately began a crack-down on prostitution, gambling, and other illegal activity. Although instances of law enforcement officials winking at the 1907 anti-gambling legislation were common throughout the state, the problem was critical in Butte where the large Chinese population dominated the city's underworld. As the following complaint from the Chinese community indicated, not all Chinese deserved the opprobrium they generally received for their illegal activities. Powerless to intervene in the situation personally, Ford forwarded the letter to the Silver Bow County Attorney who, ironically, handed the investigation to the same Chief of Police, Jere "The Wise" Murphy, against whom Wong had complained.

HELENA, MONTANA
FEBRUARY, 1917

HONORED SIR:

Trusting that you will pardon my intrusion, I am going to take the liberty of communicating with you. I am a chinese and came to Butte, Montana, from the Coast. When I arrived in Butte I naturally sought a location among my own people and located Chinatown which is a very loathsome place.

The number of gambling houses in Butte is alarming. . . . The officials of Butte, that is the County Detective and the Chief of Police pass these places up and never seem to know any thing that goes on. . . . It is

supposed that the Chinese pay heavy bribes to the Officials for their silence. . . .

As I have said before I am a Chinese and came to America for a classical Education — and not to mingle with the corrupt chinese of Butte — however, when a chinese goes to a strange town he naturally looks for some of his own nationality for friends. It was in this way that I got an insight to the vice carried on in Butte. . . .

Trusting that you will give this matter your immediate attention and assuring you that I will watch for results which I hope you can secure, I am

RESPECTFULLY AND OBEDIENTLY YOURS,

A. W. WONG

BUTTE, MONTANA
MARCH 28, 1917

HON. JOE. JACKSON
CO. ATTY.
BUTTE, MONTANA

DEAR SIR: —

You asked me to give you written report of Wong complaint of gambling in chinatown. . . . The places are all about same. There are two doors and rooms are divided off into three parts, in front part is bed, in middle tables chairs and groceries, and in back part toilet, stove, wood, coal and scattered around are dishes, teapots and the like. The chinas claim they eat, sleep and associate in these places. . . .

For a long time past we have constantly looked into these places and others inside and outside of Chinatown where complaints have been made . . . that gambling was going on. We made many arrests and have secured many convictions, as the blotter and court records will show. We are doing all in our power to suppress this evil, but it needs evidence to secure convictions. Plainclothes men and uniformed officers have gone into chinatown places several times day and night. We are nearly always given quick admission and can find no evidence of gambling for money. Sometimes we find them playing dominos and other games, but there is no money or chips in sight or passed, and they say they are playing for amusement only. . . .

We have never found any woman in any of these places only when they are in the stores buying stuff, have watched the places and followed them in. Of course lots of women go to the noodle parlors. We patrol these several times during the day and night and late Saturdays and early Sunday morning have an officer at these places constantly to check up and keep order. . . .

We have tried to get these chinas to gamble with men we have sent to their places, who are not on the force, but they have smilingly refused and responded No Gamble, just play for fun.

We will keep watch and give you a report later.

YOURS RESPECTFULLY,

J. J. MURPHY

Until 1917, Butte boasted one of the largest red-light districts in the country — all one thousand residents licensed by the city. Then Attorney General Ford closed the district, as well as all houses of ill fame in the state. A number of citizens complained that the action would only force the prostitutes out into the open (in most communities this was indeed the case) but perhaps the most unusual appeal Ford received came from one of Butte's "girls."

BUTTE, MONT.
APRIL 10, 1917

DEAR SIR:

I [just] want to drop you a line to informd you that the [Deer Lodge] sporting house is running Wide open, Music, & selling drinks.

May Carroll charge us girls $15.00 per week, & want us to stay with greeks for $2.00 & A White man for $3.00. She treats us girls like dogs. She is in Butte today gathering more girls. . . .

Its a shame to closed the rest of the sporting Houses & leave Deer Lodge run. Its put me out $1000, for I was working [in Butte.] Deer Lodge house [has] 4 to 7 girls working all the time.

All we girls want is justice. . . . I am writing to you hoping you will closed Deer Lodge or open the rest of the good towns.

I know what I am talking about because I live[d] their for two months. . . . If you are going to closed one, closed them all.

YOURS SINCERLY,

MISS GARNETT

In 1917 American entry into World War I led to an extreme nationalism that would have been humorous had it not been so destructive of individual liberties. Montana's Council of Defense, authorized by federal directives to root out pro-Germanism on the local level, proved to be one of the most zealous such organizations in the nation. The Montana Sedition Act of 1918 served as the model for similar federal legislation. By the winter of 1917-1918 the state was so well organized that even the smallest community had its local council and the public, generally favorable to the growing disregard for civil rights, had learned to be alert for enemies within.

HARLEM, MONTANA
APRIL 3, 1918

THE MONTANA STATE COUNCIL OF DEFENSE
HELENA, MONTANA

GENTLEMEN:

As a member of the County Council of Defense I desire to call your attention to some strong Pro-German parties in this Town and to one whom many think is a German Spy. The one referred to as a probable spy is a young man . . . who came into town last fall from no one seems to know where. For a long time he did nothing but walk around the streets with good clothes and spending lots of money making himself a good fellow. A little later he begun giving music lessons. He seems to be very proficient in music and now has classes organized in Harlem and Chinook, going to Chinook once or twice a week.

He still spends much more money than he makes. Some person who talks German has visited him at least a couple of times in the last two months and to this man he talks only German. This man only stopped between trains each time. The last time he was here a party who understood German heard them talking in German and went over and set down near them when one said to the other that they had better stop talking as they might be understood. . . .

A couple of nights ago a steel covered warehouse here was burned, containing 35 new grain binders and other new machinery. . . . Inside was found a new oil can still containing a small quantity of kerosene. . . . It seems certain that the building was set on fire. . . .

After a meeting held here by a number of the business men I was asked to take the matter up with you to see if there could not be a secret service man or detective sent here to look this fellow up and also look up three or four others who are known to be pro-German.

YOURS VERY TRULY

THOS. M. EVERETT

In 1918, the hatred of all things German carried the Montana Council of Defense to concerns far from its original mandate. Through a series of seventeen orders, the Council not only forced adherence to the war effort, but established a social order of unquestioning conformity. Order number three banned all use of the German language in schools, churches, and private gatherings. This rule was particularly tragic for some Montanans, because it deprived the state's German-speaking immigrant groups of the free exercise of their religious liberties.

PLEVNA MONTANA
JUNE 19, 1918

DEAR GOVERNOR STEWART:

I wish to write to you Mr. Stewart of something which lies deep in my heart. Sometime ago the State Council of Defense made an Order preventing the use of the German language in schools and churches. . . . In reply you gave me the answer that on May the 27th several church representatives expected to appear before the State Council of Defense. In regard to this meeting I have as yet, not received word of its result. . . .

To tell the truth our churches are growing very weak on account of that order. We have many . . . who are unable to understand the English language and it's hard for these people . . . not [to] be able to understand a word of what the Gospel of our Lord brings to them.

Every Sunday when I preach in English to these true citizens of our dear country my heart turns sad for they are in tears and their hearts are heavy because they cannot understand what I say.

Concerning myself, Mr. Stewart, I would not have to plead concerning this order, for I am able to preach in the English language. . . . But for these poor stricken emigrants, my heart bleeds. . . . Our church here is a praying church and what they miss more than anything else is their prayer meetings and if our preaching shall be in English cannot we hold our prayer meeting in German? . . .

Wishing the best for the welfare of our glorious Country. . . . I remain

MOST SINCERELY YOURS,

REV. J. E. SCHATZ

Exhibiting both naive sentimentality and patriotic enthusiasm, almost 40,000 Montanans went off to "whip the Kaiser." One of these doughboys was Kyle Jones, a graduate of Montana State College and by 1918, a bank cashier in Bynam. When he wrote his father from training camp in May, Jones was still looking forward to duty with the Quartermasters' Corps, but the Army assigned him to the 347th Machine Gun Battalion. During its brief eighteen days in the front lines of France, this unit sustained heavy losses. In one engagement Jones saw a man literally blown to bits and was wounded himself, although not critically. Like many other soldiers, Private Jones returned to Montana shorn of his enthusiasms for war.

CAMP LEWIS, WASHINGTON
MAY 6, 1918

MY DEAR FATHER:

To-day we all had the second inoculation against typhoid fever. It made me pretty sick for a while and I

actually fainted once. . . . My vaccination took fine and made me sick for three or four days, but I kept right on drilling and working just the same.

We have been issued complete uniforms and also our rifles. They are using the Remington Military Model of 1917 here; it is a beauty but is heavy weighing nearly 10 pounds.

Also today we have practically finished the [physical] examination. . . . I am exempted from trench service on account of my eyes. So unless I am taken in the next officers' training school here I shall not see any trench work. They will transfer me to the Quartermasters' Dept. tomorrow and, they say, will likely start me out writing insurance for the soldiers. The government furnishes cheap insurance for all the men. This is to take the place of the old pension system. . . .

I have been accepted into the service, so I guess I'll be with the army until the war is over. I made a preference for the Quartermasters' Dept., overseas Service. When they found out about my banking experience, they at once told me I would be drawn from this Company into the Quartermasters' Dept. . . .

I hope everything is fine there. I haven't received any mail from that way yet. I shall be feeling fine as soon as all these inoculations are over.

AFFECTIONATELY,

KYLE JONES

Late in September, 1918, Spanish influenza, already an epidemic in other parts of the nation, made its first appearance in eastern Montana and quickly spread through the state's urban communities. During November the number of cases rose rapidly after the long-awaited armistice brought thousands of rural residents to town for victory celebrations. Vaccination was still in the experimental stage and no control measures — even the quarantine efforts at the State Normal College in Dillon — were of any avail. Before the epidemic spent itself, over 1,000 Montanans had died.

DILLON, MONTANA
OCTOBER 21, 1918

TO: CHANCELLOR EDWARD C. ELLIOTT
SUBJECT: CONTAGIOUS DISEASE, CLOSING NORMAL COLLEGE

As indicated in my telegram this afternoon we closed the Normal College at noon to-day by order of the health officer. . . . On Saturday night, October 19, we held a meeting in the City Hall . . . to discuss the best plan of preventing an epidemic of influenza. . . .

It was found that there were five authentic cases of influenza in the county, four of which were in the vicinity of Dillon. None had developed in the Normal College. It was decided that preventive measures should be undertaken. . . . To accomplish that, all churches, schools (except the Normal College), clubs, and the theatre should be ordered closed. Private social parties were forbidden, saloons put under restriction of six people in the room at a time and those to be moved immediately after being served, extra policemen were provided to see that the order was enforced. All chairs, settees and places for lounging were removed from the mercantile establishments and hotel lobbies. It was directed that all in attendance at the Normal College should be housed in the residence halls or on campus and the order was to go into effect for all places Monday morning. . . .

Doctor Walker gave it as his opinion that unless cases of influenza developed in the residence hall there was no need of stopping the school. Yesterday, however, one of the girls became ill and this morning a well developed case of influenza appeared, another one with somewhat suspicious symptoms. Although at the first appearance of illness those girls were isolated, yet we feared that with the large number in the hall serious conditions might develop. For the reasons given here Doctor Walker directed that we close.

While the conditions here in so far as general health and sanitation are concerned and also from the amount of influenza prevalent, I believe we are in better condition than almost any other portion of the state. . . . Yet I agree with Doctor Walker that this is the thing to do. . . .

All of the students, with the exception of those who had the slightest chance to be exposed by the case which had developed are leaving for home this afternoon. . . . The staff are all here and all in good health. They are all subject to order. . . .

J. E. MONROE, PRESIDENT
STATE NORMAL COLLEGE

In 1920, presidential candidate Warren G. Harding called for a return to "normalcy," thus capturing in a phrase the national longing for a return to the bucolic, pre-war world Americans thought they remembered. In Montana nothing so clearly typified the nostalgia for the simple life as did the state fair. Each September crowds gathered in Helena from all over the state for one gala week. As Governor Sam Stewart indicated in his invitation to the 1919 festivities, the main attractions were the agricultural and livestock exhibitions, but the fair also boasted a variety of wholesome entertainments.

To the Citizens of Montana:

It becomes my pleasant privilege, . . . to direct your attention to the relationship of the *State Fair* to the development of the agricultural resources of Montana. . . . It is through the Fair that the State seeks to educate the public mind to a clearer understanding of the importance of agriculture, and to show the relation of the successful farmer to the basic financial fabric of the commonwealth. . . .

The State Fair stands as the great clearing house for the exchange of ideas, the exposition and study of the latest developments of agricultural science and the demonstration of the newest inventions and labor saving devices. . . . The State Fair this year will have a greater significance and mark a new epoch in Montana's development when, after the successful weathering of the three years of drouth, Montana will gather one of her biggest harvests. It will be the great jubilee of the staunch and true farmers whose sturdy allegiance to the Treasure State has been richly rewarded. . . . I urgently request all citizens of this great commonwealth to loyally cooperate with the Montana State Fair by exhibiting and attending.

S. V. STEWART
Governor

The decade of the 1920's was a contradictory period for Montana as it was for the nation as a whole. Beset by agricultural depression, the state's largely rural population experienced the Jazz Age to a lesser degree than other parts of the nation; nevertheless the frivolity of the flappers and bootleggers was as much a part of the era as the tragedy of the honyockers. Typifying the contradiction was the 1923 prize fight between the controversial Jack Dempsey and Tommy Gibbons for which Shelby, flush with nearby oil discoveries, put up over $500,000. Because state law required the profit to go to veterans organizations (there was to be none because of small attendance) a reluctant Loy Molumby, commander of Montana's American Legion, was put in charge of arrangements. Although there was considerable doubt that the fight would take place, few Montanans were critical of wasting so much money when thousands in the state were in acute financial distress.

GREAT FALLS, MONTANA
FEBRUARY 19, 1923

COMMANDER OF THE SHELBY POST
OF THE AMERICAN LEGION
SHELBY, MONTANA

DEAR SIR:

Mr. Dwyer of your post . . . asked me to express the opinion of the State Department in the adviseability of a Legion Post staging a fight in which the notorious slacker Dempsey will participate. . . . Personally I have no hesitancy in telling you how I feel. I believe that Jack Dempsey is champion heavy weight fighter of the world, the same as . . . Jack Johnson was and the sooner he is whipped the better I will like it. I feel that he will never be whipped if he is never fought and I also feel that if he fights often enough some . . . man will whip him and that therefore it ought to be the desire of everybody to see him fight as often as possible. . . . If he is ever licked I don't know anyplace in the world I would rather see him licked than at Shelby, Montana.

However, I would like to caution the post about being very careful about any entertainment that might be provided for this bird. . . . If you must entertain somebody I believe that Gibbons, in spite of the fact that he is not champion, is more entitled to consideration.

YOURS VERY TRULY,
LOY J. MOLUMBY

Prompted by a disintegration of the traditional authority of both church and family, the 1920's witnessed a revolution in manners and morals. The status of women was particularly altered as younger women openly smoked and drank, cut their hair and shortened their skirts, or — even worse — wore trousers! Thirty-year-old Irma Brown was a high school teacher in Big Sandy during the later years of the decade. While she disapproved of some of the student behavior she witnessed, her own life was quite different from that of her mother's generation.

MONDAY, JULY 4 [1927] — We surely had some time in the last two days. The morning of the Fourth we left early for Fort Benton. . . . We made it to town [Big Sandy] in three minutes under an hour and we were in Benton in another hour and fifteen minutes. I tried to buy me a shirt in Powers Store, but the clerks were too busy. Then we chased around looking for Dad. During our search we saw the parade — band, two cowboys, three or four decorated cars, combined harvester and two bicycles. The next event was the speech by former Attorney General Slattery of Great Falls. After the speaking we ate lunch. That fried chicken was mighty good. Benton treated all to ice cream and lemonade. We had a rhubarb pie, but we had forgotten to put in any forks or spoons, so didn't eat it. The band played until about two, when the ball game was to have started. Meanwhile black clouds had been rolling up across the river and light began to grow dimmer and dimmer. Finally we pulled out from the ball diamond — just in time to avoid paying for the game and headed down town. By the time we were there the rain began to fall hard. . . . As soon as the storm let up . . . we put on chains and curtains and started out. . . . The trip home — we left about three P.M. — is now just a nightmare. I don't believe I ever was so scared. . . .

TUESDAY, AUG. 2 [1927] — Most of today has been spent away from home. All but Mom went to town in the forenoon. I bought goods for [making] two pairs of pajamas and picked out the dress that Mom is giving me for my birthday. Furthermore, I had my hair cut. . . . The wheat and other crops between here and town are beautiful in the promise of their harvest. Everyone is spending on his prospects.

June 11 [1928] — We went to Havre and I shot five dollars "into the air, but I know where" — to paraphrase Longfellow slightly. I believe I have a Canadian nickle left. . . . It was circus day in Havre, and everybody and his boy were in town. We wanted to stay, but we would have been so late getting home. I never did get over the kid thrill of a circus in town.

SATURDAY, JUNE 16 [1928] — In the order of their accomplishments I did the following things: turned the milk thru the separator - 10 min.; made a batch of cookies - about an hour; did the ironing - about two hours; turned edges of my diamonds - 15 min; hemmed my sheet - 10 min; located diamonds on the sheet - 20 min; got up the cows - 1 hour; fed while Harold milked - 1 hour. . . .

SATURDAY, AUGUST 25 [1928] — I was just thinking today of how little of world interest [we avail ourselves], or even any interest outside of our immediate home; I am reflecting here. The Sat. Evening Post has taken a political stand — for Hoover — for the first time we know of. Prohibition is an outstanding bone of contention. . . . Shall the farmers get legislative aid? News sent in by radio. Aviators going over land and ocean — and ice. The world is teeming with events...

OCT. 28, [1928] — . . . After dinner Harold brought me to town. I have a nice room here at Fleenors. It's a north dormer, good-size, nicely furnished. I've written Fred and caught up this diary. Now I believe I'll go to Church. . . . Later . . . there's a couple in a car out front and a couple in the dark in the parlor down-stairs. I don't approve of all dark sessions myself.

OCT. 30, 1928 — . . . Had my hair marcelled tonight and now feel more civilized. Made out a few grades. . . .

TUESDAY, JANUARY 15 [1929] — Judged some extemporaneous speeches this morning. It was hard work too. . . . The Trepina kids have little money with which to buy their exercise tablets for English. I have just decided they can work for me after school correcting exercises to pay for them. It's just to keep their self-respect. . . .

FRIDAY, JANUARY 24 [1930] — We left Havre on schedule, arriving here [in Harlem] about nine-thirty. . . . We loafed all afternoon. . . . The games were good hot ones, but Harlem rallied in both cases and won by nine or ten points each. Our guards — girls — played very well. . . . This trip is fun, except that I can't keep the boys out of the girls' rooms. I don't think it looks right. . . .

FRIDAY, APRIL 11 [1930] — Parent-Teachers election. I'm so tired I didn't go. Consequently I was elected secretary.

TUESDAY, DECEMBER 9 [1930] — Had a devastating day today. First a session with Emil Trepina. He wanted to open a window. I refused. Then he wanted to leave the room. That I refused. He began to tease and then talk to other members of the class, all with the intent to make me send him from class. I didn't bluff, but finally attempted to slap him. He fought me; so I stopped. . . . We all had a session with Emil at noon. The kid went yellow under a threat of Reform School.

WEDNESDAY, JANUARY 14 [1931] — This has been a busy day. . . . Lions presented the kids with medals for scholastic achievement over six months or a year ago. Kids figured it all a bunch of hooey.

A second tremendous change came to Montana society as a result of the introduction of the automobile which liberated rural inhabitants from isolation and brought all Montanans into closer contact with the outside world. At the same time, the automobile brought the world to Montana, and the tourist trade flourished. After marrying Gene Reeder, Irma and her husband managed some tourist cabins near Yellowstone Park during the 1930's. Her diary disclosed that although much revolutionized, travel was still not without its hazards.

TUESDAY, MAY 30 [1933] — So far this has been our banner day — six cabins filled. If we can keep this up a while, we should get caught up. . . . Scores of cars have gone by toward Gardiner this A.M. and are now returning. Hope some are tourists who will stop here on their way back [from Yellowstone Park] . . . .

JANUARY 16 [1934] — Did dishes and bed and went down town for haircuts. Bought tobacco and a cigarette roller. Found $30.00 in the Five and Dime Store. No one around seemed to have lost anything so we kept the money. Goodness knows we can use it. . . .

JUNE 22 [1934] — Washed. Discovered bed bugs in No.

17. Got government prescription filled and sprayed 17 and 16. . . .

JULY 1 [1934] — Turning people away. Had the camp filled by three thirty [today.] Hope this keeps up all this month. Found more bugs in 17. Gene fumigated the place and 16 today. Therefore we can't rent them tonight. . . .

JULY 14 [1934] — Boy! What business! Full again tonight. Even rented No. 17, and turned away 4 or 5 cars. More compliments on the camp. . . . Heard this morning we have a reputation for courtesy. One of the [Yellowstone] Park rangers recommended us.

For thirteen years, the nation experimented with Prohibition; Montana tried the "noble experiment" for an even longer period, but with no greater success. In 1916, perhaps as a result of the newly-enfranchised female vote, Montana overwhelmingly banned the sale and manufacture of intoxicating beverages after December 31, 1918. The following month, the Nineteenth Amendment also achieved ratification. From the first, Prohibition was unpopular among a significant number of Montanans, particularly urban and immigrant groups, and during the 1920's the law was violated with increasing impunity. By 1932 repeal had gained such popularity that presidential candidate Franklin Roosevelt included it in his platform. At his urging, Congress repealed the Volstead Act (thus permitting 3.2 beer) and passed a resolution to repeal the Nineteenth Amendment. By December, 1933, the necessary thirty-six states had ratified. Contrary to the hopes expressed by Livingston hotel proprietor Babbitt to Senator Burton K. Wheeler, the Montana Legislature put liquor under government control.

FRIEND WHEELER: —

I want your careful personal attention to a very important matter. . . . When beer and wine and other liquors come back the great fight will be HOW will it be handled. . . .

I assume that you had a sunday school education along puritan lines as I did. . . . You agree the "Saloon must not come back" BUT A PUBLIC DRINKING PLACE WITHOUT A SCREEN IS *NOT* A SALOON. THE SCREEN *WAS* THE SALOON.

The old puritan idea is, if sin exists HIDE it so we cannot see it, compromise with it, by restricting and segregating sin and get as much money as possible out of it. . . .

I am [also] very much opposed to government sale in government places. This would build up a great bureaucracy and be a nuisance. The whole idea in drinking at all is the sociability that men and women crave. I am opposed to restricting the sale to hotels and eating places. That is class legislation. . . . There should be no discrimination of this sort.

The manufacturers should sell direct to the retailer and any liquor or wine should be allowed to be consumed on the premises. . . .

Bring it out into the open. . . . The screen does make the dyed in the wool puritans suspicious that some girl is being raped, someone murdered or robbed within. . . .

It seems to me that this would strike a popular response from the laboring man, all classes of society who enjoy an innocent drink making a little sociability possible and that it would please those who are fed up on bureaus. . . . At the same time it would mollify the fanatical drys because they could at all times see rather than surmise. . . .

VERY TRULY YOURS,

ARTHUR BABBITT, PROP.
PARK HOTEL

After 1929 Montana's agricultural depression blended with the national financial crash, and the low prices, high unemployment, and hard times continued. Because of its substantial government work force, Helena escaped the worst of the Depression. Instead, that city's disaster was natural in origin. From October 3, 1935, to February 22, 1936, over 700 earthquakes shook Helena. Although the majority were only weak tremors, a quake of major proportions occurred on October 18. Many buildings were severely damaged and hundreds of residents were forced into the streets to sleep in automobiles or hastily constructed emergency shelters. Fortunately the loss of life was minimal. On October 28, just as the city was beginning to return to normal, Helen Piper reported the experiences at the Montana Deaconess School to the institution's friends. Ironically, two days later an equally violent quake again shook the city and did even more damage.

HELENA, MONTANA
OCTOBER 28, 1935

DEAR FRIEND:

I feel quite sure that all of our friends are anxiously awaiting news of our most remarkable deliverance. . . . On the night of October 18th, all of the ladies were downstairs at our weekly meeting. There had been one heavy quake just a short time before we came down. . . . Just one week before we had quite a severe one which made many cracks on the walls. In about an hour there came a crash and with the crash the weaving of the building. Truly, the walls went in and out in a most indescribable way. Plastering fell and the lights went off.

Our children were on the upper floors. We called to them to be quiet, that we were coming. Some went up and the old gardener and myself went to the basement to get candles. The boys on the fifth floor had been organized and . . . when the housemother went down in the evening she told the boys that if anything happened to get their teams together.

The walls went out on the fifth floor. Radiators came down. Those brave youngsters jumped out of bed and got their teams together. We could hear them calling to each other to be quiet and not get excited. . . . One of the boys who was quite nervous started to run and his captain said, "You stand still in line, or I'll knock the tar out of you." . . . The little girls were aided by the older girls and some of the teachers. I know you will all be quite proud of our school management when I tell you that in six minutes time in a dark house the children were all taken out and not one child cried.

The next morning when we looked at the building and saw how huge granite blocks were hanging on the edge of the fire escapes, we felt more than ever that our Father was taking care of us. . . .

Just a few minutes after we were out the yard seemed to be filled with people. The neighbors and members of our Board rushed to our aid. The children were quite comfortable, because those of them who were not dressed had on their bathrobes. . . . The men went to the third floor and threw out mattresses and bedding. . . . We moved the autos out of the garage which is steam-heated and placed the mattresses on the floor. It was early morning before the children quieted down. . . .

That night we moved our children to a dance hall near the school. This hall is a quarter of a mile from a man who used to attend the school. He opened his house to us and we had all of our meals there. People in Helena provided the food.

On Sunday morning, one week ago today, I came to [this] building and went over it and worked out a floor plan. I got in touch with the plumber and electricians. Everybody was busy because of the torn down condition of Helena, but how good everyone was to us, putting others aside so our children could be taken care of.

I am sure we were directed to this building. I am just as sure that our Father means for us to carry on, for there is no other place in Helena in which we could be housed. So today we are forgetting the past and are pressing on more determined than ever. . . .

HELEN C. PIPER

During the 1930's federal relief programs brought a number of significant changes to life in rural Montana. Nevertheless, an out-migration continued as areas outside the state seemed to provide greater opportunities. Against this background, educator Eva Cable wrestled with the practical ramifications of upgrading the qualifications of teachers. Her arguments, which were not untypical of letters received from rural residents, persuaded the legislature to postpone the change until the 1940's.

RED LODGE, MONTANA
FEBRUARY 8, 1939

SENATOR H. A. SIMMONS
HELENA, MONTANA

DEAR SENATOR SIMMONS:

I learned just yesterday of House Bill 261. Again I am opposed to the M.E.A. I feel this bill unfair for the following reasons:

(1) This will eliminate many a good teacher who for financial reasons cannot get 144 credits. . . . In my opinion, the best teacher is one who has had to work her way to the top. The average young person who has education handed out to her by parents of means does not realize the hardships present in most of the homes of the children she must teach.

(2) Then, often they are educated too far above the little minds with whom they are daily in contact, and find it impossible to come down to their level. . . .

(3) How many persons graduated from a college or university would accept a position as teacher in a rural school? . . . I am sure you can recall in your own education your best teacher (the one able to impart the most knowledge to you) was not a teacher with a degree of any kind.

(4) This sounds like a bill backed by the greater universities to insure their progress. . . .

Granted, we have some poor teachers holding certificates to teach, but would a degree of any kind improve them in that field? I believe not. They just aren't teachers and the colleges should detect that early in their training and lead them into other fields, instead of taking their money and graduating them into a field of work for which they are not suited. . . .

YOURS VERY TRULY,
MRS. EVA CABLE
COUNTY SUPT. OF SCHOOLS

Although war clouds had been gathering for years, the Japanese attack on Pearl Harbor on December 7, 1941, took all Americans by surprise. Fortunately, several months earlier, the Montana legislature had provided for a state preparedness program. Despite the problems sketched out in this letter from Governor Sam Ford to the region's military commander, the plan went into operation without the hysteria which had characterized United States entrance into World War I.

JANUARY 28, 1942

MY DEAR GENERAL BENEDICT:

. . . I realize you are extremely busy with many important problems before you but I want to give you somewhat in detail our condition, hoping that this information will be helpful. . . .

Montana is a large State, 739 miles by highway east and west and 414 miles north and south, with a population of little more than half a million people.

Eastern Montana is largely devoted to farming and live-stock, while in the western part are found our mines, smelters, hydro-electric installations, and lumbering industries, all essential to the successful prosecution of the war.

Montana is traversed by three transcontinental railroads [and several local lines]. . . . The destruction of these or their serious damage would result in the interruption of transportation for a considerable period of time. While the Northern Pacific is now being guarded by Federal troops, it is my opinion that there is every reason why the other railroads should likewise be provided with adequate guards.

We have two . . . highway systems extending . . . through the state. . . . As in the case of the railroads there are many large bridges . . . and [their] destruction . . . would result in the complete interruption of highway transportation. . . .

Large smelters are located at Great Falls, Anaconda and East Helena. These are treating strategic metals, essential in the prosecution of the war. . . . Our copper and other mines are being worked to capacity and producing substantial quantities of strategic minerals. It would be a very serious blow to our war efforts should [they] be damaged or destroyed.

There are in Montana eleven hydro-electric dams, with power lines providing electrical energy for the operation of mines, smelters, and other essential industries in the State. . . .

We have no State troops or home guard of any kind since the National Guard is now in the Federal Service; furthermore, no money is available to State and local authorities to provide protection for the industries indicated above. . . . We have made a rather exhaustive survey to determine whether sufficient guards could be obtained in Montana to adequately protect the installations enumerated. From the information at hand I am convinced that these guards are not available. . . .

I sincerely hope that this information will prove helpful.

CORDIALLY YOURS,

SAM C. FORD
GOVERNOR OF MONTANA

Embarrassed by their behavior during World War I, Montanans exhibited little animosity toward the resident German population during the Second World War. The Japanese, a more readily identifiable minority, were another matter. In 1942 the federal government evacuated Japanese "enemy" aliens from coastal states to more isolated areas. Montana, whose colleges, CCC camps and military posts were slated to receive many evacuees, reacted sharply. Despite this protest, Montana willingly joined in the war effort and looked ahead hopefully.

MISSOULA, MONTANA
APRIL 13, 1942

HON. S. C. FORD
GOVERNOR OF MONTANA
HELENA MONTANA

DEAR GOVERNOR:

I called you by phone yesterday because I was anxious to stop any possible reaction which might occur in this community from Dr. Melby's suggestion that Japanese students might be accepted at the University of Montana. . . .

Dr. Melby's statement came out in the morning *Missoulian* on the same day when the Missoula County draft numbers were announced and in the draft numbers were a great many young University students . . . who have either been taken out of college or have voluntarily left in anticipation of the draft. One woman whose son has a low draft number and is a Junior at the University thought that her son would be called immediately before he could finish this year and she was quite hysterical about the prospect that a Japanese might be permitted to come here to more or less take his place. . . .

I am sure that many people in Montana will be reluctant to send their children to college where Japanese students are invited or accepted. It is pretty generally felt that the American educated Japanese have been largely responsible for the strategical advantage the Japs have had over us in this war and of course people who are paying taxes will no doubt feel that if there is any money available for education . . . the funds ought to be devoted to better education for our own students. . . .

SINCERELY YOURS,

HOWARD TOOLE

P.S. In fact there is just plain hell-to-pay in this town about Dr. Melby's statement.

ISOLATION CONFRONTED

LZADA TO YAAK, Helena to Washington, D.C. — the mileage separating each never changed. Externally and internally, distance was the predominant physical feature of Montana. As Nineteenth Century Montanans struggled with the vastness of the land and their separation from centers of commerce and government, each technological improvement — steamboat, stage, railroad — served to mitigate distances. Improved transportation enhanced population and economic growth. Experiments in flexible, dependable mediums of transport produced, among many things, the electric street car, the bicycle, and the internal combustion engine. Of them all, the latter had the most profound and significant impact on Montana and on the nation as a whole.

Automobiles and airplanes answered most problems of distance. As these developed, and accompanying facilities such as roads and airports improved, a consequent decline beset several rival modes of transportation. Proliferation of the automobile cut into street car and bus revenues with terminal effect in all but a few communities. Cars, trucks, airplanes, and long distance buses also eroded railroad profits, leading to abandonment of service on many nationwide lines. Developments in Montana transportation patterns mirrored national successes and failures.

Advances in communication, likewise, did nothing to reduce the physical distances and remoteness of Montana, but they broke down the psychological and social exigencies of isolation. Initially, the tasks of providing public information and contact fell on telegraph and newspapers. Technology personalized communication, adding successively, the telephone, radio and television. Each new method of transportation, each more sophisticated means of communication, facilitated the flow of people, ideas, and culture within Montana and from without. The entire process led to a social and ideological homogeneity throughout the nation — a trend which became increasingly apparent with each decade.

Agricultural policies, political issues, business regulations, humanitarian and environmental concerns, along with their associated philosophies or debates, now had a national flavor, not one particular to Montana. The physical distances did not change, but Twentieth Century advances in transportation and communication brought ideas and life styles into close proximity. Montanans became less and less unique, more and more uniform.

The Boulder-Helena Road, c. 1920

205

ISOLATION CONFRONTED
Transportation and Communication in the 20th Century

Automobiles appeared in Montana before the street and highway improvements necessary to accommodate them. Better roads came slowly everywhere, and not until 1913 did the Legislature create a highway department to oversee improvements in Montana's road network. Short trips challenged fledgling motorists; long excursions presented almost insurmountable obstacles. Good highways were lacking, but the sense of adventure was not for widow Frances Rumsey and her three teen-age children. She bought a Model T Ford, which the family dubbed "I Own A," and during the summer of 1916, embarked on a Seattle-Boston vacation. Thirteen-year-old Margaret kept a diary of the motoring adventure.

JUNE 25 [1916] SUNDAY — When we got to St. Regis Pass we really had trouble. The snow was about five feet deep and the mud was up to the hubs.... We helped four other cars through. We were the only ones with a shovel and blocks and tackle. Crossing over into Montana ... we met and saw several cars of drunken people with women in them who were smoking. About five times we kept seeing the same man on horseback. We would pass him, then he would pass us when we would get stuck.... Drove in chains today and only made 27 miles so you can judge for yourselves the state of the roads. We were told we were the best equipped car that crossed the Pass....

JUNE 28, WEDNESDAY — The boys are fixing a blow out, so I'll write my diary so I can mail it home when we get to Butte. Yesterday ... we had an accident. We were coming down a steep hill and onto a little low plank bridge with no sides; a sign on the bridge read — "Condemned" — .... A car coming down the hill on the other side just kept coming on down and drove right onto the bridge too, altho everybody could see the bridge was too narrow for passing, so we stopped and he glided right into us with a cracking sound. He told us he had put his brakes on — on the hill — but that when they did not hold, he had no place to go but onto the bridge and that he had purposely hit us dead center, otherwise both cars would have been sent off the bridge and into the river. By this time our radiator was leaking everywhere, our fender injured and several rods were bent; his front axle was broken. Our new radiator cost us $22.00 in Walker, but we had a dandy dinner in that burg and a wonderful hot cake and sausage breakfast....

JULY 1, SATURDAY — ... For 20 miles at sunset we drove beside mountain streams thru the Rockies and the scenery was beautiful. We took a wrong road out of Basin, so had to back track back to Basin where Mother and I could get a room in the hotel but the boys had to sleep in the car....

JULY 6, THURSDAY — Cousin Lottie said she would like to go through Yellowstone Park with us and we all thought that would be fun too having her along. We all had a little shopping to do.... We bought new tires all around for we had had so many blowouts we wanted to play safe in Yellowstone. $14.00 per....

JULY 18, TUESDAY — So as not to scare the horses who have never seen autos, the coaches have a schedule and the autos have a schedule for touring in [Yellowstone] park, called Control. When Control leaves camp, if you're not packed and ready, you have to wait over for the Control the next day.... If you were late coming into camp because of a blowout or engine trouble, the fine was $25.00 for having a car on the road which might scare a horse who would rear and cause the other Coach horses to run. Our Control left camp at 6:45. ...

JULY 19, WEDNESDAY — Had fun feeding the bears last night before going to bed in the moonlight. In the Park gas is 50 cents a gallon, a loaf of bread is 25 cents!!!! At 4 p.m. we got in line and left for Old Faithful Camp. ... At 10 P.M. we all went to Old Faithful Geyser, and she went off on schedule at 10:10, 200 feet in the air. The search light shining through the spouting waters in the sky created thousands of beautiful colors. ...

JULY 28, FRIDAY — By 8 o'clock we had made our way [to] Miles City.... After we left town, the roads were a fright and we waltzed all over them. The dirt in this part of the country is "gumbow dirt," and you can imagine with a name like that how sticky the roads are. At Terry we stopped at the garage to have a new tire put on.... There they told us that "gumbow" was easier to drive on when wet, for when it got drier, a car would really get glued to the road.... After we got about a mile out of town we returned to the Kempton Hotel for the night, Ham could not hold the car on the road....

Holsmans were fine, high-wheeled automobiles, and surely no lady would object to riding in one. Butte physician Thomas A. Grigg could not convince his wife of the Holsman's advantages, all the same. Progress took some adjustment.

DR. T. A. GRIGG   CHICAGO, ILLINOIS
BUTTE, MONTANA

DEAR SIR:

... We are very sorry that your wife has formed her opinion of high-wheeled cars by what she has seen of the other makes you mention, for we know if she was in a position to see one of our cars her opinion would change. There is nothing about the Holsman car to cause prejudice. It is very handsome in appearance and it is one that no lady would have any objection to riding in behind horses, and simply because we have not the horses but use a motor instead, should not make it less desirable. There is nothing in the other cars that can be compared in any way, shape or manner with the Holsman. We do not say this with the intention of running down the other cars, but we are stating actual facts. We do not claim that our car is free from all faults ... but we do claim it is free from most of the faults automobiles are subject to....

We should like very much to secure your order for one of our H-11 cars on the cash basis.... As this car will cost you $965, without top, we would suggest ... you send us your check for $200 and place your order, and pay the balance at the rate of $100 per month until such a time as we are able to make shipment, and then when the car is shipped we can draw on you for the balance due. We suggest this because we are behind in deliveries and will not be able to make deliveries for some three or four months of orders placed now, and by that time your order will be in line for a 1910 model....

VERY TRULY YOURS,

THE HOLSMAN AUTOMOBILE COMPANY

Good roads meant better business and social connections. Every part of Montana competed for limited federal and state funds to improve primary and secondary routes into or out of their communities. Spring thaws and rains made the problems more immediate; the best dirt roads were bad, the more primitive were impossible. Good Roads Committee Chairman L. K. Hills of the Baker Commercial Club was not in good humor during the spring of 1936. He sent an angry letter to the Governor describing the deplorable condition of the Baker-Wibaux road.

                              BAKER, MONTANA
                              APRIL 2, 1936
HONORABLE ELMER HOLT,
GOVERNOR OF MONTANA,
HELENA, MONTANA.

DEAR GOVERNOR:

The Baker Commercial Club has made a great effort for many years to obtain the designation of the road between Baker and Wibaux upon the Seven Per Cent System.... [There are many] reasons why this road deserves early attention. The Spring thaw has emphasized this by making this road practically impassable to cars.... The Agricultural College Band gave a concert here recently and were scheduled to play in Wibaux the following day. The condition of this road for 44 miles required them to cancel the engagement.

It is our firm belief that this Baker-Wibaux road is too important a highway to build as a piece-work project and that it is in fact a very necessary link of a complete Federal System in this part of the state.

In a spirit of fairness I would like to impress upon the members of the Highway Commission that Fallon County has contributed a very large expenditure in good road construction directly to the Federal system, which roads have been used for many years and are only now requiring rebuilding. . . . This mileage was built in the days of very high costs and have been made a part of the Federal system without expense to the state except for some reconditioning and maintenance. Since that time the roads constructed by the state have not exceeded 27 miles in this county. . . .

SINCERELY,

L. K. HILLS

Highways grew in importance with each decade of the Twentieth Century. Initially, only the Montana Highway Department handled road-related matters; but soon new laws and agencies came into being, coinciding with the proliferation of automobiles and trucks, and fragmenting administration. Vehicle registration came in 1923, motor carrier regulation in 1931. Building highways was, however, the major burden. In a large, sparsely populated state, revenues were stretched thin to cover the system of roads necessary to link scattered communities. Federal funds came in increasing amounts, but with them came responsibilities for matching funds and meeting mandated standards. The difficulties intensified in the post-World War II period with greater traffic volumes, rapidly deteriorating highways, and a paucity of funds exacerbated by inflation. Governor John Bonner appointed a special committee to assess conditions and plan remedies to maintain the state's vital road network.

REPORT TO THE GOVERNOR:

DECEMBER 1, 1948

It is the Committee's opinion that Montana's highways, streets and roads have a position of more than major importance in the present economic and social structure of our state. It is expected that they will continue to serve that structure in the future. In order that their contribution to our standard of living may be realized to the utmost extent, it is imperative that our present highway system be maintained and expanded as rapidly and economically as is consistent with users' needs and available finances.

Many portions of our present constructed system materially deteriorated during the war years because of lack of funds, equipment and manpower. Postwar flow of traffic over Montana's highways, appreciably greater than prewar traffic, and unfavorable weather conditions have also contributed to road deterioration. The subsequent necessity for a heavy program of maintenance, construction and reconstruction at today's high costs has depleted highway finances to such an extent that all sources of highway revenue, including the sale of the remaining authorized highway debenture bonds, will be inadequate. . . .

These conditions make it imperative that highway revenues be increased at this time. The longer construction and reconstruction are deferred, the greater becomes the necessity of increased maintenance operations. Such a condition will entirely eliminate construction operations from our highway program. Since federal aid monies may be applied in the main to construction only, we will definitely lose federal aid funds allocated under the 1948 Highway Act, unless additional highway revenue is secured. The loss of federal aid money from any allocation would be a serious blow to our highway program because 57.05 percent of all construction is paid for by federal funds.

Your Committee is unanimously agreed that the most urgent problem is that of obtaining an additional 2½ million dollars per year of highway revenue to insure matching of federal aid funds allocated under the 1948 Highway Act. Current highway income, plus additional income from the sale of the remaining authorized debentures available for actual highway expenditures, will be totally consumed in carrying out the presently programmed construction, reconstruction and maintenance operation. . . . After the sale of the remaining debentures, our entire highway income will be expended for retirement of debentures and maintenance operations. Because of its immediate importance, your Committee devoted the major portion of its deliberations to ways and means of securing additional revenue by the fairest and most economical manner possible. . . .

MONTANA HIGHWAY PLANNING COMMITTEE

President Dwight D. Eisenhower envisioned Interstate highways as a nationwide, multi-laned remedy for what ailed truck and auto travel in the country. From the program's inception in 1956, new monies became available to each state for nationwide implementation of the system. With the funds, however, also came new regulations, bigger bureaucracies, and multiple problems. Initially, state and community leaders competed for Interstate routes with the same vigor their predecessors exhibited over railroad lines in the previous century. When and where completed, the new highways became "taken for granted" improvements in transportation, but as construction proceeded, enthusiasm sometimes waned or was clouded by cost and building complications. Governor J. Hugo Aronson and State Senator Ben Stein responded to the negative aspects of Interstate highways.

HELENA, MONTANA
OCTOBER 14, 1960

HONORABLE FREDERICK H. MULLER
SECRETARY OF COMMERCE
WASHINGTON, D.C.

DEAR MR. SECRETARY:

[A number of Democratic politicians have] charged that we had deliberately constructed a part of the interstate system in [an area] which would be eventually inundated by water due to the construction of a dam. . . . Our engineering studies did not, at the time, indicate, nor has information secured since that time led us to believe that such a dam would be built. . . .

It is charged that projects are being let to contract without proper acquisition of right of way. As you are aware, the interstate program in Montana was not contemplated prior to 1956 to the high standard that it is now being designed. We, in Montana, have been designing and building our highways to a standard sufficient to carry the traffic presently imposed upon them. . . . When the 1956 Act went into effect, . . . we . . . had to make new surveys and raise our design standards to the degree requested by the interstate highway program. . . . In a number of cases we let contracts for construction projects where, in all cases, right of way matters had not been completely consummated. This was strictly in accordance with regulations. In all cases where this procedure has been followed the right of way has since been acquired and the cost to the State and the

Federal government has not been increased, because of that procedure. We have, however, eliminated this practice almost in its entirety at the present time.

We have also been accused of setting engineers' estimates in excess of the going contract prices. Engineers' estimates are strictly confidential and are used primarily for the purpose of setting aside funds at the Federal level under which the contract can proceed. . . . We cannot find a single case where contract prices may have been regulated due to these estimates.

We have also been accused of not doing adequate sub-surface exploration of soils prior to letting projects to contract. . . . The selection of the interstate route between Livingston and Billings has [also] been under constant study for quite some time. The Highway Department, together with Bureau personnel, has worked continuously to assure that the taxpayers' dollars are used to the best advantage for the traveling public as well as the State of Montana. Every study that we have made has indicated that the route, as selected, is to the best interests of all concerned. . . .

I have enclosed for your further inspection, certain newspaper clippings which . . . will further indicate to you the magnitude of this issue in Montana and why we are so concerned about soliciting your assistance to inform the Montana voters that these charges are no more than political expediency.

VERY TRULY YOURS

J. HUGO ARONSON

FEBRUARY 12, 1963

I hope you have your lunch with you because this could turn into a filibuster. I'm wired for sound today, mostly because when our committee considered this measure before, we were hopelessly misquoted by the

press. . . . I'd like to read this:

"WHEREAS, the Wolf Creek - Missouri River Canyon contains scenic areas which are unexcelled in the northwest . . . [and] widely recognized and utilized for their superlative fishing resources; and

WHEREAS, reasonable access may be denied to portions of both streams because of the limited access nature of Interstate Highway 15 . . . [and]

WHEREAS, construction costs of Interstate Highway 15 through these canyons is and will be astronomical; and

WHEREAS, alternate routings [exist] which would not only shorten the distance between Helena and Great Falls . . . but also may involve markedly lower . . . costs . . . [and]

WHEREAS, the hearings held by the Montana Highway Department on the routing of Interstate Highway 15 were . . . inadequate to gain comprehensive public opinion. . . .

Now, the great difficulty with our Highway program is that it's just running cross-grain to public interest and public feeling. The public is bamboozeled from beginning to end by these petty-clogging, paper shufflers and . . . the kind of language they talk. . . . The flow of business through this building across the street [the Highway Department] starts over at [the] . . . Interstate Section, then it goes to Pre-construction Section, then to the Office Engineer Section, then to the Bureau of Public Roads Division office, then the Office Engineer Section. . . There's a Plan Section, Bridge Division, Pre-construction Paving Engineer and way over here someplace it gets on to an Appraisal Section. Well, the negotiation goes in here and comes out here and by the time these paper shufflers get through with it, they're talking a language that a person out in the field can't even understand. . . .

In [our] type of democratic government . . . we want a responsive bureaucracy — if we have to have a bureaucracy, and it looks like we have them — this Highway Department [is] the biggest one. . . . I'm referring to the fact that they say as long as they comply with the letter of these laws, that they're beyond reproach. And that, Senators, is pure unadulterated violation of common sense. . . .

STATE SEN. BEN STEIN
PARK COUNTY, MONTANA

Barnstormers brought the first airplanes into Montana during 1910. The novel machines and their daring pilots attracted large crowds at state and county fairs all across Montana, as they did throughout the country. Development during World War I transformed the airplane from a novelty to a utilitarian device for transportation. Visionaries anticipated a vital and lucrative future for air travel, air freight, and air mail during the 1920's, 1930's, and beyond. J. W. Hesser's letter illustrated his personal aspirations and Governor Sam Stewart's reply demonstrated he was also attuned to the potential: "I feel confident that the airplane is, within a very few years, to work a revolution in transportation in this country. . . ." The Governor was right.

BUTTE, MONTANA
DECEMBER 4, 1919

HON. S. V. STEWART,
GOVERNOR OF MONTANA
HELENA, MONTANA

DEAR SIR:

The Inland Empire Aerial Training Corporation is composed of ex-service men who have done their full bit in the late world war. Our company is incorporated under the laws of Montana and our intentions are to commercialize aeronautics in this State similar to other enterprises in eastern States.

We have arranged for a chain of fields thruout the State and will endeavor to influence cross country trophy fliers as well as cross country liners to avail themselves of our facilities, thus bringing air routes thru Montana, causing considerable publicity for our State and numerous other advantages.

It is my intention, with your kind permission, to submit for your approval a memo, stating our position relative to future laws regarding aviation, believing that I am in a position to intelligently summarize necessary restrictions and safeguards for the future flyer, as it is only a short time now until laws will be enacted regarding commercial aviation.

Personally I feel that no more important civic step can be taken by towns and cities than to provide adequate landing fields. . . . Would you be so kind as to advise me your views on aeronautics in general and as applied to our state.

YOURS VERY TRULY,

J. W. HESSER

Commerical aviation began in Montana when National Parks Airways inaugurated regular service from Salt Lake City to Butte, Helena, and Great Falls in 1928. Governor Stewart had been correct nine years earlier — the airplane shrunk Montana's distances and revolutionized transportation. Responding to the growth of air travel within the state, Montana's 1945 Legislature created a state Aeronautics Commission to exercise a modicum of administrative and regulatory control over public and private operations. Public carriers were essentially interstate in nature and, as with state-to-state rail, truck, and bus traffic, the federal government quickly came to exercise the dominant hand in regulation. As a result, the Aeronautics Commission often found itself in an advocacy role in Montana's commerical air service.

HELENA, MONTANA
SEPTEMBER 27, 1957

HON. LEE METCALF
CONGRESSMAN FROM MONTANA
HOUSE OF REPRESENTATIVES
WASHINGTON, D.C.

DEAR LEE:

... As you know, the Montana Local Service Case concerns airline service to the entire state of Montana. ... There are two types of airline carriers involved in this case: ... local service carriers and the ... trunk line carriers. Generally speaking, local service carriers offer service over short distances, with many stops, and trunk line carriers offer service over long distances, with fewer stops. Local service carriers, generally speaking, serve smaller communities than do trunk line carriers.

The local service carriers involved in this case are Frontier Airlines and West Coast Airlines. The trunk line carriers are Northwest Airlines and Western Airlines. ... Northwest presently serves, in Montana, the cities of Kalispell, Missoula, Helena, Butte, Bozeman, Great Falls and Billings. ... West Coast Airlines does not serve any communities in the state at

the present time. Frontier Airlines presently serves Billings, Miles City, Glendive, Sidney, and Wolf Point.

The Montana communities which presently have no air service at all would like to see either Frontier or West Coast granted a complete circle route around Montana, serving all communities, thus setting up a practical and economical plan for local service carriers. The larger communities ... have no opposition to the hi-line communities securing service, or any other Montana community, for that matter, but they do not wish it to be at the expense of loss of trunk line service to them. The Montana Aeronautics Commission has taken the position that it opposes trunk line suspension at any Montana community, but wishes service to be granted to those communities which do not presently have it. At any rate, there is a conflict in feeling in the state, as to whether local service would be better than the combined local service and trunk line service we presently have....

With kindest personal regards.

VERY TRULY YOURS,

HENRY LOBLE, ATTORNEY
MONTANA AERONAUTICS COMMISSION

Frank Wiley's background in aeronautics was extensive, stretching from the early barnstorming days and the first years of commercial aviation within the state, to the United States Army Air Corps. After his discharge from the service, he returned to Montana as head of the state's newly-formed Aeronautics Commission. His experience gave him unique insights into not only the development and sophistication of air travel, but also to its particular application for Montana's needs. Frank Wiley's suggestions for the state's stockmen pointed to the expanded role of the airplane in Montana affairs.

The light airplane today has more utility for the rancher than the horse. A four passenger airplane can be operated at the same cost per mile as a medium-priced car, ... will carry a pay load of 800 pounds and will cruise at over 150 miles per hour, covering a distance between town and ranch ... unaffected by road conditions. ...

If you are under 60 years of age you can learn to fly this airplane yourself safely and successfully with 20 to 50 hours of dual instruction and with from 100 to 200 hours of supervised solo flying. ...

We have in Montana about 500 enthusiastic and competent ranchers and farmers who are airplane owners and pilots. . . . Chauncey Flynn, a rancher near Chinook, uses his airplane on skiis to spot lost cattle and to fly feed to isolated stock. . . . Gordon Sands, a rancher near Havre, uses an airplane more miles per year than he does his car or truck. . . . The Etchart Brothers near Tampico tend their sheep camps with an airplane and fly all over the United States on business trips in buying and selling livestock. . . . Repeated use is made of the ranch airplane to haul supplies and bring medical help to the rural areas isolated by blocked or damaged highways. . . .

Big corporations recognize the value of an airplane for executive travel because of the economy. Your ranch is a business like any other corporation. . . .

FRANK W. WILEY
MONTANA AERONAUTICS COMMISSION

Extending streets and highways, along with expanding air routes, constricted passenger traffic and profits for other means of transportation. In the urban setting, mass transit facilities suffered ruinous competition from private autos and "jitneys" — predecessor to the taxi. Street railways provided dependable transportation, but they lacked flexibility to adapt to changing urban traffic patterns. As a result, throughout the United States, trolley lines began to give way to buses. Seven Montana cities had street railway service at one time, but like their national counterparts, they suffered financial reverses as automobiles appeared on city streets in growing numbers. From the 1920's onward, Montana's street cars yielded to buses, but trolley service in Anaconda lingered until 1951, more than a decade longer than any other city in Montana, because of the Anaconda Company's subsidy. When Charles McLean, secretary of the local Mine, Mill and Smeltermen's Union protested abandonment, he added his voice to a long list of those who stormed in vain against the progression of urban transportation.

The removal or discontinuance of the street railway system in Anaconda would create an undue hardship upon the residents of Anaconda and the employees of the Anaconda Copper Mining Company. In the event that the service was discontinued, another means of transportation would have to be furnished so that the workers could reach the smelter. The contemplated transportation, no doubt, would be busses. Any private operator . . . could not possibly furnish transportation at a cost as reasonable as the Anaconda Company. The fare would be very much in excess of the present fares charged, and this would amount to an actual pay cut to the Smeltermen. The Smeltermen, who do not work under very good conditions on account of working in a smelter, need a means of transportation that should provide them with a good comfortable ride back and forth to work. After facing the heat, dust and gas conditions that exist on the smelter, a man is in no mood to be packed into a bus like a bunch of sardines in order to get home from work. This would be the case because it is the case everywhere where busses are in operation. We are all familiar with the chant of the bus operator "To the rear please" and to the sight of hard working men hanging onto the bus on every conceivable thing to hang on is a condition that we do not want to impose on the workers in Anaconda. . . .

The street railway . . . at present, has a heating system which is adequate in the cold winter months, and the street cars provide a decent warm place to ride which the workers need after working under hot conditions. This the busses could not provide because the small area inside a bus with the doors opening and closing continually would cause a continual draft . . . which would be injurious to the health of the Smeltermen. . . .

We think there is a serious condition existing at the present time as far as the driving of . . . private cars to the plant. . . . That is, we think there is particularly unsafe conditions as far as parking is concerned, as far as the way that the men operate their own cars themselves going to and coming from work. There hasn't been any particular accidents but that is no sign there may not be. If the trend continues I think the company will have to put in restrictions in regard to driving private cars back and forth.

The company contends they are losing money on the operation of the street cars; we think those provisions can be worked out between the employees and the unions representing the employees and the company. We don't think it is necessary to discontinue the street car service.

The people say that they are behind times, street cars in Anaconda, not keeping up with large cities. Well, in some cases we would rather be behind times because it provides the men a comfortable means of transportation.

Buses answered every city's transportation needs, or so claimed proponents of such service upon discontinuance of street car lines. Before approving trolley abandonments, Montana's Railroad Commission required bus service as a substitute, yet in all but a few of these cities, the bus companies realized all too quickly the nemesis of auto competition. Twenty-five years after Great Falls street cars gave way to buses and cars, the bus itself yielded to progress, economics, and the automobile.

The Great Falls City Lines and the Western Transit Systems, Inc., who are presently doing business as Great Falls City Lines, have . . . operated a bus line in Great Falls for a great many years. During part of the past, their operations were fairly successful. During the last eight or ten years, they have been pretty much on the verge of breaking even, with very little return from the investment. . . . At various times during the past ten or fifteen years we have found it necessary to ask for increases in fares, [we have] always realized . . . the result is that we lose certain amounts of passengers. . . .

In 1952 the operating income of the company, after income taxes, was $22,400. In 1953, [it] was $5120.00, . . . and in 1954, $316.00. . . . In 1955 there was a loss of $14,952.00 . . . and in 1956 a loss of $37,865.00. . . . The bus company is presently operating at a loss of approximately $200.00 a day. . . .

We have full coverage of the city of Great Falls, of the population of approximately sixty thousand people,

and that community can't support the present bus line. . . . Our experience has been that in serving new areas it is very difficult to produce enough riders to off-set the cost of operation. . . . If the line can be extended with the present equipment that is being operated, without additional equipment or additional drivers, the cost is much less and under those conditions sometimes an extension can be made and enough revenue produced to off-set the cost. However, new areas are extremely difficult to develop principally because of the people having their own means of transportation. . . .

We took steps last winter . . . to circularize the entire City and reached all the residents and bus patrons, and former patrons, and we noticed no physical results from it. We have tried various means of approaching different communities and our experience has been that once the passengers get away it is extremely difficult, if not impossible, to get them back because they produce their own means of transportation. . . .

As air and auto use burgeoned passenger revenues on the nation's railways deteriorated. The trend became apparent during the 1930's, but the prosperity induced by a world war staved off economic disaster for a few years. After 1945, United States railroads began an intensive examination of their passenger business and the result was modified service — abandonment in some instances, alteration in others. Great Northern Railway Company actions typified nationwide developments, for in all instances, suggested service changes brought loud responses from affected communities and individuals. Predictably, each reaction varied according to self-interest. When the Great Northern proposed discontinuing feeder runs between Great Falls and eastern Montana communities in 1951, and substituting improved transcontinental service, the Electric City's response was enthusiastic. When the railroad asked the Interstate Commerce Commission to approve the cessation of Great Falls/Butte trains less than ten years later, among the protestants was Mrs. John Hall. The Great Northern's actions and Montana's reactions typified national developments. So did the Interstate Commerce Commission's ruling — it approved both modifications.

DECEMBER 1, 1951

The Chamber of Commerce of the city of Great Falls is supporting the Great Northern Railway Company in its application . . . to change train schedules which will

cause . . . the Western Star, to run through Great Falls and to . . . establish buses which will run between Great Falls and Havre to connect with . . . the Empire Builder. For many years the people of Great Falls have endeavored . . . to induce the Great Northern to run one of its transcontinental trains through Great Falls and it now appears their efforts may be successful. . . .

The size and importance of Great Falls in the State of Montana is now about to be recognized by the Great Northern in its proposal to run one of its transcontinental trains through the city. The importance of the city is emphasized by its population and its growth. It is now the largest city in the state, its population being 39,214. This does not include the . . . suburbs which if included would make the figure 45,727. These figures are United States Census figures for the year 1950.

. . . If one were to entrain on the present trains serving Great Falls and destined to any point west of Shelby, one would arrive at Shelby 30 or 40 minutes ahead of the scheduled arrival of the Western Star. Now imagine, if you will, a woman . . . carrying on one arm a baby, in the other hand her bag and overnight bag, with a hat on her head, trying to find her way from the station at Shelby to about the 12th car on the Western Star — she has a sleeper reservation.

With all that wind blowing and snow blowing in the winter time, gales and inclement weather, there is no redcap service or service of any nature at all. Imagine that at night a passenger trying to get on the Western Star — hat blowing every direction, scarf over her face, can't see her way and there is no nice tiled roadway or walkway to the station back to the 12th car or sleeper on that train. To that kind of person this new schedule is a necessity and there are a lot of such persons. It is not an isolated instance at all. Imagine an [older] man, for instance, with two grips trying to do the same darn thing, walking back along there in the winter time to [his] sleeping car in that train. . . .

For many years Great Falls has suffered because it has not been on what might be termed the main line. We have been passed up by all kinds of good shows, orchestras. . . . Helena gets them, Butte — Great Falls never — and Billings gets them too. They won't come into Great Falls because there is no through train service. . . . Often they have a great amount of baggage and it is an inconvenience — they just won't come — community concerts and the likes. We have felt that we have been slighted all these years.

AUGUST 3, 1960

I am Mrs. John Nelson Hall. . . . I am an elected alderman of the City Council of Great Falls. . . . I have a letter here officially signed by the Mayor which simply states that on Monday, a week ago, at a regular Council meeting, the Council unanimously went on record as opposing the abandonment of these trains, and while this letter doesn't state it, they also went on record for me to represent them. . . .

In addition to my interest in the continuation of Trains 235 and 236 as a member of the City Council of Great Falls, I also have a personal interest. One of our state institutions, the Montana State Training School and Hospital, is located at Boulder, Montana, on the Great Northern route. I have a handicapped son who is in that institution. . . . These children are not allowed to go home except for Christmas vacation and summer vacation — Christmas is almost invariably bad. I'll tell you we watch the weather man pretty hard, always, because we just don't know whether we are going to make it or not, and I'm sure we won't make it if this train goes off.

In 1958 there were complete blizzard conditions from about December 23 until January 6, the roads were dreadful, and the Highway Patrol pointedly told the people to stay off of them if they possibly could. I used the train both going and coming. . . . Both times the train was filled to capacity, and when we were returning on January 2 . . . they were standing in the aisles. . . .

There are over 800 children in that school. The majority of them are from poor families and broken homes. . . . A great many of these children are not only mentally handicapped but also physically handicapped. . . . They have to be given medicines at certain times, and I mean sometimes every hour; they must have a rest room. . . . Frankly, the train is our only out. You can't even put them on a private plane; most of them have high blood pressure, hypertension.

This is a humane problem, I will admit that. I don't know anything about who is losing money and who is making money, but I do know the great need, at Christmas time particularly, for the people to go and get those children. . . . They will travel . . . all the way from Wolf Point, because I have sat right behind a woman who did it. She had a little Mongoloid girl who became ill while riding on the train, and she couldn't possibly have traveled with her in any other way. . . .

In Montana when the roads are bad, and if you are traveling by car with these children you must have two people in the car. If you have a flat tire, or if the child becomes ill, one person can't handle the situation and make sure that the child can be taken care of. . . .

MRS. JOHN N. HALL

Montanans welcomed the Northern Pacific and the Great Northern railroads in the 1880's, then in subsequent decades, cursed them as domineering and monopolistic. When the lines combined under the Northern Securities Company at the turn of the century, even the United States Supreme Court scrutinized the relationship and concurred with critics, forcing the corporation to dissolve. The high court's assessment in 1904 was correct; at best only minimal competition existed during that period. A half century later the picture had changed dramatically. Truck, bus, auto and air competition existed in vigorous form — so vigorous, in fact, that the Great Northern and Northern Pacific (plus allied companies) looked once more to merger as a way to increase efficiency and cut expenses. Along the lines of the affected railways protest arose under the spectre of the former Northern Securities monopoly and the fear of economic hardship for particular locales. Montana's legislature passed resolutions opposing the merger, including one in 1961 which State Representative John Melcher supported. The railways persisted, however, and the Interstate Commerce Commission approved the combination, as did the Supreme Court. In March, 1970, the Burlington Northern became a reality in Montana.

FEBRUARY 21, 1961

. . . We made an effort to impress upon the membership of the House the magnitude and effect of this railroad merger upon our State, and our efforts failed, because many of the members in the House refused . . . to weigh in the balance what could happen and undoubtedly will happen to the State of Montana if this merger is permitted: that we are to have fewer train crews, we are . . . to have fewer freight trains, and . . . less service in the State of Montana.

First of all, I think you are aware that after the merger, very likely there would be a gradual decrease in the tax base for the railroads involved. . . . This is becoming a matter of concern to many people throughout the State, school boards, cities, counties. . . .

But my chief concern is not with the tax base. My chief concern is the continued economic development of Montana, and the part that railroads play. . . . Many of us, including myself, have watched the Milwaukee diminish in the past few years. There are fewer freight trains and fewer passenger trains running. There has been a decrease in freight service. Now we have reached the point, if you are a livestock shipper, you have a tough time being sure that the day you deliver your livestock, that the Milwaukee train will stop and pick up the shipment. This has been a real problem the last couple of years.

In regard to the proposed merger of the Burlington, Great Northern and the Northern Pacific, management tells us the main line traffic will be on the Great Northern from Sandpoint, Idaho to Casselton, North Dakota. On the Northern Pacific we are used to good freight service. After the merger, according to management spokesmen, there will be a 59% decrease in freight traffic from Billings east on the Northern Pacific. . . .

On January 19, 1961, Vice President Burgess stated that there will be 304 less employed in Montana as a result of the merger. . . . Some people think [the figure] will be much higher. . . . Do you not agree that that would, and probably does mean 60 train crews of 5 men each? . . . That's what I mean when I say that less train crews means less freight trains and less service. . . . I contend . . . that after the merger there will be one good time freight per day from Billings east. I contend that that will not take care of our needs. It cannot possibly compare to the service we now have, with four or five fast trains each day going each way. . . .

The Northern Pacific is a land grant railroad. I would like to quote the Governor of the Montana Territory, B. F. Potts, on July 12, 1871, who states: "All that has heretofore been written about this superior land-grant of the Northern Pacific in Montana, scarcely gives an adequate conception of the extent and true value of the grant. The company will receive 25,600 acres of our best agricultural and grazing land for every mile of road that is built. I have no doubt that these lands will not only cancell the entire cost of building the railroad, but will leave a surplus to the company." . . .

I believe that after 75 years in Montana, the Northern Pacific should continue to help us develop our state. I hope that the merger is opposed here in the Senate. I hope that the Interstate Commerce Commission will take note of the strong opposition; [and] rule that the Northern Pacific must continue to give us service. . . .

REP. JOHN D. MELCHER
ROSEBUD COUNTY

Telephones, radios, and finally television became the electronic marvels of communication in the Twentieth Century. Commercial radio broadcasting began as a means of public communication in Pittsburgh, Pennsylvania, on November 2, 1920. Wireless "bugs" appeared immediately to enjoy the new media and by 1922 the number of licensed stations grew to 286 nationally. Among them was radio KDYS, Montana's first. The Great Falls TRIBUNE sponsored the effort to expand its audience beyond the newspaper's circulation limits and met with immediate success. The medium of radio broadcasting cut sharply into the psychology of isolation across the breadth of the state, giving Montanans a sense of immediacy and proximity to social, cultural, and political happenings throughout the rest of the state and nation.

LOHMAN, MONTANA
MAY 12, 1922

DEAR SIR:

I am writing this by your request to let you know I heard you last night (May 11) coming in very good. With a two-step amplifier I could hear you 125 feet away from "phones" without any sort of loud speaker.

About 8 o'clock you were liable to be on any wave length from 300 up to 400 meters but suppose you were testing. At 9 o'clock it came in the best without any change of wave length whatever. In behalf of the radio "bugs" of my district I will say that we certainly appreciate having a broadcasting station near here, where before we have had to strain our ears to tell whether we were hearing music or static, especially in the summer. I would be very much obliged if you would let me know your schedule when you get squared around.

YOURS TRULY,

ARLYN F. EVEY

Radio's utility, like newspapers, went beyond dissemination of news to open new avenues for advertising and editorial expression. Lines of propriety and policy in public expression of opinion were subjective at best, often stirring controversy and accusations of censorship. The decision of Great Falls radio station KFBB not to renew the Farmers Union Grain Terminal Association contract for air time was a case in point. Station policy limited discussion of controversial issues to donated public interest time, and the concensus of KFBB directors opposed the Association's liberal views. These two reasons combined, leading station manager Joseph P. Wilkins to cancel the particular program, thus evoking the wrath of the local Farmers Union secretary.

DECEMBER 31, 1943

MR. M. W. THATCHER
FARMERS UNION GRAIN TERMINAL ASSOC.
ST. PAUL, MINNESOTA

DEAR MR. THATCHER:

I wrote the attached letter . . . and requested Mr. Wilkins to sign a statement that it was substantially correct. Mr. Wilkins refused. . . . He agreed that the letter correctly outlined our conversation, but stated it would be as much as his job was worth to sign any statement as to why GTA was being refused the use of KFBB. . . .

It is true that many people complain about Gordon Roth's voice . . . but I am also satisfied that this complaint had nothing to do with withdrawing our broadcast. The reason we are not going to be allowed to purchase time on KFBB during the coming year is because someone who controls the broadcasting station does not want us on the air discussing matters of public interest. . . . I believe we should start a storm of protest to KFBB from the country. If it is possible to do anything in regard to bringing pressure from the Federal Communications Commission, I think we should.

Mr. Wilkins . . . stated that they would be very happy to have the Farmers Union Grain Terminal Association purchase advertising time providing we used it in extolling the virtues of some product of GTA, but we must not discuss legislation, acts of Congress, or any other matters which can be construed as of public interest. . . . I think this is just part of a nation-wide movement against liberals and all ties in with the plans of reactionaries to get control of the federal government in the election of 1944. . . . I hope that all our Farmers

Union papers will participate in a campaign to publicize the action of KFBB. . . .

VERY TRULY YOURS,

Farmers Union Grain Terminal Association
HAROLD M. BROWN

"A new age in Montana journalism began June 1, 1959," was the view of MONTANA STANDARD Editor Bert Gaskill. That year, Lee Newspapers, a midwestern chain head-quartered in Iowa, purchased Fairmont Corporation holdings in Montana. The Fairmont Corporation was a perpetuation of Montana's captive press, begun during the War of the Copper Kings. When the Anaconda Company consolidated copper mining activities in Montana it also unified control of the state's more prominent newspapers. Later, Anaconda codified this arrangement under the aegis of the Fairmont Corporation, a wholly owned subsidiary which controlled seven daily and two weekly newspapers. Alone, those figures were unimpressive, but combined, Fairmont papers accounted for over half of Montana's circulation, covering two-thirds of the state. Translated to political reality, the situation meant Anaconda Company officials dominated Montana journalism from their Butte offices. Declining revenues and ever increasing criticism prompted Anaconda to sell the papers to Lee Enterprises. Robert E. Miller, Duane Bowler and Bert Gaskill, all former Fairmont newspapermen, described the restrictions of Anaconda control and the "new age" under Lee ownership.

. . . Before the 1930s I was in the position of a lowly reporter of local news and I did not know what orders my superiors operated under. After I became a desk man about 1935 . . . the editor . . . took care of newspaper policy. Once, however, I ventured close to the point of knuckle-rapping. [Editor] Lynn Young was on vacation and I was designated to write the editorials during his absence. . . . The gold dredge was digging up the land at the lower end of Last Chance Gulch, just north of the Helena city limits, leaving huge piles of gravel. . . . I wrote a vigorous editorial pointing to the results and asking: Is a Gold Dredge an Asset to the Community?

When Mr. Young returned from his vacation he was called to visit headquarters in Butte and when he came back he told me that the rule was that no company paper ever questioned any aspect of the mining industry.

Not too long after that I was transferred to Livingston to be editor of the *Enterprise* and I have often wondered whether the transfer was a promotion or a demotion. In Livingston I was not close to company politics or policies. I knew enough about it so that I did not violate the rules. Every morning my first task was to read the *Montana Standard* very thoroughly and determine how many controversial matters had been handled. Thus I was able to follow company instructions without any day-to-day instruction. . . .

ROBERT E. MILLER

What was it like to work for the *Montana Record Herald* and *Helena Independent Record* under the ownership and control of the Anaconda Company? This must be taken in context. . . . A reporter first joining the *Montana Record Herald* in 1941 as I did, a year or two out of the Montana University Journalism School, had little frame of reference. I had grown up in Montana and was accustomed to its newspapers.

Truthfully, in those early days, they weren't all that bad, unless one knew the inner workings. . . . When I first went to work for the Anaconda Company papers the news I wrote was printed, some of it even somewhat daring for the day. It was not until one day when I uncovered a case of embezzlement in the county courthouse at Helena that the long arm of the benefactor became evident. The story was killed on orders from Butte because the malefactor, who was removed from office, had performed a useful errand some years before and had been promised protection. His job wasn't saved but his public name was.

Unless these incidents arose on one's run or a fellow reporter told you about them on his, there was little noticeable [trace] . . . of a heavy hand. It was not until I started desk work in about 1944 that the controls became evident. Union matters, industrial disasters, cost of living, consumerism . . . [were] given little or no attention. The legislature was played straight. No speculation, no interpretation. . . . Silicosis came under the euphemism of "industrial hygiene." Certain political figures' talks were given preminence, others didn't exist. . . .

You may well ask what happened to these newspapers, what caused them to fade? What made them deteriorate, lose an aggressiveness for which they were widely known? . . .

You ask, how did the change come about? The quickest answer is — owners were not newspapermen, owners who were not dependent upon the economic success of the newspapers for their profits. . . . Running the corporation were miners, metallurgists, lawyers and bookkeepers. They wanted good newspapers but they just didn't know how to let them be that. . . .

There were taboos. We didn't play up mine accidents or industrial diseases or labor troubles or the cost of living. But as far as news coverage went, at the time I went to work in Helena we pretty much wrote what we saw, heard or could uncover.

The attrition of coverage was a slow one, not something you could put your hand on day to day, but an accumulation.

The owners never made any great secret of who owned controlling interest but as time went by more and more people learned of it. As they learned, they found they could exercise an influence on what did or did not appear in the daily press. . . .

To make it short, editors of the company papers found their life was easier when the Sixth Floor — a name given to the company headquarters in Butte, Montana — received the fewest calls from politicians, lawyers, business (and just about anyone else) who didn't like something that was about to appear. . . .

The editors took the line of least resistance — stay away from the controversy at a state and local level unless it was found appropriate (by the Sixth Floor) to cut loose on some uncooperative individual. . . .

I firmly believe the owners didn't give a hoot whether the politicians liked the newspapers or not. They did care how they voted. They were not worried about the newspapers but were highly vulnerable in other quarters. . . .

I am sure the owners recognized this, too. I am sure they did not like what was happening. I believe this may have been a deciding factor in their decision to sell. . . .

DUANE W. BOWLER

My journalism school dean urged me not to leave the University of Montana to go to work for a "company" paper. Dean James L. C. Ford had his convictions, and I had mine, so I went to the company press. . . . I decided *The Standard* would be a fine place to get about five years experience. . . . So on the Ides of March in 1949, I began work as the night police reporter.

Butte became a home. It was an ugly mining town, but its people were great, and it wasn't far from choice fishing holes. . . .

Most Montana newsmen were paid shoe clerk wages. We stayed on the job because we liked Montana, not the pay. . . .

But, for dedicated newsmen, the Lee arrival in Montana meant more than wages; there was a new-found freedom of expression. People who wanted to criticize the Anaconda Company found the newsmen willing to listen — when complaints weren't just from crackpots. And, Anaconda's sacred cows weren't able to call the Sixth Floor (Anaconda's headquarters in the Hennessey Building in Butte) to keep their names out of the paper.

Much news critical of the Anaconda Company became Page 1 news. We new employes of Lee did everything we could to show the public the Anaconda Company's copper collar was gone. There weren't any real abuses, however, because the newsmen involved were good newsmen: they weren't conducting witchhunts, or running vendettas. The critical news would have been on the front pages of many papers free of outside influence.

Many Butte persons were hard to convince that Anaconda still didn't control the press. They also were critical of Lee because they believed local policy was dictated by Iowa "carpetbaggers." The widespread difference in editorial policies of the Lee newspapers has largely dispelled the latter idea.

Other benefits immediately accruing with the Lee purchase included some denied by tight-fisted Anaconda executives who wanted the papers to make money, or at least not to spend it. You didn't have to telephone everyone that would accept collect; you could use the phone for legitimate newsgathering without question. You didn't have to beg to hire a commercial photographer to take a news picture. Anaconda had no trained photographers on its staff in Butte, and few elsewhere. Lee immediately put in a photographer, added a darkroom, and bought good camera equipment. . . .

Newsmen were isolated from their peers in the Anaconda days. There were no inter-office workshops for Anaconda newsmen, no meetings, no seminars, no outside training. In fact, when the Montana Press

Association convened in Butte, the city's newspapers weren't represented at the sessions, and little appeared in the company press about what was going on. It was many years after the Lee takeover before the state press group came back to Butte.

Lee believes in training its people: workshops, seminars, American Press Institute, press association gatherings — anything that might be of value. Its publishers, general managers and editors frequently get together to discuss mutual problems and work out programs of benefit to all. . . .

A new age in Montana journalism began June 1, 1959, with the Lee purchase. Montanans in general, as well as Montana newsmen, are well aware of this. And, they are thankful those "carpetbaggers from Iowa" liked the potential they saw in the company press.

ALBERT (BERT) GASKILL

Television erased isolation and nutured national homogeniety to a remarkable degree. Technologically it represented the latest advance in public communication as the second half of the Twentieth Century began, but socially, the impact of television was more profound than the scientific expertise which made it possible. From individual to family, community or country life, an irrevocable change took place. No one could entirely ignore or avoid its influence. As with any medium, quality and opinions regarding program content varied from cultural enrichment to moral debasement. Most important, however, was the source of regulation, major programming, and impact — national or regional, not local. Good cable TV, canned programs, bad advertising, and relief — all subjects of E. G. Lee's letter — came from outside Montana's borders. Television exhibited the theme that came to dominate all aspects of Montana life during the Twentieth Century — social, cultural, political and economic images reflected on the face of the state had inspiration and origin from without, not within.

HELENA, MONTANA
OCTOBER 20, 1959

TO: FEDERAL COMMUNICATIONS COMMISSION,
    WASHINGTON, D.C.
HON. SENATOR JAMES E. MURRAY
HON. SENATOR MIKE MANSFIELD
HON. CONGRESSMAN LEE METCALF
HON. CONGRESSMAN LEROY ANDERSON

About a year and one-half ago, Mrs. Lee and I decided to invest in a television set after seeing the excellent picture and wide selection of programs brought into Helena by cable from the city of Spokane. . . . We bought a 21" set and invested in cable installation in the amount of approximately $450.00. We have enjoyed our television very much because the picture was crystal clear and we have had a wide selection of programs. . . .

[Our] pleasures came to a sudden end when the management of local TV stations KXLF Butte and KXLJ Helena decided . . . to force our Helena TV Inc., operating the Television Cable from Spokane channels to discontinue this service.

When the FCC made this ruling we were deprived of good television. Now, our picture is disgustingly poor, it rolls for long periods of time and cannot be cleared for good viewing. The programs are three to four weeks old. The local television announcers intersperse their programs with statements informing us that we are watching free television. . . . We say instead of free television, we get Nothing for Nothing. . . .

We do not care for the advertising on TV. . . . We do not drink beer or liquor and believe that the continuous barrage of beer advertising over TV from morning til night is having a terrible effect on our young people. . . . We do not want Free television where the tab is picked up by the beer and cigarette manufacturers.

We urge you to devise a plan where all television sets can be licensed on the same basis as our automobiles and a fee established for [their use]. Confine the programs to the main networks and supervise the type of programs that are offered to the public. Cut out all advertising [except] one announcement: "This program is presented by . . .", period.

VERY SINCERELY YOURS,

E. G. LEE

AGRARIAN ADAPTATION

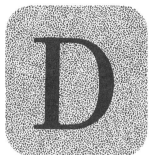

RAMATIC CHANGE characterized Montana's agriculture after the turn of the century. Dryland farming gained wider acceptance and livestock owners altered their operations toward more general agricultural practices. Aided by federal reclamation programs, farmers looked to irrigation to increase yields. The livestock industry gradually increased production, but still overgrazed some range. Enlarged homestead laws, increased World War I demands, mechanization, and improved farming methods created an agricultural boom, which ensuing drought and falling postwar markets ended. Between 1917 and 1939, Montana recorded seventeen years of below average moisture. Adverse conditions forced more change. Agriculturists established cooperative irrigation districts and federal involvement took on greater importance.

Massive dust bowls during the 1930's convinced farmers and ranchers that many areas were best left to natural grasses, while extension specialists encouraged new practices of summer fallowing and strip farming. Significantly for the livestock industry, the Taylor Grazing Act of 1934 removed the public domain from homestead entry, established grazing districts, and classified lands unsuitable for leasing. In 1935, Montana created its own Grazing Commission to administer range land for stockmen and farmers. The dry years broke many farmers, but also encouraged consolidation into larger, more efficient agricultural units.

New Deal agricultural programs, while successful to a degree, left many fundamental problems unsolved. United States entrance into World War II and a return of the wet cycle eased conditions and allowed farmers and stockmen to expand operations. Although stabilized by the mid-1950's, Montana sheep production experienced a postwar decline. Higher returns seemed to be in cattle. There were fundamental changes in American eating habits, and synthetic fibers came into wide use to challenge the market for wool.

Postwar prosperity, however, generally intensified the state's agricultural growth. Many producers saw advantages in diversification. Changing world markets, application of new technology, and continued consolidation highlighted the period. Correspondingly, production increased, due to improved varieties of grain, weed control, and further mechanization. In more recent decades, rural electrification, better farm-to-market roads, newly devised sprinkler systems, and feed lots all contributed to agriculture's status as Montana's leading industry.

Conversely, as technology and production advanced, farm population dwindled. Changes in rural life-style occurred, marking the decline of the family farm, and the emergence of the corporate farm. Thus the diminution of the classic rural culture created fresh concerns and prompted a re-evaluation of contemporary Montana.

PLOWING IN THE GALLATIN VALLEY, C. 1925

AGRARIAN ADAPTATION
Agriculture in the 20th Century

Like many newcomers to Montana's plains, James Fred Toman spent many hours "grubbing" (pulling) sage. The state's southeastern portion contained miles of brush that had to be cleared before cultivating. At the age of 25, Toman did not lack energy for the work, but his diaries, kept on his Little Powder River farm, reflected the tedium. They also reflected changes that were the key to agriculture's future — crop diversification and irrigation.

FRIDAY, [JAN.] 6 [1911] — Stormy all day. Caught our horses & rode home. Sick of our wolfers camp as we were sick in it most of the time. . . .

SATURDAY, [Jan.] 7 — Blizzards of wet rain and snow during day with Chinook between. Grubbed sage all day. . . .

MONDAY [Jan.] 9 — Steady chinook all day. . . . We grubbed sage all day. Made quite a showing. Played pitch in evening.

TUESDAY [Jan.] 10 — Bitter cold. Light snow in A.M. Grubbed sage again today. . . .

WEDNESDAY [Jan.] 11 — Cold. Grubbed sage in the forenoon. Hauled a load of wood in the afternoon. . . .

SATURDAY [JAN.] 28 — Warm. Snow melting. Grubbed sage. Finished reading Irving's Sketch Book. . . .

THURSDAY [FEB.] 2 — . . . Turned bitter cold at night. Grubbed sage. Have cleared about three acres on the bottom & it has taken 15 days work. Not long hours, however, only about five a day. . . .

JAN. 22 [1913] — Spent last week helping Bert put up ice. Then rode down little Powder River to Alfred Rues to buy some alfalfa seed. Spent a pleasant evening with them. . . .

SATURDAY, MARCH 15 — Have been working around home. Daubing my grub house & raising it. Hewed out a back bolster for the wagon. . . . Framed up Articles of Agreement for a partnership with B.H. Mitchell & sent them to him by mail. . . .

MONDAY, MAY 11 — Finished planting my spuds, sowed my alfalfa & disced it in then plowed the balance of the week. Rode down to Powder river yesterday to see my girl but couldn't locate her. . . . Rode home this morning and plowed a while but it was too dry to plow satisfactorily so I went at it to build my ditch, being anxious to try my new go-devil which I made Saturday afternoon, and also to test the surveying which Shorty & I did a week ago. After finishing the ditch I hitched to the disc and used it till supper time. After supper I turned the water into the ditch and found it flowed down just perfectly. . . .

World War I placed ranchers and farmers in unusual circumstances. Increased demands for meat and grain called for expansion. Montana producers willingly obliged, often gambling with their own financial stability. Larger yields meant more equipment, additional fuel, and rapid repairs. During wartime, new technology and military demands had far outstripped the country's ability to supply domestic machinery. More than one farmer experienced the same predicament which led T. F. Finch to write Governor Stewart for help.

BOX ELDER, MONTANA
MAY 18, 1917

GOV. S. V. STEWART
HELENA, MONTANA

MY DEAR GOVERNOR &c

Can't you help us out just a little bit. Within sound of our farm there are twenty tractors and . . . there is not one gallon of gasoline in Box Elder. There is one half dozen tractors standing still for the want of some small repair. One of our own tractors has been standing in the field all spring. We wired Helena for repairs and it was fourteen days before we received them. We run for about two hours and broke another small casting. We wired for it two weeks ago and have not received it yet. . . . We [also] ordered a small repair for our automobile six weeks ago and have not received it yet and we need it badly every day.

Now I tell you my dear Gov., that the farmer is as anxious as you, or the state, or the nation to get in all the crop we can and will say right here that we [are] being knocked out of the use of one of our tractors and our auto. . . . [It] will cut our crop short two hundred acres.

We have in now between 500 and 600 acres and should have in 800 instead.

Now we are not writing this for our own account. Could get two hundred men to back us up in this request in two hours if we had our car. . . . Please see if you can't help us a little.

YOURS TRULY,
T. F. FINCH

From the perspective of the farm boom, from 1910 through 1916, some Montanans viewed agricultural problems as momentary setbacks. Dillon banker A. L. Stone had little sympathy for agrarians. At a 1918 conference of farmers in Lewistown, called to address agricultural problems, Stone expounded on the farmer's advantages. Failing to encompass agriculture's deteriorating situation, his arguments were not popular with the assembled audience.

MARCH 13, 1918

Did you farmers ever stop to think how blessed you are at the present time? We hear so much of the troubles that the farmers suffer, and I wonder if any one has ever told you of the advantages which you have? Has it ever occurred to you, for instance, that the Government has given you the land; that the Government is financing you; that you can borrow money cheaper than any class of men in the whole country today; that the State has duplicated what the Government has done; that the State has gone further, it has provided seed for those who are unable to secure it otherwise. The Government has granted you immunity from the Sherman Anti-Trust law. You can hold anything you have as long as you want to. You can organize any kind of an institution or corporation in restraint of trade and not have it questioned. . . . No one can drive you into bankruptcy. . . . Did it ever occur to you that you are the greatest profiteers that the country has —

Irrigation seemed Montana's answer after years of drought. Securing federal involvement often resulted in unwarranted optimism and eventual frustration over poor planning. These obstacles did not turn farmers from irrigation, but made them more determined to secure water — as efficiently and rapidly as possible. John Survant, who headed the Lower Milk River Water Users Association, typified the frustration as he sought backing from Governor Dixon.

MALTA, MONTANA
MARCH 9, 1922

HON. JOS. M. DIXON, GOVERNOR,
HELENA, MONTANA

DEAR GOVERNOR:

Some twenty years ago the U.S.R.S. came into our Valley and started the Milk River Irrigation Project. It was represented at that time by U.S. employees that the valley could be irrigated at a cost of $15.00 per acre, and that in no contingency would it exceed $25.00 per acre. Under the representations made at the time myself and others went out and induced land owners to relinquish their water rights and sign up the land to be irrigated by the United States. . . . *The Lower Milk River Water Users Association* was formed, and the par value of each share of stock was $25.00, and one share represented an acre of land.

After twenty years the project manager informs us that the work is only three-fifths completed, and the estimated cost of the work complete is $90.00 per acre. . . . Then, to add insult to injury along comes one Dr. Newell who . . . tells us that the project will never prosper until there are several first-class funerals in the valley, and the Land Hogs are holding the valley back by refusing to sell their lands at a profit, etc. . . .

No country was ever settled by a more honest and sturdy lot of men and women than the Milk River Valley.

223

. . . Many of them are gone to their reward, and those of us who are left are without hope of relief from the U.S.R.S.

Shall we, the pioneers of this valley who are left, surrender or fight on to attain that which we have acquired by self-denial, hard work and thrift? By surrendering we would be false to our co-workers who have gone before and the spirits of Thos. O'Hanlon, H.A. Reeser, George Clanton, B.W. Brockway, H. H. Nelson, Eugene Coleman and others from the spirit world would cease singing and cry SHAME so loud as to drown the chorus of the Heavenly Hosts.

We are getting old, but are in hopes of getting matters in better shape before passing them on to our children, and what we want is help, and lots of it. Are you with us? If so, give us some suggestions as to how to proceed. . . .

YOURS TRULY,

JOHN SURVANT

As Montana's irrigation moved away from individual ditch diggers, irrigation companies formed. Larger developments called for irrigation districts and bonding land to finance construction. More costly projects required federal involvement. Continued drought in the 1930's convinced Montana's agriculturalists that federal support was the answer. These programs became so widespread that by 1937 over one-quarter of Montana's farms and ranches had whole or partial irrigation. One example, the Buffalo Rapids Project on the Yellowstone River, was planned to cover 18,000 acres. Backed by the Works Progress Administration, under the Bureau of Reclamation, the program had the support of Montana's entire Congressional delegation. Project organizer and Glendive attorney, Desmond O'Neil, attempted to enlist the aid of outside potential friends, including an Arkansas Senator.

DAWSON COUNTY
JUNE 18, 1937

HON. JOSEPH ROBINSON
WASHINGTON, D.C.

MY DEAR SENATOR:

May I ask you to confer with Senator Murray concerning the various water projects in Montana and the need of varying rules under which the WPA may work in different parts of the United States. . . .

We can well appreciate that what is advisable in your locality or in the Northeastern States would not apply to the great plains States. We also appreciate that a great number of Eastern Senators do not realize what irrigated land really is, or the necessity of irrigation in this territory. . . .

Irrigated farms here do not compete with farms in the central or Eastern states. Grain crops do not provide sufficient return for the work and expense required, but the production of sugar beets and forage crops on irrigated land make good money. The people in this territory . . . all the farmers and stockmen in Eastern Montana — will benefit by such irrigation. One has only to go to the Sidney territory or the Billings territory to know how the stockmen farm and the business men benefit by irrigation. One worth while irrigation project will bring more lasting benefit to the entire Eastern Montana than all the roads, play grounds, parks or other things provided by the WPA could possibly do. . . .

I beg of you that such an amendment be authorized as to permit the President to have authority to designate WPA labor in promoting the water project in Montana, and particularly the one we are so vitally interested in, the Buffalo Rapids Project.

RESPECTFULLY YOURS

DESMOND J. O'NEIL

To a child growing up in rural Montana, the livestock industry presented a variety of experiences. Bill Armington, Malta area rancher, not only worked in the wool industry at its peak, but shared in the last colorful days of the open range cattle business as a horse wrangler.

One of the first jobs I ever had I was about ten or eleven years old. I had a job washing combs and cutters out here [in Malta] at the shearing pens . . . and I got a dollar a day for my work. All the kids in town was mad at me and jealous because I was making too much money.

I remember they had a . . . machine plant and they

had a gasoline engine they powered it with, and they had an expert to run this gasoline engine. Ordinary guy didn't know anything about them, and if anything would happen, why they had to get this expert in there, and God, we'd look at him like he was some kind of magician! There was a lot of trail bands went out through here at that time. J. B. Long ran a lot of sheep up here, . . . and they'd bring these wintering bands about shearing time, which was usually the last of June and in July, and then they'd trail them on down to Dakota and ship them out of there. . . . They'd have about three bands of sheep and one camp tender, and he'd have about three trail bands of them, pretty big bands most of them, about 2,000 to 4,500. . . .

There was mostly professional sheep shearers. . . . Some of them was what they called "high rollers" and they'd knock out a couple of hundred a day there. Some of them would count out 200 strings in the morning and when they got their 200 knocked off, they'd quit, and sometimes they'd quit four o'clock in the afternoon, some of them. . . .

I washed the combs and cutters — that is, part of the clippers. . . . [I'd] brush them in cans of water and I had to wash them up before they could grind them. They got gummed up from the grease from the wool.

Well, I graduated from that pretty early. One summer was all I put in. My heart wasn't in the business. I wanted to get to punching cows as soon as I could. . . . I went to work for the Circle Diamond as horse wrangler in 1909. . . .

Frank Brock was cooking, and I was horse wrangler, and old Frank was a fine feller. . . . I used to have to flunkey for him and help him wash the dishes and chop wood and pack water to him besides watch those horse herds. . . . I remember Frank was quite a philosopher. One day he was making what they called a son-of-a-gun-in-a-sack. . . . It was really a suet pudding, and Frank was always kidding me and talking to me, and he said, "Now kid, I'll tell you something, kid. The meat might be burned or the biscuits might not be just right, but you give them something to taper off on and keep the sweet taste in their mouth, and then you get away with it all right. If you have dealings with a man, even if you have to take a little the worst of it, why, leave him with a sweet taste in the mouth." . . .

As early as the 1880's, before the use of internal combustion engines, some Montana ranchers raised horses exclusively. These animals gained acclaim for their stamina and quality, and the outbreak of World War I placed a premium on their supply as artillery and cavalry mounts. European army representatives attended the Miles City horse market — one of the world's largest — to fill their needs. Helena banker Samuel McKennan visited the community and enlightened T. C. Power on the brisk international sales.

HELENA, MONTANA
APRIL 23, 1915

One of the interesting sights which came to my attention at the Miles City stockyards was the inspection of horses by representatives of the French Government. . . . The morning I was present they were selecting light weight horses for the cavalry and were paying an average price of $135 per head for horses approved. As the horses were led into the yards, the officers looked them over critically and after say five minutes examination either accepted or rejected the animal. If accepted, they passed immediately into the branding chute, where they were branded with the proper brands of the French Army. They are able to pass on from 40 to 60 horses per day, I am told. . . .

Last week was an interesting one at the yard. Three countries were purchasing — Great Britain, France and Italy. Great Britain and France were purchasing artillery horses at an average price of about $175 per head and Italy was purchasing lighter horses at about $140. The stock was first offered to the English inspectors and all those not accepted by the English were then offered to the French and those not accepted by the French were later offered to the Italians. The result was that . . . over 900 horses were accepted during the week. At an average price of $140 per animal, the week's purchases amounted to $126,000. . . .

Approximately 225,000 horses have already left the United States for the foreign countries now at war. The average life of a horse, they tell me, is but seven days from the time it enters the army service at the front.

S. McKENNAN

After the buffalo vanished from the plains, predatory animals increasingly plagued stockmen. A long program of eradication began, aimed primarily at wolves and coyotes, with the state even paying bounties to hunters. This was only mildly successful and stockmen devised other methods for removal, including the dispersal of selected animals infected with mange or other diseases. Thomas C. Power wrote his representatives at the Judith Mercantile and Cattle Company detailing how to distribute several infected animals. This method, too, proved to be unsuccessful.

HELENA, MONTANA
OCTOBER 18, 1913

GENTLEMEN:

Will ship you Wednesday afternoon by Express, One (1) Big Strong Grey Wolf, in a single cage, and three cages of Coyotes, containing 9 Coyotes. . . .

Be extra careful in handling the Wolf as he is a bad one, and is liable to put up a fight and a good one too. . . . Place the cage on the ground at the point you desire to unload him, open the cage door and drive away for 15 or 20 minutes and give him time to get out and away.

Believe you had better start distributing the Coyotes from the 79 ranch, as the hub of a wheel, and a common center, distributing them South, east and west there from, a few miles apart in locations where there are no settlers.

Would advise the immediate distribution of these infected Coyotes as they have been penned up some time. Spare no expense, sending only good reliable men, interested in the stock business, that will see to it that the work is thoroughly done.

Remember the Bounty hunters will be after these Coyotes in order to kill them wherever possible to prevent the spread of the infection.

Make no noise about this distribution . . . and ask every one connected with the distribution to keep the thing quiet.

Coyotes to be fed but once a day on raw meat and watered while in captivity. . . .

VERY RESPECTFULLY,

T. C. POWER

Small family cattle operations declined during the 1920's, but after the catastrophic failures of the homestead period, the remaining cattlemen expanded operations. Many had no pity for those who went bankrupt, maintaining that the homesteaders had failed because of their own stupidity and cupidity. Quick to criticize, but quicker to capitalize, stockmen eagerly bought up tax-forfeited homestead land. Robert T. Pound, Lavina cattle rancher, wrote Evan Hall, newly appointed Milwaukee Railway agricultural agent, about livestock's economic role in Montana.

LAVINA, MONTANA
NOVEMBER 17, 1926

DEAR MR. HALL:

Individuals connected with this firm have been running livestock in Montana since 1886. Our experience is that natural grass has no superior as an income crop. . . . The short grass sections . . . of the state are best grazed by sheep, while the longer grass goes best with cattle. . . .

Perhaps the most remarkable thing we can say

about livestock in this section, or in Montana for that matter, is that cattle and sheep are today paying the losses of men who have been engaged in banking, storekeeping, oil drilling, mining, and a dozen other enterprises that suffered in the post war deflation. The livestock business is the major enterprise of this section of the country, and doubtless will remain so. . . .

YOURS SINCERELY,

ROBERT T. POUND

William H. Donald's struggle epitomized the plight of Montana cattle ranchers during the Depression. On his Melville ranch he bred Hereford stock and augmented his income with a dude ranching operation. Besides contending with the "usual" bad weather, Donald faced the problem of most Montanans — a lack of money. Continued confrontations with banks and federal loan officials compounded Donald's concerns. His diary disclosed a trying ten years and reflected more contact with bureaucrats than cows.

FRIDAY, MAY 6, 1927: Snow, Slush, Mud & Hell. Coldest & wettest spring that ever I saw. Rode thru G. cows. Thank God no cow presented this fiendish weather with a calf, though Fannie lay down in front of me & had a fine foal. . . .

SATURDAY, MAY 7, 1927: Weather man still turning loose a lot of snow. You'd think the son of a bitch would run out of stock some time. Stumbled thru G. cows in storm. Tagged three wet & chilly calves. . . .

SUNDAY, MAY 8, 1927: WOW! BASTARDLY BLIZZARD. Never Saw a Storm Like This In May Before. Blinding, Whirling, Howling Snowstorm On. One poor chilled calf dropped but seemed to be doing well. Storming so hard did not dare leave shelter of brush for fear of being lost. Sat around house & cursed weather. . . .

MONDAY, MAY 9, 1927: Weather Broke!!! Thank God!!!

SATURDAY, MAY 28, 1927: Rain! God Damn It, Rain!!! Started out with Herb to move yearlings on Upper Ranch. . . . New man up there, some cowboy. Doesn't care which side of a horse he gets on or off nor does he know a cow from a steer. Cold, wet, slippery work. Couldn't get out the cattle we wanted but after a lot of trouble put 176 head in Sec. 33. . . . Lunch U.R. & home wet, cold & tired. Warm house with furnace going . . . sure made a person appreciate a cozy home.

MONDAY, NOVEMBER 18, 1929: Up to Upper Ranch in Truck, worked calves around and started them out for Big Timber, 111 head. Cold raw day. John met us at 10 mile with truck and cooked lunch. John went with calves and I took truck and went on in to B.T. leaving boys [to] bed at Hathaways. . . .

TUESDAY, NOVEMBER 19, 1929: Got car started early and down after calves. Picked them up a few miles out from Big Timber. Took horse in tow and went on to bridge where I took horse and helped cross river and R.R. tracks. Led horse with car up to Stock Yards, set gates and got cattle in. Weighed up one load. Sure would of lost my shirt had I sold . . . by the pound. . . .

MONDAY, DECEMBER 9, 1929: Haircut. In and saw Eddie Phillips for a while. Talked with accountants keeping Ranch Books, and then in to see my "Big Hearted (?!*) Bankers." Same old story. I am carrying too big a load and got to cut down loans. . . . Came right down to it, though, the bull market is a bit slow. I really am just about holding my own despite a pretty poor year in the cattle business and I take quite a bit of comfort in that. . . .

SUNDAY, APRIL 20, 1930: Easter. Pretty nice day outside. . . . It was about as blue a day as I put in all winter. Not having Billy I guess is what made it seem so extra cheerless. . . . Money is awfully tight and business is rotten. Have over $4,000 worth of stuff to sell and can't move a thing nor have I paid a bill in the last three months. Last week was a particularly discouraging one. Billy getting the measles was discouraging enough. Losing 7 head of cows and four of them registered did not help much. . . . On top of that had a very discouraging talk with the Scandanavian-American Bank. . . .

SUNDAY, NOVEMBER 11, 1934: Chicago. We come racing in to Chicago & land at the Stock Yards at 9:20 A.M. Best & fastest run I ever had in to Chicago. Up to Walters & Dunbar Office, Get mail, Change clothes. Out in yards . . . get Sam Scott to inspect my cattle. Cut out Bangs reactors. Lunch. Up to Hotel, bath & cleaned up & feel fine. Wander around & invest in a few drinks. It beats the band the way all these cocktail bars are crowded — and high priced drinks too. . . .

MONDAY, NOVEMBER 12, 1934: Chicago. Out to yards fairly early. It is a rotten market. Few top cows at 4¢, top calves 5¢. Don't weigh. Most of cows around [$]2.75. . . .

TUESDAY, JULY 13, 1937: Cow Camp. Got the crowd out by 4 A.M. sharp. Bkfst 4:30 & riding by 5:15. Had cattle all corralled & cows cut from calves by 9 A.M. 5 extra cars down there & about 18 extra people. . . . Grand chicken dinner about 5:30. Big and noisy ball game. Most of the crowd went home in cars but about 12 of us still in camp.

WEDNESDAY, JULY 14, 1937: Breakfast at 6 A.M. By 7:30 we broke camp & riding home. It began to rain & everybody got well soaked. Home 10:30. Stormy looking day. Looked around ranch. Tried to nap. . . .

TUESDAY, AUGUST 24, 1937: Dam, badly worried: Regional Agr[icultural] Cr[edit] Corp. notified me a new man in Helena Office & come in & see him. Same time Federal Land Bank notified me they are so exasperated at Regional turning down my interest & taxes they are starting foreclosure. Whew! . . . Start [to] Helena in car about 10, in by 2. . . . See Gribble (new man in Regional). Nice enough guy, but put in there to be tough & he is. Politely assures me he is quite certain Regional will not renew in fall & will have to sell out. Will let me know later. Leave Helena. . . .

WEDNESDAY, SEPTEMBER 15, 1937: Helena. Lit out after breakfast for Helena. Raced the North Coast Ltd. from Big Timber to Livingston. Helena 10:30. Talked with Paul Raftery. Doc Butler is sure fighting with me against the Regional. Has U.S. Sen. Jim Murray all lined up too. . . . In to see Gribble, of the Regional at 3. Between he & Kitting from Washington was with them till 6:30. Very unsatisfactory. My chief desire was to get the Land Banks foreclosure on the lands stopped. They would not allow me the money out of sales to stop that & only conclusion I could draw was they were doing it for the deliberate purpose of forcing me to sell my cattle to protect my land thus being able to say "We never foreclosed on Bill Donalds cattle." Sure mad when I left there. . . .

WEDNESDAY, OCTOBER 27, 1937: . . . Having this summons & complaint slapped on me regarding the foreclosure on my land — in which there is a big equity — certainly looks like the RACC would have me sacrifice that so they could say it was the Federal Land Bank closed me out & not the RACC. Yet it was the RACC put the Land Bank in position where they had to do something. Fight drought & grasshoppers for 3 years. Buy feed & pasture to hold the herd together. Then this God Damned RACC is going to have me foreclosed because I borrowed too much money to buy feed & pasture.

MEMORANDA — 1937: Was a tough one & a year of great disappointments to me. First place, was just beginning to get around pretty well on my broken leg. Had flu & a bad relapse again. Nearly cut a finger off & rendered it useless in a buzz saw. Another bad infestation of grasshoppers cut down my summer pasture badly. We had a fair number of Dudes, but strung out very erratically & when I came to figure out how I had done, found I was in the hole. Didn't charge enough. In late August the RACC nearly put me out of business entirely & tried to force me to sell out. Had a mean automobile wreck where a fellow ran in to me. Bill came down with appendicities & had to be operated on. Cattle market was good up to Oct. 1st, but I overstaid my market & did not get in on the good market. Calves still unsold [because] the RACC, the Fed. Land Bank started an action to foreclose my lands. Only consolation I had was Billy was able to be with me till Xmas. One Hell Of A Year Says I.

As the Milwaukee Railroad's agricultural agent, Evan W. Hall was headquartered at Miles City. Besides promotion work, his main assignment was the development of sound agricultural techniques on land served by the railway. Poor range conditions, overgrazing, abandoned homesteads, drought and hard winters had denuded 108,000 acres between Mizpah and Pumpkin Creeks. Hall suggested to stockmen that this public domain be blocked off and leased. They agreed, and formed a cooperative grazing district, with authority of federal legislation. This was a significant step toward intelligent management of the public domain, and proved so successful during dry years that Congress used it as an example when it passed the Taylor Grazing Act in 1934.

MR. ALVA A. SIMPSON
U.S. FOREST SERVICE
DILLON, MONTANA

DEAR ALVA:

R. W. Reynolds tells me that you are contemplating writing a brief history of the Mizpah-Pumpkin Creek Grazing Area, on which the legislation incorporated in the Taylor Bill was based.

It is very interesting to note the progress which has been made in the past eight years to bring about this legislation which has been needed so long. Our original aim has been accomplished . . . to establish a demonstration which would show the western states and prove to Congress that the Public Domain which was strictly grazing land, could be handled in a practical way by using the grazing district method.... It has certainly served its purpose in bringing about the passage of the Taylor Bill.

The day on which the Mizpah-Pumpkin Creek Grazing Area was originated was Wednesday, June 16th, 1926. I had suggested to Paul Lewis, County Agent for Custer County, that we call together four or five substantial farmers and stockmen, to get their suggestions as to the real needs in Custer County and southeastern Montana in order that I might work intelligently on the problems facing us.... The things that came up most often [were] the need for more grass,... better control of grazing,... [and] stabilizing... business by control of grazing land at a reasonable cost....

The thought came to my mind "why not get this district under control and have the Public Domain blocked, with the private ownership and lease on a ten-year basis to the stockmen along the two creeks?"...

I presented the idea to the stockmen... to... Congressman Scott Leavitt, and... in December, 1928, to... E. C. Finney, Asst. Secretary, Department of Interior.... The support given [by] Congressman Leavitt [and] E. C. Finney was what finally secured the passage of the legislation making the Mizpah-Pumpkin Creek Grazing Area possible.... [They] performed a real service to the livestock industry by putting over the Mizpah-Pumpkin Creek Grazing legislation....

Sincerely,

EVAN W. HALL

By mid-century, trail drives and cowboy traditions were dim memories, but survivors of the open range era attended reunions to relive vicariously the old times. On July 1, 1951, the Montana Cowboys Association held a roundup and "branding bee" on a horse ranch near Glasgow. At the gathering were cattlemen and cowpunchers from outfits out of Montana's past, such as the Circle Diamond, XIT, 76, N-N, Turkey Track, Mill Iron, and others. Ailing Con Price could not attend, but acknowledged his regrets.

NAPA, CALIFORNIA
JUNE 2, 1951

FRANK MESSENGER
SECRETARY-DIRECTOR
MONTANA COWBOYS ASSOC.
GREAT FALLS, MONTANA

DEAR FRANK:

Well, you tell me they are going to have a big blow out in Glasgow July 1st. And how I would like to be with you all, and go among you fellows and squeeze your old Paws, and even look at your old hoofs to see if you were getting tenderfooted.

Sure will be lonesome to-day thinking of you old Scalawags. I knew most of you from the Rockies to the Dakota line, from Canada to Wyoming. But Hell, my saddle is wore out, and that part of my body that I used to sit on it, is about wore out too, so I can't make the trip. If I were there, the only sadness I would feel, would be in working the old herd. I would miss so many of the old

bunch that has crossed the big Devide, but damn it, I can't feel they are gone forever. They just went to work for another outfit on another range.... May have to go to work over there myself before too long. I am sure the big Range Boss up there has cut that old Montana Herd in a bunch by them selves. I feel there is no State in the U.S. that has your brand of people. And if it wasn't for your tough winters, I sure would go back there and finish my last roundup.

But old Dad time has put his Hobbles on me, I couldn't even trot fast enough to keep warm and I don't seem to shed off anymore, you old boys know that is a bad sign.... Guess I better unsaddle and quit.

Hoping the Sun shines on all of your trails to the jumping off place. Wishing you health and happiness all the way. So Long — Good Bye — and Good Luck.

Sincerely,

CON PRICE

Adaptation and diversification have always characterized Montana agriculture. Livestock owners expanded and changed to keep pace, and theirs became a significant industry, rather than a romantic interlude as it was during parts of the Nineteenth Century. Ralph Miracle, as Secretary of the Montana Stockgrowers Association, discussed the evolution and local dependence on the livestock business.

I think everybody realizes how much the cattle industry meant in the early days of Montana, that it was the cattle industry primarily and the livestock industry as a whole that built Montana. . . . But that was a long time ago — been a lot of changes since then — the industry's changed — everything's changed . . . but in the process . . . the cattle and livestock industry is even more important today. . . . And it involves more people.

In the real early days of the open range we had a few large cattle owners that utilized the range. . . . Today, almost everybody that has a ranch or farm property owns some livestock and has some cattle and has a cattle brand and utilizes the facilities that have developed over the years for marketing their cattle and utilizing the information that's available to them from their educational institutions, and from the organizations that serve the industry. . . .

When you start talking about the importance of the cattle industry you're not only talking about the value of the ranches and the value of the cattle and the value of the equipment that they have, but you're also speaking of all the people and all the businesses that are related to that industry. . . . If you take in the related industries, the amount of equipment and the amount of fertilizer and the amount of feed and all the different supplies that go into the cattle industry, it becomes a tremendous industry affecting so many people. . . .

We hear many people talking today about urban and rural conflict, that they're entirely different kind of people and put their hats on a different way and they don't get along with each other and they're opposed. But when you get to Montana, and you start talking about urban Montana, we're really talking about people who are just about as close to the ranch as they can be without living on it. They're in the automobile business, they're in the hardware business. If it's feed, or if it's any other type of business, or even if it's hotels and motels and all the other things that are combined, they're real close to the industry which is agriculture and which livestock is the big part of it in the state of Montana. . . .

Exportation of goods has historically been essential to bolster markets for Montana's agricultural products. Better foreign markets meant more production, particularly for high protein wheat. Bob Brastrup of the Montana Department of Agriculture addressed the export issue before the Senate Finance and Claims Committee in 1974. His support of a portion of H.B. 746 called for funding of an eighteen-month foreign export study, and reflected the state's search for new market opportunities. Despite Brastrup's testimony, the bill failed to pass.

I appear today to support [a portion of] House Bill 746. . . . I'm really not here as a matter of self-interest, because of all Montana's products, agricultural and otherwise, wheat already produces practically all of the dough in Montana's present export trade. . . . Of $208,900,000 worth of agricultural commodities exported from Montana in fiscal year 1972-73, . . . 72 percent was represented by wheat alone. . . . In effect, then, what I'm saying is that as far as the export market is concerned, Montana has been living by bread alone. For nearly 10 years, wheat has represented two-thirds of the total exports from Montana. . . .

As promised in the Governor's State of the State address, the Foreign Trade Potential Committee will develop the information necessary for all Montana products — not just wheat — to take better advantage of expanding opportunities in international markets. It is certainly true, as the Governor said, that increased foreign export offers a definite possibility of improving the state economy. [We need to] . . . inventory products suitable for export, locate markets, improve transportation arrangements and apply innovative new approaches in foreign commerce. . . .

I say to you as strongly as I can that I am a "true believer" — we are and have been selling at least 60 per cent of our wheat to foreign nations. I'm afraid the only alternative in many past years would have been to plow it up. Certainly Montana should explore the possibility of selling its various other products in the same manner and quantity. The market awaits our action. . . .

Many have viewed rural life as more healthful and wholesome than an urban existence, and have deplored the decline of a pastoral way of life. Yet in Montana, as elsewhere, the move away from the farm has been a constant reality. In 1945, a Lewistown group under the auspices of the Montana Study, met to evaluate the situation in that community and heard Ann Mather, a farm wife, voice her feelings.

Quite often city folk consider farm folk peculiar, but the farmers are just like anybody else. . . . [I do feel] that moral, religious and educational standards are easier to maintain on the farm than in town, because neighbor children live farther away, frequent meetings do not occur and discipline is easier. . . . Most farm children are kept busy by chores and cannot get into trouble. . . .

[I] worked during the depression in the Roundup area with farm families who were in need of loans. In these families, many lacking the necessities of life, [I] found that the wives were very devoted to their husbands. With so few material comforts . . . they might be expected to find fault, but . . . they did not. . . .

The farm woman . . . is tremendously important. A farm wife who desires a social life in the city cannot be a successful partner. Many farm wives are forced to move to the city for the education of their children, thus causing a disruption in the normal activities of the farm family. Nine of the twelve months are thus spent away from the real home. . . .

Rural children should consciously be taught the value of their birthright. Urbanization brings a decay in the moral fibre of people. . . .

Formal religion has . . . largely disappeared from the rural community because of the disappearance of the "little red school house." Rural community clubs and other activities have [also] grown less active because of [its] disappearance. . . . Now many organizations take the time of farm people [and] draw them away from the farm to the city. Young people are drawn away in the same manner, leaving the old folks on the farm.

Small farming and livestock interests were not always compatible. Often at issue was the conflict of life-style and economics. In 1973, the Montana Legislature saw the groups in opposition over this question — farmers speaking through the Farmers Union versus the livestock associations. House Bill 132, referred to as the Family Farm Act, attempted to place control on corporate farming, calling for limits on corporation shares, a return to family control, and an end to factory-type operations. Theoretically, it would have preserved Montana's rural environment and helped slow the out-migration of the state's young people. Clyde Jarvis spoke unsuccessfully for the bill's approval at a committee hearing.

The Montana Farmers Union supports House Bill 132, the Montana Family Farm Act of 1973, both from an economic and a philosophic basis. This legislation not only will prevent economic injustices, but also it will preserve the social benefits of rural life. . . .

The family farm or ranch . . . provides the best rural environment for the growth of individual personality and character, for stability of family life, and for the strength of the rural community and all of its institutions — churches, schools, businesses and local governments. . . .

This legislation would stop tax-loss farming by so-called conglomerates and prevent them from putting excess profits into large agricultural operations as a tax shelter. . . . It is aimed at stopping corporations from buying farms or ranches for an investment. . . .

These major corporations . . . put extremely little back into Montana from a financial viewpoint, yet are capable of using unlimited funds from out-of-state to compete against young Montanans seeking agricultural livelihoods. Thus, our own young people are squeezed out despite the fact they have the expertise. [Montana] has the resources, and the financing could be found, to permit them to stay and flourish in the Treasure State.

From yet another economic viewpoint, it is significant in considering this legislation to note many studies indicate smaller units in agriculture are the most efficient and economical. Almost all such research shows well-managed one- and two-man farms and ranches are the most efficient when measured by the cost per unit of output. . . .

With these observations on the Montana Family Farm Act of 1973, I have no hesitancy in recommending that your committee support its passage. . . .

CLYDE JARVIS, PRESIDENT
MONTANA FARMERS UNION

photo by N. B. Cresswell, Kansas City *Journal Post*

COLLISION OF INTERESTS

HE PATTERN OF personal constituencies and the dominance of corporate interests continued to color the fabric of Montana politics during much of the Twentieth Century. Comprised of diverse elements and subject to a host of disruptive influences — including considerable voter independence — both major parties were but loosely structured. The result was that if politics in the state were frequently unpredictable and fraught with a kind of schizophrenia, they were always complex. For many years, the Anaconda Company, often in concert with other corporate interests, wielded overwhelming influence on politics in the state. Although eminently successful in its objectives, this corporate influence was unlike that of the traditional political bossism, for it cut across party lines with such subtlety that the influence was sometimes barely perceptible. It was a domination that continued, albeit in more benign guise, well into the century.

Beginning in the 1940's, however, changing internal conditions brought corporate politics into competition with other highly influential pressure groups, including farm, labor, education and other sectors. With reapportionment still in the future, rural areas continued to wield a large influence, much of it generating a conservatism and a demand for economy and reorganization in state government.

In contrast with the generally conservative tinge of politics at home, Montana voters elected a host of liberals to national office. Because of the political affiliations of such men as Senators Thomas J. Walsh, Burton K. Wheeler, James E. Murray, Mike Mansfield and Lee Metcalf, Montana reaped proportionately more from federal spending programs than it paid out in federal taxes. At the same time, the state's congressional delegations have a number of times risen to great influence and renown in national affairs, out of proportion to the small electorate they represented.

Recent improvements in communication, together with the "liberation" of the state press, permitted national influences to become an increasingly prominent foundation for state decision making. The resultant focus upon issues rather than personalities and a number of important structural changes, including a new constitution, pointed to the development of a sophisticated political alignment more in tune with national patterns.

B. K. WHEELER CAMPAIGNING FOR THE VICE-PRESIDENCY, 1924

COLLISION OF INTERESTS
Politics in the 20th Century

[*Montana's political history has traditionally been a complex of varying ideological beliefs, interests, and factional loyalties — all intertwined to weave a tangled network. Although he spoke with reference to presidential politics of 1948, the attitudes of Missoula lawyer Emmet Glore were equally applicable to Montana politics during most of the century.*]

MISSOULA, MONTANA
OCTOBER 10, 1947

MR. PRESCOTT COOKINGHAM
PORTLAND, OREGON

DEAR MR. COOKINGHAM:

Our mutual friend has asked that I write you briefly concerning the . . . situation in Montana as it may affect Senator [Robert] Taft's possible candidacy for the republican presidential nomination. The Montana political situation stinks; and not briefly. Unless Montana's few delegates and votes are imperative to Senator Taft, in my opinion he will be better advised to seek his support elsewhere. . . .

Montana politics can be understood only by Montana politicians. This is a rugged state. So are its politics. So far as I know, only one [columnist] had even a passing conception of what was going on in the Wheeler-Erickson senatorial shuffle that ended, to the amazement of all hands, with the election of Zales Ecton. . . . The republican people's governor [Ford], a potent Baptist every Sunday, is a company-bound disciple of the ex-democrat senator [Wheeler] . . . who was originally elected as the people's advocate and promptly went over to the company. This ex-senator was defeated last fall in Montana, by one Leif Erickson because his opinions on Germany offended some of the wealthy Jews in New York City. All the Butte chaws and cousin-jacks voted for Erickson. Does this make sense? Absolutely in Montana. [Wellington Rankin, a republican] now expects to defeat the incumbent democrat [Murray] with the assistance of [Ford] and this same ex-democrat senator's machine, which, incidentally, elected this republican people's governor. . . . It's all fascinating and on one's better days, hilarious. . . .

If he must have Montana, my advice to Senator Taft is to buy it: from B. K. Wheeler, Sam Ford, Wellington D. Rankin and J. Burke Clements, and from the Monopoly. In Montana politics, that approach is most direct, least expensive and best understood.

YOURS FOR HONEST ELECTIONS,

EMMET GLORE

During the early decades of the Twentieth Century, Montana politics took on a new variety that caused consternation in many quarters. Primarily centered in the mining regions and paralleling the concern of agrarian radicals in eastern Montana, the Montana Socialist Party became a sizeable minority which served as a framework for social criticism. Although many of its ideas are today routinely accepted, the party was undeniably radical in its time, and at the peak of its influence it found an able spokesman in Lewis J. Duncan. When he wrote the following letter to Utah Socialist William Brown in 1911, Duncan had just won a resounding victory in the race for mayor of Butte. A decade later, the Socialist Party in Montana was all but extinct.

APRIL 12, 1911

WM. THURSTON BROWN
SALT LAKE CITY, UTAH

DEAR COMRADE:

My election will make a vacancy in the office of state secretary. . . . I want you to have the position, and I know the comrades at Butte and Great Falls will nominate and try to elect you, if you will consider the proposition.

To mention the least important matter first, the salary is ˙. . . $100.00 per month. The really important matter is the cause in Montana. This I am certain will appeal to you. For the first time, the socialists have [an] opportunity to demonstrate their methods and efficiency before the people of Montana. This demonstration will be in the strongest organized labor town in the state, where, if we make good, we shall be able to get the practical support of the industrial organizations in our political efforts. It was the labor vote that carried us into power this time and it can do it every time if we can retain the confidence of the workers. This situation is going to result in a clear class alignment in future political fights—organized labor with the socialists on one side and the Amalgamated with the old political machines on the other side. . . .

This condition will center the attention of the whole state on the socialist administration in Butte. . . . We have a fine body of workers that are enthusiastic . . . but we are short handed for speakers and writers. We mean to keep up the education at even greater pace than during the last four months. We want to make the paper a weekly. We want to carry on weekly propaganda meetings in the local and outside the local. I am about the only one competent to take the platform with the kind of propaganda message that is required, and the duties of the mayoralty, will be even more onerous and time consuming than those of state secretary. Another man of culture is needed and you are the man we want. . . .

Should we prove convincing in city affairs, we shall be able to get the county at the next election and send representatives to legislature. We might even be able to get state officers next year. We have got to have men for these positions. We must import and make them. We want you first of all as one of those to assist in developing the right kind of material in the ranks of the comrades and of organized labor. . . .

Yours Comradely,

DUNCAN

After a long struggle, Montana women won the vote in 1914, part of the victory attributable to the Progressive crusade to make political institutions more representative. A majority of the responsibility, however, lay with Jeannette Rankin who formed a sophisticated organization and marshaled a host of dedicated campaigners to visit every part of the state. During the campaign, Rankin reported on the progress to Anna Howard Shaw, president of the National American Women's Suffrage Association. Although the suffragists — and their opponents — declared that women would reform and/or vastly change politics, women as members of the electorate altered the character of Montana politics very little.

[DEAR DR. SHAW,]

I had been asked to come by the suffrage workers [but after] I consented they found that the people did not want me on the program because they did not want a political speech. However, the governor was billed to speak so I said I would go anyway and if there was a chance alright and if not alright. When I arrived it was still said that I would not be allowed to speak, but there were several men very determined so when the speaking was over they called "Miss Rankin." The men helped me on the platform but the chairman shook his head so I got down. Then they started to call again and as the chairman had left and the crowd started to leave, I got up and a man introduced me and the crowd came back. I talked a few minutes telling my best stories and the people thought it was a great joke that I finally got on, and they were all very good-natured. . . .

We had an interesting time in a little . . . village where we held an open air meeting. There were very few people in town [as] they were preparing for a big celebration the next day. The men sat around the saloons and insisted they would not come to hear the speaking, but a few women and children mixed in with our crowd made a beginning and after that the men gradually came until we had a good audience. . . . We did not try to take up a collection but told them we had some Votes for Women buttons to sell. A woman in the audience who was the assistant postmaster came out in front and said, "Here, come buy these buttons," and the men came up and we sold all the buttons we had. We felt that we had gained quite a victory.

The country districts are coming forward most wonderfully. We had a very interesting time at our State Central Committee at Lewistown. . . . Women from all parts of the state made their first suffrage and open-air speeches at the same time and the audiences enjoyed them very much. There was one anti in Lewistown. . . .

One woman . . . said that the antis reminded her of the old jingle about the purple cow: — "I never saw a purple cow. I hope I never see one, but I can tell you anyhow, I would rather see than be one."

[JEANNETTE RANKIN]

The Progressives' desire to reform government gained momentum from the enthusiastic boosterism of the period to produce the phenomenon known as county-splitting. As Montana population sky-rocketed during the homestead era, the creation of additional counties seemed an admirable idea, one calculated to bring people closer to their government while providing impetus for economic development. Thus, from 1910 to 1925, Montana counties frenetically divided and redivided until twenty-eight new government entities emerged. With the onset of drought and depression the population trend dramatically reversed, leaving a legacy of overly expensive local government.

Nov. 2, 1922

Flathead county has been much excited, perturbed, agitated and aggravated recently over the matter of county division, as well as a wild scheme to remove the county seat from Kalispell to Whitefish — or elsewhere. . . .

The movement started in Polson to create a new county out of portions of Flathead and Missoula counties . . . which the people of this vicinity generally recognized as a fair division, and little if any opposition was made.

But the county divisionists had a specialist on the job, who gets so much per division, and the next move was a petition to bring the north boundary of the proposed county of Lake nearly to Somers, and to . . . [propose] the creation of still another new county out of northern Flathead and eastern Lincoln counties, removing the county seat from Kalispell entirely.

The Columbian designates this threat . . . as a "form of reprisal," . . . to force the people of Northern Flathead to accede to the proposed new line of division near Somers.

County division fights are always nasty, and this one is no exception. Already it is beginning to bear fruit in the way of abuse and criticism, just at a time when the different communities should be working together for the common good.

As we see it, the people of the southern part of the county want, and are entitled, to a county seat. There has always been complaint of the hardship of traveling the fifty-odd miles to Kalispell during the winter months. . . . But conditions would not be improved if a division were made whereby the people from . . . the north end of Flathead lake were compelled to travel to a county seat at Polson. . . .

The only logical division would be about midway of Flathead lake, . . . and it impresses us that the sane method of procedure would be for the factions to get together and agree upon a division which would be reasonable and best for the interest of all concerned.

The division is bound to come some day, and we may as well have it over and done with it. . . .

L. D. SPAFFORD, EDITOR
KALISPELL INTERLAKE

In the heat of hysteria during World War I, there was an ever-present threat to personal liberties throughout the country. It was especially apparent in Montana, where the Council of Defense sat in Helena to enforce sedition laws and stave off what it considered anti-American action. As the following letter indicated, Attorney General Sam C. Ford became increasingly alarmed, and although his complaint dealt solely with juridical matters, Ford perceived that the Council, together with many of its zealous supporters, possessed a dangerous potential for crushing all political dissent.

MAY 27, 1918

MONTANA COUNCIL OF DEFENSE,
HELENA, MONTANA

GENTLEMEN:

As Attorney General of the State of Montana, I feel it my duty to call to the attention of your honorable

body, recent violations of the state constitution and laws in a number of counties of the state . . . which in my opinion, are matters of tremendous importance to every citizen of the state.

The right of free speech [has] been denied individuals . . . by violence and in direct violation of law. . . .

Furthermore, it is common knowledge that in many cases members of county councils of defense participated in these unlawful proceedings. . . . The persons so misused have been met by self-constituted committees and informed that they would not be permitted to make addresses. . . . If they attempted to make addresses they might subject themselves to violence. . . .

The freedom of the press, and the unrestricted right of public assemblage and free speech are absolutely necessary for the maintenance of a republican form of government. . . . It is true that we are at war and that the life of the nation is at stake; and that these conditions may so effect the minds of over-zealous patriots and persons of hysterical tendencies as to lessen their power to clearly analyze civil rights; and to perceive the importance of the strict respect that should be given the same; nevertheless, it is also true that the primary purpose of this war is to uphold the fundamental principles of freedom and to prevent autocratic groverment, the rule of might, from being established on this continent.

A cloud has arisen upon Montana's horizon that threatens dire consequences to the people of the state. Class is being arrayed against class, and . . . if the lawlessness cited is not put down, and the right to free speech is not rescued from the disrepute thrown upon it, in my opinion, conditions may follow that will do the people and the fair name of the state incalculable injury. . . .

I am constrained to suggest to your honorable body that you take steps to reinforce and assist the ordinary authorities in repressing those engaged in these infractions of the law and in the punishment of the offenders. . . .

SAM C. FORD
ATTORNEY GENERAL

During the early years of the century, corporate influence was still dominant in Montana politics. To achieve legislative goals, their methods included bribery, election fraud, almost total control of the state's press and both major parties. The result was even further complication of an already involved political alignment. In 1919 a group of Butte Republicans, parroting the Company "line," ironically raised the issue of election fraud in order to challenge an anti-Company slate which had captured the Democratic nomination.

At a meeting called for the purpose of . . . informing the public as to the conditions of political affairs and frauds perpetrated for the sake of securing so-called Democrats immunity in office, [the Republicans of Silver Bow County stated the following facts:]

Butte . . . filled up in past days with adventurous souls to whom the lure of the silvery dollar appealed in raucous tones. . . . Time has passed and Butte has changed, and — for the better — as to morals, but not as to elections. . . .

Matters have so come to pass with us that secret jugglery of the ballots, forgeries, the casting of ballots by dead men and women, purposeful miscounts, . . . have developed. A political democratic machine, nearly as efficient as that of Tammany has been built up, and its leaders are influenced by money or ambitious designs for power. . . .

The Republicans, numerically inferior in Silver Bow County, aided, however, at times by popular sentiment when things became too "raw" have been the backbone . . . of the forces fighting for principles. . . . Our men and our women candidates for office have at all times been people of most excellent citizenship and seldom, if ever, has one been chosen against whom reproach could be cast. . . .

The last Election presented strange anomalies here. One man . . . was declared elected. . . . Then the voters seem suddenly to have switched and . . . votes went in overwhelming numbers to his antithesis. . . . Only peculiar methods could produce such peculiar results. . . . We believe desperate methods were resorted to to accomplish some of the results. . . .

We believe the great majority of public sentiment here demands that the Republicans, . . . particularly every Republican in the Senate and House of Representatives of this state, "go through" to the finish on this question of fraud. . . . This is not a partisan issue but a matter of good citizenship. . . . We now ask the Legislative Assembly to . . . stand against hydra-headed fraud in Elections, and help us stamp into the ground the viperous heads raised treasonably against good government. . . .

LEE HAWLEY
D. J. CHARLES

Progressive ideas tended to disrupt both major political parties. Such fragmentation is well exemplified by the career of Joseph M. Dixon, one of Montana's most outstanding but overlooked politicians. As a United States Senator, Dixon split with orthodox Republicans in 1912 to support Theodore Roosevelt's Progressives. Although he later rejoined the party, conservatives were loath to forgive Dixon, even after he won the governor's race in 1920 in a heated campaign against B. K. Wheeler. In a letter to Congressman Carl Riddick, Attorney General Ford, himself a disappointed aspirant to the governorship that year, urged that the party put factionalism behind and move forward as a united party.

HELENA, MONTANA
DECEMBER 23, 1920

HON. CARL RIDDICK
MEMBER OF CONGRESS
WASHINGTON, D.C.

MY DEAR CARL,

. . . Under ordinary conditions I think perhaps your plan would work out fairly satisfactory but we should not forget that extraordinary conditions prevail in Montana. The republican party is as much divided to-day as any. We still have the old would-be leaders, the most reactionary set of men to be found in the state, whose interest in politics is largely personal and selfish and who have seldom, if ever, assisted a party in the state. And there is a young progressive element who believes in honesty and fair dealing in politics. . . . [who] resent the unscrupulous and contemptuous method of the old wing and believe that party interest should come before personal interest. In 1912, some, but by no means all, of the more liberal in the party joined the progressive party and during the campaign just closed an effort was made

to get these republicans back into the party. . . . Now that they are back are we going to keep them or drive them out by surrendering all to the reactionary crowd? . . .

Some of the prominent republicans throughout the state are ready, willing and anxious to trade off the entire ticket from president down in order to save Senator Dixon. . . . Personally I cannot subscribe to such a policy. I would never permit these men who have no interest in you or Senator Harding to make a single appointment but on the other hand those who honestly and conscientiously did their part should receive due consideration. . . .

If we use just a little common sense we can reach no other conclusion but that the future success of the party in Montana depends upon a progressive, forward-looking set of men and the sooner we get the elements which you propose to give recognition to . . . the sooner the party will be on a firm foundation with bright prospects for the future. . . .

SAM C. FORD
ATTORNEY GENERAL

In contrast with the generally conservative aspect of politics within Montana, the state's voters sent a long line of liberal representatives and senators to Congress. One of the most distinguished was Thomas J. Walsh, who served in the Senate from 1912 to 1933. A superb politician, Walsh proved adept at bending to the company at home — as evidenced in this letter to Bozeman newspaperman Walter Aitkin — while furthering liberal legislation in Washington. Perhaps best known for his exposure of the Teapot Dome scandal in 1923, Walsh was appointed Attorney General by Franklin Roosevelt, but was denied this honor by a fatal heart attack.

WASHINGTON, D.C.
APRIL 8, 1932

MR. WALTER AITKIN
BOZEMAN, MONTANA

DEAR WALTER:

. . . I am in a rather embarrassing position concerning . . . Penwell. . . . Miles Romney has been my consistent friend and supporter, in person and through

his paper, ever since I have been a seeker after public office. He was belligerently so at Livingston in the convention of 1910, a crucial test. In the campaign a year ago last fall I twice appealed to Erickson to take the stump for me. In both instances he responded with alacrity. Under these circumstances, intimate as my relations with Penwell have been, I do not feel warranted in throwing the weight of any influence I may have in favor of him as against either of the other two.

Then another situation is embarrassing to me. No one conversant with the matter can hesitate in the belief that the Anaconda Company and its allies have been exercising a dominating influence over our public life. I had to encounter that opposition to come to the Senate in the first place. I dare say it and the Montana Power Company have been escaping their just share of the heavy burden of taxation . . . but I am not keen just now to assail the Anaconda Company when every day the probability grows more and more imminent that it will be forced to shut down. . . . I think every one must realize that since copper fell below seven or eight cents at least all of its operations have been carried on at a loss. If it were making money I should have every disposition to get into a fight to compel it to bear its fair share of the cost of government, by whomsoever the effort to attain that end might be led. As it is, as indicated, I am not keen about a fight on them just now.

SINCERELY YOURS,

T. J. WALSH
U.S. SENATE

In theory, appointive powers permitted an elected official to reward his friends and strengthen his party; in practice, patronage tended to please only the few, while disappointing the many. In this case, the rivalry between eastern and western portions of the state disrupted Governor Cooney's attempt to carefully balance all significant interests.

GLENDIVE, MONTANA
APRIL 21, 1933

HONORABLE F. H. COONEY
HELENA, MONTANA

DEAR MR. COONEY:

In reply to your letter of April 19th concerning the appointment of a gentleman from Missoula to the State Highway Commission. I must say that the people of Eastern Montana feel deeply hurt at your action.

If you will take a map of Montana and draw a line East of Butte and Great Falls, Montana, you will find that over half of the State of Montana was overlooked. . . . I assume that you selected an able man, yet it has been my experience that people in Western Montana have never realized what Eastern Montana is. . . . I am writing you in this manner for I feel undoubtedly three years from now you'll be a candidate to succeed yourself, and political experience and policy should suggest to you that Eastern Montana must at all times be considered. . . .

YOURS VERY TRULY,

DESMOND J. O'NEIL

Senator Burton K. Wheeler, one of the most powerful politicians in Montana's history, possessed an unblemished reputation as a liberal during the early years of his career. After jousting with the Anaconda Company and the Council of Defense, Wheeler won election to the Senate in 1922. Within two years his fame was such that he received the vice-presidential nomination on Robert LaFollette's Progressive ticket. Senator Wheeler at first staunchly supported the New Deal, but he later broke with Roosevelt, first over the court-packing issue and later over foreign affairs. Wheeler's isolationism was unquestionably based on principal, but it, along with this break with the President, convinced many Montanans that he had become a reactionary with pro-German sympathies. In 1946 Wheeler lost his bid for re-election in the Democratic primary, an event foreshadowed before the fact in Walter Aitken's letter.

BOZEMAN, MONTANA

MR. BURTON K. WHEELER
UNITED STATES SENATOR
WASHINGTON, D.C.

MY DEAR SENATOR:

I have received from you a copy of "The United States and the Peace." . . . Perhaps you are right in assuming, as you do in your covering letter, that the inclusion of your speech in a compilation of other speeches and documents of real importance is something of a compliment to you, but it seems more likely that the real purpose is to enable readers to make comparisons and contrasts with speeches by other senators on the same general subject. . . . If that is done it is not going to enhance your reputation either as a speaker or a patriot. . . .

Your speech was not intended to be helpful in devising some workable means whereby the world may hereafter be reasonably free from the scourge of war, but to put obstacles in the way of accomplishing that most desirable purpose. . . . Considering the satisfaction with which that speech and some others by you have been received, quoted and used by the enemies with whom our country has been and is now at war . . . the conclusion is logical [that your statements are] close to, if not actually and legally, treasonable.

Of my own knowledge there are many among your Montana constituents, formerly your political friends and supporters, who now regard you as a traitor. . . . Many . . . myself among them, distrust you for the friends you have made, in Montana, throughout the Nation and abroad. . . .

[We recall] one of your early [statements], "When they support me, my friends, you may be sure that I have betrayed you." . . . They are supporting you and praising you, Senator, those predatory special interests in this state which you at one time so roundly and vehemently denounced as public enemies and worse and who in turn characterized you as . . . a "Russian-loving communist," "political upstart," "dangerous demagogue, agitator" and other familiar epithets. . . .

If and when you again become a candidate in Montana for re-election . . . it will be a test of whether the people of Montana, including the farmers and the railroad employes, regard material profit or genuine patriotic loyalty as the higher and more enlightened self-interest. . . . There are many Montana voters who have voted for you three times, including myself, and some of them four times, but who nevertheless have good memories and, remembering, are "fed up" with you. They no longer trust you or believe in your sincerity or loyalty to anything but your own not over-scrupulous self-aggrandizment and self-seeking, and you are going to have a hard time fooling them again. . . .

WALTER AITKEN

Although the New Deal produced a political realignment in the nation as a whole, in Montana the impact of Roosevelt's New Deal politics was only temporary. During the first years of the 1930's, Montana Democrats experienced solid victories and an ideological shift to the left. This trend culminated in the 1936 election to Congress of Jerry J. O'Connell, who represented the extreme left-wing of the party. In subsequent years, however, the liberal coalition collapsed as a result of state and national pressures and the party reverted to a more typical pattern of personal constituencies. Ironically, the same 1940 election which marked O'Connell's second unsuccessful try for re-election, also witnessed the appearance of Mike Mansfield, who was to establish the greatest political constituency in Montana's history.

HAMILTON, MONTANA
APRIL 9, 1940

H. S. BRUCE, EDITOR,
THE PEOPLE'S VOICE,
HELENA, MONTANA.

DEAR CAP:

. . . I do not know whether you have been following Caverly's paper. . . . If you have you will notice that Tom time and time again, has taken little pot shots at me in a rather clever way. This is obviously because he is for Mansfield for Congress. Naturally I resent it, particularly because on the basis of my record I feel I do not deserve it even for somebody like Mansfield, who is absolutely untried and has no record. . . .

If you fellows get together and decide who the liberal candidate for Governor is, what assurance have I that you have not already done so as far as the congressional race or any other race is concerned. From present indications, it looks pretty much to me that you have already decided on Mansfield, untried, no political experience, and God only knows what he would do if he were elected. I know he says he is a liberal, but why doesn't he run for the state legislature, show us what he's got, and then if he withstands the heat, let's give him his chance. In the face of all this, I have only one conclusion to make, and that is that your crowd has decided to write me out of the picture; if that is so then I have only one alternative, to take the situation to the rank and file of the progressive organizations, and I think you know I can do a fair job. . . .

SINCERELY YOURS,
JERRY

As a result of her unpopular vote against involvement in World War I, Jeannette Rankin, the first woman to serve in Congress, was defeated in a try for the Senate in 1918. After the loss, she retired to a farm in Georgia to devote herself to feminist and pacifist causes. During this period she returned to Montana only occasionally. The advent of the intervention debate as an important national issue during the late 1930's, however, prompted Rankin to re-enter Montana politics. Despite sentiments such as those expressed by Mrs. Friday, she won re-election to Congress in 1940. A consistent dove, Jeannette Rankin cast the sole dissenting vote against the country's entry into World War II.

MANHATTAN, MONTANA
NOVEMBER 11, 1940

TO THE PEOPLES VOICE:

I see you have Jeannette Rankins picture in your paper as a winner in the Election. I don't think that is anything for any of us to be proud of, for She hasn't lived here for 24 years that I know of and when she was sent to Congress 24 years ago she cried like a baby. The people that sent her this time better donate some sheets to catch her Tears. Another thing, she is past 60 years Old. We have enough Old people in the White House now. We need new younger blood, people with up to date Ideas, & Another thing, we have to many Women taking Jobs away from men.... The machine age is a whole lot of our trouble today. Senator Wheeler is one of the biggest kickers against Our president, also a Third term, but he didn't turn down a fourth term tho; Why shouldn't a president have a third, fourth or 5 term if he is good. Mont sent a know nothing do nothing Nazi 2 years ago & what does Rankin know about the needs of Mont.... I think the whole state of Montana needs a good House cleaning & suppose Mont will be the laughing stock of the Congress this coming year again.

MRS. MARY E. FRIDAY

In the first years after women won the vote, Montanans elected several women to the state legislature, but as the years passed, women gradually assumed a passive role in electoral politics. During the 1920's and 1930's only an occasional woman sought election to the legis-lature, and then only to the lower house. In 1944 Ellenore Bridenstine broke the barrier to the state senate in a move that she hoped would initiate a new era of political responsibility for women. In a radio broadcast in 1945 she commented on the past session, revealing not only her views about women in politics, but also the lack of sophistication concerning the legislative process that was common among the electorate.

LADIES AND GENTLEMEN:

I have been asked a number of times since coming to Helena, how it feels to be the first woman Senator. My answer to that question is that it is a very nice feeling.... But in addition to being an honor, it is a big responsi-bility; [it] carries with it an obligation to do an ex-ceptionally good job. . . .

Women, it seems to me, are just beginning to wake up to the fact that they have been accepting the privileges of full voting citizenship for a good many years without accepting any of the responsibilities of government. . . .

The process of law making is rather awesome and seemingly intricate to a newcomer, but as the weeks go on it begins to look clearer from the inside. It would be fairly simple except for the usual variations of personali-ties. People are all so very different and each person thinks differently about the same thing. . . . Before coming up to Helena, I was led to believe that there would be much more rough-and-tumble disagreement than there has been. There have, of course, been some arguments both on the floor of the Senate and in commit-tees, but I love a good argument, especially when there is some right on both sides which is the case more often than not. I have been much impressed and pleased to see that such arguments, when finished, are com-pletely over and as far as I can see, leave no bitterness behind them. . . .

The casual visitor might think the state was wasting money paying a group of people for coming to Helena for sixty days from all over the state to just sit and listen to something read rapidly from the desk. They cannot, of course, see the hours spent in the study of these bills and what they might mean to the state. When the casual visitor sees us reading newspapers or just talking among ourselves, while the roll call is being made on the final vote, they cannot know the time, effort and thought that has gone into the decision. . . . The casual visitor cannot see the long hours of research, the time spent in

answering letters from constituents, or hours spent in stuffy committee rooms listening to testimony . . . but I have learned during this my first session, that the legislators really work, and work hard. . . .

ELLENORE M. BRIDENSTINE
REPUBLICAN, PRAIRIE COUNTY

As the state government increased in size and scope during post-war years, it spawned an ever increasing number of committees, agencies, commissions, and bureaus. To the over-burdened taxpayers the activities of such bureaucratic groups often seemed more illusory than real.

TROY, MONTANA
FEBRUARY 3, 1956

MR. GEORGE SCHOTTE, CHAIRMAN
MONTANA FACT FINDING COMMITTEE
  ON HIGHWAYS, STREETS & BRIDGES
BUTTE, MONTANA

DEAR MR. SCHOTTE—

Should your committee happen to stumble onto any kind of a fact or anything that looks like one please send it along to me.

ALLEN GOODGAME
REPRESENTATIVE FROM LINCOLN COUNTY
MONTANA HOUSE OF REPRESENTATIVES

Unlike B. K. Wheeler, Senator James E. Murray never broke with Roosevelt and never lost his liberal constituency. Throughout a quarter century of service in Washington (1935-1961), Murray remained popular with farm and labor organizations by working diligently to secure federal spending for Montana. In 1960, the 84-year-old Murray attracted two strong opponents from among the younger leadership of the party — Congressmen Lee Metcalf and LeRoy Anderson. When it appeared he might not be physically able to carry on a vigorous campaign, Murray resigned, thus precipitating yet another example of the intra-party bitterness that was so common in Montana's politics.

WASHINGTON, D.C.
MAY 10, 1960

DEAR FRIEND:

As you know, I have withdrawn from the primary in response to the repeated urgings of my family and because of the political situation which has developed in Montana.

My sons had urged me to withdraw on the grounds that, in my twenty-five years of service, I had fully discharged my obligations to the people of Montana and that I had won the right to enjoy a less arduous and more rewarding life. This I was reluctant to do because I believed that the seniority and influence in the Senate which my quarter of a century of service had won for Montana was far too important to the people of our State for me to throw away just so I could retire to a life of ease. That is why I announced my candidacy. . . .

Then the situation changed. . . . Casting both

personal and political loyalty to the winds, Anderson and Metcalf decided to run for my seat in the Senate. Metcalf did so after announcing that he could not oppose me because we stood for the same things and I could get them done better! . . .

I was advised that to win reelection I would have to shirk my work here in Washington and race them around the State in an endurance contest aimed at seeing who could shake the most hands and who could out-villify the others. Apparently they believe it's brawn, not brains, that a Senator needs. . . . I was willing and eager . . . to put all the energies I have left to me at the service of Montana, but I most certainly would not [take] part in the type of primary campaign which both Anderson and Metcalf must have known would have to be waged when they decided to run against me.

It is for this reason . . . that I bid a political goodbye to my many friends in Montana. . . . I hope too that my many friends . . . will join me in supporting a man who . . . has proved his unwavering loyalty to his friends and to his party. . . . I hope and ask that all Montana's Democrats rally round and bring victory in the primary and in the final election to John Bonner. . . .

SINCERELY YOUR FRIEND,
JAMES E. MURRAY
U.S. SENATE

Despite the strife resulting from the nomination fight, Lee Metcalf proved to be a fitting heir to Murray's Senate seat. Closely tied with the liberal wing of the Democratic Party, Metcalf's career reflected the growing influence of national issues (in Metcalf's case, primarily energy and the environment) in state politics. The following letter to one of Metcalf's supporters indicated the degree to which the national anti-communist hysteria of the 1950's was reflected in Montana.

ANACONDA, MONTANA
JUNE 9, 1960

DEAR L. HART

Since Metcalf has won the nomination for U.S. Senator, I'd like to call your attention to a characteristic of Metcalf's career that I, as well as many others, do not agree with. Here it is in a nutshell: Why is it that Metcalf never speaks out against Communism? Is this fact just an accident or is it intentional on his part? I think the voters have a right to know the answer to this important question. . . '.

Perhaps you folks in Stevensville there, have no Communist subversion to worry about. However, we here in Anaconda and Butte are plagued by the Mine Mill Union which has Communists for leaders. In Anaconda there is a battle going on against the traitors who head the . . . Union. I am helping in every way that I can. The recent terrible and long strike was actually caused by these . . . Reds, not the rank and file at all.

I wrote Metcalf during the strike and told him the tough situation we were in and how intense was the suffering from the strike. I also told him I protested his appearance as a speaker at a [Union] convention because of the Communist domination of the union. He wrote back and I'll give him credit for that (Murray has ignored my letters). . . . Metcalf wrote back that he did not believe [they were communists] or he never would have consented. . . . Well Metcalf evidently doesn't do any research on Union leaders or he would know that Clark [head of the Mine-Mill Union] plead the fifth Amendment . . . urges trade with Red China, and asked Harry Bridges to be guest speaker at the last . . . convention. If Clark isn't a Communist then he sure is a doggone poor American. It's my opinion that Metcalf had best refuse to go along with [the Union] any longer.

EDNA PETERSON

In earlier days a legion of lobbyists for corporate interests descended upon Helena during every legislative session. If their methods tended to be ruthless, they were highly effective. In more recent times the number of interest groups sending lobbyists to Helena has proliferated. The methods of the new style lobbyists were both sophisticated and subject to regulation, and the legislators themselves developed a certain sense of humor about the phenomenon.

FEBRUARY 28, 1961

SENATE RESOLUTION XX
INTRODUCED BY PAUL E. BRENNER
DEMOCRAT, JEFFERSON COUNTY

WHEREAS: By the 58th day of the 37th Session of the Montana Legislature, some of the Lobbyists attached thereto have shown courage above and beyond the call of duty;

AND WHEREAS: The amount of blood, sweat and tears shed in the field of foreign bars, calls for some distinctive recognition and special notice similar to the Purple Heart.

THEREFORE BE IT RESOLVED: That the Senate authorize the designing of a medal to be struck in horse feathers and to embrace a design of trading stamps . . . same to be awarded where actual physical, mental or moral damage can be established.

One of the most conspicuous and effective of special interest groups in recent years has been organized labor. Although not one of the more powerful unions, the carpenters joined the liberal chorus which administered a resounding defeat to the sales tax proposal in a 1971 referendum.

KALISPELL, MONTANA
JANUARY 31, 1967

MEMBERS, 40TH MONT. LEGISLATIVE ASSEMBLY
LADIES AND GENTLEMEN:

We oppose a Sales Tax on plain and simple and honest grounds. It is intended to tax and will tax people whose pitiful Social Security checks, Workman's Compensation checks and unemployment checks are not now subject to Income Tax. Thus, it is a tax imposed on the needy. . . . It is imposed on the sick or injured disabled working man or farmer with, perhaps, no income at all or, at the most, a Workman's Compensation check. It is a tax imposed on widows and orphans and the beneficiaries of Life Insurance Policies, no matter how small the payment might be. It is a tax imposed upon the elderly. . . . It is a tax imposed on the student who finds it necessary to earn a few hundred dollars to keep himself in school. In short, it is a tax imposed upon the most needy and for the benefit of those of us who have an income and who may desire to reduce our taxes by passing them on to those less able to pay. . . .

We oppose sending Sales Tax Legislation out for a referendum, for the very simple reason that those least able to pay the tax are, also, unable to protect themselves with the paid advertising and even unpaid political propaganda that the rich will use to buy the votes to put it over. . . . The sole protection of the general public, and your constituents, lies in your refusal to enact such legislation. . . .

VERY TRULY YOURS,

ROBERT C. WELLER, EXEC. SEC.
MONTANA CARPENTERS DIST. COUNCIL

Erosion of the population of eastern Montana during the 1920's and 1930's resulted in a maldistribution of legislators to favor underpopulated rural areas. This imbalance was partially responsible for the traditional conservative orientation of the legislature even after corporate influence declined. Although the rural-urban migration continued, reapportionment did not take place until a federal court order in 1965. Even then the intransigence of rural legislators led to an impasse that had to be worked out by a special court panel. Despite the fears of people such as Representative William Mather of Musselshell County, reapportionment did not radically alter legislative patterns, although it did provide for a more equitable position for the state's growing urban majority.

FEB. 11, 1965

Let's stop and look at this just a minute. Before any plan we should adopt here, it has to meet two . . . basic requirements. First, it must be constitutional; second, it must be acceptable to the people of the state of Montana. . . . Let us first discuss the constitutionality of this. The Leuthold plan which we are discussing here today, is based upon one senator for each 13,500 population. . . . Let's just take our two top counties, Yellowstone and Cascade, for illustration. Yellowstone county, according to the last census, had a 79,000 population; Cascade county had a 73,400 population or a difference of 5,600. . . . In other words, Cascade county will have one less senator than Yellowstone county but they only have 5,600 population less. . . . The additional 5,600 people in Yellowstone county are getting an additional senator. . . .

Will this be acceptable to all of the counties and to the state and to the people as a whole? . . . If you just go through House Bill 84 you will find that twelve counties . . . will control our state senate. . . . In other words, we have forty-four counties which we left entirely without representation and I don't believe . . . that forty-four of us from forty-four counties can go home and say, people, you are suddenly left without representation in our state senate.

Let's look at it another way. The Leuthold plan breaks us into twenty-eight districts. . . . Out of each district there is necessarily going to be one predominant county. That means there are going to be twenty-eight counties which are going to be subordinate counties. They are not going to have the privileges of government. They are not going to have the right of representation, the right of spokesmanship, the right to be heard in committee and on the floor in the state senate. . . . Is this what we want to present to the people of the state of Montana? . . .

Over the years a growing number of legislators and civic groups realized that effective state government required not piecemeal amending of the unwieldy 1889 constitution but comprehensive structural revision. Toward this end, the legislature established a Constitution Revision Commission in 1969. After study, this group recommended that a constitutional convention be proposed to the voters. To encourage support, the group's administrative assistant contacted all Montana newspapermen. In 1972 the convention assembled and drew up a new constitution. Narrowly approved by the voters, that document served as the new basis for political decision.

MISSOULA, MONTANA
FEBRUARY 13, 1970

DEAR SIR:

This year, 1970, will be an historic year in Montana. For the first time ever, the people of the state will vote on the question of calling a constitutional convention to revise, alter, or amend the constitution which was adopted in 1889. . . . Because of the importance of this vote to the future of Montana state and local government, the Montana Constitution Revision Commission wishes to encourage wide public examination of the issues involved. . . .

As Montana looks to the future, it is shackled to the past by a constitution that [has been criticized as:]

1. not written in clear . . . language;
2. not reasonably short and simple;
3. not restricted to fundamentals;
4. not flexible enough to meet present needs and to adapt to future requirements of our people;
5. reflecting lack of confidence in popular control of government;
6. containing many ill-advised limitations on state legislative power;
7. lacking a strong . . . executive;
8. failing to provide adequate reapportionment;
9. providing for an out-of-date inferior court;
10. denying local governments control of their own affairs;
11. containing outmoded approaches and procedures that are costly and inefficient; and
12. hampering reasonable revisions.

The 1967-1968 Legislative Council study of the Montana constitution concluded that less than one-half of the provisions of the Montana constitution are adequate. . . . The Legislative Council concluded that 124 sections are adequate as presently written. . . . In addition, 53 sections should be revised, and 85 sections should be repealed. Some of these should be replaced by statute. Included in the portion that the Council felt should be repealed are four entire articles. . . .

Only five state constitutions dating from the 19th century have been amended fewer times than the Montana constitution. . . . The number of amendments proposed in the legislature has increased sharply since reapportionment, and has averaged thirty in each of the last three legislative sessions. . . . Responding to the increased pressure of proposed amendments . . . in 1967 legislation for creation of a Constitution Study Commission was introduced, [and] the Legislative Council was instructed to study the Montana constitution to determine its "adequacy." . . .

The interest in constitutional revision appears to be broad enough to substantiate a belief that the people will vote to hold a convention if the need is fully explained to them. . . . A convention at this time makes sense because it is the best method of obtaining full and public reconsideration of the Montana constitution. A convention can look at the entire document without being restricted, as is the Legislative Assembly, by the three-amendment limitation and without being distracted by the problems and pressures of a session of the Legislative Assembly. The convention would be representative of the people of Montana. . . . A convention devoted to the single purpose of considering constitutional revision would have every opportunity to produce a worthy product. The convention can be expected to propose moderate, realistic and appropriate changes in the constitution because it . . . is subject to searching coverage by modern communications media and is tempered by the necessity of seeking ratification of its efforts by the voters. A significant by-product of the convention would be the opportunity for all people of Montana to focus on the constitutional foundation of our state. . . .

The Constitution Revision Commission urges you to join us and other Montana citizens in this endeavor to familiarize Montanans with the Montana constitution, its impact on the everyday functioning of government, and the need for its modernization. . . .

DALE A. HARRIS

246

EXTRACTIVE ECONOMY

MINING AND SMELTING continued to dominate Montana's economy and politics. Technological change and consolidation shaped the industry to more efficient patterns. Standard Oil, the nation's largest trust, began major consolidation in the copper industry by purchasing majority ownership of the Anaconda and forming, in 1899, the Amalgamated Copper Company. This copper trust largely controlled Butte, and Montana, until court action, instituted by federal "trust busters," forced dissolution of the combine in 1915. After that date, the Anaconda Copper Mining Company, divorced from the Standard Oil trust, assumed the pre-eminent role in the industry. By 1930, this company owned all significant ore bodies in the Butte region, smelters, a supportive railroad, vast tracts of timber throughout the state, coal mines, and most daily newspapers. Its mineral production made the Anaconda a major asset in the two world conflicts that exploded in the Twentieth Century. The paternalistic influence of this corporate giant provoked political controversy, public relations embarrassment, and the animosity of many state residents.

Checks on Anaconda's domination came only from national and international economic trends or periodic opposition of organized labor. The ability of copper industry unions to effectively confront Montana mining companies declined from the position of power and influence enjoyed at the turn of the century. Unlike the steady progress enjoyed by labor in other trades and industries, mining unions suffered internal dissension and massive, united company opposition which robbed them of effectiveness until revitalized by federal actions in the Depression era. Labor's renewed militancy partially influenced Anaconda's decision to turn heavily to production from mines outside Montana. By the 1960's, adverse economic trends forced the contraction of Anaconda's operations and allowed agriculture to replace mining as the dominant Montana industry.

Technological change and general expansion in mining, lumbering, agriculture, and recreation/tourism, forced further growth and diversification in supportive commerce and industry. Most significantly, other power sources emerged as a result of industrial and public necessity. Electricity, gas, coal and oil, modified all facets of existence and their production drastically altered Montana's economy. Other sectors, too, changed to meet shifting, growing emphases. In a rapidly maturing economy, "Main Street" in Montana communities supplied goods and services unheard of a quarter century earlier.

With this maturation came an even closer correlation between Montana's economy and national trends and events. Changing markets, war booms, postwar inflation, national depression, international competition, and governmental manipulation and regulation forced responses from the region's business and industry. The state's continued reliance on extractive industry intensified this situation. Closely tied to marketplace vagaries, extractive industry also, by its nature, left an indelible mark on the land. Increased awareness of the finite nature of the environment, another national trend, compounded Montana's economic problems. Questions deriving from multiple demands on the state's resources dominated Montana's recent past and suggested a variety of responses for the future.

GOING TO WORK, ANACONDA, C. 1940

EXTRACTIVE ECONOMY
Business and Industry in the 20th Century

> *Butte avoided the tumultous labor conflicts which rocked the nation in the 1890's. The city's Miners Union, Local No. 1, Western Federation of Miners, held a powerful position while the Copper Kings competed for the good will of the workers. The Amalgamated Company's defeat of F. Augustus Heinze in 1906 ended the owners' conflict and signaled the decline of the Butte union. Amalgamated and the other copper companies soon established dominance over the union and its conservative leadership. Militant members, with support from the syndicalist Industrial Workers of the World, revolted, rifled the safe at Union Hall, exchanged shots during which one man was killed, and dynamited the union building. Insurgents formed a new union but continuing violence gave authorities justification for bringing in troops. The new union collapsed while the old local existed only as a skeleton. Clearly, labor's divisions cost the miners representation, and every Butte citizen resented the troops, the violence, and the rumors which followed.*

BUTTE, MONTANA
SEPTEMBER 14, 1914

GOV. S. V. STEWART
HELENA, MONTANA

DEAR SIR:

It has occured to me that you might be interested in the opinion of the common laboring people regarding the situation in Butte. . . . We feel that we have been dishonored and disgraced in the eyes of our whole country, for we are not a lawless or degraded class, but industrious law abiding citizens. . . .

Now in our simplicity we think that there never was a time when it seemed so unnecessary to have big guns trained upon us . . . who have no thought of breaking any laws. . . . In our ignorance, we simply look upon this whole business as a move to put down Socialism and the power of the unions in Butte.

Letters have come from the East telling us how sorry they are for us; "that the streets of Butte are running with miners' blood" and that "all the business district is in ashes, blown up by the miners." We are dishonored and disgraced, [for we are] a hardworking, lawabiding and progressive people who only demand a wage to keep us living like human beings, and sanitary conditions to work in and to bring up our children to become good American citizens not slaves. It is our educational advantages that have given us the power to think and frame our own conclusions; that makes us indignant at our being forced at the point of the bayonet to come under the power of money or political intrigue. . . . The power of mind, of thought, of principal, are the forces we hope to use, and these forces awaken with [new] vigor when people feel they have been outraged. . .

A VOICE FROM THE PEOPLE
MRS. ADA DAWSON

> *Montana's rivers and the mining industry's demands for power presented opportunity to enterprising men willing to explore the potential of hydroelectric power generation. Begun in the 1890's, several small companies erected dams and transmission lines to service mines, smelters and communities. Competition and corporate influence eventually forced Samuel T. Hauser's Missouri River Power Company to combine with corporations controlled by the Amalgamated, producing the Montana Power Company. John D. Ryan, long president of the Anaconda Company, recounted the intertwining of mining and electricity and the formation of the power company in a letter to H. H. Cole of the Boston News Bureau.*

MAY 1, 1923

DEAR MR. COLE:

In reply to your letter of yesterday asking for information . . . as to the business of The Montana Power Company with the Anaconda Company. . . . I will say that the proportion of the gross revenue of The Montana Power Company derived from business with the Anaconda Company and all of its subsidiaries in Montana . . . varies from twenty to thirty-three per cent of the total gross of the Power Company. . . .

In 1908 The Missouri River Power Company's dam at Hauser Lake on the Missouri River, near Helena, which had been supplying the Butte mines with power, collapsed and was entirely destroyed, and only a small amount of power . . . was available for mining operations.

The Amalgamated Copper Company then owned . . . control of the Anaconda Company and various other mining corporations, and also owned about a million dollars of the bonds of the Missouri River Power Company and a considerable block of its preferred and common stock. . . .

If the Mining Companies had [to use] steam power they not only would be tremendously affected in the matter of costs, but the inconvenience in the use of steam power as compared with electric power in their operations would have added greatly to operating difficulties. . . .

With this knowledge . . . I endeavored to get Mr. H. H. Rogers, then President of the Amalgamated Company [and] . . . that Company to take some action that would result in the development of power . . . but the experience of the Company in its investment in Missouri River Power securities caused them to decide not to go any further into hydro-electric development. . . . I then told Mr. Rogers that I was satisfied that I personally could raise the money to buy the [James J.] Hill interests [at Great Falls] and could finance the development of power sufficient to meet the needs of the Mining Companies if I had a contract with the Mining Companies. . . . As a result of long negotiations . . . a contract was drawn up which Mr. Rogers insisted should

be for the life of the mines. . . . As a part of the contract I took over at the cost to the Amalgamated Copper Company all of its interests in the securities of the bankrupt Missouri River Power Company.

The first development of the Rainbow Falls . . . commenced in 1909, finished in 1910, and power was being delivered in eighteen months from the time the stock of the Water Power & Townsite Company was purchased from Mr. Hill. Power was sold to the Mining Companies at $30. at Butte for which they had formerly paid $50. to the Missouri River Power Company, and the Power Company bound itself to make additional developments required to meet the estimated needs of the Mining Companies over a long period of years, all of which options have been exercised and the terms of the contract carried out to the fullest extent.

When the contracts were made . . . no member of the Board of [the Amalgamated] excepting myself, had any interest whatever in the Power Companies. . . . If there is any criticism on the part of any shareholder of the Anaconda Company of the relations between The Montana Power Company and the Anaconda Copper Mining Company, I have never heard it, and I do not believe . . . that anything but benefit to the Anaconda Company has resulted in the relations of the two Companies. . . . The Montana Power Company, thanks to the good sense used in planning it, the brains in engineering it, and the large quantities of power which it has been able to sell from the day development was finished, has been a profitable enterprise. . . .

SINCERELY YOURS,

JOHN D. RYAN

Conflict over the use of Montana's natural resources appeared between farmer and miner with increasing frequency in earlier decades. The most noted case, the suit of Deer Lodge Valley farmers against the Washoe Smelter of the Anaconda Trust, set national precedent. A conservation-minded president, Theodore Roosevelt, led the federal government to join litigation to halt timber and grass destruction resulting from fumes escaping from the smelter's stack. The 1911 finding against Amalgamated did not satisfy area farmers but their opposition demonstrated remedies for similar future problems. Boulder Valley farmers, in appealing to government authority, acted as aggressively to protect their use of the land and water.

BASIN, MONTANA
MARCH 11, 1917

S. C. FORD, ATTORNEY GENERAL
HELENA, MONTANA

DEAR SIR:

We have your favor of March 6th calling our attention to . . . information to the effect that we have

been dumping debris and tailings from our works into Boulder River and that by reason thereof, the property of the State has been greatly damaged and that the injury to this property will become greater unless prompt action be taken. . . .

We wish to express our sincere appreciation of your . . . method of bringing this matter to our notice . . . but before proceeding any further we feel that in all fairness we should acquaint you with our side of the dispute.

In June 1914, the writer commenced the retreatment of the tailings dumps at Basin.... The writer was well aware of the trouble between the Boulder valley farmers and the old Basin Reduction Company.... He personally visited the farmers around Boulder, where at periods of high water the tailings from the reduction works had overflowed the banks of the river and materially damaged the property of the farmers. He called the attention of the farmers to the fact that whereas the Basin Reduction Company, and later on the Butte & Superior Copper Company had been treating in the neighborhood of 1,000 tons of ore per day, that he was milling less than 150 tons a day and did not believe that any damage would result.... He ... assured them that if they ever found that the tailings from his mill were causing the least damage to their property that he held himself ready and willing to commence impounding these tailings at the concentrator.... They have always assured him that they had no complaint to make whatsoever.... For this reason there has been no attempt made to impound the tailings....

We are just as unwilling now as we have always been to cause any damage to the farmers of Boulder valley.... The farmer's lot is a hard one at best and far be it from us to want to add to his burden, but the impounding of tailings is an expensive matter and unless the farmers can show a bona fide cause for complaint or unless you order it, we do not believe it the fair thing to compel us to incur this extra expense.

We believe that Boulder Valley has profited to no small extent by our operations at Basin.... We feel sure that there is nothing put into the water that would endanger the life of cattle drinking from the stream and that the sands and slimes dumped into the river are of such a small quantity and have settled to such an extent by the time they get to the farms that there can be nothing more serious to complain of....

We beg that you give this matter your consideration and instruct us further, and we desire to assure you that every effort will be made to comply with your instructions in the matter.

> BASIN SALVAGE COMPANY
> M. W. ATWATER, President

Depletion of timber in the east and upper midwest turned lumbermen westward. Their operations in Montana, after the turn of the century, greatly expanded this sector of Montana's economy. Accompanying this rapid expansion were attendant abuses and shortcomings in the employer-labor relationship. After 1907, the Industrial Workers of the World — known as "Wobblies" — played an increasingly militant role in labor conflict in the lumber industry, as the loggers' frustrations with conditions mounted. The disputes of 1917 capped I.W.W. efforts to organize lumber camps. Champ Hannon, a government forester at Darby, witnessed the clashes of that period.

[I lived in] these logging camps [with] as many as 200 men. I've been in those [logging] bunk houses with 50 or 60 men. And wet socks hanging up over them old barrel heaters. And you know what they had to sleep on? They had a pile of straw in a log bunk.

So the Wobblies came along. When the Wobblies got through they had beds, mattresses, sheets and shower baths. And so my sympathies are all with the Wobblies. Because they forced the logging companies to make a lumberjack a human being. When we were in Idaho none of those lumberjacks were married.... They came out there and lived like animals in those camps, sleeping on lousy straw for maybe 6 months. Then they'd go out [to town] and in 3 days they'd be broke,

and they'd be back.... And they were just like grizzly bears. You meet one of them along the road and speak to him, he'd just grunt at ya. I mean you can't wonder at it. They were tough, they were tough characters.

[But the I.W.W. changed their way of living], you bet they did. They forced the logging companies, they forced them to put in showers, baths, and sheets. And the men, when we were there, the lumberjacks carried their beds. Their blanket ya know, they had their soogans.

[They also went into helping straighten out] everything connected with making the conditions, the working conditions better for the lumberjacks there.... As far as I'm concerned it was one of the best organizations ever.

Clashes during the summer of 1917 created bitterness on both sides of the issue. Patriotism of World War I translated into opposition to strikes and militant unionism, promoting accusations of treason and obstructionism from lumber owners. Montana's chief executive called out the militia to preserve peace and allow lumbering operations to proceed. The I.W.W. became "villains" in the confrontation and were jailed or driven from the camps and villages of the timber country. Depending upon the interests involved, two views of the roles and methods of the "Wobblies" existed, and Governor Stewart received them both.

KALISPELL, MONTANA
JUNE 27, 1917

GOV. S. V. STEWART
HELENA, MONTANA

MY DEAR SIR:

Your valued communication of the 25th received, and you have relieved my mind entirely, for I was a little disturbed when it was reported to me . . . that the . . . prosecuting attorneys of Flathead and Lincoln Counties . . . were starting an investigation to ascertain who had made unreliable reports to you in regard to conditions in this section. . . . Everything that was reported was the absolute truth. . . . The business men in general here were more or less alarmed over conditions and felt that an emergency existed and were very anxious to do their duty. . . . They seemed to feel that actual crimes had to be committed before any arrests could be made. . . . It seemed that there was only one alternative, this being the troops, and although I have no knowledge whatever of how the troops were ordered to our section, I think I can voice the sentiments of the vast majority when I say the troops have saved the situation. . . .

I believe I told you that possibly thirty I.W.W.'s, a great many of them being agitators, were in Kalispell, and had opened up headquarters. However, day before yesterday our Sheriff and Chief of Police felt that these headquarters should be either curbed or removed and [had] . . . five or six leaders . . . arrested for some offense, the headquarters closed up, and the "element" disbanded, and we are indeed very grateful to Sheriff Metcalf for taking this action. . . .

The I.W.W.'s methods of destruction are various. . . . In one logging camp they had sawed about 1,500,000 feet of logs four inches short of the marks. . . . Some are reported as having mis-labeled cans and cases in a cannery, crippling horses in the feed stables, dropping sour milk into fresh in a condensory, dropping acid on goods in clothing stores. A favorite stunt is to hit a steel rail with a heavy ax; another is to break shovel handles as fast as they get them, to lose or hide tools, to saw trees so that they will break, polluting wells by throwing in old boards, etc. I heard that one I.W.W. was caught with a tin box full of cockroaches, after he had let a lot more loose in a cook house and dining room. Another was found to have placed a lousy shirt in each bunk.

On the farm they tell of tricks done during harvest such as disabling threshers, throwing a piece of iron in the engine, slashing the ends of bales of new grain sacks, and even putting matches in bundles of wheat.

The average lumber-jack is a first class man, honest, and square, and ready to do the right thing, [and] if he joins the I.W.W. he does it only because he thinks it will help him to better conditions. . . .

YOURS TRULY,

F. D. BECKER, SECRETARY
MONTANA LUMBER
MANUFACTURER'S ASSOC.

THOMPSON FALLS, MONTANA
AUGUST 15, 1917

HON. SAM V. STEWART, GOVERNOR
HON. SAM C. FORD, ATTORNEY GENERAL
HELENA, MONTANA

DEAR GOVERNOR AND [ATTORNEY] GENERAL:

. . . I have interviewed Mr. W. B. Russell, a lumber operative of Plains, [and] Mr. Russell says that the I.W.W. men who are on strike at Plains, many of whom were formerly employed by him, are all good men and law abiding. He has no kick to put in about them and hoped to again employ them.

I also talked to Company representatives from the west end of the county who state to me that the *I.W.W.s are all quiet and law abiding.* I have interviewed several of the laborers myself and find no spirit of lawlessness. . . . A group of them have rented a house at Plains and will permit no liquor of any kind on the premises; they have taken cards of the organization from men who became unruly, and drunk — so I have been told. They patronize the local grocery stores and pay cash. . . . I have a number of reports that the *I.W.W. men made excellent farm hands.* One large rancher reported that they had the best haying crew they ever employed and they were mostly of the striking I.W.W.s.

The sentiment about Plains and other portions of the county seems to be that the I.W.W. here is not of the lawless brand that is being advertised in the daily papers.

WADE R. PARKS
SANDERS COUNTY ATTORNEY

A period of harsh conflict between labor and management in Butte began in 1917. The Speculator Mine disaster left 164 dead, I.W.W. activity and the lynching of "Wobbly" organizer Frank Little aggravated emotions, draft resistance and the anti-British feeling of Irish and German miners heated tempers, and active resentment focused on Anaconda's rustling card system of employment. All these elements combined to promote formation of a militant new union. The Metal Mine Workers, as the organization was styled, called a strike that halted production just as war's necessities demanded increased copper output. The introduction of federal troops forced a settlement of the strike by mid-September, 1917, but unrest continued in the city until 1920. Radical sentiment remained, but the Anaconda Company also fomented trouble by insisting that all strikes were treasonous and that any dissension was the product of "outside agitators." The Company dismissed as "radical" even legitimate grievances, ignoring financial problems stemming from postwar inflation. General acquiescence by state officials reinforced the Company's attitude. A miner's wife, Catherine Penney, protested and offered solutions, but conditions in Butte remained unchanged and labor's demoralization continued into the Depression.

[As] a miner's wife, I would say that the unrest and dissatisfaction that is showing itself in Butte . . . has been smouldering for years. . . . The great factor that . . . has caused the recent outbreaks has been the "Rustling Card" with its accompanying gunmen and spy system.

Now, the "Rustling Card" is a very simple and harmless thing in itself, but the way it has been used to secure and maintain absolute control of local affairs, political and economic, makes it a most formidable weapon for intimidation, . . . creating and keeping alive dissensions and feelings of distrust, [and] preventing united action on any issue. . . .

The Local and State papers owned or controlled by the big corporations constantly and consistently misrepresent everything relating [to] labor and politics. The psychological effect of all this cannot be exaggerated. . . . Any one who dares to voice his sentiments, can and will be punished through the "Black List." . . .

The constant increasing cost of living, without a corresponding increase in wages, of course adds to the feeling of dissatisfaction. There have been several successive raises in wages since the beginning of the War, but the advance has always been anticipated [by increases in the cost of living] . . . so that the wage-earner has never netted a cent. . . . In many cases he is worse off than before. . . . People feel that they are being

exploited to the limit in Butte.

Attempts [to] alleviate this condition by co-operative buying has been met by fierce opposition from the "Chamber of Commerce." . . . The Bulletin is the only paper in Butte through which labor can express itself, and the persistent opposition it has encountered together with the arrest and prosecution of its staff has had anything but a soothing effect. . . . "Patriotic" committees . . . tell the workers what amount they should contribute to the numerous funds for patriotic and other purposes, and brand as pro-german or disloyal, all who do not come up to their requirements. . . . To most miners, the mine inspection as it is done at present, is a joke—the compensation law is far from satisfactory also. All these and many less prominent causes contribute to a feeling that must sooner or later express itself in open revolt.

Now as to remedies: I believe that Government control of the mines (ownership would be better) . . . would be a great step towards better feeling. . . . Shorter hours of labor rather than a raise in wages, would prevent the profiteers from further enriching themselves at the expense of the workers. . . . [we also want] free press and free speech. . . . We want at home the real democracy that our sons are fighting for in France.

In conclusion, I would say that if Uncle Sam would take hold of Butte—men—mines—foodstuffs and all things essential to the production of the much needed copper, our men would dig in in such a manner that the charge of disloyalty so loudly made by their accusers would be silenced for all time.

CATHERINE J. PENNEY
BUTTE, MONTANA

Changes in communications, transportation and the exigencies of war altered operations of large and small commercial firms. During the spartan days of World War I, federal officials looked upon the home delivery of groceries, a product of urbanization and competition, as wasteful. In Red Lodge, consideration of savings, coupled with the ambitions of an advantageously placed competitor, prompted a spirited defense of home delivery. "Cash and Carry" did not survive after the war but it did triumph in the supermarket era, fifty years later.

RED LODGE, MONTANA
MAY 25, 1918

MR. C. D. GREENFIELD
SECRETARY STATE COUNCIL OF DEFENSE
HELENA, MONTANA

DEAR SIR:

. . . The subject of non-delivery has been discussed pro and con in this city for sometime, with the result that it is the opinion of we merchants that it is not feasible. This is taken very much to heart by Mr. Hough, who happens to be district Food Administrator and he has handed the writer a veiled threat that he will see that we do away with delivery. . . .

The desire of Mr. Hough to see that we do away with the delivery, is purely selfish. . . . He has recently put the Carbon Trading Co., of which he is manager, on the cash and carry basis and from what investigations we have made, we are of the opinion that it is not working out satisfactorily. . . . To save himself, he, as Food Administrator is trying to put the rest of the stores in Red Lodge in the same class.

At the time he put this system into effect, he advertised an approximate saving, to the trade, of about five per cent, but recent comparisons by us show that the saving in delivery to the store, gave the people no advantage in prices and reduced his sales to the point where he could not hold his prices below ours. Our volume takes care of the extra expense caused by delivery and our trade is such that they demand this service.

The matter of co-operative delivery has been taken up [but] . . . every store in this city does enough business to keep one man busy all the time, so that even by going on a co-operative basis, we doubt if there would be a saving in man power. . . .

We are willing to do all in our power to further the winning of the war, to eliminate extra expense, use as few men as possible and place our goods before the public at the least possible cost, but in the matter of delivery, we cannot see any way in which it would benefit the government, the people or ourselves, to do without it. . . .

YOURS RESPECTFULLY,
HOME TRADING CO.
A. H. KREMER, MGR.

Severe dislocations to Montana's economy followed the end of World War I. Market depression, inflated prices and a disrupted labor force created havoc in all sectors. Disillusion, drought and labor unrest compounded financial worries. For a marginal operation, such as the Yogo Sapphire Mines, which had been forced to close during the war, the postwar situation made operation nearly impossible. Mine manager, Charles T. Gadsden, regularly reported to the firm's chairman in England on operations and local conditions.

DEAR MR. WOOD:

DECEMBER 16, 1918

. . . I stayed over in Great Falls on my way back [from Seattle] and found a few idle men around the employment agencies, but they were ranch hands. I think that there will be quite a few men idle this winter if they return many soldiers which I don't think they will, but not many miners. . . .

There is much unrest in Seattle where there are about 40,000 shipbuilders over the wages award and the Mooney incident. . . . Many men have gone [to Seattle] from Montana on account of the high wages, but the bulk of the shifting labor west . . . is very much of the I.W.W. Our best supply was farmer's sons for outside work and carmen but I am afraid that as the country is now settled up there will not be so many coming out now there are no homesteads to look for.

With regard to mining labor, we are and shall be very badly up against it. Our best men were men who started here as carmen and learnt mining here. . . . Now since we shut down all of our men went to Butte on account of the high wages. I have tried some back since when we were working last time but they are entirely spoilt and won't do 50 per cent of the work they used to or take any interest in it. One man on whom I rather depended . . . has gone to the bad there. He worked here steady for years, since 1907. . . .

The influenza too is still around. Several have died and we have no doctor now nearer than Moore, 36 miles, also we have prohibition in full force, which means that we cannot buy anything even antiseptic with more than 2% alcohol, so that it is now impossible to buy Listerine,

which we used . . . with peroxide for tonsilitis of which we get quite a number of cases among the boys. [We cannot get] iodine or any other antiseptic, neither can any doctor's prescription carry more than 2%. Likewise if we had an accident and I gave anyone a little brandy to keep them going until a Dr. got here I should be fined and imprisoned. . . .

At the present time the police in Butte are watching seven imported Bolsheviki agitators, but I don't think they need import any. There are enough home raised ones, and the peculiar part is that they are not all laboring men either. So many of these farmers are just as bad; in fact, there are whole colonies of them. North Dakota has gone solid for the Non-Partisans from the Governor down, and it is getting a big hold in Montana. . . .

YOURS VERY SINCERELY,
C. T. GADSDEN

Postwar financial problems caused the Sixteenth Legislative Assembly (1919) to appoint a State Efficiency and Trade Commission. This group investigated Montana trade and industry, giving particular emphasis to reasons for the prevailing high cost of living. While the Legislature displayed commendable concern, the inability to cope with national economic trends doomed the effort. In the group's hearings, concerted interest focused on the coal industry, then a major source of industrial and home heating fuel. Edward Davies, a Roundup coal miner, testified before the Commission about his living costs.

We can average between 9 and 10 ton [per day] providing we get cars. From 6:45 we go down the mine and are outside by 3:30 p.m. Some days we may get 12 tons of coal . . . but that means perpetual motion you might say. That's the limit.

You understand our labor is not simply confined to loading this coal. The room we work in is 26 ft. wide and the truck is 4 ft. wide and there is 11 feet on either side that a man has to clean up, and that involves moving the coal twice. It's not merely a question of loading 10 cars and finishing it.

[Tools are] a small expense, hardly worth mentioning. They charge us for sharpening our tools, whether we have them sharpened or not, they take 1% of our wages for sharpening our tools. Perhaps you won't take a pick out once in three months and you may have gone as high as $90. a half, then you would have to pay 90¢ for getting your drill sharpened and you have not given them any labor. You actually pay the wages of the blacksmith and he is supposed to be working for the company. The labor he does sharpening tools takes him about an hour a day.

[Powder] costs us if we work steadily from $3.00 to $3.25 for two weeks on this machine proposition; and it may go up as high as $15.00 for two weeks with pick work. Probably about 25% [of our mining is pick work.]

We worked 5 days last week; we averaged 3 days a week since the first of the year with the exception of one week. In the busy season we are able to work full time [from] about the first of September generally to April before our slack time commences. . . .

I am able to earn enough now under present conditions to cover our family expenses. I have two children, but I own my house, but if there is anything extra like sickness [I] generally have to take a few dollars from the bank. . . . My wife usually goes out about once a week and gets an order. She buys eggs and butter from the ranchers about once a week. There is a store right next door to us but we do very little business there as we can come down to a store in town and buy a little cheaper. . . .

I have averaged probably $400. or $500. a year to put away, but I never drink or waste any money. I own my own house, and that is included in that of course.

*Change in the postwar years coincided with exploration and development in a new industry —
oil. The presence of oil in Montana had been known since the 1860's, but there had been no
necessity to exploit it. Technological advances and the rapid emergence of the automobile
caused new interest in western oil deposits. In Montana, Cat Creek was one of the first fields
drilled and made commercially profitable, and Curly Meek participated in the initial strike.*

We came into Winnett in October [1919]. . . .
Because of a threatened coal strike we were held there . . .
seven weeks before we could get out to the well. . . . The
coal strike hit the first part of November, by the 8th the
trains had been curtailed. Where there had been one
train every day before to Winnett, there were now only
two a week. In those days the railroad was the only
transportation except wagons and horses. There were a
few cars, but there were no reliable roads.

Before we got this rig out we had to change over
from coal to wood. . . . To pump the water we lay pipeline
on top of the ground and built fires all along the pipeline. That way we could pump water even when it was
40° below, and 1919 was one of the longest and hardest
winters that we ever had in Montana. . . .

This well was started in December. It came in in
February, 1920. We got a little oil. Then the excitement
started. They tried to keep it a little quiet because it was
all government land then. . . . There was no such thing as

a lease law until they passed it on February 26. That is
why they wanted to keep it a little quiet, but it was kind of
hard. When I sent a wire to Frank Franz, the president of
the company in Denver, I sent it to him in a code. . . . The
wire read, "Pine trees grow tall here, come ye men of
war." They had it fixed up that way. "Trees grow tall"
meant a big well, "small" meant a small well. If it didn't
grow, there was no well at all, and "come ye men of war,"
meant to bring a number of men.

There was a lot of excitement around Winnett.
Everybody tried to get me drunk and everything else to
try to find out if they got a well. In the meantime the well
had filled up and run over. . . . It would have looked
much better if they had let it flow because it wasn't pure
oil. There was quite a little water with the well. But when
they came up they saw there was water with it but they
backed away and went to get the mining claims in good
standing. They didn't drill the well until April 4th. It
came in with about 50 barrels. . . .

*Joseph Russell, a Butte gasoline dealer, also testified before the State's Efficiency and Trade
Commission in 1919, his statements reflecting the impact generated by the internal combustion
engine. The automobile provided flexible personal transportation and gave rise to several
industries. It spurred oil development and the marketing of fuel — notably gasoline — took on
increased significance as the number of cars on Montana's roads and trails increased. The
impact first felt in this era expanded with the decades, radically altering all phases of life
in Montana.*

Before I started in the gasolene business I was
driving a pleasure car. I found when I went to Missoula
that Continental would pour gas in my car at thirty to
thirty and a half cents [per gallon]. When I came back to
Butte I tried to get the same people to sell me gasolene.
They referred me to the garages. They told me that they
had an agreement with the garages not to sell to the
public. I went to the Texaco people, and they told me the
same thing, that they didn't handle it in a retail way, that
if I wanted to buy gasolene I would have to go to the
garages and pay thirty-four or thirty-five cents.

I finally decided to start in the gasolene game and
put in a filling station. After getting my location, and

making all the arrangements to start, . . . one of the
dealers [asked] me if I was going into the gasolene
business he would like to know what prices I was going
to sell it at. I told him I didn't know; I hadn't got into the
game; I didn't know what it was going to cost me, and I
didn't know what I could sell it at. After I got at it, got
half way through putting in my station, they cut the
price down to thirty cents. Whether it was an intimidation to try to scare me out I can't say.

But after I got started I adopted their price, which
was twenty-nine and a half cents wholesale, and thirty
cents retail, and I thought I could at least take their
prices that they had cut to in order to intimidate me and

keep going, and make a fair price. After thirty days the business men of Butte commenced to patronize me to the extent that I was taking their business from them, and they cut to twenty-eight cents retail and twenty-seven cents wholesale, the same men who was charging thirty-four and thirty-five in July. Now, during that period . . . the big companies had only reduced the price of gasolene one cent wholesale; in other words, they had cut the carload price from twenty-six down to twenty-five cents. . . .

To many Montanans, particularly in the western portion of the state, the Anaconda Company was a villain, the root cause of all their troubles and disappointments. Its employees wore the "Copper Collar" and measured their morality by the firm's interests. Neither the extreme antipathy of many company enemies nor the sanction of all the company's actions were justified. The Anaconda's presence had many positive features but usually little credit accrued to it or its officers for their contributions. W. C. Whipps, a former mayor of Kalispell and community businessman, gave credit where it was due.

KALISPELL, MONTANA
MAY 2, 1929

HON. J. E. ERICKSON
HELENA, MONTANA

MY DEAR GOVERNOR:

The bronze plate for Gov. Smith's monument is here and. . . . I am enclosing a copy of a letter I am to-day mailing to Mr. Wiggin thanking him and the A.C.M. . . .

The A.C.M. do many generous, creditable things. They have furnished the D.A.R. several plates for marking historical spots within the state. . . . [They]

hardly get even a "thank you" from most people who are favored. It seems to be the nature of a great many people to never say anything good of a large corporation. As a matter of fact the A.C.M. have done more for the development of Montana than any other dozen corporations or individuals within the state . . . and one rarely hears a good word spoken of them. This is a rank injustice. . . . They . . . should receive the publicity for them to which they are entitled. . . . So far as I am concerned I am perfectly willing to have you hand my letter to Mr. Wiggin [and] to the papers for publication.

W.C. WHIPPS

Labor dissension in 1914, and again in 1917-1919, destroyed union effectiveness in Butte. Low prices and cheaper copper from other Anaconda Company mines caused shutdowns and reduced labor forces through the mid-1920's. In this period, negotiation and strikes gained nothing for the miner, and troops sometimes forced strikers back to work. Limited recovery in the late 1920's provided increased jobs and wages, but the stock market crash of 1929 sent Butte's economy plummeting again. Only the favorable outlook and encouragement of the Roosevelt Administration gave labor the impetus to organize once more. Butte's local of the Mine, Mill and Smeltermen's Union, with a membership frustrated by twenty years of futility, and suffering from the Depression's effects, struck in 1934. The stoppage, involving all mine-mill and craft unions in Butte, Great Falls, and Anaconda, was the most peaceful the industry experienced since the turn of the century. Company supporters called for troops to halt the strike, but the Governor resisted and the strike ended through mediation on September 21, 1934. Four and a half months of solidarity achieved a generally favorable contract. This, combined with increased copper production as a result of military requirements, allowed prosperity and good labor relations to prevail in the Montana copper industry for over a decade.

AUGUST 6, 1934

GOV. FRANK H. COONEY
HELENA, MONTANA

MY DEAR GOVERNOR:

. . . [I] am writing a personal appeal to you, not to be disturbed by anything you may hear from us over here. I

have made Butte my home for nearly thirty-six years, been a part of its educational and civic life and a heavy taxpayer for most of the time. I would like to say . . . that in all the years I have spent in Butte, I have never seen such tactics used as are being resorted to in the last two months by the A.C.M. to "Bring the troops to Butte." . . .

They will stop at nothing to discredit the miners. . . .

I have never seen greater evidence of patience, tolerance and suffering self-control than I have witnessed day after day among the workers of Butte. Neither have I ever seen more concerted effort on the part of Corporate interests and their Company-owned press . . . to besmirch or to destroy the worker than I have seen in this strike. As one of the great middle class . . . I am sure . . . that this same large middle class is in sympathy with [the strikers].

The Company never has played square and they never will. They do not know the meaning of the word fairness. . . . These devils are stopping at nothing to incite the men to trouble. . . . I can't see for the life of me how the strikers have refrained as well as they are doing.

Please do not be drawn into their nefarious maneuvering to involve you and to force you into sending armed men for the protection of their property. The life of one of our striking men is of more consequence a thousand times than the A.C.M. or the Montana Power has ever meant to Butte. . . .

MARGARET LOUGHRIN

Wages dominated most labor disputes, but working conditions became an increasing concern of labor in Montana and the nation. Unions demanded safety programs, insurance coverage, and employer responsibility for industrial accidents and disease. The main fear of the hardrock miner, silicosis, continued to be excluded from early industrial insurance compensation. Victims of the disease served as reminders of the danger of underground labor, and miners continuously agitated for protection and coverage. Liberal labor periodicals, such as the SUNDAY ALL AMERICAN, *led the protest which did culminate in silicosis coverage. Publicizing George Burch's death, in 1936, was a part of that campaign.*

"If I hadn't taken awfully good care of myself, I'd have been buried long ago. All the rest of the boys I worked with are gone." It was a frequent statement . . . of George P. Burch, [once] secretary of the FERA Workers' Union in Butte. . . . Burch throughout his life took pride in the superb physical endowment which at one time earned recognition for him as an expert in athletic feats. . . . [He was] a man who . . . lived cleanly, refused drink and evil associations, took regular physical culture. This man, George P. Burch, died at Galen recently [circa 1936] at the age of 47. Why?

Simply because he had filled his lungs so full of rock during his twenty years of labor in the Butte mines that there was no room left for air. Even before his final illness, when he still looked the picture of robust and beautiful manhood, George Burch could not arise from his chair and tack a leaflet to the wall without puffing.

He could not walk a block down grade without puffing. He was a beautiful, robust man, but his lungs had been stuffed up "with globules of dust," . . . a condition which is experienced by every Butte miner in the course of time, a condition that leaves him helpless before the approach of pneumonia, tuberculosis or any other disease. . . .

Burch was a good miner, a conscientious worker, a hard worker. He made "good" money in the mines — ten or twelve dollars per day in some places. . . . George took "good care of himself." He used to work [with] a wet sponge over his nose to keep out as much dust as possible. George counted on that sponge. "The boys that worked with me are all gone," said Burch a year [before his death] in defense of the sponge as a protection. But the sponge failed George. It didn't keep out all the dust. . . .

Champ Hannon, retired Darby forester, worked for the Forest Service all his life. He resented more recent timber management practices which he felt destroyed decades of work. The lumber industry's demands on privately held forests rapidly outstripped available yield and timber on the public domain had to be cut to meet market necessities. Policy for harvesting timber experienced several changes through the decades after the inception of the Forest Reserve system in 1891. Pressures on this resource remained low before World War II, but need increased with the heavy postwar housing boom. These stringent demands further complicated the Forest Service's management policy and led to concerns mirrored in Hannon's criticisms.

. . . In 1918 I went to work for the Bitterroot National Forest at Alta as a guard, and I worked two seasons, 1918 and 1919. I went through that big 1919 fire season, as a guard at the West Fork Ranger Station.

Then I went to the Selway and I worked the summer 1920 and 1921. . . . I went to school over in Bozeman, until '24. . . . In '26 my wife and I were married. . . . Then the depression hit. I didn't go to work any more for the forest service until '35. In the mean time they had passed the regulation where only forestry graduates could hold ranger jobs. So I didn't get a ranger job. I went to work on the Lofthorse Road as a time keeper. . . . Then I went to work for Timber Management — and I have worked in Timber Management ever since.

The first sale we had after I went to work in Timber Management was the Robbins Gulch sale. . . . And that was a well managed sale because we followed the instructions exactly on making out the sale and everything. . . . We had an ax and a U.S. stamp [on] every . . . log and the stump. That's something they don't do any

more because I think they don't have anybody who can handle an ax. . . .

[In 1943] when the private timber was beginning to play out we started in on Laird Creek. We got less than $4 a thousand for that timber. . . . I started marking timber, then for the next 15 years I marked, that's what I did most of the time, marked timber on various sales. We marked 50% of the Yellow Pine. We actually had the forest service policy on a sustained yield basis. Now sustained yield means to me that you cut the timber in such a way that you can cut without reducing the cut for all time to come. . . . The forest service now has completely abandoned that in the Bitterroot. . . .

They have gone back over 95% of the timber we marked and have cut it clear for all practical purposes. They've taken out everything. . . . The 15 years work that I did for the forest service was just thrown away. And I wore my legs out marking timber, trying to do a good job. I feel pretty badly about it . . . that's all.

Recovery from the Great Depression could not be traced to the New Deal but to the demands of a world arming for war. Pre-war and wartime armament purchases had a particularly salutary effect on the copper industry, raising manpower needs in mines, smelters and fabrication plants. Young men, new to mining, found jobs where none had existed before. Bill Burke, Butte journalist and a one-time "greenhorn miner," described, in a fictional account, the novice's first day at the shaft.

They told me when I at last made up my mind to give the Butte mines a whirl that it would be a cinch. "All you have to do," they encouraged, "is to go up and get yourself a rustling card — go down to the Union Hall for a list of mines that are hiring — then go up to one of the mines listed and tell the foreman that you are a miner, and he'll tell you to come out that night or the next morning."

Only I wasn't a miner or had never been down in a mine in my life. I got the rustling card okay. I had to fill out a questionnaire giving my life history and where I worked for the past ten years. The last was easy. I worked on the old man's farm before the dust had got both the farm and the old man.

There was a long list of mines hiring posted on the Union Hall bulletin board. It also told the hours of rustling each mine. I decided on the Mountain Con because it was close to my boarding house. The time for rustling the Con was twelve, noon.

I was feeling pretty happy. I was on my way to being a hard-rock miner. Six or eight bucks a day looked like a jackpot after a winter of $52 a month on the WPA.

I hurried up the hill to the Mountain Con. It was about five minutes to twelve when I got there and there was a long line of rustlers ahead of me. I was the last one in line when the noon whistles blew and the line started moving past the foreman's little window stuck in the center of the big red fence.

That line was moving fast and it didn't look like he was hiring very many. I noticed that most of the rustlers in the line were well dressed, warm and neat. They didn't have that hang-dog, down-at-the-heels look like the factory rustlers have in the East. These miners were happy and laughed and joked, and didn't seem to care if they landed a job or not.

The line slowed up and it looked like the foreman was hiring several from the middle of it. I could see them handing in their rustling cards through the window. It slowed up again and two or three more were hired, then started moving fast once more and before I knew it, the guy in front of me was asking if there was any show for a miner. The foreman looked him over and shook his head. It was my turn next.

I was nervous. It seemed like my innards were trembling and trying to turn over. I hate like hell to get caught in a lie. I had my head in the window, and the foreman, a big, gruff, red-faced man was sizing me up.

"Any show for a miner?" I gulped, and the words were sticking in my throat. He was still giving me the once-over but he shook his head, and then glancing behind me and seeing I was the last in line, he called me back.

"Did you say you were a miner?"

I nodded my head. Here it comes, I thought. He'll catch me in a lie sure as hell. But he merely grunted, "Let me see your rustling card."

Boy, I guess I was lucky. I handed him the card and he copied down my name and number and told me to take it over to the timekeeper's office to sign up, and for me to report to a shift boss named McDougal at eight o'clock the next morning.

Well, I landed a job, and at ten minutes to eight the next morning I was at the shaft of the mine, all changed into my work clothes; rubber shoes with hard toes, heavy underwear, waist overalls, cardboard hat with an electric light on front of it, a battery strapped on my back and a jumper coat. . . .

A big swarthy-skinned miner pointed out to me [the] shift boss, a strapping fellow with a red nose and a yellow mackinaw. I walked over to him and told him I was to report to him. He had a pleasant kind of face and looked like he might be a good head. He took out a little book and asked me my name. I told him.

"Miner, eh?" he said, and I could feel him looking right through me.

I guess my face must have turned red, but I did manage to mutter "Yeah."

He looked out over the crowd of miners gathered around the shaft, and then gave me the once-over again. My heart was thumping.

Then he closed the book and said, "See that little, weazened fellow sitting on that bundle of wedges and

tying his shoe? That's McCarthy. His partner's off on a bender. Work with him today."

"And, say," he added as he gave me a wise sort of look, as if he knew damn well I was lying, "stick close by him, and do what he tells you, and be careful. The two of you get off at the thirty hundred."

I walked over to McCarthy. He had finished tying his shoe, and was filling his stump of a pipe with an evil looking brand of tobacco. He looked like he might be about sixty years old.

I was wishing I wasn't so damn timid and nervous, but I stammered, "Mister McCarthy, Mister McDougal told me to work with you today."

He looked up at me with a start. I guess those "Misters" must have given him a jolt. He eyed me up and down.

"Hm-m, all new clothes — a greenhorn," he grumbled. He had a little touch of brogue. I wish I could show you how he talked, but I'm no good at taking anyone off. "You never worked in the mines before, and I'm damn glad you're honest enough to own up to it."

Before I could say anything, he went on, "I don't mind working with a greenhorn if he'll admit it. It's those smart alecs who think they know it all, that burn me up. You've a good pair of shoulders on you, and you look smart. Stay by me and I'll make a miner out of you in no time at all. . . ."

I was getting more jittery every minute. A big burly worker was loading the miners on the cages. He packed nine men on a cage, tight up against each other like sardines. . . . Then he gave a pull on a signal rope, and the cage was lowered about ten feet. Then the cage on top of the first one was loaded the same way. . . . He gave another signal and the whole business dropped out of sight into the darkness of the shaft. . . . Another cage was coming up on the other side of the shaft, making a hell of a noise like it was being shook to pieces. . . . There was a rush for the cage. McCarthy pushed me ahead of him. . . . I was bellied up tight against the fellow in front of me. . . .

Whis-s-h! the cage was dropping. And when I say dropping, I mean just that. For a moment my heart almost stopped. . . . Talk about express elevators in sky-scrapers — they don't travel any faster than a mine cage in Butte. And noise! You'd think the whole shaft was coming in, the way those steel cages pounded and rattled. Then — Swish! Bang! the cage had stopped, then sprung up and down in the shaft for a minute or two. . . .

McCarthy said, "Here's where we unload, lad," and we stepped out into the light. We were in a big, concrete room with a high-powered electric light overhead. McCarthy said it was the station. He was starting my schooling early. He pointed out a big hole in the center of the station as the skip chute and told me all the ore from the level was dumped into it. . . . He showed me how to light my battery lamp and filled a canvas water bag with water and gave it to me to carry. He also gave me a half dozen little, white "salt pills." . . . He said they were in case I got heat cramps.

McCarthy led the way into the place where we were going to work. . . . It was solid rock all over with no timber. In places water was dripping off the top . . . and the farther in we walked, the hotter it was getting. I was sweating and could feel my undershirt getting damp. . . . I was thinking to myself: This is a hell of a place to earn a living. You could hear the rock making funny noises like maybe it was going to cave. . . .

We started to work. . . . "Barring down," [McCarthy] told me, was the most important part of the shift, as it made the place where we worked safer. He said we couldn't take a chance on a loose slab or boulder

crashing down on our heads. . . . He wasn't satisfied until the ground over our heads had a clear, ringing sound when hit with the bar. . . .

McCarthy told me we were going to drill and blast that shift. . . .

[We stopped for a smoking break and] when we finished . . . McCarthy told me to go down and turn on the air. When I came back that old drill was vibrating on the bar like it would shake itself to pieces. McCarthy hadn't turned on the little drill valve on the machine yet, and with all that compressed air waiting to be turned loose, the drill reminded me of a race horse . . . raring to run its legs off. McCarthy put in a short drill steel in the machine, a "starter" he called it; attached one of the drill bits; set the drill against a place in the ore he had marked; and turned on the valve. Boy, was there some noise. You couldn't hear yourself think. . . . We had three seven-foot holes all finished when McCarthy looked at his watch and said it was dinner time. The time sure had gone fast. . . .

Finished changing clothes, I passed McCarthy on the way to the timekeeper's office. He said, "Well, I'll see you in the morning, lad," — and I knew he'd see me there alright, and the next morning too — and the next — and the next — I knew I was going to be a miner.

Anaconda's Washoe Smelter operated nonstop throughout the war years. Workers on "The Hill" recognized the dangers inherent in such employment but the necessity of war production kept them on the job. Edward Reynolds, Works Progress Administration writer, captured the flavor of work in the giant smelter in a fictionalized account.

Butte and Anaconda were booming and we all had jobs. Far down underground in Butte men were digging ore from the veins of the "richest hill on earth" and over in Anaconda men were boiling that ore down into molten copper that glowed a bloody red. "Sinews of war," the editorial writers call it; "bread and butter," say the miners and smeltermen.

"Yes," they agree, "war is hell. But work is hell, too, and starving to death is a damn sight worse."

So we won't talk about that because we all had jobs. Sodbusters from North Dakota, cowhands from Eastern Montana, Okies from the dust bowl, boomers from the southland, the east and the west — and home town boys, too, who were given first preference. . . .

Above us towered the 585-foot smoke stack, largest in the world. All around us stretched huge buildings, interlaced with a network of roads and steel tracks over which roared trucks and automobiles or ore trains drawn by snorting little air engines. We had punched the time clock and taken our cards. Now we were looking for the Zinc Tank House and wondering if our jobs were to be steady or if we'd have to keep on rustling until we found a permanent spot. . . .

We went into the office and found the rest of the rustlers. . . . [There the foreman] doled out rubber boots and overshoes. "What are we going to do, work in a lot of mud and water?" a rustler asked. "Naw. Electricity. If you didn't have these rubber shoes on you'd be hopping around like a jitterbug." . . . When we got our boots fitted, [they] gave us wire masks and showed us how to place gauze in them.

[Then we went] upstairs to the tank floor. A wide corridor split the building with mathematical precision. Tiny railroad flatcars clattered over miniature tracks with switches and sidings like a model railroad. . . . On either side were double rows of large rectangular tanks, four deep. . . . Massive copper bars, charged with electricity, stretched along the outside of the tanks. Alternating lead anodes and galvanized steel cathodes with copper side arms contacted the bars and hung down into a solution containing zinc. This zinc, through an electrolytic process, collected on the cathodes and was stripped off in sheets.

Tiny bubbles danced through the effervescent solution like champagne. They exploded at the top and leaped into the air to form an acid-fog that hovered over the tanks and crept through the room. . . . The acid pelted and stung my face like tiny needles shot from minute blowguns. The mask grew warm; my nose started to run. I raised the mask to blow my nose. The inhalation sent me gasping and choking out of the door into the open air. "You'll get used to it," the foreman laughed. . . .

I returned to where the others had gathered ready for work. . . . Alabama manned the power hoist and raised large wooden boxes from the basement. Irish and I swung them onto the little flatcars and wheeled them to the cascade. A couple of other rustlers manipulated chain hoists. . . . They would pull a box over to a tank and lower it to a rustler clad in hip boots and standing in the soupy muck. The man in the tank would fill the box while Irish and I went back for more empties. When the box was filled, the hoist man placed it on a flatcar and Irish and I hustled it back to Alabama to be lowered again to the basement. Here, it was placed on another flatcar and pushed over to the Zinc Leaching Plant to be used over again in making the solution.

It was hard work but we didn't ease up; we wanted to make a good impression. . . . The rustlers were really making their shovels fly. . . . "For God's sake, watch what you're doing," a sodbuster from North Dakota screamed. One of the rustlers shoveling had splashed some muck in his eye. . . . "Anyone who gets the slightest hurt should let me know," [the foreman warned after taking North Dakota to the emergency hospital], "We have to send everyone to the nurse. Watch your step." We worked more carefully after that. It's no fun to get acid in your eyes. . . .

After about three hours work we finished cleaning the tanks and went downstairs to eat. . . . We went into the locker room where [a man] was selling milk. "What's the big idea of milk?" a fellow from Colorado asked. . . . "Acid," [the man] answered. "Milk counteracts the acid. If you don't drink it, your teeth will fall out."

"Nice pleasant place here, isn't it. Sounds like a guy's a fool to work here."

"Naw. You'll get used to it. There's lots worse." . . .

"Well. It's no worse than that dust back in North Dakota," exclaimed the sodbuster. "At least you get paid for this."

"Yeah, and ah think it's bettah than down South," said Alabama, "although Alabama's a mighty nice place. Ah'd suah like to go back there on a visit sometime with a lot of money in mah pocket."

"Where're you from, Irish?"

"I'm from Butte. Born in Dublin Gulch. I left there about five years ago. Got fed up on the mines."

"Well, this $6.30 ain't so hard to take. What's the thirty cents for, Steve?"

"Clothes. This acid eats 'em. You'd better get some aprons. Get that old canvas off the filters. Otherwise you'll go broke."

After lunch we sat around smoking and talking until 8 o'clock when Steve routed us out to go upstairs and cleanup. We put the empty boxes away and washed everything down with hoses. Then we placed the copper bars along the clean tanks, gathered up our tools and returned to the locker room. It was just 10 o'clock and we still had two hours until the end of the shift. Most of the boys were stretched out taking naps when Steve came in.

"Well, boys, you're no longer rustlers. You're on steady. The boss says you're okay, so come back tomorrow."

Gone were all remembrances of the acid-fog; gone were doubts raised by the extraordinary precautions of emergency nurse and milk drinking; gone was the fear of empty stomachs and ejection from lodgings.

"Boy, the depression's ovah," shouted Alabama.

"And how," chimed in Colorado.

"By God, I oughta get drunk on that," said Irish. "A fellow oughta be able to establish credit, now that he's gotta job."

North Dakota kicked his feet in the dust and grinned.

War required expanded production in all sectors. Often work went forward under hazardous conditions and calamity sometimes resulted. Disaster struck the Smith Mine on February 27, 1943. Seventy-four men died from explosion and gas in the Montana Coal and Iron Company mine. It was the worst coal mining accident in Montana history and resulted in increased safety legislation and inspection. General Manager J. M. Freeman reported the disaster to Charles E. Dunlap, a company officer.

MARCH 4, 1943

DEAR MR. DUNLAP:

I regret that during my absence on a recent trip to the coast we had a very serious mine explosion, which trapped 74 men and damaged our mine fans so that we could not get air to the men in time to save their lives.... I held off writing to you hoping to have something definite as to the cause of the accident, but up to [now] have been unable to discover [the cause]....

The explosion was not a major one but it did remove all of the oxygen from the mine and the men died from asphyxiation. We have had a little trouble with gas occasionally . . . but our mine was not considered gaseous. Since the Federal inspectors were here in November we have been unusually cautious. . . .

It appears that the men all died within five minutes of the explosion. We had rescue crews and rescue equipment and did everything possible to save them but our efforts were in vain.... I have definitely decided not to reopen the old mine in the future but will increase the capacity of the new mine at Foster Gulch.... For a few months our production will be down but as the demand for coal during the summer months is not heavy our annual production will not suffer. We were fortunate in that there was no fire after the explosion. . . .

Regretting that this unpredictable and unexpected catastrophe had to happen and hoping that you will not worry too much about it, I am as ever,

J. M. FREEMAN

Reflecting the drastic changes stemming from the Depression, New Deal programs and World War II, power for home and industry emerged as a leading concern for postwar Montana. Hydroelectric power and other uses of Montana's vast water resources promised a better, more productive life. Efforts of the federal Rural Electrification Administration emphasized the necessity of effective water and power utilization. This program, in combination with other circumstances, acted as a major cause of significant postwar expansion of power sources in Montana. Governor John W. Bonner, in setting forth his views on the REA and allied concerns, spoke to issues which continued to concern the state and its residents.

HELENA, MONTANA
AUGUST 11, 1949

DEAR MR. BILLINGS:

. . . I want it plainly understood that I am 100% for Rural Electrification and I will lend every effort within my power to procure Rural Electrification to the greatest extent for the people of this state. I want it further plainly understood that I am for *cheap* power developed in this state to be used by and for the people of Montana. I have said many times that the greatest resource we have is our water. I reiterate that statement now. We have the two great water sheds in this state. Our duty is to see to it that these waters are developed for power and for irrigation for Montana people. Our duty as Montanans is to see to it that these waters are not taken away from us. I am convinced that the salvation of this state lies in its

waters, and that these waters should be developed for our farmers and ranchers and power created in order that we may procure new industries.... With the dams that are being constructed, we must [also] have cheap power for pumping . . . because . . . a dam is useless [for] irrigation . . . unless we can pump the water . . . at a reasonable cost to the farmers and ranchers. I believe also that one of the greatest things we can have happen in Montana is to have more small dams.

I do hope that we are successful in developing cheap power for Montana and that Montana people are absolutely assured of first priority from the power produced in this state. . . .

JOHN W. BONNER
GOVERNOR

Copper, with war demands ended, responded to more normal forces for the next several years. The period included market changes, labor confrontation, technological innovation and diversification. Significant in the changes Anaconda experienced was the work undertaken, in 1955, on the Berkeley Pit on the eastern end of Butte hill. Pit mining, new to Montana, allowed the exploitation of vast quantities of low grade ore with an appreciable reduction in labor costs. As labor forces dropped in Butte and Anaconda, technological change seemed an increasing threat to the workingman. The Berkeley operation became the most obvious example of such change. Anaconda Company officials attempted to allay the fears of their working force.

BUTTE, MONTANA
DECEMBER 12, 1957

DEAR EMPLOYEE:

Has the Berkeley Pit hurt Butte more than it has helped? . . . Would more underground vein mines, such as the Mountain Con and Belmont, be operating under present metal market conditions if there were no Berkeley Pit? No!

The reason for this is that total costs of all operations are taken into consideration. An economic operation at the Berkeley helps carry higher-cost mines in these times. Without the Berkeley Pit's low costs, the Kelley, Leonard, Anselmo and Emma mine total costs would be seriously increased. . . . The Berkeley Pit helps to stabilize Butte's overall mining picture.

There is also some feeling that the Berkeley will eventually eliminate all of Butte's underground vein mining. This is not true. The Mountain Con, Belmont, etc., cannot possibly be mined by the open pit method because the veins are too narrow, too deep, and the wall rock is *waste*. The Berkeley is in a geologic zone in which the *wall rock does contain low grade ore values sufficient for open pit mining only.* . . .

Present Berkeley plans show that [it] . . . can be mined only by the open pit method. All of the high grade veins in this same zone were mined out many years ago by underground methods. . . . Remining this zone . . . definitely adds to what Butte has. It is like finding money in an old suit.

E. I. RENOUARD

THE ANACONDA COMPANY

National recession, falling copper prices and union demands combined to force a record length strike in 1959-1960 with devastating effects on the economy of Butte and all Montana. Begun on August 19, 1959, the stoppage ended February 11, 1960, with a cost of $17,000,000 in lost wages alone. Both sides made some concessions but neither gained substantially from the prolonged confrontation. The strike compounded the company's slumping financial outlook, contributed to reductions in Anaconda's Montana labor force, and strengthened its reliance on other, cheaper sources of copper. E. I. Renouard set forth the company's bargaining position in a letter to Montana Governor J. Hugo Aronson.

BUTTE, MONTANA
DECEMBER 18, 1959

DEAR GOVERNOR ARONSON:

In view of your . . . efforts . . . to encourage an early settlement of the devastating copper strike in this state, I would like to advise you of the latest developments.

In response to your appeal . . . the Anaconda

Company formulated a proposal which would have allowed our Montana workers to return to work before Christmas. As we advised you, the Company was willing to resume operations immediately and continue negotiations if labor would agree to remain at work for a six-month period. . . . Our workers would have had jobs and pay checks while the negotiators for both sides were resolving their contract differences. . . .

This back-to-work-while-we-negotiate program drew immediate favorable response from Montana people in all walks of life.... On Thursday, the Company was notified by the Joint Negotiating Committee that the proposal had been rejected by the Union membership. ... In view of the urgent desire of most working people to resume their jobs, it would appear that this rejection resulted more from the coercion of the Union leadership rather than the free choice of the Union membership.

While the Union's action killed hopes of an immediate resumption of operations, ... Local Union No. 117 ... representing the Anaconda Smeltermen, voted to negotiate separately with the Company, and meetings have been conducted with officers of that Union this week.... The company is optimistic that this opportunity for free choice will result in a favorable vote on the offer.

The Company finds it hard to understand why the Joint Negotiating Committee persists in its stubborn insistence upon excessive demands and refuses to recognize the realities of our Montana operations. The action taken by the men at Anaconda is proof that the Committee's attitude is dictated more by outside Union leadership than a concern for the best interests of Montana workers....

The Anaconda Company wishes to assure you that it will continue to strive for an early settlement of this strike. Our only concern is to obtain a contract which will allow us to employ the most men possible under the best conditions possible within the economic limits of our Montana operations.

VERY TRULY YOURS,

E. I. RENOUARD

Controversy over the establishment of power sites on the Clark Fork River typified many of the concerns such development fostered. The opposing sides in the Paradise/Knowles-Buffalo Rapids clash debated public or private power development, environmental fears, corporate domination, and jobs/progress or farms/lifestyle. The Corps of Engineers' Paradise/Knowles alternatives clashed with the Buffalo Rapids plan, proposed by Montana Power Company. Groups aligned behind these dissimilar projects as their interests warranted. From the first suggestions in the late 1940's until the issue faded in the 1960's, the controversy over site and size of dams on the Clark Fork colored political campaigns, led to virulent rhetoric and animosity, and accomplished little in the field of hydroelectric power development. S.R. Logan, a retired educator living near Charlo, and Sam B. Chase, Montana Power Company executive, voiced opposing views. Their arguments on this matter addressed problems which continued to disturb Montanans in their search for answers to similar, if more complex, problems of land and resource utilization.

BUTTE, MONTANA
APRIL 28, 1958

SEATTLE DISTRICT ENGINEER
U.S. ARMY CORPS OF ENGINEERS
SEATTLE, WASHINGTON

DEAR SIR:

We have read the Information Bulletin ... on the Corps of Engineers study of the proposed Knowles Project on the Flathead River in Montana and desire to comment on the proposal.... The reasons which led us to oppose the Paradise project convince us that it is necessary to oppose Knowles. These reasons will be briefly summarized as follows:

1. It would flood thousands of acres of valuable agricultural land, hay land and grazing land....

2. It would displace approximately 2700 residents who make their homes and conduct their businesses in the reservoir area.

3. It would cause irreparable damage to business, agriculture and industry in the region and would result in the loss of thousands of dollars a year in tax revenues in Lake and Sanders counties.

4. It would flood out and force relocation of the railroad between Ravalli and Paradise and would threaten the existence of railroad service to Polson....

5. Due to the limitations of the water in the Flathead River, the plant would produce power at low load factor and at extremely high cost per kilowatt-hour.

6. The drawdown on this reservoir would ... be detrimental to the attractiveness and recreational value of the Flathead valley....

7. It would preclude construction by The Montana Power Company of the Buffalo Rapids Project which would develop power for the area without extensive flooding and dislocation and which would result in the payment of additional taxes in Lake and Sanders counties. . . .

In view of this situation, The Montana Power Company favors the construction of the Buffalo Rapids site and is opposed to the construction of the Knowles Project. . . .

SINCERELY,

SAM B. CHASE

LAKE COUNTY, MONTANA
SEPTEMBER 15, 1962

HON. CLIFFORD DAVIS, CHAIRMAN
SUBCOMMITTEE ON FLOOD CONTROL
HOUSE OF REPRESENTATIVES
WASHINGTON, D. C.

DEAR MR. DAVIS:

. . . I think at least 90% of the opposition to this Knowles-Paradise project has been manufactured by the Montana Power Company. This has been accomplished largely through misrepresentation, arm twisting, and large-scale expenditures financed by their captive customers. . . .

The company's management has waged an unceasing 15-year war against the Knowles-Paradise project. . . . In recent months the company has kept one or more of its officials campaigning in the counties immediately affected . . . as part of a well-coached team of four or five speakers. . . . They have also solicited and secured permission to speak to all kinds of organizations and groups. Local assistants have been enlisted to canvass every community, every organization, and every citizen. . . . The company's agents and officials have assisted in the preparation of fantastically exaggerated and cunningly contrived estimates of losses, . . . omitting all gains. . . . High company officials have continuously held top offices in the state chamber of commerce, and have succeeded in keeping many local chambers in line. . . .

It is interesting to note, however, that the total membership of [their] organizations . . . is but a small fraction of the total membership of the organizations which have consistently supported the Knowles-Paradise project. . . . In addition, the Montana Democratic platform for years has included specific endorsements . . . and Democratic candidates . . . have stressed . . . this plank.

There is reason to believe that the company does not seriously expect to secure a license to build at . . . Buffalo Rapids which would block multi-purpose, full

development permanently. Its promises of prompt construction, large additional taxes to Lake County, and large rental payments to the Indian Tribes who own the sites are probably a ruse to enlist local support to kill or delay the Knowles project. . . . The company's last ditch opposition to Hungry Horse and its fifteen year war on the Knowles-Paradise project are due to the determination of its officials to keep low-cost, prime power out of Montana as long as possible, and to strengthen its domination not only of the electric power business, but of business and government generally. As a means of acquiring and maintaining such domination, its officials strengthen their hold on political parties, candidates, chambers of commerce, the utilities commission, the legislature, the state administration, the media of communication, educational institutions, and all groups which might be useful to it. . . .

Finding the national level of our federal system of government less manageable than state and local levels, the company's propaganda impugns the integrity and competence of Congress, the Executive and our National governmental institutions generally. . . . Its supporters capitalize on geographical and class suspicion and jealousy, implying that supporters of multi-purpose, full development are indeed "socialists" and "socialism is communism in a white collar." . . . A monopoly, with the governmental power to condemn and take property, it poses as a paragon and champion of free, private enterprise, fighting a rapacious, far-away government to preserve . . . property and freedom. . . .

I advocate both public and private development of our rivers, but I deplore the success of the "private" power monopolies in brainwashing so many businessmen into believing the nonsense that regulated monopoly is "tax-paying, free, private enterprise." Through public participation in the development of our public-owned rivers, we promote both competition and conservation and we foster and multiply free, private enterprise. . . .

RESPECTFULLY,

S. R. LOGAN

NEW PERSPECTIVES

PROBLEMS AND CONTROVERSY have always been corollary to progress, and so it has been in Montana. Indian and white squared off over land and life; railroads vied for territorial favors; laborer and mine owner confronted each other about working conditions; farmers struggled with the land and government for generations; residents, politicians and power companies bickered over electric generating facilities — Hauser Dam, Paradise/Knowles, Colstrip 3 and 4. Isolation and distance turned Montana's perspectives inward during the Nineteenth and early Twentieth Centuries. Given economic verities, it was an incongruous point of view. Because of its predominantly extractive economy (everything from fur, to gold, to coal) Montana has been unusually subject to national or world market and economic conditions.

Improved transportation and communication broke down the isolation and expanded the point of view. Montanans became more aware of broader currents and followers of, or participants in, national trends, debates and controversies. This transition became exceedingly apparent in the decades following World War II.

Obscured or illuminated, the issues which have brought controversy to Montana have invariably included a thread of conflict involving land utilization. The theme continued and became increasingly dominant after 1945, augmented by a new consideration — preservation. Simplified, the new dichotomy was this: retention of state heritage, beauty and isolation on the one hand, continued development of her resources, economic progress and future prosperity on the other. Concerns regarding the environment, education, and life style orbitted about the central conflict. The broader perspectives were not necessarily antithetical in purpose, but neither were they synonymous in prospect. Similarly, there were no absolute answers — only differing suggestions.

Participants chronicled each issue in letter, speech, petition, and diary. Their accounts documented the most recent chapter of Montana's past, but the phrases carried no conclusions, only questions and searchings. Central among the queries was the one of utilization or preservation. Had Montanans really mastered the land?

HOERNER-WALDORF PLANT, MISSOULA, 1966

NEW PERSPECTIVES
Considerations for Today and Tomorrow

Urbanization began early in the United States and by 1920 more Americans lived in the city than in rural areas. The trend continued and with it came political, economic and social decline in small communities throughout the nation. This had acute implications for rural Montanans. Following World War II, the Rockefeller Foundation financed the Montana Study to examine extant phenomena and seek remedies for small community dilemmas. Montana Study Director Baker Brownell and most participants in the program saw the project as a positive, enriching experience — a chance to reflect on the state's heritage and its future.

MISSOULA, MONTANA
JANUARY 8, 1947

DR. RAYMOND B. FOSDICK
PRESIDENT, ROCKEFELLER FOUNDATION
NEW YORK, NEW YORK

DEAR DR. FOSDICK:

. . . It is true that [the Montana study] provides a threshold to the problem . . . [of] excessive drainage of population from the rural regions to urban industrial centers. . . . The youth and wealth of Montana drain not only to the cities but entirely out of the state. Many small communities not only are static or declining but have disappeared entirely and the State as a whole is somewhat less in population than in 1920. [Montana] shows dramatically all the signs of a colonial economy and many of the signs of a colonial culture in general. . . .

[This] is part of a critical problem that confronts the nation and indeed the entire western world. That problem is the increasing lack of balance in western culture between urban and rural life. Central in that problem is the decline of the small community. I doubt if the way of life that we call democratic, Christian or liberal can survive except in relation to the small community. . . . Its decline as a functioning, influential group has been accompanied by social and moral disaster. Its continued decline will be accompanied by general economic failure and reduced population. . . . Unless more people in the urban centers realize their own stake in vigorous and well-distributed community life in the rural regions and do something besides facilitating the drainage of youth and wealth away from them the whole modern structure, urban and rural, will collapse. . . .

What can be done about it? . . . I believe that I can recognize the problem . . . and I can see that it must be answered in terms of a way of life and human values, not in terms of various manipulative instruments. . . . I feel that I should make clear that our work in Montana was on a small scale, mostly experimental. . . . The work, I think, was definitely worth while, but we cannot claim that it changed the face of Montana or finally solved the problem of rural decay. . . . We concerned ourselves, so far as we could, with the intimate problems of the small community. We worked in and around these communities and drew in members of them as our most valued advisers and helpers. We organized what we called community study groups, wrote a study group guide called *Life in Montana, as Seen in Lonepine a Small Community,* and concerned ourselves — always with the close cooperation of the community group concerned — with learning about that community, its social structure, its ethnic, religious, family, historical, economic background. We studied its problems and their relation to the problems of the region, the state and the nation. We made special studies with recommendations as to the development of small businesses in the community, recreation, education and the like. Although these study groups were not themselves meant to be action groups, action groups did bud off from them leading to recreational, educational, artistic, and small business programs of great value to the community. . . .

The problem of The Montana Study in regard to fields of operation and projects was for the most part a matter of deciding what we could undertake, and where, with the limited facilities that we had. First in importance was the field work in the small communities themselves. . . . Our organized field work had roughly two divisions: first, a community study group devoted to the study of the community and its problems by persons from all levels of the community. Second, and usually following the first, a group was organized about some form of community expression. . . .

A second field of operation is the establishment of training centers and short courses for prospective community leaders. . . . Our problem in Montana, however, was, first, to find teachers able to do the training; second, to find ways of selecting likely leaders to train; and, third, to set up a simple program of training within reach of the different communities of the huge State. . . .

Although The Montana Study has not been an adult education project, it has continually been in contact with these problems. One of the more important instruments in the stabilization and enrichment of the small community will be the development of the school as a continuous service and center, alike for young people and adults all through their lives. The community centered school . . . a cultural service center, could become of great significance in the development of this country. . . .

SINCERELY

BAKER BROWNELL

While the Montana Study infused small, existing communities with a sense of heritage and worth, their antithesis sprang up in the promise of vast federal expenditures at Hungry Horse Dam. Author Joseph Kinsey Howard captured the optimism and enthusiasm of these and other new communities — an exuberance not at all dissimilar to that of boom towns during Montana's territorial days.

JANUARY 22, 1947

DEAR MRS. PRITCHARD:

. . . Up in northwestern Montana, just south of the western entrance to Glacier National Park, is Hungry Horse, site of a long-projected dam development on the Flathead river, well up in the Rocky Mountains. On and around the dam site a group of "boom towns" living solely on beer and hope have sprung up. There has been no actual work on the dam, and due to recent Congressional economy campaigns, God knows when there will be. . . . Funds for the job have not yet been granted and in the last session they were cut.

Nevertheless, the towns of Hungry Horse, Martin City, etc., are flourishing. Their people must have brought some money from war work, etc., because they haven't anything else to live on. These towns are the youngest and brashest boom towns I ever saw. Martin City, for instance, is busily planning a "Pioneer Days" fete in the spring to honor its "oldtimers"; the town will be a year old then. Its correspondent for the *Hungry Horse News*, a year-old newspaper at Hungry Horse (and a damn good one, run by a skilled newspaper man with tongue in cheek) is providing weekly interviews with "pioneers." The correspondent for another of the towns is a girl of 14 who has given the editor orders not to cut her stuff so he runs it without change and it's the frankest news column . . . on record. . . .

Front page feature of the *Hungry Horse News* this week was two large letter O's, side by side, explained as the answer to an inquirer who wanted to know what a mountain goat looks like in that country at this time of the year. . . . The letter O's represented "for all practical purposes, a binocular view of a Billy on Mount Brown's slopes last week." . . .

Martin City occasionally sings hymns of praise to its pioneer "business men" — barkeeps; it has seven bars and that's about all it has. . . .

The country in which all this is happening is high and remote, pretty well isolated all winter. Nearest town of any size is Kalispell, population normally 6,000, which . . . is building a couple of big (for Montana) hotels; it installed parking meters (to the glee of the whole state) and had a pitched battle with the company which made them when it insisted on taking them out and installing another type. . . .

The area is among the most beautiful in the northwest, with several mountain ranges in close proximity and two or three big lakes. . . . It is currently attracting interest as a winter sports area, due to efforts of two or more paratroop veterans who are building ski lodges in the Glacier Park vicinity. Suppose HOLIDAY or the POST might be interested?

SINCERELY

JOSEPH K. HOWARD

American Indian ideologies and heritage fell victim to advancing white culture in Montana and throughout the United States. On the reservation, too, the Montana Study provided a vehicle for expression of these older values. Flatheads, through the words of Conko, expressed resignation toward the progress of white ways and the apparent dissolution of their Indian way of life.

The old people have their old customs that they had way back in the days before the whites. Now our ways and customs are altogether different. We have new tools, such as axes, lawn mowers, rakes, and new inventions like cars and airplanes and highways, and food, for which they had no words because there were no such things in their day. In the same way, they had tools and kinds of food and ways of living which we don't have any more and the words they used for them are gone because we don't have a written language. . . .

Now at present almost every boy is in school. Every one of this young generation think they like the white customs. Everything that they knew and learned is almost forgotten. We might as well say we are just moving rapidly on. It won't take very long. . . . All of the Indian customs in not many years will melt away. Very few of us still have our braids and whenever that custom passes away the old Indians will be gone. . . .

Indian policy reflected personal whims and prevailing Congressional attitudes. As a result, the course of federal policy periodically underwent dramatic changes. Major recodifications encompassed the Dawes Act of 1887 — to "civilize" Indians and convert them to individual, land-owning farmers; the Wheeler-Howard Act of 1934 — promoting tribal organization and identity; and Termination, initiated in 1953 to abolish the Indian's reservation residence and status. Views on the wisdom of each course differed. The Termination controversy had a national forum, but had particular significance on Montana's seven reservations. Montana Congressman Wesley A. D'Ewart (1945-1955) and Blackfeet Secretary Iliff McKay viewed the means and goals of Termination from opposing perspectives.

Well, there is five or six tribes here in my district and some of them have beautiful reservations. . . . Good reservations. They're well managed and the Indians are doing a good job on them . . . but they're never happy no matter what you do. Work as hard as you can and when you get back it's "why didn't you do this," and "why didn't you do the other," and there's always a partisan group in every tribe. . . . I was up at Browning one time meeting with those people up there and I met with the tribal council and so on and I walked up the street and here was an old Indian sitting on a bench, says: "Don't believe a word those fellows say, they're crooks." That's the way Indians are. . . . So, it makes it difficult. I visited practically every reservation from the Seminoles in Florida, Palm Springs, the Eskimos in Alaska and really made quite a study of Indian problems and tried to help, but I was a little bit ahead of my time. I thought that an Indian who had been to the army and . . . college for a while, . . . ought to be on his own, not a ward of the Federal Government. . . . They don't want it at all. I got a bill through towards that end. The principle of the bill was that after an Indian was . . . twenty, he would become an independent citizen, not a ward of the government. In the meantime, if some Indian wanted to be an independent citizen he would go before the county commissioners and apply for full citizenship. That's the way I called it. And the welfare people could go and protest, his tribal council could go and protest, anybody could go, very much like a citizenship hearing. I got that through and then Truman vetoed it on invading presidential prerogatives. . . .

WESLEY A. D'EWART

———————————

BROWNING, MONTANA
MAY 16, 1958

HON. GLENN L. EMMONS
COMMISSIONER OF INDIAN AFFAIRS
WASHINGTON, D.C.

DEAR COMMISSIONER EMMONS:

I have read with real concern an account of your recent news release regarding your policies on Indian land sales wherein you stated, "Under the system of free democracy, few concepts are more centrally important than respect for individual property rights. This is in sharp contrast with the situation in the Soviet Union and other Communist countries where individual property rights are either not recognized at all or regularly and systematically subordinated to the interests of the state or the larger group." . . .

The inference which can be readily (and I hope mistakenly) recognized in this statement [is] that you consider that all those who oppose the present policy of allowing individual Indians to sell their land to the highest bidder for cash at sales supervised by the Indian Bureau, are persons or groups of Communist thinking.

As you know, the Blackfeet, as well as many other Indian tribes, have opposed this policy. We have been joined by many members of Congress and many students of Indian affairs in this opposition. I therefore believe that in order to minimize the possibility of the public

being misled by such a statement, you should issue a release stating that it was not your intention to brand as Communists all those who oppose your Bureau's present land sale policies.

I know it was not your intention to disparage the loyalty or impugn the motives of the oldest and most loyal minority group in the United States — the American Indians. But it seems to be fashionable these days, when all else fails to win an argument, to brand those who don't agree [as] Communists. . . . I beg of you, Commissioner, let's argue policies affecting Indians on their merits rather than resorting to name-calling. . . .

ILIFF McKAY, SECRETARY
BLACKFEET TRIBAL COUNCIL
BROWNING, MONTANA

Heritage and future hinged on the course of education for the Indian. At issue were two points: state or federal jurisdiction, and the quality of education about and for Indians. Members of the Rocky Boy Reservation faced the first dilemma and its personal impact in 1958 when, under the broad philosophy of Termination, federal officials decided to close reservation schools and bus Indian students to nearby Havre. Montana's legislators addressed the second question, quality education, in 1973 with a measure to require six college credits in Indian culture for any reservation teacher.

DECEMBER 12, 1958

TO EACH CONGRESSMAN AND SENATOR FROM MONTANA:

It appears that a grave injustice is being done to the Rocky Boy children. . . . We have been informed that it is the plan to transport Rocky Boy High School children to the Havre High School about 30 miles from Rocky Boy Agency.

This action has been taken without the consent of a majority of the people of Rocky Boy. At a meeting of the Chippewa Cree Tribe we were told that we could decide if we wanted a Bureau School or a Public School, and the vote was overwhelmingly for a Bureau School, but someone has turned against us and now we must have a public school.

We are afraid that under the public school, the children of many of our families who are in desperate circumstances during the winter months, will suffer because of a light lunch taking the place of the good

meals the children now receive, that would mean even lower nourishment and even more sickness.

We do not want our young people to go to Havre High School because our children are not made welcome there. We are not able to dress our children as the people of Havre dress their children, furthermore our children have not been prepared to compete on the level of those in the Havre School, and so big a school, they are soon far behind and finally completely out. . . .

We request that we may . . . have a High School at Rocky Boy, where the eligible young people who would like to go to High School might have a chance. There are now over 250 children enrolled in the grade schools at Rocky Boy, and there are now from 40 to 65 young people eligible for High School, if there were a High School where they could go and be with others on their own level. . . .

[SIGNED BY 90 MEMBERS OF
ROCKY BOY RESERVATION]

MARCH 3, 1973

In respect to HB 343 which this committee has before it for consideration, . . . It is an appalling fact that between 50% and 60% of all Indian children drop out of

school. In some areas the figure is as high at 75%. This stands in sharp contrast to the national average of 23%. A full generation of Indian adults have been severely damaged by an unresponsive educational system. At a time when economic survival in society requires increasing comprehension of both general knowledge and technical skills, Indians are lost at the lowest level of achievement of any group in our society. . . .

First, let me point out that this bill will not add to the cost of state government. Quite the contrary, it has real economic merit, not only for the Indian people but for the whole state of Montana. Anyone lacking educational skills will be among the underemployed with no means of survival except welfare. . . .

A second point for the committee's consideration is the fact that our new constitution has made a commitment to recognize and preserve the cultural heritage of the American Indian. This bill will be a first step in keeping this commitment.

The third point I ask the committee to consider carefully is the relationship between our state government and the Tribal governments. As "nations within a nation" by federal definition, the state does not have jurisdiction over these governments. Nevertheless, there are areas where mutual cooperation is needed to solve problems. It is certain that cooperating to help Tribal governments solve their problems will be mutually beneficial to all of us. . . .

FRANCES SATTERTHWAITE
LOBBYIST, INTER-TRIBAL POLICY BOARD

School districts constituted a basic unit of local government for all Montanans from the first days of the Territory to the present. Local boards represented not only the most basic exercise in community organization, they also meant jurisdiction (within broad state accreditation limits) over the dissemination and perpetuation of knowledge and values. Advocates of small school districts saw in those schools and their governing boards the bulwark of democracy and a center of rural life. Opponents pointed to needless duplication of effort and resultant inefficiency, suggesting remedy through consolidation. House Bill 220 during the 1961 Legislature proposed such consolidation and provoked heated debate before its death later in the session. Russell Mercer from Richland County and Jim Graham of Custer did not agree on the results of proposed district unification.

JANUARY 27, 1961

RUSSELL MERCER STATEMENT

In 1946 the Montana Committee on Public Elementary and Secondary School Organization and Finance reported to the 30th Legislative Assembly. . . . "The present pattern of school organization does not provide a continuous program of education from the first grade through high school. The school districts of Montana are too small and too inefficient to provide a modern program of education." . . . The same is true today.

At one time the state had about 3,000 school districts. This was during the homestead period, when it was desirable to have small districts. In 1900, 10% of our children attended high school; today 90% attend high school. Education today is no longer grades 1 to 8; it is 1 to 12; and for a larger percentage each year it is becoming grades 1 to 12 and college. . . .

With our modern educational requirements, there's no time for duplication of effort, or wasting of the children's time teaching them what another administrative unit should have taught.

At the present time, Montana law recognizes seven types of school districts. . . . In many cases, students in the first grade are under the control of one board of trustees, and are under the control of another in the 7th, 8th and 9th grades, and in high school, under another. . . . A school system that controls grades 1 through 12 will eliminate these discrepancies. . . .

The Montana Constitution states: "It shall be the duty of the Legislative Assembly of Montana to establish and maintain a general, uniform and thorough system of public, free, common schools." . . . We cannot have equal opportunity for children and equal taxation unless the number of administrative units are cut. At the present time, we do not have a uniform system of schools, nor equal educational opportunity, nor do we have all people contributing equally toward that system.

It is our hope that we have devised a method of improving the present system, where the people will solve the problems themselves at the county and local level, a method that will establish a more uniform system, and still retain the freedom of choice so vital to the people. . . .

JIM GRAHAM STATEMENT

I represent the people of Custer County. . . . First, I want you to know that I can't say that I attended this university or that one. I studied on my own. If, by any chance, you detect a slight quiver of the voice, I'm not going to sing. It's indicative of the battle going on here between the me that would enjoy sitting in the back row, and the me that feels a deep responsibility that we have facing us on this matter. . . .

I would like to explain one of the main reasons that we are opposed to this plan: because it calls for the centralization of government. This is something that we, as American citizens, have always shunned. . . . There is a tendency, however, now . . . to lean more in that direction — centralization of government. In other words, the responsibilities of the people at the local, grass roots level, are gradually being taken away from us. In so doing, it is also spoiling the people, in that they have become so accustomed to it, they are beginning to look to the State Legislature and to Washington for the support that they could very easily carry on at the local level. . . .

Take, for example, our own County of Custer. It would automatically become a one-district county, whereas today we have 21 districts. We would become a one-district county, with one high school, which we have, and a junior college, under the supervision of a seven-member board of trustees. We are told that the elementary schools in the rural areas will remain as they are; . . . that these elementary schools will continue to have local control. The only local control that they would have would be, by chance, to have one member on this seven-member board, and only one school would be represented there. . . .

I'm a member of the local school board. We take great interest in our school. We mop the floors, paint the building, and I guess we'll continue to clean the privies, too. We hire the teachers. We try to pick the best teacher available for our children. Let me ask you, in the county-wide district under a seven-member board, what chance have we got for better teachers in our school? Our elementary schools in the far reaching areas of the district would actually become a dumping off place. . . .

As far as finances are concerned . . . let's look . . . very carefully [at] equalization of finances. . . . New school buildings will have to go up. What happens next? School buses have to be bought, and maintenance equipment for the rural roads, because certainly our county doesn't have it to spare. That's where this equalization of finances will come into it. It will be equalized all right, but it sure will be digging into your pockets, and don't forget it.

I would like to stress this point with you: we are primarily concerned with our children. That's the number one factor. Finances and all of the other things come later. The number one factor is the children. . . . No matter how these gentlemen feel and think . . . [consolidation] can have a terrific rebound on all of us who pay the bills, and on our little kids who have to suffer the consequences.

Public awareness increased not only in matters as finite as local school districts, but with issues as expansive as Montana's land and air. Attention quickly focused on industry, old and new. Lumber mills, refineries, smelters, and generating plants were central to the controversy. They provided jobs, prosperity and problems. Montanans had long enjoyed fresh air and resented its violation; yet employee, merchant, and farmer welcomed salaries and tax revenues from industrial investments. Vocal groups and individuals encouraged plants to build or stay, but demanded they not pollute land, air or water. Environmentalists sometimes expected more than existing technology could produce. Democratic National Committeewoman Mrs. S. Rae Logan and Frank J. Laird from the Anaconda Company represented the essence of the problem. She objected to air pollution produced by pulp plants and lumber mills in Missoula; he protested unrealistic or inflexible expectations.

CHARLO, MONTANA
MAY 26, 1967

You might suppose that living, as we do in the Mission Valley . . . we would not be affected by air pollution. But my husband and I have noted the unmistakable rotten-egg smell of the pulp plant north of St. Ignatius. We have seen the drifts of its smoke coming across Ravalli Hill and the southern end of the valley. When the wind is from the north, smoke from the lumber mills at Polson or Pablo hazes our view of the Mission Mountains.

Nor are we immune from economic effects of smog.

Twice when flying east in winter we have incurred the added expenditure of time and money, driving to Great Falls over icy mountain roads and staying overnight, to make sure of getting aboard a plane. Both times we learned the plane we might have taken at Missoula was unable to land.

We feel entitled to speak as persons directly affected [by pollution] as well as because of [our] citizen concern for a serious problem of national scope. A layman cannot speak in technical terms of specific pollution standards, but can talk in terms of principles on the basis of which standards should be set. . . .

No one owns the air, or any part of it. No one has a right to damage what is not his, to cause illness and loss to his fellow citizens. Standards, then, should . . . guarantee the right of the public to see that the air we all must breathe is healthful, free from noxious, toxic fumes and particles, and the right to stop, instantly, anyone who violates those standards. . . . Since no one has a right to pollute the air, the cost of keeping it clean should be a part of the cost of doing business, or owning an automobile.

In other parts of the country thermal power plants have been major air polluters. At the recent hearing on water pollution standards, electric utilities objected to proposed standards of thermal pollution below their coal-fired generating plans. Presumably they will wish to continue to pollute the air by smoke from their stacks. As power is a necessity of civilized society and the demand doubles every decade, utilities pose a problem for most of the nation.

Montana is fortunate. Hydro-generation of electricity causes neither thermal pollution or water nor air pollution from burning coal or oil. . . . There still remains a tremendous potential for development of power without pollution of either water or air. And with low cost hydro-power available for use by industry, for home-heating, for whatever use power is needed, air pollution can be reduced.

With such an advantage Montana should be able to set and maintain higher standards than the rest of the Nation, and to keep its Big Sky clean.

MRS. S. RAE LOGAN

———————————

FEBRUARY 2, 1972

I am Frank J. Laird, Jr., Director of Environmental Engineering for the Anaconda Company. . . . The purpose of our appearance today is to generate some imput which might assist you in your difficult task in writing Montana's constitution regarding man and his environment. . . .

Anaconda has a commitment to environmental quality and established this department in 1965 with overall responsibility to achieve this end. It is aware of its responsibility to the public interest and is committing dollars to satisfy reasonable demands. At the Anaconda Smelter alone, over $30 million will be spent for environmental controls in the next few years. It must be remembered that these are "capital" expenditures and that the annual operating costs will be of major significance. In some instances our involvement has been accelerated by standards and in other instances . . . has been strictly voluntary. These are the general areas of concern to Anaconda in Montana and will be discussed in detail only if you so desire.

Everyone would like clear, concise data from which meaningful standards concerning the atmosphere could

be drawn. Unfortunately, such data is not yet available. It has been said that at least 70% of the atmospheric contaminants are unidentified and their biological effects unknown. In lieu of something better, standards have been set to incorporate an adequate margin of safety. . . . It is believed that Federal standards best represent the current state of knowledge. . . .

Many of the complexities will be resolved and standards will probably be reset — both up and down — as more knowledge is acquired. In my opinion, our existing legislative and judicial systems have the inherent flexibility to cope with such changes.

People have a right to clean air and where health is concerned there can be no compromise. If standards are set, however, with no other purpose than a "zero emissions" concept then we may be myopic in our desire for the pristine environment. A basic law of physics states that the mass of any substance entering into a physical or chemical reaction can never be changed. We can change its form but not its mass. The control of atmospheric emissions produce other control problems either in the form of solids, gases or liquids. It is conceivable that in our haste we can create environmental problems far exceeding the benefits. . . .

National energy problems and policies called attention to a significant energy source in eastern Montana — coal. The low grade deposits necessitated strip mining to be economical, while Montana's low population density and alternative power sources meant little coal was needed for statewide use. Consequently, the bulk of the product left the state by train to fire generating plants elsewhere or it stoked nearby generators and left Montana via high voltage transmission lines. Neither alternative escaped controversy. Montana's legislature and state agencies spent the 1970's dealing with problems of strip mining, generating plants, power transmission lines, and the like, listening to opponents as diverse in origin and outlook as the myriad problems they foresaw in coal development. To Harry Billings the process was yet another case of industrial abuse in the state; for Montana farmers, strip mining and related industries debauched the environment and meant terminal land or water use; for Dr. C. D. Vermillion, it was a journey to the environmental degradation of the eastern United States from which he had recently escaped. In testimony heard before the House Natural Resources Committee, arguments were emotional or reasoned, personal or philosophical, national or local, but the feelings were intense.

JANUARY 25, 1973

MR. CHAIRMAN, MEMBERS OF THE COMMITTEE:

My name is Harry L. Billings and I represent the Montana State AFL-CIO. . . .

Not too many decades ago . . . a bill such as House Bill 127 would have been considered visionary in the extreme. That was before a substantial part of the population realized that we cannot continue indefinitely defiling our land, water and air resources at an accelerating rate and still maintain a liveable habitat for man and beast.

With our great, wide-open spaces, many thought it just couldn't happen in our Montana. For generations, we looked at odors and poisons emitted by the Anaconda and East Helena smelters, — by a handful of oil refineries, — by a scattering of livestock yards — as simply local problems to be put up with by the citizenry, the best way they could.

Then, some thirty years ago, various environmental questions were given wide currency by the State's largest private utility as it vainly sought to block construction of the publicly-owned Hungry Horse Dam. While most of the ecological concerns which were so assiduously propounded proved more fantasy than fact, the advocates had inadvertently cracked the seal on a "pandora's box." Some of the more farsighted began to think and talk in terms of the total environment. The realization gradually spread that industrial development, profits and jobs were not the only considerations.

This realization has been furthered in the years

since by the establishment of a fluoride-emitting phosphate plant at Garrison, a pulpmill of dubious aromatic value west of Missoula, a mountain side laid largely barren by poisonous fumes from an aluminum plant at Columbia Falls, by an air-befouling steam electric plant in Billings, and, until recently, smoke-belching teepee burners all over northwest Montana.

Now, the prospect of several monstrous coal-fed power generating plants in eastern Montana holds promise of further [harm to] our air resource, [consumption of] inordinately large quantities of our limited water resource . . . [and] potentially irreparable damage to the surface of tens of thousands of acres of agricultural and grazing lands.

We have come full circle from the early "environmental" campaign launched by that utility for its own purposes. We are now considering a piece of legislation which will, if enacted, make this and other energy companies prove the extent of damage to the total environment [which] any new electric or gasification installations may bring. . . .

This legislation is overdue. The public interest must be the first consideration. This objective can only be accomplished by establishing guidelines which must be met BEFORE a permit to proceed with construction is granted.

House Bill 127 sets the rules. They are fair rules. The energy companies can live with them and still make a profit. Yet, they are rules which place the public interest paramount. . . .

Thank you.

I am Terry Murphy of Cardwell, Montana, appearing today to speak for myself and as a member of the board of directors to speak for the Montana Farmers Union. . . . We strongly support . . . a moratorium on further coal strip-mining and the attendant facilities. . . . The present and future growth of coal mining and related activities might well herald the most profound changes — economically, sociologically and politically — that Montana has ever seen. Land will be involved. Water will be involved. Air will be involved. And, most importantly, people will be involved. . . .

Any development in our state which disturbs the land surface or changes the use of that land should be evaluated ahead of time as to its possible effect on agriculture. . . . Consider carefully the role of agriculture in Montana. We produce about $750,000,000 worth of food, feed and fiber every year. This is new wealth and the production will recur next year, and the next, on and on. All from the same land.

Agriculture is by far the largest dollar-producing business in Montana and the fact we deal exclusively in renewable resources must be emphasized. Agriculture has been, is and will continue for the forseeable future to be the economic and social foundation for Montana — regardless of other developments.

Exploitive industries might appear extremely attractive on the short-term economic scene, but they do come and go — and they can go just as quickly as they come. Agriculture will be here always, producing the things we all need. That is, it will be here always if it isn't dug, blown, dried or polluted out of business.

Just as vital as agriculture is to the Montana economy, so is water vital to agriculture. . . . Already we know that in some of the strip mines water is draining into the pits and being pumped out into streams which eventually enter the Yellowstone River. . . . The waters of the Yellowstone and its tributaries are used on 23 per cent of Montana's total irrigated acreage of cash crops.

With sufficient water, the Yellowstone basin will bloom and produce abundantly — from now on, if need be. Without sufficient water, the economy of the area will suffer sharp reverses. . . .

An acre of crop or range land produces its wealth every year. An acre mined of its coal will never produce coal again. The agricultural land needs only care — which the farmer and rancher provides, and good, clean water which we have. Coal mining and power generating use up and dirty that water. . . .

It is not just agriculture, either. Another clean, renewable, growing industry in Montana is tourism. Why do tourists come here, spend money, leave and hope to return again? Do they come to see barren pits, dry or dirty streams, a sky brown or gray from power generating facilities? I think it's more probable they come for the abundant clean water we have presently — — for the fish which thrive therein — for the clear sky through which they can see for distances unheard of where most of them come from — for the air they can breathe without the stench burning their nostrils or the grit of ashes settling in their lungs. Those alternatives they get now in the industrialized "advanced" areas from which they come. . . .

We need time to see the results of research, studies and some experimentation already under way. . . . There will be no second chance. We must do this right the first time. Failure could mean a desert Appalachia in that vast, pastoral, tranquil area of eastern Montana. . . .

A moratorium is a must. If we act now in haste, we shall continue our long history of colonial subservience to exploiters. In a few short years, we will have more than land to reclaim; we will have a state economy and a rural society to rebuild. . . . The coal has been there thousands of years. Its potential has been known many years. It will not spoil — it will still be there, safe in the ground, while we take the time to make the right decision. . . .

BILLINGS, MONTANA
FEBRUARY 1, 1973

MR. ARTHUR SHELDEN, CHAIRMAN
NATIONAL RESOURCES COMMITTEE
HOUSE OF REPRESENTATIVES
HELENA, MONTANA

DEAR MR. CHAIRMAN:

. . . I am Doctor Dale Vermillion and I am currently practicing in Billings. Prior to settling in Billings, I grew up in Kansas and have lived in Boston for the last ten

years. Since I grew up enjoying hunting, fishing, and outdoor activities in general, it was soon apparent that the industrialized East was not where I wanted my children to grow up. . . . Montana seemed unique to us in that it was sparsely populated and combined mountains with open prairies. . . . In short, it seemed to offer . . . an unspoiled environment. Unfortunately we settled in Montana thinking it would remain that way. . . .

Let me state at this point that I am a Republican and have generally been in agreement in the past with those advocating industrial expansion. . . . Therefore it is somewhat of a surprise, perhaps, that I have recently become so opposed to the industrialization of eastern Montana. . . . It seems unlikely to me that strip mining can ever ultimately be stopped given the coal resources that are there. However, the devastation that it seems likely to create . . . hardly seems worth what the coal companies offer, namely, short-term prosperity for a small portion of Montana and a very big profit for a very small sector of the Montana business community. It seems to me that Montana should demand, if their coal is to be mined, that these companies reclaim the land according to very stringent reclamation rules. I think these rules should include the State's right to deny mine permits in cases where reclamation seems doubtful, reclamation of land to a condition equal to its premined state, the right of the State and/or citizens to sue these companies if they do not fulfill their obligations, no mining or construction of energy producing plants until all permits and questions have been answered to the public's satisfaction and the right of the owners of the surface to prohibit strip mining on their land if they so choose. In short, if they are to strip mine Montana, let's make sure we have control over it, and that we do it right, and that the coal companies pay a fair price for it. If the coal companies feel that it is just too expensive this way, that's fine. The coal will keep for a few more years and some day it will probably be put to a better use than just being burned. . . .

I would hope in the future that the State, through its laws, would be able to encourage the power companies to build their power plants elsewhere. This power is obviously intended for other areas' industrial needs and thus it seems only fair that they should pay for their prosperity by also accepting the pollution that their energy needs require. . . . To pollute Montana's air and country-side to provide Omaha with air-conditioning and Kansas City stockyards with sewage purification plants must certainly seem like a good deal to them and a pretty poor one to Montana. . . . I think Montana should proceed slowly, . . . to seek a better and more just solution for Montana and its citizens. . . .

C. D. VERMILLION, M.D.

No less intense were proponents of coal/energy development in Montana, who argued economically and environmentally sound development could take place. They were certain that employment, tax revenues, and prosperity could grow with adequate environmental safeguards. When legislative committees and state boards held their hearings, some Montanans argued for development of coal reserves. Dolph Harris was among them.

FEBRUARY 5, 1971

I am Dolph Harris, president of the Economic Development Association of Eastern Montana. Our organization came into being in 1970 and encompasses 18 counties and 2 Indian reservations. . . . We . . . like to think that we represent the economic interests of some 93,000 people in eastern Montana. We are concerned that in the last ten years we are experiencing an exodus of people to the tune of 13% or some 14,000 people. Our economy is agriculturally orientated and we have lost in the last ten year period a larger percentage of farms. Our employment rate dropped off some 14.2%. . . .

To encourage the economic and social development of this state, it is the purpose of the Eastern Montana Development Association to promote the location of industry and businesses in the state, especially electric power production facilities on Montana coal fields as a better alternative for the state than the shipping of this coal to other states. . . . It is our conviction that mine mouth generation plants will create far more jobs for Montanans, [and] will provide additional revenue to state and local governments. . . .

In the face of the serious and continuing shortages of electric power in many parts of the country, we believe that the upper great plains will increasingly become a major energy center of the nation, providing low cost abundant electric power to utilities of all kinds and to power critical industries. . . .

Finally, we believe that . . . power production agencies can [meet] . . . the highest standards with respect to environment. . . .

We are endorsing the concept of developing our coal resources in Montana. We do favor the idea of locating generation facilities in Montana. We do feel we can reap real economic benefits from related industries that depend upon an adequate and efficient source of power. . . . Utilization of our coal resources in Montana for the profit of Montanans is all we ask. . . .

Mountains, distance, and broad, unmarred vistas once frustrated settlement in Montana. Yet less than a century later, these same physical features drew tourists. National Parks, Chambers of Commerce, advertising departments, and travel agencies encouraged the influx, and visitor revenues soon rose to become one of Montana's leading industries. Dollar signs and prosperity were attractive; increased litter and growing crowds were not. "Welcome to Montana," "Invite a Friend to Montana," "The Last of the Big Time Splendors" — tourist promotions varied in title and so did opinions of the efforts. Glacier Park Company's C. K. Walbert favored it; KFBB television newsman Ken Dunham of Great Falls did not.

APRIL 19, 1962

We sincerely appreciate the opportunity of gathering with our good friends, all of whom are so vitally interested in the Montana Tourist Industry. We hope this is the beginning of continued meetings of this type [to] evaluate our combined efforts, create new ideas and re-dedicate ourselves to the most pleasant task of promoting travel to the great and glorious State of Montana. . . .

We must impress upon all of our people who perform a service for our guests that they make that extra effort — a broad smile and a hearty Montana Welcome, proof that Montanans are a warm and hospitable people. . . .

What an opportune time to kick off this "Welcome to Montana" campaign. All indications point to a banner year for all of us. . . . Let's put out the big Welcome Mat and send these good people home with the real Montana Story. This done, we will have thousands on our public relations staff spreading the good word. . . .

C. K. WALBERT
GLACIER PARK, INC.

MAY 29, 1973

I disagree with the current state advertising campaign, entitled . . . "Invite a Friend to Montana." What we are getting in the state are great hordes of tourists who do nothing but cheapen our quality of life, and add a few dollars to the state's economy. The average Montanan, unless he is in the tourist or recreation business, benefits little from the tourist trade directly. What he gets for the state's campaign is crowded fishing streams, littered camping areas, and a tourist under every rock.

I can't see how the state of Montana can justify spending public funds to attract visitors to the state. The priorities should be examined . . . and the money spent instead on keeping the few residents we have from moving . . . after being educated in the state's schools. . . . Montana would benefit more from tourism only if there were fewer tourists, with more money. . . . Let's take a look at our quality of life, a life style we fiercely defend, but sell down the river for the sake of a few bucks from an out of state population hungry for our uncrowded spaces.

KEN DUNHAM

Montana infatuated visitor and native alike. To escape urban crowding, resident and non-resident looked to the vacant mountain sides and valleys for a residence or a cabin site — "a place in the country." Particularly in growing, valley-bound communities like Missoula and Bozeman, conditions were right for subdivision growth. Land was available, at a price, and agriculture in the fertile valleys suffered in consequence. At issue were questions which transcended Montana — rights of property and pursuit of happiness. In both 1974 and 1975, legislators considered a moratorium on subdividing agricultural land. Hank Deschenes and Charles Bradley represented the opposing views and emotional values involved.

FEBRUARY 8, 1975

My name is Hank Deschenes. For the past ten years I've been a ranch and land broker out of Missoula. I'm here to voice total opposition to . . . the Agricultural Protection Act which as we know when stripped of its misleading title, is nothing more than another sub-division moratorium. . . .

My concern is that this bill completely neglects the caretaker of the land that its proponents claim they want so badly to protect and, in doing so, defeat the alleged intention of this bill. I submit to you that a great number of the backers of this bill . . . [have no] knowledge of or interest in agriculture. . . . This bill . . . constitutes another burden on agriculture as well as being a definite obstacle to man's God given right of life, liberty and the pursuit of happiness.

When you tell a man he can't do something and cause him economic hardship at the same time, you take . . . his incentive. Heart and incentive on the part of the American farmer — have been the backbone of this country since its beginning. . . . Most . . . people are in agriculture because they chose it as their means of [making] a living. . . .

Here again its going to be the little guy, the family farmer who is going to be hurt the most, whether all or part of the family income is from that farm. Traditionally agriculture has been far from the best way of making a living money-wise because of low profit margin. The only time this man really gets paid for his labors is when he sells his farm or part of it. How much he gets paid is of course determined by the value of the land. This bill is going to devalue [the] land. . . . The lessening of value results in less collateral for loans . . . loans this man is operating on while producing food and fibre. . . . If he cannot get enough operating capital, he goes under and you have lost a farmer. . . .

If more financing is not possible he might be able to sell a 10 acre piece of the place off for a homesite which will enable him to go on. Under this act he can't! And this is common practice today!

Presently agriculture needs every advantage it can get to survive, let alone prosper. We must consider the man who is caring for the land, for without him the land cannot flourish to feed and furnish some of these people who want to protect it so badly. . . .

There is some rancher support of this bill and I sympathize with some of their thinking and I hope they were honestly informed of all of the implications of this thing. But I have to ask myself how many of these are the Montana rancher as we know and respect him and how many are the rich eastern kid whose daddy bought him a chipmunk farm up the Blackfoot Valley and calls himself a rancher? . . . Many of the proponents just got here from some place else. Why don't they learn first how we live before trying to tell us how? The majority of the ranchers I have talked to don't want this kind of bill. We're going to get into land-use controls, but I hope carefully and intelligently by knowledgeable people. Please keep the politicians and government out of agriculture and we will find our own way out of our troubles as we always have! I love and want to protect Montana. . . . But the only snow job I want is that which I can see by looking out of the window! I sure thank you.

BOZEMAN, MONTANA
FEBRUARY 11, 1974

MR. ARTHUR SHELDEN
CHAIRMAN, COMMITTEE ON NATURAL RESOURCES
HOUSE OF REPRESENTATIVES
HELENA, MONTANA

I am appearing in support of H.B. 875. . . . As a boy I just happened to grow up around people who considered land ownership to be a privilege, not a right. This was before the day when "land stewardship" had become a popular cliche. When I was a young man I had the privilege of working on a Montana ranch over on the Boulder. Among the important things I learned was that there were two kinds of ranchers. There were those who worked with the thought of passing the ranch on to their children. And then there were those whose life style consisted of buying a ranch, mining it for a few years and moving on. I suppose the moral of this is that it sharpens your vision of the future to know and love the person who will have your land when you are gone. . . .

Today we are a much more crowded nation. Land is suddenly terribly precious. What we as individuals do to it has much farther reaching consequences for the public than it used to.

I am quite aware that H.B. 875, though aimed at a specific land problem, will, if passed, become a precedent for further limitations on private property rights. In supporting the bill I wish there was no conflict between my idealism and the pragmatic side of my make up. My idealism shrinks a little from another proposal to erode another increment of my personal freedom and put it in the hands of the state. My pragmatic side notes the truth of subdivisions. . . . They are growing like a cancer on some of our best agricultural land, our most scenic areas, areas of primary resources. They are growing without regard to long range public values. They are growing without concern for the fact that they often wastefully and unnecessarily compound the resource shortages that are facing us today and will deepen tomorrow. . . .

The pragmatic side of me also notes that while

wisdom is not yet wholly concentrated in the state, by and large there is a persistent and growing attempt on the part of government to do a better job of involving and representing the whole public rather than just the corporate interests. . . .

The same cannot really be said for developers, well-meaning though some of them are. There is no denying any longer that the sum total of what the developers do has a profound, lasting, and often detrimental effect upon matters of public interest and consequence. . . .

CHARLES C. BRADLEY

Montana's 1889 Constitutional Convention denied women the right to vote. J. Fred Toman homesteaded along the Little Powder River in 1911 and grubbed sage by hand. Both instances reflected traditional attitudes and actions — traditions which underwent dramatic changes in subsequent years. Catalysts for the transitions in life style were predominantly national in origin, but the ramifications had real and personal application for Montanans. As Congress gave final deliberation to the Equal Rights Amendment preparatory to submitting it to the states for ratification, Constitutional Convention delegate Virginia Blend of Cascade County pushed to have the ideologies of the national movement codified in Montana's Constitution and statutes. Likewise, Fred Toman was part of Twentieth Century advancements from the capsule which dispelled his stomach pain, to his television and automobile. Regardless of origin, "progress," new ideologies, and each technological advance chipped away at traditions, molded heritage into slightly different forms, and meant controversy or questions.

FEBRUARY 2, 1972

To: BILL OF RIGHTS COMMITTEE

My proposal reads "Equality of rights under the laws shall not be abridged by the state of Montana on account of sex." I have underlined "under the laws" for this is the crux of the proposal. My proposal is an exact copy of the proposed amendment to the constitution of the U.S., with the words "state of Montana" inserted instead of "by any state". . . .

The general effect on federal and state laws and official practices would not nullify all distinguishments on the basis of sex, but would require that the law treat men and women equally. Equal treatment can be accomplished either by extending the law which applies only to one sex [or] to the other sex, or by rendering the law unconstitutional as denying equality of rights to one sex. I am not sure that this premise is fully understood by all women involved in what is referred to as "Women's Lib", nor to men not involved in the practice of law or the dispensing of it. However, it is my opinion that freedom involves responsibility. . . .

Special restrictions on property rights of married women would be invalidated. They could engage in business as freely as men and manage their separate property such as inheritances and earnings. This has not been a problem in Montana, but as late as two years ago a woman, single, divorced or widowed, could not purchase an automobile, home or open a charge account unless she had a male to cosign.

The status of homemaker would not change, but depend upon individual circumstances. It would give new dignity to these roles, and the status of traditional women's occupations would be enhanced, for these would become positions accepted by women as equals, not as roles imposed on them as inferiors. This is a problem of social mores and tradition.

State protective labor laws would apply not only to women. The weight lifting, working hours, night work, employment in particular occupations would be invalidated. Men would share in any advantages provided.

The Equal Rights Amendment on the subject of employment would restrict only government action, prohibiting discrimination by it as an employer in federal, state, county and city including school boards. Private employment would not be effected. It would require equal pay for equal work only for employees of government.

In the area of education, it would prohibit public institutions from requiring higher standards for admission for women (or for men if such exist). . . .

In the U.S. and Montana we say we are one class of citizens. The Equal Rights proposal I urge you to include in the Bill of Rights grants equality to both sexes which is what we think we now have, but do not. I urge this Committee to give its best consideration to my proposal.

VIRGINIA H. BLEND
DELEGATE, DISTRICT 13

JANUARY, 1969

[JAN.] 1 - WEDNESDAY — This was a lazy day. I wrote a letter in the morning, shovelled some snow off the patio after breakfast, again after dinner. Got most of the patio cleaned off. Listened to the Rose Bowl parade in the forenoon and the football game in the afternoon. Ohio State won over Southern California, 24 to 16. . . .

[JAN.] 5 - SUNDAY — I was up early, took a bath, did a little writing before . . . breakfast. Just at breakfast time I felt a gas pain coming on and took a capsule to dispel it. . . . I spent some time lying down, but this didn't seem to help greatly. . . . I dressed for church.

[JAN.] 7 - TUESDAY — Drove around past the Congregational Manse in the forenoon to see if our new minister had arrived and saw a U-Haul truck, a U-Haul trailer, and a car with Oregon license on it backed up against the house. . . .

[JAN.] 20 - MONDAY — This was the big day in the nation's capital, the inauguration of Richard Nixon as president of the United States. Rose and I had little else to do and we spent much of the day watching the ceremonies on TV. Unfortunately, though, we get no color now on the Rapid City station, the only good station we have to watch. The Billings station shows color but that station is not plain, never has been. . . .

[JULY] 2 - WEDNESDAY — We put in the day as usual. I attended a TAC (Technical Action Panel) meeting in the Federal Building in the afternoon. Among other things we discussed a suggestion of a month ago, when the Broadus County-City Planning Commission (whatever that is composed of) "stressed the need for better relations with the Belle Creek community." Our opinion was that we have extended the friendly hand to Belle Creek . . . but the oil interests there . . . just don't want to be bothered with us. They can get most anything they want without consulting us and their only concern is that the people of the county don't tax them too much. . . . The oil interests supply 7/8s of our tax income. And here we allowed them to defeat the recent bond issue for a hospital in Broadus.

DECEMBER 25 - THURSDAY — Our Christmas at the ranch: Rose and I left Broadus fairly early, arrived at the ranch about nine-thirty. Never had better roads to travel on — hard and dry. . . . Our gifts went under the tree until they could all be together, after we had finished dinner. . . . We read Christmas letters, sang carols, visited all afternoon. Mike got out a recorder . . . and recorded our singing, then played it back. . . . He also took a number of pictures with a new Polaroid camera. . . . Rose and I drove back to Broadus. It was a happy day for all of us. . . .

History is the record of man's past — the lineage, the diary, the collective memory of a state, a nation, or a civilization. Historic preservation took many forms from the printed page to all the possible and personal expressions of experience. In Montana, as elsewhere, reflections of the past appeared in diverse form. Two Montana historians reflected the broad scope of historical consideration in the state. In both instances the subject of the letters did not come to fruition — Meadow Lark Country Club did not personalize its golf course, and the Montana Board of Education did not approve the deletion of history requirements in public schools. The words of both Joseph Kinsey Howard and K. Ross Toole attested, however, to the breadth and depth of Montana's heritage — a heritage grounded "not in precious metals alone."

MAY 1, 1950

DR. C. E. MAGNER, CHAIRMAN
GOLF COMMITTEE
MEADOW LARK COUNTRY CLUB
GREAT FALLS, MONTANA

DEAR DR. MAGNER:

Your choice of names for the holes on the Country Club course will have to be predicated upon whether you want authentic Montana names . . . or names which are nationally known and therefore would be interesting to visitors. I'd think the latter would be preferable and so most of those I list are in that classification. For

instance, the first white man in Montana (1802-03) was Charles LeRaye . . . but no one save a very few historical scholars has ever heard of him.

You could work up a historical progression if you wished from the first hole to the eighteenth. In that event the first hole probably should be Jefferson; he never saw Montana but had it not been for him it would never have become part of the United States. Next, of course, would be Meriwether Lewis and William Clark. . . . Then Sacajawea if you wished, and perhaps her worthless . . . husband, Charbonneau. . . .

Next probably should be David Thompson, great British geographer and explorer. And Manuel Lisa, of St.

Louis. They introduced the fur trade. . . . Then we come to the period of the mountain men, of whom the greatest and one whose name you certainly should use was Jim Bridger. He camped on approximately the site of the Country Club. . . .

John Mullan, who built the trail through here to Walla Walla, should be honored and perhaps the two great Jesuits, Jean DeSmet and Anthony Ravalli, though neither actually worked in the Great Falls vicinity. . . .

Coming down to Montana Territorial days, take Granville Stuart, one of the discoverers of gold, with his brother James. . . . For the Vigilante era the notables are of course the outlaw leader Henry Plummer . . . the prosecutor Sanders and the Marshals, James Williams . . . and Biedler, the famous John F. X., but he was pretty much a phony so I'd skip him. General Thomas Francis Meagher, the great Irish rebel who was acting Governor, might be used; or the actual first Governor, Sidney Edgerton, though he skipped out as soon as he could. In the copper era the greats were Marcus Daly, W. A. Clark and F. Augustus Heinze. If you try anything much later you'll run into modern political controversy.

The Indian war period would bring up such names as George Armstrong Custer, Nelson A. Miles and Oliver O. Howard. . . . Greatest of all Indians to frequent Montana was undoubtedly Joseph. Then there was Sitting Bull (real name Sitting Buffalo but nobody knows it, so don't use it), Crazy Horse, Two Moons, and Gall, all of them Sioux except Two Moons, a Cheyenne. They licked Custer.

If you have a dog-leg hole, whatever that is (I don't play golf) you might want to use Scannon, the dog which accompanied Lewis and Clark and was the first one ever to make a "transcontinental" trip — from St. Louis to Pacific and back.

This will give you plenty of choices. Since the Lewis and Clark expedition camped very close to the Country Club you may want to use several of the names of its personnel. If you want to bring it up to comparatively modern times you'd have to pave the way by using someone like Edgerton or Sanders (latter was much the bigger man and has some local connection) . . . and then use Jim Hill of the Great Northern, who actually was the founder of Great Falls though Paris Gibson, who worked for and with him, laid out the town. . . .

SINCERELY

JOSEPH K. HOWARD

MISSOULA, MONTANA
JUNE 13, 1975

JAMES BURK, SUPERVISOR, SECONDARY EDUCATION
OFFICE OF SUPERINTENDENT OF PUBLIC INSTRUCTION
HELENA, MONTANA

DEAR MR. BURK:

A few weeks ago rumors reached the Department of History at the University of Montana that American history might be deleted from our high schools as a required course. . . .

I do not intend to dwell on the awesome implications of your recommendation. It is unconscionable to entertain the thought that high school students in Montana should not be required to study the history of their country. If curriculum reform (which all of us agree is desirable) is to be based on the deletion of such vital and imperative core disciplines, the already frightening acceleration of the production of functional illiterates from our high schools can only reach uncontrollable velocity.

Our universities in America, however varied in excellence (and however troubled by their own great need for reforms), are now being inundated by high school graduates who neither read nor write nor think. But even more frightening is the increasing number of students emerging from our high schools who have not the remotest idea of what kind of country they live in. . . . These, then are rootless, rudderless and deeply ignorant young men and women. . . .

The reform needed, Mr. Burk, is not to delete American history as a requirement from your curriculum; it is, on the contrary, to teach more of it, better and more often. . . . What you propose is not reform, it is a flight from the hard fact of things. . . . Santyana was quite right when he said, "A people who ignore their history are doomed to repeat it." . . .

We are, perforce, much too concerned about this matter to accept soft blandishments that it is merely a matter under study. . . . The strong words in this letter reflect only our deep and abiding concern about a proposal which we consider to be dreadfully inimical to and destructive of the best interests of the young people of the state of Montana. . . .

K. ROSS TOOLE
HAMMOND PROFESSOR OF WESTERN HISTORY
UNIVERSITY OF MONTANA

NOTES ON SOURCES

BOOK I

Chapter 1 PRELUDE TO SETTLEMENT
Exploration, Fur Trade, Missionaries, 1804-1861

p. 4 — Thomas Jefferson to Meriwether Lewis, July 6, 1803. Jefferson Letter, Montana Historical Society (hereafter cited as MHS).

p. 5 — Pierre Menard to Pierre Chouteau, April 21, 1810. Chouteau Collection, MHS.

p. 6 — Alexander Ross, diary, 1824. Ross Diary (typescript copy), MHS. Original in Hudson's Bay Company Records, Manitoba Provincial Archives. Originally published in, Alexander Ross, *Fur Hunters of the Far West* (London: Smith, Elder & Co., 1855).

p. 8 — J. Archibald Hamilton to Pratte, Chouteau and Company, July 18, 1835. Fort Union Letter Book (typescript copies), MHS. Originals owned by the Missouri Historical Society.

p. 9 — Unknown to Alexander Culbertson, May 5, 1835. Fort Union Letter Book, (typescript copies), MHS. Originals owned by the Missouri Historical Society.

p. 10 — John F. A. Sanford to William Clark, July 26, 1833. Sanford Letter (typescript copy), MHS. Original owned by the Missouri Historical Society.

p. 12 — Crow Chiefs' receipt to Alfred J. Vaughan, Sept. 18, 1854. Vaughan Papers, MHS.

p. 13 — Alexander Culbertson, report to the Bureau of Indian Affairs, circa 1854. U.S. Washington Superintendency of Indian Affairs Records (microfilm copy), MHS. Originals in the National Archives.

p. 14 — Andrew Dawson, journal entries, 1854-1856. Pierre Chouteau, Jr. and Company Journals, MHS. Originally published in MHS, *Contributions*, Vol. X, 1940.

p. 16 — Pierre Jean De Smet, writings, 1841. From *Letters and Sketches with Narratives of a Year's Residence Among the Indians* (New York: Fithian Publishers, 1843).

p. 18 — John Owen to E. R. Geary, Dec. 21, 1860. U.S. Washington Superintendency of Indian Affairs Records (microfilm copy), MHS. Originals in the National Archives.

p. 19 — Alfred J. Vaughan to unknown, July, 1856. Vaughan Papers, MHS.

p. 20 — Thaddeus Culbertson, diary, 1850. Culbertson Diary (portion), MHS. Published in the *Annual Report of the Smithsonian Institution*, 1850.

p. 22 — John F. Dodson, diary, 1852. Dodson Diary, MHS.

p. 22 — John Owen to Doty, April 25, 1857. U.S. Washington Superintendency of Indian Affairs Records (microfilm copy), MHS. Originals in the National Archives.

p. 24 — P. M. Engle, report, Jan. 8, 1860. Included in *Report of Captain John Mullan* (Washington: U.S. G.P.O., Ex. Doc. 43, 37th Cong., 3rd Sess., 1863).

Chapter 2 THE RUSH FOR GOLD
First Major Migrations and Settlement, 1862-1867

p. 28 — F. M. Thompson, promotional statement, July 26, 1865. Thompson Collection, MHS.

p. 29 — Daniel H. Weston, diary, 1866. Weston Diary, MHS.

p. 31 — W. K. Thomas, diary, 1866. Thomas Diary, MHS.

p. 32 — James Fergus to James L. Fisk, Jan. 1, 1863 (recopied by Fisk, Nov. 19, 1889). Fergus Papers (microfilm copy), MHS. Original owned by William Bertsche.

p. 33 — F. E. W. Patten, diary, 1863. Patten Diary (typescript copy), MHS. Source of original unknown.

p. 35 — Emily R. Meredith to "Father," April 30, 1863. Meredith Family Papers, MHS.

p. 36 — Andrew J. Fisk, diary, 1866. Fisk Family Papers, MHS.

p. 37 — James H. Morley, diary, 1864. Morley Diary, MHS.

p. 38 — E. M. Morsman to "Father" (M. J. Morsman), Jan. 20, 1865. Morsman Collection (typescript copies), MHS.

p. 39-40 — Thomas Conrad to Mary Conrad, Oct. 2, Oct. 11, 1864, Jan. 15, 1865. Conrad Papers, MHS.

p. 41-42 — Franklin Kirkaldie to "Family," Dec. 6, 1864, Jan. 24, 1865, Aug. 30, Dec. 16, 1866. Kirkaldie Papers, MHS.

p. 42 — Homer Thomas to Isabella Thomas, Dec. 17, 1864. Thomas Collection (typescript copy), MHS.

p. 44 — Henry J. Bose, reminiscence, circa 1865-1869. Bose Reminiscence (photocopy), MHS. Original owned by Elizabeth Rodolf.

p. 45-46 — Mary Edgerton to "Sister," Jan. 1, 1864, Mar. 6, 1865. Edgerton Family Papers, MHS.

p. 46 — James H. Morley, diary, 1862-1864. Morley Diary, MHS.

p. 48 — Wilbur Fisk Sanders to "Sister," Dec. 26, 1863. Loaned for publication by owner of original, Wilbur F. Sanders.

p. 49 — Cornelius Hedges to "Parents," Sept. 13, 1865. Hedges Family Papers, MHS.

BOOK II

Chapter 3 INDIAN - WHITE RELATIONS
Encounter, Conflict, and Subjugation

p. 54 — Elk Head, drawings, circa 1883. Gros Ventre Heraldic Art, MHS.

p. 55 — Mary Sdipp-shin-mah reminiscence as recounted by Pierre Pichette. "Story of Mary Sdipp-shin-mah," *Montana Study Publications*, Vol. III, 1947, item #51.

p. 56 — Victor to Sidney Edgerton, April 25, 1865. Edgerton Family Papers, MHS.

p. 57 — Frank Elliott to "Father" (George Elliott), May, 1867. Elliott Papers, MHS.

p. 58 — Gustavus C. Doane, report, 1873. Doane-Pease Report with appendices (typescript copies), MHS. Originals in the National Archives.

p. 59 — Benjamin F. Potts to Columbus Delano, Nov. 9, 1872. Montana Governors Papers, MHS.

p. 60 — Military Department of Dakota, report, 1870. Heavy Runners Heirs' Claim Records (microfilm copy), MHS. Originals in the National Archives.

p. 60 — Bear Head, statement, 1915. Heavy Runners Heirs' Claim Records (microfilm copy), MHS. Originals in the National Archives.

p. 61 — Benjamin F. Potts to Secretary of the Interior, Sept. 8, 1871. Montana Governors Papers, MHS.

p. 62 — Flathead Chief, statement, 1876. From Missoula, *The Missoulian*, April 26, 1876.

p. 63 — Thomas J. Mitchell to J. Q. Smith, Sept. 25, 1876. U.S. Bureau of Indian Affairs; Montana Superintendency Records (microfilm copy), MHS. Originals in the National Archives.

p. 64 — E. G. Brooke to Martin Maginnis, Dec. 6, 1877. Maginnis Papers, MHS.

p. 65 — George S. Browning to James S. Brisbin, Dec. 18, 1878. Brisbin Papers, MHS.

p. 66 — Charles A. Broadwater to Martin Maginnis, Dec. 6, 1881. Maginnis Papers, MHS.

p. 66 — Blackfeet Tribal Code, 1875. Blackfeet Confederacy Collection, MHS.

p. 67 — James S. Brisbin, writings, Dec. 18, 1889. Brisbin Papers, MHS.

p. 68 — Thomas O. Miles to Joseph K. Toole, Nov. 22, 1891. Montana Governors Papers, MHS.

p. 69 — T. J. Morgan to Peter Ronan, April 23, 1892. Worlds Fair Managers Board Records, Montana State Archives, MHS.

Chapter 4   THE MILITARY EXPERIENCE
             Contrasts in Adventure and Boredom

p. 72 — Hezekiah L. Hosmer to Samuel T. Hauser, June 24, 1865. Hauser Papers, MHS.

p. 73 — Martin E. Hogan to Andrew O'Connell, Aug. 25, Sept. 17, 1866. Hogan Papers, MHS.

p. 74 — Edmond R. P. Shurly to James S. Brisbin, n.d. Brisbin Papers, MHS.

p. 76 — Philippe deTrobriand to O. D. Greene, Sept. 9, 1869. DeTrobriand Papers, MHS.

p. 77 — Philippe deTrobriand to Simmons, Thompson, et. al., Oct. 6, 1869. DeTrobriand Papers, MHS.

p. 78 — Philippe deTrobriand to O. D. Greene, Feb. 2, 1870. DeTrobriand Papers, MHS.

p. 78 — Phillipe deTrobriand to O. D. Greene, Feb. 2, 1870. DeTrobriand Papers, MHS.

p. 79 — Matthew Carroll, diary, 1876. Carroll Collection, MHS. Originally published in MHS, Contributions, Vol. II, 1896.

p. 80 — George Crook, report, Sept. 25, 1876. U.S. War Department; Department of the Platte Records (microfilm copy), MHS. Originals in the National Archives.

p. 80 — Edwin M. "Trumpeter" Brown to John Penwell, 1876. Brown Diaries, MHS.

p. 81 — William R. Sellew to "Mother" (Hansey A. Sellew), Dec. 9, 1876. Sellew Papers, MHS.

p. 82 — John P. Martens, diary, 1877. Martens Diary (microfilm copy), MHS. Source of original unknown.

p. 83 — Thomas M. Woodruff to "Mother," Oct. 15, 1877. Woodruff Letter, MHS.

p. 84 — Samuel T. Hauser to Martin Maginnis, Dec. 11, 1877. Maginnis Papers, MHS.

p. 85 — Unknown Harper's correspondent, unpublished article, circa 1878. Brisbin Papers, MHS.

p. 86 — Andrew McKeon to Patrick McKeon, Sept. 20, 1886. McKeon Letter, MHS.

p. 87 — C. S. Otis to Commanding Officer, Fort Custer, Aug. 3, 1888. Fort Assiniboine Records, MHS.

p. 88 — Fred S. Yaeger to Mrs. Eugene French, April 18, 1899. Eugene French Collection, MHS.

p. 89 — J. L. Bagley and Joel Cooper, statements, Aug., 1902. Fort Assiniboine Records, MHS.

Chapter 5   FOOD FROM THE LAND
             Livestock and Agriculture in the 19th Century

p. 92 — Thomas W. Harris, diaries, 1860-1867. Harris Papers, MHS.

p. 94 — Joseph Bumby to "Family," May 21, Aug. 4, Aug. 20, 1871. Bumby Family Papers, MHS.

p. 95 — John P. Martens, diary, 1877. Martens Diary (microfilm copy), MHS. Source of original unknown.

p. 96 — P. B. Mills to Editor, Rocky Mountain Husbandman, Dec. 13, 1876. From Diamond City, Rocky Mountain Husbandman, Dec. 21, 1876, p. 6.

p. 96 — S. S. Huntley to P. B. Clark, Nov. 22, 1877. Huntley Letter, MHS.

p. 97 — H. J. Rutter, reminiscence, 1884. Harold J. Rutter Reminiscence (written 1931, typescript copy), MHS. Original owned by Harry J. Simons.

p. 98 — Granville Stuart to Samuel T. Hauser, Sept. 10, 1884. Hauser Papers, MHS.

p. 98-99 — Granville Stuart to Samuel T. Hauser, June 28, Dec. 6, 1881. Hauser Papers, MHS.

p. 100 — Grace Marron, reminiscence, 1884-1885. Grace Marron Gilmore Papers, MHS.

p. 100 — John H. Stoutenburg, reminiscence, 1878-1880. Stoutenburg Reminiscence, MHS.

p. 101 — James H. Blake to C. E. Stone, Mar. 24, 1881. John M. Blake Papers, MHS.

p. 102 — Montana Stockgrowers Association, secretary's report (Russell B. Harrison), April 19, 1887. Montana Stockgrowers Association Records, MHS.

p. 102 — Albert Ronne to James Fergus, Nov., 1892. Fergus Papers, MHS.

p. 103 — Paris Gibson to R. B. Smith, April 2, 1900. Montana Governors Papers, MHS.

Chapter 6   SPANNING THE DISTANCES
             Transportation in the 19th Century

p. 106 — Joseph C. Walker, reminiscence, Dec. 6, 1864. Walker Papers, MHS.

p. 107 — Wellington Bird to J. H. Simpson, June 18, 1866. U.S. Interior Department Records (microfilm copy), MHS. Originals in the National Archives.

p. 108 — Achilles Lamme to Martin Maginnis, Feb. 9, 1876. Maginnis Papers, MHS.

p. 109 — David G. Browne to H. S. Cummings (includes itemized claim), Feb. 23, 1886. Browne Papers, MHS.

p. 110 — I. P. Baker to T. C. Power, July 12, 1884. Power Papers, MHS.

p. 110 — Alma Coffin, reminiscence, 1878. Alma Coffin Kirkpatrick Reminiscence, MHS.

p. 111 — Walter Burke to T. C. Power, July 4, 1882. Power Papers, MHS.

p. 112 — Charles Higgenbotham, reminiscence, 1866-1890. Higgenbotham Manuscript, MHS.

p. 113 — H. K. Weeden to T. C. Power and Brother, May 7, 1886. Power Papers, MHS.

p. 114 — O. B. O'Bannon to Samuel T. Hauser, Mar. 13, 1876. Hauser Papers, MHS.

p. 114 — "Prospector," writings, 1882. "Prospector" Manuscript (handwritten copy), from an unidentified eastern newspaper, MHS.

p. 115 — Roy M. Cobban to "Mother," diary, 1880. Cobban Papers, MHS.

p. 117 — W. R. Sellew to "Mother," June 21, 1888. Sellew Papers, MHS.

p. 118 — E. D. Edgerton to N. P. Terall, Oct. 4, 1889. Helena, Hot Springs and Smelter Railroad Company Records, MHS.

p. 207 — L. K. Hills to Elmer Holt, April 2, 1936. Montana Governors Papers, MHS.

p. 208 — Montana, Highway Planning Committee, report, Dec. 1, 1948. Montana. Highway Planning Committee Records (microfilm copy), MHS.

p. 209 — J. Hugo Aronson to F. H. Muller, Oct. 14, 1960. Montana Governors Papers, MHS.

p. 209 — Ben Stein, testimony on Senate Resolution #2, Feb. 12, 1963. 38th Legislative Assembly Records, RS 13, Montana State Archives, MHS.

p. 210 — J. W. Hesser to S. V. Stewart, Dec. 4, 1919. Montana Governors Papers, MHS.

p. 211 — Henry Loble to Lee Metcalf, Sept. 27, 1957. Metcalf Papers, MHS. Permission to publish granted by Lee Metcalf.

p. 211 — Frank Wiley, article, 1956. Aeronautics Commission Records, Montana State Archives, MHS. Originally published in *The Montana Stockgrower*, Mar. 15, 1956.

p. 212 — Charles McLean, testimony, 1951. Public Service Commission Records, Montana State Archives, RS 107, MHS.

p. 213 — Art Jardine, statement, 1957. Public Service Commission, RS 107, Montana State Archives, MHS.

p. 213 — Lawrence F. Nichols, testimony, 1951. Public Service Commission, RS 107, Montana State Archives, MHS.

p. 214 — Mrs. John N. Hall, testimony, August 3, 1960. Public Service Commission, RS 107, Montana State Archives, MHS.

p. 215 — John D. Melcher, testimony on Senate Resolution #13, Feb. 21, 1961. 37th Legislative Assembly Records, RS 12, Montana State Archives, MHS.

p. 216 — Arlyn F. Evey to "Sir," May 12, 1922. From *Great Falls Tribune*, May 21, 1922, p.9.

p. 216 — Harold M. Brown to M. W. Thatcher, Dec. 31, 1943. Montana Farmers Union Grain Terminal Association Records, MHS.

p. 217-219 — Robert E. Miller, Duane W. Bowler, and Albert Gaskill, reminiscences, 1930-1959. Don Anderson Collection, MHS.

p. 219 — E. G. Lee to Federal Communications Commission, *et. al.*, Oct. 20, 1959. Lee Metcalf Papers, MHS. Permission to publish granted by Lee Metcalf.

Chapter 14   AGRARIAN ADAPTATION
Agriculture in the 20th Century

p. 222 — James Fred Toman, diaries, 1911-1913. Toman Papers (photocopies), MHS. Originals owned by J. Fred Toman.

p. 222 — T. F. Finch to S. V. Stewart, May 18, 1917. Montana Governors Papers, MHS.

p. 223 — A. L. Stone, statement, Mar. 13, 1918. Montana Farmers Tax Conference Minutes, MHS.

p. 223 — John Survant to Joseph M. Dixon, Mar. 9, 1922. Montana Governors Papers, MHS.

p. 224 — Desmond J. O'Neil to Joseph Robinson, June 18, 1937. Buffalo Rapids Irrigation Project Records, MHS.

p. 224 — Bill Armington, reminiscence, 1908-1909. Armington Reminiscence (microfilm copy), MHS. Original owned by Homer Loucks.

p. 225 — Samuel McKennan to T. C. Power, April 23, 1915. Power Papers, MHS.

p. 226 — T. C. Power to C. W. Frields and Frank Palmer, Oct. 18, 1913. Power Papers, MHS.

p. 226 — Robert T. Pound to Evan W. Hall, Nov. 17, 1926. Hall Papers, MHS.

p. 227 — William H. Donald, diaries, 1927-1937. Donald Diaries (microfilm copy), MHS. Originals owned by William Donald.

p. 228 — Evan W. Hall to Alva A. Simpson, June 25, 1934. Hall Papers, MHS.

p. 229 — Con Price to Frank Messenger, June 2, 1951. Paul Campbell Scrapbook (microfilm copy). MHS. Original owned by Paul Campbell.

p. 230 — Ralph Miracle, statement, 1974. Montana Historical Society Livestock Industry Oral History Project, MHS.

p. 230 — Robert Brastrup, testimony on House Bill #746, 1974. 43rd Legislative Assembly Records, RS 18, Montana State Archives, MHS.

p. 231 — Ann Mather, statement, 1945. *Montana Study Publications*, Vol. II, 1945, item #24.

p. 231 — Clyde Jarvis, testimony on House Bill #132, 1973. 43rd Legislative Assembly Records, RS 18, Montana State Archives, MHS.

Chapter 15   COLLISION OF INTERESTS
Politics in the 20th Century

p. 234 — Emmet Glore to Prescott Cookingham, Oct. 10, 1947. Lee Metcalf Papers, MHS. Permission to publish granted by Lee Metcalf.

p. 234 — Lewis J. Duncan to William T. Brown, April 12, 1911. Montana Socialist Party Records, owned by Terry McGlynn.

p. 235 — Jeannette Rankin to Anna Howard Shaw, circa 1913. Montana Suffrage Club Records (typescript), MHS.

p. 236 — L. D. Spafford, county division editorial, Nov. 2, 1922. From *Kalispell Interlake*, Nov. 2, 1922. Also in Lake County Creation Scrapbook, MHS.

p. 236 — Sam C. Ford to Montana Council of Defense, May 27, 1918. Council of Defense Records, Montana State Archives, MHS.

p. 237 — Lee Hawley and D. J. Charles, statement, 1919. Attorneys General Records, RS 76, Montana State Archives, MHS.

p. 238 — Sam C. Ford to Carl Riddick, Dec. 23, 1920. Attorneys General Records, RS 76, Montana State Archives, MHS.

p. 238 — Thomas J. Walsh to Walter Aitken, April 8, 1932. Aitken Papers, MHS.

p. 239 — Desmond J. O'Neil to F. H. Cooney, April 21, 1933. Montana Governors Papers, MHS.

p. 239 — Walter Aitken to Burton K. Wheeler, circa 1945. Aitken Papers, MHS.

p. 240 — Jerry O'Connell to H. S. Bruce, April 9, 1940. *People's Voice* Records, MHS.

p. 241 — Mary E. Friday to the *People's Voice*, Nov. 11, 1940. *People's Voice* Records, MHS.

p. 241 — Ellenore M. Bridenstine, statement, Feb. 24, 1945. From *The Radio Story of the 29th Legislative Assembly*, KPFA, Helena, 1945.

p. 242 — Allen Goodgame to George Schotte, Feb. 3, 1956. Factfinding Committee on Highways, Streets and Bridges Records, Montana State Archives, MHS.

p. 242 — James E. Murray to "Friend," May 10, 1960. Frances Logan Merriam Papers, MHS.

p. 243 — Edna Peterson to L. Hart, June 9, 1960. Lee Metcalf Papers, MHS. Permission to publish granted by Lee Metcalf.

p. 243 — Senate Resolution #20, introduced by Paul E. Brenner, Feb. 28, 1961. 37th Legislative Assembly Records, RS 12, Montana State Archives, MHS.

p. 244 — Robert C. Weller, testimony on House Bill #333, Jan. 31, 1967. 40th Legislative Assembly Records, RS 15, Montana State Archives, MHS.

p. 244 — William Mather, testimony on House Bill #84, Feb. 11, 1965. 39th Legislative Assembly Records, RS 14, Montana State Archives, MHS.

p. 245 — Dale A. Harris to "Dear Sir," Feb. 13, 1970. Constitution Revision Commission Records, Montana State Archives, MHS.

Chapter 16   EXTRACTIVE ECONOMY
Business and Industry in the 20th Century

p. 248 — Ada Dawson to S. V. Stewart, Sept. 14, 1914. Montana Governors Papers, MHS.

p. 248 — John D. Ryan to H. H. Cole, May 1, 1923. Public Service Commission Records, RS 107, Montana State Archives, MHS.

p. 249 — M. W. Atwater to S. C. Ford, Mar. 11, 1917. Attorneys General Records, RS 76, Montana State Archives, MHS.

p. 250 — Champ Hannon, oral reminiscence, 1917-1918. Hannon Interview, MHS.

p. 251 — F. D. Becker to S. V. Stewart, June 27, 1917. Council of Defense Records, Montana State Archives, MHS.

p. 251 — Wade R. Parks to S. V. Stewart, Aug. 15, 1917. Montana Governors Papers, MHS.

p. 252 — Catherine Penney to Attorney General, Circa 1919. Attorneys General Records, RS 76, Montana State Archives, MHS.

p. 253 — A. H. Kremer to C. D. Greenfield, May 25, 1918. Council of Defense Records, Montana State Archives, MHS.

p. 253 — Charles T. Gadsden to Mr. Wood, Dec. 16, 1918. New Mine Sapphire Syndicate Records, MHS.

p. 254 — Edward O. Davies, testimony, April 12, 1919. Efficiency and Trade Commission Records, Montana State Archives, MHS.

p. 255 — Curly Meek, oral reminiscence, circa 1919. Meek Interview, MHS.

p. 255 — Joseph Russell, testimony, Jan. 21, 1919. Efficiency and Trade Commission Records, Montana State Archives, MHS.

p. 256 — W. C. Whipps to J. E. Erickson, May 2, 1929. Montana Governors Papers, MHS.

p. 256 — Margaret Loughrin to Frank H. Cooney, Aug. 6, 1934. Montana Governors Papers, MHS.

p. 257 — "George Burch Martyr," article, circa Jan., 1936. From Butte Sunday All-American.

p. 257 — Champ Hannon, oral reminiscence, circa 1918-1960. Hannon Interview, MHS.

p. 258 — Bill Burke, article, "Greenhorn Miner," 1941. Montana Works Progress Administration Records, MHS.

p. 260 — Edward Reynolds, article, "Blood and Bread," 1941. Montana Works Progress Administration Records, MHS.

p. 262 — J. M. Freeman to Mr. Dunlap, Mar. 4, 1943. Montana Coal and Iron Company Records, MHS.

p. 262 — John W. Bonner to Harry Billings, Aug. 11, 1949. People's Voice Records, MHS.

p. 263. —E.I. Renouard to "Employee," Dec. 12, 1957. Lee Metcalf Papers, MHS. Permission to publish granted by Lee Metcalf.

p. 263 — E. I. Renouard to J. Hugo Aronson, Dec. 18, 1959. Montana Governors Papers, MHS.

p. 264 — Sam B. Chase to U.S. Corps of Engineers, April 28, 1958. Montana Governors Papers, MHS.

p. 265 — S. R. Logan to Clifford Davis, Sept. 15, 1962. Frances Logan Merriam Papers, MHS.

Chapter 17   NEW PERSPECTIVES
Considerations for Today and Tomorrow

p. 268 — Baker Brownell to Raymond B. Fosdick, Jan. 8, 1947. Joseph Kinsey Howard Papers, MHS.

p. 269 — Joseph K. Howard to Mrs. Pritchard, Jan. 22, 1947. Howard Papers, MHS.

p. 270 — Conko, statement, 1947. Montana Study Publications, Vol. III, 1947, item #51.

p. 270 — Iliff McKay to Glenn L. Emmons, May 16, 1958. Lee Metcalf Papers, MHS. Permission to publish granted by Lee Metcalf.

p. 271 — Wesley A. D'Ewart, statement, circa 1947-1954. Montana Historical Society Livestock Industry Oral History Project, MHS.

p. 271 — Rocky Boy Members to Montana Congressional delegation, Dec. 12, 1958. Lee Metcalf Papers, MHS. Permission to publish granted by Lee Metcalf.

p. 271 — Frances Satterthwaite, testimony on House Bill #343, Mar. 3, 1973. 43rd Legislative Assembly Records, RS 18, Montana State Archives, MHS.

p. 272-273 — Russell Mercer and James Graham, testimony on House Bill #220, Jan. 27, 1961. 37th Legislative Assembly Records, RS 12, Montana State Archives, MHS.

p. 273 — Mrs. S. Rae Logan to State Board of Health, May 26, 1967. Frances Logan Merriam Papers, MHS.

p. 274 — Frank J. Laird, Jr., testimony before Natural Resources Committee, Constitutional Convention, Feb. 2, 1972. Constitutional Convention Records, Montana State Archives, MHS.

p. 275 — Harry L. Billings, testimony on House Bill #127, Jan. 25, 1973. 43rd Legislative Assembly Records, RS 18, Montana State Archives, MHS.

p. 276 — Terry Murphy, testimony on House Bill #492, 1973. 43rd Legislative Assembly Records, RS 18, Montana State Archives, MHS.

p. 276 — C. D. Vermillion to Arthur Shelden, Feb. 1, 1973. 43rd Legislative Assembly Records, RS 18, Montana State Archives, MHS.

p. 277 — Dolph Harris, testimony on House Bill #534, Feb. 5, 1971. 42nd Legislative Assembly Records, RS 17, Montana State Archives, MHS.

p. 278 — C. K. Walbert, statement, April 19, 1962. Department of Agriculture Records, RS 26, Montana State Archives, MHS.

p. 278 — Ken Dunham, statement, May 29, 1973. Greater Montana Foundation Collection, MHS.

p. 278 — Hank Deschenes, testimony on House Bill #319, Feb. 8, 1975. 44th Legislative Assembly Records, RS 89, Montana State Archives, MHS.

p. 279 — Charles C. Bradley to Arthur Shelden, Feb. 11, 1974. 43rd Legislative Assembly Records, Montana State Archives, MHS.

p. 280 — Virginia H. Blend, testimony before Bill of Rights Committee, Constitutional Convention, Feb. 2, 1972. Constitutional Convention Records, Montana State Archives, MHS.

p. 281 — J. Fred Toman, diary, 1969. Toman Papers (photocopies), MHS. Originals owned by J. Fred Toman.

p. 281 — Joseph Kinsey Howard to C. E. Magner, May 1, 1950. Howard Papers, MHS.

p. 282 — K. Ross Toole to James Burk, June 13, 1975. Montana Historical Society Records, MHS.

INDEX